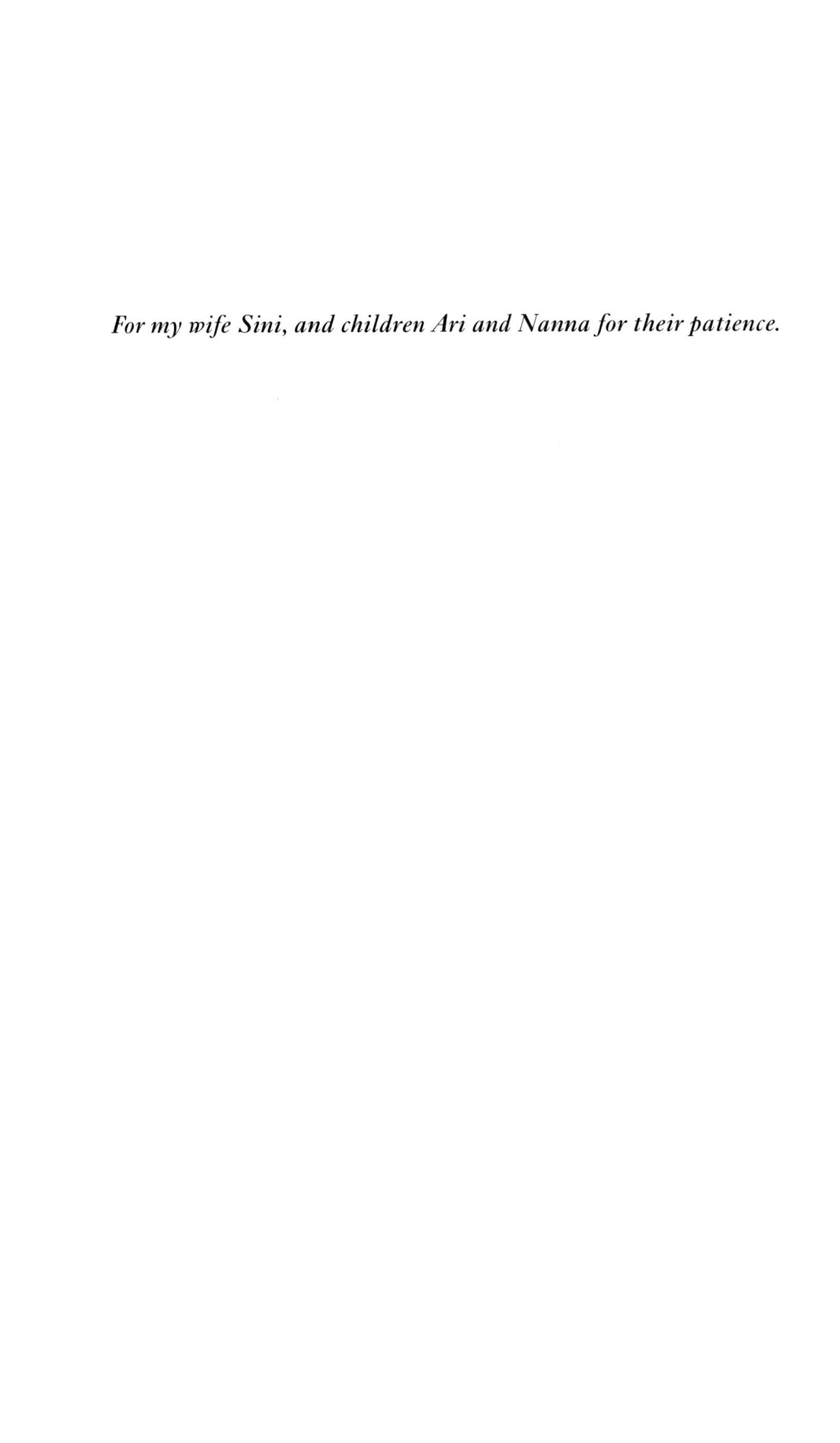

For my wife Sini, and children Ari and Nanna for their patience.

Caracalla

A Military Biography

Ilkka Syvänne

'Be harmonious, enrich the soldiers, and scorn all other men!'
Septimius Severus to his sons Caracalla and Geta according to Dio, tr. by Cary.

'It is of course an ancient maxim that teaches us to try to assault the enemy without ourselves suffering any injury'. The Strategikon, late sixth century, tr. by Dennis p.93

Pen & Sword
MILITARY

First published in Great Britain in 2017 by
Pen & Sword Military
an imprint of
Pen & Sword Books Ltd
47 Church Street
Barnsley
South Yorkshire
S70 2AS

Copyright © Ilkka Syvänne 2017

ISBN 978 1 47389 524 9

The right of Ilkka Syvänne to be identified as the Author of this Work has been asserted by him in accordance with the Copyright, Designs and Patents Act 1988.

A CIP catalogue record for this book is available from the British Library

All rights reserved. No part of this book may be reproduced or transmitted in any form or by any means, electronic or mechanical including photocopying, recording or by any information storage and retrieval system, without permission from the Publisher in writing.

Typeset in Ehrhardt by
Mac Style Ltd, Bridlington, East Yorkshire
Printed and bound in the UK by CPI Group (UK) Ltd,
Croydon, CR0 4YY

Pen & Sword Books Ltd incorporates the imprints of Pen & Sword Archaeology, Atlas, Aviation, Battleground, Discovery, Family History, History, Maritime, Military, Naval, Politics, Railways, Select, Transport, True Crime, Fiction, Frontline Books, Leo Cooper, Praetorian Press, Seaforth Publishing and Wharncliffe.

For a complete list of Pen & Sword titles please contact
PEN & SWORD BOOKS LIMITED
47 Church Street, Barnsley, South Yorkshire, S70 2AS, England
E-mail: enquiries@pen-and-sword.co.uk
Website: www.pen-and-sword.co.uk

'... It [Rome] had grown through its struggles from Romulus to Septimius and by then, because of the policies of Bassianus [Caracalla] it stood at its peak, so to speak.'

Sextus Aurelius Victor, *Liber De Caesaribus* 24.8, tr. by H-W. Bird p.27.

Contents

Acknowledgements viii
List of Plates ix
List of Maps xi
Introduction xii
Abbreviations xiii

Chapter 1	Background	1
Chapter 2	Youth and Education	79
Chapter 3	The Military Education: the Campaigns of 207–211	92
Chapter 4	The Joint Rule: Antoninus (211–217) and his Hapless Brother Geta (211–212)	124
Chapter 5	Antoninus Caracalla Takes Power	132
Chapter 6	German Campaign 212–213: Antoninus Imperator, Germanicus Maximus, Pacator Orbis, Magnus	154
Chapter 7	Caracalla's Anabasis Phase 1: Caracalla the *Geticus* and the Preparations in 214	190
Chapter 8	Caracalla's Anabasis Phase 2: Caracalla Arrives in Asia to make Further Preparations	212
Chapter 9	Caracalla's Anabasis Phase 3: Campaigns in Armenia and Alexandria, 215	220
Chapter 10	Caracalla's Anabasis Phase 4: Campaign Against Artabanus in 216	235
Chapter 11	Caracalla's Anabasis Phase 5: Army at Winter Quarters and the Death of Caracalla, 216–217	266
Chapter 12	The Apogee of Rome: The Reign of Caracalla Magnus, 'The Ausonian Beast' (211–217)	277
Chapter 13	An Epilogue: The Reign of Macrinus the Effeminate, 217–218	282

Appendix I: The Family of Caracalla 309
Appendix II: Julius Africanus and Severan Military Science 311
Appendix III: The Georgian Chronicles and Caracalla's Campaign in Armenia 326
Select Bibliography 330
Index 336

Acknowledgements

First of all, I would like to thank the Commissioning Editor Philip Sidnell for accepting the proposal for this book, which had been waiting on my 'bookshelf' for several years. He also deserves a big 'thank you' for his patience. Special thanks are also due to the Copy Editor, Marketing and other staff of Pen & Sword for their stellar work and for the outstanding support they give for the author. I would also like to thank Prof. Geoffrey Greatrex for having recommended an unknown historian to Pen & Sword in 2011.

I would also like to thank many of my friends, such as Perry Gray (who read one chapter in full and extracts from others), who have contributed to this study by reading a chapter or two or with their specific comments or otherwise. The latter includes the testing of views through role-playing games in which I have acted as a gamemaster. It goes without saying that they are not responsible for any mistakes that may remain. Similarly, it is quite probable that they do not share all of my ideas and conclusions regarding the reign of Caracalla.

The Finnish re-enactor Jyrki Halme deserves particular thanks for the contribution of his photos and comments regarding equipment. He possesses a truly vast amount of expertise in many matters related to re-enacting of various periods and continues to surprise me with his vast range of re-enacting equipment and photos. I appreciate your help tremendously. If there are any mistakes left, those are the sole responsibility of the author.

List of Plates

A bust of Septimius Severus. Source: Bernoulli.

Another bust of Septimius Severus. Source: Bernoulli.

A bust of Julia Domna from two angles. Source: Bernoulli.

A bust of Plautianus. Source: Bernoulli.

A bust of Geta. Source: Bernoulli.

A bust of Caracalla at Berlin from two angles. Source: Bernoulli.

A statue of Septimius Severus at the British Museum. Photo by the author.

A bust of young Caracalla. Photo by the author.

A copy of the Naples bust of Caracalla. Photo by Jyrki Halme.© Jyrki Halme.

A bust of Caracalla in the British Museum. Photo by the author.

A drawing of a bust of Caracalla at the Metropolitan Museum at NY. © Dr Ilkka Syvänne 2014.

Another bust of Caracalla at the British Museum from two angles. Photo by the author.

A copy of the Naples bust of Caracalla. Photo by Jyrki Halme. © Jyrki Halme.

Author's drawing of the Naples Caracalla. © Dr Ilkka Syvänne 2016.

Finnish re-enactor Jyrki Halme in period equipment (Theilenhofen helmet). Photo by Jyrki Halme.© Jyrki Halme.

Finnish re-enactor Jyrki Halme in period equipment (Niederbieber/Friedberg helmet and lamellar armour). Photo by Jyrki Halme.© Jyrki Halme.

A drawing of Caracalla as a duellist. © Dr. Ilkka Syvänne 2014.

Two Roman cavalry helmets at the British Museum. Photo by the author.

A bust of Caracalla. Photo by Jyrki Halme.© Jyrki Halme.

A drawing of Caracalla imitating Alexander the Great during his last days. © Dr Ilkka Syvänne 2014.

A drawing of a centurion or officer ca. AD 180. © Dr Ilkka Syvänne 2014.

Author's drawing of Caracalla with radiate diadem. © Dr Ilkka Syvänne 2016.

A drawing of a *praefectus pratorio* or *tribunus praetorio*. © Dr Ilkka Syvänne 2014.

A drawing of an auxiliary footman. © Dr Ilkka Syvänne 2014.

A Sasanian segmented helmet at the British Museum. Photo by the author.

A drawing of a statue of Caracalla imitating Alexander the Great. © Dr Ilkka Syvänne 2014.

Caledonian spearheads and spearbutts at the British Museum. Photo by the author.

A drawing representing a marine of the Misenum Fleet and a cavalry decurion. © Dr Ilkka Syvänne 2014.

A drawing of a multipurpose horseman using a *xyston/lancea pugnatoria*. © Dr Ilkka Syvänne 2014.

A drawing of Caracalla attacking with his lions. © Dr Ilkka Syvänne 2016.

A drawing showing a multipurpose horseman using shower archery and a Worthing helmet. © Dr Ilkka Syvänne 2014.

A coin of Caracalla at the British Museum. Photo by the author.

A Theilenhofen helmet. Photo by Jyrki Halme.© Jyrki Halme.

A drawing of a *speculator* with the Vecten and Ostrov helmets. © Dr Ilkka Syvänne 2014.

A drawing of three praetorians, shields and two spearheads. © Dr Ilkka Syvänne 2014.

A drawing representing Marcus Cincius Nigrinus of the XI Urban Cohort with his servant. © Dr Ilkka Syvänne 2014.

A drawing representing a *trierarches* (captain) of the Misenum Fleet. © Dr Ilkka Syvänne 2014.

A drawing of an Osroenian cataphract. © Dr Ilkka Syvänne 2014.

Nineteenth-century reconstructions of the third-century Danish warriors on the basis of bog finds. *Maailman historia* and Sophus Müller. (*Vor Oldtid*)

A statue of Elagabalus. Source: Bernoulli.

Coins of Vologaesus/Vologaeses V or VI, and Artabanus V. Source: Rawlinson 1893.

A statue of Julia Soaemias. Source: Bernoulli.

A statue of Julia Mamaea. Source: Bernoulli.

A statue of Diadumenianus. Source: Bernoulli.

A statue of Alexander Severus. Source: Bernoulli.

A statue of Maximinus Thrax. Source: Bernoulli.

List of Maps

Locations of Legions in 211	xiv
Persia	xv
Neighbours of Rome	xvi
Rhine Frontier	xvii
Caucasus and Armenia	xviii
Danubian Frontier	xix
Strategic Mobility	45
Roman Empire c. AD 215	46
Roman Naval Deployment	62
Britain in 208–211	95
Roman Marching Camps in Scotland/Caledonia	106
Forts and Camps at Ardoch	107
Roman Campaign in Scotland in 209: Alternative 1	108
Roman Campaign in Scotland in 209: Alternative 2	109
Roman Campaign in Scotland in 210: Alternative 1	114
Roman Campaign in Scotland in 210: Alternative 2	115
Caracalla's Caledonian Campaign in 211	118
Imperial Palace	125
The City of Rome under Caracalla	133
Black Sea	165
Supply Routes to Germania	167
Caracalla's German Campaigns in 212–214	178
Locations of Caracalla's Activities in 214–215	194
Hatra	195
Alexandria	223
Ancient Yemen	228
Antioch	235
Seleucia and Edessa	236
Caracalla's Parthian and Armenian Campaigns in 216	257
Artaxata	258
Takt-e Solayman	259
Tabriz	259
Rayy	260
Syria	304

Introduction

The aim of this book is simply to reassess the reign of Caracalla (AD 211–217) and offer a new revisionist interpretation of the sources and events. The interpretation of the evidence doesn't follow the standard philological methodology adopted by the vast majority of Classicists, but adopts the methodology employed by military historians, which includes some analytical tools employed by intelligence services to assess unreliable sources. The narrative also includes colourful language and presents its case with 'warts and all', but it should still be stressed that I use the terminology employed by the period sources to do this. I do not believe that a politically correct approach to the sources would serve any good. It is only a form of censorship in which difficult topics are not raised, analyzed and discussed. The aim of every historian should be to seek the truth wherever it leads them to such an extent as is humanly possible – one cannot entirely separate oneself from the study, which is always an image of its author. In short, all research is subjective, but every effort should be made that it is as objective as possible. It is unfortunate that the current research culture among the social sciences and history in the western universities is not conductive for truly novel ideas thanks to the atmosphere of political correctness. It is far more typical for the system to reward those who follow the established consensus opinion or the majority opinion and to ostracize those who attempt to challenge this. As such this is very strange because these very same persons usually praise the courage of Galileo Galilei when he challenged the established truths. On the other than this is obviously a very human thing to do. It is very rare for us humans to be glad if someone states that we are wrong. Consequently, I am afraid that the same reluctance to adopt new ideas will persist in one form or another, but I would still urge greater tolerance to dissenting voices, even unpopular ones, because that it is what academia is supposed to encourage. It is high time that we academics look into the mirror and ask ourselves the question: are we encouraging the rise of new ideas or are we stymieing these?

I have also included a long analysis of the Roman military system and intelligence-gathering apparatus and Caracalla's reforms, because this is a military biography. This analysis will offer several new conclusions and will also correct some very common misunderstandings regarding the Roman armed forces.

The book has been a long time in the making. I wrote most of the material up to 2009, but then shelved the project in 2010 to write other articles and monographs. I took it off the shelf to finish it at the suggestion of my wife in the autumn of 2014.

The maps are usually based on the outstanding Barrington Atlas.

Abbreviations

PIR   *Prosopographia imperii romani saec.* I. II. III. Berlin (1897).
Ref 1   The Roman Eastern Frontier and the Persian Wars (AD 226–363), compiled and edited by M.H. Dodgeon and S.N.C. Lieu. London and New York (1991).
SHA   *Scriptores Historiae Augustae* (Augustan Histories).

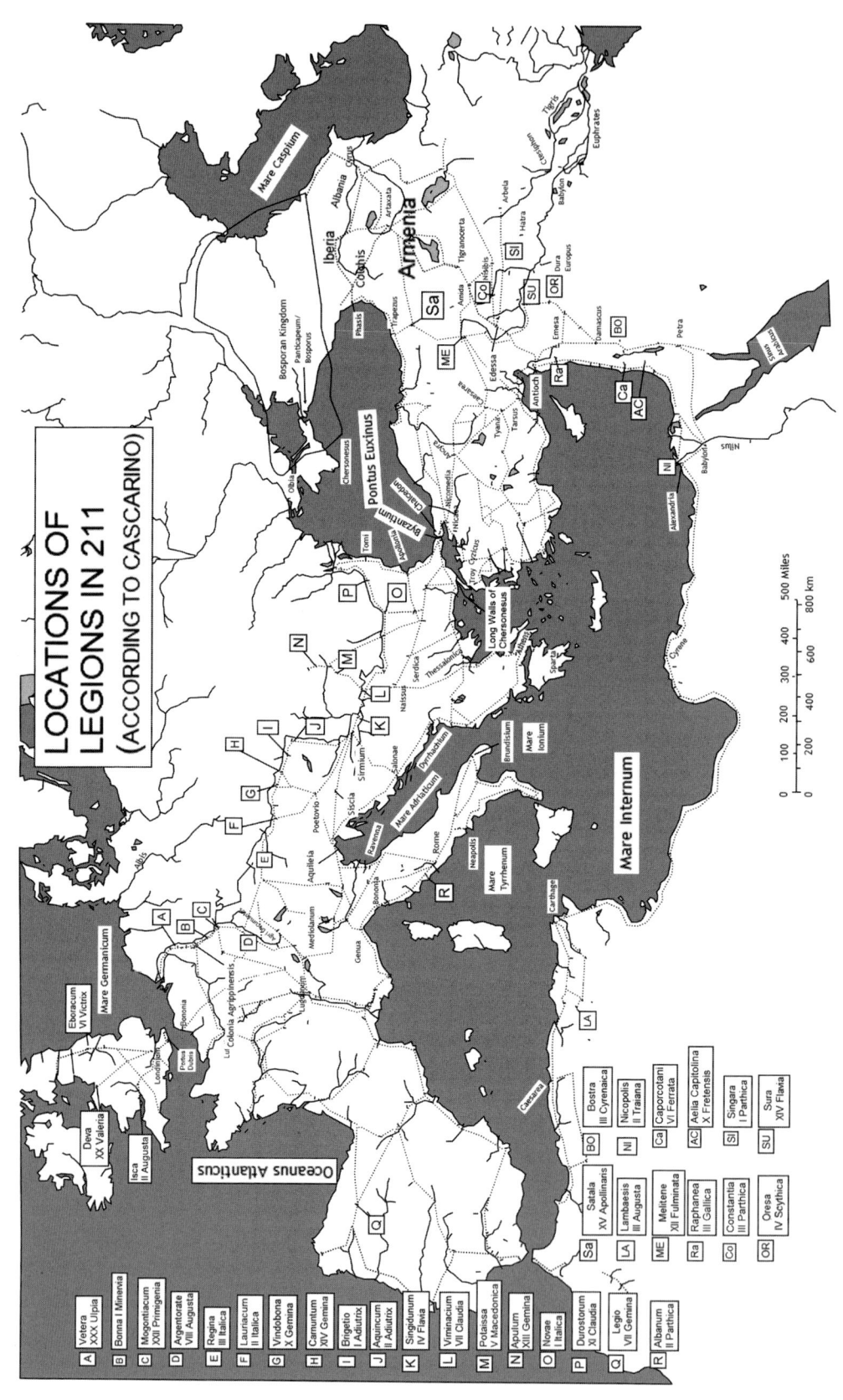

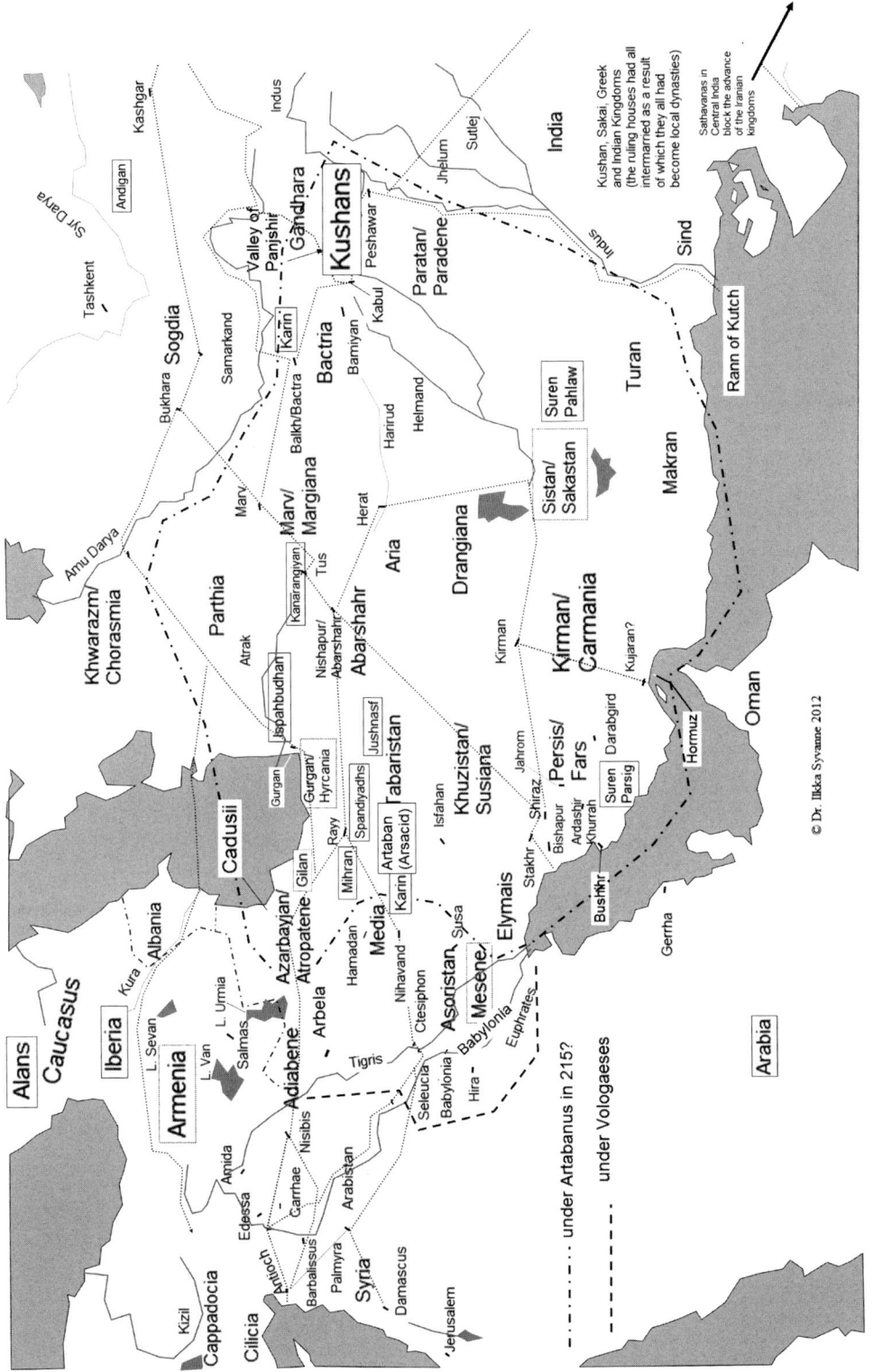

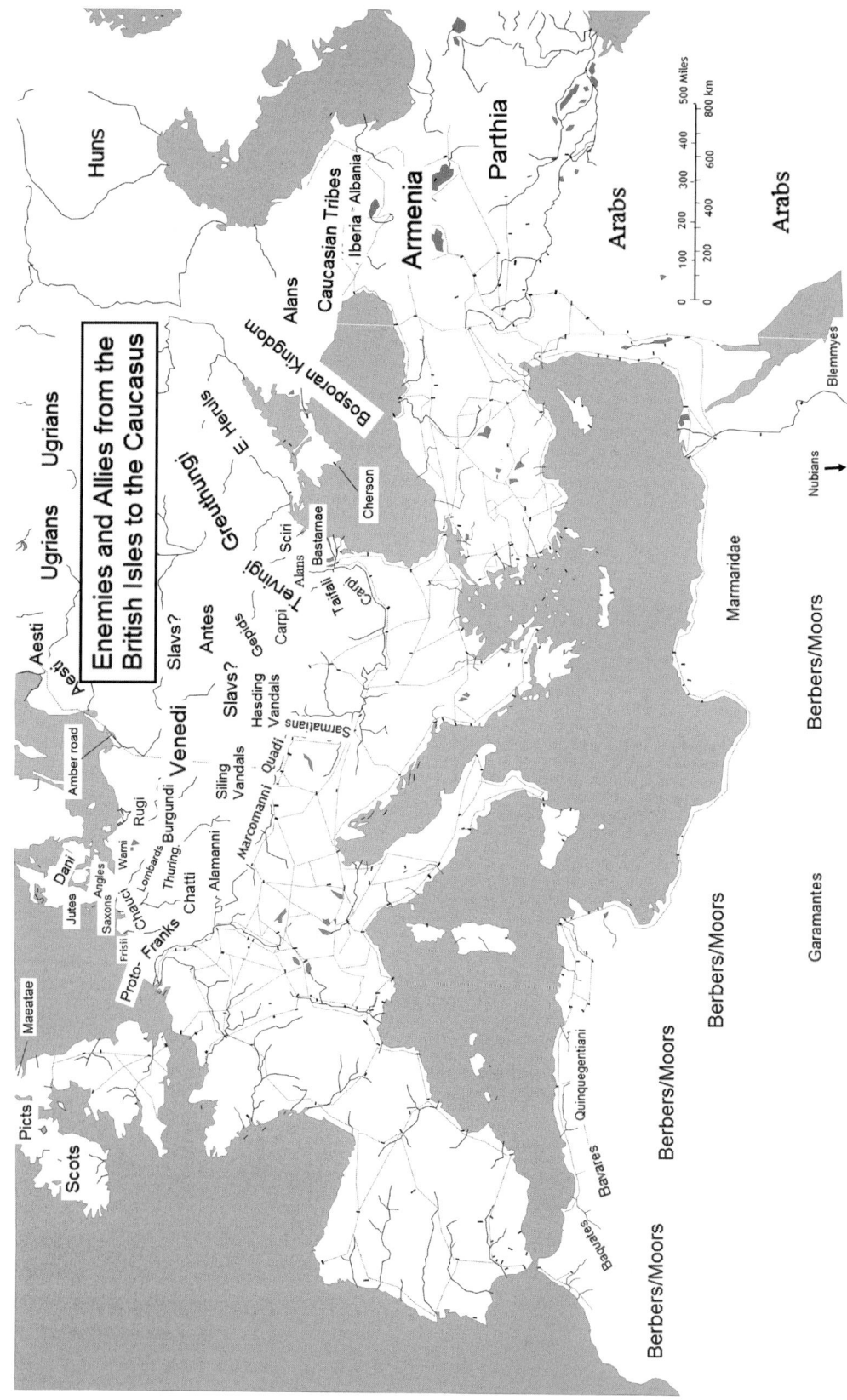

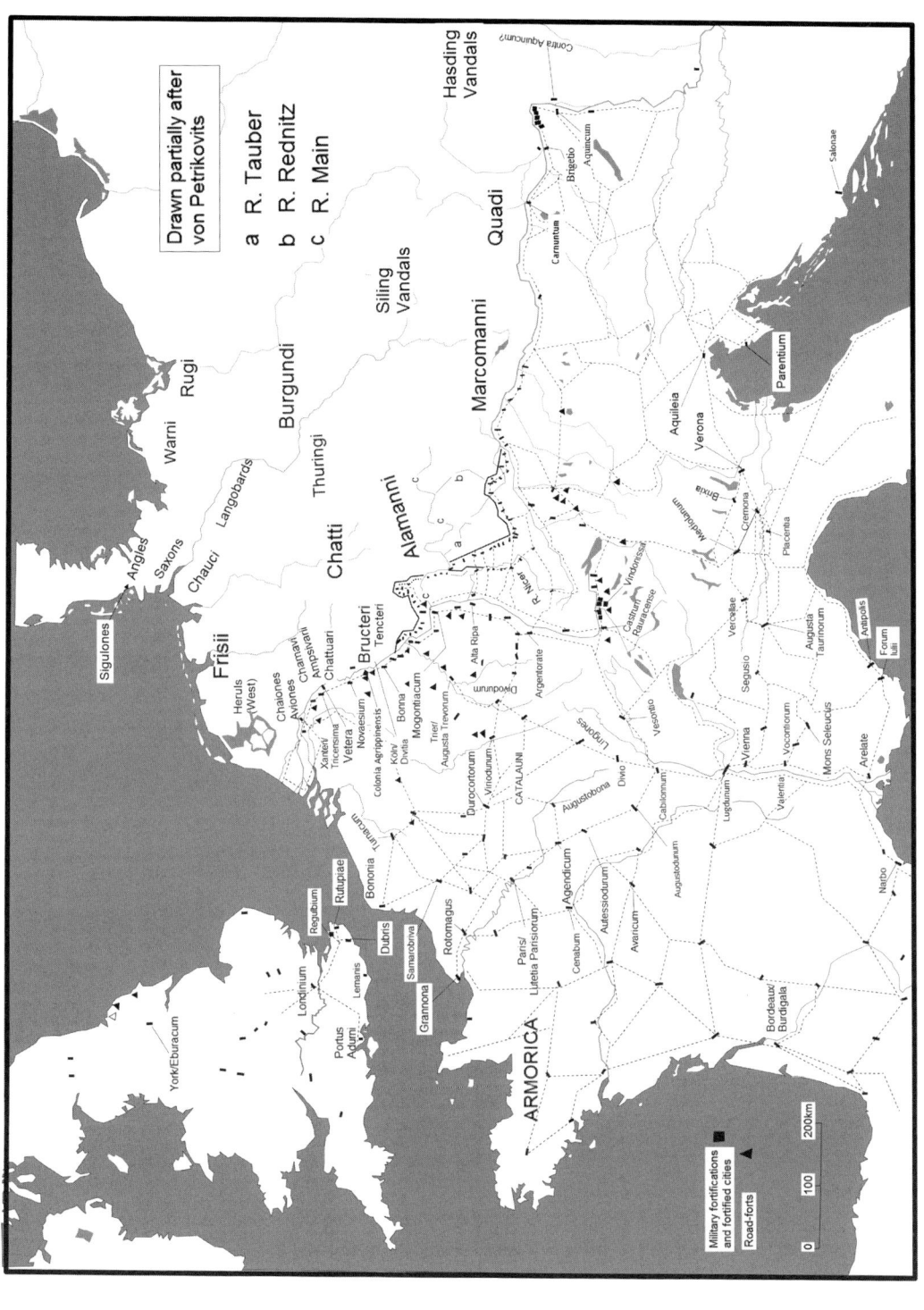

Chapter One

Background

1.1. Roman Society

Roman society was a class-based society that consisted of judicial and social hierarchies. The judicial hierarchy divided the populace into freemen and slaves. The freemen in their turn consisted of freeborn men and freedmen, with the former consisting of Roman citizens and tribesmen with varying rights. Slaves could become freedmen when they either managed to buy their freedom or their master granted them freedom. The freedmen had no political rights, but their children were freeborn men with full rights. In addition to this, there existed a third class of freeborn: the provincials, who did not have Roman citizenship. Their legal position varied greatly according to the treaties their nations or cities had made with Rome and according to the legal systems they had in place in their own territories.

The official social categories consisted of the senatorial order, the equestrian order and the plebs. The senatorial order was hereditary but could receive new blood when the emperor so desired. Its members consisted of Roman citizens with a minimum property of 1 million sesterces. The most important military and civilian offices of the empire were the privilege of the senatorial class. One of the ways in which the emperors rewarded their supporters was to nominate them as senators. As a result of this, most of the senators consisted of provincials by the beginning of the third century AD. Since it was dangerous for emperors to allow the wealthy senators to be anywhere near the legions, senators had an obligation to reside at Rome and to invest one third of their property in Italy. Senators were allowed to travel away from Italy only with the approval of the emperor. Senators wore *toga laticlavius* (broad-stripe) as a sign of their social standing. They were liable to pay only donatives (paid every five years, or when the army campaigned, or to celebrate some important occasion) and very small inheritance taxes. This meant that the wealthiest citizens, who owned most of the property, contributed only a very small proportion of the imperial taxes.

The equestrian order was a non-hereditary order, the members of which consisted of Roman citizens with a minimum property of 400,000 sesterces, who had successfully applied to be enrolled into its ranks. The reason for the willingness to be enrolled among the order was that some of the positions in the imperial administration and armed forces were reserved for equestrians. The most successful of the equestrians could hope to be enrolled among the senatorial order.

2 Caracalla

The equestrians consisted of those who had inherited money or who were self-made men. They wore the *toga angusticlavius* in public as an indication of their rank. Ever since the first century, the emperors had promoted the relative position of the equestrian order vis-à-vis the senatorial order by increasing its role in the imperial administration and the military. The reason for this was that the emperors considered the members of the heterogeneous equestrian order to be generally more loyal and professional than the senators. The most important demonstration of this was that the emperors had reserved the most important military positions – the two or three praetorian prefects – for the members of the equestrian order. As we shall see, the trust that the emperors placed on the loyalty of the equestrians and praetorian prefects was entirely misplaced.

The vast majority of the free population consisted of the plebs. This order included both rich and poor. The richest members of the plebs (decurions with citizenship) were allowed to wear the *toga praetexta* to separate them from the middle-class and poor. The rest of the plebs consisted of the rich (businessmen, merchants and bankers etc.), the 'middle-class' plebs (artisans, boutique keepers, merchants, bakers, artists, intellectuals/philosophers etc.) and the poor plebs (peasants, carriers, labourers etc.).

The civilian and military officers followed in theory the so-called *cursus honorum*. This system reserved certain posts for the members of the senatorial order and others for the equestrian order, with the very highest posts the prerogative of the former. However, in practice the emperors often bypassed these requirements and appointed equestrians or even imperial freedmen to the highest offices. Even more importantly, the top military commands of the empire, the posts of the praetorian prefects, were reserved for members of the equestrian order, as noted above. The same was true with the very important post of the prefect of Egypt and with the new prefectures of the three Parthian legions created by Septimius Severus.

In truth, the class structure of society was not as clear as the official divisions would imply. In practice, the emperor and the imperial family formed a separate privileged class above the rest, just as did the members of the former imperial families. The friends of the emperor – who could consist of senators, equestrians, freedmen and even trusted slaves – and the imperial women could also wield unofficial power far in excess of their official standing, thanks to their closeness to the emperor. In addition to this, from about the mid-second century onwards, the old judicial and social standings and divisions started to disappear. The older divisions were superseded partially by a new form of class division which divided the people into *honestiores* and *humiliores*. The *honestiores* consisted of the senators, equestrians, veterans and decuriones. They had legal privileges and exemptions from the harsher punishments to separate them from the *humiliores*. This is believed to have resulted from decisions undertaken by Hadrian, Antoninus Pius or Marcus Aurelius. At about the same time as the emperors created the *honestiores* class, they also created honorary ranks with judicial privileges. It is usually assumed that

Marcus Aurelius was the first emperor to do so, but it is possible that this decision was already made under Hadrian. The praetorian prefects obtained the rank of *viri eminentissimi*, the senators the rank of *clarissimus* and the officials of the court the rank of *perfectissimi*. The aim of this policy was clearly to reward those members of society who contributed most to the state in the form of taxes and/or administrative and military duties. The goal was to secure their loyalty to the emperor. This was very important in light of the fact that an emperor's position depended on his ability to retain the loyalty of his military officers and administrators, and his ability to collect taxes through the civilian decurions. The latter position was becoming less and less desirable in the eyes of the rich city dwellers because the members of the city councils were required to pay any tax arrears.

Agriculture formed the basis of the Roman economy, but in contrast to most of its neighbours the empire also had very significant artisan and merchant classes. This meant that most of the tax income was collected from the peasants through the city councils for use by the imperial administration. It was thanks to this that the Romans were always eager to settle foreign tribes within their borders to till the land and provide soldiers. The emperors could not rely solely on the taxes obtained from the peasants, because it varied from one year to another depending on the size of the crops. It was due to this that the emperors tapped other sources of income. These consisted of the produce of the imperial estates and mines, donatives, extraordinary taxes levied when needed, confiscation of the property of the rich with various excuses like faked charges, conscription of soldiers (or its threat to produce money) and tolls and customs (collected from internal and external trade). The customs collected from long-distance trade with Arabia, Africa, India and China formed one of the most important sources of revenue for the emperor. It should not be forgotten that the emperors needed money for the upkeep of the imperial machinery and armed forces, the latter of which consumed most of the revenue. If everything else had failed, emperors even resorted to the selling of imperial property or on loans or forced loans from the wealthy senators, equestrians and bankers.

1.2. Governing the Empire

The Emperor
The Roman Empire was officially a republic in which the emperor, the *princeps* (the first among equals/first citizen), possessed executive (proconsul) and legislative powers (people's tribune). He also acted as commander-in-chief of the armed forces (proconsul and *imperator*) and was the high priest of the empire (*pontifex maximus*). In addition to this, the emperor possessed informal power over the senators and people, which was publicly recognized under the name *auctoritas* (influence) and with the official surname *Augustus*. On his death, the emperor would also become a god. In practice, the emperor therefore possessed the executive, legislative and judiciary powers, and controlled Rome's foreign policy and military forces, appointed all civil

4   Caracalla

and military functionaries, proposed and legislated imperial legislation and acted as the Supreme Court. However, in truth, the emperor's powers rested solely on his control of the military machinery. The soldiers had already learnt in the first century AD that they could nominate their own commanders as emperors. The latest example of this was obviously the rise of Septimius Severus.

There were several inherent weaknesses in this system, but the most important were: 1) the principate did not establish an orderly system of succession; and 2) the emperors could not place any gifted commander in charge of large military forces without the risk of being overthrown by this general. It should still be stressed that even if the emperor's right to rule rested solely on his control of the military forces, as was so well understood by Septimius Severus and Caracalla, it was still necessary for the emperor to court the important members of the senatorial and equestrian classes because their members still formed the moneyed elite of the society, members of which filled up almost all of the important administrative and military positions. The emperors could achieve this by showing proper respect to tradition.

The Central Administration
The imperial central administration of the Roman Empire was initially only an extension of Augustus' own private household, which was located at his palatial residence on the Palatine Hill. Consequently, the central administration of the empire consisted of the emperor, imperial family, *consilium* (private council) and the household staff. Therefore, the private council of the emperor was also initially only an informal body of advisors, but at some point during the second century AD it was reorganized to become an official body of advisors. It is usually thought that this reform was the handiwork of Hadrian.

The advisors of the emperor consisted of persons considered competent and loyal, but outsiders could also be called in to attend meetings when needed. The advisors were initially only given the titles *amici* (friends) or *comites* (companions), but after the council became an official body of permanent advisors they could also be called the *consiliarii* (counsellors/advisors). The *comites* formed an inner circle of trusted friends who also accompanied the emperor on his travels and military campaigns. The *consilium* advised the emperor on matters of domestic and foreign policy, on all military matters, and in cases requiring legal expertise. It is therefore unsurprising that the counsellors usually included well-known jurists (often one of the praetorian prefects). It is not known whether the *protectores* (bodyguards) of Septimius Severus and Caracalla were already considered part of the emperor's *comites*, as they were during the latter half of the third century. The emperor and his body of advisors can roughly be considered to have been the Roman equivalent of the modern government, with ministers and prime minister/president, but with the difference that it was the emperor who made all the decisions. It should be stressed that even though the members of the *consilium* had official positions as advisors of the emperor, his decisions could also be influenced by 'outsiders', the most important of whom were his wife (when he had one), relatives, the staff of the imperial bedchamber and others, depending on the situation.

The next administrative layer below the emperor and his advisors consisted of the emperor's household staff, which was essentially an imperial chancellery consisting of bureaus, departments and ministries. The chancellery/household put into effect the wishes of the emperor so that the empire's resources and military forces were allocated where desired. The household staff originally consisted solely of domestics (imperial freedmen and slaves dressed in white clothes), but from the reign of Hadrian onwards the heads of the departments were equestrian procurators. The staffs of freedmen and slaves below the procurators were organized hierarchically into separate decuries. The procurators of the imperial household were: 1) *a rationibus* (in charge of the imperial accounts, treasury and finances, which included the payments to the troops etc.) assisted by *magister rei privatae* (in charge of emperor's personal finances); 2) *a libellis* (in charge of the petitions to the emperor); 3) *ab epistulis* (imperial correspondence) divided into Greek and Latin sections; 4) *a cognitionibus* (hearing of judicial matters); 5) *a studiis* (preparation of files, reports and dossiers for the emperor); 6) *a censibus* (examination of the financial standing of persons seeking to become senators or equestrians); 7) *a commentariis* (archives); 8) *a memoria* (secretarial services). In addition to this, the emperor's household included many other functionaries, the most important of which were the *cubicularii* of the imperial bedchamber. Thanks to their closeness to the emperor, it was possible for the *cubicularii* (usually eunuchs) to gain considerable influence on the emperor, his wife (when he had one) and children. It should be noted that the teachers usually had the greatest influence upon the children of the emperor, which meant that their actions too had a direct influence upon destiny of the empire.

The Senate, made up of the senators, was still officially the legislative body of the empire which nominated the administrators and the emperor, and voted about treaties with foreign powers and so forth. In truth, its role had already become largely ceremonial under Octavianus Augustus. In practice, the Senate only confirmed the appointment of the emperor, and acted as an advisory body and confirmed the emperor's decisions when he so desired. Officially, the Senate retained control of Italy and the provinces left under its jurisdiction, but in truth the emperor could intervene in their affairs at his will. The emperor controlled every bit of land in the empire as he wished, so long as he retained control of the armed forces.

The Administrative Areas
The administration of the Roman Empire consisted of geographical areas: 1) Rome; 2) Italy; 3) the Provinces. The city of Rome, the capital of the empire with about a million inhabitants, was controlled and fed by the emperor through his representative, the *Praefectus Urbis Romae/Praefectus Urbi* (Urban Prefect of Rome). The feeding of the population was a massive undertaking and required a

huge logistical network to transport the necessary foodstuff from Egypt, North Africa, Sicily, Italy and other places. The city of Rome was particularly reliant on Egyptian and North African corn, which meant that the emperor sought to control and protect these sources of revenue. The city itself was divided into regions, each of which was controlled by a curator. The curators in their turn were under the control of the Urban Prefect. The Urban Prefect controlled the administration of the capital and was responsible for the upkeep of public order.

Italy, which ranked second in the hierarchy, was formally under the jurisdiction of the Senate, but this was a mirage. In practice, the emperor controlled everything through his own representatives. Regardless of this, Italy had some very real advantages over the provinces. The Italians possessed Roman citizenship and were usually not ruled by governors, and, with the exception of the naval forces and *Legio II Parthica* (after its creation by Septimius), they did not have to billet troops in their cities.

Ever since the days of Augustus, the provinces had been divided into imperial and senatorial provinces. The imperial provinces were ruled by imperial legates (*legati Augusti pro praetore*), the length of whose term was dictated by the emperor. The legates in their turn were divided into two categories: 1) senatorial legates; 2) equestrian legates. The senatorial provinces were governed by proconsuls (*proconsulares*) who were chosen by lot from among the senators for a one-year term. All provinces possessed at least small numbers of military forces to enable their governors to perform their duties, but naturally most of these were posted along the frontiers. Either Septimius Severus or Caracalla limited the number of legions per province to two to make usurpation more difficult.[1] The provinces provided the bulk of the taxes and were subjected to the whims of the often-corrupt governors, which the emperors sought to limit.

The Municipal Administration
In their administration of territories, the Romans relied on the services performed at a local level by the city councils. The city council controlled the people, taxation and movement of goods, valuables and money on their territories on behalf of the Roman state. The people living in the Eastern provinces had already been urbanized by the time the Romans conquered them, but in the West it had been the Romans who had founded new cities to perform the necessary duties. The municipal administration of all of the cities of the empire consisted of three levels: 1) the popular assembly of citizens, which was no longer functioning in the third century; 2) the municipal council or Order of Decurions (also called Senate), which consisted of the former magistrates and/or wealthy citizens with the unenviable duty of paying the taxes when those collected fell short of the requirement; 3) the magistrates with executive powers.

1.3. The Armed Forces and the Security Apparatus in c. AD 200

At the beginning of the third century AD, the Roman Empire was ruled by the Emperor Septimius Severus. He had obtained the throne through a civil war in which he had crushed his rivals with the help of his network of North African compatriots and other friends and clients. These men and women had formed Septimius' network of spies and supporters in Italy, at Rome and in the provinces. After having gained the throne, Severus secured his own and his family's position further by taking full advantage of the official arms of the Roman secret services, which consisted of the imperial messengers (*frumentarii*) and other spies (*peregrini*), and of the select trusted members of the bodyguard units. These acted as Severus' eyes and ears, and as his personal assassins. His son, Caracalla, eventually inherited this network of friends and security organs, but unfortunately for him, its loyalties were divided.

The Land Forces

After the reforms of Septimius Severus, the Roman land forces consisted of: 1) the forces posted in or near the capital; 2) regular legions (citizens); 3) regular auxiliary forces (non-citizens and citizens); 4) national *numeri*[2]; 5) veterans called for service; 6) urban and rural paramilitary militias; 7) the allies.

After the first century AD, most of the regular forces (legions, auxiliaries, *numeri*) had been posted close to the borders of the empire to provide a zone of preclusive security for the provinces and the interior. During the Late Empire, these forces were known by the name *limitanei*. The first recorded instance of the use of the term *limitanei* comes from the SHA, which states that there were *limitanei* under Pescennius Niger (Pesc. 7.7) and Alexander Severus (Alex. Sev. 58.4). Unless the term in the SHA is an anachronism, it is therefore possible that the frontier forces may already have received the nickname *limitanei* by the end of the second century, because it was actually an apt description for the forces posted close to the *limes*. The frontier forces, together with the fortifications, walls and forts posted along the border, served four strategic purposes: 1) their presence deterred would-be invaders; 2) the garrison forces could engage the enemy in the border region; 3) the garrisons could be used for surprise attacks over the border and as staging posts for major invasions/raids; 4) they gathered intelligence. The forces posted in or near the capital formed the mobile reserve army at the disposal of the emperor, the numbers of which he could bolster with detachments (*vexillationes*) drawn from the frontier armies, newly raised legions and allies.

The deployment pattern was defensive. The emperors expected that the forces posted along the borders would be sufficient for the task, but when this was not the case it required the transfer of forces from other sections of the frontier, which in turn weakened these sections. It should be remembered that the armed forces posted along the borders and the reserve forces were not the only means at the disposal of the emperor to secure the empire's borders. In addition to these, the emperor employed a network of alliances, spies and diplomacy to provide a secure environment for his subjects, and if everything else failed he sought to divide his enemies, first through diplomacy and then by employing a combination of alliances, diplomacy and military action to secure the relevant section of the frontier. When the emperor felt that his own prestige or the prestige of Roman arms required offensive military action, he usually assembled an army consisting of his bodyguard units, detachments drawn from the frontier forces and the allied forces, and then either invaded or even conquer enemy territory. The goals of Roman foreign and military policy obviously varied according to the personality of the emperor and his political needs.

When the frontier installations and garrisons proved insufficient for the task and the neighbours were able to invade or raid Roman territory, the Roman strategic doctrine demanded that fear of Roman arms had to be reinstated with punitive raids and campaigns, that also brought booty and glory for the emperor. Contrary to modern popular opinion among Classicists, the spoils of war and military glory were (and are) also valuable goals in their own right, because both served to make the position of the emperor more secure in the eyes of the army and people, and also made him look more formidable in foreign eyes. In the absence of true reserve armies, the concentration of significant numbers of men on one spot meant the dispatch of detachments of forces from other sections of the frontier. The mobile reserve forces posted in and around the city of Rome were in themselves insufficient to meet major crises. The only way to avoid this was to raise new legions in Italy, as had been done for example by Trajan, Marcus Aurelius and Septimius Severus, but the quality of these new legions was obviously not the same as veteran formations, unless the core around which each new legion was formed included significant numbers of troops transferred from existing legions. The quality of each existing legion diminished in the same proportion as they recruited/enlisted/conscripted new recruits/conscripts to replace the men they had sent to form the new legions.

Legions
After the reforms of Septimius Severus, the legionary forces appear to have been organized for combat in three different manners, all of which were based on a basic file of eight men. The reason for this was that the size of the legionary units varied according to the type of force. The legionary forces when on campaign consisted of the complete old-style regular legions, legionary detachments and the new type of legions adopted by Septimius Severus for his Parthian legions.

It is usually assumed that the regular legion had a paper strength of about 5,120 heavy infantrymen, plus the recruits, servants, horsemen and specialists. On the basis of Josephus' text, it is also usually assumed that the legionary cavalry consisted of 120 or 128 men, but this is a mistake. In truth, the relevant part of Josephus' text referred only to the number of horsemen accompanying each legion in the marching formation, but at the same time Josephus stated that there were other horsemen in front and rear. Consequently, it is more than likely that the typical cavalry component of each imperial legion still consisted of the traditional *ala* of 512 horsemen. This system appears to have been adopted when Marius (John Lydus, *De Magistr.* 1.16) reformed the legions so that they consisted of 6,000 infantry and 600 cavalry, which seems to have served as the model for Augustus when he formed his imperial legions. The 6,000 footmen and 600 horsemen would have also included recruits, servants, specialists and officers, so that the actual fighting strength of the legion would have been probably about 4,800 infantry and 512 cavalry. The size of the legion was increased during the latter half of the first century so that the first cohort of the legion became a military cohort and its actual fighting strength became the 5,120 footmen as stated above.

The referrals to the different-sized cavalry units in Pseudo-Hyginus (5.30) and John Lydus (*De Magistr.* 1.46) suggest the possibility that by the end of the second century the size and type of legionary cavalry may have varied. The reason for this conclusion is that Pseudo-Hyginus does not include any *equites legionis* for his three legions, but mentions 1,600 *vexillarii legionum*, which suggests that these *vexillarii* were the legionary cavalry of the three legions in question. Pseudo-Hyginus' figures are consistent with the 500-horseman *turmae* of mounted archers, 500-horseman *vexillationes* and 600-horseman *alae* mentioned by John Lydus (*De Magistr.* 1.46), hence the possibility that three legions may have had three different types of cavalry (*alae, vexillationes, turmae*) attached to them.

The only anomaly is Vegetius, who claims that the legions had three different totals of 726, 732 and 736 horsemen, plus the supernumeraries. My own educated guess is that the regular component consisted of 726 men (one of the figures), which was made up of twenty-two *turmae* (22 x 32 + 22 decurions) and when one adds to this figure seven centurions and a standard-bearer, trumpeter and cape-bearer, one reaches the figure of 736 (the last of the numbers), but in addition to this there would have been a separate tribune or prefect who would have served as the overall commander of the entire cavalry unit. Vegetius' figure may represent the size of the cavalry units among Septimius Severus' reformed Parthian legions, or the strength of the cavalry component after the reforms of Gallienus or the enlarged cavalry component under Gallienus' successors. My own belief is that Vegetius' enlarged cavalry component was adopted by Septimius Severus.

The traditional infantry component of the regular legion consisted of ten cohorts, of which the first cohort had 800 legionaries (plus 100 recruits and 100 servants), with the rest of the cohorts having 480 (plus recruits and servants). Each of the regular cohorts from two to ten consisted of six centuries (eighty men plus recruits and servants), which were grouped as maniples of 160 men for combat, when the men used *pila*-javelins. The first cohort consisted of five double-strength centuries of 160 men. The legion therefore consisted of fifty-nine centuries. The tent group called *contubernium* was the basic building block of the army and its combat formation. It consisted of ten men, of whom eight were grouped together to fight as a single eight-man deep file in the rank-and-file battle formation. The commander of the *contubernium* and eight-man file was called a *decanus* (commander of ten). In battle, the *decanus* served as the front ranker for the seven-man file behind him. The rest of the *contubernium* consisted of one green recruit *(tiro)* and one servant (with a mule or ass), who were usually left to protect the marching camp when the eight men advanced to fight. In addition to the soldiers making up the *contubernia*, the legions also included artillerymen, medics, doctors, clerks, logistical services, engineers, architects and artisans, among others, to support their operations.

Septimius Severus' reforms did not stop at the reorganization of the strategic dispositions and recruiting of new forces, but also included measures that improved the attractiveness of serving in the armed forces, the auxiliaries included. He increased the salary (with the donatives doubled), allowed the men to marry and allowed the legionaries to wear a golden ring which symbolized their ability to rise through the ranks to the equestrian positions. He also instituted the regular distribution of *donativa* to keep the men happy (paid when the emperor 'assumed the purple' and every five years after that; on family anniversaries like when a child was born; on the calends (first day) of January; to celebrate military victories; and just before and during a campaign to improve the loyalty and morale of the army). The normal length of service for the legionaries was still about twenty-six years, but the new privileges more than compensated for this. It is therefore not surprising that Septimius Severus managed to buy the loyalty of the soldiers for the Severan Dynasty, which after all was the principal goal of his actions.

The highest command positions in the armed forces were reserved for members of the senatorial class, and the positions below them to the equestrians. This meant that commanders of the legions were almost always senators, the exceptions to the rule being the Praetorian Guard, Parthian legions and the legions posted in Egypt, which were all commanded by equestrians. The officers of the regular legion consisted of: 1) one imperial propraetor legate (senatorial rank, in command of the legion or legions, if governor); 2) one laticlavian tribune (senatorial rank, second-in-command, a young nobleman learning the soldiering); 3) one camp prefect (third-in-command, an experienced veteran in charge of the camp); 4) five angusticlavian prefects (equestrian rank, in charge of cohorts etc.); 5) one (?) *sexmenstris* tribune possibly in charge of the legionary cavalry. The non-commissioned officers of the first cohort, in order of seniority, consisted of the centurions *primus pilus, princeps prior, hastatus prior, princeps posterior* and *hastatus posterior*. The rest of the centurions, in order of seniority, consisted of *pilus prior, princeps prior, hastatus prior, pilus posterior, princeps posterior* and *hastatus posterior*. The soldiers were also hierarchically ranked.[3] See the diagram of the organization which is based on my monograph *A Military History of Late Rome 284–361* Volume 1 and Bohec (1994).

Probable command structure of the regular legion c. AD 90–260
- 1 Legate (S) until the reign of Gallienus, who abolished the office; or prefect (E) for the Egyptian and Parthian legions. After Gallienus, the commanders were prefects (E); commander of the legion.
- 1 Laticlavian tribune (S) changed by Gallienus into *tribunus maior* (E); in charge of one cohort and second-in-command of the legion.
- 1 *Praefectus Castrorum* (camp, medics, siege equipment etc.) (E).
- 1 *Praefectus Fabrorum* (workmen, construction etc.) (E).
- 5 tribunes (E), each in charge of one cohort of 480 men.
- 1 *tribunus sexmenstris* (in charge of cavalry?) (E).
- 5 centurions of the first cohort (incl. *primus pilus* who could act as *praepositus* for the cohort).
- 54 centurions (called *centenarii* by the end of the third century):
    5 unattached centurions that could be detailed for variety of purposes; these could be used as e.g. acting *praepositi* (commanders for the cohorts of 480 men).
    9 centurions, each in charge of two centuries (2 x 80 men).
    9 x 4 centurions, each in charge of one century (80 men).
    4 cavalry centurions in charge of 128 horsemen.
- 64 infantry *decani*, one of whom was *optio*/second-in-command to a centurion (each *decanus* part of and in charge of their 8-man file/*contubernium*, in addition to which came a *tiro*/recruit and one servant used for the guarding of the camp).
- 16 cavalry decurions (each in charge of their 32-horseman *turma*).
- First cohort of 800 men (5 centuries of 160 men) plus 100 recruits and 100 servants.
- Cohorts 2–10 = 9 x 420 footmen (including the *decani*, 480) plus 60 recruits and 60 servants per cohort.
- 496 horsemen (with the decurions, 512; Vegetius may have been wrong in adding the decurions to the strength of the *turma*, because the Roman cavalry organization was based on the Greek one. However, if Vegetius is correct, then these should be added to the total for a total of 512, plus 16 decurions and about 128 servants/squires.
- At least about 715 artillerymen in charge of the 55 *carroballistae* (cart-mounted bolt/arrow shooters) and 10 *onagri* (single-armed stone-throwers).
- 10 *speculatores* (formerly scouts), but now couriers, police officers and executioners.
 Proculcatores and *exploratores* scouted the roads. It is not known whether these counted as part of the cavalry or were separate from it. In practice, the *mensores* could also act as scouts.
- Unknown numbers of military police with the title of *stator*, and unknown numbers of guard dogs. Inside each camp there was also a police station, called a *statio*, under a tribune. Some of the soldiers were also used as sentinels (*excubitores*) and there were other specific guards for various tasks.
- In addition, there were unknown numbers of other specialists and bureaucrats, consisting of surveyors, *campidoctor* (chief instructor), *haruspex* (read the entrails prepared by *victimarius*), *pullarius*, *actuarii*, *librarii* (*librarius a rationibus* also worked for the state post and could act as a spy), *notarii* (could act as spies on the activities of the commander), *commentariensis* (archivist, under a head curator), heralds, standard-bearers, *draconarii*, cape-bearers, trumpeters, drummers, engineers, workmen, artisans, hunters, carters and cartwrights, doctors, medics etc.
- the legates/prefects were also guarded by a unit of *singulares* (both infantry and cavalry), which consisted of detached auxiliaries. (Confusingly the staff officers in training could also be called *singulares*.) These bodyguards were replaced by *protectores* detached by the emperor from his staff, at the latest during the reign of Gallienus, as a safety measure against usurpations.

12   Caracalla

- The legion also included beasts of burden (depending on the units, these could be horses, asses, mules, camels or oxen).
N.B: (S) = senatorial office; (E) = equestrian office

It is quite probable that when Septimius Severus raised his three new Parthian legions in c. 193, he organized those in the manner that can be found in Vegetius. There are four pieces of evidence to back this up, but all are unfortunately inconclusive. Firstly, Dio (86.12.5) refers to a 550-man group of soldiers, which should probably be equated with the size of the 555-man cohort in Vegetius. The problem with this is that we do not know whether the 550-man group is a cohort. Secondly, Modestus includes the same legionary organization in his treatise which is dedicated to the Emperor Tacitus. The problem with this treatise is that some historians consider it a fifteenth-century forgery. Thirdly, the legion was commanded by a prefect, as were the newly raised Parthian legions. Fourthly, the Romans may have adopted from the Germans a new infantry wedge which was called *caput porci/caput porcinum* (the Viking *Svinfylking*) and was quite unlike any previous wedge because it was actually a hollow rhombus, or the array could have been invented by Septimius Severus or by one of his subordinates at a time he created the Parthian legions, or the Germans just used the unit organization they had copied from the Romans. The problem with this is that we do not know for certain when or if the Romans even adopted this formation. The later Viking *Svinfylking* consisted of 1,110 men, which would therefore have consisted of two 555-man cohorts, which does suggest the possibility that the Romans had copied a Germanic unit organization in order to be able to form the 1,110-strong *caput porcinum*, or that the Romans invented it in the second century and the Germans then copied it. Once again this is not conclusive because the evidence is late, but at least it has the advantage of explaining why the Romans would have adopted a new type of wedge with a new unit organization. The reason for the adoption of this new wedge could have been that the eastern Germans had achieved some successes with the *caput porcinum* during the Marcomannic Wars, or that it was a good formation against the Germans, but I am inclined to believe that it was actually adopted only after c. 267 as a result of Odin's conquests because the earliest and only evidence for the use of this type of formation by the Romans comes from Vegetius' text. For further details, see my Odin the Man article included on the academia.edu website. Consequently, when one keeps these caveats in mind there is reason to believe that Septimius Severus did organize his new legions according to the model presented by Vegetius and Modestus, and that it is possible that he may have introduced the hollow rhombus-wedge. This would also mean that the Marcomannic Wars would have brought home the need to increase the size of the cavalry component, because Vegetius' legions had 726 horsemen and not 500 or 600 as previously.

The following list, which is based on my monograph *A Military History of Late Rome* Vol. 1, presents the legionary organization of Vegetius.

Vegetius' Ancient Legion (Epit. 2.6ff.) with additional comments in brackets
- 1 *praefectus legionis*, formerly *legatus*; commander of the legion.
- 1 *tribunus maior*; appointed by the emperor, in charge of one cohort (probably the 1st; second-in-command of the legion).
- 1 *Praefectus Castrorum* (camp, medics, siege equipment etc.).
- 1 *Praefectus Fabrorum* (workmen, construction etc.).
- *tribuni minores* from the ranks (6 tribunes{?} put in charge of the cohorts and cavalry alongside with the *praepositi*).
- 5 centurions of the 1st Cohort (Vegetius' list differs from the other known lists of officers and is also 100 men short of the 1,100 men he gives for the 1st Cohort):
    primus pilus in charge of 4 centuries/400 men (probable standard organization and deployment of 320 heavy infantry deployed 8 deep and 80 light infantry deployed 2 deep)
    primus hastatus 'now called *ducenarius*' in charge of two centuries/200 men (probably 160 heavies and 40 light)
    princeps 1.5 centuries/150 men (probably 120 heavies and 30 light)
    secundus hastatus 1.5 centuries/150 men (probably 120 heavies and 30 light)
    triarius prior 1 century/100 men (probably 80 heavies and 20 light)
- 5 centurions for the cavalry.
- 45 centurions of the 2nd–10th Cohorts each in charge of 100 men, 'now' called *centenarii*.
- 1st Cohort: 1,105 footmen (990 footmen, 110 *decani* and 5 centurions; possible organization behind the numbers could be 800 legionaries incl. the *decani* deployed 8 ranks deep, 200 light infantry deployed two ranks deep and 100 recruits, or 880 heavies deployed 8 ranks deep and 220 light deployed 2 ranks deep plus recruits).
    132 horsemen (128 horsemen and 4 decurions; in truth, the decurions may have been part of the 128 horsemen, in addition to which came one centurion, 2 musicians and one standard-bearer; when trained to do so, the 128 horsemen could form up a rhombus so that at each apex stood one decurion).
- 2nd–10th Cohorts: 9 x 555 footmen (495 footmen, 55 *decani* and 5 centurions; possible organization behind the figures could be 400 legionaries inc. the *decani* deployed 8 ranks deep, 100 light infantry 2 ranks deep and 50 recruits, or 440 heavies deployed 8 deep and 110 light deployed 2 deep plus recruits).
    9 x 66 horsemen (64 horsemen and 2 decurions; as noted above, the decurions should probably be included as part of the 64 horsemen; the 64 men could be formed either as a wedge or two rank-and-file oblongs).
- artillerymen (55 *carroballistae*, each with 11 men and 10 *onagri* per legion), 'squires', servants and various kinds of standard-bearers and musicians, and other specialists like clerks, medics, wood-workers, masons, carpenters, blacksmiths, painters, siege-equipment builders, armourers etc. (*aquiliferi, imaginarii/imaginiferi, signiferi/draconarii, tesserarii, optiones, metatores, librarii, tubicines, cornicines, buccinators, mensores, lignarios, structores, ferrarios, carpentarios, pictores* etc.).
- On the basis of my above hypothesis regarding the organization behind Vegetius' figures, a possible overall fighting strength of Vegetius' legion may have been: 4,400 heavy infantry; 1,100 light infantry; 726 cavalry; at least 660 *artillerymen* with 55 *carroballistae* and 10 *onagri*; at least 550 recruits left to defend the marching camp, together with the servants and workmen. The extra men on top of the older paper strengths may actually represent the recruits not normally included in armed strengths, but one cannot be entirely sure of that. It is possible that the recruits also accompanied the legion into combat, as Dio's referral to 550 men does suggest this. The obvious problem with Vegetius' information and my reconstruction based on it is that we have practically

no evidence to corroborate it, but if one presents the information in this manner it does make sense and is therefore plausible. Vegetius notes that the legion could also include several milliary cohorts, which probably refers to the Praetorians (which had milliary cohorts after Septimius's reign) or to the practice of Vegetius's own day to group together different units to form 'temporary legions' that were later called *mere* by the Eastern Romans (sing. *meros*/division).

In practice, the actual fighting strength of the legions rarely reached the paper strength because of injuries, sickness, wounds, deaths and problems with recruiting, but when the Romans were planning to conduct a military campaign, they usually bolstered the numbers with additional recruits so that the units could actually be above their paper strength. However, we should still remember that the legions rarely marched out in their entirety, even when fighting close to their own base. In most cases the legions would have left at least a skeleton force behind to protect their camp, and if the legions operated further away it was far more usual for the legions to dispatch detachments there rather than march the whole legion away from its base. It is possible that the sixth-century author John Lydus describes the organization of such legionary detachments, because none of the other sources give any evidence for such an organization. On the other hand, it is possible that the list proves that the names of the units had changed to reflect the armament carried by the different legionaries so that only those who carried the heavier panoply were considered to belong to the cohorts. It is clear that his list predates Constantine the Great because it fails to mention the *limitanei* and *comitatenses* and includes the *praetoriani*. This means that we can use it to shed light on the earlier practices.

The sixth-century author Lydus (*De Magistr.* 1.46) states that the professional Roman army consisted of units (*speirai*) of 300 *aspidoforoi* (shield-bearers)[4] called cohorts, cavalry *alae* (*ilai*) of 600 horsemen, *turmae* of 500 horsemen, *vexillationes* of 500 horsemen and legions of 6,000 footmen and the same numbers of horsemen. It is likely that the 6,000 infantry and the same numbers of cavalry refer to the situation that prevailed during the reign of Gallienus, who apparently organized independently operating cavalry units consisting of cavalry detachments. The referrals to the 600-horseman *alae*, 500-horseman *turmae* and 500-horseman *vexillationes* seem to refer to the earlier situation in which each legion was accompanied by one such detachment of cavalry (see above). It also seems probable that we should round up the cohort of 300 *aspidoforoi* to 320 men, so that each detachment/cohort consisted of four centuries of eighty shield-bearers for a total of 320 men (in a depth of four or eight men). Notably, the SHA (Pert. 11.1) refers to a wedge/globe (*cuneus/globus*) of 300 Praetorians who attacked the Imperial Palace in 193. It is possible that this 300-man group should be equated with the 300-man (i.e. 320-man) cohort of John Lydus, but the problem with this is that the Epitome of Dio claims that only the 200 boldest attacked the palace. If one assumes that Dio's shortened text is accurate, it is still possible to reconcile the sources if one assumes that only 200 men out of the 300 made the final attack. Regardless, the uncertainty remains. On the basis of this incomplete evidence, I would still suggest that it is probable that in the course of the second century AD, the Romans started to separate the differently armed soldiers within the legion into different units, so that only the 320 shield-bearers were considered part of the cohort. The actual combat strength of the unit would have remained 480 men, but the light-armed legionaries (*lanciarii, sagittarii, verutarii, funditores, ferentarii*) would have been deployed behind the a*spidoforoi*. The number of light-armed troops would have been 160 so that the total remained (with four heavies and two lights, or eight heavies and four lights) the same 480 men.

Lydus' text is useful for another reason, which is that it includes a comprehensive list of various types of troops. When reading the list, it should be kept in mind, however, that the same men could be used for a variety of roles just by changing equipment, which means that in practice the same man could perform many of the different types of missions mentioned in the list. The inclusion of the *primoscutarii/protectores* in the list suggests that it dates from the third century. This suggests that the list may date from the period between Gallienus and Diocletian, but since the *protectores* are mentioned for the first time in the reign of Septimius Severus/Caracalla, it is possible that it would describe the early third-century army. The inclusion of the *ocreati, hastati/doryforoi, pilarii/akontistai, lanciarii* and *verutarii* should be interpreted to mean that the different ranks in the phalanx were equipped with these pieces of equipment. The front ranks (depending upon the depth of the formation ranks one to two, one to four or one to eight), which consisted of the *aspidoforoi*, would have been equipped either with the *hastae* as *hastati/doryforoi* against cavalry, or with the *pila* as *pilarii/akontistai* against infantry. The first rank of the *aspidoforoi* would have always been equipped with the greaves so that it was called *ocreati*, while the rear ranks would have always used some sort of javelin as the various names (*lancea, verutus*) imply. The archers, slingers and artillerymen would have been deployed behind the *aspidoforoi*.[5] The list is based on the edition and translation of Bundy (Lydus, pp.69–75) and Syvanne (*A Military History of Late Rome*), with some changes.

Lydus' Legions:

alai apo ch hippeôn	*alae* of 600 horsemen (former auxiliary cavalry)
vexillationēs apo f hippeôn	*vexillationes* of 500 horsemen (former legionary cavalry)
tourmai apo f toxotôn hippeôn	*turmae* of 500 mounted archers
legiōnes, legiones apo hexakischiliôn pezôn	legions of 6,000 infantrymen
tribounoi, dēmarchoi	*tribuni*, tribunes
ordinarioi, taxiarchoi, ordinarii	*ducenarii* and centurions?
signiferai, sēmeioforoi	*signiferi*, standard-bearers (during Vegetius' day called *draconarii*)
optiōnes, optiones	options, chosen men (centurion's deputies/vicars) or registrars

16 Caracalla

vēxillarioi, doryforoi	*vexillarii*, spear-bearing men belonging to *vexillationes*, i.e. legionary cavalry
mēnsōres	*mensores*, camp-surveyors
toubikines, salpistai pezōn	*tubicines*, infantry buglers
boukinatōres, salpistai hippeōn	*bucinatores*, cavalry buglers
kornikines, keraulai	*cornicines*, horn-blowers
andabatai, katafraktoi	*andabatae*, cataphract cavalry
mētatōres, chōrometrai	*metatores*, land-surveyors
archytēs kai sagittarioi, toxotai kai beloforoi	*arquites* and *sagittarii*, archers and arrow-bearers
praitōrianoi, stratēgikoi	*praetoriani*, praetorians, general's men
lagchiarioi/lanchiaroi, akontoboloi	*lanciarii*, lance-throwers
dekemprimoi, dekaprōtoi	*decemprimi*, heads of 10 men, *decani*
benefikialioi, hoi epi therapeia tōn beteranōn tetagmenoi	*beneficiales*, those giving medical aid to the *veterani* / veterans.
torkouatoi, streptoforoi, hoi tous maniakas foreuntes	*torquati*, torc-wearers who wear necklaces (rewarded for bravery) and those who wear arm-guards.
brachiatoi, ē toi armilligeroi, pselioforoi	*brachiati* or *armilligeri*, bracelet-wearers (rewarded for bravery)
armigeroi, hoploforoi	*armigeri*, armour-bearers/arms-bearers (hoplon-bearers)
mounerarioi, leitourgoi	*munerarii*, servants or soldiers (*munifices*) doing fatigues and services
dēputatoi, afōrismenoi	*deputati*, deputies appointed for a specific task
auxiliarioi, hypaspistai	*auxiliarii*, auxiliaries (note the use of *hypaspistai*/shield-bearers for foreign troops which is suggestive for their later use as a term for *bucellarii*)
kouspatōres, fylakistai	*cuspatores*, gaolers
imaginiferai, eichonoforoi	*imaginiferi*/*imaginarii*, image-bearers, i.e. bearers of the emperor's image
okreatoi, pezoi sidērōi tas knēmas peripefrakmenoi	*ocreati*, infantry with iron greaves to protect the calves
armatoura prima, hoplomeletē prōtē	*armature prima*, first arms service
armatoura sēmissalia, hoplomeletē meizōn	*armature semissalis*, advanced arms practise
hastatoi, doryforoi	*hastati*, spearmen
tessarioi, hoi ta symbola en tōi kairōi tēs symbolēs tōi plēthei perifēmizontes	*tesserarii*, who announce the watchword to the soldiery at the time of encounter
dracōnarioi, drakontoforoi	*draconarii*, the bearers of the dragon standard
adioutōres, hypoboēthoi	*adiutores*, adjutants
samiarioi, hoi tōn hoplōn stilpnōtai	*semiarii*, the polishers of arms
baginarioi/vaginarioi/thēkopoio	*vaginarii*, scabbard-makers
arkouarioi, toxopoioi	*arcuarii*, bow-makers
pilarioi, akontistai	*pilarii*, javelin throwers

beroutarioi, veroutarioi, diskoboloi	*verutarii*, throwers of *verutum/spiculum* javelin (Veg: shaft 3.5ft, iron tip 5in.)
founditōres, sfendonētai	*funditores*, slingers
ballistarioi, katapeltistai (katapeltēs de estin eidos helepoleōs, kaleitai de tōi plēthei onagros	*ballistarii*, catapult-men. A catapult is a kind of city-taker/siege engine; it is called by the soldiers/multitude *onager* (wild ass)
binearioi, vinearioi, teichomachoi	*vinearii*, wall-fighters or men who fought with the siege sheds
primoskoutarioi, hyperaspistai, hoi legomenoi protēktōres	*primoscutarii*, shield-bearers who are now called *protectores*
primosagittarioi, toxotai prōtoi	*primosagittarii*, first archers (i.e. mounted bodyguard or commanders of light infantry?)
klibanarioi, holosidēroi. kēlibana gar hoi Rhōmaioi ta sidēra kalummata kalousin, anti tou kēlamina	*clibanarii*, the horsemen who wear iron armour, for the Romans call iron coverings *celibana*, that is to say *celamina*
flammoularioi, hōn epi tēs akras tou doratos foinika rhakē exērtēnto	*flammularii*, who bear at the end of their spears scarlet banners
expeditoi, euzōnoi, gymnoi, hetoimoi pros machēn	*expediti*, well-girt, lightly clad and mobile, ready for battle (i.e. non-encumbered with baggage train and lightly equipped for ease of movement)
ferentarioi, akrobolistai	*ferentarii*, skirmishers
kirkitōres, hoi peri tous machomenous periiontes kai chorēgountes hopla mētō epistamenoi machesthai	*circitores*, who go about the fighters and give them arms
adōratōres, beteranoi, teirōnes	*adoratores*, honourably retired soldiers; *veterani*, those who had grown old while in service; *tirones*, recruits not yet permitted to fight.

The legionary equipment and tactics[6]

The legionary equipment of the early third century did not only vary according to the tactical role of the soldiers, but from one legion to another. The principal differences, however, always resulted from the intended use in combat. If the intention was to fight a pitched battle, the men were usually equipped with armour and heavier equipment, but if the purpose was to fight as skirmishers or in difficult terrain, the men could be equipped with lighter equipment. Therefore the legionary armour could consist of: 1) the traditional *lorica segmentata* (segmented plate armour) of the Newstead-type (the usual type); 2) the *lorica squamata* (scale armour); 3) *lorica hamata* (mail armour); 4) rigid and soft leather armour; 5) muscle armour (bronze or rigid leather); 6) a *thoracomachus* or *subarmalis* (padded coat of linen, leather or felt) was always used under the armour, but could also be used on its own; 7) no armour. It is not known whether the so-called *lorica plumata* (mail with small scales attached) was still used as it was during the first century, but one may make the educated guess that it was because all kinds of armour and ersatz armour continued to be used. It is also possible that composite armour consisting of segmented armour and mail was introduced at this time (Elliot, pp.90–92). The front-rankers could also wear a *manica* (armguard, vambrace) to protect the sword-arm, and a greave to protect the left lower leg or greaves. The *lorica segmentata* was a light and highly specialized type of armour which protected the shoulders (in particular) against downward sword cuts. It increased the mobility of the swordman. It was very costly to manufacture and maintain and was largely replaced by mail and scale armour in the course of the third century as it was increasingly difficult for the legionary armourers to find the time to produce the segmented armour when the armies were constantly on the move. In fact, the gradual abandonment of the *segmentata* armour in favour of the longer mail and scale armours was symptomatic of the trend in evidence from the Marcomannic Wars onwards. The legionaries used more and more armour, together with more protective helmets and shields.

By the early third century AD, the legionary shield (*scutum*) was usually oval in shape, but the traditional rectangular curved shield and several other types continued to be used. The traditional *scutum* (both oval and rectangular ones) had traditionally been curved, but by the late second century the curvature had become less pronounced so that the difference between the legionary shield and auxiliary flat shield had largely disappeared. In fact, most legionaries and auxiliaries were using the same slightly domed oval shields. The only difference with the earlier auxiliary shield was that the late second and third-century oval shields were slightly larger in size. According to the consensus opinion among historians and archaeologists, the heavily curved shield had meant that the legionaries had concentrated solely on fighting in close order so that the shield protected the legionary's left side and front, and he could concentrate on using a sword with his right hand.[7] The following illustration (based on Roman works of art) shows the types of shield used by the Roman infantry and cavalry during the second and third centuries.

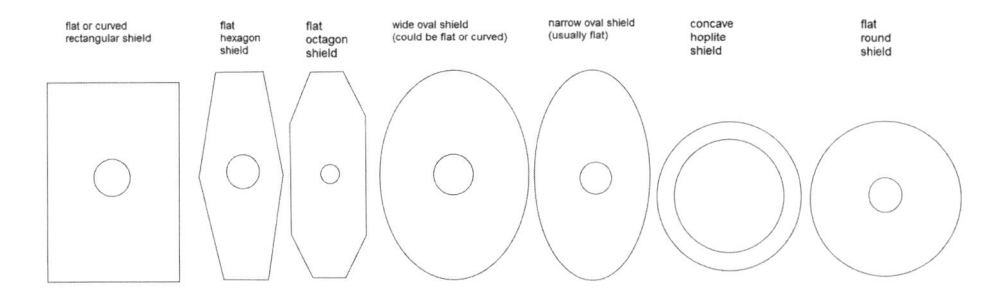

flat or curved rectangular shield | flat hexagon shield | flat octagon shield | wide oval shield (could be flat or curved) | narrow oval shield (usually flat) | concave hoplite shield | flat round shield

It is not usually noted, but the Roman shields also had three different kinds of grips:[8] 1) the single horizontal handle behind the boss which was used for punching (on the rectangular *scutum*, oval and hexagon shield, round shield); 2) the old hoplite/cavalry grips/leather straps with grips for hand/wrist and arm, which was particularly good for shield bashing and shoving and for use in phalanx with spears (oval, round, hexagon and octagon shields); 3) shields with both styles of grips (hexagon, octagon, oval and round shields). This is important to note because the difference in the grips and shields required different fighting styles, with the implication that different kinds of fighting styles were used with different shields. Each of these shield types required the use of different kinds of unit orders and combat tactics.

In my opinion, the use of the curved shields meant the exact opposite as usually suggested. Since the curvature of the shield prevented the effective overlapping of the shields, it is clear that the legionaries had always fought in a more open formation (shields usually in rim-to-rim array, each individual file occupying about 66–90cm in width) in pitched battles than the auxiliaries. On top of that, it is clear that the use of the curved shield was also better suited to sword-fighting with shortswords by individual legionaries than the flat shield used by the auxiliaries, because the curvature protected the left side of the fighter. This in turn required better fighting morale from the legionaries, who had to fight as individuals. They did not have the physical and psychological support provided by the shoulder-to-shoulder, rim-to-boss array to help them. The fact that by the late second century most of the legionaries had adopted the oval flat shield meant that the way in which the legionaries fought had also undergone a change. The flat shield could be used to form rim-to-boss arrays with overlapping shields, which means that the phalanx had probably become the standard fighting formation for most of the legions. In terms of tactics, the overlapping of the shields meant that the men were better protected against enemy missiles and that the combat formations were more orderly, but this was achieved at the cost of limiting the ability of the men to fight as individuals. In addition to this, when the array assumed the closest order (*synaspismos*, *testudo*, *foulkon*) with the the shields overlapping each other in width, it was less easy to manoeuvre the array to meet new threats. This suggests that the general standard of the legionary recruits had probably fallen from the previous period, which is not surprising in light of the fact that the salaries had stayed the same for long periods of time. The authorities no longer expected that the individual legionaries would stay and fight, if faced with a determined enemy. It was preferable to use mass formations consisting of shield-walls which prevented the possibility of easy flight, and leave the fighting in open formation to the elite of the legions and/or the specialized *antesignani/lanciarii*. The fact that the legionaries had adopted less mobile tactics also made the use of the *lorica segmentata* redundant. There was no longer need for lighter armour to increase mobility.

The legions had always included men who were used as skirmishers or as light infantry, and their role grew in importance when the rest of the men became tied up in the rank-and-file formations. All regulars were also taught the use of slings and at least a quarter to a third of the men were taught how to use bows. The early name for the elite skirmishers appears to have been *velites* or *antesignani* (those who fought before the *signa*/standards). In the early third century, they received a new name, *lanciarii* (*lancea*-bearers). Since the first known infantry *lanciarius* belonged to the Legio II Parthica, it is possible that Septimius Severus had named his skirmishers in that manner.[9] It seems probable that these *lanciarii* could also form a wedge in front of the battle line to break up an enemy cavalry charge in the manner described by the tactical treatises. When deployed for combat, the rear-rankers of the battle formations (ranks five to eight in an eight-rank formation or nine to sixteen in sixteen ranks) also consisted of these *lanciarii*. The light-armed *lanciarii*, slingers and archers could be used in front of the battle line for skirmishing, and could also be formed on the flanks to subject the enemy to crossfire. If used for skirmishing, the light-armed troops were always withdrawn behind the heavily equipped men before the melee.

The legionary helmet was also undergoing changes at the turn of the third century. The tendency was to increase the protection provided by the helmet to strikes from above and at the neck, throat and face. This is most visible in the adoption of the so-called Imperial Italic H (Niedermörmter) helmet and in the use of cavalry helmets by infantry (e.g. Niederbieber, Buch, Regensburg, Friedberg, Kalkar-Hönnepel, Dura), but the Romans continued to use other types of helmets (variants of older helmets, segmented, leather etc.).[10] The use of these helmets had implications for the way in which the legionary could fight. This was particularly true of the cavalry helmet. The use of neckguards and cheek-pieces that extended down to the neck and throat meant that the head had to be held more upright than before. Bishop & Coulston (pp.174–75) and Elliot speculate that this meant that the legionaries had adopted a more upright stance than previously to facilitate the use of the longer *spatha*-swords (plu. *spathae*, double-edged longsword), the *hasta*-spear, oval shields and cavalry helmets, but this is only partially true because the helmet did not prevent the bending of the knees, even if it did prevent free movement of the neck and head. Regardless, it is still clear that the adoption of these helmets forced a more upright posture for the neck and head in all fighting stances.

The shafted weapons of the legionaries consisted of the traditional *pilum* (heavy javelin), *hasta* (spear) and *lancea* (two variants: light javelin and thrusting spear). The *pilum* was a heavy javelin with a maximum throwing distance of about 20m, but it could also be used as a thrusting weapon. The *hasta* could be used either as a thrusting or throwing weapon. The *hasta* was a 2.5–3.74m long spear (the exact dimensions are not known),[11] which was used by the front rankers (in the eight-rank formation the ranks one to four). In either case, the standard combat doctrine against infantry was that the front rankers threw their javelins/spears and then used

Background   21

underarm grip
use: thrusts

© Dr. Ilkka Syvänne 2014
left figure drawn
partially after Elliot

overarm grip
use: throws, thrusts

longer reach with a thrust, no throwing

shorter reach with a thrust, but longer reach with a throw

legio X Gemina

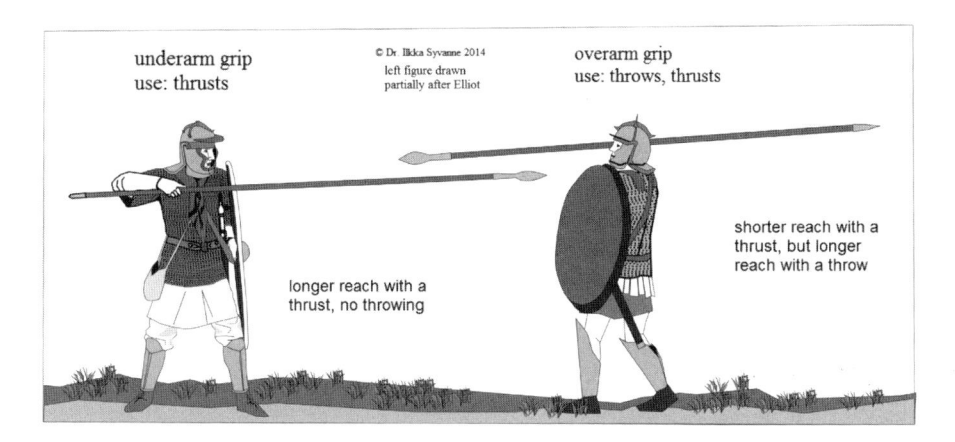

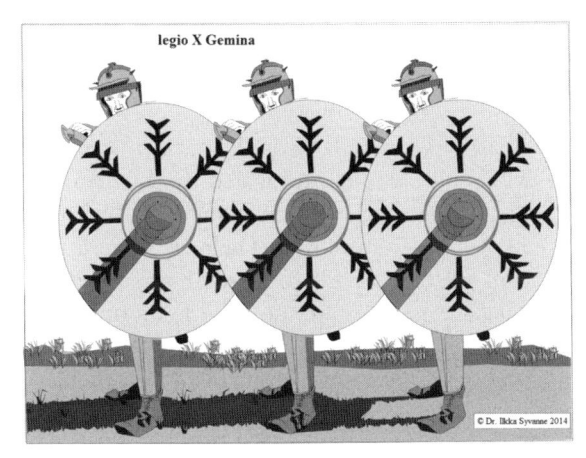

The use of the oval and round shields enabled the use of the underarm grip together with the overlapping shields. The shield emblem of the *legio X Gemina* is taken from the Notitia Dignitatum (turn of the fifth century). Compare with the bull-emblem suggested by Dando-Collins.

legio X Gemina
(emblem according to Dando-Collins)

underarm technique with the rectangular scutum = impossible to form a real shield wall with overlapping shields.

overarm technique = interlocking of the shields possible, but at the cost of shorter reach with the spear = it was wiser to throw the spear and use sword if one had the rectangular scutum.

swords, while the spearmen/javeliners behind supported them with spear thrusts or with thrown weapons. The *hasta* and *pilum* could also be used as thrusting weapons with the overarm and underarm techniques. The standard tactic against cavalry was to use the *pila/hastae/*heavy *lancea* as thrusting weapons, but these could still be thrown when needed. The light javelin *lancea* was used by the rear rankers (ranks four to eight in an eight-man file) and skirmishers. The maximum effective range for this weapon was about 30–40m.[12]

The typical bladed weapons consisted of the *spatha* (long-sword), *semi-spatha* (short-sword, the equivalent of the earlier *gladius*) and *pugio* (dagger), but *gladius* and other types of bladed weapons continued to be used. The legions had adopted the *spatha* as their primary bladed weapon in the course of the second century, so that along with the oval flat shield their fighting tactics became the same as had been with the auxiliary forces. It is usually assumed that the *spatha* became the principal bladed weapon because the legionaries were increasingly facing cavalry-based enemies, which made it necessary to use longer swords. The *spatha* was used as a cut-and-thrust sword that could be used either way. The shorter *semi-spatha* (*machaira*) was primarily used in infantry combat, and was probably used mainly as a thrusting weapon even if it was usable for both thrusts and cuts. It is possible that the *semi-spatha* meant the so-called ring-pommel swords (48cm long, originally a Sarmatian sword) which were introduced during the second century. The dagger was used only as an emergency weapon at really close quarters.

It seems probable that the Roman legionary equipment and tactics changed during the so-called Antonine Revolution, mainly as a result of the lessons learnt during the Marcomannic Wars. It was following these contacts that the Romans borrowed pieces of equipment from the Germans and Sarmatians. These included the use of trousers (German), ring-pommel sword (Sarmatian) and scabbards (Sarmatian). The fact that the Romans were increasingly facing cavalry-based enemies (Goths, Sarmatians and Parthians) had also resulted in the adoption of the *spatha* as the main infantry sword thanks to its slightly longer reach. The use of the *spatha* in turn made the curved rectangular *scutum* less useful because its straight edges hindered the use of the weapon for cuts, hence the adoption of the oval shield. The oval shield in its turn facilitated the use of the spear for thrusts and the use of the phalangial array, which was also better suited to facing cavalry-based enemies, so that the changes in equipment were mutally complementary. When the legions adopted the oval or round shield with the phalangial formation, the adoption of the cavalry helmet became useful because it provided better protection for men when they stood in a shield wall which had 'holes' in the defences resulting from the oval or round shape of the shields.[13] For the different styles of sword (thrust, cut, stab, slash) and spear fighting at close quarters, see the Adamklisi images in Chapter 6.

It should be noted, however, that there is one common mistake that needs to be corrected regarding the way in which the new pieces of equipment and the tactics to go with them came into existence among the Roman legions. It was not the result of soldiers copying from each other what was useful. At a local level, the governor could order a sometimes ad hoc adoption of new equipment and tactics to counter enemy tactics, but empire-wide changes could result only from an order of the emperor. The best proofs of this are: 1) The Romans generally used similar pieces of equipment and tactics, which suggests some central organizing body behind these; 2) Arrian (e.g. Tact. 44.1–2) clearly refers to very specific orders of Hadrian regarding the way in which the forces were to train (including weaponry and equipment) for tactical manoeuvres, which are also confirmed by inscriptions at Lambaesis. There is no doubt at all that all empire-wide changes in tactical doctrine and equipment were the result of imperial commands. In sum, all soldiers were trained to fight in the manner specified by the central government, but there were still local differences resulting from the adaptation of the armed forces to meet local challenges – a sign of flexibility.

In addition to this, the legions also included a number of other specialists, including clubmen, archers, slingers, siege-engineers and artillerymen. A quarter to a third of the legionaries were trained as archers, and all men were trained to use slings and throw stones. Depending on the depth of the heavy infantry array, the archers and slingers usually formed the ranks nine to twelve or seventeen to twenty-four (these consisted of auxiliaries when possible). When needed, the legionaries could even use spades, axes, hatchets, pickaxes and so forth. In fact, legionaries could be expected to perform a great variety of tasks as required, which was a necessity when the auxiliaries did not possess adequate numbers of archers and slingers to support the legions. The Roman bows included the recurved composite bows, wooden bows, crossbows with composite or metal construction (*arcuballista*) and torsion-powered crossbows (*manuballista*). The slingers used either the traditional sling or the staff-sling. The artillerymen employed torsion or tension-powered (steel or bronze springs) *ballistae*/catapults (dart, spear and stone throwers) and *onagri* (stone throwers) of various calibres. The siege-engineers in their turn used various other kinds of siege engines.[14]

The legionary cavalry appears to have been equipped like the rest of the regular Roman cavalry, so they could vary their equipment according to the needs of the moment. The four-horned cavalry saddle gave the riders a secure platform from which to act as javelin throwers, lancers, swordsmen, archers and crossbowmen. Arrian's description of cavalry training and the composition of the legionary cavalry prove that the legionary cavalry could be used as line cavalry, and assault and skirmish troops as needed. We do not know whether there were any differences in equipment between legionary cavalry and auxiliary cavalry, but it is possible that at least some of the former were equipped with *lorica segmentata* (shown in the Columns of Marcus Aurelius and Trajan), while the auxiliaries were not. The rest of the cavalry would have used other types of armour (mail, scale, muscle cuirass, lamellar) or padded coats of leather/felt/linen as needed. Thanks to the fluid nature of cavalry combat, the cavalry helmets had always provided more protection than the

24 Caracalla

Eastern auxiliary archers. Note the use of segmented helmets also worn by the Sarmatians and Parthians.

Legionary cavalry in the Column of Trajan (Bertoli and Bartolo, 1704). It is quite possible that the type of armour worn by the legionary cavalry was a reflection of the equipment worn by the legionary infantry so that when infantry changed its equipment so did the cavalry.

The legionaries did most of the manual and engineering work associated with the marching camps, sieges and building projects.

Various types of auxiliaries (Germanic clubmen, regular auxiliaries, Eastern archers, slingers) fighting against the Dacians in Trajan's Column while the legions watched behind.

The legions possessed also field artillery drawn by horses, which could be transported quickly from one part of the field to another as required by the situation.

Background 25

Top Left: Centurion Q. Sertorius Festus (gladius, ocreae, sagum, vitis in right hand, calceus, lorica squamata or lorica plumata); probably late 1st century; Text: Q. Sertorius, L. f. Pob. Festus, centur, leg XI Claudine piae fidelis. Source and drawn after: Lindenschmit. Centurion's cross-plumed helmet added below the man.

Top Right: Tombstone of legionary C. Valerius Crispus, Wiesbaden. According to Bishop and Coulston (pp.10-11) late 1st or early 2nd century (pilum, gladius, leather armour, scutum, possibly cavalry style helmet). Text: C(aius) Valerius C(aii) f(ilius) Berta, Menenia (tribu) Crispus, mi (les) leg(ionis) VIII Aug(ustae) an (norum) XL stip(endiorum) XXI f (rater) f(aciendum) c(uravit). Sources for the illustration and text: Lindenschmit and D'Amato.

The shield-emblem of the *legio II Parthica* is based on Dando-Collins' reconstruction, but on the basis of the extant tombstones it is likelier that the emblem was actually a cross as shown here.

there were several different types of pila some of which are shown here

Roman legionary
Legio II Parthica
- *hasta*, *spatha*, oval shield, Heddernheim helmet, greaves, manica arm-protection and *lorica hamata*.

(drawn partially after the reconstruction of A. Zimmermann in Gräf)

© Dr. Ilkka Syvänne 2014

the hasta was primarily used against cavalry, but could also be used against infantry

Roman legionary
Legio II Italica
- pilum, spatha, lorica segmentata Newstead, helmet Imperial Italica II/Niedermormter, rectangular shield.

(drawn partially after Cascarino)

a socketed *pilum* with a triple weight

the pilum was primarily used against infantry, but could also be used against cavalry

tanged pila

a socketed *pilum* with a double weight

a socketed *pilum* with a single weight, the shaft bound with a cord

26   Caracalla

legionary cavalry (?) in the Column of Aurelius (drawing by Petrus Bellorius and Petro Bartolo 1704)

A funerary relief of a cavalryman, Apulum (Alba Julia), 2nd century AD, probably *eques vexillationis* of the *legio XIII Gemina*. Equipment according to D'Amato: a helmet with an eagle metallic crest (Hedderheim-type), scale armor, sword, two javelins (à la Josephus, Bellum Judaicum 3.5.5.96). (drawn after D'Amato/Sumner).

Tombstone of C. Marius, Bonn, legionary cavalry
C(aius) Marius Lucii) f(ilius) Vol (tinia tribu) Luco Augusti Eques leg(ionis) Iannor(um) XXX stip (endiorum) XV h(ic) e(st), Sex(tus) Sempronius frater facien(dum) curavit. Drawn after Lindenschmit.

the torsion-powered crossbow was a very useful weapon for land and naval battles and for siege warfare.

infantry ones, and the same tendency continued. It was even possible to use the so-called parade helmets with face masks to complete the protective cover. The horses could also wear protective side coverings and chamfrons. On the basis of Arrian's description of cavalry training, the martial equipment used by the cavalry consisted of the various types of spears/lances (*lancea*, *xyston*, *hasta*, Gallic *contus*), *spatha* sword, *pugio* dagger, sling, composite bow and crossbow. The *lancea* and *xyston* were either thrown or used for thrusting (with underarm, overarm etc. techniques). The *hasta* and Gallic *contus* were primarily used for thrusting, but could also be thrown if needed. On horseback, the *spatha* was primarily used for cuts, but could also be used effectively as a thrusting weapon.

The military also wore and carried clothing and equipment that separated them from the rest of the populace. These included military-style belts and buckles, fittings, long-sleeved tunics, tents, tight trousers and looser trousers, military cloaks (*sagum*-cloak, hooded cloaks called *caracalla/caracallus*, which were lengthened by Caracalla, *birrus*-cloak and other types), and studded shoes (a variety of open and closed types).

The illustrations and Plates section show some of the equipment worn by the legions and other units. Note the great variety of equipment.

Auxiliaries, National Numeri and Temporary Allies
The regular auxiliaries of the Imperial period consisted of units of around 500–1,000 men. During the early period, the provincials had flocked to the auxiliary corps because it was possible to obtain Roman citizenship after service or during it by distinguished service, but by the late second century the Romans faced serious recruiting problems. Antonius Pius' Edict had ensured that the children of auxiliaries did not become citizens automatically, on top of which the auxiliaries were required to serve for twenty-eight years before discharge, not to mention the fact that a significant proportion of the auxiliaries were now citizens. This meant that service in the *auxiliary infantry* was becoming ever more unpopular in comparison with service in the legions. It was probably because of this that in the course of the second century, the Romans recruited ever-increasing numbers of so-called national *numeri* from tribesmen. The Romans wanted to retain at least the same numbers of auxiliaries as there had been before.

The *auxilia* proper consisted of the cavalry *alae* (wings), equipped with different pieces of equipment according to the combat needs or origin of the unit; 'medium' infantry, usually equipped with a basic helmet, mail, scale or ersatz armour or with no armour at all, flat shields, *hasta* spear or *lancea* spears and/or javelins, and *spatha* sword (long double-edged sword); mixed units of cavalry and infantry; foot archers; and slingers (slings and staff slings). Note, however, that some auxiliaries are known to have used typical legionary equipment. Some of the cavalry units appear to have been equipped as javelin throwers, mounted archers or as Sarmatian-style *kontoforoi*, armed with a Sarmatian *kontos/contus* (a heavy spear used with two hands), sword and bow; and at least one cataphract *ala* (armoured man and horse) is also known to have existed. The auxiliary cavalry formed the bulk of the Roman cavalry forces, and thanks to the varied training schemes could be expected to perform whatever tactical role (light or heavy cavalry, skirmishers or shock troops) the commander required. The 'medium' infantry also performed multiple roles. It was equally adaptable to scouting, skirmishing and pitched battle. On the battlefield, the 'medium' infantry could be used either as javelin throwers or as spearmen thanks to their varied equipment, while their standard battle formation was the phalanx. The light-armed auxiliaries were naturally used as missile troops, both as skirmishers and as line troops. The only role in which the *auxilia* had a clear weakness in comparison with the legions was their relative lack of artillery and siege engineering skills.

The following list, which is based on my MHLR (Vol.1) and Le Bohec (1994), summarizes the organization of the auxiliary units, but it should be noted that in practice the actual size of the units varied greatly. Thanks to the fact that the auxiliaries were organized in similar-sized units as the legions, it was possible to organize them similarly on the battlefield. The cavalry *alae* were commanded by prefects. The around 500-man *cohors quingenaria* were also commanded by prefects, but the around 1,000-man *milliaria* units were commanded by tribunes. The prefects and tribunes belonged to the equestrian class. It is probable that the tribunes were assisted by sub-prefects. The 32-horseman cavalry *turmae* were commanded by decurions. The senior decurion was called the *decurion princeps*. Centurions were placed in charge of groupings of three *turmae*. The auxiliary foot was commanded by centurions. In addition to this, the auxiliary units naturally included a great variety of support personnel (clerical staff, logistical services etc.), just like the legions.

The national *numeri* consisted of units raised from tribes and client kingdoms. The *numeri* appear to have consisted of volunteers and of men forced into Roman service as a result of defeat. Some of the units were short-lived, but others became part of the permanent military establishment. The *numeri* were therefore like mercenaries that were raised when needed and then disbanded when not needed, unless the Romans integrated these units permanently into their armed forces, for example as garrison troops. The availability of the national units added flexibility to the system. It was possible to raise these units fast and then dismiss them from service if there was no further use for them. The size (100–1,000 men) and composition could also be varied as needed. Additionally, the raising and maintaining of these units cost less than the maintaining of the regular establishment. By using the *numeri*, the Romans could also exploit the national characteristics of the recruits. For example, it was possible to avoid the very time-consuming and expensive process of training mounted archers (which the Romans did with the regular units) simply by raising new units of mounted archers in the East that cost less than the regulars. The national *numeri* were commanded by legionary centurions designated as *praepositi*, and the larger units occasionally by men of equestrian class. The NCOs appear to have consisted of Romans or Romanized provincials. In addition to these, there would have been clerks, cooks and other detached staff to support the operations. In some cases the *numeri* were grouped together with legions, or less often with auxiliaries, so they were placed under the commander of the legion or auxiliary unit.[15]

It is possible that the system of *seniores* and *iuniores* units dates from this era, because there existed a unit called *equites itemque pedites iuniores Mauri* during the reign of Caracalla (Handy, p.176). In this system, the 'mother unit', which was called the *seniores* unit, dispatched a part of its force as a detachment to form a new unit called *iuniores*. It is not known whether this practice was introduced by Septimius Severus or by Caracalla, but the reign of Commodus is also a possibility because he had Parthian archers and Moorish javeliners as bodyguards (Handy, p.176; Herodian 1.15.2). Notably, both Parthian archers and Moorish javeliners are attested among the bodyguard units during the Late Empire and both are also attested among the army which accompanied Caracalla to the East. The name implies that this system of dividing a unit was first introduced among the foreign *numeri* bodyguards because their irregular organization was better suited to this. In short, it is possible that the first *seniores-iuniores* units were already created during the late second century.

In addition to the above, the Roman armies could also include true allies, which consisted of the contingents provided by the allied tribes and kingdoms. These were not part of the Roman armed forces in any sense, but forces provided for service through a treaty relationship between Rome and its ally. The name for this treaty was *foedus*, and the allied forces (*symmachiarii*) were therefore considered *foederati*. This group of soldiers became famous only in later times, but even these became integrated into the Eastern Roman army in the fifth and sixth centuries. The following list of auxiliaries (based on Syvanne, MHLR Vol.1) does not give their organization because it varied greatly and in most cases is not even known.

Approximate size and organization of auxiliary units:

Unit	Foot	Horse	Centuries	Turmae
Cohors Quingenaria Peditata	480		6	
Cohors Quingenaria Equitata	480	128	6	4
Cohors Milliaria Peditata	800		10	
Cohors Milliaria Equitata	800	256	10	8
Ala Quingenaria		512		16
Ala Milliaria		768 (campaign strength?)		24
		1,024 (paper strength?)		32
Numeri (mercenaries)	varied	varied	varied	varied
Foederati (treaty-based allies)	varied	varied	varied	varied

30 Caracalla

The following illustrations show some of the different types of auxiliary units and *numeri*. The combat styles demonstrated by these examples were also employed by the legions and outside allies. Excluding cavalry and the units using native equipment, their equipment was often simple, task-oriented and not as 'flashy' as the legionary equipment. Additional examples of equipment and combat styles can also be found in the Plates section and in the section dealing with legions.

Funerary monument of Hyperanor of auxilia Museum of Creuznach. Hyperanor Hyperanoria f.(ilius), cretic. Lappa, Mil.(es), Cho. (hortis) T. Sag.(ittariorum) ann(orum) LX stip.(endiorum) XVIII h.(ic) s.(itus) e.(st). Drawn after Lindenschmit

A funerary monument of Licaius, an auxiliary of the I Pannonian Cohort, at Wiesbaden (drawn after Lindenschmit). Licaius Seri f(ilius) miles ex cho (cohorte) I Panonioru(m) ann(orum) XXX sti(pendiorum) XVI h (ic) s(itus) e(st) frater...

Top Right: Auxiliary line infantry.
Below Right: Roman slinger drawn after the columns of Trajan and Aurelius. Note that the Romans taught all of their regulars to use the sling, which means that this slinger could be either legionary or auxiliary.

Note the flat rectangular shield. It was typical for the auxiliaries to use flat shields even when these were rectangular in shape.

auxiliary archers in Marcus Aurelius's Column (Sarmatians?)

Background 31

Eastern archer in Trajan's Column equipped with chain mail armor, segmented helmet, composite bow, back quiver and short sword

Moorish light infantry archer (sources: Arch of Constantine; Hamdoune, 208) or alternatively Nubians/Meroites (see MHLR Vol.3). Legs, bow-string, and missing portions of the arrows emended to the illustration. Note the peculiar way of carrying the arrows around the head, which Claudian (see MHLR Vol.3) claims was typical for the warriors of Meroe presumably meaning the Nubians at that time.

© Dr. Ilkka Syvänne 2014

© Dr. Ilkka Syvänne 2013

recurved composite bow

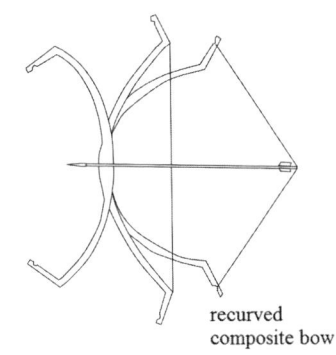

examples of different releases used in antiquity

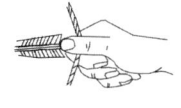

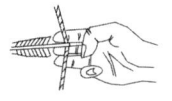

Mediterranean Release / Lock

Mongolian Release / Lock

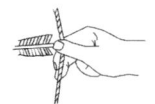

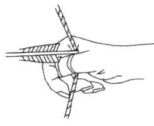

The Romans employed a great variety of different types of bows ranging from the wooden self-bows to the re-curved composite bows (short Scythian/Alan, long Parthian / "Sasanian", asymmetric long "Hunnic"), but so that the standard type of bow was the re-curved composite bow shown here. The names of the bows are misleading as all of the above-mentioned models were in use from the 1st century AD onwards in the Mediterranean. The Romans also used a great variety of different locks / releases. The various different thumb releases had been copied from the Parthians, Sarmatians and Alans while the Mediterranean Release was probably common among the peoples of the Mediterranean. The usual mistake is to assume that the thumb-lock would have allowed more powerful shots with the bow or that it would have been impossible to use shower archery with the Mediterranean Release. The Mediterranean Release was equally suited to both even if each of the different locks had its own benefits and drawbacks. The archers had to use different releases, arrows and types of bows according to their physical characteristics (height, length of arm and fingers) and type of armour worn and the great variety of bows and releases made this possible. The stiffer the bow, the stronger the man, the longer the arms and fingers, and the heavier the arrow, the more powerful would be the arrowshot. This illustration and text follows the interpretation published in the *Historia i Swiat 2015*. The original concept, however, was developed for the forthcoming *Military History of Sasanian Iran*.

32 Caracalla

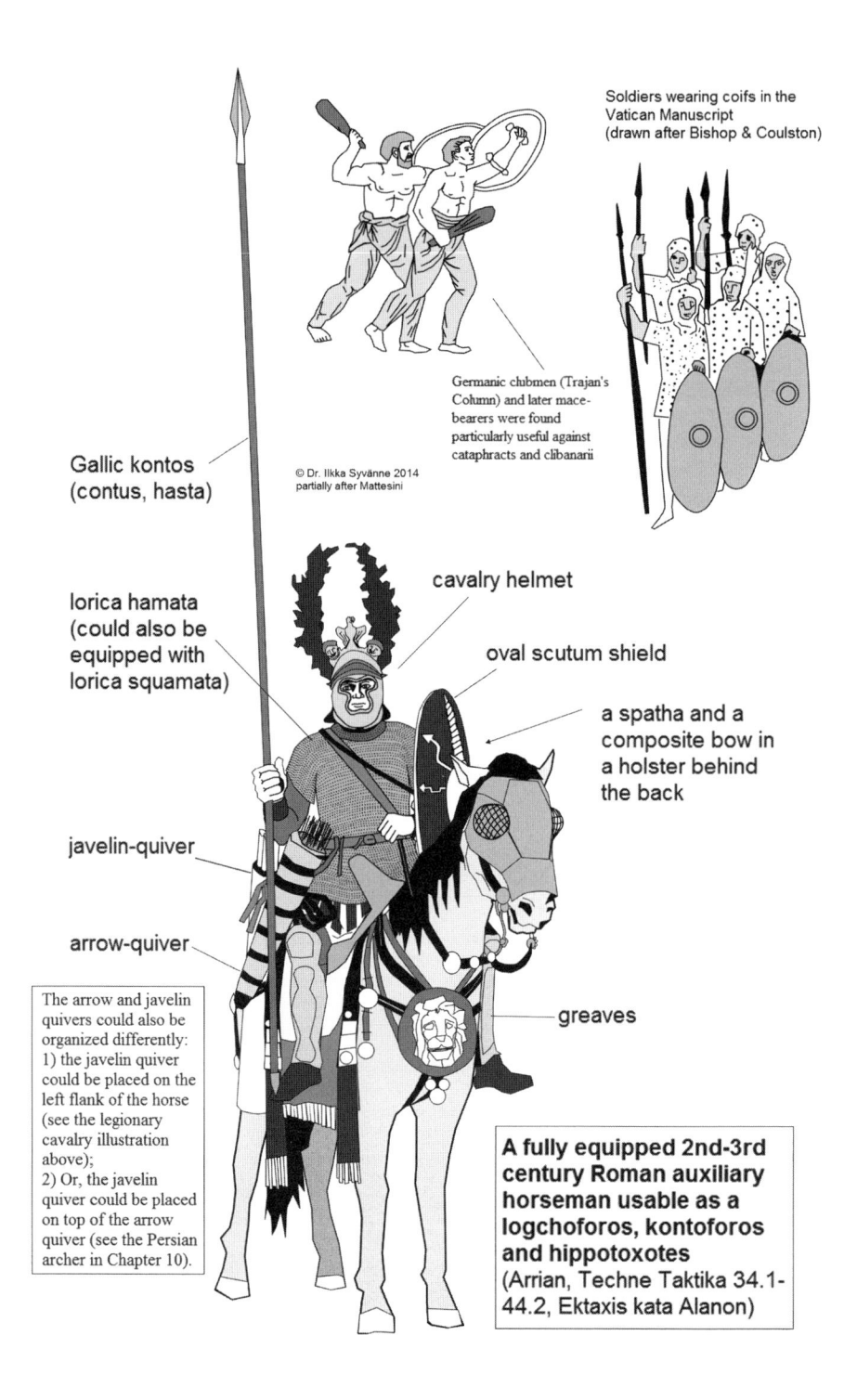

Soldiers wearing coifs in the Vatican Manuscript (drawn after Bishop & Coulston)

Germanic clubmen (Trajan's Column) and later mace-bearers were found particularly useful against cataphracts and clibanarii

© Dr. Ilkka Syvänne 2014
partially after Mattesini

Gallic kontos (contus, hasta)

cavalry helmet

lorica hamata (could also be equipped with lorica squamata)

oval scutum shield

a spatha and a composite bow in a holster behind the back

javelin-quiver

arrow-quiver

greaves

The arrow and javelin quivers could also be organized differently:
1) the javelin quiver could be placed on the left flank of the horse (see the legionary cavalry illustration above);
2) Or, the javelin quiver could be placed on top of the arrow quiver (see the Persian archer in Chapter 10).

A fully equipped 2nd-3rd century Roman auxiliary horseman usable as a logchoforos, kontoforos and hippotoxotes
(Arrian, Techne Taktika 34.1-44.2, Ektaxis kata Alanon)

Background

The over-the-shoulder technique with the spear was used for both downward thrusts and for javelin throws.

When the spear was placed in the low position it was used for downward and/or straight thrusts.

Underarm technique with the spear tucked between the arm and side, or in the armpit was used for shock and thrusts.

The two-handed technique with the Sarmatian *contus* was used for shock combat and for thrusts. The spear could also be placed along the right flank of the horse.

MOUNTED ARCHERY TECHNIQUES

- The three basic forms of mounted shooting (Saracen Archery 71-72):
a) downward; b) upward; c) shooting horizontally.

Ten Forms of Shooting by right-handed archer from Horseback according to Saracen Archery (pp.80-81):

1) To left flank, forward and downward parallel with thigh.
2) To left flank, forward and upward.
3) In horizontal plane (target roughly level with left shoulder).
4) Ahead with bow, upper limb to right, canted above horse's neck.
5) To right flank, forward and downward.
6) To left flank rear, upward or downward, with bow canted over horse's croup.
7) To left flank rear, upward or downward, with bow vertical.
8) Jarmaki of two kinds, each with four shots.
9) Beneath horse's neck from right to left.
10) Beneath horse's neck from left to right.

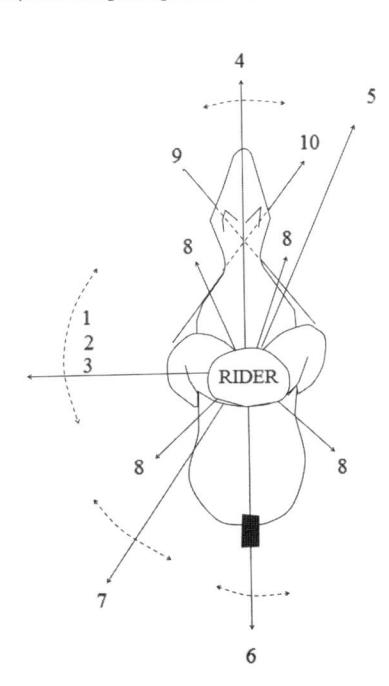

34 Caracalla

1 **Signifer Q. Carminius, auxiliary, Worms.** Q(uinto) Carminio Ingenuo Equiti Alae Hispanorum stip(endiorum) XXV Signifero, Sacer Julius (h(ere) e(x) t(testamento). Drawn after Lindenschmit.
2. **C. Romanius Mainz.** C(aius) Romanius equ(es) Alae Norico(rum) Claud(ia tribu) Capito, Caleia, an(norum) XL stip(endiorum) XIX h(ic) s(itus) e(st) h(eres) ex t(estamento) f(aciendum) c(uravit). Drawn after Lindenschmit.
3. **Roman mounted archer in Marcus Aurelius' Column.** 18th century drawing.
4. **Argiotalus, aux. Worms**. Drawn after Lindenschmit.

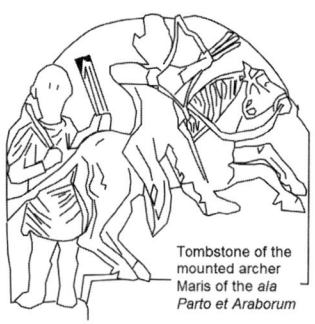

Tombstone of the mounted archer Maris of the *ala Parto et Araborum*

Note the use of the shower archer technique with three arrows on the left hand and the use of the servant behind to replenish the arrows!

Antonine tombstone of the *lanciarius* Ulpius Tertius (drawn after Bishop & Coulston)

Background 35

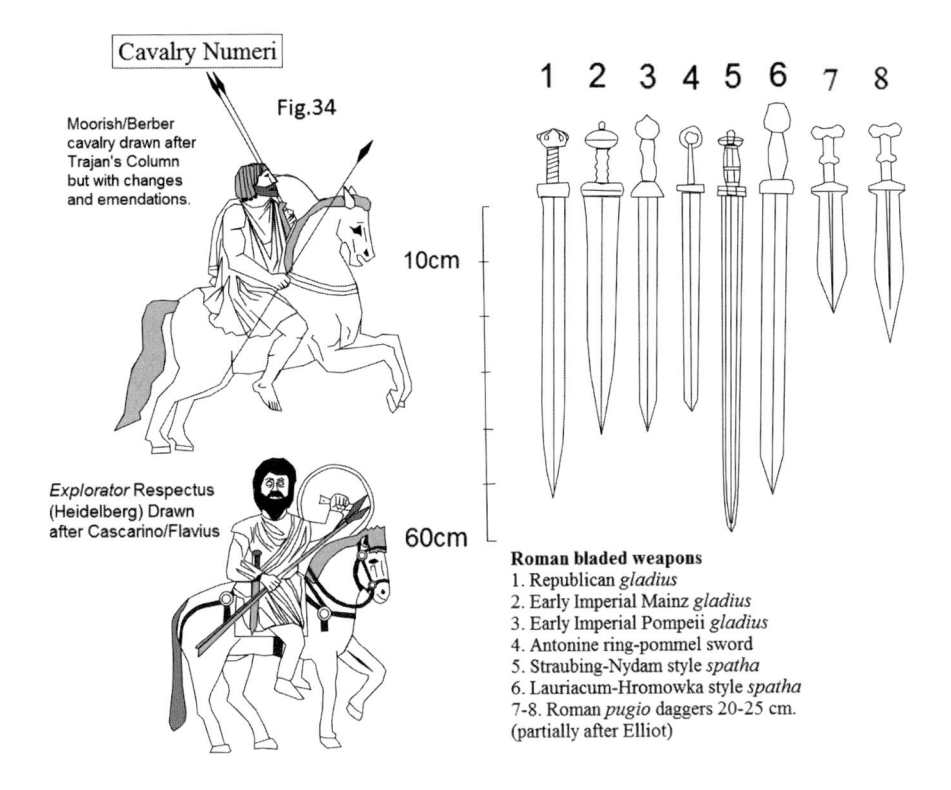

Fig.34

Cavalry Numeri

Moorish/Berber cavalry drawn after Trajan's Column but with changes and emendations.

Explorator Respectus (Heidelberg) Drawn after Cascarino/Flavius

Roman bladed weapons
1. Republican *gladius*
2. Early Imperial Mainz *gladius*
3. Early Imperial Pompeii *gladius*
4. Antonine ring-pommel sword
5. Straubing-Nydam style *spatha*
6. Lauriacum-Hromowka style *spatha*
7-8. Roman *pugio* daggers 20-25 cm.
(partially after Elliot)

The Strategic Reserve: Rome and its Surroundings[16]

When he took control of the city of Rome, Septimius Severus reorganized its defensive organization completely. The old Praetorian Guard of nine cohorts consisting of Italians was dismissed and replaced with veteran legionaries from the Danube frontier, and a tenth cohort was added to its size, which ensured its loyalty to Severus and improved its value as a fighting force. Subsequently, all legionaries who had distinguished themselves in service were rewarded with a position in the Guard. The fighting strength of each of the ten Praetorian Cohorts (*Praetoriani*) was increased to 1,000 (i.e. 1,024) so that the resulting 10,000 (10,240) men were commanded by ten tribunes and sixty centurions. The cavalry probably consisted of ten *turmae* of cavalry, with 192(?) horsemen per *turma* for a total of 1,920(?). During the reign of Severus, the Praetorians were commanded by two prefects, one of whom was a legal expert (depending on the time, there were always one to three prefects). The principal task of the Praetorian Guard was to protect the emperor and to act as his crack fighting force during military campaigns. The Praetorians also acted as special operatives for the emperor wherever needed.

The Praetorian barracks also housed 300 cavalry *Speculatores*. They were commanded by a *Trecenarius* (a centurion in charge of 300), under who served a

Princeps Castrorum. The *Speculatores* appear to have acted as personal lifeguards of the emperor, just like the later 300 *Excubitores* in the sixth century. In addition to their primary role, the *Speculatores* performed special assignments when needed. The *Numerus* of *Statores Augusti*, who acted as military police, were also housed in the barracks. Their command structure is unknown. The personal cavalry bodyguards of the emperor were the 2,000 (2,048) *Equites Singulares Augusti* (commanded by two tribunes, *Decurion Principes*, and sixty-four decurions) who consisted of barbarians (mainly Germans). In spite of being housed in the so-called New Camp, they too served under the Praetorian Prefect. The *Equites Singulares Augusti* were usually more loyal to the emperor than the other units because their position and life was entirely dependent on the goodwill of the emperor. It is possible that the staff of the Imperial Stables (*stratores*/equerries and grooms, the *Stablesiani*, under *Tribunus Stabuli*) also belonged to the cavalry bodyguards of the emperor (see Chapter 11).

In addition to this, there existed still another special imperial bodyguard unit, which consisted of the *Evocati Augusti* (veteran Praetorians who had been recalled back to service) and who served under the Praetorian Prefect. The best evidence for the existence of a separate unit comes from Dio 55.24.8, in which he states that he did not know the size of the *Evocati* which had been recalled to service by Octavianus Augustus. Dio also states that the *Evocati* of his day were still a separate corps which carried batons like centurions. Consequently, it is possible that when the sources refer to the use of centurions as imperial bodyguards or as assassins, they often meant this corps rather than the other bodyguard units.[17]

The capital also included special operations units/spies the *Peregrini* and *Frumentarii*, devoted to internal and external security missions. These units were housed at the barracks on the Caelian Hill. The *Peregrini* served as the emperor's private secret police and operated all around the empire at his whim. They were commanded by a *Princeps*, a *Subprinceps* and centurions, but that is all that we know of them. Thanks to the secrecy surrounding the unit, we do not know their overall numbers or exact organization. The *Frumentarii* were imperial couriers who were used to carry out special and secret missions, which included spying and assassinations. The commander of the *Frumentarii* was the *Princeps* of the *Peregrini*.

The city also housed two other units, the Urban Cohorts (*Cohortes Urbanae/ Urbaniciani*) and the *Vigiles*. The commander of the *Urbaniciani* was the Urban Prefect (*Praefectus Urbi*), who belonged to the senatorial class. The length of service was twenty years and it consisted of Italians. Septimius Severus may have raised the strength of each cohort to 1,500 footmen (with three tribunes and fifty-four centurions) for a total of 4,500 men. The primary mission of the *Urbaniciani* was to guard and police the city, but they too could be detached for other duties so that the emperor sometimes possessed one cohort of *Urbaniciani* when on campaign. The tombstone of Nigrinus (see image in this chapter) demonstrates the military functions of the *Urbaniciani*. They were equipped as soldiers, whereas the *Vigiles* (see the tombstone of Iulius in this chapter) were first and foremost firemen and policemen, whose principal pieces of equipment were firefighting tools and the nightstick. They only used the sword in extreme emergencies. It is probable that the *Urbaniciani* were housed in the same barracks as the *Praetoriani* up to the year 270, but it has also been suggested that they were transferred to the new barracks named after them, *Castra Urbana*, in the late second century AD. Whatever the case, the *Urbaniciani* of Rome formed cohorts X, XI and XII of the *Castra Praetoriani* thanks to the fact that they were originally housed there (the original number of Praetorian cohorts was nine). Additional Urban Cohorts were housed at Ostia, Puteoli, Lyon and Carthage to secure these strategically very important locations. All of these places had magazines to store supplies for feeding of the city of Rome, and Lyon also had a mint. By AD 69 there were cohorts IX–XVIII in existence, and Vespasian is also known to have added *coh I Flavia Urbana* to its ranks. There were Urban Cohorts in existence until the fall of Rome and Constantinople, but we do not possess any definite knowledge of how many there were and where at any given time after c. AD 69/70. All that we have are glimpses of what happened, such as the transfer of two units in the second century.[18] My own educated guess based on the material uncovered in this monograph is that Alexandria possessed probably at least one cohort, and that detachments or individual *urbaniciani* were located all over the empire to secure provisions for the city of Rome, which after all was one of the main responsibilities of the Urban Prefect. It is unsurprising that these men were also used to gather intelligence.

The fourth major force in the city were the seven 1,000-man cohorts of the *Vigiles* under the Prefect of the *Vigiles*, sub-prefect, seven tribunes and forty-nine centurions. The *Vigiles* served as night patrolmen, firemen and policemen, and just like the *Urbaniciani*, detachments of *Vigiles* could serve where needed, so that at least under Claudius there was one cohort at Puteoli and another at Ostia. The *Vigiles* were naturally equipped with the equipment needed to fulfil their duties and not to serve as a real fighting force.

In addition to this, the city of Rome also always possessed other forces. The emperor had a sort of Staff College which consisted of staff officers drawn from the ranks of the *primipilares*. It is possible that we should identify these with the unknown bodyguard units appearing in the sources at about this time. The fact that the Chronicle Paschale (ed. Dindorf, pp.501–02) and Cedrenus (ed. Dindorf, pp.451) both state that Gordian and Philip the Arab created two groups of *Candidati* (dressed in white) out of the sixth and seventh *scholae*[19] to act as personal bodyguards for the emperor suggests that the precursor of the Late Roman *Scholae* had been created before the year 238. The creation of this unit seems to predate the reign of Alexander Severus because the SHA (Sev. Alex. 23.3) states that there was an unknown bodyguard unit called *Ostensionales* (Paraders = later *Armaturae*?) dressed in bright clothes during the reign of Severus Alexander. It is improbable that it would have been created during the reign of Caracalla, because he is known to have created the *Leones* to serve as his unit of bodyguards (see Chapter 7) and it is probable that we should equate it with the *Protectores* (another late Roman bodyguard/staff unit connected with the *Scholae*) of the reign of Caracalla (SHA Car. 5.8, 7.1). The *Ostensionales/Protectores* cannot be the Praetorians, because the SHA (Max. et Balb. 13.5ff.) clearly separates the different bodyguard units from each other for the short reign of Maximus and Balbinus in 238, so that there were three groups of bodyguards: the *milites* (i.e. the Praetorians), *Germani* (i.e. the *Equites Singulares Augusti*) and the *Aulici* ('Court-troops', the *Palatini* i.e. the *Scholae/Candidati/Protectores*). In fact, it is almost certain that the *Ostensionales/Aulici/Protectores/Scholae* were created by Septimius Severus (or by Commodus?[20]) because the SHA states (Maximini 3.5) that Maximinus served in the personal court bodyguards (*corporis in aula*) of Septimius Severus.[21] On the basis of the presence of Parthian and Moorish bodyguards in the court of Commodus, it is possible that the *Aulici/Scholae* also consisted of foreigners, as the presence of Maximinus amongst them suggests. The unit structure of this special bodyguard unit was apparently based on the informal structure of the *scholae* (schools/meeting places of the officers) in the *principia* of legionary camps which Severus was first to recognize officially. This does suggest some sort of connection with a staff college/imperial bodyguard unit from which the emperor then dispatched staff officers to serve in the staffs of legionary commanders and governors.[22]

In addition to this, the city of Rome always had permanent detachments of marines/sailors from the Praetorian Fleets of Ravenna and Misenum on duty at Rome, which also accompanied the emperor during important campaigns, as, for example, Pseudo-Hyginus' treatise attests. Lastly, there were always soldiers on leave in Rome to enjoy the many entertainments that a megalopolis could offer.

One of the most important reforms of Septimius Severus was also the posting the *Legio II Parthica* at Alba (Albanum), which lay a short striking distance from the city of Rome. The presence of the *Legio II Parthica* at a distance of five hours' march away enabled the emperors to use this legion as a counterbalance against any units at Rome which showed signs of disloyalty. The only downside to this was that the new emperors also needed to buy the support of this legion and not only the support of the Praetorian Guard when they donned the purple. This naturally increased the cost of becoming an emperor.

The different units posted at the capital wore the standard equipment used by infantry and cavalry, the only likely difference being that the general quality and appearance of the Guard units was better. The Praetorians, like the other bodyguards, also appear to have worn the Attic-style helmets and sometimes the *parazonium* sword to separate them from the regulars. The light and heavy-armed

Background 39

Marcus Cincius Nigrinus
XI Urban Cohort at Rome
- Equipment: tunique, *sagum*-cloak, sword, pugio, helmet, shield, leather cuirass, greaves.
- Servant with spear

ΜΑΡΚΟΣ - ΚΙΝΚΙΟΣ - ΝΙΓΡΕΙΝΟ
ΣΤΡΑΤΙΩΤΗΣ-Χ ΩΡΤΗΣ ΕΝ ΔΕΚΑΤΗ ΣΟΡ
ΒΑΝΗΣ ΗΡΩΣ ΑΓΑΘΟΠΟΙΟΣ

© Dr. Ilkka Syvänne 2014
drawn after R. Cagnat and V. Chapot

A soldier of the Urbaniciani

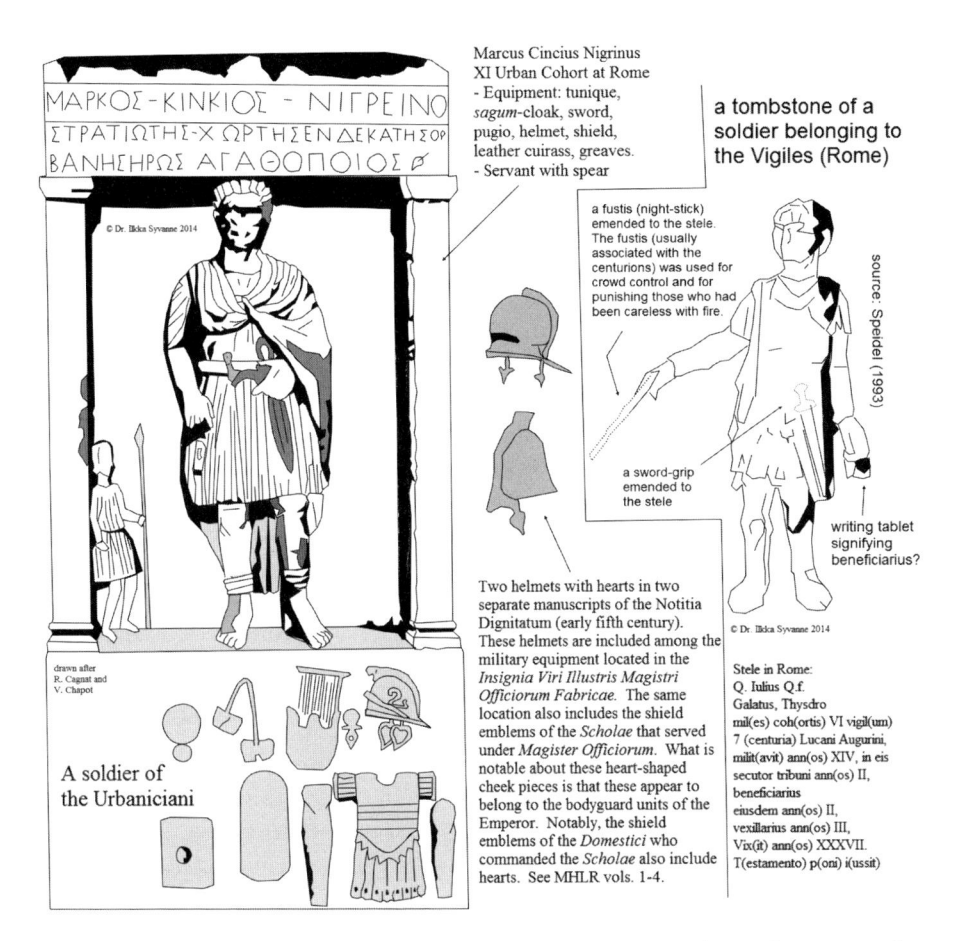

Two helmets with hearts in two separate manuscripts of the Notitia Dignitatum (early fifth century). These helmets are included among the military equipment located in the *Insignia Viri Illustris Magistri Officiorum Fabricae*. The same location also includes the shield emblems of the *Scholae* that served under *Magister Officiorum*. What is notable about these heart-shaped cheek pieces is that these appear to belong to the bodyguard units of the Emperor. Notably, the shield emblems of the *Domestici* who commanded the *Scholae* also include hearts. See MHLR vols. 1-4.

a tombstone of a soldier belonging to the Vigiles (Rome)

a fustis (night-stick) emended to the stele. The fustis (usually associated with the centurions) was used for crowd control and for punishing those who had been careless with fire.

a sword-grip emended to the stele

writing tablet signifying beneficiarius?

source: Speidel (1993)

© Dr. Ilkka Syvänne 2014

Stele in Rome:
Q. Iulius Q.f.
Galatus, Thysdro
mil(es) coh(ortis) VI vigil(um)
7 (centuria) Lucani Augurini,
milit(avit) ann(os) XIV, in eis
secutor tribuni ann(os) II,
beneficiarius
eiusdem ann(os) II,
vexillarius ann(os) III,
Vix(it) ann(os) XXXVII.
T(estamento) p(oni) i(ussit)

wore equipment suited to their tasks. This was true also of the *Urbaniciani*, who could be equipped as regular soldiers, but not of the *Vigiles*. If the Moors and Parthians formed part of the *Aulici* and *Equites Singulares Augusti*, as appears quite possible, then they probably used their native equipment. Modern research (e.g. Rankov, Praet.) claims that the appearance of the Praetorian Guard had changed, presumably as a result of Severus' reforms, so that the standard piece of armour among the Praetorian Guard was now scale armour, both for the infantry and cavalry.

When needed, the emperors possessed still another reserve force, the existence of which much modern research has forgotten, which was the populace of Italy. The best proof of this is the ability of the Italians to resist Maximinus Thrax's elite army in 238. The reason for this is that all new legions appear to have been raised initially in Italy, at least until about mid-third century, which forced the Italian societies to maintain some level of military training for this to be possible. The practice of raising new legions in Italy was partially abandoned during the chaotic third century, when the emperors whose territories lay outside Italy could not do so. The Italians and provincials were at least partially disarmed during the reign of Valentinian and Valens, when they issued a law forbidding the carrying of arms by civilians. Regardless, the citizen militias still continued to train, but the quality of military training was apparently not the same as before, because the Italians did not present similarly formidable opposition to Alaric in 408–410 as they had been able to do in the third century. However, this was not yet the case in the early third century. The Italians and Romans retained their formidable martial qualities and

Trajanic relief incorporated into the Arch of Constantine. The footmen and cavalry with the plumed helmets belong to the Praetorians. Note in particular the use of the Pseudo-Attic helmets, which were also used by Constantine's Scholarii, hence the inclusion of this relief. Source: Bellori 1690.

Equites Singulares Augusti in the Column of Trajan

Background   41

FLAVIVS PROCLVS/EQ[ues] SING[ularis] AVG[usti] DOMO/ [pi]LODELPIA AN[norum] XX/STIP[endiorum] ... H[eres] F[aciendum] C[uravit] at Mainz. Adapted from K.R. Dixon's drawing who dates the tombstone to the 1st century AD, but this is probably a mistake and the tombstone should be dated to the 2nd century AD. The artist may have mistakenly drawn the bowstring on both sides of the horse's neck, but it is also possible that the double string actually belongs to the bridle. Note the separate quivers for javelins and arrows! I have emended to the drawing with dotted lines portions that can be guessed to have existed, and I have highlighted important details (horned saddle, arrow quiver, javelin quiver, bow, bowstring, arrow) with grey color.

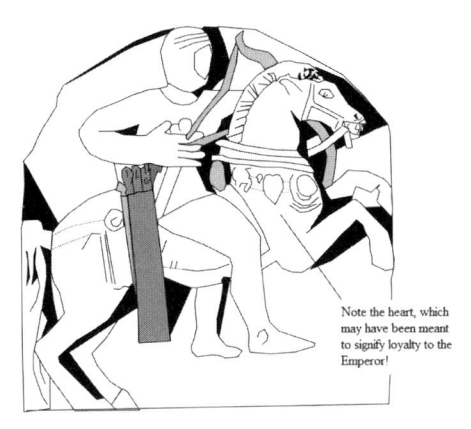

Note the heart, which may have been meant to signify loyalty to the Emperor!

The emperor Marcus Aurelius surrounded by his bodyguards (probably *Speculatores*) in the Column of Marcus Aurelius

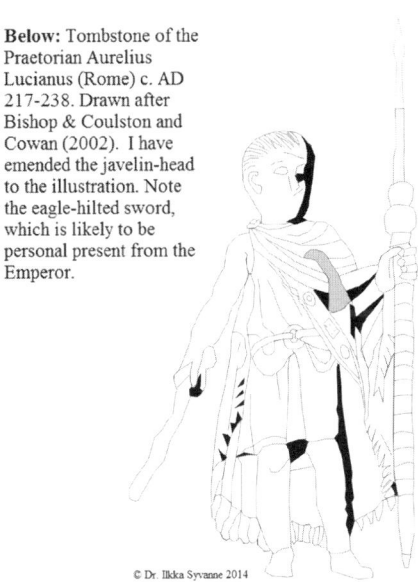

Below: Tombstone of the Praetorian Aurelius Lucianus (Rome) c. AD 217-238. Drawn after Bishop & Coulston and Cowan (2002). I have emended the javelin-head to the illustration. Note the eagle-hilted sword, which is likely to be personal present from the Emperor.

© Dr. Ilkka Syvänne 2014

could be relied on to form an emergency reserve force of conscripts which could be relied upon to defend their cities.

The Civilian Police Forces and Militias[23]

It is often forgotten that the Roman armed forces were not the only military force in existence. In addition to the professional military, there were civilian police forces and militias (paramilitary forces consisting of civilian levies) which kept the public order, chased criminals, collected taxes, prevented banditry and barbarian raids and piracy, controlled the movement of people and goods, and protected the towns and cities. The direct intervention of military forces in these fields was only needed when the civilians failed to perform these duties adequately. The most obvious example of this is Judaea, where the local civilian authorities could not be expected to control the Jews and Samaritans because most of them belonged to these religious groups. It was thanks to this that the Romans had garrisoned the area heavily. Similarly, Egypt was known to be a restless place and therefore possessed more civilian police forces and militias than any other province of the empire. The emperor wanted to be sure that all of its produce ended up in the right place.

It should be noted that all of the civilians performed all of these functions under the supervision of Roman magistrates and military detachments serving under them. The city magistrates and their staff and paramilitary forces kept the order in their cities and in the surrounding countryside, so the city walls were regularly guarded by watches, the roads patrolled, guard towers in the countryside manned and checkpoints placed on crossroads. The aim was to control the movement of both people and goods. The most efficient paramilitary forces consisted of the professional policemen who tracked and apprehended or killed criminals and bandits in the countryside. The names of the militias varied from one place to another, but there appears to have existed so-called *burgarii* or their equivalents in most border regions. The *burgarii* had a particularly important defensive role because they acted as de facto border guards for significant portions of the frontier.

The civilians were supported in their performance of duty by detachments of soldiers. The Romans established in the late second century administrative posts called *stationes* in most of the provinces. The soldiers posted at the *stationes* were commanded by the *beneficiarii consularis*. The *beneficiarii* in their turn appear to have served under the *speculatores* detached to serve among the staff of the governor or in the legions. The *beneficiarii* were originally placed under the governers of their respective provinces, but eventually became independent of them. Their exact functions varied from province to province, and included the control of traffic and collection of customs, taxes and *annona* (grain provisions for the army). In addition to this, the *beneficiarii* could also perform actual police work and surveillance duties, which included the persecution of Christians when this was the order of the day. The soldiers who were posted to the *stationes* were called *milites stationarii* (sing. *stationarus*). Sometimes these soldiers offered to the civilians an alternative route to seek justice when the civilian police/judiciary system had failed, but at the same time these soldiers could also abuse their powers. The *frumentarii* were also used for similar police duties thanks to their role as messengers between the emperor, governors and armies, but they had considerably more power than the above-mentioned detachments and could be equally corrupt. The veterans (*evocati*) who continued in service were also quite often used for similar duties as the above.

Background 43

The funerary monument of Markos Aurelios Diodoros (Marcus Aurelius Diodorus) from Hierapolis in Phrygia shows the police forces of Asia Minor and their equipment. The equipment of a policeman/ranger consisted of a leather banded *lorica*, a thick *subarmalis* underneath, spears, club and a *fustis* (?). From other sources we know that they could also use swords and shields. Some of the men were mounted while others served on foot. The dogs were used to track down bandits and criminals. The leather banded *lorica* resembles closely the leather *lorica segmentata* worn by the soldier included in the Plates section and it is likely that we are here dealing with the same type of equipment. Jyrki Halme has suggested to me that this type of armour had been copied from the chariot drivers. This sounds correct. Drawn after D'Amato.

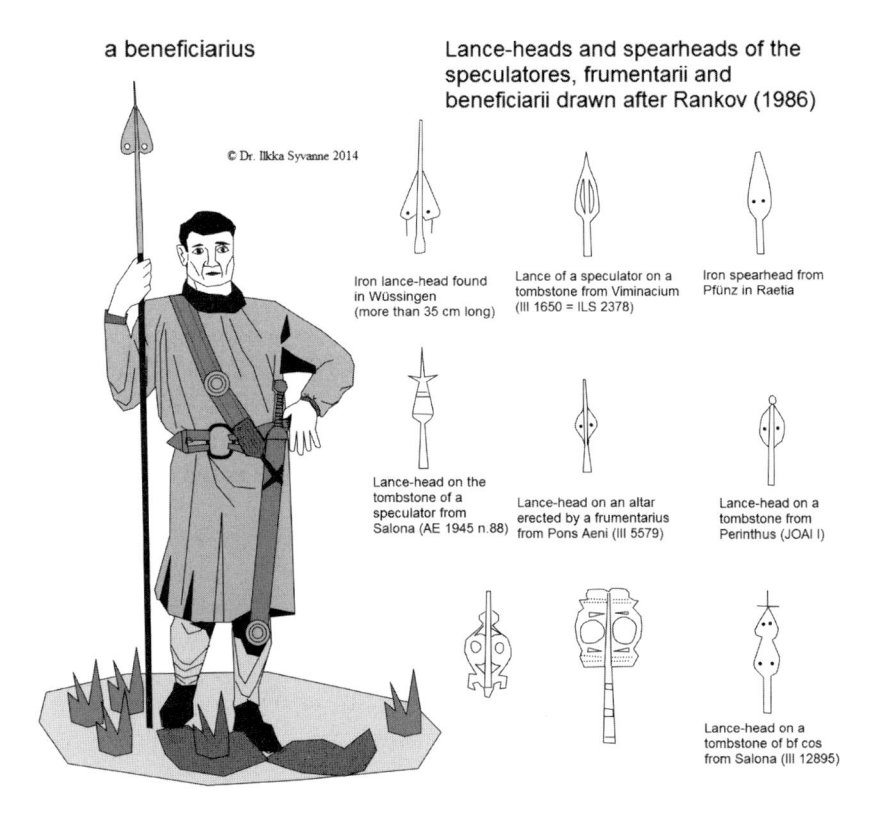

a beneficiarius

Lance-heads and spearheads of the speculatores, frumentarii and beneficiarii drawn after Rankov (1986)

Iron lance-head found in Wüssingen (more than 35 cm long)

Lance of a speculator on a tombstone from Viminacium (III 1650 = ILS 2378)

Iron spearhead from Pfünz in Raetia

Lance-head on the tombstone of a speculator from Salona (AE 1945 n.88)

Lance-head on an altar erected by a frumentarius from Pons Aeni (III 5579)

Lance-head on a tombstone from Perinthus (JOAI I)

Lance-head on a tombstone of bf cos from Salona (III 12895)

44   Caracalla

Strategy

The Roman Empire was a hegemonic empire which controlled its core territories directly and its outlying territories indirectly.[24] The Romans controlled their client states and tribes with a combination of bribery, diplomacy and threat of military action, which was sometimes demonstrated in reality. The basic deployment pattern was defensive, but those emperors who sought to improve their own standing among the armed forces and populace (or who purposefully weakened their neighbours with pre-emptive invasions) did engage in offensive warfare. When this happened, the emperor took detachments from the forces posted alongside the borders to bolster the bodyguard units accompanying him on a campaign. The same practice was also used when the enemy had managed to fight its way through on some section of the frontier, but this was always a risky proposition because the neighbours were in the habit of exploiting any weakening of the defences by invading.

The Romans had always possessed a ready reserve in Italy whenever the emperors chose to raise new legions through conscription, but the emperors were usually very reluctant to do this as it did not endear them to the Italian population. Regardless, in extreme emergencies or when new legions were needed for wars of conquest, it was typical for the emperors to raise them. Therefore, Septimius Severus' decision to post *Legio II Parthica* at Alba (Albanum) and increase the numbers of Praetorians and other bodyguard units was one of the most important reforms in the history of Rome. After this, the emperor always had at his disposal a strong reserve force of elite troops which would only need to be strengthened with detachments from other units – the levying of new legions was necessary only in extreme circumstances.

It should be remembered that the military forces did not only defend the empire, but also provided internal security. It was because of this that the emperors kept the strongest forces nearby, and Septimius Severus limited the number of legions per governor to two. He knew from personal experience that it was dangerous to give any governor larger forces. It was also dangerous for the emperors to give any competent general command of a large army, because there always existed the danger of usurpation. This meant that the emperors usually took charge of the military operations in person, which was a difficult proposition when the Romans faced two simultaneous major conflicts. This was a major strategic weakness. In fact, since the Romans possessed tactical superiority over their enemies, the emperors saw the potential usurpers as their greatest strategic and physical threat. It was the intelligence-gathering apparatus that was at the forefront of this struggle, but the many usurpations and assassinations prove this was far from perfect.

The principal reason for the placing of military units so close to the borders was that the strategic mobility of Roman armies was relatively slow. It took a really long time for the Romans to mobilize forces from one end of the empire to another if the enemy had managed to break through the defences, when one takes into account the time it took for the information to reach the emperor and then the time it took for him and his advisors to react and plan an operation, and for this plan to be put

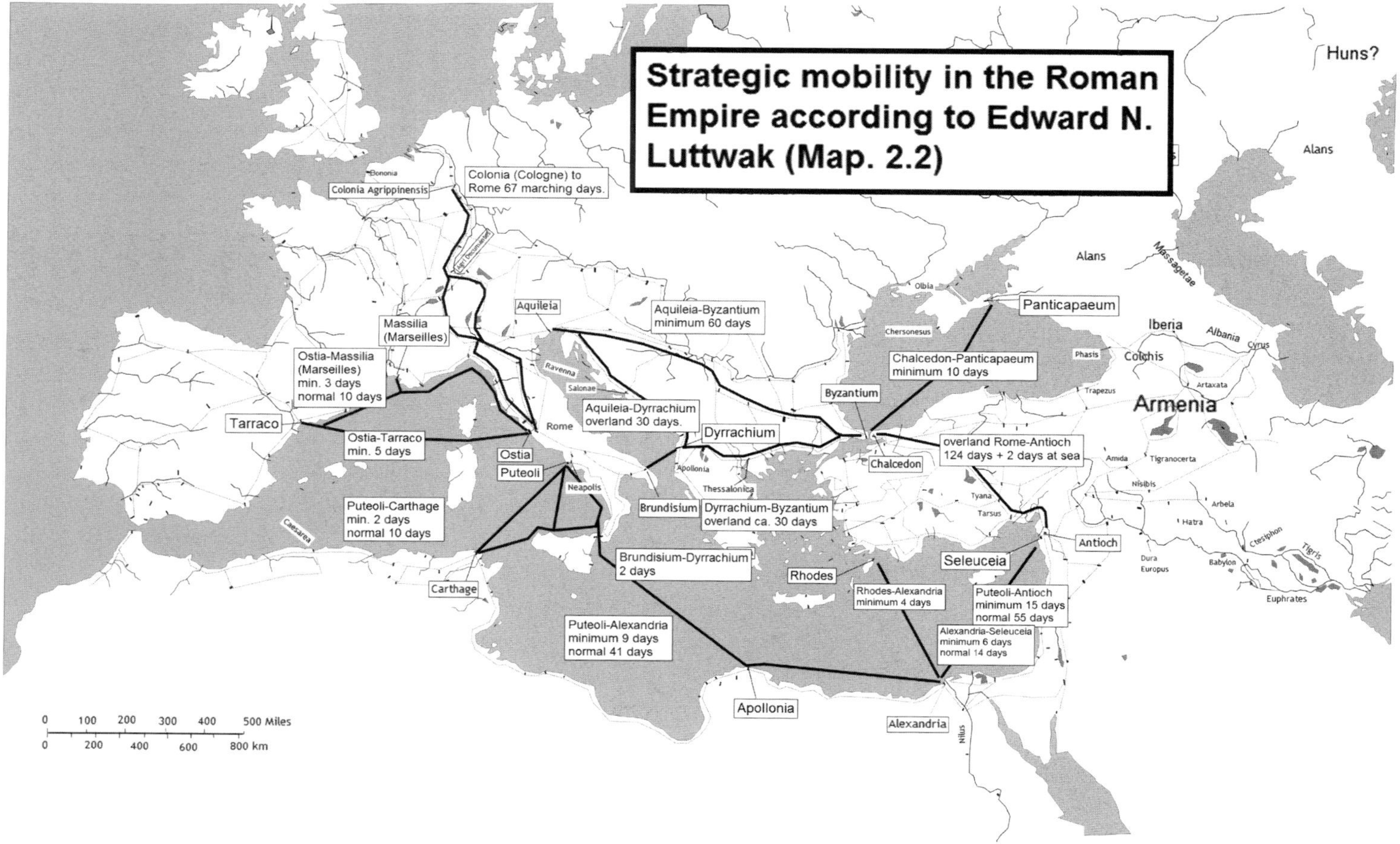
Strategic mobility in the Roman Empire according to Edward N. Luttwak (Map. 2.2)
Huns?
Alans
Alans
Massagetae
Iberia
Albania
Cyrus
Colchis
Phasis
Armenia
Artaxata
Trapezus
Panticapaeum
Olbia
Chersonesus
Chalcedon-Panticapaeum minimum 10 days
Byzantium
Chalcedon
overland Rome-Antioch 124 days + 2 days at sea
Amida
Tigranocerta
Nisibis
Arbela
Hatra
Ctesiphon
Tigris
Dura Europus
Babylon
Euphrates
Tyana
Tarsus
Antioch
Seleuceia
Puteoli-Antioch minimum 15 days normal 55 days
Alexandria-Seleuceia minimum 6 days normal 14 days
Rhodes
Rhodes-Alexandria minimum 4 days
Alexandria
Nilus
Apollonia
Puteoli-Alexandria minimum 9 days normal 41 days
Brundisium-Dyrrachium 2 days
Brundisium
Dyrrachium-Byzantium overland ca. 30 days
Thessalonica
Apollonia
Dyrrachium
Aquileia-Dyrrachium overland 30 days.
Aquileia-Byzantium minimum 60 days
Aquileia
Ravenna
Salonae
Rome
Ostia
Puteoli
Neapolis
Carthage
Puteoli-Carthage min. 2 days normal 10 days
Caesarea
Ostia-Tarraco min. 5 days
Tarraco
Ostia-Massilia (Marseilles) min. 3 days normal 10 days
Massilia (Marseilles)
Colonia (Cologne) to Rome 67 marching days.
Bononia
Colonia Agrippinensis
0 100 200 300 400 500 Miles
0 200 400 600 800 km

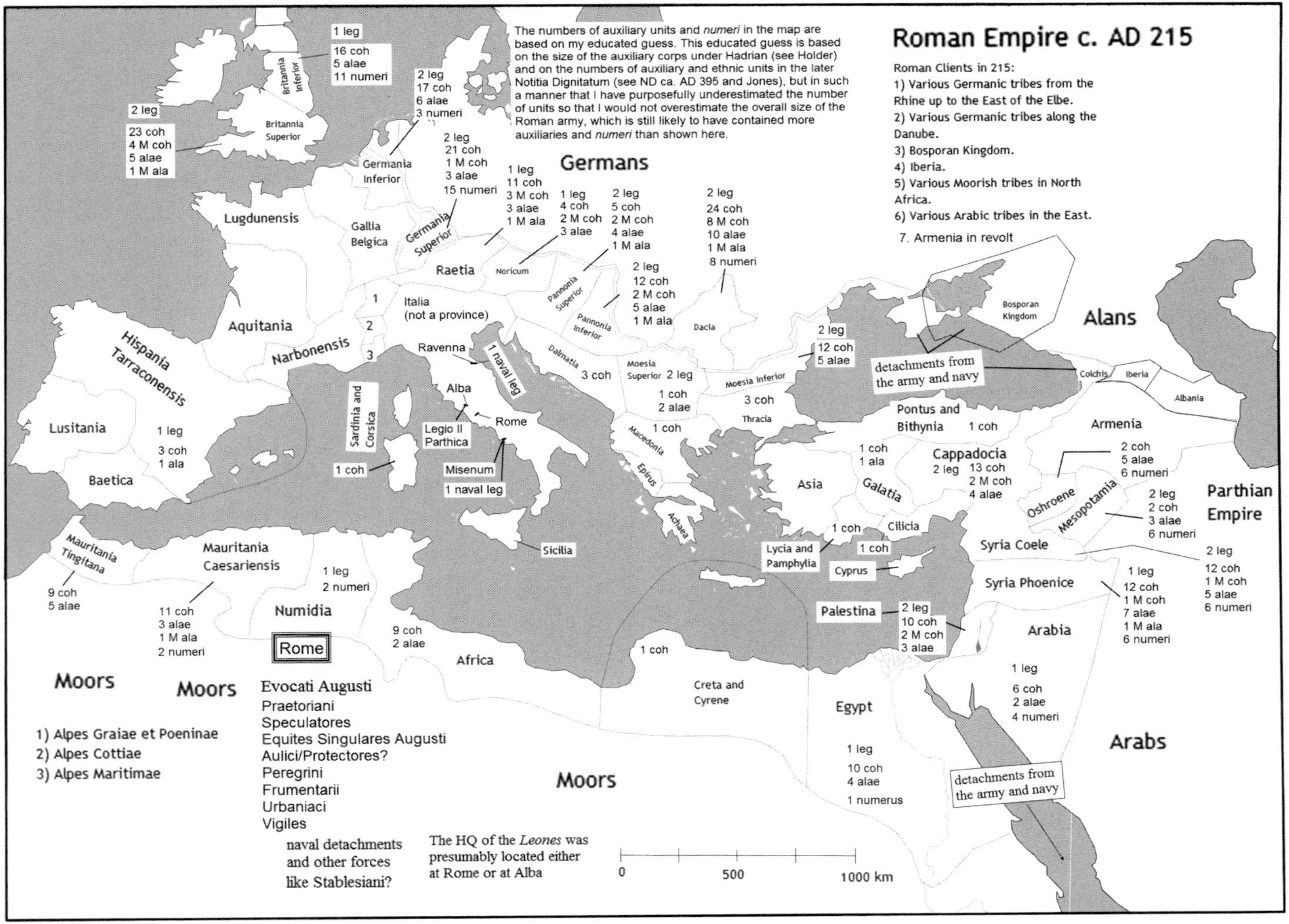

Roman Empire c. AD 215
The numbers of auxiliary units and *numeri* in the map are based on my educated guess. This educated guess is based on the size of the auxiliary corps under Hadrian (see Holder) and on the numbers of auxiliary and ethnic units in the later Notitia Dignitatum (see ND ca. AD 395 and Jones), but in such a manner that I have purposefully underestimated the number of units so that I would not overestimate the overall size of the Roman army, which is still likely to have contained more auxiliaries and *numeri* than shown here.
Roman Clients in 215:
1) Various Germanic tribes from the Rhine up to the East of the Elbe.
2) Various Germanic tribes along the Danube.
3) Bosporan Kingdom.
4) Iberia.
5) Various Moorish tribes in North Africa.
6) Various Arabic tribes in the East.
7. Armenia in revolt
Germans
Alans
Parthian Empire
Arabs
Moors
Moors
Moors
1 leg
16 coh
5 alae
11 numeri
Britannia Inferior
Britannia Superior
2 leg
23 coh
4 M coh
5 alae
1 M ala
2 leg
17 coh
6 alae
3 numeri
Germania Inferior
2 leg
21 coh
1 M coh
3 alae
15 numeri
Germania Superior
1 leg
11 coh
3 M coh
3 alae
1 M ala
1 leg
4 coh
2 M coh
3 alae
2 leg
5 coh
2 M coh
4 alae
1 M ala
2 leg
24 coh
8 M coh
10 alae
1 M ala
8 numeri
2 leg
12 coh
2 M coh
5 alae
1 M ala
Lugdunensis
Gallia Belgica
Raetia
Noricum
Pannonia Superior
Pannonia Inferior
Dacia
Aquitania
Narbonensis
Hispania Tarraconensis
Lusitania
Baetica
1 leg
3 coh
1 ala
1
2
3
Italia (not a province)
Ravenna
1 naval leg
Alba
Rome
Legio II Parthica
Misenum
1 naval leg
Sardinia and Corsica
1 coh
Sicilia
Dalmatia
3 coh
Moesia Superior
2 leg
1 coh
2 alae
Moesia Inferior
3 coh
Thracia
1 coh
Macedonia
Epirus
Achaea
2 leg
12 coh
5 alae
detachments from the army and navy
Bosporan Kingdom
Colchis
Iberia
Albania
Pontus and Bithynia
1 coh
Armenia
2 coh
5 alae
6 numeri
Cappadocia
2 leg
13 coh
2 M coh
4 alae
1 coh
1 ala
Galatia
Asia
Osrhoene
Mesopotamia
2 leg
2 coh
3 alae
6 numeri
2 leg
12 coh
1 M coh
5 alae
6 numeri
Cilicia
1 coh
1 coh
Lycia and Pamphylia
Cyprus
Syria Coele
Syria Phoenice
1 leg
12 coh
1 M coh
7 alae
1 M ala
6 numeri
Palestina
2 leg
10 coh
2 M coh
3 alae
Arabia
1 leg
6 coh
2 alae
4 numeri
detachments from the army and navy
Egypt
1 leg
10 coh
4 alae
1 numerus
Creta and Cyrene
1 coh
Africa
9 coh
2 alae
Numidia
1 leg
2 numeri
Mauritania Caesariensis
11 coh
3 alae
1 M ala
2 numeri
Mauritania Tingitana
9 coh
5 alae
Rome
Evocati Augusti
Praetoriani
Speculatores
Equites Singulares Augusti
Aulici/Protectores?
Peregrini
Frumentarii
Urbaniaci
Vigiles
naval detachments and other forces like Stablesiani?
The HQ of the *Leones* was presumably located either at Rome or at Alba
1) Alpes Graiae et Poeninae
2) Alpes Cottiae
3) Alpes Maritimae
0
500
1000 km

into effect. The accompanying map, which is adapted from Luttwak's, shows the amount of time it took to travel from one location to another. In light of the time it took to concentrate forces against a major invasion, one can justifiably say that the taking of periodical offensives against neigbours could save plenty of money while keeping the enemies too weak to contemplate invasions. This is what Caracalla did!

The other accompanying map shows my educated guess for the peacetime deployment pattern of all Roman land-based forces in 215. In practice, a significant portion of the army was concentrated under Caracalla for the campaigns (pre-emptive strikes and conquests) he conducted from 212 until his death in 217.[25]

During this period, the Roman navy possessed an absolute mastery of the seas along the Atlantic coastline, Mediterranean, Black Sea and Red Sea, and could also influence the course of political and economic events in the Arabian Sea and Indian Ocean whenever it chose to deploy naval assets there. The fleet still performed the traditional roles of intelligence-gathering, policing of the seas in anti-pirate and anti-smuggling operations, protection of shipments of men and supplies, but the opposition was practically non-existent. If Roman fleets encountered any opposition, it was very easy for them to destroy this force because the Romans possessed superior ship designs that carried professional crews of sailors and marines. It was thanks to this that the Romans possessed superior transport capability to support their land-based operations. The Romans could also exploit their naval mastery by projecting power from the sea to the land. Their enemies did not possess powerful enough artillery with strong enough fortifications to prevent this. The strategic significance of the sizeable Praetorian fleets was that these secured for the emperor naval supremacy against potential usurpers.

Campaigns

Intelligence-Gathering

The Roman foreign and military intelligence services were based on the exploitation of spies (military officers or others who posed as traders, diplomats etc.); spies/scouts (*speculatores*); scouting patrols (*exploratores*) along the frontiers; naval patrols; intelligence provided by traders and other private explorers and deserters; and use of military outposts (*stationarii* under the *beneficiarii consulares*) and civilian militiamen, fortifications and walls. The dissemination of intelligence was facilitated by the road network, public post, and fire and smoke signalling. The internal security of the empire, in other words the personal safety of the emperor, was based on the exploitation of many different agencies and systems. Most of those seem to have operated under the Praetorian Prefect who was responsible for the personal safety of the emperor. However, as will be shown later, the emperor could reorganize the intelligence services as he deemed best. There were also the clients of the emperor and those who sought his favour who were bound to do their utmost to please him. The system of rewarding informers also made others ready to betray the trust of their masters or friends. Then there were the members of the military establishment such as the *speculatores*, centurions, bodyguards and even ordinary soldiers that were used to spy upon the populace in plain clothes. The *frumentarii* (messengers, supply officers, spies etc.) and *peregrini* were also constantly travelling from provinces to Rome and back, which made them ideal for intelligence-gathering purposes. Alongside the members of the bodyguard units, the *urbaniciani*, the *frumentarii*, *peregrini* and staff officers were also used as special operatives and as imperial assassins.[26]

The purpose of the military and political intelligence was to make certain that the emperor always possessed an accurate picture of what his neighbours and potential usurpers were up to, what would be the best way to react to these and how to defeat the enemy if that was necessary.

In addition to these, there appears to have operated a network of spies based around the religious organizations of seers, astrologers and other magicians that were used to implicate those patrons who sought protection against the emperor's prying eyes or were seeking information regarding his demise. In an age of superstitious beliefs, this organization was particularly useful for the emperors. It is therefore not surprising that Roman emperors sought to prevent the arrival of new cults such as Christianity and the Cult of Isis to the city of Rome, because the conversion of upper-class citizens to foreign religions hindered the ability of the emperor to control the Roman upper classes through their network of seers, astrologers, and magicians, who acted as their eyes and ears. The probable origin of this system lay with the organization created by Caius Julius Caesar and his adopted son Augustus. Unsurprisingly, both were known for their utter lack of respect for religious predictions. The position of *pontifex maximus* enabled Julius Caesar, and then his adopted son Octavian Augustus and other emperors, to gather information from the seers, who they in the capacity of *pontifices* supervised.[27]

Roman Military Campaigns and Generalship

The Roman attitude towards generalship was schizophrenic. It depended entirely on the point of view of the observer. Some Romans admired bold risk-takers like Alexander the Great, Julius Caesar, Drusus and Germanicus, while others preferred cautious and methodological commanders such as Scipio Africanus, Pompey the Great, Tiberius and Corbulo. There also existed another divide in the attitude towards generalship, which was that while the traditional view of generalship stressed the importance of the general sharing the hardships of the soldiers so that he could endear himself to them, the Roman upper-class attitude (i.e. the senatorial view) exemplified by Dio who emphasized the importance of the hierarchial divide between the officers and rank-and-file, so that officers would be seen as superior to common soldiers. The upper class figures like Dio also did not accept the treacherous way of waging war, while this was quite acceptable to the professional soldiers.

Background 49

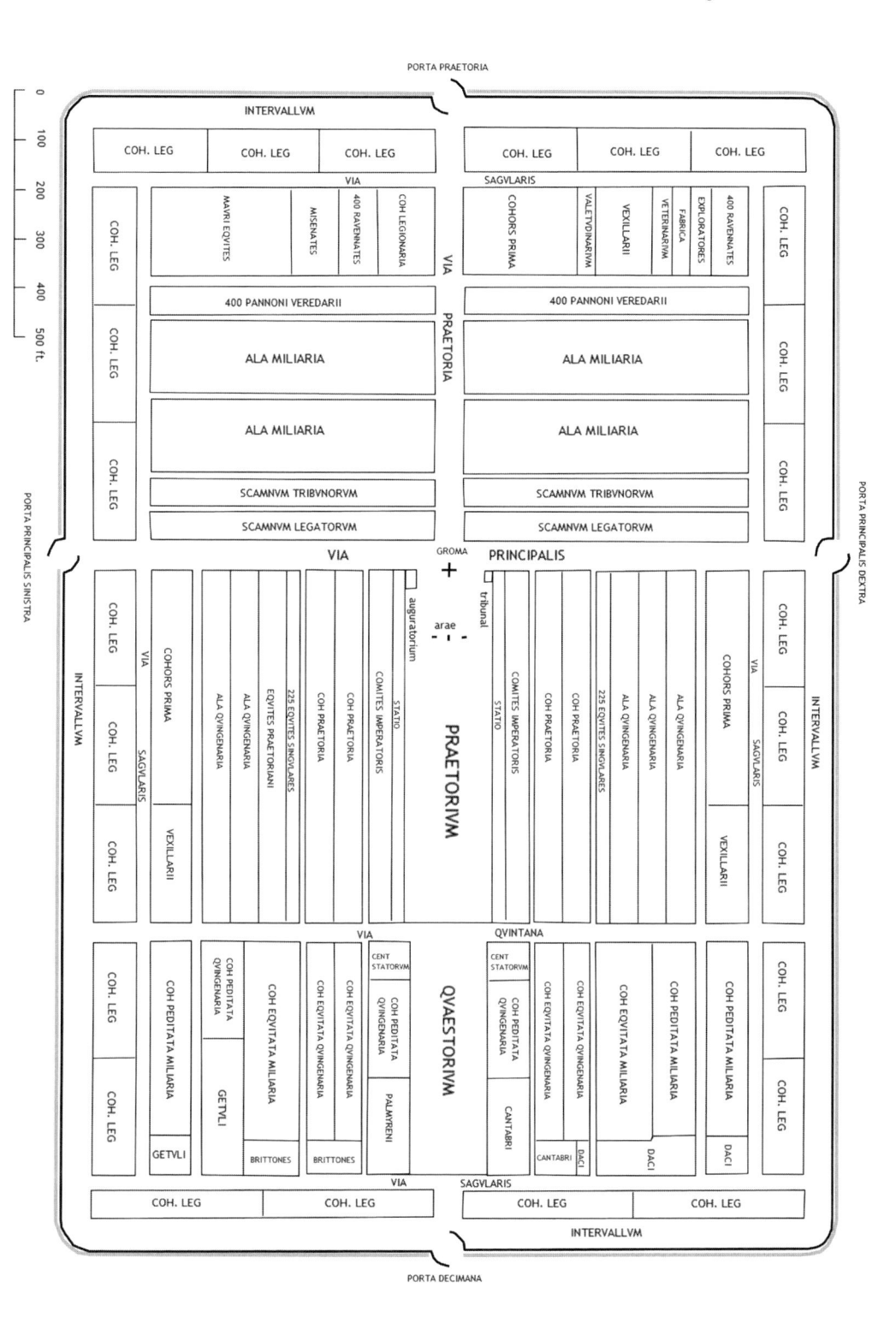

The Roman civil and military administrations ensured that taxes were used to obtain sufficient food and fodder for the armies and all the equipment they needed. The military gear and equipment was produced either by legionary specialists or by civilian artisans, where these existed. The vast logistical network ensured that the equipment and supplies were transported where needed. The soldiers in their turn received their salaries in money, from which the officers then deducted money spent on clothes, equipment and food. In times of war, soldiers would also receive supplies in kind to support the war effort, and after the reforms of Septimius Severus the soldiers could also expect to be bribed with *donativa* of money paid by the middle class and rich before and during campaigns. The soldiers consisted mostly of volunteers, but the army also included very significant numbers of conscripts and sons of soldiers pressed into service.

Roman military doctrine expected that their commanders knew everything there was to know about the enemy so that they could then take full advantage of the situation. The Romans always paid particular attention to supplies, so that they could decide when and where and how to engage the enemy. It was a sign of very poor generalship if the Romans lacked adequate supplies. Taxes provided the necessary supplies, which were then collected and transported in ships and wagons to storage houses and from there to where needed. The military doctrine also expected soldiers to be better-trained and equipped than their enemies, which meant that the Romans expected to be able to defeat their enemies even when outnumbered, but it was still recommended that battles with a numerically superior foe were to be avoided. In addition to this, the Romans possessed superior engineering and siege engineering skills, which enabled them to besiege and defend their possessions against great odds.

Roman military doctrine also called for the use of secure marching formations and fortified marching camps (see layout of the marching camp on page 49, drawn after the reconstruction of Lenoir) so that the enemy would be unable to surprise them. The marching formation in friendly areas was the marching column. In hostile areas, the army usually used the hollow square/oblong or the open half-square or wedge formations for marching, but when this was not possible they did use the column, with extra layers of scouts and skirmishers outside. All marching formations were protected by auxiliary units in front, behind and on the flanks.

Roman cavalry (legionaries, auxiliaries and *numeri*) was trained for scouting, skirmishing and pitched battles. The cavalry's primary roles were scouting, skirmishing, guerrilla warfare, protection of the infantry during marching and battles, and pursuit of the defeated enemy. The Romans very rarely used their cavalry separately from infantry – the typical instances being when it was deployed as a separate vanguard or when it pursued a defeated enemy in front of the infantry. When the time came to fight a pitched battle, the Romans could perform very complex battlefield manoeuvres to confuse and overcome the enemy, thanks to the constant drilling of the men. The cavalry consisted of five basic categories:

1) The traditional Romano-Gallic-Spanish cavalry (legionaries and auxiliaries) equipped with a shield, helmet, armour sword and javelin(s) or spear(s), but who could use crossbows and bows when needed and could also fight like the Sarmatian and Parthian *kontoforoi* and cataphracts. The horses of this type of cavalry were usually unarmoured, but could also have chamfrons and side-coverings. Most of the cavalry belonged to this highly versatile category.
2) The second category consisted of the specialist mounted archers. These consisted primarily of auxiliaries and *numeri* of eastern origin.
3) The super heavy cavalry, the cataphracts (man and horse armoured, and rider armed with a spear, shield, sword and possibly with a bow), formed the third category of troops. Most of these consisted of troops from the East. The only known unit to belong to this category during this era is the *ala Gallorum et Pannoniorum catafractata*, which is attested for the first time in the reign of Hadrian, but may have been created by Trajan. The next definite piece of evidence for a new cataphract unit (*ala nova firma catafractaria Philippiana*) dates from the reign of Philip the Arab (244–249), but it is very likely that other units of cataphracts also existed. The two known examples belonged to the auxiliaries, but it is possible that some of the Eastern *numeri* were also equipped as cataphracted mounted archers and lancers. Regardless, it is clear that their numbers remained very small because the regular cavalry could also be equipped as such.[28]
4) The fourth category consisted of the troops equipped like the Sarmatian *contarii* (*kontoforoi*/lancers) or Arabic lancers. The key piece of equipment was the Sarmatian *contus*, which was wielded with two hands. The horses of this category were usually unarmoured, but could have the Roman-style cavalry armour mentioned above. These forces consisted of the legionary cavalry, auxiliaries and the *numeri*.
5) The Moorish/Berber extra light cavalry javeliners formed the fifth group.[29] Most of them did not use any armour or helmets, and their horses were also unbridled and unarmoured. The Moors naturally consisted of the native Berbers and belonged mostly to the *numeri*-class of troops, but some of the Moors were evidently recruited into a new bodyguard corps at some point during the second century AD.

The imperial stud-farms and taxpayers provided different horse breeds for the various types of cavalry to enable them to perform their combat roles in the best possible way.

The open order was used in marching and the close order for combat. The type of unit formation depended on the type of cavalry and combat mission. The unit formations consisted of: 1) rank-and-file squares/oblongs (the standard formation, with depths varying between three and ten ranks according to the quality of the unit and number of squires in the array) which were used either as units, or so that different files advanced in its turn forward and back to skirmish with javelins or bows; 2) wedges (rank-and-file version with sixty-four horsemen) used for breaking through the enemy array; 3) rhomboids used at least by the units of eastern origin (rank-and-file array with 128 horsemen) for all-around defensive and offensive purposes; 4) irregular throngs (*droungoi*) used in scouting, skirmishing, pursuit, ambushes and for fast movement on the battlefield. The Roman cataphracts appear to have also used the massive 'regimental' wedge for the breaking up of an enemy infantry formation.[30]

The extant evidence (e.g. in the texts of Caesar, Tacitus, Arrian and Trajan's Column) suggests that when the Romans deployed their cavalry separately for combat, they always posted a second line to serve as a reserve and used a separate small vanguard in front of the cavalry array before the battle. The evidence also suggests that these arrays became the basis for the Late Roman Italian drill in the sixth century *Strategikon*. This array had three different variants: 1) a small cavalry army with less than 5,000 men in which the second line had only one reserve division; 2) a medium-sized cavalry army with 5,000–15,000 men in which the second line consisted of two reserve divisions; 3) a large cavalry army in excess of 12,000–15,000 men with four reserve divisions.

It is clear that the Romans were already using cavalry reserves well before the birth of Christ, but we do not know when the other parts of the Italian formation were added. It is clear that the outflankers and flank guards were added to the formation when it was noted that the flanks of the first line needed extra protection. Similarly, it is clear that the fill-up *banda* ('flags' of men, usually 200–400 in strength) between the divisions of the second line (medium and large versions) came into existence when it was realised that the intervals between them could be too small for the first-line divisions to pass through when retreating unless there were men to keep the divisions apart. The rear guards behind the second line would also have been introduced when someone noted the need. My own theory is that the Italian array reached its final form of development under Gallienus, and that he put in place the final missing pieces of the array. It is probable that the Drill Formation obtained its name from the fact that Gallienus placed his new cavalry *Tagmata* at Milan.[31] It is impossible to know which of the features were added by Gallienus, but I have made the educated guess in the following diagrams that it would have been the fill-up *banda* between the units of the second line, because it was during his reign that the Romans started to employ cavalry in truly large formations. When deployed with the infantry for combat, the cavalry was usually formed on the flanks so that the heavier cavalry was placed closest to the infantry and the light cavalry farthest away.

The cavalry divisions of the Italian array consisted of units of *koursores* (runners/skirmishers) and *defensores* (defenders). The normal location for the *koursores* was on the flanks of the *defensores*, but the order could also be reversed. The *koursores* were typically used for skirmishing and pursuit in irregular order (*droungos*). In contrast, the *defensores* in the centre of each division always maintained their close order so that they could perform frontal attacks safely and protect the *koursores* when needed. The other tactical alternative was to use the entire cavalry line for a charge in close order. Regardless of the way in which the attack was conducted, the Romans always sought to outflank the enemy with wings or ambushers, and if that failed (e.g. because they were outnumbered), then they attempted to crush the enemy centre while the wings were kept back.

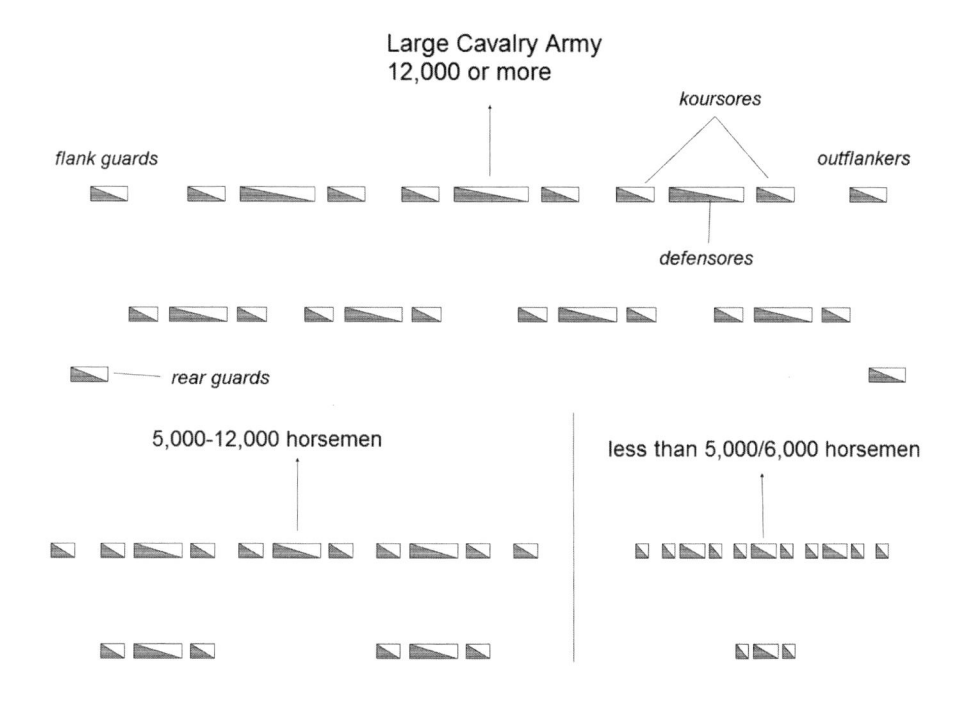

Large Cavalry Army 12,000 or more

flank guards — *koursores* — *outflankers*

defensores

rear guards

5,000-12,000 horsemen | less than 5,000/6,000 horsemen

The information in Arrian's *Taktika* and *Ektaxis kata Alanôn* proves that the Italian array cannot have been the only type of cavalry formation in use. The latter includes a formation in which the cavalry pursues Alans, which is likely to be the same as when the horsemen would have been deployed separately from infantry. The wings of the front line consisted of the Armenian *symmachiarii*, which means that these units were composed of *katafraktoi* (cataphracts, possibly used as a front rank), *kontoforoi* (*contarii*) and *hippotoxotai* (mounted archers). The six *lochoi* of auxiliary *alae* posted in the middle consisted of the *hippotoxotai*, who, despite being called mounted archers, were probably regular *alae* also equipped with javelins, swords and shields. The posting of mounted archers in front was naturally very good for pursuit. The two wing reserves appear to have consisted of the legionary cavalry, which was either divided into units of lancers (*kontoforoi, machairoforoi*) and javeliners (*logchoforoi, machairaforoi, pelekoforoi*), known in Greek military

54 Caracalla

theory by the term *elafroi* (light-armed); or their units consisted of all of these elements, so that the *kontoforoi* formed the two front ranks and the *lonchoforoi* the next two in a formation of four ranks. The information regarding the 200 *equites singulares* (elite auxiliaries), the bodyguards of the governor Xenophon (Arrian) which were posted as a reserve behind the centre, is unfortunately not conclusive because the extant extracts fail to state unequivocally whether the bodyguard also joined the rest of the cavalry in pursuit. It is possible that they remained behind the infantry. What is particularly noteworthy of this array is that it is conceptually quite different from the Italian formation, which included the *koursores* and *defensores* in all of the divisions. In Arrian's array, the whole front line can be considered to be the equivalent of the *koursores*, so that the units of the second line formed the *defensores*.

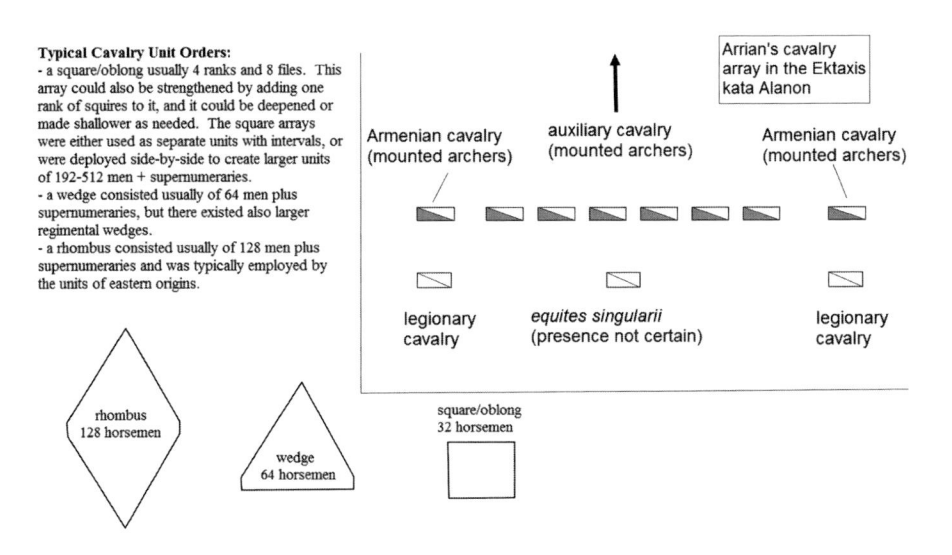

Typical Cavalry Unit Orders:
- a square/oblong usually 4 ranks and 8 files. This array could also be strengthened by adding one rank of squires to it, and it could be deepened or made shallower as needed. The square arrays were either used as separate units with intervals, or were deployed side-by-side to create larger units of 192-512 men + supernumeraries.
- a wedge consisted usually of 64 men plus supernumeraries, but there existed also larger regimental wedges.
- a rhombus consisted usually of 128 men plus supernumeraries and was typically employed by the units of eastern origins.

Arrian's cavalry array in the Ektaxis kata Alanon

Armenian cavalry (mounted archers) — auxiliary cavalry (mounted archers) — Armenian cavalry (mounted archers)

legionary cavalry — equites singularii (presence not certain) — legionary cavalry

rhombus 128 horsemen

wedge 64 horsemen

square/oblong 32 horsemen

The infantry combat formation included the cohortal arrays, with one to four lines of cohorts, and the phalangial formations, in which the cohorts were placed side by side as a single line that could be divided into two lines of phalanxes. Traditionally, the Romans placed their auxiliaries (a heavy infantry front with light infantry behind them) in front of their legions, but as the legions gradually became equipped like the auxiliaries this practice was abandoned. The final death blow to this system came when Caracalla granted citizenship to all freeborn men (see page 141). The depths of the cohorts (with light infantry behind) and phalangial arrays varied from six (four heavy infantry, two light), twelve (eight heavy, four light) and twenty-four (sixteen heavy, eight light), to fifty-two (thirty-two heavy, sixteen light). When the baggage train followed the army, it was placed behind the battle array.

The phalanx proper had three divisions if there were less than 24,000 men and four divisions if more. If the rear was unprotected (no baggage train, camp, artillery, hill etc.), the phalanx was divided into a double phalanx by forming the rear ranks of each unit into a separate line to protect the rear. The standard phalangial division combined features taken from both the Roman and Macedonian inheritance. The heavy infantry division/phalanx consisted of 4,096 men and the light infantry behind them 2,048 men, so that the division/phalanx consisted of about 6,000 men like the traditional legion.

The traditional Imperial battle order with the auxiliaries placed in front of the legions

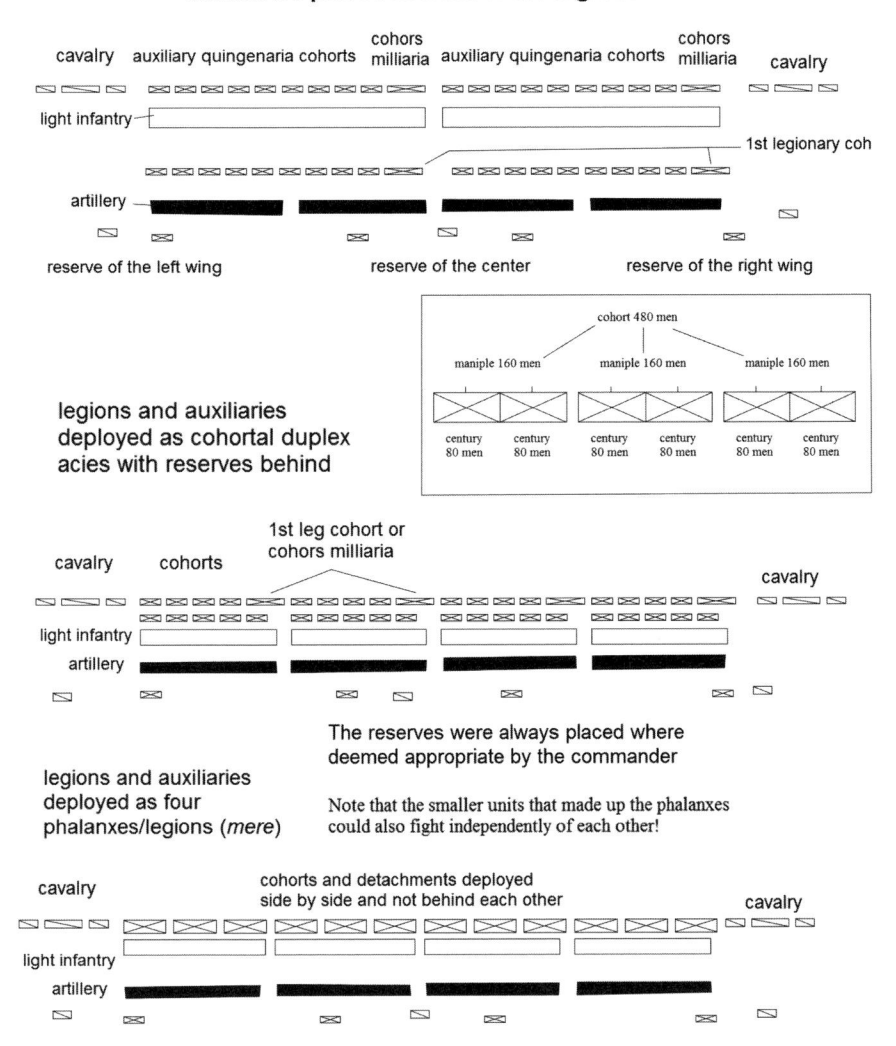

legions and auxiliaries deployed as cohortal duplex acies with reserves behind

cohort 480 men
maniple 160 men
century 80 men

The reserves were always placed where deemed appropriate by the commander

legions and auxiliaries deployed as four phalanxes/legions (*mere*)

Note that the smaller units that made up the phalanxes could also fight independently of each other!

cohorts and detachments deployed side by side and not behind each other

All of these arrays could be used for outflanking on one or two sides with various kinds of manoeuvres, of which the following diagrams present the standard ones mentioned by Vegetius and other sources (see Syvänne, 2004). The cavalry was usually posted on the flanks and behind as a reserve, but their location in the battle array could be varied according to the tactical needs. The location of the light infantry could also be varied so that these men were posted either behind, in front or on the flanks of the heavy infantry, or between the heavy infantry files or units of the heavy infantry. When the Romans used field artillery (*carroballistae and onagri*), these were placed behind the light infantry.

At a unit level, the infantry combat units could be deepened (to break through the enemy array, or to prevent a breakthrough), shallowed/widened (to outflank the enemy, or to prevent outflanking), divided in half so that the rear ranks faced the rear (the two-faced *orbis/amfistomos* array), the ranks of the units could be divided into two units to form a double phalanx, or the enemy could be harrassed by using the *serra* (saw) formation in which alternate units advanced and retreated. The units could also be used to form a wedge (*cuneus, embolon*; or to form a hollow rhombus *caput porcinum* with the help of reserves?) to break through the enemy line, be formed as a hollow wedge (scissors) against an enemy wedge, or the array

simplified versions of the standard infantry battle formations

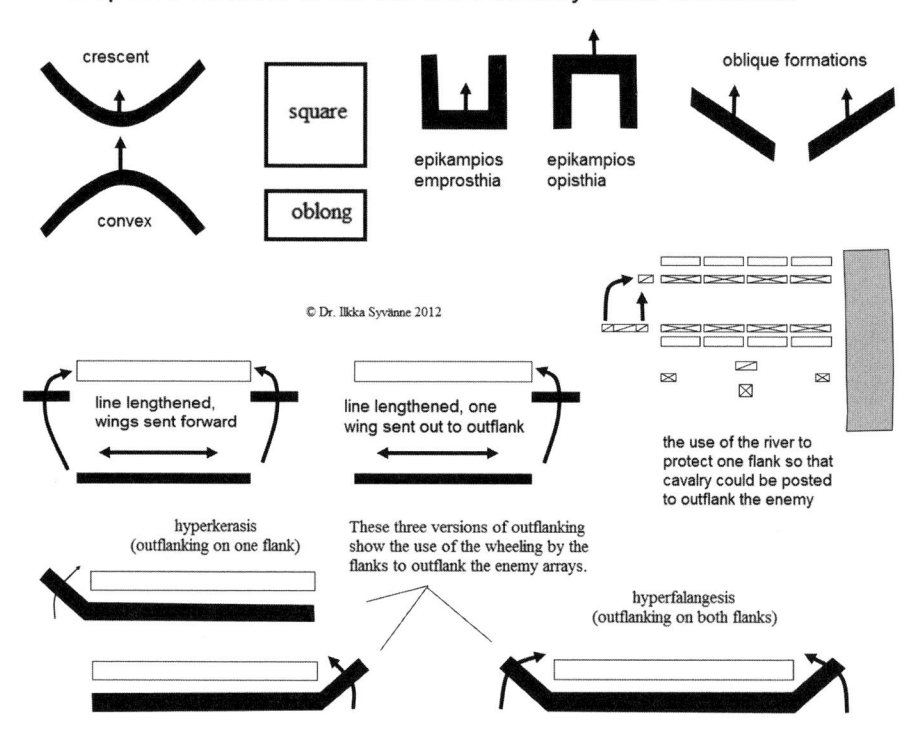

© Dr. Ilkka Syvänne 2012

hyperkerasis (outflanking on one flank)

line lengthened, wings sent forward

line lengthened, one wing sent out to outflank

These three versions of outflanking show the use of the wheeling by the flanks to outflank the enemy arrays.

the use of the river to protect one flank so that cavalry could be posted to outflank the enemy

hyperfalangesis (outflanking on both flanks)

could be opened up to let enemy cavalry/elephants/chariots through between *antistomos* phalanxes (two phalanxes facing each other). The units could also be formed into independently, operating irregular *globi* (sing. *globus*; globe, often an irregular wedge or rhomboid in shape) against the enemy. It was also possible to form a separate wedge of infantry in front of the phalanx proper to break up the impetus of the enemy cavalry charge, or use club-bearers in open formation for the same purpose. The fact that each of the cohorts consisted of three maniples (with

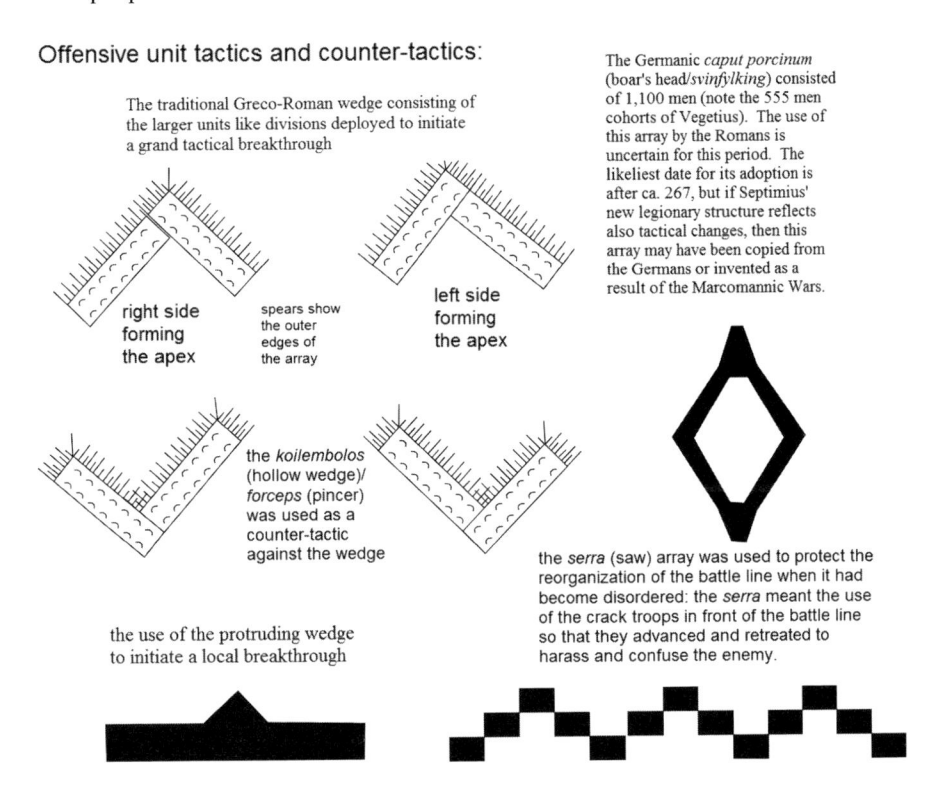

Offensive unit tactics and counter-tactics:

The traditional Greco-Roman wedge consisting of the larger units like divisions deployed to initiate a grand tactical breakthrough

right side forming the apex

spears show the outer edges of the array

left side forming the apex

the *koilembolos* (hollow wedge)/ *forceps* (pincer) was used as a counter-tactic against the wedge

the use of the protruding wedge to initiate a local breakthrough

The Germanic *caput porcinum* (boar's head/*svinfylking*) consisted of 1,100 men (note the 555 men cohorts of Vegetius). The use of this array by the Romans is uncertain for this period. The likeliest date for its adoption is after ca. 267, but if Septimius' new legionary structure reflects also tactical changes, then this array may have been copied from the Germans or invented as a result of the Marcomannic Wars.

the *serra* (saw) array was used to protect the reorganization of the battle line when it had become disordered: the *serra* meant the use of the crack troops in front of the battle line so that they advanced and retreated to harass and confuse the enemy.

The defensive unit arrays when the enemy had managed to outflank the Romans:

The *amphistomos* (double-fronted) array used to face enemy behind **(left)**. The Roman name for this array was *orbis* because in practice the array faced all directions simultaneously **(right)** if there was a need for this.

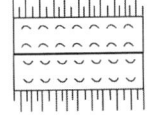

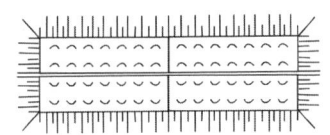

the difalangia array (double phalanx) was used to face the enemy from two directions when there was enough time to form it.

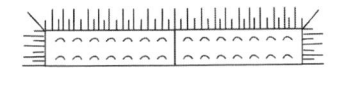

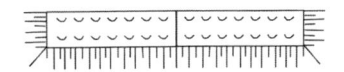

58　Caracalla

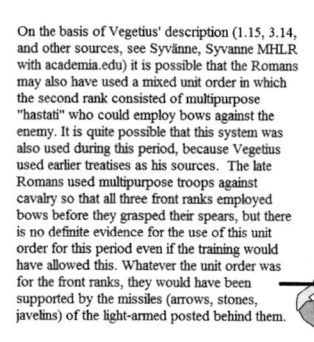

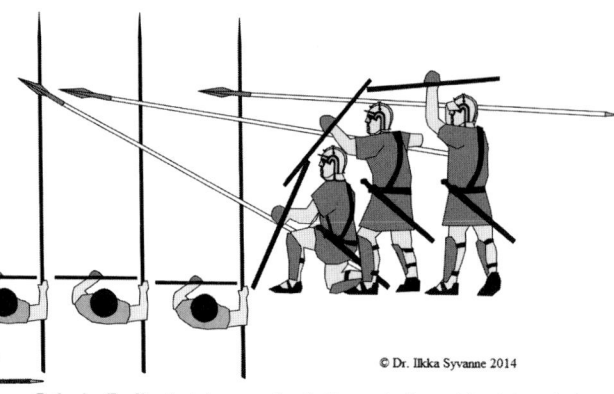

On the basis of Vegetius' description (1.15, 3.14, and other sources, see Syvänne, Syvanne MHLR with academia.edu) it is possible that the Romans may also have used a mixed unit order in which the second rank consisted of multipurpose "hastati" who could employ bows against the enemy. It is quite possible that this system was also used during this period, because Vegetius used earlier treatises as his sources. The late Romans used multipurpose troops against cavalry so that all three front ranks employed bows before they grasped their spears, but there is no definite evidence for the use of this unit order for this period even if the training would have allowed this. Whatever the unit order was for the front ranks, they would have been supported by the missiles (arrows, stones, javelins) of the light-armed posted behind them.

Defensive Foulkon/testudo vs. cavalry. In this array the front rank kneeled to make it more difficult for the men to flee while the width was kept more open so that the men were able to place the bottom of their spears/javelins against the ground. Note the difference in reach between the *hasta* (top) and *pila* (bottom). This could be very important for psychological reason, but not decisive when the soldiers consisted of steadfast men. If the men had the will to stay in place, the javelin throwers, slingers, and archers provided long range missile fire against the approaching cavalry. The openness of the formation enabled the front rankers (or the light-armed behind them) to charge forward at the horsemen who would have been forced to stop just in front of the array. This unit order could also be used with curved rectangular shields.

Offensive Foulkon/testudo
In this array the shields were interlocked both in width and depth. The standard way to hold javelins and spears in this array was to use the underarm grip so that the javelins or spears could be used as missiles just prior to the attack with swords. This array was usually employed only against infantry, but it could also be used against cavalry (the version shown below), if it was necessary to obtain extra protection against enemy missiles, or when the Romans had no time to adopt the defensive *testudo* vs. cavalry. If it was used against cavalry, then the front rank probably used the underarm grip to obtain longer reach. This unit order was not particularly well-suited for units using the curved rectangular shield.

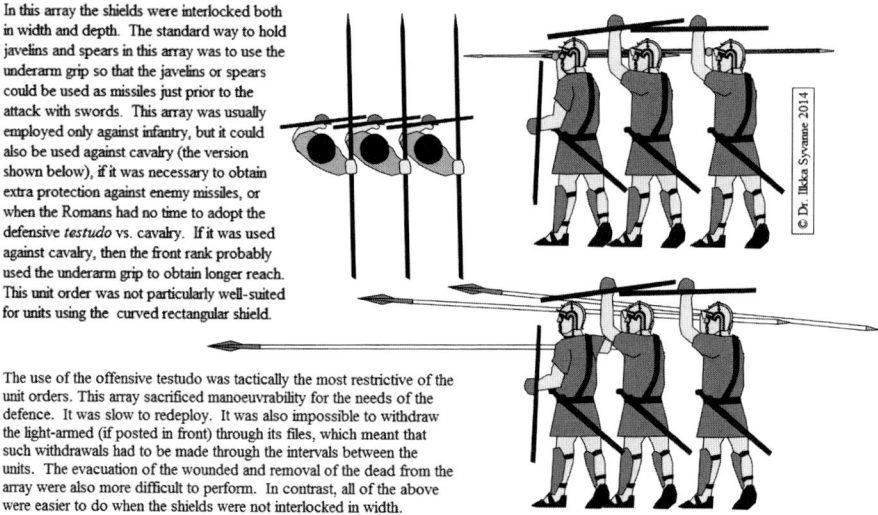

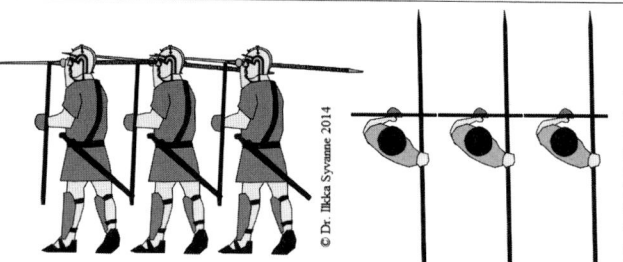

The use of the offensive testudo was tactically the most restrictive of the unit orders. This array sacrificed manoeuvrability for the needs of the defence. It was slow to redeploy. It was also impossible to withdraw the light-armed (if posted in front) through its files, which meant that such withdrawals had to be made through the intervals between the units. The evacuation of the wounded and removal of the dead from the array were also more difficult to perform. In contrast, all of the above were easier to do when the shields were not interlocked in width.

Close order (shields rim-to-rim) used in combat when the men were fully armoured. This array (men armed with either javelins or spears) could be used against both infantry and cavalry (in this case some of the men would probably have used the underarm grip) even if it was more typical to use this order against footmen. This unit order could also be used by men using the curved rectangular shield.

two centuries each) enabled the different maniples of the cohorts to fight separate battles, which was also true to a lesser extent for the separate centuries. For combat mechanics/face of battle, see my *The Age of Hippotoxotai*, articles at academia.edu, Appendix 2 and *MHLR*.

The infantry units could be deployed in four different unit orders: 1) open order used for marching; 2) close order (*pyknosis*, shields in files placed rim-to-rim) for attack; 3) tortoise order, with a shield-roof which had three variants (*synaspismos/testudo/foulkon*, shields locked rim-to-boss against archers; an assault *testudo* against fortifications with shields rim-to-boss, which could have some men kneeling to help others behind mount the formation; and *foulkon/testudo*, used against cavalry, in which the front rank kneeled and the following three ranks interlocked their shields with the ones in front, the shields in files placed almost rim-to-rim to enable the pointing of spears by the three to four ranks); 4) irregular order (*droungos*, a throng). The standard combat tactics were to use the *pyknosis* (when there was no need for extra cover from shields) and *synaspismos* (when extra protection was needed against missiles) order against infantry. The tortoise array with a kneeling front rank was naturally used to face cavalry charges. The standard tactical doctrine was to throw the spears and javelins and then use swords when facing infantry, and to use spears or *pila* for thrusting when facing cavalry. In all variants, the light infantry and artillery supported the attack or defence with volleys of missiles. The irregular order was naturally used when the terrain required this or when it was necessary to move the men from one locale to another very fast.

Siege Warfare
Romans possessed the most sophisticated siege engines and techniques available at the time and had an absolute superiority over all of their enemies in these fields. Consequently, the Romans could expect to be able take any enemy fortification they wanted if they possessed enough provisions for the operation, while also being able to defend any and all of their major fortified places. Roman siege equipment consisted of artillery (*ballistae, onagri*), cranes, siege towers, battering rams, siege sheds, pickaxes, drills, sambucas (counter-weight tubes), *helepolis* ('city-taker'), a sort of flame-thrower operated by bellows used against stone walls, mantlets and various kinds of ladders. The artillery could shoot fire-darts, fire-bombs, stones, arrows, darts and spears. Offensive siege techniques included assault, undermining of walls, clearing of the enemy from walls with missiles (e.g. with artillery pieces mounted on siege-towers and/or mounds) and blockade to starve the enemy. Defensive siege techniques included the use of all the above-mentioned pieces of equipment, along with counter-mining, padding to protect the walls, counter-mounds and towers and relief armies.[32]

60 Caracalla

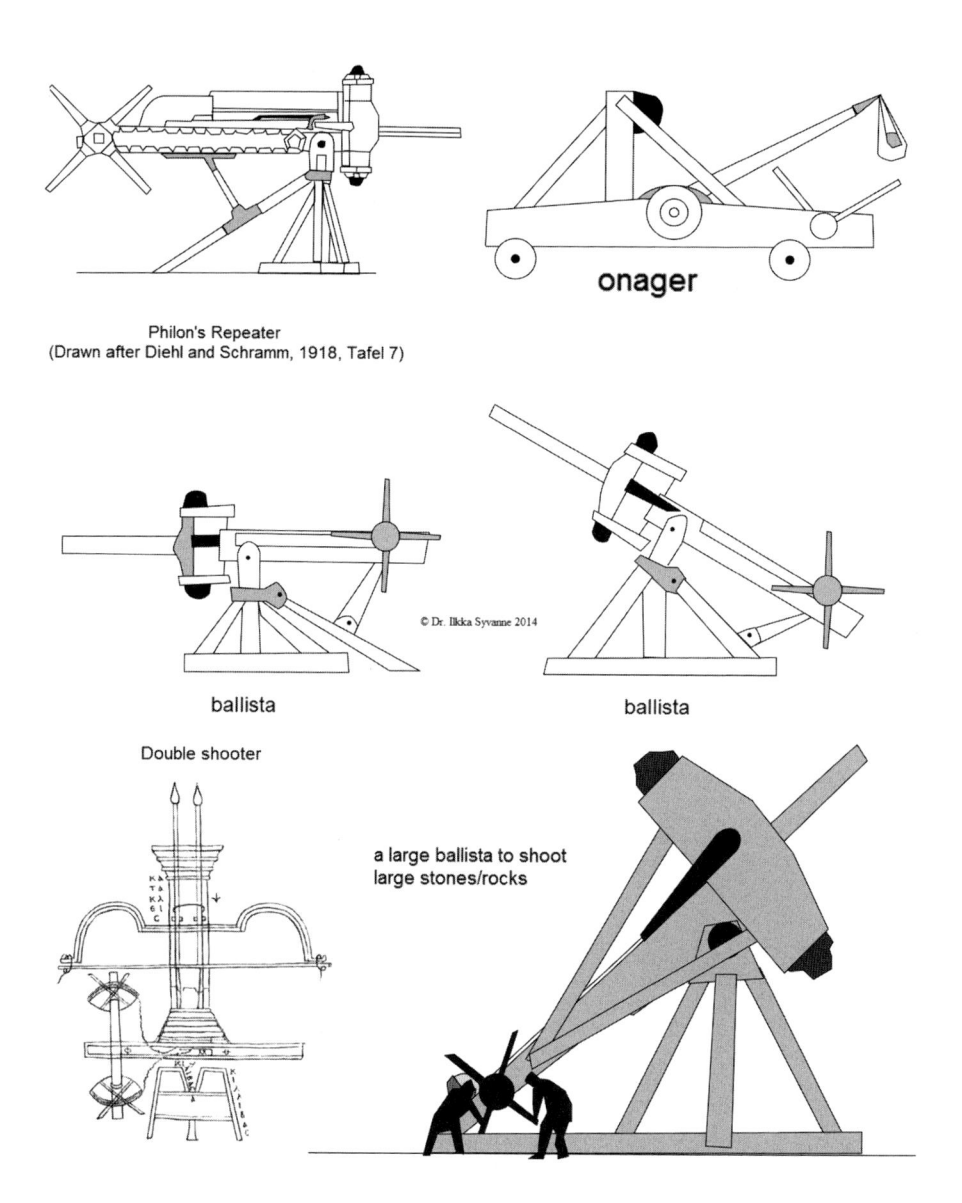

Philon's Repeater
(Drawn after Diehl and Schramm, 1918, Tafel 7)

onager

ballista

ballista

Double shooter

a large ballista to shoot large stones/rocks

The Imperial Navy[33]

The Imperial Fleet consisted of two classes: 1) the Praetorian fleets of Italy; 2) the Provincial fleets posted in the provinces. The two Praetorian fleets were *Classis Praetoriae Misenatium/Misenatis* and *Classis Praetoriae Ravennatum/ Ravennatis/Ravennas*, both based in Italy. The Provincial fleets consisted of the *Classis Alexandrina, Classis Syriaca, Classis Nova Libyca, Classis Germanica, Classis*

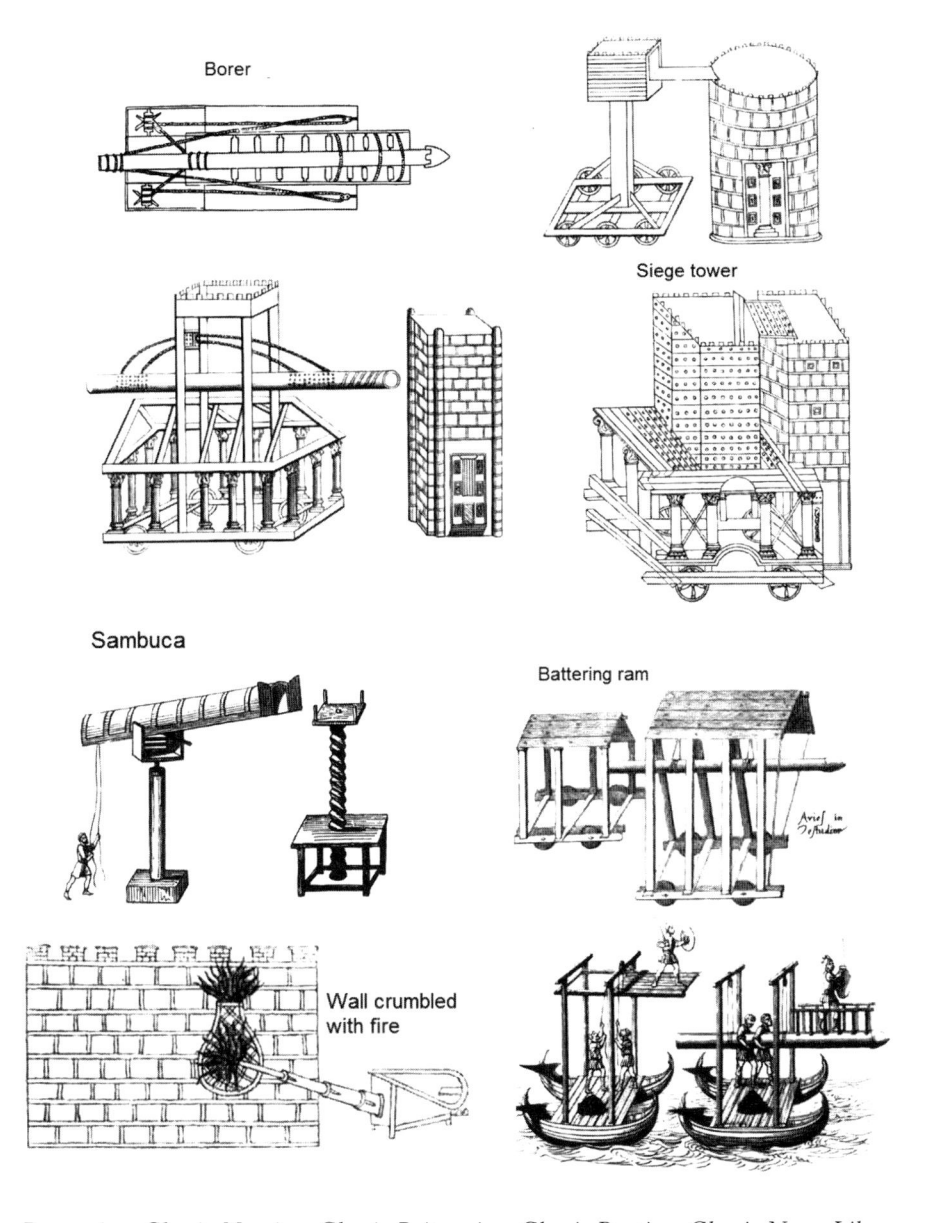

Pannonica, Classis Moesica, Classis Britannica, Classis Pontica, Classis Nova Libyca and *Classis Africana*.[34] The coast of Mauretania may have possessed a separate small fleet called *Classis Mauretanica* (of thirteen *liburnae*) to prevent attacks by Moorish pirates, but most researchers think that it consisted of detachments of Syrian and Alexandrian fleets, or alternatively of a detachment just of the latter. In my opinion, it is more than likely that there was also a separate fleet to protect the Mauretanian

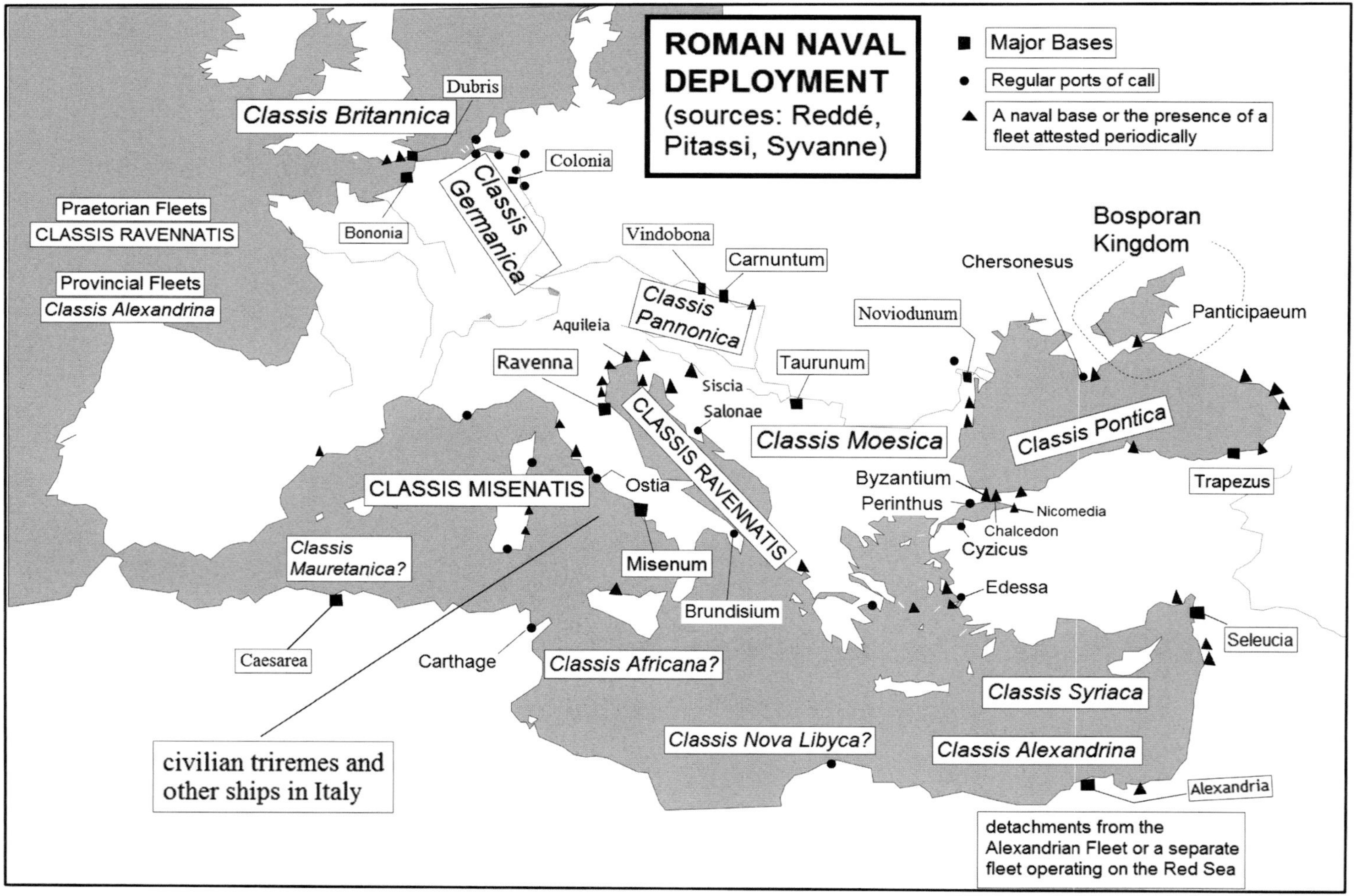
ROMAN NAVAL DEPLOYMENT
(sources: Reddé, Pitassi, Syvanne)
Major Bases
Regular ports of call
A naval base or the presence of a fleet attested periodically
Praetorian Fleets
CLASSIS RAVENNATIS
Provincial Fleets
Classis Alexandrina
Classis Britannica
Dubris
Bononia
Colonia
Classis Germanica
Vindobona
Carnuntum
Classis Pannonica
Aquileia
Ravenna
Siscia
Salonae
Taurunum
Classis Moesica
Noviodunum
Chersonesus
Bosporan Kingdom
Panticipaeum
Classis Pontica
Trapezus
Byzantium
Perinthus
Nicomedia
Chalcedon
Cyzicus
Edessa
CLASSIS RAVENNATIS
CLASSIS MISENATIS
Ostia
Misenum
Brundisium
Classis Mauretanica?
Caesarea
Carthage
Classis Africana?
civilian triremes and other ships in Italy
Classis Nova Libyca?
Classis Syriaca
Seleucia
Classis Alexandrina
Alexandria
detachments from the Alexandrian Fleet or a separate fleet operating on the Red Sea

coast. The reason for this is that it is difficult to see why Syrian and Egyptian fleets would have been used to protect the Mauretanian coast when there existed separate fleets for the provinces of Africa and Cyrene.

The accompanying map shows the naval deployment at the turn of the third century. It demonstrates clearly how the Praetorian fleets were used as strategic reserves while the day-to-day defence and protection of the sea lanes and rivers was left in the hands of the Provincial fleets.

The ways in which naval forces were used depended on the needs and goals set up by each emperor for each particular period of time. This meant that the use of the naval assets usually formed only one aspect of the overall strategy. In order to achieve a particular political, economic or military objective, emperors could employ simultaneously (for example) any combination of trade embargo, diplomacy, alliances, threats of military action, special operations and actual military action. Regardless of this, some general conclusions regarding the use of naval power can be made. Depending on the type of fleet and the size and type of vessel used, the fleets were typically used for five major missions: 1) to control the seas and rivers (if there existed any naval threat, it was either defeated in combat and/or forced to remain inactive); 2) to project power ashore with amphibious operations, blockades and active siege operations; 3) to raid enemy coasts and shipping when necessary (this was true only on the Irish, North, Black, Red and Arabic Seas and on the Indian Ocean, because the Mediterranean was a Roman lake); 4) to protect shipments and trade routes; 5) to protect cities, coastal areas and other frontiers. It was the navy that enabled the Romans to collect taxes, to transport men and supplies so that their land forces could overcome the enemies on land, and to control the trade networks. In short, the Roman ability to maintain their empire was entirely based on their control of the seas. The Romans also projected power from land to sea in two ways: 1) they captured places that could be used as harbours and thereby denied the enemy access to the sea; 2) their own harbours were protected by walls and artillery, which means that their unsophisticated foes could not threaten these unless they could gain access to them through surprise or treachery.[35]

Coastal defence consisted of passive/defensive measures (forts, towers, fortified cities and towns along coasts and rivers) and active/offensive measures undertaken by the fleets. The defence (control of harbours, collection of tolls/taxes, prevention of smuggling and wrecking, guarding of coasts against piratical attacks) was performed mainly by the civilian police/paramilitary forces (probably under the so-called *limenarchae*), with the support of military forces detached for this duty, while the active/offensive defence was mainly performed by fleets, with the possible help of corvéed civilian ships used for active anti-piratical duties. If there was a special emergency resulting from piracy, special prefects (*praefectus orae maritimae*) could also be appointed to take control of all defensive and offensive measures needed to protect a section of the coastline. During the Principate, such prefects were appointed for example for the coasts of the Black Sea, Mauretania, Hispania

Tarraconensis and the Red Sea. Herodian's text suggests that the Italian cities at least were still required to possess triremes with crews as they did during the Republican era, which the emperor could order to be mobilized for military purposes. These triremes formed a similar last-ditch reserve as the civilian conscripts of Italy were for the legions. The provinces were also required to contribute warships, and one may assume that they could also be ordered to man them.[36]

Despite the fact that the navy was absolutely indispensable for the Romans, they still considered it an auxiliary service, so the main recruiting ground for the Misenum fleet lay in the East, and for the Ravenna fleet in the Danubian and Illyrian provinces. Unsurprisingly, the vast majority of the staff of the provincial fleets also consisted of provincials. The sailors and marines of the Praetorian fleets received the same salaries as *equites cohortis* of the auxiliary forces, while the regulars of the Provincial fleets received the same salaries as the *milites cohortis* of the auxiliary forces (Bohec, 2000, p.212). The lowly status of the navy is also apparent in that it included significant numbers of freedmen. The length of service for seamen/marines/mariners was twenty-eight years, at the end of which the men were granted Roman citizenship. In general, naval officers belonged to the equestrian class, but some of the emperors also appointed freedmen and foreigners as admirals.

Each of the Praetorian fleets had a single naval legion attached to them (Vegetius 4.31). In contrast to the rest of the navy, it seems probable that the naval legions had similar terms of service as their comrades on land, with the exception that their commanders belonged to the equestrian class. It was thanks to this that the Praetorian fleets were always combat-ready and could transport a legion wherever needed. According to Vegetius, the fleet of Misenum protected the western shores of Italy and formed a reserve fleet for Gaul, Spain, Mauretania, Africa, Egypt, Sardinia and Sicily, and the fleet of Ravenna protected the Adriatic and formed a reserve fleet for Epirus, Macedonia, Achaia, Propontus, Pontus, the Orient, Crete and Cyprus. In practise, however, the fleet of Misenum saw service all over the empire, because it was the most powerful fleet in the Mediterranean, and detachments of both fleets could be sent wherever needed. In addition to this, both fleets posted detachments of sailors/mariners in the city of Rome to operate the canvas awnings of the Colosseum and stage mock naval battles with gladiators. Detachments of mariners could also be sent to assist the field armies, as Pseudo-Hyginus' treatise proves. Besides their regular duties, the Praetorian fleets also acted as deterrents against would-be usurpers. Under Septimius Severus, and presumably also under Caracalla, the Praetorian fleets were united under a single prefect (see PIR2 Cn. Marcius Rustius Rufinus), which means that both fleets were used to support the imperial campaigns.

Modern calculations suggest that the Misenum fleet consisted of at least one six (*sexteres/hexeres*), one five (*quinquereme*), ten fours (*quodriremes*), fifty-two triremes and fifteen *liburnae*, while the Ravenna fleet had two fives, six fours, twenty-three triremes and four *liburnae*. The port of Ravenna could apparently hold 250 ships

(Jordanes Get. 29, after Dio), which suggests that the harbours also possessed naval transports and supply ships in addition to their warships.

The provincial fleets were primarily used for the suppression of piracy and the transport of personnel and supplies. In order to enable them to perform these missions, the provincial fleets had lighter and more mobile vessels: 1) one trireme which served as a flagship for the commanding prefect; 2) *liburnae*; 3) blue-coloured scouting ships (*scaphae exploratoriae*); 4) other smaller vessels and boats. The provincial river fleets possessed specialized river versions of the *liburna*. Later evidence from the Theodosian Code (7.17.1 in January 412) suggests that the river fleets could consist of large numbers of vessels. According to this document, the areas which in the third century were controlled by the *Classis Moesica* had 225 *naves lusoriae* in 412.[37] It is unlikely that the figures would have been smaller in the third century.

The command structure of each of the fleets appears to have consisted of the following: Fleet Prefect (*praefectus classis*); 2nd-in-command *subpraefectus*; *navarchi*, each in charge of several ships; *trierarchi* (captains of ships). The *navarchi* were also graded, so the most senior of the *navarchi* was *navarchus princeps*, whom we may possibly equate with the *tribunus maius/subpraefectus*. The *navarchi* and *trierarchi* were also classed according to the ranks held by the regular army, so the *navarchi* were classed either as tribunes or highest-ranking fleet centurions (*centuriones classiarii*), while the *trierarchi* were classed either as *optiones navaliorum* or *suboptiones* depending upon the size of the vessel under their command. The NCOs on board the ships consisted at least of: armourer (*armorum custos*); standard bearers (*signiferi*); trumpeters (*tubicines* and *cornicines*); a helmsman (*gubernator*), a bow-officer/helmsman's adjutant (*proreta/proretus*); *nauphylax* (supply officer or ship-guard, or both?); a man to give timing for the oarsmen (*hortator*); and a musician to give the rhythm to oar movements (*symphoniacus*). The *liburnae* and larger ship also had two doctors/medics (*medicus, subunctor/strigilarius*), attendants to the sacrifices (*victimarii*) and other attendants.[38]

Each of the fleets also possessed administrative staff consisting of the *quaestores classici* (pay, equipment and supplies), *cornicularius* (officer), *beneficiarius* (appointee), *actuarius* (clerk), *scribae* (writers) and *librarii* (librarians/archivists). The fleet paymaster (*dispensator classis*) and *tabularius* (clerk) were not considered to be on active service because they were freedmen or slaves. Other naval specialists included pilots (*gubernatores*), rowers (*remiges*), sailors (*nautae*), marines/soldiers (*milites*), specialist elite *propugnatores* (front-rank fighters), *balistarii* (artillerymen), *sagittarii* (archers), *urinatores* (divers), craftsmen (*fabri*), sail-trimmers/makers (*velarii*) and rowing masters (*celeustae* or *pausarii*).[39]

The fleets, just like the land forces, could be required to contribute detachments for campaign purposes, as happened for example during the British campaign in 208–211 (see Chapter 3). These forces had temporary commanders who were graded according to their rank of importance. The naval detachments which included units

66   Caracalla

from the Praetorian fleets were commanded by a *praepositus vexillationis*, who was usually a very high-ranking person. The detachments consisting of provincial forces were put under a *praepositus classis/classibus*, the rank of whom was commensurate to the importance of the mission. According to Reddé, the Romans introduced a new title, *praepositus reliquationis*, for a *primus pilus* left in temporary command of a naval base when its fleet was on a campaign.[40]

Ships
All estimations regarding the size of the Roman navy are educated guesses, and therefore it is not surprising that modern researchers have been unable to reach a consensus opinion. My own estimate is that the Roman navy consisted of at least one six, two fives, 14 fours, 83 triremes, 523 *liburnae* and 1,776 patrol boats.[41] Unfortunately, it is impossible to make any accurate estimation for the overall size of the fleet because historians have not reached any consensus regarding the number of ships, and the estimates for the sizes of the crews vary so much that some believe the crew of a *liburna* to be about eighty to 120 men while others estimate that the *liburnae* had crews of 200–220. My own very rough 'guesstimate' is that the navy consisted at least of 75,000–120,000 fighting men and seamen, but that it may have had considerably more men than this because this figure does not include the

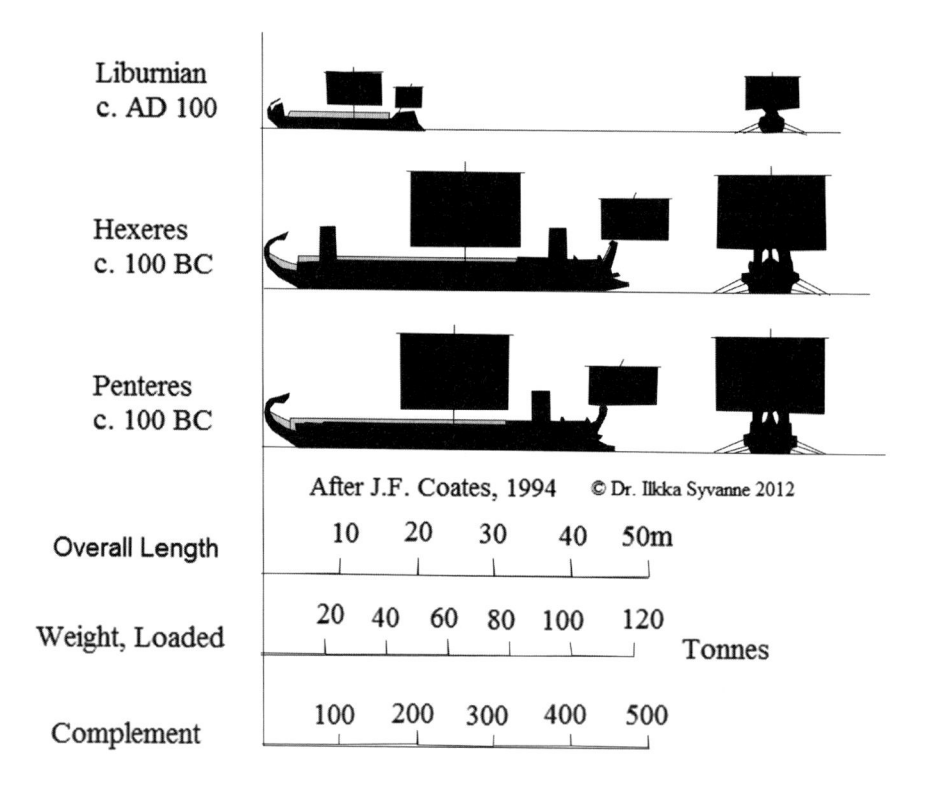

workforce needed to maintain the navy. The maintenance of the fleet was clearly a major undertaking, but well worth it.

The Romans used a great variety of ships, boats and rafts for all sorts of needs. Their fleets possessed specialist transport ships, for example for the movement of horses and military gear, but the bulk of the transports would have always consisted of the corvéed civilian transport ships. The standard Roman warship was a galley, which came in many sizes and shapes, but the vast majority of the warships consisted of the *liburnae*, which were the real workhorse of the navy. The *liburna* was a fast ship, ideally suite to chasing pirates and still large enough to encounter any enemy ship with the expectation that the *liburna* would prevail. My own view is that the *liburnae* would have had two ranks/remes of oars, so that each side would have had two banks of twenty-five oars for a total of 100 oars. The reason for this conclusion is that the later bireme *dromones*, which were based on the *liburna* design, had this number of oars. The Romans did still possess some behemoths, but their numbers were drastically reduced from the days of Actium because the Romans now had absolute naval mastery. The *hexeres/hexeris* (six), quinquereme (five) and quadrireme (four) were definitely equipped with both *onagri* and *ballistae*. It is also probable that the triremes (three) and *liburnae* could carry both *onagri* and *ballistae*,

Roman merchant ship used to transport supplies (source: Lamarre)

Below: Roman war galley (source: Lamarre)

a spear shooter?

so that river fleets could employ both to clear landing beaches, even if it is likelier that both of these classes of ships carried primarily *ballistae*. The majority of these war galleys were equipped either with rams or what I have called hybrid-ram/spur-bows, a transitional version of the spur.[42]

Naval Tactics[43]

The general rule of thumb for ancient naval warfare is that sailing was usually avoided in winter and in bad weather, but, as always, there were exceptions to the rule. In addition to this, knowledge of winds, tides, locale and signs of weather played a far greater role than on land.

Naval combat followed the same principles as on land. Scouting boats and ships were used for intelligence-gathering so that commanders could plan their own action. If possible, the Romans attempted to surprise or ambush the enemy, but if this was not possible then they could employ their superior ships with superior crews against them. None of their enemies possessed ships that would have been a match for Roman war galleys, which meant that the Romans could expect to beat any enemy fleet, even when they were outnumbered.

The standard naval battle formations were: 1) the crescent formation, with the best ships and men posted on the flanks to outflank the enemy; 2) the convex array, in which the best ships and men were placed in the centre to break through the enemy array; 3) a double convex array for greater safety; 4) a line abreast with reserves behind; 5) a double line abreast for maximum safety, if there existed enough ships for that; 6) a defensive circle. The two standard naval tactics were: 1) penetration of the enemy formation with a *diekplous* manoeuvre, in which one galley rushed forward into the interval between two enemy galleys, and was then followed up by other galleys so that the first sheared the oars and the second rammed the immobile ship; 2) *periplous* manoeuvre, in which the flank galleys extended their line to outflank the enemy line.[44]

When the Romans used larger ships, they started to bombard the enemy with *ballistae* and bows at a distance of about 300–600 metres. The *onagri*, slings and staff-slings joined the action at a distance of about 150 metres. The *onagri* could be used to fire stones and fire-bombs, while the *ballistae* were primarily used to shoot incendiary arrows. At a distance of about 40 metres, the Romans started to throw light javelins, and at about 20–30 metres they threw heavy javelins. At a ramming distance, Roman ships either rammed, sheared the enemy's oars or grappled the enemy vessel for boarding.

The fighting component onboard each ship consisted of the marines/soldiers (*milites*), sailors (*nautae*) and oarsmen (*remiges*), with the possible addition of land forces to bolster their numbers. Sailors and oarsmen had a double duty, as they were also expected to be able to fight. Modern research (e.g. Bishop & Coulston) suggests that marines wore the same pieces of equipment as land forces, but Vegetius' account (4.44) actually suggests that naval soldiers were better-protected than average

Arrian's *Ars Tactica* 43.1 proves that the horsemen also trained to use crossbows and/or torsion hand-bows from horseback. It is unfortunate that Arrian (or any other source) fails to tell us how the horsemen drew their crossbows, but there are two probable ways this could have been done. The Romans certainly knew the cranequin and could have used it, but I have made the educated guess that they would have used the simpler method of just using a stirrup in the crossbow so that the archer could place his foot in the stirrup and draw the cord back. The sources also fail to tell us how the Romans used their mounted crossbowmen in combat. One possibility is that these were used for a single salvo just before the other horsemen charged or that the crossbowmen protected retreating cavalry with their bolts or that these were used as snipers or that the horsemen just trained to use this weapon just in case it was needed for example in sieges.

legionaries and auxiliaries as they wore cataphract-armour or *lorica* (coat of mail?) with helmet and greaves, and had *scutum* (shields) which were stronger and larger than on land to withstand enemy stones. Just like their comrades on land, marines could expect to defeat their enemies in hand-to-hand combat thanks to their better training and higher quality equipment.

1.2. The Sources

When interpreting the information provided by ancient sources, one has to keep in mind that most of the ancient historians were very hostile towards Caracalla. The reason for the hostility is that Caracalla was conceived as an arch-enemy of the senatorial class and most of the ancient historians either sought to please the members of the senatorial class in the hopes of gaining their favour, or belonged to it themselves. As a result, one has to take almost everything they wrote about Caracalla with a grain of salt. This perceivable hostility is most visible in the reluctance to give Caracalla any credit for the very many successes of his foreign and military policies, as a result of which his reign can justifiably be called the apogee of Rome, after which the Roman Empire began its long, tortuous decline. My intention is to correct this injustice.

Another of the reasons that Caracalla has received such a bad press is that our extant sources have also been tainted by pagan bias. The reason for this hostility is that Caracalla ended the persecution of Christians and Jews and did not persecute homosexuals.[45] It is unfortunate that modern historians have not taken into account the bias caused by the later pagan 'counter-reform' against the Christians so clearly visible in these pagan sources. Ironically, the same tendency also appears to have received additional impetus from the propaganda of Constantine the Great and his successors, who found it in their interest to claim that it was the House of Constantine alone that was the true benefactor and protector of the Christians. Consequently, it was politically expedient to forget that Caracalla, Alexander Severus and Gallienus had all showed tolerance towards Christians (and Jews), and that Philip the Arab appears to have been a Christian himself. In the case of Gallienus, the falsification of history is at its most extreme, because his murderer Claudius II (supposedly an ancestor of Constantine) was given the credit for the victories won by Gallienus, as has been well demonstrated by Alföldi.

The principal extant sources for the life and reign of Caracalla are: *Scriptores historiae Augustae* (SHA Aelius Spartianus: Severus; Antoninus Caracallus; Antoninus Geta; and Opellius Macrinus, Maximini, Gordiani and by Julius Capitolinus; Elagabalus by Aelius Lampridius); Dio 78.1–79.10.3; Herodian 4.1–14.3; coins and inscriptions. Other less detailed sources are: Anonymous (sometimes credited to Sextus Aurelius Victor), *Epitome de Caesaribus* 21; Sextus Aurelius Victor, *Liber de Caesaribus* 21; Eutropius, *Historiae Romanae Breviarium* 8.20; Festus, *Breviarium Rerum Gestarum Populi Romani* 21; Orosius 18; Zosimus 1.9–10; Synkellos (Syncellus) AM 5701ff; Bar Hebraeus; Moses Khorenat'si; Michael Syrus (the Syrian, or the Great). It should be noted that some of these lesser sources include very important pieces of evidence that in places allow the correction of disinformation provided by the more detailed sources. In fact, the Latin tradition is in general slightly more favourable to Caracalla than the Greek tradition and includes additional variant versions of his life, which suggests that an alternative, more favourable tradition concerning the reign of Caracalla existed in antiquity, which was later suppressed. These sources include: SHA (Severus 18.8, 20.2; Car. 10.1–4, 11.5; Geta 7.3–6); Anon., *Epitome de Caesaribus* 21, sometimes ascribed to Sextus Aurelius Victor; Sextus Aurelius Victor, *Liber de Caesaribus* 21; Eutropius, *Historiae Romanae Breviarium* 8.20; Michael Syrus; Bar Hebraeus.

Unfortunately, despite acknowledging Dio's bias against Caracalla, most modern historians still seem to accept at face value Dio's characterization of Caracalla as a sexually depraved cowardly psychopath, because Dio was a very high-ranking contemporary (senator, governor and a member of the Emperor's Council) and eyewitness to the events he describes. These historians have failed to take fully into account the very intense hostility of Dio towards Caracalla, which taints his whole work. Dio's text is actually a prime example of what I have repeatedly stated: that historians should not assume that period sources are always better than later ones. The later sources can preserve traditions that the period authors suppressed. It is actually very easy to demonstrate the bias and falsification of the facts by Dio by analyzing the gross inconsistencies in his own work, some of which may, however, have resulted from inaccurate editing and shortening of the text by the Byzantine compilers (e.g. Xiphilinus, Zonaras, Exc. Val.). I will henceforth call all of these collectively Byzantine epitomizer or epitomizers, or similarly. Even if one can never be absolutely certain of the quality of such compilations, I have here made the assumption that the later Byzantine compilers would still have faithfully preserved the tone and content, so that all of the inconsistencies and biases would have also been present in the original text. In fact, it is quite easy to see that Dio has been carried away by his own hostility to such an extent that he even failed to streamline his text to take into account his own falsifications. On the basis of these inconsistencies, it is easy to see that Dio cannot have possessed any greater than mediocre abilities as a historian and military commander (as was recognized by Caracalla, who treated him and his senatorial ilk in a very high-handed manner).

The following analysis will make it abundantly clear that Dio was himself a liar who did not understand anything about military matters, tactics or strategy, or of the way in which Caracalla manipulated him and those around him. The other alternative is that Dio simply chose to distort the truth, even when he knew the facts behind the fiction, but did this with very little skill as he left so many inconsistencies in the text.

There are some notable and noble exceptions among modern historians to the tendency to see Caracalla through the coloured lens of Dio and his ilk.[46] These include, for example, C.R. Whittaker, B. Levick and P.A. Garcia, who all note the flagrant bias of Dio and the slightly less flagrant bias of Herodian against Caracalla. This realization has led Levick (pp.89–90) to suspect in her outstanding biography of Julia Domna, rightly in my opinion, that there may be something behind the complaints of Caracalla that it had been his brother who had been plotting against him. She also points out other instances. It comes, therefore, as no surprise that the expert of period military Ross Cowan (2009, p.29) calls Dio a bitter senator who was so hostile towards Caracalla that he was ready to even lie to blacken his memory. In the following reconstruction of Caracalla's reign, I will go even further in the rehabilitation of the man and his rule.

Very much contrary to common practice, I also consider the SHA a very important source not to be overlooked or dismissed with disdain, as is too often done. Every source, even those written by the worst liars, can and should be used to shed light on ancient events – note that the same historians who disdain the SHA are in the habit of using Dio, who is no better as a source. One should only analyze their version with even greater diligence! The modern, commonly accepted opinion among historians is that the SHA is a forgery that was written by a single unknown author in the late fourth century AD. It is possible that this is true, but the evidence for this is far from being as certain as usually presented in modern research. It is basically the opinion of one very influential nineteenth-century German historian, whose theory others have repeated like parrots ever since. The SHA is admittedly full of outright falsifications, inventions and disinformation, a case in point of which is its treatment of the reign of Gallienus, but with judicious use, the source can give us important pieces of evidence. The SHA is actually so carelessly written that the text abounds with inconsistencies, which can be used to reconstruct the likely truth behind the rubbish. The treatise is also tainted by various layers of pro-pagan, pro-senatorial class and pro-Constantine propaganda present in the sources used by the unknown author, authors or compiler. But once again, when one takes these biases into account, one can reinterpret the information provided by the SHA. In fact, when read carefully, it becomes apparent that the SHA contains important bits and pieces taken from a source or sources more favourable to Caracalla that has later been falsified. Therefore, these parts of the SHA act as a corrective to the more hostile tradition present in the same treatise.

Just like Dio, Herodian was a contemporary of Caracalla and therefore in a position to know the gossip of the day. Unfortunately, we know next to nothing about Herodian, which means that we cannot assess whether he was in a position to know the facts. Our knowledge is entirely based upon the information he provides of himself in his histories. However, two things make his account very valuable for the reconstruction of Caracalla's reign: 1) he has preserved alternative versions of events not found in Dio; 2) his account is slightly less biased against Caracalla.

Sextus Aurelius Victor's *Liber De Caesaribus* offers the best corrective to the otherwise overly hostile tradition based on the pro-senatorial sources. He lived and wrote during the fourth century. Victor was born on a small farm in North Africa a little after AD 320. Despite the fact that Victor's father was not a man of wealth, he managed to have his son educated. As a result of this education and personal talent, Victor was able to rise up the bureaucratic and social ladder so high as to reach the position of governor under Julian and urban prefect in 388/9 under Theodosius I. It is no wonder that Victor, who was a self-made man, felt sympathy towards such an emperor as Caracalla, who was quite ready to promote the careers of those whom he considered talented, no matter what their background.

Background 73

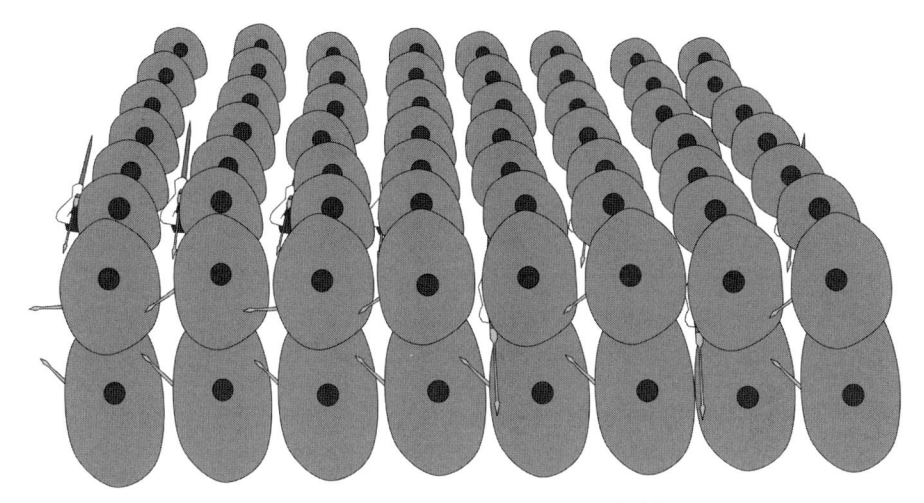

This illustration shows in a slightly simplified form how the *testudo* (which was meant for use against cavalry) would have looked from the front when the men were armed with *pila* and oval shields.

Notes

1. Legates and proconsuls naturally possessed staffs besides the regular military units posted to their province to enable them to perform their functions. According to A.H.M. Jones (pp.563–64), these included a centurion as *princeps officii*, six senior non-commissioned officers (three *cornicularii* and three *commentariensis*), twenty *speculatores* (intelligence officers), sixty *beneficiarii* (detached officers serving under the *speculatores*, see Syvänne ASMEA 2015), *stratores* (equerries in charge of levying horses for the court and cavalry) and other staff, and a bodyguard of *equites singulares* and *pedites singulares* (chosen elite units of auxiliaries). The *stratores* appear to have served collectively under the *Tribunus Stabuli*. A full summary of the personnel of each of the governors and officers with personnel left out here can be found in Le Bohec (2000, pp.53–56).
2. The national before the *numeri* is meant to separate the ethnic tribal *numeri* from the regular units, which could also be called *numeri* for a number of reasons. For details of the term *numerus/numeri*, see Southern (1989). I will give the national *numeri* henceforth the title *numeri*.
3. See for example Bohec (1994, pp.19–67).
4. *Aspidoforoi* = *skoutatoi* = *scutati* = *scutum*-shield-bearers (large rectangular, round or oblong shields).
5. It is possible that the *hastati*, *principes* and *triarii*, which still existed, used these different types of equipment and weapons so that each of these groups occupied certain ranks in the formation. In light of Vegetius, it is possible that in the second- to fourth-century version the *principes* formed the first rank (or ranks), contrary to the Republican practice. The continued use of these names at least until the fourth century

and the description of military drill by separate units of *hastati*, *principes* and *triarii* for the reign of Hadrian has led some historians (myself included; I gave a lecture in 2008 in which I suggested this on the basis of Speidel's book) like Speidel (2006), Cowan (2009, p.34) and Arguin (pp.289–291) to suggest the possibility that the Romans may still have continued to use their legions in the manipular manner. However, in light of the fact we have no specific evidence for the use of manipular tactics anywhere in the sources, whereas we have quite specific evidence for the use of units with different equipment for the different ranks, I would suggest that the different ranks were not used in the chequerboard manipular order, but as separate ranks in cohorts that could be advanced and retreated as needed. This could e.g. mean that the javeliners and lightly equipped men advanced in front to skirmish, then retreated back through the files of those who stayed behind (as long as the files were at least 80-100cm in width it was possible to advance and retreat through them). The other possibility is that the cohorts which consisted of three maniples (each of which had two centuries of eighty men) were indeed still separated as maniples when needed for combat, but in this case the resulting array would have been based on the original cohortal formation and not on the chequerboard manipular array of the Republican period. If this is the case, then the *hastati*, *principes* and *triarii* would have belonged to separate cohorts, but all extant evidence suggests that each of the cohorts actually consisted of all these three groups, which would then imply that the different ranks in each of the maniples/centuries would have reformed as separate units of *hastati*, *principes* and *triarii* – a thing which would have taken much longer to do than the separation of existing maniples of each cohort as separate lines, and which is therefore quite improbable. In my opinion, however, the most likely alternative remains that the *hastati*, *principes* and *triarii* should rather be seen as different ranks of the same unit.

6. For the equipment used during this period, see the conclusions included in this narrative together with the illustrations. See also D'Amato, Arguin (esp. p.159ff.), Bishop and Coulston, Cascarino, Elliot, Feugere, Mattesini and Stephenson. My interpretation of the equipment used during this period is based (but does not always follow their views) on their studies and narrative and visual sources.
7. Bishop and Coulston, p.257; Elliot with James, p.182ff.
8. As far as I know this has been noted first by me in vol. 1 MHLR.
9. Cowan (2003, pp.24–27); Syvanne (2011) (Caesar).
10. For a fuller discussion, see Bishop and Coulston, Cascarino (2008, esp. pp.121–22), Stephenson and Elliot. For the equipment used during this era, see the same studies with D'Amato (2009a) and the discussion in this book.
11. For a discussion of the various spear lengths in the sources, see Dawson. In my opinion, however, it is very probable that the Romans employed two basic spear lengths, 2.5m and 3.74m, the latter of which was meant for use against cavalry. The best proof of this is the spear lengths in the military treatises and the fact that the Danish bog finds (dated second to third century) have produced spears that match these sizes exactly. See my *Britain in the Age of Arthur*.
12. See Syvänne (2004) with Syvanne MHLR.
13. Elliot with Bishop and Coulston with Stephenson (2001) and James p.182ff., p.212ff.

14. See Vegetius 1.15–16, 3.14 with Syvänne (2004), Syvanne *MHLR* and academia.edu articles.
15. Based on Southern's (1989) analysis.
16. See Syvanne (MHLR Vol. 1); Le Bohec (2000, p.20ff.; 2009, pp.24–26); Arguin, pp.70–85.
17. See for example Dio 55.24.8, 58.2.2–3, with chapter 11.
18. Arguin, pp.80–81; Le Bohec (2000, pp.21–22); Webster, pp.98–99. Le Bohec (e.g. 2009, p.30) has argued that the *Urbaniciani* passed from the control of the Urban Prefect to the control of the Praetorian Prefect in the course of the second century. I have certain reservations regarding this conclusion. It is quite probable that the Praetorian Prefects as the highest ranking officers of the military establishment could indeed take control of the corps, but I would still suggest that the Urban Prefects retained control over the corps in some form or manner, because the Urban Prefects, and under them the *praefecti annonae* (there was usually only a single *Praefectus Annonae* at any given point in time for the city of Rome), were in charge of the supplying of the city of Rome and it would be very odd if the Urban Prefects had no control over the urban cohorts that were posted to protect this supply network. Furthermore, as will be made quite clear in this monograph, the Urban Prefects clearly controlled some troops in the provinces from which they obtained information regarding potential usurpers. The likeliest candidates for these troops remain the urban cohorts. On top of that, the Cilo affair makes this absolutely certain! He had been the commander of the *Urbaniciani* as their prefect.
19. The *Scholae* were units of cavalry bodyguards mostly of foreign origin which are for the first time securely dated to the reign of Constantine the Great, but it is clear that they date from an earlier era because the cavalry *scutarii* (sing. *scutarius*) referred to bodyguards, the origin of which can be dated to the third century. Notably, the *scutarii* are always associated with the *scholae* so that when one started a career in the *Scholae* as *scutarius* one was then promoted from there to the '*protectores*' units. E.g. the Emperor Maximinus Daia progressed from the position of *scutarius* (i.e. from *Scholae*) to that of *protector*. See Syvanne (MHLR Vo.1).
20. In fact, it is possible that the Parthian and Moorish bodyguards could date from an even earlier date. The Moors definitely had an important role in the Roman armed forces at least since the reign of Trajan, and the Romans definitely obtained *numeri* of Parthian archers as a result of their victories under Trajan and Marcus Aurelius/Lucius Verus. If you are interested in the life of Commodus in general, see Hekster with McHugh.
21. It is possible that the *Aulici* were created even before this because these appear to have existed under Pertinax and Commodus, and may have consisted of barbarian freedmen. See SHA Pertinax 8.1, 11.5–6, 13.9, 14.6.
22. See Syvanne (MHLR Vol.1).
23. This chapter is based on the outstanding studies of Fuhrmann (civilian policing esp. pp.2187) and Isaac (1990) and my additions to their conclusions in Syvanne MHLR Vol.1. For the role of the *beneficiarius consularis*, see Fuhrmann, Austin and Rankov, and Rankov (1986).
24. For further details, see the indispensable Luttwak with Syvanne/Syvänne (2004, MHLR). Some of the generalizations that Luttwak has made do not stand closer

scrutiny, but all the same it provides the best overview of the different kinds of strategies adopted. I recommend it highly.
25. I have based my educated guess on the locations of the legions, mainly in the information provided by Arguin, and I have placed the auxiliary units where Holder and Notitia Dignitatum place them.
26. For additional information, see the outstanding study of Roman intelligence services by Rose Mary Sheldon (2005), esp. p.143ff., together with Austin and Rankov and Syvanne (MHLR) and my forthcoming analysis of the role of *Pontifex Maximus*. After having written this book, I have also discussed these matters in greater detail in a research paper 'The Eyes and Ears: the Sasanian and Roman Spies AD 224–450', generously supported by a research grant by ASMEA in 2015 and published by Historia i Swiat.
27. See my presentations at academia.edu. Consequently, when one reads in Plutarch (Caesar 63) information regarding the warning given to Caesar by a seer that he would be killed on the Ides of March and that the seers serving him also stated the same after having made sacrifices, we should see in this the workings of an intelligence-gathering network that had been disguised as prophesying. The instance in which the teacher of Greek philosophy Artemidorus had become familiar with the plot to kill Caesar in the course of his teaching, as a result of which he tried to warn Caesar, should probably be interpreted as an early example of the private informer acting on his own initiative for the good of the ruler rather than a secret network of official spies, but one cannot be too regimented about this conclusion (Plutarch Caes. 65). It is still possible that he and other persons of similar position were also used for intelligence-gathering purposes as part of a secret organization. We are in no position to know the facts. This raises the interesting question whether there are similar systems operating in modern societies. We know that in the past the Jesuits acted as spies of the popes when they heard confessions, that the Soviets had thoroughly infiltrated the Russian Orthodox Church and that Opus Dei still acts in the interest of the Vatican, but are there also other similar religious organizations and systems that spy upon their own members for the benefit of some other organization? It should also be noted that the Russian Orthodox Church is a successor of the Byzantine Orthodox Church, that its emperors used as one of the tools of imperial control of the populace and clergy. The latter fact is usually overlooked by modern researchers of the Byzantine Orthodox Church, who usually merely concentrate on the different religious controversies and their political importance. This overlooks the most important reason behind such policies, which was to ensure control over the religious rhetoric used to control and manipulate the populace and soldiers, and at the same time to ensure the availability of intelligence of the activities of religious upper-class persons who could pose a threat to the emperor.
28. For additional information regarding the Roman cataphracts, see Syvanne/Syvänne (2004, MHLR); Eadie; Mielczarek; Coulston; Bishop and Coulston.
29. The Moors were most famous as lightly equipped ferocious mounted javeliners, but they also included mounted archers and infantry javeliners and archers. In general, see Hamdoune together with e.g. Herodian 3.3.4–5, MHLR vols.13 and chapter 13 of this book.
30. Based on Syvanne (MHLR Vol.1) with academia.edu material.

31. Several research papers and presentations since 2008, which I presented in greater detail in Slingshot (2011–2012). The same presentations and articles also prove that the Italian Array was already used in the first century AD.
32. For a fuller discussion, see Syvänne (2004) and Syvanne MHLR. The siege techniques remained largely unchanged from the third century BC until the twelfth century. The only significant new piece of equipment was the trebuchet, which was introduced by the sixth century. The siege techniques and tactics remained unchanged.
33. Based on Zahariade (2011), D'Amato (2009b), Rankov, Reddé (highly recommended), Pitassi (2009, 2011), Bounegru and Zahariade (Danubian Fleets), Starr, and Syvanne/Syvänne (2004, 2013–2014, MHLR).
34. The *Classis Nova Libyca* was created by Commodus to protect the corn shipments from Egypt. It is also probable that Commodus (SHA Com. 17.7) created a *Classis Africana* to protect the coastline along the province of Africa. Modern researchers usually think that the author has confused *Classis Africana* with the *Classis Nova Libyca* or that it was a temporary fleet to alleviate problems of food supply from Egypt. In my opinion, the SHA is likely to be true because the *Classis Nova Libyca* would have protected the coastline of Libya (Province of Cyrene/Cyrenaica) and the *Classis Africana* the coastline of the Province of Africa.
35. This chapter has been excerpted and adapted from my research paper/presentation held at Norfolk in 2014, which was partially based on my research paper presented at Annapolis in 2013.
36. This chapter has been adapted from my research paper/presentation held at Norfolk in 2014, which was partially based on my research paper presented at Annapolis in 2013. See also Herodian 2.14.6–7. For the measures undertaken to defend the coasts, see Starr (1943 with 1960). Septimius Severus and Antoninus Caracalla had exempted the discharged soldiers from the duty of contributing to the construction of ships, and they were also exempted from the duty of acting as tax collectors unless they had voluntarily enrolled into the city councils. See Paulus in Digest 49.18.5 (Levick 2, p.75). This suggests that the requirement to build warships extended also outside Italy proper.
37. For the fleets of the Danube, see the standard work by Bounegru and Zahariade, together with Zahariede's 2011 introduction to provincial fleets.
38. Based on Reddé; Rankov; D'Amato (2009b); Pitassi; Syvanne (2013–2014, MLHR). It should be noted that their views are slightly different from each other and that I have also made my own changes to the list.
39. Reddé; Rankov; D'Amato (2009b); Pitassi; Pitassi; Syvanne (2013–2014, MLHR). The problem with my interpretation is that Vegetius (4.32) provides contradictory evidence. He states that each of the praetorian fleets (with a legion apiece) was commanded by a prefect, under who served ten tribunes each in charge of a cohort and *navarchi* as captains of individual *liburnae* of varying sizes. This leaves out the *trierachi*, whom we know to have served as captains of ships because this is attested by inscriptions and other sources. One possible explanation could be that the practice had changed by the time Vegetius wrote or that Vegetius has mistakenly called the captains *nauarchi* when he should have called them *trierarchi*. This would mean that the ten tribunes of Vegetius were actually the *nauarchi*. Still another possible solution would be to equate the *trierachi* with the tribunes, but this salutation is the most problematic of the alternatives.

40. See Reddé, Syvanne (2013–2014, MLHR).
41. My estimate is based on Reddé's calculations as well as on the number of scouting boats given for the fleets posted in the area of former *Classis Moesiaca* (225 *lusoriae*, sixty-eight *judiciariae*, 154 *agrarienses*) in the Theodosian Code (CTh 17 on Jan. 28, p.412). I have made the educated guess that the Romans would have employed river *liburnae* in the third century rather than the *lusoriae* type of ships so that there would have been on average sixty-three *liburnae* per provincial fleet as suggested by Reddé, and that in addition to this they would have had smaller river patrol boats (the equivalents of the *judiciariae*) and inshore patrol boats (the equivalents of the *agrarienses*).
42. Syvanne presentations 2013–2014.
43. This is based on Syvänne (2004) and my presentations 2013–2014.
44. Based on Pitassi; Syvänne (2004); Syvanne (MHLR Vol.1).
45. Bar Hebraeus, p.55; Michael Syrus (p.60, 119). Contrary to the majority of Christian chroniclers who themselves seem to have fallen victim to the pagan propaganda, Caracalla indeed seems to have been quite tolerant of other religions, as even the SHA (Car.1.6–2.1) admits was the case in his boyhood. Dio actually goes so far as to accuse Caracalla of corrupting the youth because he did not persecute homosexuals (the Exc. Val. 394–396 fragments of Dio, Loeb/Cary ed. 78.24).
46. Even Adrian Goldsworthy, whose work I greatly admire (in particular his studies of the Roman army and generals, Late Republic and Principate), has fallen victim to this same tendency in his *The Fall of the West* (p.70ff.). However, I recommend all Goldsworthy's works because these always include erudite conclusions and out-of-the-box thinking. This recommendation includes his *The Fall of the West*, even if it becomes immediately obvious to anyone who reads our works that I do not agree with the conclusions presented in that work.

Chapter Two

Youth and Education

Lucius Septimius Bassianus or Julius Bassianus (Marcus Aurelius Severus Antoninus = Caracallus/Caracalla) was born on 4 or 6 April in 174, 186 or 188. His father was the future Emperor Septimius Severus. As regards his mother, there are two versions in the sources. The most commonly accepted version, or probably even the only accepted version among modern historians, is that Bassianus' mother was Julia Domna, the second wife of Severus and the future mother of Bassianus' brother Geta. It should be kept in mind that this is the official version. One should not jump to the conclusion on the basis of this that it is a fact. We simply do not know. For example, modern historians have dated the marriage between Septimius Severus and Julia Domna to have taken place in the summer of 187, on the basis that it must have taken place then if Caracalla was Julia Domna's legitimate son who was born on 4 or 6 April 188.[1] The years 174 and 186 would naturally imply that Julia Domna was a stepmother.

According to the other version preserved by the Latin sources, Caracalla and Geta had different mothers, the former having been born of the first marriage of Septimius Severus with Paccia Marciana.[2] In other words, Julia would have adopted Caracalla. According to this tradition, after having murdered his brother Geta (in this version his stepbrother), Caracalla then lustily married his stepmother with the latter's full consent. Unfortunately, contrary to the commonly held view, in my opinion it is impossible to decide with certainty which of the versions is correct because Severus was certainly in a position to falsify the evidence to suit his own needs. One thing, however, is certain. Contrary to what Dio claims, Julia Domna maintained a very good and close relationship with Caracalla, even after the latter had killed Geta – we just do not know the exact reasons for this, but one of the reasons could certainly have been an incestual relationship, as claimed by the Latin tradition.

In my opinion, there are actually three possible things that support the version that Bassianus was born from the first marriage in 174 or 186: 1) the age difference of three or more years would explain why it was that Caracalla was promoted more quickly to become heir apparent and why there was a distinct difference in personal authority between the brothers; 2) if the brothers had different mothers, it would also make the subsequent sibling rivalry even more understandable, even if sibling rivalry is deemed present in all families; 3) it is more difficult, though not impossible, for a woman to become impregnated immediately after the birth of the first baby, as would have been the case if the age difference was only about 12 months between the brothers Bassianus and Geta. According to Levick (p.32), Geta was probably born on 7 March 189, while the SHA claims 27 May 189. The fact that Caracalla's original name in the sources was Bassianus, which was the name of Julia's father and a common name in her family, is not conclusive. Severus might have married a second time into a family that had members bearing the same name as his son, or it is even more likely the boy could have been renamed immediately after the second marriage at the same time as he was adopted by the mother. In theory, it is possible that Severus could also have had an extra-marital affair with Julia Domna, as a result of which Bassianus was born to Julia Domna while Severus was still married to his first wife, or that Septimius married Julia only after she had given birth to a son because he needed a man to succeed him, and that the date of birth was hidden in order to hide his status as a bastard. Herodian's claim (4.9.3, with Whittaker's note) that the Alexandrians jokingly called Julia Domna 'Jocasta' (Oedipus' mother) could actually be used to support this theory. Jocasta had two other sons, one of whom had a legal claim for the crown and another who did not.

Barbara Levick suggests that the story of an earlier date of birth from the marriage with Paccia Marciana would later have been purposefully spread by Caracalla to make him look more mature. She also suggests that the public at large wanted to believe in such stories, because these helped them better to understand the hatred between Caracalla and Geta and the claimed incest between mother and son. She also suggests that tales of adultery and incest are to be expected when one deals with stories of the imperial family and should be considered implausible.[3] I am more reserved than she and many other historians. Sometimes the rumours have a solid founding in facts. I would not entirely discount the possibility that there could have been an incestuous relationship between the mother or stepmother and the son. What is certainly known is that they were to have a very close relationship when Caracalla became the ruler, and he never remarried after he divorced Plautilla.

A good place to start the analysis of Caracalla's character and reign is the description of his youth in the SHA (Aelius Spartianus, Antoninus Caracallus 1.1–2.11, tr. D. Magie, pp.3–7, with additions and comments in square brackets):

> 'The two sons left by Septimius Severus, Geta and Bassianus [*The name was changed to that of Marcus Aurelius Antoninus in 195 or 196, but he is better known with his later nickname Caracalla/Caracallus*] both received the surname Antoninus, one from the army, the other from his father, but Geta was declared a public enemy, while Bassianus got the empire. … He [*Caracalla*] himself in his boyhood was winsome and clever, respectful to his parents and courteous to his parents' friends, beloved by the people, popular with the senate, and well able to further his own interest in winning affection. Never did he seem backward in letters or slow in deeds of kindness, never niggardly in largesse or tardy in forgiving – at least while under his parents. For example, if ever he

saw condemned criminals pitted against wild beasts, he wept or turned away his eyes, and this was more than pleasing to the people. Once, when a child of seven, hearing that a certain playmate of his had been severely scourged for adopting the religion of the Jews, he long refused to look at either the boy's father or his own, because he regarded them responsible for the scourging. It was at his plea, moreover, that their ancient rights were restored to the citizens of Antioch and Byzantium, with whom Severus had become angry because they had given aid to Niger [*one of Severus' enemies during the civil wars*]. He conceived a hatred for Plautianus because of his cruelty [*note that the author or authors of the SHA have been unable to present his lies consistently and that in the Life of Geta quoted later he claims that Bassianus and Plautianus were both equally cruel and supportive of each other*]. And all the gifts he received from his father on the occasion of the Sigillaria he presented of his own accord to his dependants or to his teachers [*note that according to the SHA, Geta did not give away any of his presents; see the quote below*].

'All this, however, was in his boyhood. For when he passed beyond the age of a boy, either by his father's advice or through a natural cunning, or because he thought that he must imitate Alexander of Macedonia, he became more reserved and stern, and even somewhat savage in expression … Alexander the Great and his achievements were ever on his lips, and often in a public gathering he would praise Tiberius and Sulla. He was more arrogant than his father; and his brother, because he was very modest, he thoroughly despised.

'After his father's death, he went to the Praetorian Camp and complained there to the soldiers that his brother was forming a conspiracy against him. And so he had slain his brother in the Palace … He also said in the Camp that his brother had made preparations to poison him and had shown disrespect to their mother. To those who had killed his brother [*probably centurions of the Praetorian Guard and/or the evocati*] he rendered thanks publicly [*however, see my discussion below!*], and indeed he even gave them a bonus for being so loyal to him. … The senate received his speech with little favour, when he said that although he had granted his brother every indulgence and had in fact saved him from conspiracy [*note that the claim is that Caracalla has in the past saved his brother, who now repaid the help by conspiring against him!*], yet Geta had formed a most dangerous plot against him and had made no return for his brotherly affection.'

The picture painted by the above quote is actually quite believable, and also receives circumstantial support from other sources. It shows Bassianus Antoninus to have been a dutiful and gifted boy who had a big heart towards those who were treated with harshness. In other words, he felt empathy towards the oppressed. He was no psychopath. The reason for his later more reserved behaviour and stern look was simply that when he grew up, he became ever more aware of the harsh realities of

82 Caracalla

Roman upper-class life and more and more disappointed in humans. It is practically certain that his father also advised his son not to show to others what he thought. As regards Antoninus' relationship to his brother, it appears that he did indeed feel brotherly love towards him, which Geta betrayed, as will be shown below. However, this should not make us blind to the other half of Antoninus Caracalla's personality, which was his belief that it was his right to be the sole successor to his father. Antoninus also seems to have been the typical elder sibling who was closer to the value system of his parents, while Geta, as the younger sibling, seems to have been more easily subjected to outside influences provided by the attendants and sycophants.

Dio (78.11.2–7) has the following to say about Bassianus Antoninus Caracalla's education and habits (tr. by Cary, pp. 301–05, 357, with additions in square brackets):

> 'Indeed, he had no regard whatever for higher things, and never learned anything of that nature, as he himself admitted; and hence he actually held in contempt those of us who possessed anything like an education [*The other evidence shows this to be untrue. In truth, Caracalla appears to have despised the likes of Dio, who clearly did not understand anything about warfare or the finer points of governing the empire and also suffered from stupid superstitions that could readily be exploited, and who in all was possessed with quite mediocre intellect, and Dio was quite aware of Caracalla's view. Caracalla did not overlook the finer arts. He even learnt to play the lyre later in life, as Dio admits at 78.13.7, p. 310*]. Severus, to be sure, had trained him in absolutely all the pursuits that tended to excellence, whether of body or of mind, so that even after he became emperor he went to teachers and studied philosophy most of the day [*in light of what Dio states here, his above claims are just incredible*]. He used to be rubbed dry with oil, and would ride on horseback as much as a hundred miles [*i.e. Caracalla was in top physical shape and a good rider, and therefore able to move fast from one place to another if needed, as was expected from a general*]; and he practiced swimming even in rough water. In consequence of these pursuits he was vigorous enough in a fashion, but he forgot his intellectual training as completely as if he had never heard of such a thing. And yet he was not lacking either in ability to express himself or in good judgment, but showed a very shrewd understanding of most matters and talked very readily [*Dio contradicts himself once again*]. For thanks to his authority and impetuosity, as well as to his habit of blurting out recklessly everything alike that came into his head and of feeling no shame at all about airing all his thoughts, he often stumbled upon a happy phrase [*Dio seems to stumble into a happy contradiction here*].
>
> 'But this same emperor made many mistakes because of the obstinacy with which he clung to his own opinions [*i.e. he did not pay proper respect to Dio's opinions!*]; for he wished not only to know anything [*i.e. he was intellectually

curious] but to be the only one to know anything [*knowledge is power! It is no wonder that Caracalla employed spies*], and he desired not only to have all power but to be the only one to have power [*i.e. he did not listen to the advice of Dio and other similarly mediocre men of the senatorial class. He did not respect the Senate even for the sake of appearances*]. Hence he asked no one's advice and was jealous of those who had useful knowledge. He never loved anyone, but he hated all who excelled in anything [*It was basically dangerous for the emperor if there were men of senatorial class who were gifted generals; it was because of this that Caracalla often appointed men of lowly origins to high places; consequently, Dio's statement is misleading. Caracalla promoted gifted men, not only from the senatorial class but also from the lower classes*], most of all those whom he pretended to love most; and he destroyed many of them in one way or another.... I [*Dio*] also recalled that when he was giving us a banquet in Nicomedeia at the Saturnalia [*in 17–23.12.214?*] and had talked a good deal, as was natural at a symposium, he had called to me, as we rose to depart, and remarked: "Well and truly Dio, has Euripides said: 'O the works of the gods – in manifold wise they reveal them; manifold things unhoped for the gods to accomplish bring. And the things that we looked for, the gods deign not to fulfill them; And the paths undiscerned of our eyes, the gods unseal them, So fell this marvelous thing.'" [*Once again Dio's own words betray him! Caracalla did not forget his education and remained interested in the finer things in life including poetry, music and philosophy. It is also clear that this refers to a disagreement between Dio and Caracalla in which the latter tried to sooth the former*].

As can easily be seen, Antoninus Caracalla received an excellent and well-rounded education and was also intellectually curious, which even the poisonous pen of Dio has been unable to hide. The real source of the hostility is that Dio and his ilk were men of senatorial class and/or pretentious intellectuals (or rather fools who pretended to be intellectuals), whose quite mediocre intellect the quite bright emperor failed to respect even for the sake of appearances.[4] Antoninus knew better, but it should still be noted that despite his superior intellect, Antoninus was still ultimately removed by the people whom he did not respect enough. It was certainly unwise for Caracalla to show his disrespect, but for a man with supreme power this sort of behaviour is understandable.

Bassianus was renamed Marcus Aurelius Antoninus and appointed as Caesar in 195 or 196, and from 196 or 197 onwards he was called *imperator destinatus* (Emperor designate). On 28 January 198, Antoninus was declared a co-ruler and Augustus and Septimius started to groom his son as his successor. In 202, Antoninus was married to Plautilla, the daughter of the Praetorian Prefect Plautianus. Plautianus was a very close friend of Severus and, according to the gossip of the day, was also the gay lover of Septimius. The goal of the marriage was to unite the two families.

84   Caracalla

Top Left: Septimius Severus on a coin.
Top Centre and Right (reverse): Julia Domna on a coin.
(Drawn after Cohen)

Left: Young Antoninus (Caracalla on a coin)
Right: Young Geta on a coin.
- Note the difference in the way how the hair is represented: curly vs. straight. Did the brothers have different mothers? Drawn after Cohen

This was not to be, because Antoninus felt intense dislike towards his wife and her father. Antoninus considered the latter to be much too cruel a person and his daughter to be a whore – and in fact Antoninus was right in both cases. In addition, Plautianus kept meddling in Caracalla's affairs. It is unsurprising that Severus' wife, Julia Domna, also hated Plautianus – the rumour that Plautianus had at one time been Severus' gay lover would have been reason enough for any wife. The story was certainly believable in light of Severus' favouritism and because Plautianus'

Septimius Severus
(source: Piranesi 1805)

Plautilla
(source: Piranesi 1805)

own sexual behaviour, which included the abuse of both boys and girls for his own perverted pleasures, made this quite believable.[5]

Antoninus' instincts about Plautianus served him well. In 205, Plautianus seems to have formed a plot to kill both the son and father. Dio (77.3.1ff.) claims that there was no plot and that it had been invented by Antoninus, but he betrays himself as a liar by contradicting himself (e.g. 77.4.4). Dio (77.4.3–4, tr. by Cary) states: 'But Antoninus, as Plautianus was making denial and expressing amazement at what was said [Plautianus was accused of a plot to kill Severus and Antoninus], rushed up, took away his sword, and struck him with his fist; and even wanted to kill him with his own hands, after the other had remarked, "You have forestalled me in killing".' But being prevented by his father, Antoninus ordered one of the attendants to slay Plautianus. It is the words of Plautianus that betrayed him, just like these words betray Dio's bias. The incident also proves nicely how Antoninus was already a man of action from an early age.

Dio seems to have been among those senators who had too close contacts with Plautianus, as a result of which he was very fearful for his life. According to the story spread at the time, it was Severus' brother, Geta, who first warned Severus of the evil designs of Plautianus when he lay on his deathbed. It was apparently as a result of this that Plautianus' powers were significantly reduced, so he began to plot against Severus and his son, although he may already have been so doing. The person who uncovered the plot to assassinate Severus and Antoninus was the centurion or tribune Saturninus (i.e. a member of the imperial bodyguard), who was helped by Antoninus' tutor, Euodus. According to Dio's falsified story, Antoninus ordered Euodus to persuade Saturninus and two other centurions to tell a story according to which Plautianus would have ordered ten centurions (including the three of them) to murder both Severus and Antoninus. Plautianus was apprehended. Severus and Antoninus interrogated Plautianus in person in the palace, after which took place the incident described above which ended in the death of Plautianus. All those whom Severus or Antoninus suspected of being involved in the plot were killed or exiled. After this, Antoninus promptly divorced Plautilla and exiled her and her brother.

Notably, one of Plautianus's clients was the lowly-born (future emperor) Macrinus, but his life was spared when Cilo, the Urban Prefect, appealed for his life. Macrinus was subsequently made *Procurator rei Privatae* (Procurator of the Emperor's Private Property, the office of which was created by Severus) by Severus, and in this capacity he appears to have forged a good rapport with the future emperor Antoninus. For the future, it is important to note that at the time, Antoninus, unlike his brother Geta, was already heavily involved in the day-to-day administration of the empire and in its internal security functions. Antoninus' ability to command the loyalty of the centurion/tribune Saturninus and to order the attendants/boyguards to kill Plautianus and other plotters prove that he had already forged very close relationships with the junior and senior officers of the Praetorian Guard, especially with its elite branch, the *Speculatores*, and other units of the bodyguards. There was no attempt by the Praetorians to defend their prefect. This also proves that Antoninus had become quite familiar with the murky affairs of internal security and spying, and even if Dio was right that Antoninus fabricated the charges against Plautianus (which is quite improbable), it would even then prove that Antoninus had become familiar with the methods (i.e. use of disinformation) used by the intelligence apparatus to further his own goals. Barbara Levick (p.80) suggests that in truth Septimius Severus was behind the killing of Plautianus and just used his son to carry this out. This is possible, but there is no definite evidence for it.

The Plautianus affair can also be used to shed light on the disinformation techniques used by the hostile sources, of which the following quote from the SHA (Geta 4.1–5.3) provides a very good example (tr. by Magie, pp. 39–41, with additions in square brackets):

> 'As a youth, he [*Geta in the SHA*] was handsome, brusque in his manners, though not disrespectful, incontinent in love, gluttonous, and lover of food and of wine variously spiced. There is quoted a famous remark of his in his boyhood; for when Severus was planning to kill the men of the opposite factions [*the supporters of the rival emperors*] and said to his family, "I am ridding you of your enemies", Bassianus gave his approval, even declaring that should he be consulted, their children too should be slain, but Geta, it is said asked how large was the number of those to be put to death. When his father informed him, he asked again, "Have they parents, have they kinsmen?" And when answer was made that they had, he remarked, "Then there will be more in the state to mourn than to make merry at our victory." And he would have carried his point, had not the prefect Plautianus, or rather Juvenalis, stood out against him in the hope of proscriptions, from which they became enriched. They were also encouraged by the great brutality of Bassianus [*note that the other sources are explicit about the fact that Antoninus hated Plautianus and considered him much too cruel! It is also worth noting that Severus didn't actually kill the children of his enemies, so the opposite opinion won the day for the moment.*]. He, in the course of his argument, urged, half in jest half in earnest, that all those of the opposite factions be slain together with their children; whereupon Geta, it is said, exclaimed, "You, who spare no one, are capable even of killing your brother" – a remark which received no attention then, but afterwards passed for an omen.
>
> 'In his literary studies he held fast to the ancient writers [*note that it was actually Antoninus Caracalla who emulated ancient heroes!*]. He was ever mindful of his father's sayings, always regarded his brother with hatred [*on the basis of this, one may ask why it was then that it was actually Antoninus who was raised to become emperor and not Geta?*], more affectionate than his brother toward their mother, speaking with a stammer though his voice

was melodious. He was very fond of bright clothing – so much so, in fact, that his father would laugh at him [*it is not impossible that Geta would have liked bright clothing, but it is noteworthy that it was actually Antoninus who became famous for a piece of clothing as Caracalla!*]. Whatever he received from his parents he used for his own adornment, and he never gave presents to any [*undoubtedly real characteristics of Geta!*].

'After the Parthian war, his father, who was then at the height of his glory and had named Bassianus partner in the imperial power [*note that Antoninus was considered better suited to rule the empire by his father*], gave Geta the name of Caesar and, according to some, of Antoninus also.'

I would suggest that the above quote is a very good example of the way with which the endearing qualities of Antoninus Caracalla have been transferred to his brother. It is quite clear from the contradictory evidence that it was actually Antoninus who opposed the needless shedding of blood and who hated Plautianus for his extreme cruelty. One may indeed ask why it was that Septimius Severus raised Antoninus as his successor and involved him in all his policy decisions while leaving out Geta, if it really was Antoninus who did not respect his father's views? The obvious answer is that the person who did not respect his father's views was actually Geta, who therefore was a typical younger sibling. According to modern research, younger siblings typically do not share the value system of their parents to the same extent as elder siblings. It was precisely for this reason that Severus did not involve the much-too-cruel Geta in policy decisions.

According to Dio (77.7.1ff.), after the killing of Plautianus, both Antoninus and Geta felt that they were no longer restrained by anyone, with the result that they outraged women and abused boys, embezzled money and made gladiators and charioteers their companions. They were rivals in everything: when one cheered for one chariot team, the other cheered another. There were four factions (white, red, blue and green); Caracalla appears to have favoured the blues and Geta the greens. The fun ended when the brothers were both driving chariots and Antoninus fell out of his two-wheeled chariot and broke his leg. Was this accident an attempt by Geta to kill Antoninus? The support of ruffians (roughly the equivalents of the modern biker gangs or football hooligans[6]) could be used to great effect in urban fighting, and it is therefore possible that both brothers were seeking supporters for their eventual fight for the throne.

The accompanying illustration of a painting in Herculaenum by Piranesi shows how the brothers would have spent some of their spare moments – something that all young men would like to do. The Roman nobility made love quite publicly, and when the lovebirds wanted some music in the bedroom, musicians were brought there. It is probable that if Antoninus slept with Julia Soaemias and Julia Mamaea during this period, that there were several witnesses to the fact. This illustration is still quite decent in content. The brothels and bedrooms could contain paintings that were far more graphic in their description of sex scenes.

I would suggest that both teenagers were simply acting like typical careless teenagers with too much money and free time on their hands, and that Dio has exaggerated the seriousness of their youthful escapades. However, I would still find plenty of truth in Dio's statement that when Severus witnessed the loose living and quarrels of his sons, he felt that he had to do something. It is here that Herodian's text

A reconstruction of the Roman barracks at Pompeii by Saint Non. During peactime the Roman soldiers lived in relative comfort even if they were constantly drilled for combat.

Tombstone of Flavius Trypho, tesserarius, *legio II Parthica*, Apamea, (ca. AD 215-218 according to Cowan)

Lucius Septimius Viator, *lanciarius* of Legio II Parthica

adds an important piece of information. According to Herodian (3.10.4, 3.13.1–6), the attendants and sycophants sowed discord between the brothers and encouraged their bad behaviour. On the basis of the list of people executed after Antoninus gained power, the attendants included the tutors of both brothers. Severus' solution was to separate the brothers from their sycophants and the corrupting influence of the capital city, and what better way to do that than fight a war under his personal tutelage? A healthy dose of military life was sure to correct the behaviour. Not unnaturally, the worried father wanted to reconcile his sons back into agreement (Herodian 3.10.4, 3.13.3–6). He knew that the attendants were trying to turn the brothers against each other. I would suggest that at the root of the problem was that Geta, or rather his sycophants, were not willing to play second fiddle to Antoninus, and Antoninus was not willing to share his power with his brother. The problem was that Septimius Severus had designated Antoninus as the heir apparent with the title of Augustus and had given Geta only the title of Caesar. The Roman Empire and the emperors prepared for combat.

Notes

1. Birley, p.77; Levick, p.31 with their endnotes. A papyrus found in the temple of Artemis at Dura Europos retains a calendar of official supplications made by the XX Cohort of the Palmyrenes to the emperors during the reign of Alexander Severus. See Levick 2 (pp.13436). This list includes two supplications for Antoninus the Great (Caracalla): an ox to the deified Antoninus the Great for his imperial power on 4 February and an ox to the deified Antoninus the Great on his birthday, 4 April. This suggests that 4 April was the official birthday. Magie (SHA vol.2, p.2) suggests a name Julius Bassianus.

90 Caracalla

2. Sources collected in PIR Septimius Bassianus, e.g. Sextus Victor, *Liber De Caesaribus* 21.23; SHA Car. 10 etc.
3. Levick, pp.32-33, 98-99.
4. Potter (pp.141–42) includes some enlightening examples of Antoninus' dealings with rhetors. Contrary to Potter, I do not think that his behaviour would have been self-congratulatory. Rather, in my opinion these examples prove that Antoninus was justifiably very impatient with incompetence while he was also ready to reward true excellence or courage when he encountered it. The example in which Antoninus stated impatiently that such a legal case should never been brought before him because the previous edict is so clear, only shows his impatience with the incompetence of the judges – a similar attitude should always be shown when one encounters incompetence, which unfortunately is not usually the case. Antoninus' overturning of the privileges of the teachers of rhetoric in a fit of temper at a hearing should not be seen in the worst possible light as something that resulted only from a sudden burst of anger. It is actually quite clear that he must have previously pondered the justification of such privileges for such an outburst of shouting to occur at that moment. It was indeed ethically unsound to exempt the teachers of rhetoric from public service on the basis of their trade, and Antoninus' decision to revoke these should be seen as well-justified. The instance in which the rhetor Heliodorus Arabs had the audacity to stand up against Antoninus actually proves the greatness of the man. When this took place, Antoninus sprang up from his seat and said that this sort of behaviour was unheard of etc., but then rewarded Heliodorus with the equestrian rank and bestowed it also on his children and nominated him *advocatus fisci*. See also Philostratus, *Lives of the Sophists*, Loeb ed. pp.300–315, for additional details. This proves that Antoninus appreciated courage and was ready to reward such. The instance in which Antoninus ordered two senior advocates to argue who should be the high priest at a local temple and then interrupted both does not show Dio's arguments to be true – rather it shows that Antoninus had equally little respect for these two advocates as he did for Dio and other mediocre men. He actually appears to have distrusted those in particular who flattered him, as effeminate men were prone to do (see chapter 11). In sum, there is every reason to believe that Antoninus never forgot his education, but was just impatient with stupidity, incompetence and slavish flattery. For an alternative view, see Potter's excellent study, a superb piece of research and highly recommended reading even if we disagree on some points; but it should be noted that I agree on most of his points even if it is not immediately apparent here because I interpret the evidence regarding Antoninus differently.
5. Principal sources for the Plautianus affair are: SHA Sev 14.79, Car. 1.7, Geta 4; Dio 14.1ff.; Herodian 3.1ff.; with Levick p.74ff.; Birley, p.161ff. In this context, I would like to point out that there is a very unfortunate tendency among the conservatively thinking Classicists (this obviously is not true of every Classicist, note e.g. my studies) to downplay the importance of sexual behaviour in history and to show their critical attitude to the sources by claiming that all extraordinary or somehow reprehensible sexual behaviour would not have taken place, which is very odd because in order for one to do that one would have to turn a blind eye to all similar behaviour in our own day – were the people of the past really somehow better than us? Here it suffices to draw attention to the sexual

behaviour of Stalin, Enver Hoxha, Mao, Saddam Hussein and their entourages. In short, there is no reason to doubt that Plautianus was a cruel child molester who deserved to die. As regards the sexual behaviour of the spouses in antiquity, the fact that Plautilla made Antoninus a cuckold was a humiliation that he could not stand. This brings up the probable double standards of the ancient (and modern) world, namely that it was acceptable for the husband to cheat but not for the wife. It is very unfortunate that we do not know when Antoninus began his womanizing because that would tell us whether he started it before he learnt of the cheating of his wife or only afterwards as a form of revenge. The extant evidence suggests that the latter is the case, because the first instances of sleeping with other women mentioned by the sources appear to have taken place in 204 (Soeamias and Julia Mamaea). Some historians and numismatics (e.g. Mattingly) have claimed on the basis of coins of Plautilla, which have a child on the reverse that it is possible that Caracalla had a child (daughter) with Plautilla in about 204 and that this child was later executed together with the mother. Even though one cannot entirely rule out this possibility, it is still very unlikely because it is very difficult to see how the very hostile sources would have failed to mention it, especially so if Caracalla had this child executed later. My own educated guess is that the coins represented either a hope of future offspring or that the child died at birth (or as a result of miscarriage) or that the father of the child was actually someone else and a proof of Plautilla's infidelity. If the last is true, then it is possible to think that the alleged sleeping with Soaemias and Julia Mamaea in 204 resulted from this. See also Garcia's (p.40ff.) analysis of the same coins and situation.

6. It should be noted that Dio 78.10.1-3 implies that Caracalla supported the Blues because he wore their costume while driving a chariot. However, Malalas 12.24 claims that he supported the Greens. I have preferred the former interpretation because Malalas is usually very unreliable for this period. Note the modern unholy alliance between the KGB and mob before 1991, and after1991 the alliance between the FSB and Mafia, and the alliance between Putin and biker gangs, and the creation of the assassination squad to kill Fidel Castro by the CIA and Mafia. The official security organs have always seen the use of the Mafia as a useful tool in their arsenal, and it comes as no great surprise that this same phenomenon can also be observed in antiquity.

Chapter Three

The Military Education: the Campaigns of 207–211

The suitable excuse for war came from Britain. The situation there had been tumultuous ever since 196, when Albinus had withdrawn most of the Roman forces from Britain to fight against Septimius Severus. In my opinion it is clear that the Romans still considered the so-called Antonine Wall as the border because the southernmost enemies in the following campaigns were the Maeatae, who lived just north-east of the wall. Most historians suggest that the Antonine Wall had already been abandoned and the border moved south to Hadrian's Wall, but in light of the evidence this is unlikely. After his victory over Albinus at Lyon in 197, Severus had dispatched a new governor, Virius Lupus, with an army to secure Britain.

Virius Lupus was forced to buy peace from the Maeatae, but this failed to stabilize the situation. The Maeatae allied with the other major tribal confederation of north-east Scotland, the Caledonians, and resumed the war. The Romans achieved a number of successes and were able to repair or rebuild barracks and forts along Hadrian's Wall in 206 under Valerius Pudens and in 207 under L. Alfenus Senecio. Severus' strategy appears to have been to abandon the territory north of Hadrian's Wall, and repair and refortify the wall. He followed the same policy in Raetia, where dendrological studies have established that the wood of the walls was cut in 206–7. Both wall-building projects proved insufficient to contain the threat. The British defences were the first to collapse. The reason for this appears to have been the revolt of the Brigantes just south of Hadrian's Wall in 207, the probable cause of their rising being that the governor had used them as a corvéed workforce for the rebuilding of the forts. Another possible reason for the revolt was persecution of Christians. The governor, Alfenus Senecio, reported that the situation had become so grave that it required the sending of reinforcements.[1] Note that this situation is in agreement with the information provided by the British tradition. This British tradition suggests that both the governor of Britain and the rebel leader died in battle near Eboracum (York), after which the Britons were forced to flee to Scotland.

The tribal rebels appear to have been able to put the city of Eboracum under siege. The revolt of the Brigantes is confirmed by two altars in Britain which mention a Roman victory over the Brigantes. This proves correct Dio's claim that one of the reasons why Severus wanted to campaign in person was that other people were winning wars in Britain, not him or his sons.[2] Once again this is in agreement with the British tradition, which states that the Romans defeated the rebels near York, and that the Roman commander and the enemy leader both died as a result of the battle. The defeat of the Brigantes and their allies, and the death of their leader, explain why there was no military threat at the time the emperors arrived in Britain, and why the Maeatae were ready to negotiate.

Consequently, according to Dio, Severus took his sons and an army to Britain in 208 and launched an invasion of Scotland (Caledonia) in 209, but Herodian implies (3.14.9) that Geta was summoned to Britain only after preparations for war were complete. What better way to separate the sons from bad influences and to teach them the necessary military skills than fighting a glorious war? There was also the expectation that the campaign would increase the glory of the ruling house and thereby secure its standing among the army. The timing was also lucky because Severus felt that his elite legions were becoming too accustomed to peace.[3]

Nicholas Reed, Stephan Bender, Anthony R. Birley and many others suggest that Caracalla was already actively campaigning in 207. The consensus opinion among numismatics is that the Romans minted coins in 207 which showed Caracalla with either Mars or Virtus (both demonstrated military prowess), and even more importantly with captives and a river-god. This suggests that Caracalla had been active in some province already in 207. Reed suggests Britain and Bender Raetia, while Birley says the Middle Danube. All are plausible. The Middle Danube is the likeliest candidate because the governor of *Pannonia Superior*, Egnatius Victor, and legate of the V Legion, Claudius Piso, made a dedication at Arrabona in which they referred to the victory of the emperors and of the *Legio I Adiutrix Antoniniana*.[4] This can be seen as an early indication of Antoninus' eagerness to advertise the loyalty of his men. It is less likely, but possible, that the young Caracalla was rushed off to Britain in the company of some experienced general when the Roman governor was killed, as suggested by the British tradition, and then returned later in the year to Rome. It is also possible that Severus had dispatched Caracalla to Raetia to oversee the strengthening of the Raetian *Limes* with a new wall in 207 while the governor of Britain performed similar functions along Hadrian's Wall. In this case, the river would obviously be the Main and the captives those Alamannic tribesmen who had opposed the strengthening of the *Limes*. In fact, it is possible that the strengthening of the *Limes* had included some show of force even before it started, to ensure that the building project could be performed without danger to the building parties. This would actually suggest the possibility that the building projects in Raetia and Britain were meant to form a secure base of operations for further advances into the Barbaricum in the following years, especially because one of Septimius' governors (whose names are not preserved) built new granaries at Banna (Birdoswald), Cilurnum (Chesters), Vercovicium (Housesteads), Coria (Corbridge) and Arbeia (South Shields). The latter was converted into a supply depot which could hold enough corn for 40,000 men for three months. With the other granaries, the size of the invading force would have been considerably larger than 40,000 men. Daquet-Gagey has also noted that several roads in Gaul that eased the marching to Gesoriacum were renovated and improved during 202–207/9, which suggests the possibility that Severus was already planning to launch a major campaign in Britain well before 209.[5] I would still suggest that the likeliest location for Antoninus' campaign in 207 would have been the Middle Danube, on the grounds of the title *Antoniniana* for the *Legio I Adiutrix*.

The problem with the claims that Antoninus campaigned in 207 is that the dating of the coins is not absolutely secure and, even if the dating was accurate, it is still possible that the images were just used as imperial propaganda without any basis in truth, or that some general had achieved successes that the emperors appropriated for their own use. In addition, the reason why some researchers have suggested a campaign in Raetia or the Danube in 207 is that the Arval Brothers[6] gave Caracalla the titles of *victor felicissimus* and *Germanicus maximus* on 20 May 213, and papyrus (dated 29 August 212–29 August 213) confirms this. There is actually no need for such postulations, because Caracalla could have received the the title *Germanicus* as a result of some success achieved by his general or because he would have begun his German campaigns already in 212.

In sum, it is entirely possible that Antoninus fought a campaign in Pannonia in 207, but if he did, he still travelled back to Rome, from whence he and his father Severus travelled together to Britain.

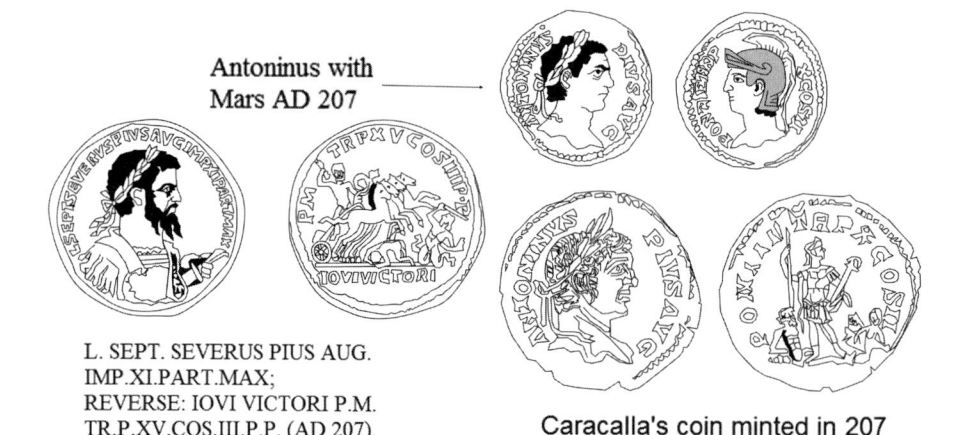

Antoninus with Mars AD 207

L. SEPT. SEVERUS PIUS AUG. IMP.XI.PART.MAX;
REVERSE: IOVI VICTORI P.M. TR.P.XV.COS.III.P.P. (AD 207).
Drawn after Cohen.

Caracalla's coin minted in 207 with a river god and prisoners

Italy was not without its own troubles, because it was severely harassed by a brigand called Bulla during 206–207 until he was apprehended by a tribune of the bodyguards[7] who managed to convince a mistress of Bulla through her husband to betray the brigand. There would also have been other problems in 207 and 208, as

The Military Education: the Campaigns of 207–211   95

there are inscriptions at Ephesus in Asia and at Sicca Veneria in *Africa Proconsularis* which refer to the defeat of insidious plots in these regions. The latter is securely dated to 208. The coins (a female figure of Africa with an elephant which has a lion at its feet) from 207 have sometimes been used to suggest that Severus crushed the plots in Africa in person, but there is no firm evidence for this interpretation. There was a revolt in Gaul which was suppressed by the *dux*[8] Julius Septimius Castinus (also *legatus* of the *Legio I Minervia*), with the help of detachments drawn from all four legions of the two Germanias (*I Minervia*, *XXX Ulpia*, *XX Primigenia* and

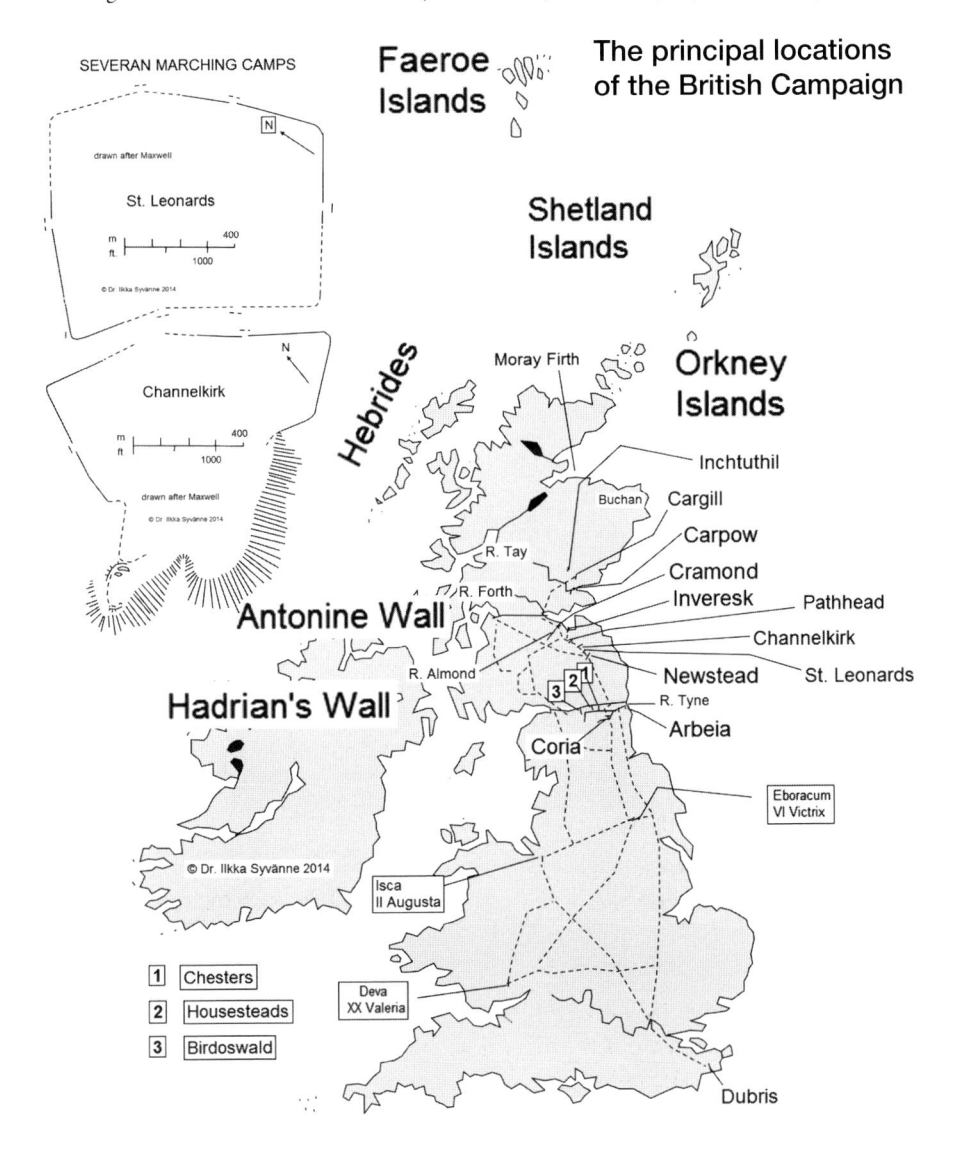

VIII Augusta) against defectors and rebels, which resulted in the 12th imperial salutation for Severus.[9] It is possible that soldiers from further away, who had been enervated by a long period of peace, revolted when they reached Gaul en route to Britain, or that the Gauls revolted against the extra taxes and corvéed labour resulting from the forthcoming war in Britain, or that the defectors and rebels consisted of Gallic soldiers who had deserted their colours when the news of the forthcoming war reached them. Unfortunately, it is impossible to know what was happening. Consequently, there is a lot that we do not know about the events that took place between 206 and 208.

Roman planning for the upcoming war in Britain was very thorough, because according to Dio, Septimius' goal was nothing less than a complete conquest of the entire island. The above-mentioned granaries were clearly meant to support sizeable forces in the field. It is probable that the corn and other foodstuffs meant for the army were shipped in a constant stream from the south of Britain, Aquitania (south-west Gaul) and the Rhineland to these locations during this period. Birley has suggested that it is probable that the Tigris bargemen were relocated to Arbeia at this time and gave their name (Arabia) to the town. The presence of Tigris bargemen suggests that these bargemen possessed suitable skills to construct the right kind of rafts for the Tyne River to ship the supplies from Arbeia to Coria. The remains of the Roman marching camps from Hadrian's Wall to Cramond suggest that Severus' main army marched along the road that ran from Eboracum via Coria and Newstead to Cramond. It is probable that the granaries meant for this army consisted of those built at Arbeia and Coria, while the rest of the granaries supplied forces that garrisoned the wall. It is not known whether the bargemen would also have built barges for the fleet to tow to Cramond on the Forth, or whether the fleet had its own transport ships for this purpose.[10]

The loading of supplies to ships and from ships to a supply depot would have looked something like shown below in Trajan's Column (seventeenth century drawings).

The Military Education: the Campaigns of 207–211 97

Birley has aptly noted that before embarking on his campaign, Septimius would have first convened his council of advisors for the planning session. It was after this initial meeting that the detailed planning would have been started. Severus and Caracalla would have been accompanied by their *comites* and administrations. These would have continued to advise both during the campaign. In addition to this, the Imperial Family would have taken with them a very significant portion of the central administration so that the empire could be ruled from Britain. The sources mention two administrators: Castor the *Cubicularius*, who acted as *a memoria* for Severus, and Euodus. In addition to this, the emperors would have been accompanied by their bodyguard units and at least one Preatorian prefect, Papinian. Inscriptions prove that one unknown man (his name is missing from the inscription) served as commander of the provincial fleets of Britain, Germania, Pannonia and Moesia (*classes Britannica*, *Germanica*, *Pannonica*, and *Moesica*), while another man was put in charge of the granaries at Coria. It is clear that the Germanian, Pannonian and Moesian fleets sent only detachments and not their entire force. The Germanian fleet would have sailed from the Rhine to Britain, but the other fleets would have journeyed truly remarkable distances. They would have sailed first along the Danube to the Black Sea and then to the Mediterranean, then through the Straits of Gibraltar to the Atlantic and from there to Arabeia. The presence of these fleets suggests that the land forces posted along the Danube and Rhine also contributed detachments and units for the campaign. It is possible that some of these troops were shipped by the fleets of their respective areas, but it is still more likely that most of them would have been marched to Gesoriacum/Bononia (Boulogne) and then shipped to Dubris (Dover) in Britain. It is probable that the fleets in question were primarily used to protect the transports carrying the supplies.[11]

It is also highly likely that the *Classis Misenatum* (and possibly also *Classis Ravennatis*, because both were commanded by a single prefect) accompanied the emperors, even if we do not possess any similar inscriptions to prove it, as it would be strange that when the emperors were in Britain they would not have been accompanied by their Pretorian fleet. The emperors would also have taken with them the *Legio II Parthica* (c. 5,000 foot, 500 horse), most of the *Praetoriani* (c. 8,000 foot, 1,500 horse), *Equites Singularis Augusti* (c. 2,000 cav.), possibly *Aulici* (c. 2,000 cav.?), one cohort of the *Urbaniciani* (c. 1,500 foot) and detachments from the *Peregrini*, *Frumentarii* and *Speculatores* (c. 300 cavalry). This would have given the emperors a core of about 14,500 foot and 6,300 horse. In addition to this, the emperors would have drawn vexillationes from the European legions; each legion probably contributed about 2,000 foot and 200 horse, and the auxiliaries about the same number of foot and probably at least three times as many horse. With sixteen legions, this would add up to 32,000 infantry and 3,200 cavalry, while the auxiliaries would have contributed about 16,000 infantry and 9,600 cavalry. It should also be noted that it is possible that Septimius raised new legions to occupy Caledonia, because this was the standard practice when new territories were added to the empire, and recruited additional *numeri* among the Moors to increase the number of horsemen, but unfortunately there is no definite evidence for this. The expeditionary force would also have drawn detachments from the two legions posted in Wales (c. 6,000 foot, 600 cavalry) while most of the the legion posted in Eboracum (c. 5,000 foot and 500 cavalry) would have joined the campaigning army. In addition to this, it is probable that at least half of the auxiliaries (11,500 foot, 5,000 cavalry) would have joined the expedition to the north. Daquet-Gagey (p.424) estimates the size of the Roman army in Britain to be 30,000–50,000 fighting men, which would make it even stronger than my conservative estimate. My own estimations would add up to 85,000 infantry and 25,200 cavalry for the main field army, which would probably be quite close to the figures needed to achieve the goals set by Septimius.

The following interpretation of the campaign is based on the consensus opinion among archaeologists regarding the extant remains of Roman marching camps found in Scotland, combined with the sparse accounts provided by the narrative sources. It should be remembered that interpretation of the archaeological evidence is in most cases a hazardous task, and in this instance is made even more difficult by the fact that most of the camps do not include anything concrete to date them. Therefore, the interpretation has been based on a number of educated guesses without taking into account the full set of evidence. Hanson has listed these problems in his article. The most important of the failings of the consensus opinion is that it does not take into account the fact that there were other major campaigns in Scotland besides those of Agricola and Severus. There were large-scale campaigns in Scotland in the 140s, 180s, 305–6, 342–3, 364, 367–8, 382 and the 390s. The camps that have been tentatively dated to the campaigns of either Agricola or Severus form only a small sample of the evidence, because by 1989 archaeologists had found over 200 marching camps in Scotland.[12] Regardless of these problems, I have here made the assumption that the consensus opinion is correct as it is the best that we have at the moment. However, there are many ways to interpret this archaeological evidence, and in this I have not followed the consensus opinion.

Consequently, we can estimate the size of the main Roman army from the sizes of the extant large marching camps between Hadrian's Wall, Cramond and the Antonine Wall. There were two major Roman roads between Hadrian's Wall and the Antonine Wall, and the extant large camps were built along the eastern one of those. The size of these camps (Newstead, St Leonards, Channelkirk and Pathhead) is about 165 acres (67ha), and when one uses the typical range of estimates (350–480 men per acre) one has an army of 57,750 to 79,200 men.[13] We should not forget that it is unlikely that the marching camps mentioned would have housed the entire force taken on the campaign. In addition to this, we should add the men who supported the main army, which included people in charge of logistics, artisans, the navy and administrative staff. It is also probable, as suggested by Maxwell (p.28), that the fleet would have sailed alongside the main army, while another Roman force would have advanced along the other, western Roman road leading from Hadrian's Wall to the Antonine Wall so the Romans would have reoccupied the entire area between the walls. On the basis of the above, my educated guess is that the detachments from Wales and the British auxiliaries (c. 20,000 foot, 6,000 horse) advanced along the western road, and the rest of the forces, the main army (60,000 foot and 20,000 horse), advanced along the eastern road to Cramond and the Antonine Wall. I would suggest that the emperors left part of the force to protect their supply bases and posted the remainder on ships that would have been sailed to Cramond.

The year 208 began with a joint consulship of Antoninus (the third time) and Geta (second time), and nothing suggested that Severus would have wanted to promote Geta as Augustus. The coins show Severus riding off to war, but Herodian's text suggests that he was carried on a litter for most of the journey because of gout or arthritis. The arrival of the emperors in Britain panicked the Britons. The Britons sued for peace, but the emperor was hell-bent for war and glory and refused to grant peace or even truce. One of Severus' coins from 208 shows a stone bridge over a river, and it has been suggested that he had a stone bridge built over either the Forth or the Tay in that year. On the other hand, Daquet-Gagey (p.425) suggests that Severus built the stone bridge over the Ouse at Eboracum. One of Antoninus' coins from 208 or 209 shows a bridge built of ships (pontoon bridge) over a river, and it has similarly been suggested that it represents a bridge built over the Forth or the Tay. In the absence of reliable archaeological finds, it is impossible to know where the bridges were built. The only thing that is known with certainty is that there existed a small bridgehead camp on the north shore of the Tay at St Madoes opposite a polygonal camp (63 acres) just south of the permanent Severan base at Carpow. This has led Maxwell and others to suggest that this is the location where Antoninus had his pontoon bridge built in 209. In my opinion this sounds correct. This means that Severus' stone bridge must have been built over either the Forth or some of the rivers south of it. This would once again seem natural, because it is likely that the permanent stone bridge was built when there was no serious fighting.

The following illustration from Trajan's Column shows the massive stone bridge over the Danube built by the engineer/architect Apollodoros (eighteenth-century drawing). It shows well what type of bridge Severus would have built, even if it was not quite as long. Septimius' coin is an earlier example depicting a bridge.

Septimius and the stone bridge (source Cohen)

Antoninus' pontoon bridge of ships would have looked something like shown below in the Column of Marcus Aurelius (eighteenth-century drawing).

When the emperors reached Britain, the Maeatae appear to have allowed the Romans to march north to the Antonine Wall without any attempt to harass them. After all, this was Roman territory. The emperors left part of the force at Cramond to build a permanent base there, and then marched to the Antonine Wall, apparently garrisoned some of the forts there and built a stone bridge over the Forth. The fleet would have met the emperors at the safe harbour provided by the mouth of the River Almond near Cramond, after which they would have helped in the building

The Military Education: the Campaigns of 207–211 101

of the bridge.[14] It is probable that the other Roman army would have simultaneously occupied the western portion of the Antonine Wall and started to rebuild forts along it.[15] The following illustration from Trajan's Column (eighteenth-century drawing) shows the legionaries at work while the auxiliaries stand guard. This is how the legionaries would have also built the permanent stone forts under the Severans.

When Septimius Severus began his campaign in 209, he left his son Geta and wife Julia at Eboracum, which was to serve as the base of operations for the entire campaign. The administration of the empire was officially left in the hands of Geta. He would have received hands-on guidance from his mother Julia Domna and a group of senior advisors. This left Severus and Antoninus free to begin their campaign against the Maeatae and Caledonians. The aim was to teach to Caracalla the art of leading an army on a campaign. The emperors apparently marched their army across the River Forth over the stone bridge, but what happened then is subject to various interpretations.

Dio provides a good description of the type of enemy the Romans were facing (77.12.1–4, tr. by Cary, pp.263–65, with my comments in square brackets):

> 'There are two principal races of the Britons, the Caledonians [*Kalêdonioi*] and the Maeatae [*Maiatai*], and the names of the others have been merged in these two. The Maeatae live next to the cross-wall [*Antonine Wall*] which cuts the island in half, and the Caledonians are behind them. Both tribes inhabit wild and waterless mountains and desolate and swampy plains, and possess neither walls, cities, nor tilled fields, but live on their flocks, wild game, and certain fruits; for they do not touch the fish which are there found in immense and inexhaustible quantities. They dwell in tents, naked and unshod, possess their women in common, and in common rear all their offspring. Their rule is democratic for the most part, and they are very fond of plundering; they go into battle in chariots, and have small,

swift horses; there are also foot-soldiers, very swift in running and very firm in standing their ground. [*In other words, the Britons are credited with great staying power in the field. This suggests an ability to fight in a shieldwall phalanx formation, and also stands as proof that the Caledonians and Maeatae engaged the Romans in prolonged pitched battles.*] For arms they have a shield and short spear, with a bronze apple attached to the end of the spear-shaft, so that when it is shaken it may clash and terrify the enemy; and they also have daggers. They can endure hunger and cold and any kind of hardship; for they plunge into the swamps and exist there for many days with only their heads above water, and in the forest they support themselves upon bark and roots, and for all emergencies they prepare a certain kind of food, the eating of a small portion of which, the size of a bean, prevents them from feeling either hunger or thirst [*clearly a drug similar to the coca leaves or khat*].'

A member of the Caledonian warrior elite in front of his chariot insulting and challenging the Romans to a duel. He is naked to show his bravado. He also wears tattoos all over his body in the expectation that these would protect him magically against the enemy weapons.

Herodian (3.14.5ff., tr. by Whittaker, p.359, with my comments in square brackets) says:

'A particular effort went into intersecting the marshy areas with pontoons to permit the troops to advance safely crossing them and so to fight on a firm standing of solid ground. ... The barbarians usually swim in these swamps or run along in them, submerged up to the waist. Of course, they are practically naked ... They also tattoo their bodies with various patterns and pictures of all sorts of animals. Hence the reason why they do not wear clothes, so as not

The Military Education: the Campaigns of 207–211 103

to cover the pictures on their bodies [*the Picts who later occupied these same areas became famous for the same, but similar practices were also followed in the Steppes*]. They are very fierce and dangerous fighters, protected only by a barrow shield and a spear, with a sword slung from their naked bodies.'

The Maeatae and Caledonians clearly practised the traditional forms of British warfare and still used war chariots, like their compatriots in Ireland. The histories of Dio (78.12ff.) and Herodian show that there had not been any major changes in British fighting tactics since the first century AD. However, in the field of strategy there were two major changes. Firstly, in contrast to the previous era, the Britons now seem to have concentrated on guerrilla-type warfare and avoided pitched battles as much as possible. Secondly, and most importantly, the Britons had learned that in numbers lay strength, and therefore they had started to cooperate against the invaders. The picture of the British fighting methods given by Dio suggests that the only real change after the first century was the introduction of a new type of spear. It is obviously possible that Dio could have copied an early source like Tacitus, but as a contemporary high official he was in position to know the facts. Vitally, he also provides new information not mentioned by Tacitus (new weaponry, new tribal confederations, new details of guerrilla warfare etc.), which proves that he was not merely plagiarizing. Additionally, as I have said repeatedly, one of the standard literary tricks was and is to quote an older piece of text because it is an accurate reflection of reality, and even if Dio had used Tacitus as his source this does not prove his text is unreliable. The waging of wars actually remained practically unchanged throughout antiquity thanks to the limitations imposed by the weaponry.

Even though the Britons certainly had ships and boats, the sources do not mention any naval warfare. Therefore it is probable that the Britons avoided combat at sea, unless surprised by the Romans' fast *liburnae* before they could flee. The Romans possessed superior ship designs[16] and it would have been idiotic to attempt to engage them in naval combat. Consequently, it is fair to say that the Romans possessed an absolute and complete naval mastery in the region which enabled them to ship in supplies and troops wherever needed.

Despite the massive preparations, the war did not progress as planned because the enemy refused to fight a decisive pitched battle and resorted to the use of guerrilla warfare. Dio tells us (77.13.1–4, tr. by Cary, with my additions in square brackets):

'Severus, accordingly, desiring to subjugate the whole of it, invaded Caledonia. But as he advanced through the country he experienced countless hardships in cutting down the forests, levelling the heights, filling up the swamps, and bridging the rivers [*the extant coin/medallion credits Antoninus with this operation too*]; but he fought no battle and beheld no enemy in battle array. The enemy purposefully put sheep and cattle in front of the soldiers for them to seize in order that they might be lured on still further until they were

The sources do not mention any sea battles between the Romans and Britons, but even with the seagoing liburnae it would have been an easy task for the Romans to sink the types of ships/boats (small clinkers and curraghs) employed by the Britons at this time. It is possible that some small scale action took place if the Romans managed to surprise the Britons before they could flee.

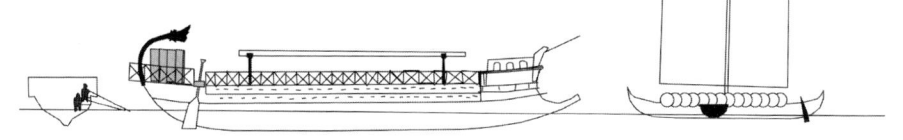

Seagoing Liburna
length 42m; each side 50 oars in two ranks/remes for a total of 100 oars.
Crew: 1 captain, 3 officers, 6 sailors, 24 marines, 50 upper rank rowers; 50 lower rank rowers; total 134.

Skuldelev 5, c. 1050, 26 men, 17.4 x 2.6 x 1.1m

© Dr. Ilkka Syvänne 2014 (source for the *liburna*: Pitassi)

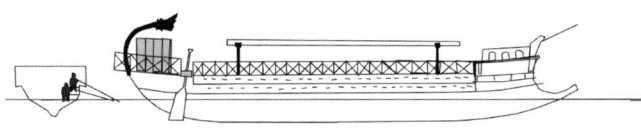

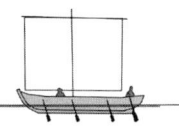

Curragh ca. 16-18 men

worn out; for in fact the water caused great suffering to the Romans, and when they became scattered, they would be attacked. Then unable to walk, they would be slain by their own men, in order to avoid capture, so that a full fifty thousand died. [*This is a massive exaggeration of the number of casualties among the Romans, but if this would refer to the number of casualties among the Maetae and Caledonians then it would be credible. It is hardly believable that the Romans would have lost most of their men and still be able to conquer the territory. In fact, it is possible that it originally did refer to the people of Scotland, because it is entirely possible or even probable that the Byzantine epitomizer has made a mistake when shortening the text. The other alternative is that Dio's hostility to Septimius and Caracalla has crept into his account.*] But Severus did not desist until he had approached the extremity of the island [*likely to mean that he reached the sea at the north-east corner of Scotland as he marched up to the Moray Firth*]. Here he observed most accurately the variation of the sun's motion and the length of the days and the nights in summer and winter respectively. [This i*mplies that Severus stayed there until the start of the winter. His aim was clearly to occupy the land.*] Having thus been conveyed through practically the whole of the hostile country (for he actually was conveyed in a covered litter most of the way, on account of his infirmity), he returned to the friendly portion, after he had forced the Britons to come to terms [*i.e. Severus' persistence forced the enemy to submit*], on condition that they should abandon a large part of their territory. [*Since the Severans built a permanent stone fort at Carpow, the Maeatae lost at least part of their coastal territory and one may make the guess that the Caledonians would also have lost part of theirs.*]'

The above gives a good general description of the type of fighting the Romans faced in Scotland,[17] but Dio fails to give us any details of the route taken by the emperors. It is here that the archaeological evidence of the extant Roman marching camps comes in handy. There are several ways to interpret the evidence. The usual interpretation, adopted for example by Maxwell, is that after the crossing of the Forth the emperors divided their armies into two divisions (two sets of camps of 63–65 acres = c. 23ha), so that Antoninus probably marched closer to the coast, if it is accepted that he built the pontoon bridge close to Carpow, while his father marched further inland. Each of the 63-acre (23-ha) camps had a separate smaller external annex/camp about 2–3 acres (c. 1ha) in size. Maxwell suggests that these smaller camps may have housed native scouts, hostages/prisoners or detachments to maintain the defences of the main camp for later use. Hanson explains this annexe as a later or earlier feature. My own suggestion is that the external annexe is likely to be similar in concept to the Persian use (which is also attested for the Romans) of a separate detachment of soldiers outside the camp which could be used to attack in the flank any force threatening the main camp. The sizes of the camps suggest that each emperor had a maximum of 32,000 men.

The map (drawn after Maxwell and Hanson) shows the marching camps that archaeologists consider to date from the Severan period. In my opinion, it is incomplete, because I agree with Birley that Severus must have marched at least up to the Moray Firth for the conditions detailed in the sources to be met. The stone forts at Cramond and Carpow appear to have served as logistical hubs, to where the fleet transported supplies. Considering the likelihood that Septimius marched all the way up to the Moray Firth, it is probable that there would have been at least one or two other logistical hubs for the fleet to bring supplies north, possibly built out of wood. I have also included the large (c. 110 acres/44.6ha) marching camps with supposed Flavian provenance in the map, because, as noted, the dating of the camps is an uncertain task. Considering the fact that the Severans are said to have suffered serious losses as a result of the defenders' guerrilla war, and would also have needed to leave detachments behind to build the forts, it would be only natural for the size of the marching camp to diminish from 130 acres (55ha) to 110 acres (44.6ha), which would represent a loss of about 15 per cent of the force. Durno is the largest camp so far found in Scotland, and it has been suggested that it was the site of Agricola's Battle of Mons Graupius in AD 84,[18] but since it is known that the Romans varied the size of the camp slightly according to the lay of the land and needs of the moment, this is not certain. Other possibilities include that this large camp would preserve the size of the army under Antoninus in 211, or that the emperors had temporarily increased the size of the force with reinforcements from the navy (e.g. with one naval legion) just prior to the decisive moment that led to the surrender of the Caledonians to the Roman army in 209.

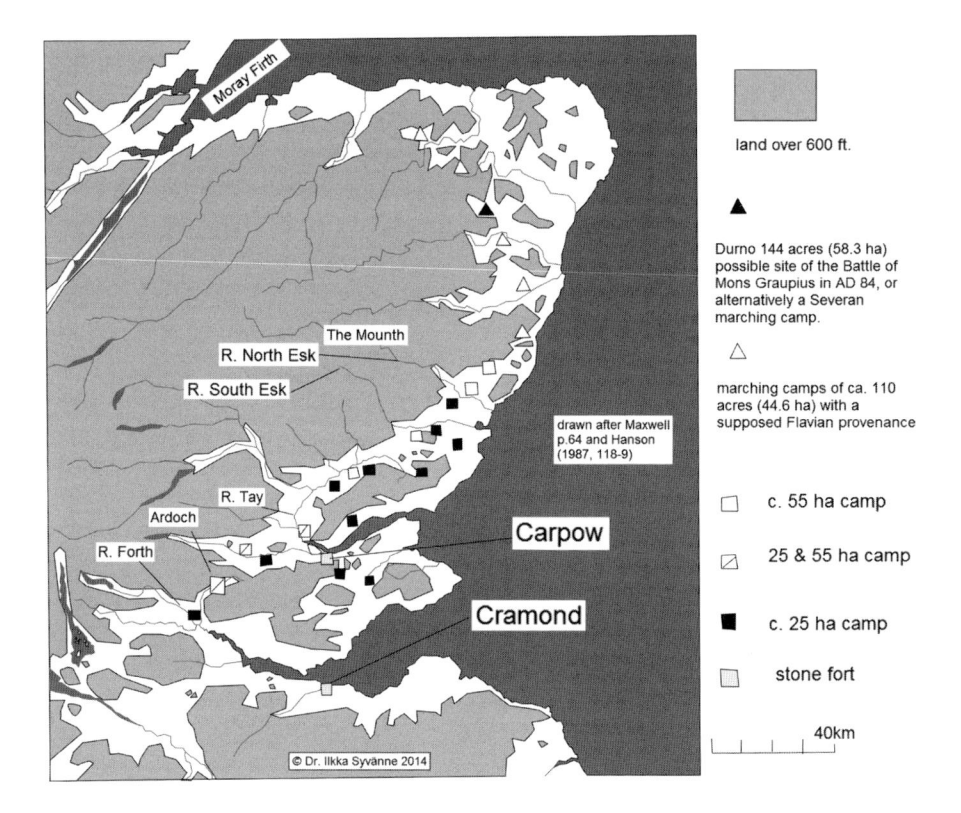

If the army was divided, as is usually suggested, then it is clear that Severus would have given his son some generals to instruct him, but subsequent events proved that he did not need their help. The march would have progressed as stated by Dio until both emperors reached the Tay. It was here that Antoninus appears to have left part of the army and part of the fleet behind to build a permanent base at Carpow, while some of the fleet was used to construct a bridge over the river at some point close to it. It is possible that Caracalla reinforced his land force with naval forces, because the sizes of the marching camps remained the same and we know that Carpow was built by two legionary detachments belonging to the British legions of *VI Victrix* and *II Augusta* (Birley, p.182). It was a stone fortress which had an internal area of 24 acres/9.6ha and outer defences covering 27.6 acres/11ha (Birley, p.182). It is possible that both emperors united their army, because there is one c. 55ha camp on the other side of the Tay, but it is equally possible that this camp dates from the next year's campaign.[19] The other possibility is that each of the emperors built separate pontoon bridges for their respective forces.

Maxwell (p.65–66) and Hanson (p.146, but he notes that the evidence is not certain) suggest on the basis of the archaeological research that since the camps at

Forts and camps at Ardoch
(drawn after Hanson, 122)

- titulum
- camp with possible Severan provenance
- 300m

The so-called Stracathro camps with the clavicula have traditionally been dated Flavian, but in my opinion these are likely to be late Roman/Byzantine. Compare with the sixth century camp below (Syvänne, 2004).

clavicula

Stracathro
425m X 370m
38 acres/15.7 ha

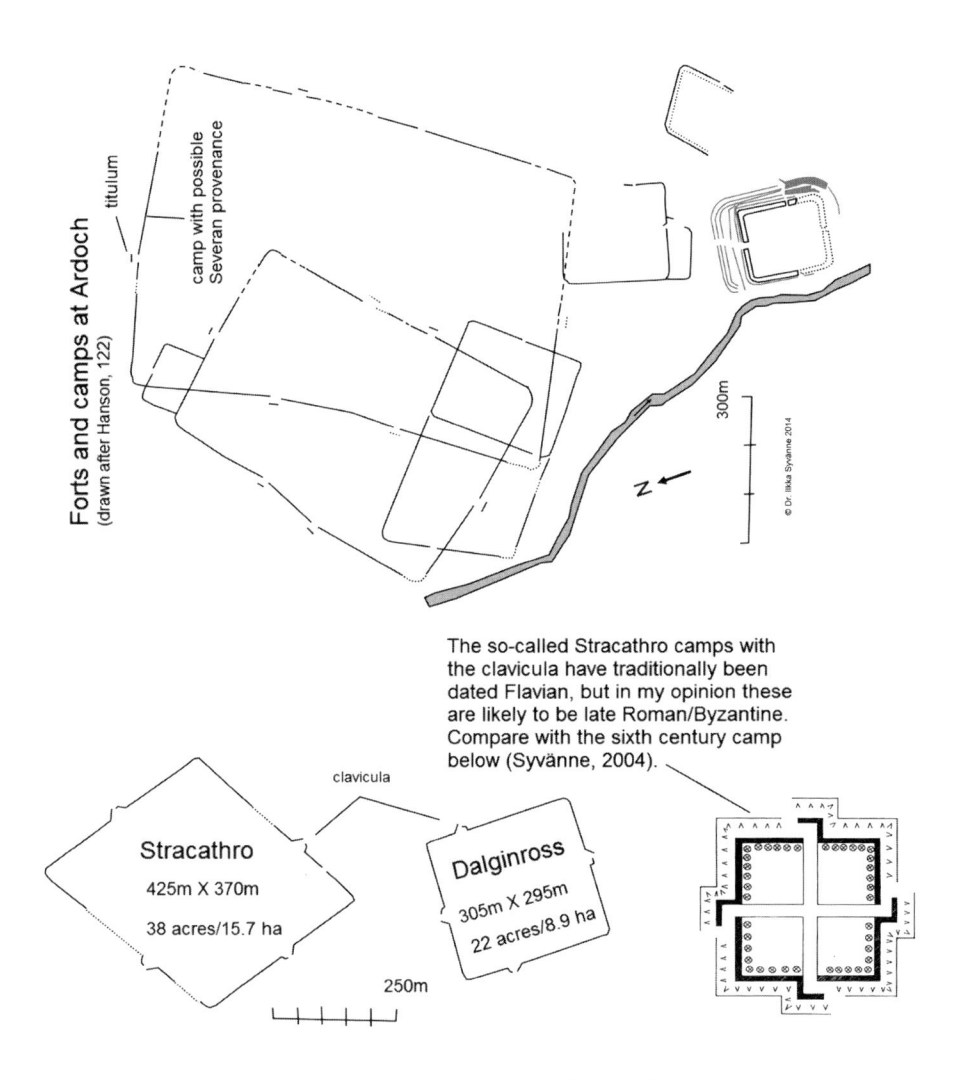

Dalginross
305m X 295m
22 acres/8.9 ha

250m

Ardoch are of 63 acres and 130 acres, of which the latter is later, that the larger camp was used by Antoninus in 210. This is possible, but it does not take into account the possibility that the latter camp would have rather been used in 211 or any of the other possible datings. The drawings of the marching camps found in Scotland demonstrate the problems quite well. Ardoch, for example, includes several camps, and the dating of these on the basis of the size and outward features is at best only a good guess. The so-called Stracathro camps (traditionally dated Flavian) also demonstrate the dating problems quite well, because in my opinion these are actually likely to be Late Roman on the basis of their structure. The square shape with the *clavicula* was more typical for Late Roman and Byzantine camps than for Principate camps, which were typically elongated squares in shape.

108   Caracalla

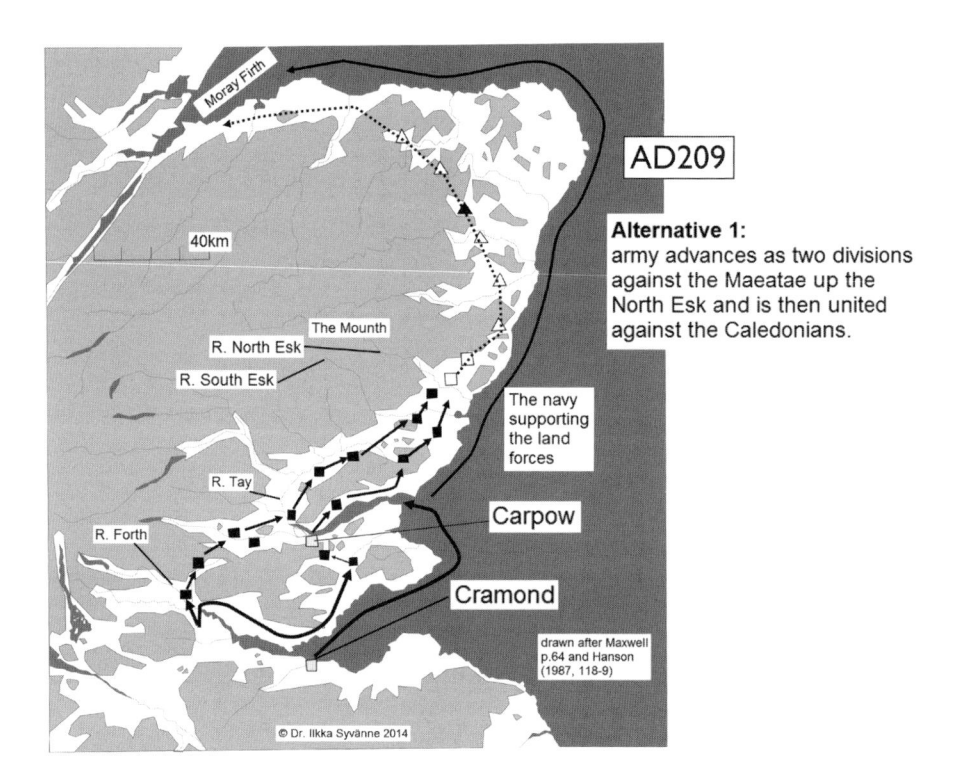

Most historians believe the emperors divided their army after they crossed the Forth and then marched north in separate columns, crossed the River South Esk and North Esk and then turned around near Kair House on Bervie Water, where the 63–65 acre (23–25ha) camps end just before Mounth, because it was supposedly unduly difficult to march beyond Kair House as it would have embroiled the army in a prolonged campaign against the tribes of north-east Scotland (Maxwell, p.66). It should be noted that this is precisely what Dio says happened Severus did embroil his army in a lengthy campaign.

In sum, if the consensus opinion is correct that the Roman army marched in two divisions up to the North Esk, then it must have reunited and marched northwards up to the sea just north of Buchan or all the way up to the Moray Firth, as suggested by Birley (p.181). The reasons for this are based on Dio's statements that Severus reached the sea, and that Antoninus and Severus were campaigning together and were present in the same camp.

This brings up the second alternative, which is that the emperors did not divide their army at all in 209, because Dio nowhere states this, but rather shows them to be campaigning together in the same camp. In my opinion, this alternative is inherently more likely than the current consensus opinion among historians. The fact that the enemy used guerrilla warfare against the Romans in fact supports this,

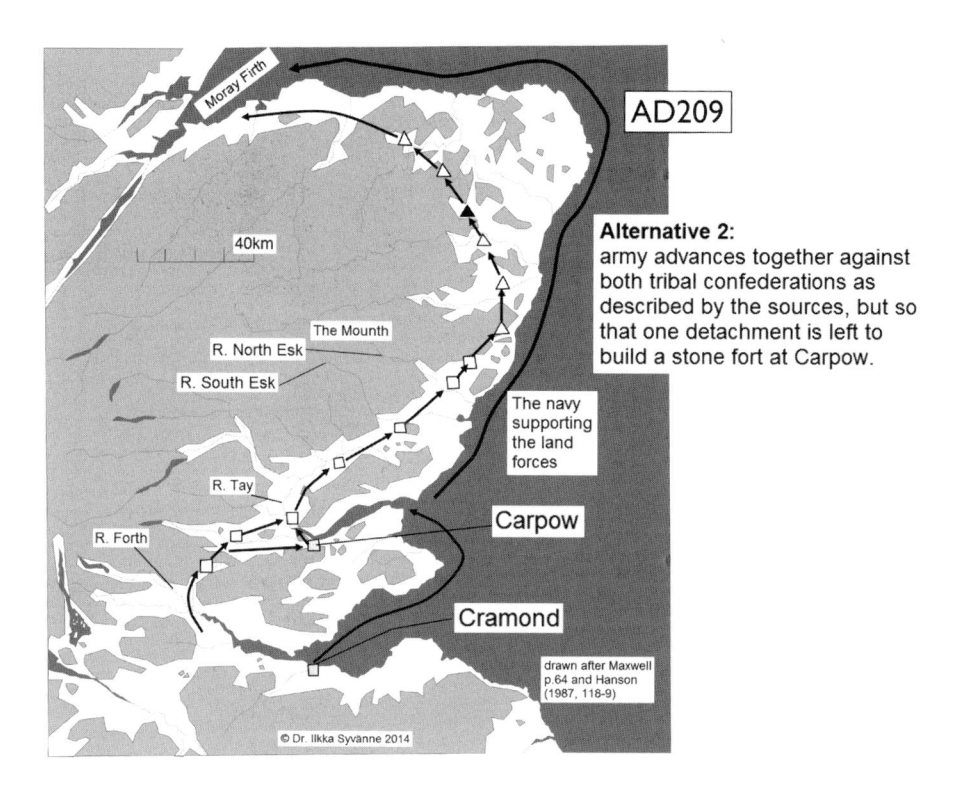

The Military Education: the Campaigns of 207–211 109

Alternative 2:
army advances together against both tribal confederations as described by the sources, but so that one detachment is left to build a stone fort at Carpow.

as do the details of the next year's campaign. The fact that it was very dangerous for the Romans to venture far from their main army because of the fear of being ambushed speaks also of a need to keep close together. The reason for the failure of this tactic against the Romans was that they were not dependent on local supplies but brought their own in ships and wagons. It was this that enabled them to outlast the willingness and ability of the enemy to stay together. In contrast, the locals were living off the land that the Romans were pillaging and torching. Indeed, information provided by the sources makes it certain that the Roman tactic against the guerrillas was to build a base camp from which they would send detachments to pillage the surrounding area, after which they moved forward to repeat the same until the enemy would submit. Despite heavy casualties, this tactic worked because we know that in the end the Britons were forced to surrender. Dio describes only the surrender of the Caledonians, which suggests that the Maeatae had reached a separate treaty with the emperors before this.

Dio (78.14) describes two incidents that took place during the campaign which in his opinion proved that Antoninus was attempting to kill his father. In my opinion, it is more likely that these instances are outright lies based on real events that have been used as a basis for a false story. After all, the best lie is one that includes things that are true.

110 Caracalla

The first of the lies is that Antoninus wanted to murder his father with soldiers posted just outside Severus' tent. Since this incident is placed before the surrender of the Caledonians, it must have happened somewhere north of the River Forth. According to Dio, Antoninus had placed his own soldiers in readiness to begin a tumult outside his father's camp when he attempted to enter his father's tent. It was then that Antonius ran out of his father's quarters, shouting that he was wronged by Castor, who was a freedman, secretary (*a memoria*) and chamberlain (*cubicularius*) of his father.[20] As a result, some of the soldiers outside started to shout until Severus himself came out and punished the loudest. Dio's story is simply implausible. If the purpose was to assassinate Septimius with the help of the soldiers posted outside, then the soldiers could have done that when he emerged from his quarters. What this incident actually shows is that when Severus was clearly already sick or that the succession issue was being discussed, his son Antoninus wanted to see him, but was prevented by Castor. Like any son, he was not prepared to put up with such behaviour. He ran outside to get the support of his bodyguards and other soldiers.[21] It was doubly important for him to make certain that his father received the best care available and that the attendants could not form a plot that would allow them to claim that Severus' last wish was to appoint the more malleable Geta as the senior emperor.

We know from a military diploma dated to 7 January 210 that Geta had been appointed as Augustus while Septimius and Antoninus were still campaigning against the Maeatae and Caledonians.[22] If such a move was being discussed in the imperial quarters, it is easy to see why Antoninus would have reacted in the manner described above. He would have certainly wanted to be present. One can only speculate about what motivated Severus to take such a move. Perhaps he simply attempted to reconcile the brothers, as claimed by the sources. On the other hand, from the fact that among Antoninus' first actions after the death of his father were the executions of the *Cubicularius* Castor and Euodus, and the dismissal of Papinian, one can conclude that he accused these men of the promotion of his brother. One cannot escape the possibility that the mind of the elderly and ailing emperor could have been influenced by his closest advisors, who saw in Geta a person whom they could use as their puppet, or that Severus just wanted to satisfy Geta's lust for the title and thereby try to make him more ready to recognize his elder brother's superior position as the elder Augustus, or that the father just tried to save his younger son somehow. One can also easily guess that when news of the promotion of Geta was brought to Antoninus, he would have been livid. Until then he had been the sole successor to the throne.

The second of these instances describes the scene of the surrender of the Caledonians, which means that it probably took place in late 209. When both Severus and Antoninus, with their well-ordered army following them in silence, were riding forward to meet the Caledonians and receive their arms as part of a peace treaty, Antoninus supposedly reined his horse and drew his sword to strike his father in the back. The others who were riding with them shouted, with the result that Antoninus did not carry through his intent. It was then that Severus turned and saw the sword. He said nothing and stepped on to the tribunal. According to Dio's version, it was only afterwards at the headquarters that Severus accused his son of hostile intentions in the presence of Papinian and Castor. Dio claims that Severus placed a sword within easy reach of Antoninus and told him either to use the sword or order Papinian to murder him.

The unfortunate thing in all this is that it is next to impossible to say whether this account has any basis in truth, because Dio is guilty of so many lies. If there is, then Antoninus must have felt that his father had betrayed him and deserved to die, but then hesitated at the very last moment. It is also possible that Severus believed that Antoninus had intended to kill him with the sword, but the whole account becomes suspicious when one remembers that Severus still gave Antoninus command of the whole army in the following year. In fact, it is easy to see that behind the whole story lies what was to become the favourite military trick of Caracalla the emperor. What actually seems to have happened is that Antoninus was about to give an order with his raised sword for the troops to charge and kill the practically helpless enemies without the prior approval of his father, just as he was subsequently to do several times against enemies who had foolishly placed themselves before his army when he was emperor. Antoninus simply could not understand why it would not be acceptable to kill the vulnerable enemies who had been lured into a trap. Future events would prove this judgment sound. In his opinion it was the apogee of generalship to defeat the enemy when it was least expecting to be killed. Roman history has many examples of this kind of behavior.[23]

There is another possible explanation for the alleged behaviour of Antoninus, which is the Oedipus complex. The SHA (Sev. 18.8, 21.8; Car. 10.1–4) and Victor (p.21) both claim that Julia Domna was Antoninus' stepmother and an adulteress whom Antoninus married after the death of his father. If this tradition is correct, it can be seen as a possible explanation for the sibling rivalry and the events that unfolded. This line of reasoning can be developed further when one remembers that Julia Maesa (Julia Domna's sister) and her daughters Julia Soaemias Bassiana and Julia Avita Mamaea claimed that Antoninus had slept with them and had begat sons with them. This raises the possibility that Julia Domna had also 'pimped' the daughters of her sister to her stepson or son in order to keep him under control. These stories are usually taken to represent a hostile tradition that tries to blacken the reputations of both Antoninus and Julia Domna, but this is by no means certain. The imperial families lived in a twisted reality. The perverse sexual lives of Tiberius, Caligula, Claudius and Nero demonstrate quite well that incest within the Imperial Family was by no means impossible. It should still be remembered that in light of the evidence that we have it is still improbable that Antoninus would have attempted to kill his father as the hostile tradition claims, for the reasons stated above and others I will go on to relate, but if the stories of incest with his mother/stepmother

112   Caracalla

are true (as they probably are because the more favourable Latin tradition claims this to be so), then it would be quite easy to understand why Septimius Severus would suddenly have wanted to nominate Geta as Augustus against the wishes of Antoninus, if his advisors told him of this behaviour.

It was probably after this surrender of the Caledonians that Severus marched to the extremity of Britain (i.e. to the shore of the North Sea, probably somewhere in the Moray Firth) and observed the sun's motions in summer and winter. It was therefore already winter when the emperors returned to Eboracum, where they spent the rest of the winter and early spring of 210.

The SHA (Sev. 18.9–11, tr. by Magie with slight changes and comments) also includes an incident that took place during the campaign of 209 or before that of 210:

> 'On one occasion when he [*Severus*] so suffered from gout as to delay a campaign, his soldiers in their dismay conferred on his son, who was with him at the time [*209–210*], the title of Augustus. Severus, however, had himself lifted up and carried to the tribunal, summoned all the tribunes, centurions, *duces* [*generals in charge of detachments*] and cohorts responsible for this occurrence, and after commanding his son, who had received the name Augustus, to stand up, gave orders that all the authors of this deed save only his son, should be punished. When they threw themselves before the tribunal and begged for pardon, Severus touched his head with his hand and said, "Now at last you know that the head does the ruling, and not the feet." And even after fortune had led him step by step through the pursuits of study and of warfare even to the throne, he used to say: "Everything have I been, and nothing have I gained."'

This incident proves nicely how frustrated the soldiers were becoming at the slowness of the emperor and how the old emperor still possessed the authority to take command of the situation when necessary. It also proves that Severus did not suspect that Antoninus would have been plotting to oust or kill him. Even after incidents like this, in which the soldiers demonstrated their loyalty to the son rather than to the father, Severus was quite prepared to place the entire field army under the command of his son. There is clearly no basis in truth to the claims that Antoninus would have attempted to murder his father.

Birley (2000, pp.179–80) has made a suggestion that it might be possible to detect one instance of Geta's independent activity in Britain during 209, if one places the martyrdom of St Alban to this year. According to the *Passio*, after St Alban had been killed, the most impious Caesar halted persecution in the name of the emperors because it only increased the numbers of Christians. Birley's claim actually receives support from the British tradition, which claims that the leader of the Britons who had started the revolt was a Christian. This would explain quite well why the Romans would have launched their persecution, and also why the revolt had started in the first place. It would have been the result of the persecution of Christians launched by Septimius Severus in 203. Severus and his mostly North African advisors were intensely hostile towards Jews and Christians, and it is therefore not at all surprising in these circumstances that Geta would have initiated a persecution of Christians, but would have stopped it when he and his advisors noted that the killing only increased the numbers of Christian converts, the result of the cult of martyrdom.

Despite his gout and poor health Severus was not prepared to rest once he had returned to Eboracum. The SHA (Sev. 22.4–5) says that on his arrival he inspected Hadrian's Wall; when he was inspecting the wall at Luguvallum (Carlisle), he met an Ethiopian who belonged to a *numerus* which had clearly been posted to guard the section of the wall. The Ethiopian shouted: 'You have been all things, you have conquered all, now victor be a god.' These words and his black skin colour were considered bad omens, according to the SHA.

The peace achieved in 209 proved ephemeral, as the Maeatae apparently revolted almost immediately after the emperors had left. The probable reason for this is that the peace terms had been harsh, and when the main army had left the natives once again felt strong enough to revolt. Birley (p.186) notes that it is highly likely that the tribal centre of the Maeatae was right next to the fortress of Carpow, because the later Pictish capital of Abernathy was only a mile or so away. This time Severus gave Antoninus command of the troops, because he was suffering from poor health and he had already noticed that his son had learnt the tricks of the trade. It was time to give him the chance of leading the troops alone. Both Dio and Herodian try to blacken Caracalla's skills as commander and his motives. Herodian claims that he was not interested in generalship but in canvassing the soldiers' support, as if the latter would not be part of any general's repertoire.[24] Regardless of the bias, it is still undoubtedly true that one of Antoninus' goals was to gain the military's support for himself. This was particularly important for the future because he knew that his father was in poor health.

On the basis of future events, it appears probable that in the course of the 210 campaign Antoninus succeeded in gaining a significant amount of support among the rank-and-file, the junior to middle-ranking officers and even from the top brass. He was also able to consolidate his support among a very significant portion of the Praetorians and other important military units. One of those who became an ardent supporter of Antoninus was the future Emperor Maximinus Thrax, who appears to have served in the *Aulici/Protectores* or in the *Equites Singulares Augusti*, probably implying the general attitude of that corps, and then under Caracalla as a cavalry officer, rising to the status of centurion (in the *Leones*?).[25] Most importantly, Antoninus managed to gain the support of Laetus, the senior Prefect of the Guard and its de facto military commander, because the other prefect, Papinian, was a lawyer. Significantly, he also seems to have been able to corner the support of Oclatinius Adventus. Adventus appears to have started his career as a mercenary

114 Caracalla

(probably as a non-citizen auxiliary) and advanced to the position of *speculator*,[26] centurion of the *frumentarii*,[27] *Princeps Peregrinorum*[28] and finally procurator of the emperors. In the latter position he had evidently been in charge of military intelligence-gathering and preparations in Britain in advance of the campaign.[29] Consequently, Antoninus had managed to obtain the support of the most important section of the bodyguards and those who were in charge of various intelligence-gathering organizations and operations.

The events of 210 proved that it would have been better to butcher the helpless enemy when the Romans had a chance to do so in 209. Severus ordered his soldiers, now operating under Antoninus, to invade and kill everyone they met. The nature of the mission suggests that it was now that the Roman army adopted the use of at least two or possibly three divisions to fulfill the wishes of the emperor. This time, however, the terror tactic failed miserably, inciting the Caledonians to revolt. When they witnessed the butchery of their fellow Britons, they naturally became fearful that this fate would also await them. It is also possible that if the Romans had garrisons in Caledonia (implied by the handing over of lands to the Romans), these now marched against the Maeatae, which would have created a power vacuum for the Caledonians to exploit.

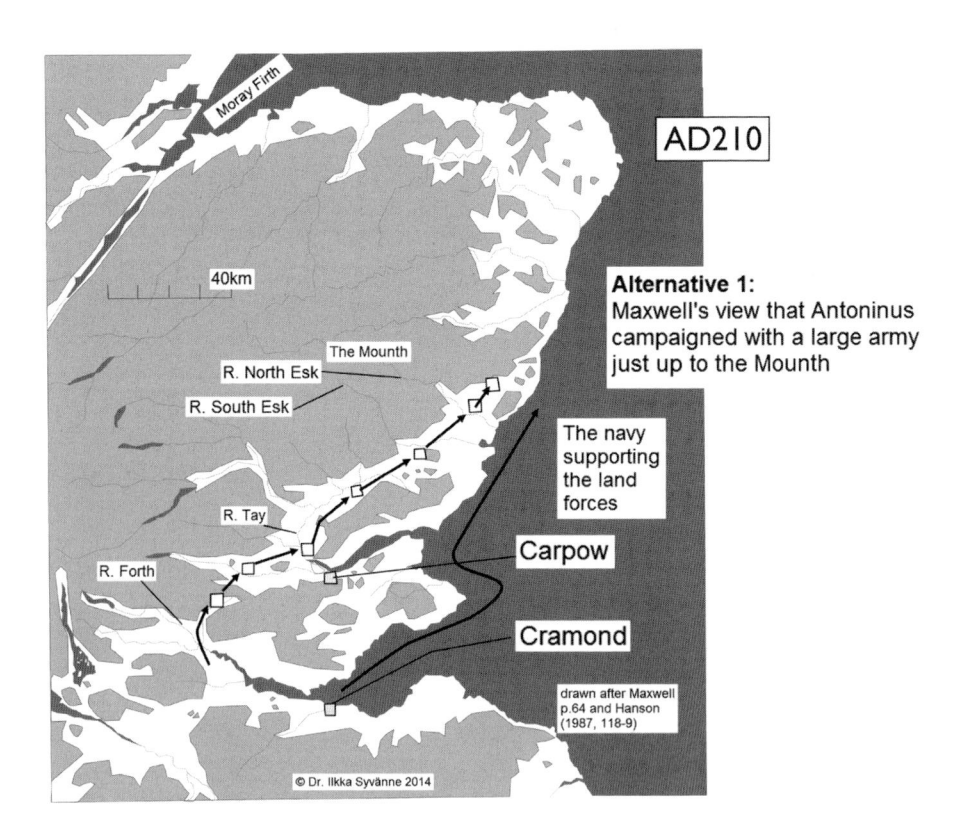

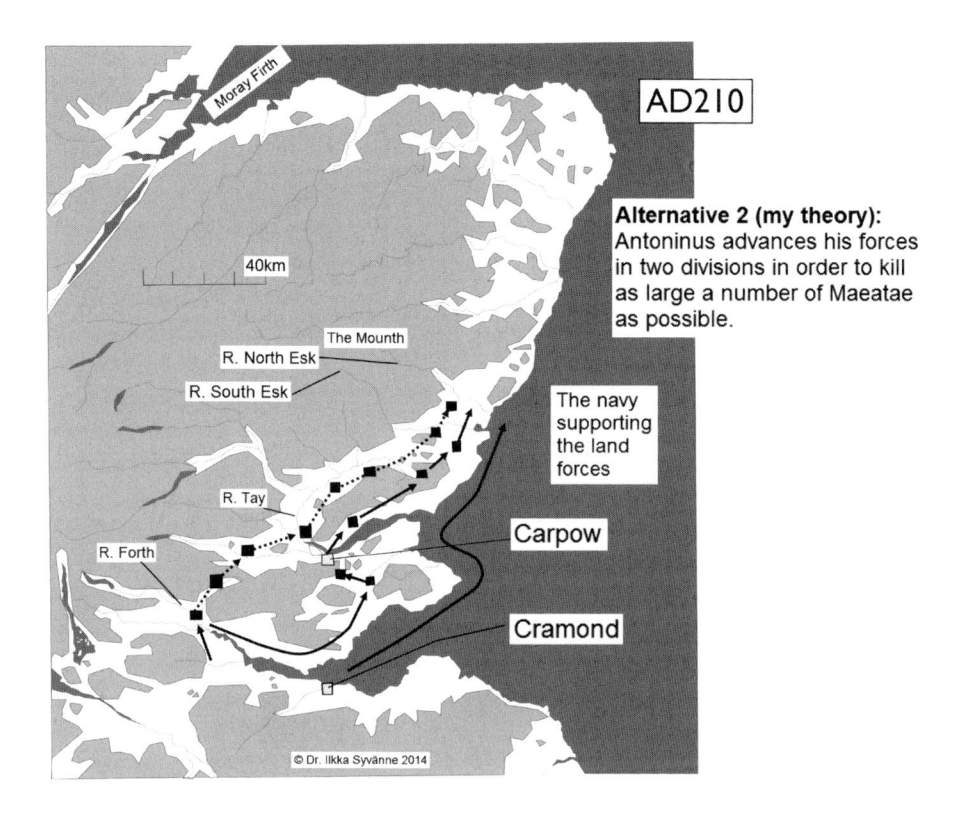

The Military Education: the Campaigns of 207–211   115

Alternative 2 (my theory):
Antoninus advances his forces in two divisions in order to kill as large a number of Maeatae as possible.

The navy supporting the land forces

Antoninus appears to have stopped his campaign at the border of Caledonia, after which he retreated. Consequently, Severus began to prepare to lead a campaign against them in person next year, but it was not his fate to carry it through. On 4 February 211 Severus died of illness, which the hostile tradition implies was helped along by Antoninus. The calumniators of Antoninus claim that he attempted to bribe the doctors to poison his father and then, after his death, killed the doctors because they had not obeyed him. Anne Daguet-Gagey suggests the possibility that what Antoninus had in mind was actually a form of euthanasia to put an end to the suffering of his father. This is possible, but we will probably never know for certain what happened. It was on his deathbed that Septimius Severus gave his famous advice for his sons, which has in my opinion been quite needlessly thought of as suspect: 'Be harmonious, enrich the soldiers [*stratiôtai*], and scorn all other men.'[30] The fact that Severus had followed a similar policy proves its accuracy. Severus had showered the soldiers with favours and used prefects as commanders of his new legions. Antoninus appears to have followed his father's advice to the letter, which is not surprising considering the fact that he was the elder son, and eldest siblings usually share the values of their parents. Antoninus certainly enriched the rank-and-file soldiers and scorned all other men, and as the following account makes clear, he also sought harmony with his brother in such a manner that the latter would accept his superior position, just like Severus' brother Geta had accepted his superior postion; Geta had obviously not held the title of Augustus, but the similarity of position cannot have escaped Antoninus' attention. The following coin is a good example of this attempt to find harmony.

Caracalla's Concordia coin with Geta a. 211. Note that the emperor on the left (presumably Caracalla) gives a baton or scroll to the one right. This probably implies a superior position. Drawn after Cohen.

After the death of their father, the brothers patched up their differences for the moment because their immediate goal was to secure the throne.[31] Regardless, Caracalla's greater strength of character appears to have been visible from the start, as Dio claims that Antoninus immediately assumed the full reins of power. Caracalla was certainly ready to follow his father's advice, if Geta would accept his superior position as elder Augustus. Consequently, Antoninus dismissed the Praetorian Prefect Papinian, whose replacement was Patruinus, and had Euodus, his (and Geta's) tutor, *cubicularius* Castor, Proculus Torpacion and others killed.[32] It appears probable that Antoninus considered these people to have been behind the promotion of Geta. It is therefore clear that Antoninus had already managed to secure for himself the full support of the Praetorian cohorts and other military units guarding the emperor. After all, he was the senior emperor. However, on the basis of the SHA (Caracalla 3.2ff.), it would appear that Papinian, Laetus (or Laenus/Laelius) and Patruinus were all still in the office as three prefects of the Praetorians at the time of the murder of Geta, which is problematic in light of what Dio claims (if his account has been preserved correctly). Dio's own statement (78.4.1a) that the Praetorians demanded the killing of Papinian and Patruinus also suggests that both were still in office. The likeliest answer, that also reconciles the sources, is that Papinian had indeed been dismissed and replaced by Patruinus, but may have been reinstated into office by Geta immediately after Antoninus had left Eboracum and joined the army. It is therefore quite possible that there were three prefects in office at the time of Geta's murder. Victor (*Liber 22*) preserves an alternative tradition, according to which Papinian was in charge of Antoninus' secretariat at the time he was killed, but Victor himself preferred the version according to which Papinian was Praetorian Prefect at the time of his death. However, I have accepted here Dio's

The Military Education: the Campaigns of 207–211   117

version, according to which Antoninus was the de facto ruler immediately after the death of his father, and therefore in a position to dismiss and kill high-ranking military men and administrators, because all the extant evidence points in this direction. This suggests that Antoninus had managed to gather significant support from among the rank-and-file Praetorians, and from their centurions and tribunes. It is also likely that Antoninus had managed to endear himself with the Germanic *equites singularii Augusti*, because he subsequently trusted his personal safety to his Germanic bodyguards.

Considering Antoninus's ability to order killings and dismissals of the most powerful men present at the court, it is particularly notable that he did not immediately order the killing of his brother, which suggests that it was not he who was responsible for the events leading to Geta's death. Notably, the defence put into the mouth of Antoninus in the SHA (Caracalla 2.10–11) immediately after the killing of his brother stated that he had in fact given his brother every indulgence possible and had even saved him from a conspiracy, only to be betrayed in his brotherly love. Given the circumstances, his defence sounds right. The conspiracy against his brother must have been formed by someone in Geta's inner circle in order to please Antoninus, which Antoninus must have exposed when he learnt of it.

After having secured his position by removing the enemies present in the Imperial Court, Antoninus rejoined the army to secure its loyalty and carry on the war.[33] His principal aims were to win over the commanders (legates, prefects, *duces*) to his side with promises and bribes, and at the same time to bring the northern war to a successful conclusion. It is important to note that most of these commanders belonged to the senatorial upper class that in general seems to have favoured Geta, which made it difficult for Antoninus to obtain their support. When it became apparent that most of the higher-ranking commanders would respect Severus' last wish of joint rule, he desisted from his attempts for a while. According to Herodian (3.15.6), Antoninus granted a peace to the barbarians in return for 'guarantees', which means that he had defeated the enemy and they had given him hostages as a guarantee. After this, Antoninus left their territory and marched back to Eboracum. The fact that Severus had planned to conduct a campaign against the Caledonians in 211 means that the enemies whom Antoninus subjugated were the Caledonians, and that he had advanced as far north as needed for this. According to the hostile Dio (78.1.1), Antoninus concluded a peace with the enemy, retreated from their territory and abandoned the forts. In other words, Dio implies that Antoninus bought the peace. As is obvious, Dio once again reveals his antipathy towards Antoninus. Even Herodian was ready to admit that Antoninus had defeated the enemy. Maxwell (p.36) notes that Dio's claim that the forts were abandoned immediately is also false.[34] He states that Dio has here either telescoped the events or was guilty of libel. I would opt for the latter if this has not resulted from poor compiling by Byzantine authors.

118 Caracalla

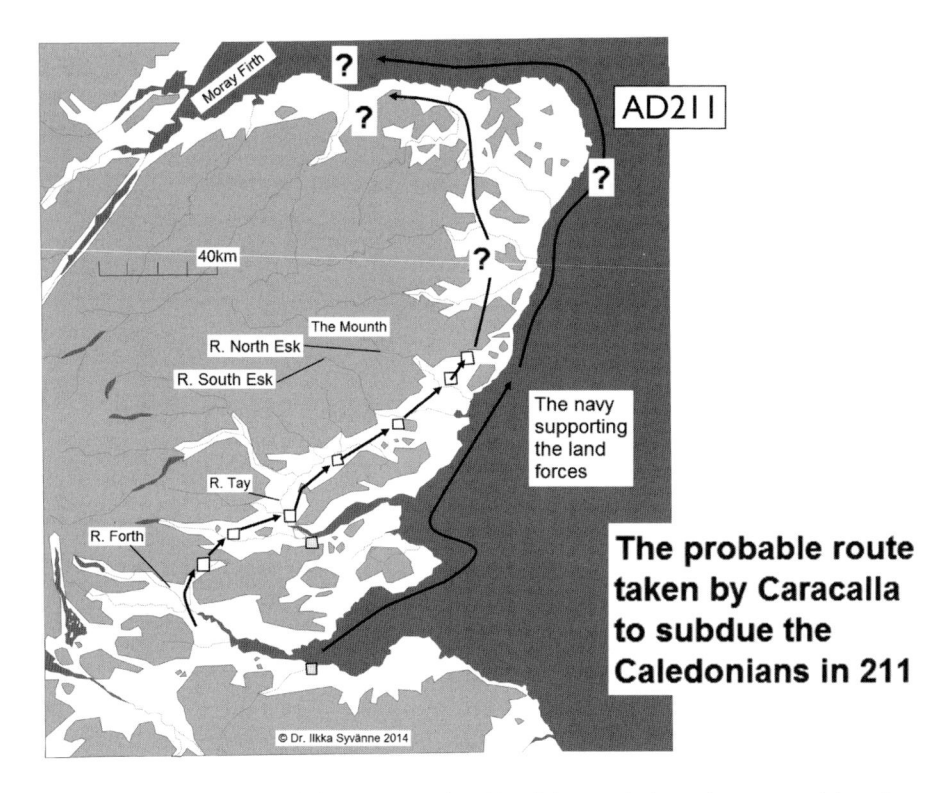

The probable route taken by Caracalla to subdue the Caledonians in 211

Contrary to the usual opinion among the Classicists, Dio is no better as a historian than the much-hated author or authors of the SHA. The campaigns conducted by Septimius Severus in 209, and in particular by Antoninus during two seasons (210–211), and Antoninus' skillful settlement secured peace for the North of England for decades to come, as is also noted for example by Salway (p.181). If the British revolt had been fuelled by the persecution of Christians, the ending of this first by Geta and then by Antoninus would certainly have contributed to the willingness of the Britons to come to terms with him. The new system of defence appears to have been based on a combination of alliances formed with the defeated tribes (*foederati, socii*) and the presence of garrisons in these areas. The building activity at Carpow continued under Antoninus. It is not known when this project was abandoned and the fort demolished, so that the Roman military presence in the north consisted of the garrisons of Hadrian's Wall and forward outposts (at Netherby, Bewcastle, High Rochester and Risingham) north of it, but in my opinion it is very unlikely that this would have happened during his reign.[35]

Antoninus' decision not to continue the war after he had forced the enemy to admit defeat and hand over hostages was a wise policy decision. He rightly concluded that it would have been a waste of men and money to fight over the barren northern wastelands while the brothers still needed to secure their position among the Senate and populace.

The Military Education: the Campaigns of 207–211   119

The British Tradition
The British campaign of Septimius Severus has also found its way into the British historical tradition, in a very garbled manner, but it is possible to attempt to find possible additional pieces of evidence from this tradition to explain the events described above. According to Nennius (22), Lucius, the king of the Britons, converted to Christiniaty in 167. It was after his reign that Severus recovered the province from barbaric invasions, and ordered a wall and rampart with a length of 133 miles to be built from sea to sea to protect the Britons from the Scots (the Irish Scotti) in the west, and Picts (anachronistic, meaning the Caledonians) in the north (Nennius 23). Bede's version of events (Chronicle AM 4163, Ecclesiastical History 5) is that after having recovered the provinces from invasions, Severus dug a great trench and constructed a rampart of sod which was topped with a wooden palisade that had towers placed on top of it at regular intervals. The rampart was built from sea to sea and had a total distance of 132 miles. It is clear that both accounts are based on the same tradition.

Geoffrey of Monmouth (4.19–5.2) provides an account which is even more badly muddled. The following is a summary of the contents, with my comments inside parentheses. Geoffrey claims that the Britons had converted to Christianity when Eleutherius was Pope. When Lucius died in Gloucester with no heirs, the Britons started to fight against each other, with the result that the Senate sent Severus as a legate with two legions to restore peace. (This would presumably mean the legate Virius Lupus in 197.) The Britons tried to oppose the landing, but were defeated and forced to retreat from Deira (south of Hadrian's Wall) into Albany (the area north of Hadrian's Wall). Severus (Virius Lupus?) took with him the Romans and large numbers of Britons as allies and advanced into Albany against Sulgenius, who was the leader of the rebels. (This was a follow-up action by Virius Lupus or by one of his successors.) Sulgenius inflicted immense slaughter on the attackers, but was defeated thanks to the numerical advantage possessed by the Romans. According to Geoffrey, the casualties annoyed the emperor (Severus has now changed from a legate into emperor in Geoffrey's account), with the result that he ordered a rampart to be built between Deira and Albany. The building of this rampart was paid by the taxpayers. (This would refer to the rebuilding of Hadrian's Wall and possibly also to the rebuilding of the Antonine Wall, because the next enemies mentioned by Roman sources, the Maeatae, were north of the latter.)

The defeated Sulgenius crossed into Scythia and sought help from the Picts. (In this case the Picts probably mean some of the Caledonian or Irish tribes. According to the tribal tradition preserved by Geoffrey and other sources, the Picts arrived from Scythia [presumably from Scandinavia if true] and were then, after their defeat, settled in the northernmost corner of Scotland. When the Caledonians refused to give them wives, they obtained those from the Scots/Irish and obtained settlements also from north-east Ireland. It seems very probable that the Picts migrated from Scythia at the same time as Odin was making his trek to Scandinavia so that they arrived in Albany at some point during the 270s or 280s. The other alternative, which is that they arrived in the late second century as a result of the tumult created by the Marcomannic Wars, is less likely (but still possible) on the grounds that the Roman sources mention the Picts for the first time in 297. The Picts reinforced Sulgenius with their young ones. (It was typical for all European barbarians to send their youth to war to prove their manhood before they could marry.) Sulgenius crossed back into Britain with a huge fleet and besieged York (Eboracum). When the rest of the tribes learnt of this, they deserted Severus and joined Sulgenius. (This would probably refer to the massive revolt of the various tribes in 207 which led to the plea for help. The principal tribe to revolt was the Brigantes, and it is quite possible that they would have been eager to join the cause of the Christian Sulgenius when Septimius Severus was persecuting Christians. It should be noted that it is in this area that Geta subsequently launched his campaign against the Christians.) Severus (i.e. the governor) assembled the Romans and Britons who had stayed loyal, marched to relieve the siege and fought against Sulgenius. Severus and many of his men were killed, while Sulgenius was mortally wounded. (If the people who were killed in battle were the Roman governor and the rebel leader, then this would explain why the situation was stabilized by the time Severus arrived in 208.) Severus was buried at York and succeeded by Bassianus and Geta, the former born to a British woman and the latter to a Roman woman. (This part of the account appears to confuse the events that took place under Severus' legate and under his own command. It is notable that Geoffrey also claims that Caracalla and Geta had different mothers. After this, Geoffrey's account becomes even more muddled as he hopelessly confuses the events that took place in the course of the next 100 years.)

Even though this is ultimately unprovable, it is possible that these British accounts preserve some garbled tribal memory of real events, so that there really existed one Lucius and Sulgenius, and that the latter led a revolt against the Roman authorities from c. 197 until his death in c. 207, and that it was during 206 and 207 that Severus' two governors rebuilt the two Roman walls separating Roman Britain from Scotland. It is also quite possible that the Christian faith of Sulgenius could have played a role in the revolt. If the Britons included significant numbers of Christians, it would be quite easy to see why they would have been willing to conclude peace with Antoninus. The problem with this is that the period sources tell us that most of the tribesmen were using tattoos with pagan motifs, which proves that these were in all probability pagans. Regardless, one cannot entirely dismiss the possibility that these tribes could have included significant numbers of Christians amongst their ranks, as suggested by the British tradition. If these referrals are correct, then it is not known what happened to these Christians in the aftermath of the rise of the Pictish Confederacy in the latter half of the third century, but it is more than likely that they either converted into the heathen faith or were killed. After all, the defeat suffered at the hands of Severus and Antoninus would have undermined the position of the Christians. Perhaps some of the stone monuments with Christian motifs, that have been considered to belong to the Pictish period, actually date from the Caledonian period. The casualties suffered by the Caledonians weakened them to such an extent that the Irish Annals of the Four Masters claim that the Irish High King Cormac mac Art conquered them in 240. It is also notable that the Irish sources claim that Cormac was the first ruler to convert into Christianity, which does lend support to the British referrals to early Christian influence in the isles. If Sulgenius really brought the Picts from Scythia (presumably Scandinavia) to assist him at this time as is claimed above, their arrival would have resembled the much later arrival of Saxons who also initially served as mercenaries – the main difference being that the Picts would have become completely assimilated through their marriage with Celtic women.

Notes

1. Birley, pp.170–72; Daquet-Gagey, pp.415–18. I do not agree with Birley that we should reject Herodian's story about the governor's letter which pleaded for help as pure invention.
2. Birley, p.172.
3. Dio77.11ff.
4. Reed, pp.98–99; Bender, p.106, Birley p.176. The relevant inscription can easily be found in Campbell (p.134).
5. The referrals to the building of new granaries and roads in Birley, p.173, and Daquet-Gagey, p.419.
6. A religious cult with twelve priests that worshipped in official capacity the fertility goddess Dea Dia established by Augustus. It included the emperor and members of the imperial family.
7. Dio's '*chiliarchon tôn sômatofulakôn*' does not specify the group of bodyguards, but it is probable that the Praetorians are meant.
8. A 'general' with a temporary command of units, which clearly suggests that the title of *dux* was already becoming more common than the *praepositus*. According to Saxer (pp.122–23), the Romans started to employ the title *dux* for the first time during the Marcomannic War. Before this the commanders of detachments were *legatus Aug. vex.*, *praefectus vex.*, *praepositus vex.*, *tribunus vex*. During and after the Marcomannic War, the titles were *dux vex.*, *praepositus vex.* and *tribunus vex.*
9. Dio 77.10.1ff.; Birley, p.176; Daquet-Gagey pp.413–18; Pollard and Berry, p.71; Saxer, p.48 (includes the actual inscription).
10. Birley, 173; Daquet-Gagey, 419ff.
11. Birley, pp.174–75; Daquet-Gagey, pp.419–24.
12. Maxwell, pp.38–67; Hanson (1978); Birley, p.170ff.
13. Hanson (1978) camps: Grillone 480 men per acre; or 380 men per acre; Hanson's average, 350 men per acre. Maxwell calculates the size as follows: 40 acre/16ha = 15,000–20,000

122 Caracalla

     men. Note, however, that some researchers prefer considerably smaller numbers (see e.g. Kamm, p.126), but in my opinion this is a mistake.
14. Maxwell, pp.61–63.
15. It is probably for the same reason that the Romans posted detachments of *II Augusta* and *XX Valeria Victrix* at Carlisle to protect Hadrian's Wall in the early third century. The western portion of the frontier also required the presence of legionary forces. The presence of detachments from these two legions at Carlisle during the early third century is noted in Pollard & Berry, pp.89–92, 104.
16. Syvanne, research papers 2013–2014.
17. The name Scotland comes from the later Irish settlers called the *Scotti* (Scots).
18. This is not the only theory. For an example of another quite possible alternative, see Fraser.
19. For the locations of the camps and use of two divisions, see Maxwell (p.60ff.) with Reed and Hanson (1978), and the accompanying map here drawn after Maxwell. Note, however, that my interpretation of the evidence differs from theirs.
20. During the Late Roman period, one of the eunuchs of the *cubiculum* was responsible for the carrying of the emperor's sword and/or his military equipment. This eunuch was called *spatharius* (*spatha*-sword-bearer). By the reign of Zeno/Zenon, the *spatharii* (*spatharioi*) of the *cubiculum* (bed chamber) had become bodyguards of the emperor. However, it is quite possible that the Late Roman instution of *spatharii* (*spatha*-sword-bearers) had been created during the late second century, the likeliest candidate for the creation being Commodus. The first attested mention of a *spatharius* dates from 443 or 448, but as noted by Delmaire (p.167), it is very probable that the instution was older. I would suggest that Castor was indeed Severus' *spatharius* and *cubicularius*, and thereby in charge not only of the staff of the imperial household, but also of the *spatharii* eunuchs/servants who guarded the emperor's life in his bed chamber.
21. It is only natural for a son to demand to be allowed to see his father. A good modern example of this comes from an unnamed European country, in which a female nurse is alleged to have prevented the son (I do not name the person, because he is a public figure and very upright person, perhaps even too upright) from seeing his father so that she was able to make the father sign a will that gave her the entire estate. This was overturned in court, but before that happened the woman was alleged to have stolen a sizeable sum of money (millions) through such means that it was impossible to convict her and her accomplices. As is usual in Hollywood films, any resemblance to living or deceased persons in this case is merely accidental. Antoninus was not ready to put up with this sort of behaviour.
22. Birley, p.274, Daguet-Gagey, pp.427–28, Levick, p.83.
23. See e.g. Syvanne MHLR vols.1–2.
24. British campaign in Dio 77.11.1ff.; Herodian 3.14.2ff.
25. Jordanes 15 (83–88, esp. 87–88); SHA Maximi Duo 2.1ff. According to Jordanes and the SHA, Maximinus' father was a Goth and his mother an Alan. He joined the cavalry, from which Severus raised him to the rank of *stipatores corporis* (bodyguard, probably among the Germanic cavalry) and under Caracalla he became an officer of the Centuries or Centurions (i.e. of the *Leones?*) or in the *evocati*. When Caracalla was murdered,

The Military Education: the Campaigns of 207–211   123

Maximinus left the army in disgust and returned to Thrace, where he was considered a friend of the Goths and Alans, which suggests that he was one of the persons behind the subsequent attack of the Goths against Macrinus. When Elagabalus had overthrown Macrinus, he rejoined the army to serve under the son of his beloved Caracalla. When it became apparent that Elagabalus was a degenerate, Maximinus did his best to avoid any contact. However, when Alexander assumed power, Maximinus was again ready to lend his helping hand to the new ruler, who readily promoted so loyal a supporter through the ranks, only to pay the price for such foolish trust when Maximinus usurped the throne.

26. Presumably a member of the mounted elite unit of the *speculatores Augusti* of the Praetorian Guard used as scouts, intelligence officers and personal bodyguards that quite probably had the rank of centurion.
27. Imperial messengers, spies and assassins. It is probable that as centurion of the *Frumentarii*, and as a former *Speculator*, Adventus acted as a sort of double agent to observe the activities of the couriers.
28. Commander of the *Frumentarii* and *Peregrini*.
29. For the career of Adventus, see: Dio 79.14.1–3, 80.8.2; Birley (2000) p.171.
30. Dio 77.15.1–2. Tr. by Cary, pp.271–73.
31. The following is based on: Dio 78.1.1ff.; Herod. 3.15.4ff.
32. Dio 78.1.1; Levick, p.86; Birley suggests (*BBC TimeWatch*, April 2006) that the decapitated bodies found near York are among the first victims of Caracalla's purge, that includes Castor etc. According to Dando (pp.483–84), the York Archaeological Trust has concluded that the corpses date from four different periods, which makes it probable that (if some of the corpses date from the period in question) they would be a group of Praetorians who were punished. However, even this is uncertain because other views have been given recently, which can be found with a web search by those who are interested.
33. The following is still based on: Dio 78.1.1ff.; Herod. 3.15.4ff.
34. The existence of an inscription recording building activity at Carpow in 212 or a little later suggests that Antoninus did not immediately abandon the conquests (Breeze and Dobson, p.142; Salway, p.176). Regardless, Breeze and Dobson suggest that Carpow did not survive long after Caracalla's departure, but was abandoned and demolished, probably together with Cramanon and Newstead. In my opinion, in the absence of dateable evidence, it is improbable that this would have taken place under Caracalla (note the building activity in 212 or later) but should be dated to the period after him.
35. See Breeze and Dobson (p.142ff.).

Chapter Four

The Joint Rule: Antoninus (211–217) and his Hapless Brother Geta (211–212)

After Antoninus had returned to Eboracum, he, together with his mother Julia Domna, brother Geta, distinguished citizens and his father's friends, held a joint discussion in which Antoninus apparently tried to convince the others that it was his birthright to be the senior emperor, while the others tried to reconcile the brothers. When it became apparent that most were unanimously opposed to Antoninus, he was compelled to accept Geta as his equal. Consequently, it was decided that both should sail to Gaul and then take the ashes of Severus to Rome.[1]

When the new emperors arrived in Rome, they divided the palace buildings and staff, and bricked up the connecting passages. It is unfortunate that the sources do not specify exactly what buildings were in question, because there were several 'palaces' on the Palatine Hill (*Palatium*). However, in light of the fact that the brothers bricked up the connecting passages, the likeliest alternative is that they lived in the three-building group on the south-east corner of the Palatine Hill which included the Domus of Septimius Severus, so that the brothers and the mother would each have had one building – see the map of the *Palatium* below (grey shows the extent of the hill). The closeness of the circus gave both brothers ready access to the muscle provided by the circus factions, and it is therefore not at all surprising that both sought to gain their support.

The following illustration (source: Piranesi) shows the ruins of the Imperial Palace from the direction of the Circus Maximus, and hence the likely location

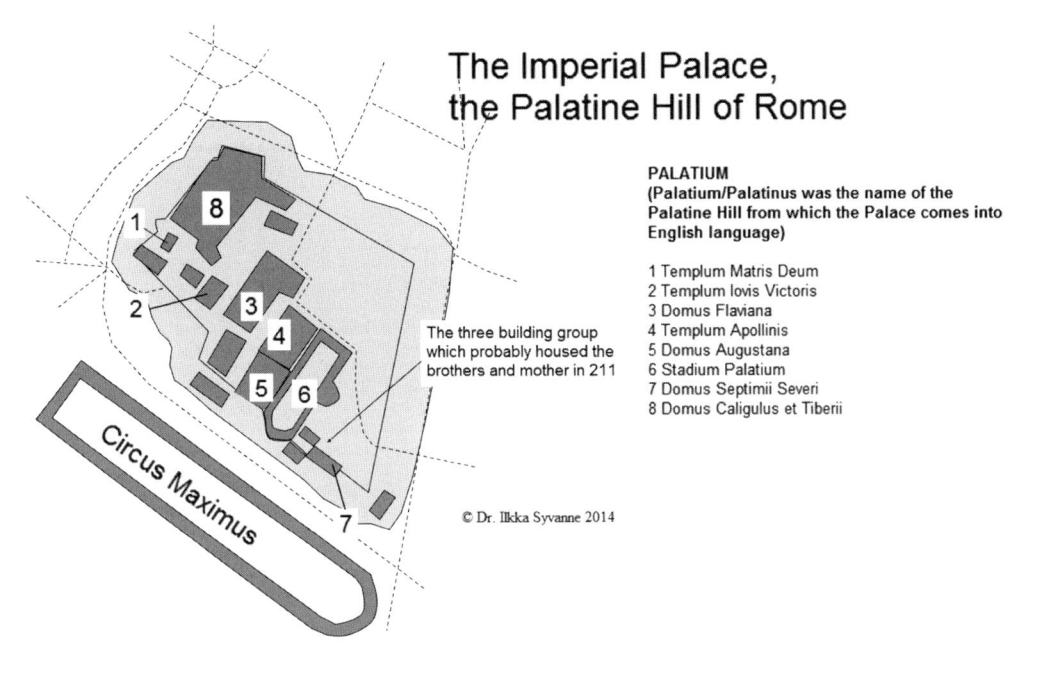

The Imperial Palace, the Palatine Hill of Rome

PALATIUM
(Palatium/Palatinus was the name of the Palatine Hill from which the Palace comes into English language)

1 Templum Matris Deum
2 Templum Iovis Victoris
3 Domus Flaviana
4 Templum Apollinis
5 Domus Augustana
6 Stadium Palatium
7 Domus Septimii Severi
8 Domus Caligulus et Tiberii

The three building group which probably housed the brothers and mother in 211

© Dr. Ilkka Syvänne 2014

where the murder of Geta took place. The Imperial Palace complex was truly impressive and it is no wonder that the barbarians were duly impressed when they witnessed the glory of Rome in its full extent.

At the same time as they quarreled, both Antoninus and Geta continued to gather as much support for themselves as possible from the ranks of the army, Praetorians and other bodyguards, Senate, civil service, circus factions and populace so that they could challenge the position of the other emperor. It was not long, however, before Antoninus, the more forceful and resourceful and probably also the more violent of the two, began to gain the upper hand, as is usual in the power struggles for dictatorships. He sacked the Prefect of the City, Fabius Cilo, because he had advised the brothers to patch up their differences and replaced him with Sextus Varius Marcellus, whom he considered more loyal to him. He held the title of Acting Prefect of the *Urbaniciani*. This secured the *Urbaniciani* for Antoninus. Caracalla also appointed Marcellus as Acting Prefect of the Praetorians. After 4 April 211, Marcellus was also put in charge of the imperial private property (*ratio privata*), a very important position for the purposes of canvassing support through bribery, including the Praetorian Guard. Antoninus also managed to place Q. Marcius Dioga in charge of the general treasury (*a rationibus*). Consequently, he had secured for himself the two most important treasuries of the empire. Antoninus had now a stranglehold on all imperial decisions that required financing. It was in this situation that the famous charioteer Euprepes made his foolish decision to side

126   Caracalla

with Geta. Antoninus had him killed to prove that Geta could not even protect his own supporters.[2]

The court seems to have become divided into two factions: the African faction that supported Geta and the Syrian faction which supported Antoninus. Marcellus, who was the husband of Julia Domna's niece Soaemias, and therefore belonged to the Syrian faction, was steadfastly loyal to Antoninus. The evidence suggests strongly that the North African advisors of Severus were behind the power struggle and the rise of Geta. It is quite possible that they had never forgiven Antoninus' role in the downfall of Plautianus. They had turned first Severus and then Geta against Antoninus and Julia Domna. The Africans wanted to put Geta on the throne because they considered him more malleable. In contrast, Julia Domna and her relatives and friends supported Antoninus because they knew that Geta listened to the advice of others. In short, Geta was no longer ready to recognize his brother's superior position and was following the advice of Severus' mostly North African compatriots against the supporters of Antoninus and the extended family of their mother. It is also within the limits of possibility that Varius Marcellus may have gained his career advancement as a result of 'pimping' his wife Julia Soaemias (Sohaemias), Antoninus' cousin, to Antoninus, because her mother Julia Maesa (sister of Julia Domna) was later to claim that both of her daughters (Julia Soaemias and Julia Mamaea, the mother of Alexander Severus) had slept with Antoninus Caracalla, and that Soaemias' and Marcellus' son Elagabalus was in truth the biological son of Caracalla![3]

Geta's medallion with radiate head proclaiming British victory. Geta did also proclaim the loyalty of the troops in his coins, but in practice he relied more on the support of the African clique of the senatorial class than on the support of the army.

Antoninus's coin 208-211 proclaiming generocity of Augustus to the troops

Caracalla's aim was to court the soldiers as his father had adviced

Geta's coin proclaiming British Victory in 211 which had in truth been achieved by his brother Antoninus.

Geta's long beard was probably meant to associate him with Marcus Aurelius and thereby gather supporters for his cause from the senators

all coins drawn after Cohen

Note the early example of the use of sideburns in imitation of Alexander the Great, which was soon replaced by a full beard to please the soldiers. The sideburns returned when Antoninus had endeared himself with the troops.

Julia Domna on a coin. Note the military style clothing meant to endear the Augusta with the troops!
(Drawn after Cohen)

Antoninus (211–217) and his Hapless Brother Geta (211–212) 127

According to Herodian, Antoninus obtained his supporters mainly because he was seen to be ruthless and violent, while Geta got his due to his friendly and mild character. A more flattering tradition is represented by the *Liber de Caesaribus* 21, according to which Antoninus Caracalla was the more patient, accessible and calmer of the two.[4] One may ask why else would he have been able to gather as many supporters as he did among the army and administration? It is clear that his supporters must have considered him to be trustworthy and true to his word and not at all unpredictable in his behaviour. Regardless, it is still quite clear that the more ruthless and opportunistic elements among the military and Roman elite, and the outsiders, the oppressed, easterners and those of humbler origins were supporting Antoninus; they saw that by backing him they had better chances of advancement than had they supported Geta, who appears to have been following the advice of those who had risen to the top positions during the reign of Septimius Severus and therefore consisted of the more conservative and traditional elements within the Roman elite (i.e. those advisors appointed by Severus to guide his sons). In fact, the two views of Antoninus' personality are not incompatible. It is entirely possible for the same person to be simultaneously patient, accessible, calm, violent and ruthless. In short, it was thanks to his behaviour and control of the treasury of the state that Antoninus secured the necessary support among military forces in the capital to overthrow Geta. However, Geta and his supporters had not been idle either. The majority of the senators backed him, and he was guarded night and day by his loyal bodyguard of soldiers and athletes.[5]

The brothers could not agree on anything and both tried to secure their own nominees to the offices. In order to stop the impasse, both decided to divide the empire in half, with the blessing of Severus' council, so that Antoninus would receive Europe and North Africa up to Libya, while Geta would get the East. According to Herodian, it was only the passionate intervention of Julia Domna that put an end to this project. She tried to reconcile the men, but with no success.[6] I would suggest that Julia's aim had been to try to persuade the members of the council and Geta to accept Antoninus as the senior emperor, which indeed also appears to have been Severus' intention considering the order of promotions.

Eventually the situation became intolerable. On the basis of the fact that the sources are clearly biased against Antoninus, it is impossible to determine the course of subsequent events that led to the murder of Geta with definite certainty, which in the case of conspiracies would already be difficult enough to untangle without additional complications. It would have been entirely within the character of Caracalla to have lured his brother away from his bodyguards so that he could be assassinated, and then claim innocence. On the other hand, it would also be similarly in character for Antoninus to have tried one more time, with the help of the mother, to bring about a reconciliation with Geta, if he would just recognize Antoninus' seniority. I find this latter alternative much more plausible, since the accounts that accuse Antoninus are full of inconsistencies. Regardless of which of these versions is correct, I would suggest that the ultimate guilt for the tragedy rests solely with Geta, who was unwilling to accept his brother's superior claim to the throne. It was his attitude and actions that made reconciliation impossible.

According to the hostile tradition, both brothers were constantly attempting to kill each other, but all attempts to poison or assassinate the other had failed. According to this tradition, it was Antoninus who first tried to assassinate Geta just after the Saturnalia on 25 December 211, and when this failed he decided to use their mother to lure Geta away from his own portion of the Palace. Consequently, the following day he suggested to Geta that they meet that evening at their mother's quarters without bodyguards. According to Dio, when Geta arrived, he was ruthlessly killed by the centurions (presumably *Speculatores* and/or *Peregrini*, *Aulici* and *Evocati*) accompanying Antoninus, and he died on his mother's breast, but Dio contradicts (probably without realizing it) this version later by claiming (78.23.3) that Antoninus dedicated to Sarapis the sword with which he had slain his brother. Consequently, there is a clear discrepancy in his account which makes his version unreliable. According to Herodian's version, it was Antoninus himself who killed Geta. The mother was supposedly forced to show no emotions about the horrific murder, because she feared what her borderline psychopathic elder son would do if she did so.[7] As noted before, there is also a Latin tradition according to which Antoninus Caracalla and Geta had different mothers, the former having been born of the first marriage of Septimius Severus. According to this tradition, after having murdered his brother Geta (in this version his stepbrother), Antoninus then lustily married his stepmother with her consent.[8] If this tradition was correct, then one can guess that the stepmother could have actually cooperated with Antoninus in the murder of her own biological son, because she is said to have used her charms to get Antoninus' attention.

As is typical with sources that attempt to falsify the evidence, they fail to create a consistent account, so that the SHA (Car. 8.4) actually notes that when Antoninus had accused Geta of treachery, Papinian pleaded on behalf of Geta so that Antoninus would not put him to death. This suggests three things: 1) it was actually Geta who had made the first attempt on Antoninus' life; 2) Antoninus could have had Geta killed by the soldiers if he had wished to do so; 3) Papinian had been successful in his plea, which demonstrates the unheard of clemency of Antoninus towards his brother.

It should be noted, however, that if we are to believe Dio's version of Antoninus' life, despite all his ruthlessness, deviousness and cruelty demonstrated in the field of international politics, he was later to suffer severely from a guilty conscience. Dio's version is actually quite persuasive and finds additional support from the SHA (Geta 7.5–6), which claims that Antoninus always wept for the death of Geta whenever he heard his name or saw his portrait or statue. Dio stated that the burden was so heavy that Antoninus had to try placating every possible god to obtain relief from the effects of his bad conscience. Dio (78.16.1–2) also claims that some witnesses alleged that Antoninus eventually lost his sexual desire (i.e. became impotent) and thereafter satisfied his sexual desires in a different depraved manner, and that his example was followed by others who had similar inclinations and claimed to behave in that manner because they cared for Caracalla's health. If Dio's version is correct, and not included just to blacken Antoninus's reputation, then we can say with some confidence that despite all the cleverness and ruthlessness Antoninus had shown in the power struggle, it was too much for his own psyche to bear. Dio's account is internally coherent. It is easy to see how someone with a bad conscience would start to have sex with all kinds of women and would start to drink too much, all of which would ultimately cause impotence. However, it is doubtful that Dio's account would be correct in all respects, because he is clearly guilty of falsifying the successes and accomplishments of Caracalla into failings. This is particularly true of the supposed impotence of Caracalla, even if Dio's version is plausible. Heavy drinking would certainly have led to impotence, at least when the person was hopelessly drunk, but this if anything would still seem like a standard way to blacken the memory of a hated emperor. It is a direct attack on his very manhood. Furthermore, if the other accounts which claim that Caracalla married his stepmother are correct, then this would quite easily explain why he suddenly lost interest in other women. It should be noted, however, that the marrying of a stepmother could be considered depraved sexual behaviour.

This leads us to the other alternative, which is that Antoninus was actually innocent of the murder of his brother, as he himself claimed all along, and suffered from guilt for the reason that he really loved his brother. If one interprets the events this way, then one can make the educated guess that the supposed wish of Antoninus to assassinate Geta on Saturnalia (Dio 78.2.1) is actually the very conspiracy from which Antoninus subsequently claims to have saved his brother, or that it was then that Geta had attempted to murder Antoninus, which was the reason for the above-mentioned plea by Papinian. After this conciliatory gesture that should have won Geta's confidence, Antoninus asked their mother to request both to come to her quarters for a meeting to reconcile the differences. Then when both arrived, Geta once again attempted to murder his brother.

According to Antoninus' own version of events, presented in Herodian (4.5.4–5), when he was already with his mother and without any bodyguards, Geta arrived, accompanied by several men, and attacked him with a sword, and Antoninus only defended himself. Since Herodian (4.4.2–4) and Dio (78.23.3) both credit Antoninus with the killing of Geta and the killing was done with one sword, which Antoninus subsequently dedicated to Sarapis, it appears very likely that Antoninus had either drawn his own sword or had taken his brother's sword, with which he then killed him. It is here that the version in the SHA (Caracalla 2.5) comes in handy, even if the author falsely claims that Geta was killed by the Praetorians only after Caracalla had fled to their camp.

According to the SHA, Antoninus claimed to the Praetorians that Geta had not only tried to kill him, but had also showed disrespect to their mother. When one adds to this piece of information the fact that Julia Domna had received a wound in her hand, while supposedly protecting Geta from the centurions (Dio 78.2.4), the picture becomes clearer. It is probable that Julia Domna had actually protected her son/stepson Antoninus from Geta's attack, and had as a result received a wound in her hand (i.e. Geta had disrespected her). As a result, Antoninus was either able to disarm Geta and use Geta's own sword against him or drew his own sword and killed Geta. The laughter of Julia Domna (Dio 78.2.5) would have simply been hysterical laughter after the horrible tragedy caused by Geta. After the killing of Geta, the innocent Antoninus indeed had to run for his life, as he himself claimed. The centurions who had accompanied Geta were still trying to kill Antoninus. Herodian's version of events (4.4.3ff.) suggests that Antoninus had arrived without bodyguards and was therefore the first to jump out of the mother's chamber. Herodian claims that Antoninus ran through the palace unaccompanied by anyone, while shouting that he had escaped from great danger. He declared to the Praetorians who were guarding the palace that he was in great danger and would be killed unless they escorted him immediately to the safety of the barracks of the Praetorian Guard. According to Herodian, the Praetorians believed him, because they did not know what had happened inside Julia's chamber and therefore immediately escorted Antoninus to their camp. According to Dio, Antoninus hysterically cried all the way that there had been an attempt on his life. When Antoninus reached the camp, he went before the shrine of the camp and offered thanks for having been saved by the gods. When news of this reached the Praetorians, who were either taking their baths or sleeping, as it was already night, they sounded the alarm and armed themselves.[9] However, it was not yet the time to mourn the death of his brother or dwell on what had happened. It was time to secure the loyalty of the Praetorian Guard, Urban Cohorts and other units posted in the capital or nearby. For the strategic situation facing Antoninus at this time, see the map of Rome in the next chapter.

Notes

1. Herod. 3.15.6ff.
2. Based on Dio 78.1.1 ff.; Herod 4.1.3 ff. Info regarding Marcellus and Dioga based on Levick, p.73, and Christol, p.40.
3. Dio 79.30.2–31.4; SHA Elagabalus 2.1; Herod. 5.2.211. Barbara Levick (p.147) notes that Sohaemias was indeed at Rome in 204 at the time of Elagabalus' birth, which means that the story may be true.
4. The Latin tradition is in general slightly more favourable to Caracalla than the Greek tradition and includes variant versions of his life. These sources include: SHA, Sev. 18.8, Sev. 20.2, Car. 10.1–4, Car. 11.5, Geta 7.3–6; Sextus Aurelius Victor, Epitome de

Caesaribus 21; Sextus Aurelius Victor, Liber de Caesaribus 21; Eutropius, Historiae Romanae Breviarium 8.20.
5. Based on Dio 77.1.1 ff.; Herod. 4.1.3ff.; Potter (2004), p.135.
6. Herod. 4.3.4–4.1.
7. Herod. 4.4.23; Dio 78.1.3–2.2. The date in Potter (2004) p.135. For other alternative dates, see Whittaker's comments in Herod (392–3, n.1) with Levick (p.89 with n.17).
8. Sextus Aurelius Victor, Epitome de Caesaribus 21; Sextus Aurelius Victor, Liber de Caesaribus 21; Eutropius, Historiae Romanae Breviarium 8.20; Festus, Breviarium Rerum Gestarum Populi Romani 21; Orosius 18.
9. Dio 78.3.1; Herod. 4.4.3ff.

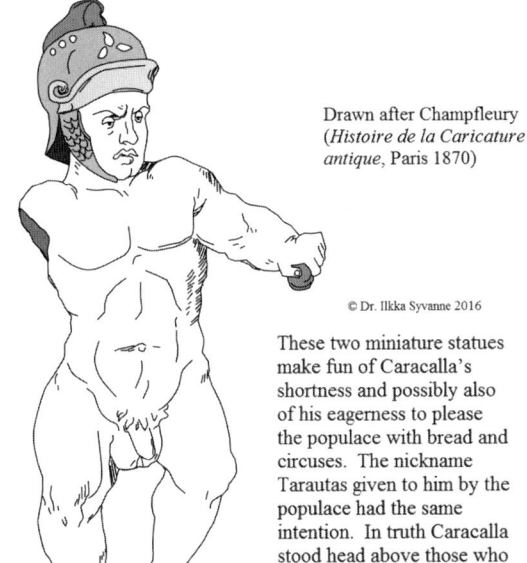

Roman caricature of Caracalla the Warrior

Roman caricature of Caracalla either as an apple-seller or bread-seller

Drawn after Champfleury (*Histoire de la Caricature antique*, Paris 1870)

© Dr. Ilkka Syvänne 2016

These two miniature statues make fun of Caracalla's shortness and possibly also of his eagerness to please the populace with bread and circuses. The nickname Tarautas given to him by the populace had the same intention. In truth Caracalla stood head above those who ridiculed him and he truly deserved his name Antoninus Magnus (the Great) that separated him from Antoninus Pius.

Chapter Five

Antoninus Caracalla Takes Power

5.1. The Securing of Power: the Purge and Bribery

After he had offered his thanks to the gods for saving his life, Antoninus followed a predictable course by trying to secure the support of the Praetorian Guard.[1] Antoninus explained that he had been forced to defend himself by killing his brother. According to Dio (tr. by Cary, p.283), Caracalla uttered the famous words: 'Rejoice, fellow-soldiers, for now I am in a position to do you favours.' Caracalla promised a large donative to gain the support of the Praetorians and the *Urbaniciani* housed in the same camp (see below). The size of the bribe silenced even those who held some suspicions. It is possible that the Acting Prefect of the *Praetoriani* and *Urbaniciani* Marcellus helped Antoninus to obtain the support of the tribunes, officers, NCOs and rank-and-file. The soldiers were told to go to the temples and treasuries and to obtain what had been promised. In addition to this, Antoninus bribed the Praetorians with the promise that they could vent their anger towards Papinian and Patruinus. These men were clearly unsuited to their tasks if they had managed to become so hated that their own men wanted them dead. Their deaths suited Antoninus, as both appear to have been supporters of Geta, but as we shall see Antoninus was still prepared to pardon Papinian if he would just agree to change sides. Antoninus' loyal bodyguards (and assassins?) also received thanks and a large bonus.

Antoninus Caracalla Takes Power 133

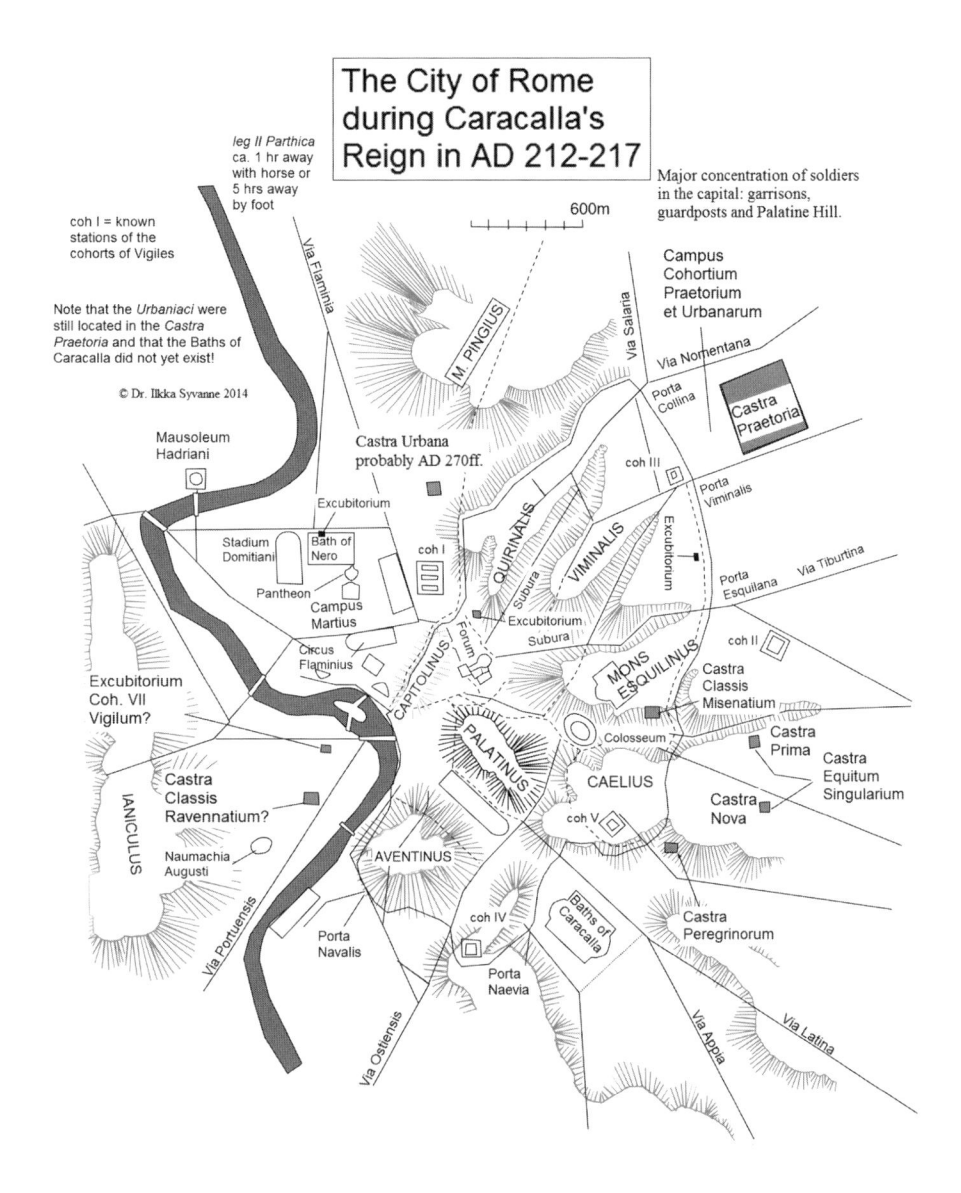

In the morning Antoninus went to Alba to gain the support of the *Legio II Parthica*, but here he was at first refused admittance to the camp, as a result of which the legion failed to obtain the epithet *Antoniniana*, which was reserved only for loyal legions. The use of this epithet *Antoniniana* by Antoninus to reward the loyalty of those units that supported him can be considered similar in intent as Roman crowns and modern medals of honour – a cheap but effective way to reward the men. It appears likely that the legionaries of this legion (or at least their commander) had been among the supporters of Geta and were therefore quite prepared to extort money and promises from Antoninus before granting him their backing. After their demands had been satisfied, Antoninus was admitted inside and given their reluctant support.

In addition to the donatives, Antoninus increased the army's salary by 50 per cent, the total extra cost to the treasury being 70 million *denarii*, which it could ill afford, even after the frugal fiscal policy of his father. After Antoninus' pay increase, the salaries alone cost the treasury annually 140 million *denarii* (or 560 million sesterces), in addition to which came other expenses such as food, fodder, equipment, medical expenses, entertainments and lodgings.[2] The fact that Antoninus' supporters had been placed in charge of the two imperial treasuries was of utmost importance for his ability to fulfill his promises, as was his readiness to allow the looting of the temples! However, as will be seen, Antoninus wisely transferred most of the permanent extra costs so created on to the shoulders of the rich senators, the only men who could really afford to pay such taxes.

The following table, which is based on Le Bohec's outstanding studies, gives the approximate salaries in sesterces of each different type of regular soldier in service and how much Caracalla raised the salaries. It is based on the few known salaries, but readers should keep in mind that the table is still only the best educated guess.[3] It shows well how the *Praetoriani* and *Urbaniciani* received better salaries than all the rest, thanks to their importance for maintaining security.

	Augustus	Domitian	Septimius Severus	Caracalla
Praetorianus	3,000	4,000	8,000	12,000
Urbaniacus	1,500	2,000	4,000	8,000
Vigilis	750 ?	1,500?	3,000?	6,000?
Eques legionis/alae	1,050	1,400	2,800	4,200
Miles legionis	900	1,200	2,400	3,600
Eques cohortis	900	1,200	2,400	3,600
Miles cohortis	750	1,000	2,000	3,000
Praetorian Fleet	900	1,200	2,400	3,600
Provincial Fleet	750	1,000	2,000	3,000

Now that Antoninus had gained the support of the armed forces inside and in the neighbourhood of the capital, he went to the Senate to present the *fait accompli* to them. Antoninus was accompanied by the entire Praetorian Guard, which was armed for combat contrary to custom. When Antoninus appeared before the Senate, he had a *lorica* underneath his senator's robes and was accompanied by large numbers of guards, who then formed a double line around the benches. The presence of the double line and the referral to *Capitolium* by the SHA suggests that the Senate was not convened in its regular location in the *Curia Iulia*, which was far too small for a large gathering, but on the Capitoline Hill (*Capitolium/Collis Capitolinus*).

When the senators were seated and the guards were in place, Antoninus explained what had happened and presented his demands. The Senate had no other alternative than to accept the fact that Antoninus was now their emperor. Antoninus ordered the return of all exiles, including even those banished for religious reasons. His goal was to gain the support of the exiled senators, equestrians and others against those senators and equestrians who had remained steadfastly loyal to Geta and who had formed the 'African clique'. In recalling these men, Antoninus appears to have miscalculated badly, as will be seen later. Regardless, the actions Antoninus undertook immediately after the death of Geta prove that he was a skilled and ruthless plotter when necessary.

Just like his father, Antoninus the history buff was an avid admirer of Sulla, who with his proscriptions provided an example to emulate.[4] Consequently, because there was really no other alternative available, Antoninus ordered an immediate purge of Geta's servants and supporters.[5] As a result, according to Dio, 20,000 were massacred in Rome, with not even women or children spared.[6] Antoninus had formed his plan well before he marched his Praetorians to the city centre, and it appears to have consisted of three separate operations: 1) the securing of the support of the Senate; 2) the securing of the Palatine Hill; 3) the arrest or killing of people who could pose any risk to Antoninus. The Praetorians must have taken positions to accomplish the occupation of the Palatine Hill while Antoninus was still in the meeting of the Senate, and probably launched their attack while the Senate was still in session. When Antoninus emerged from the meeting, he threw away his senatorial garb and joined his soldiers. The first to fall victim to the attack were the members of Geta's household and bodyguards. At the same time as this was taking place, the Praetorian hit squads spread throughout the city to seek the high-ranking persons and other supporters of Geta on the list prepared by Antoninus and his advisors.

The sources provide contradictory evidence of what happened, as was also recognized by the SHA (several versions in Car. 8.1ff., with the other information relating to the killings in Car. 2.4ff and Geta 6.1ff.). The list of people to be apprehended naturally included all those who could command the support of some sections of the military forces in or near the capital, and therefore included at least the praetorian prefects Papinian (Papinianus) and Patruinus, and the former Urban Prefect Cilo. Antoninus did not stop there: his hit list also included anyone suspected of being a supporter of Geta.

The sources mention the arrest of Papinian and Cilo by the Praetorians, both of whom appear to have been ordered to be taken to the *Palatium* by Antoninus. However, both men were brought before Antoninus when he was still en route from the *Capitolium* to the *Palatium*. According to Dio and the SHA, Antoninus would also have ordered the death of Cilo, because he had counselled reconciliation

Antoninus in a military uniform as he would have appeared when he led the Praetorians and Urban cohorts in the streets of Rome. Note also the signs of the Zodiac. (Statue by Montfaucon).

The Praetorians bringing Dacian (or Parthian) prisoner to Trajan in the Arch of Constantine. Excluding the fact that Antoninus was wearing military garb, this is how the scene would have looked like also in Rome. Drawing by Bertoli, 1690.

between the brothers, if the populace and Urban Cohorts would not have shown their support for Cilo. According to Dio, when the Praetorians were already close to the *Palatium*, they abused Cilo, tore off his clothing and bloodied his face with punches. When the *Urbaniciani* saw this, they raised an outcry, with the result that Antoninus, in his military garb, rushed to the scene and shielded Cilo with his cloak. Dio claims that Antoninus had the tribune and the Praetorians escorting Cilo killed, not because he loved Cilo, but because the Praetorians had not killed him. It is quite easy to see that the truth is probably the exact opposite of what Dio claims. Antoninus must have loved Cilo, because he had really tried to reconcile the brothers. He only vented his anger and vengeance against those who had encouraged Geta to act against him. This incident involving the *Urbaniciani* and *Praetoriani* had another root cause, which was the mutual hostility and rivalry of the two units.[7] In light of this, it is not at all surprising that the *Urbaniciani* moved to protect their former prefect against the *Praetoriani*. It is in fact a sign of great persuasive skill that Caracalla managed to make these two units work together.

There are several versions of what happened to Papinian. According to one preserved in the SHA (Car. 3.2), when Antoninus went from the *Capitolium* to the *Palatium*, he did so by leaning on the arms of Papinian and Cilo. It is probable that this took place only after the soldiers had brought both men to the scene. This suggests that Antoninus had actually ordered that both Papinian and Cilo were to be brought to the *Palatium* unharmed so that he could then grant them mercy if they would accept the situation. The reason for Antoninus' readiness to pardon these two men was that they had earnestly attempted to reconcile the brothers. Antoninus clearly sought to punish only those who had incited the brothers to quarrel and was prepared to pardon those who wanted reconciliation. When Antoninus then reached the palace, he saw Julia Domna and other women weeping for Geta. Dio and the SHA both claim that he forbade the mourning on pain of death. It was after this that Antoninus organized the trial of Papinian mentioned by the two versions preserved in the SHA. According to these versions, Antoninus ordered Papinian to explain to the Senate and people why he, Antoninus, had killed Geta; to which Papinian answered that it was easier to kill a brother than to explain it away. According to the third version preserved by the SHA, which is also Dio's version, Antoninus had Papinian killed simply because he was a supporter of Geta, but as noted above, the discrepancies in the sources suggest that Antoninus was actually seeking to pardon Papinian if only he would be reconciled with him, even when the Praetorians were accusing Papinian and Patruinus of 'certain things'.[8] The accusation must mean that both men were supporters of Geta. The refusal of Papinian to support Antoninus sealed his fate. Antoninus ordered the Praetorians to kill him, but contrary to his wishes the man who executed the prefect did not use the sword (*xifos*) but hacked him to pieces with an axe (*axinê*). The use of the sword would have presumably been more humane and better suited for a former commander of the Guard.

The case of the Praetorian Prefect Laetus (or Laenus) is also very problematic, because the sources have several different versions. The SHA (Caracalla 3.4) claims that Antoninus ordered Laetus to kill himself with the poison he sent him, but that he afterwards regretted this decision. This order is odd, because Laetus had been Antoninus' loyal supporter and the first man who had advised the killing of Geta, unless of course Antoninus was executing those who had incited the brothers against each other while attempting to preserve the lives of those who had wanted reconciliation. This conclusion finds support in the SHA (Caracalla 3.5), which notes that many who had been similarly disposed as Laetus and had urged Antoninus to murder Geta were also killed. This suggests Antoninus' first actions were not entirely calculated, but based on an emotional reaction to the events that had taken place. The only rational explanation for the killing of Laetus is that Antoninus would have suspected his loyalty on the basis of his readiness to act against Geta. Regardless, it was still very unwise to execute one's own supporters, and it is no wonder that Antoninus regretted his initial decision. But there is an alternative tradition which is also supported by extant inscriptions and which appears to preserve the real version of events. The information in the SHA is contradicted by Dio (78.5.4 Exc. Val. 357), who claims that Antoninus would have ordered the killing of Laenus (the name should be read as Laetus, as has been done by most historians) had he not been so ill, and then explained his decision before the soldiers by stating that this was the reason for not killing him. It is also known from inscriptions that Laetus belonged to Antoninus' Official Council of *amici* (friends) and *comites* (companions), remained *Praefectus Praetoriani* until 215 and was also nominated as ordinary consul for 215, which means that he was not killed but promoted (Okon, 2013, p.258). It is quite obvious that the sources have to and can be reconciled by simply assuming that the regret in the SHA referred to Antoninus' initial decision to kill Laetus and that he never sent the poison to Laetus. Antoninus' defence of his decision not to kill Laetus before the soldiers should be seen as an excuse in a situation in which the soldiers had demanded his killing, presumably because he had been a hated disciplinarian. In other words, Antoninus kept this loyal friend among his innermost circle. In fact, Quintus Maecius Laetus may have been the only Praetorian Prefect during 212–214, but this is not known with definite certainty because we do not know when Antoninus appointed Adventus and Macrinus as prefects.[9]

The firm securing of the throne demanded other measures too, which included the killing of anyone who could be thought to have a claim to the throne on the basis of a family relationship to former imperial houses. By killing them, Antoninus made certain that these persons could not become figureheads for the senators opposing him. Consequently, Cornificia, daughter of the Emperor Marcus Aurelius, and her son were killed in the name of the greater good. The killed also included Antoninus' former wife Plautilla and her brother Plautius – Antoninus had two reasons for this: she had not been faithful, and both could serve as rallying points for others. There were several other Roman notables who perished, but most of the names are lost to history because the Byzantine epitomators of Dio (77.6.3, 78.1.1ff.) left out their names. The persecution of Geta's supporters and potential supporters was eventually extended to the provinces, and all real or imagined enemies were purged with ruthless efficiency.

The prompt and effective purge of all potential enemies throughout the empire secured the throne for Antoninus. He did not have to fight a civil war against a usurper, either in the capital or in the provinces. This bespeaks well for the efficiency of the Roman secret services, consisting of the so-called *Frumentarii*, *Speculatores*, *Peregrini*, Praetorians and other bodyguards, Praetorian tribunes and centurions (probably the *Evocati*) and of the personal clients and henchmen of Antoninus, the latter of which can be called his informal Mafia of supporters.

What is notable about the details is that none of the sources mention the presence of the members of the *Equites Singulares, Frumentarii, Peregrini, Vigiles* and *Legio II Parthica* among the soldiers taking part in the purge inside the city of Rome. The sources mention only two groups, the *Praetoriani* and *Urbaniciani*, both of which were probably housed in the same garrison, the *Castra Praetoria*.[10] Just like the other loyal units, the urban cohorts were rewarded with the title *Antoniniani* (e.g. *cohors I urbanae Antoninianae*).[11] This suggests several things. Firstly, it is clear that Antoninus considered the *Legio II Parthica* disloyal and left it in its garrison. Secondly, he clearly fully trusted only the members of the *Praetoriani* and *Urbaniciani* who served under Marcellus. We do not know the stance adopted by the *Equites Singulares Augusti* or other bodyguard units and the *Vigiles*, but the fact that Antoninus did not seek their support after he had gained the backing of the *Praetoriani* and *Urbaniciani*, and proceeded straight to the camp of the *Legio II Parthica* at Alba/Albanum, suggests that he had managed to gain their support, or at least their neutrality. It is unlikely that Antoninus would have gone straight to Alba if these units were not secured. The subsequent trust that Antoninus showed towards the Germanic bodyguards suggests that the *Equites Singulares Augusti* and *Aulici* must have been steadfastly loyal to him. The likeliest reason for not using the Germans and other foreigners in the purge must have been that it was politically unwise to use foreigners for such purposes. The use of native Romans and/or Roman citizens was less offensive. It should still be noted that this is an argument from silence. It is possible that foreigners were still used, even if not recorded by the sources. As regards the *Vigiles*, these were probably not used because they were not considered soldiers but policemen and firefighters. Even if they were composed of soldiers, the *Frumentarii* and *Peregrini* were not real combat units, but rather intelligence officers. Consequently, it is not too surprising if Antoninus relied solely on the combat-ready Praetorian and Urban cohorts as suggested by the sources.

The initial phase of the purge of Geta's supporters appears to have been a great success, because Caracalla allowed his loyal supporter Marcellus to give up his post as *Praefectus Urbi* to the new consul C. Julius Asper before 1 January 212. Marcellus was rewarded with a position in the Senate and dispatched to pacify Numidia, which was divided between the supporters of Caracalla and Geta. Asper, however, proved to be a disappointment for Caracalla. According to the SHA (Geta 6.4), the *Urbaniciani* mutinied, with the result that their tribune was either killed or exiled. My interpretation is that we should either connect this with the poor performance of Asper in office, or that the SHA has confused events so it actually referred to the incident in which the Praetorians mistreated Cilo and their tribune was then executed. The latter is more likely. The Cilo incident would have taken place on the same day as Caracalla spoke to the Senate and not after 1 January 212. Consequently, I would suggest that Asper was exiled to his native town of Tusculum later, perhaps in late 212 or even in 213–214. It is actually probable that Asper had himself asked Caracalla to relieve him of his post and retire him to Tusculum, because Dio specifically refers to this.[12]

If we are to believe Dio, Antoninus' bad conscience resulting from the killing of his brother led him to drink too much alcohol and have too much sex with women, eventually leading to impotence. This supposedly had two consequences: 1) Antoninus sought to punish all adulterers and those who violated their religious vows, such as the Vestal Virgins,[13] who had engaged in sex, in some cases with Antoninus himself (note that Antoninus had had personal experience of unfaithful women in Plautilla and was therefore very likely to punish such behaviour when in position to do so!); 2) Antoninus supposedly sought to find a remedy for his impotence and bad conscience from all possible supernatural sources, deities and gods, and therefore always sought to visit shrines dedicated to these if such were close by.[14]

Once again I would suggest that the sources paint an image of Antoninus that is utterly or at least partially false. The punishment of adultery was something that all so-called good emperors had done in order to promote stability in society, and it is therefore just another instance of the sources trying to paint everything that Antoninus did in the worst possible light. As regards Antoninus' frequent visits to shrines during military campaigns, these probably had at least four different purposes: 1) such visits were undoubtedly used as ploys to reassure the soldiers that their emperor was seeking supernatural help against the enemies; 2) despite Antoninus' general personal cynicism towards established religions (he refused to be called a god),[15] it is possible he still felt some sort of superstitious need to obtain supernatural help to cure the breast cancer of his mother (or stepmother)[16] and/or a cure for his own impotence (if true, but this is very doubtful) and to obtain some sort of redemption from the killing of his brother; 3) Antoninus appears to have used such visits for the cynical purpose of supposedly receiving supernatural advice on the identities of his enemies etc., when he in truth received envoys bearing intelligence reports; 4) it is also possible that just before he assassinated his enemies or fought a war, Antoninus wanted to say prayers to the gods of healing. The third of these is by far the likeliest, as will be made apparent later. The downside with visiting the shrines was that his enemies within the ranks were quite aware of the route the emperor would take!

Antoninus needed money to keep his promises. Consequently, he made the rich senators pay the bulk of the extra expenses in various ways. The policy of massacring enemies and potential enemies created a windfall of cash that Antoninus sorely needed in order to fulfill his immediate promises to the army and his supporters, but more was needed for the following years. The practice of giving a part of the loot so gained to the informer(s) created the necessary motivation of gain for the greedy. The punishment of adultery created a similar windfall in money to the state coffers, as those who were thereby punished always belonged to the upper classes. However, even confiscation of the property of wealthy enemies proved insufficient

These two busts advertise the military side of Septimius Severus and the type of armour he would have worn on the battlefield. (*Source: Bernoulli*)

Julia Domna, Louvre. (*Source: Bernoulli*)

Top Left: Plautianus. (*Source: Bernoulli*). **Top Right:** Geta. (*Source: Bernoulli*).

Below: Bust of Caracalla in Berlin. (*Source: Bernoulli*)

Left: A statue of Septimius Severus, father of Caracalla. (*Author's photo, British Museum*)

Above: Young Caracalla. (*Author's photo*)

Below: A copy of the Naples bust of Caracalla. (*Photo by Jyrki Halme. © Jyrki Halme*)

A bust of Caracalla in the British Museum. (Photo: Author)

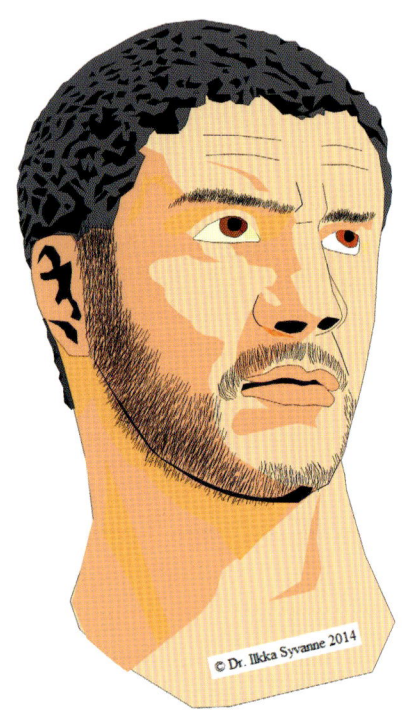

Head of Caracalla modelled after the bust in the Metropolitan Museum, New York. The curly hair shows his African and Syrian roots.

Another bust of Caracalla at the British Museum. Note the kind facial expression and the untypical way he wears the cloak. (*Author's photo*)

A copy of the Naples bust of Caracalla from a different angle. (*Photos by Jyrki Halme. © Jyrki Halme*)

Top Right: Author's drawing of the Naples Caracalla.

Jyrki Halme in period Roman equipment. Note the belt, shoes and the cavalry helmet found at Theilenhofen. (© *Jyrki Halme*)

Jyrki Halme in period Roman equipment. He wears lamellar armour, which was not typical for the era, but still used like all the other armour variants. Note also the harpoon-javelin, belt, shoes and the Niederbieber/Friedberg style helmet. (© *Jyrki Halme*)

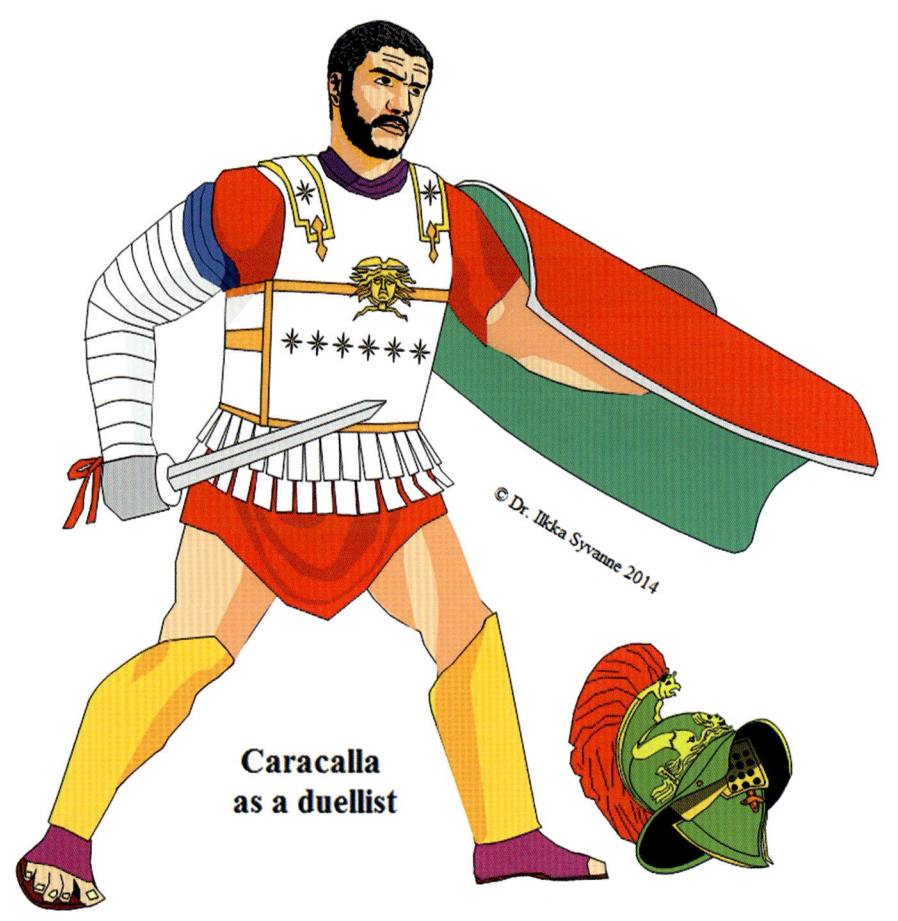

Caracalla as a duellist

My educated guess of how Caracalla would have looked when he fought single combats against enemy leaders. My reconstruction is based on the fact that Caracalla trained to fight as a gladiator and often wore linen armour in combat. (Dio 78.13.2, p.312 in Loeb ed. with 78.17.4, 79.3.1–3)

Two cavalry helmets with visors in the British Museum. (*Photos: Author*)

A copy of the Naples bust of Caracalla. (*Photo by Jyrki Halme. © Jyrki Halme*)

The beardless Caracalla during his final days in Syria. He imitates Alexander the Great and is wearing Germanic clothing, a purple cloak (which could also have a white stripe in the centre, or just a stripe of purple in the centre; I have made the guess that the cloak was the Caracalla) and linen-armour which was presumably white (Dio 78.20.1, 79.3.2–3). This illustration is partially based on the statue, bust and medallion of Caracalla.

Centurio or officer of *cohors volontariorum* in the Portonaccio Sarcophagus (Rome). Drawn after D'Amato and the original work. The sarcophagus belongs to a general of Marcus Aurelius so it describes the equipment used in c. 180 AD. The man wears a Hellenistic helmet and leather *lorica segmentata*, which had probably been copied from the leather cuirass of the chariot drivers (this was kindly suggested by Jyrki Halme). Note also the resemblance with the armour worn by the civilian policemen which I have included in the text.

ANTONINUS MAGNUS (CARACALLA) 211-217
WEARING THE RADIATE DIADEM OF THE SOL

Praefectus Praetorio or Tribunus Praetorio (drawn after a person in a relief located in Louvre, dated usually either 1st or 2nd century AD)

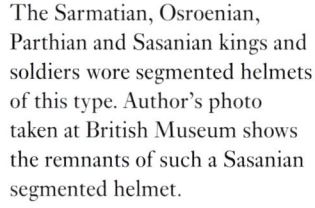

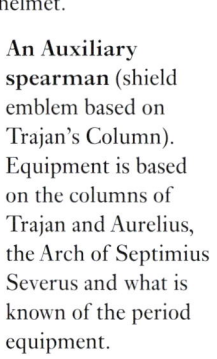

The Sarmatian, Osroenian, Parthian and Sasanian kings and soldiers wore segmented helmets of this type. Author's photo taken at British Museum shows the remnants of such a Sasanian segmented helmet.

An Auxiliary spearman (shield emblem based on Trajan's Column). Equipment is based on the columns of Trajan and Aurelius, the Arch of Septimius Severus and what is known of the period equipment.

A Statue of Caracalla
Drawn after the line drawing of Guhl and Koner with the addition of colours and the spear. If this statue really represents Caracalla and not Alexander the Great, it must be one more instance of Alexander imitation because it is well-known that Caracalla wore his hair short even at the time when he was already imitating Alexander in all other manners, like shaving the beard. It is also possible that this statue represents the young beardless Caracalla.

© Dr. Ilkka Syvanne 2014

The archaeological finds confirm the use of apples at the end of the spear shaft. The use of small shields was undoubtedly related to the use of spear that could be used like a staff/spear. The Britons were clearly ill-equipped to face the armoured Romans in pitched battles. It is therefore not at all surprising that the brave Britons resorted to the use of guerrilla warfare to counter the advantages that the Romans had.

Iron spearhead and Cast bronze sprea-butt, found at Crichie in Scotland. Cast bronze spear-butts, Lisnacrogher, Skerry, County Antrim. (*British Museum*)

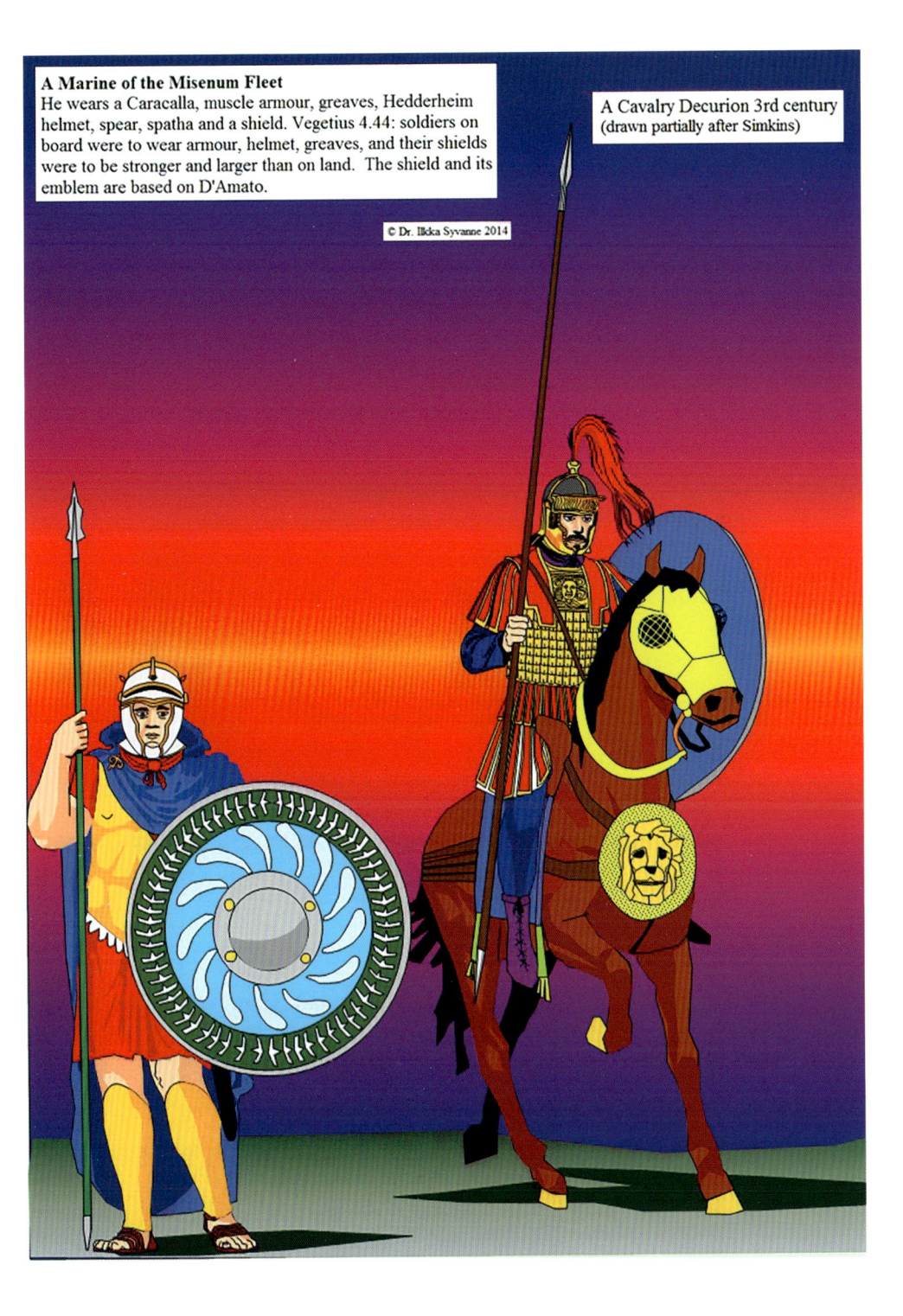

A Marine of the Misenum Fleet
He wears a Caracalla, muscle armour, greaves, Hedderheim helmet, spear, spatha and a shield. Vegetius 4.44: soldiers on board were to wear armour, helmet, greaves, and their shields were to be stronger and larger than on land. The shield and its emblem are based on D'Amato.

A Cavalry Decurion 3rd century
(drawn partially after Simkins)

© Dr. Ilkka Syvänne 2014

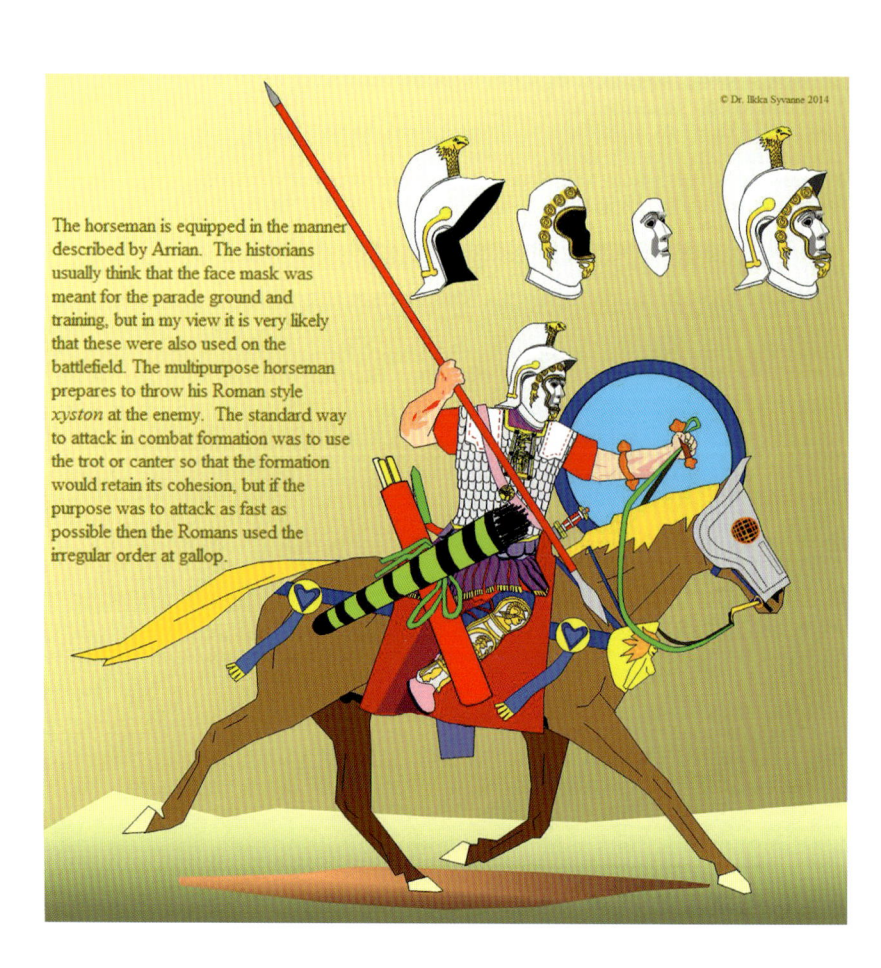

The horseman is equipped in the manner described by Arrian. The historians usually think that the face mask was meant for the parade ground and training, but in my view it is very likely that these were also used on the battlefield. The multipurpose horseman prepares to throw his Roman style *xyston* at the enemy. The standard way to attack in combat formation was to use the trot or canter so that the formation would retain its cohesion, but if the purpose was to attack as fast as possible then the Romans used the irregular order at gallop.

This scene depicts Caracalla with his lions attacking the Parthians. In Caracalla's case the lions meant both his Germanic / 'Scythian' bodyguards (Dio 59.6.1, Loeb ed. p.342, 350; SHA Car. 6.4) who were called Leones/Lions, and his actual pet lions. The scene is based on Rubens' painting. Note also the use of the metal slippers/sandals by the Roman cavalry that were needed when the Roman cavalry used caltrops. Similarly, note the use of the make-up by two of the 'Parthians' (Plutarch, Crassus 24.2).

Caracalla's head used as a model for the beardless Caracalla

Bronze helmet of the Worthing type drawn after Mattesini.

A Roman multipurpose horseman described by Arrian. In the illustration the horseman uses the trot, but when necessary the Romans could also use the gallop to achieve greater mobility on the battlefield

© Dr. Ilkka Syvänne 2014

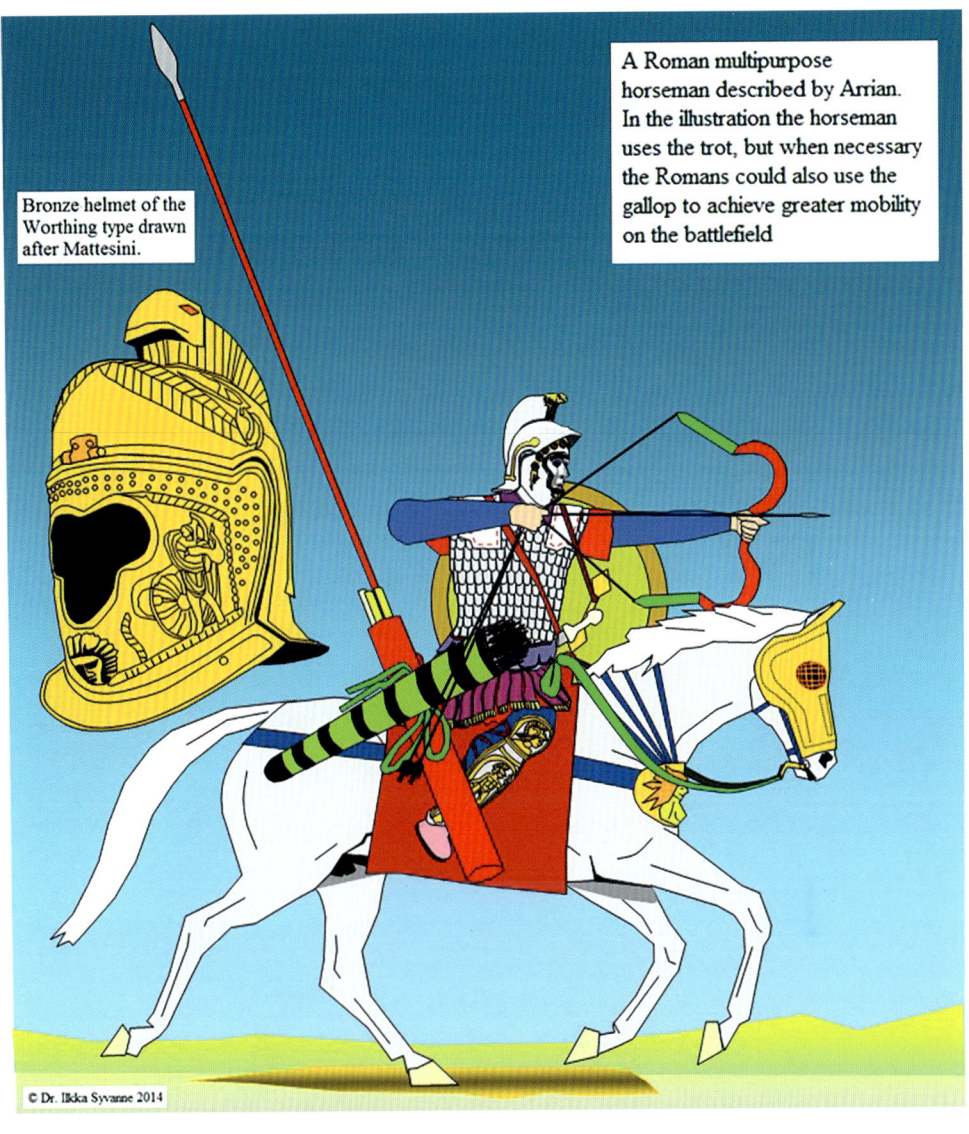

A coin of Caracalla in the British Museum. (*Photo by the author*)

The cavalry helmet found at Theilenhofen. (© *Jyrki Halme*)

Cavalry helmet found at Vechten with the addition of a visor (2-3rd Century AD) drawn after Mattesini.

a *speculator* (imperial bodyguard) mounted on a horse

Ostrov-helmet 2nd century AD, my reconstruction is based on Mattesini's reconstruction.

A Praetorian in typical period legionary equipment. This legionary is modelled after the troops shown in the Arch of Septimius Severus. This arch shows troops equipped with various types of armour (most with the *lorica segmentata*) and using curved rectangular, oval and hexagonal shields, most with the same shield emblem with slight variations in the position of the lightnings. It is probable that all of these men belonged to the Praetorians. In the reconstruction I have used the Imperial Italic H-helmet and the Newstead *lorica segmentata*. It should be noted, however, that the Praetorians may actually have worn the Attican helmets, and that they usually used scale armour during this period.

Below: A Praetorian footman in scale armour, which was typical for the period Praetorians.

Below right: Two spearheads in Caracalla's medallions, which continued in use at least until the seventh century (see MHLR). It is probable that these were principally used by the cavalry so that the spear was easier to draw back for another thrust.

Right: A Praetorian horseman with the scorpion emblem on the shield and helmet. He is equipped with scale armour, *spatha*-sword, three *lanceae*-javelins and Gallic *contus*-spear. Note the use of the Attic-style helmet, which the Praetorians continued to use until the fourth century. The three flat shields (hexagonal, octagonal and oval) show some of the emblems used by the Praetorian horsemen.

Marcus Cincius Nigrinus with his servant. XI Urban Cohort at Rome.

Trierarches of the Misenum Fleet. Armour drawn after Mattesini and the shield after D'Amato. Note the colouring of the shield.

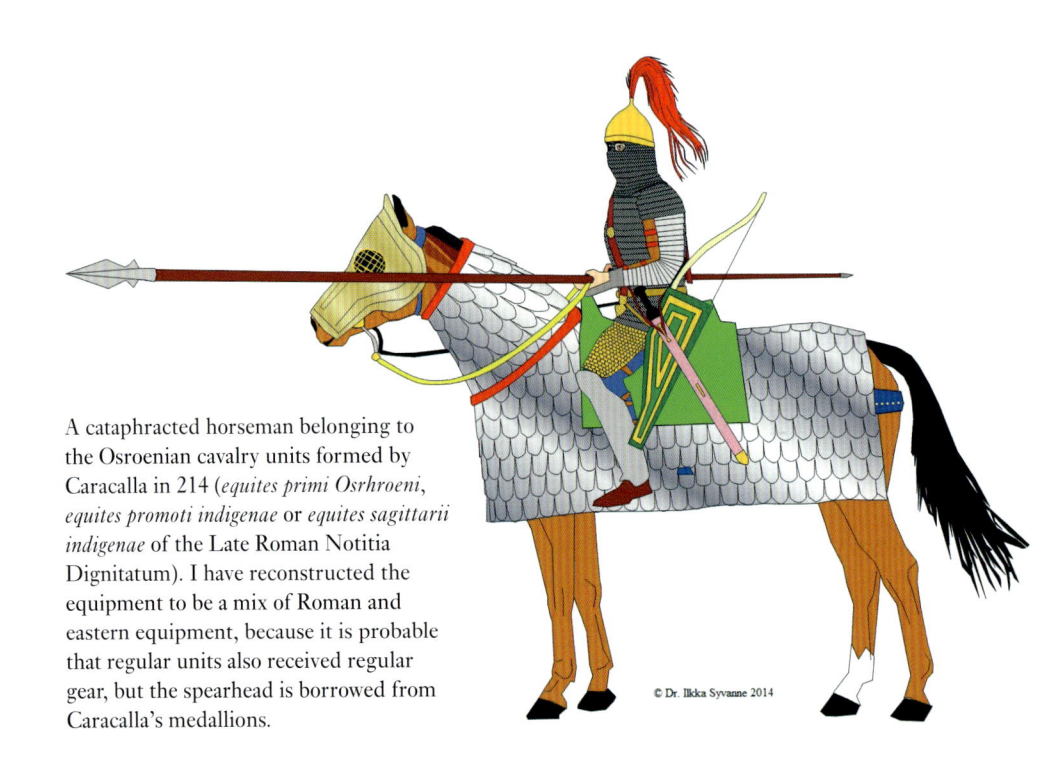

A cataphracted horseman belonging to the Osroenian cavalry units formed by Caracalla in 214 (*equites primi Osrhroeni*, *equites promoti indigenae* or *equites sagittarii indigenae* of the Late Roman Notitia Dignitatum). I have reconstructed the equipment to be a mix of Roman and eastern equipment, because it is probable that regular units also received regular gear, but the spearhead is borrowed from Caracalla's medallions.

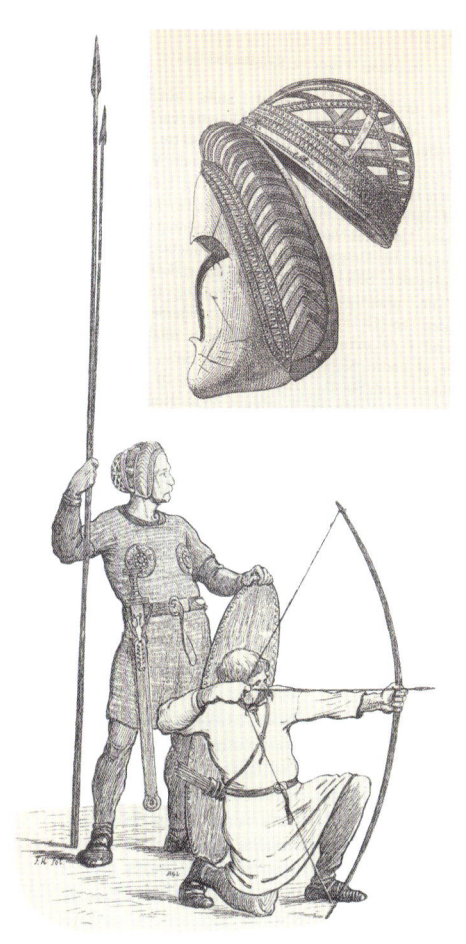

Nineteenth-century reconstructions of the third-century Danish warriors on the basis of bog finds. The equipment worn by these warriors reflects the standard equipment worn by the North Germanic warriors during the third century, who appear to have worn armour quite regularly. Note the length of the spears, which resembles closely the Roman practice of using one type of spear against cavalry and another against infantry. Sources: *Maailman historia* and Sophus Müller. (*Vor Oldtid*)

Elagabalus. (Bernoulli considers him to be an unknown youth).

Coins of Vologaesus/Vologaeses V or VI, and Artabanus V. Source: *Rawlinson 1893*.

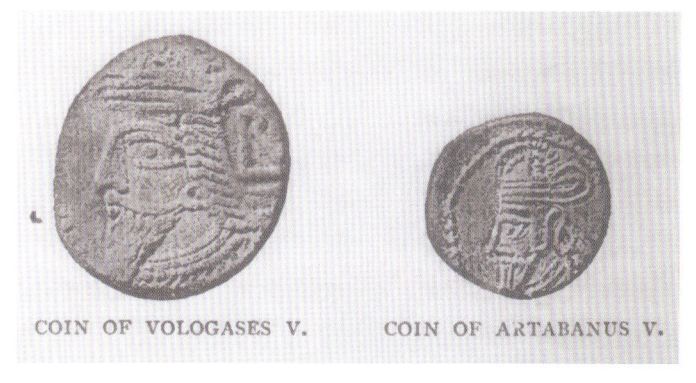

COIN OF VOLOGASES V.   COIN OF ARTABANUS V.

Julia Soaemias. (*Source: Bernoulli*)

Julia Mamaea. (*Source: Bernoulli*)

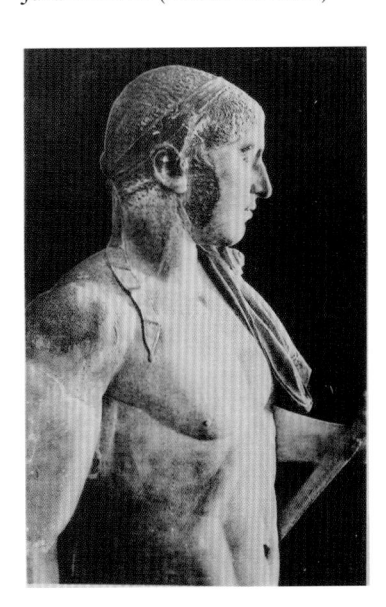

Above Left: Diadumenianus.
Above Right: Colossal statue of Alexander Severus, which tried to represent him as a man with a warrior's physique. It is indeed quite possible that he did have a physique like that, but it did not hide from the soldiers the fact that he was a 'mama's boy' who followed the wishes of his mother. His replacement was Maximinus Thrax, a born hard soldier like Caracalla.
Below Left: Maximinus Thrax. Maximinus was a bulky, tall and brave warrior, but he was not Caracalla. His weaknesses were his lowly birth and poor education. In contrast to him, Caracalla was a man who (despite his short stature) was not only a skilled soldier, but also a very skilled and learned commander. It was education and birth that separated the men. Caracalla had received a very thorough schooling in history and the art of war to enable him to perform his duties as emperor. As a member of the imperial family, he was also more acceptable to the people and Senate. (*Source of photos: Bernoulli*)

to meet the promises made by Antoninus. Consequently, the next step he took was to grant citizenship with the *constitutio Antoniniana* to all free inhabitants of the empire in 212. The so-called *dediticii* (defeated barbarians settled within the empire as farmer-soldiers) were not included. This decision added inheritance tax to the other taxes already paid by the provincials. Antoninus also raised inheritance taxes and some other taxes, and debased the silver coinage in order to increase the number of coins so that he could pay salaries of his troops. See Chapters 6–9. The granting of citizenship had the additional political benefit of joining all new citizens in name with the emperor, because it was customary to add the sponsor's name to the name of new citizen. All new citizens now bore the name Antoninus. Therefore the empire and its citizens became ever more closely linked with the emperor.[17]

The granting of citizenship to freemen had another very important consequence for military efficiency. It made service in the auxiliary forces less attractive than before, because the length of service and salary in such forces was less appealing than in the legions. The possibility of receiving Roman citizenship after service could no longer be used as an inducement for joining the auxiliary forces. It seems probable that Antoninus recognized the difficulties his decision entailed for his ability to recruit auxiliaries, and therefore lengthened the length of service to twenty-eight years (Bohec, 2004, p.64) so that the number of men leaving the service just before his planned military campaigns in the East would be fewer. It is unfortunate that we do not know the date when this decision was taken, because it must have been very unpopular, but probably not overly so because Antoninus remained very popular among the rank-and-file, even after his death. Regardless, we still know that the granting of citizenship did cause recruiting problems to the commanders of auxiliary units that became visible only after Antoninus' reign; the navy appears to have become undermanned by the reign of Alexander Severus.[18] The fact that the auxiliary units could not obtain enough recruits meant that in the course of the third century, the Romans recruited ever-increasing numbers of new non-citizen tribal units and temporary allies to allieviate the manpower problems. In addition to this, the Romans started to use other means of obtaining men for the army when the volunteer-based system failed to obtain enough recruits: 1) the sons of serving soldiers were forced to become soldiers; 2) the use of conscription became ever more usual. Regardless, it is still probable that the raising of salaries and the improvements in conditions of service instituted by father Severus and son Caracalla improved the general standard of recruits seeking service in the armed forces.

In 212, according to the hostile tradition, Antoninus sought to repair his damaged relationship with the people of Rome. His intention was to achieve this by giving the populace presents and a string of shows at the circus and amphitheatre. These same sources claim that Antoninus failed miserably in spite of his good intentions, because he was still a young man in his twenties who now had absolute power over life and death. According to these sources, Antoninus could not resist the lure of being able to drive chariots in the costume of the Blue Faction with the radiate diadem of Sol/Helios and to hunt beasts in person (see Plates, page 7). His aim appears to have been to emulate the behaviour of Commodus and thereby humiliate the senatorial aristocracy. His goal was to endear himself to the common man – he cared very little what the conservative senators thought. According to this hostile tradition, the audience was not amused by the behaviour of their emperor and showed its dislike openly. At one point the hot-tempered Caracalla supposedly even ordered his soldiers to arrest and kill all those who had jeered at a charioteer favoured by him, with the result that soldiers killed people in the audience indiscriminately. If true, this was not a popular move, but the hostility of the sources makes this suspect. In the end the supposedly frustrated Caracalla decided that it was time to leave the capital, but before he did so, he characteristically showed his power over the populace on several occasion by posting his soldiers in the stands to silence the crowds.[19] If this version is correct, which is highly doubtful, it would show that Antoninus knew that he could openly show his contempt towards the people and senators so long as the Praetorians and soldiers remained steadfastly loyal to him. This would not have been wise and would have shown his youth.

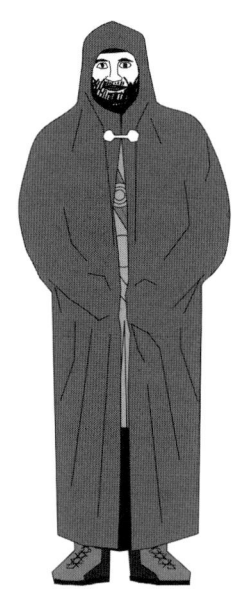

compare the cloaks!

© Dr. Ilkka Syvänne 2014
"Antonine" Caracalla

However, it appears very likely that the image painted by the hostile sources is once again utter rubbish. This hot-tempered version of Caracalla painted by Dio is contradicted by the other tradition, which claims that Antoninus Caracalla was a patient, accessible and calm man. This same tradition also finds support from the subsequent hostility of the population towards Macrinus and his son Diadumenianus, the killers of Caracalla, the darling of the people, which even Dio had to admit.[20] This tradition paints an entirely different picture of Caracalla; one who was loved and adored by the populace in general. Consequently, it is clear that Caracalla achieved what he aimed for. Only Dio and his ilk among the senatorial class felt intense hostility towards Caracalla. Unsurprisingly, Sextus Aurelius Victor's *Liber de Caesaribus* 21 presents a far more flattering tradition of Caracalla's achievements. According to him, Caracalla won over to his side the Roman populace with measures that the populace had never before witnessed. The most notable of these was the distribution of Gallic cloaks of a reddish hue ('*coloris russei*', according to the SHA, Diad. 2.6.8) called Caracalla/Caracallus which reached down to the ankles, from which he got his nickname. I will therefore henceforth call Antoninus either Antoninus Caracalla or just Caracalla. It is quite probable that the inspiration for the so-called Antonine Caracalla cloak actually came from the Celtic god Telesphorus (usually a drawf whose head was always covered with a cap, see the illustration) who was the son of Aesculapius and the god of youth and healing.[21] It should be remembered that Caracalla regularly visited the temples of Aesculapius in his mission to seek healing (or rather information) and that some of Caracalla's ancestors were Gauls. This suggests the possibility that Antoninus Caracalla's Gallic roots formed a very strong component of his identity, which led him to adopt the use of the Caracalla cloak which was connected with Telesphorus. It is quite probable that the adoption of the Caracalla cloak was a form of self-parody, because Caracalla, just like the god Telesphorus, was not tall. According to Dio (79.9.3, Loeb. p.358), some of the people called Caracalla Tarautas, after a gladiator who was ugly, reckless and bloodthirsty. What is notable about this is that Dio does not claim that this would have caused Caracalla to react violently against those commoners who used this nickname. The ability to laugh at himself and his own weaknesses suggests a very strong self-esteem.

Caracalla initiated another project to endear himself with the populace for which he is justly famous – he built the celebrated *Thermae Antoniniana* (Baths of Caracalla) in Rome, the remains of which are still visible. Even the SHA (Car. 9.4) noted this project. Caracalla therefore clearly cared for his people.

5.2. Internal and External Security

The single most important factor in the mind of any Roman emperor, Caracalla included, was the maintenance of internal security, which consisted of many methods for the different levels of society. As was so well recognized by father and son, the loyalty of the army formed the basis of the emperor's power. Considering Severus' advice to secure the loyalty of the army, it is unsurprising that Caracalla did more than any other emperor to retain its support. In fact, he did this so brazenly that he antagonized even those senators who could have otherwise lent their support to his rule. Caracalla knew full well that he needed the backing of the army in order to keep the senators in order.[22]

However, Caracalla's system of maintaining internal security was more complex than that. He also wanted the support of the populace (*humiliores*) and wealthy middle classes (equestrians), which he gained with various policies, the most important of which were the opening up of higher office career paths to freemen, freedmen and equestrians, and the bribing of the masses with various gifts and mass amusements. The granting of citizenship to all freeborn inhabitants of the empire made Caracalla the most popular emperor ever among the provincials. This decision was to have truly far-reaching consequences, as it made every freeborn man and woman in the empire part of the empire they lived in. Caracalla was also wise enough to end the persecution of religious minorities and embrace other religions in order to gain the goodwill of all religions towards his rule. Like other emperors, Caracalla also used coins, sculptures, pictures and buildings to project his imperial propaganda and power, and in this he seems to have been very successful, since the stern facial expression in his sculptures has even affected our perception of him.[23]

Despite the recognition that the sources are biased against Caracalla, most modern historians seem to have been misled into believing that Caracalla was somehow more brutal than other emperors, and the stern images put up by him throughout the empire must have played their part in the birth of this image. Indeed, Caracalla seems to have been very successful in his projection of the outward image of a soldier emperor who protected the Roman soldiers and people from enemies both outside and inside the empire.

However, in order to survive in the hostile world, Caracalla could not rely solely on the goodwill of the soldiers and populace. He also needed internal security agents and informers. In fact, circumstantial evidence suggests that Caracalla maintained a very effective network of informers and spies, and could have even survived the final plot to kill him, had he had the sense to take additional security measures when he suspected his Praetorian Prefect Macrinus of plotting against him, and he should not have kept a man (Martialis) whom he had mistreated among his closest servants and bodyguards. Caracalla's only mistake was to assume that the freedmen and equestrian military officers would remain loyal to him, because they owed their position to him. As we shall see, after the purge of Geta's supporters, most of the senators remained loyal – even the hostile ones!

The scattered pieces of evidence in the sources allow us to reconstruct the rough outline of Caracalla's internal security organization. The sources make it clear that Caracalla had in his service secret agents, informers and assassins (mostly centurions from unspecified units, which were likely to be the bodyguards and/or the *Evocati*) who could be used to kill his enemies throughout the empire either openly, secretly (where death was made to look accidental) or with poison. In addition to this, he had a network of private informers, most of whom appear to have consisted of opportunists. The informers included both senators and commoners. Dio mentions specifically three senators: Manilius, Julius and Sulpicius Arrenianus. The most efficient of the private informers appears to have been Lucius Priscillianus, a brave man particularly known for his unassisted fight against a bear, panther, lioness and lion at the same time – this would certainly have gained Caracalla's admiration, even without the other services. Dio claims that Priscillianus levelled false charges (were these really false?) against both equestrians (knights) and senators, and was amply rewarded by Caracalla so that he eventually became governor of Achaia. This implies that Priscillianus probably employed very effectively a private network of undercover operatives, consisting of his clients and servants, on behalf of the emperor. It should be noted that the private informers did not only disclose matters of imperial importance, but also acted as whistleblowers against the corrupt or otherwise suspect practices of their superiors. Caracalla rewarded such whistleblowers amply and undoubtedly improved the efficiency of the state apparatus in this way.[24]

On the basis of the sources, the eight most important organizations and sources of information used for these purposes probably consisted of: 1) members of the regular army who were seconded as secret agents; 2) the 'centurions', who were probably either members of the imperial bodyguard units (Praetorians, *Speculatores, Equites Singulares/Protectores/Aulici* and later *Leones*) and/or alternatively the special unit of *Evocati Augusti* consisting of the reservists recalled to service; 3) the *Frumentarii* and the *Peregrini*, who performed special missions alongside their regular duties; 4) the Urban Cohorts and other units (could also include Praetorians and *Vigiles*) who were placed under the Urban Prefect to act as an internal security force in the capital when Caracalla was not in Rome; 5) seers, astrologers, oracles, augurs and fortune-tellers who acted as informers on those who had sought their advice on matters of imperial importance, that appear to have operated under the general jurisdiction of the *pontifices*, of whom the most important person was the emperor himself as *Pontifex Maximus* (high priest), and that included among its ranks the Praetorian prefects (see below), but who at least under Caracalla seem to have reported to the Urban Prefect when he was not at Rome; 6) private individuals who acted as informers for their own benefit or because they felt that there were persons who threatened the emperor; 7) the staff of the sacred bedchamber, the *cubicularii*; 8) the staff of the *scrinium memoriae*.[25]

It is also possible that the *Fratres Arvales* were involved in intelligence-gathering, because its members included members of the Imperial Family and *amici* of the emperor, and it received and publicized military information at Rome, but evidence for this is uncertain. The same concerns the role of the priests of the temples of certain deities (in particular those of Apollo Grannus, Asclepius/Aesculapius

146   Caracalla

and Sarapis/Serapis[26]). Caracalla's constant visits to those temples and the daily use of couriers going back and forth, in particular before killings, may imply that he employed these priests among his clandestine undercover organizations. The problem with this is that it is very likely that at least the followers of Serapis in the city of Alexandria were actually enemies of Caracalla, but it is still possible that Caracalla pretended to be their friend and used them until the day he destroyed them. For more on this, see Chapter 9. It cannot be stressed too much that most of the evidence regarding the intelligence system employed by the emperors, Caracalla included, is circumstantial and quite often also impossible to prove without doubt.

Dio (78.17.1–4) also implies that there was a special organization within the military, employed as Caracalla's eyes and ears to terrorize senators, whose commander was actually the *Praepositus Sacri Cubiculi* Sempronius Rufus, who appears to have been the successor of Festus (see Chapter 8). It is notable that Caracalla had placed his freedmen and members of his own household in charge of security operations. Caracalla also unified the posts of the head of the *Scrinium Memoriae* (Bureau of Memoire) and *Praepositus Sacri Cubiculi* (Commander of the Sacred Bedchamber), which appears to have meant that the same person (a freedman and/or eunuch) was in charge of both potential sources of intelligence and also had the power to employ regular soldiers as his spies. Interestingly, before his appointment to that position, Rufus, who was by profession a poisoner (drug/poison seller) and sorcerer/wizard/juggler/enchanter, had been exiled to an island by Septimius Severus. Rufus' role as intelligence operative is not surprising, because as a former sorcerer/poisoner he was certainly familiar with the workings of the state security apparatus, which brings us to the next claim made by Dio.[27]

Dio claims that Caracalla trusted blindly in astrology, oracles and other supernatural interpretations to determine who were his enemies and his friends, and appears to claim that even in the case of Macrinus the prophecy was true (see Chapter 11). What this actually proves is that Caracalla was very successful in hiding his network of private and official informers behind the veil of supernatural predictions. Dio (79.21) suggests that Caracalla may have either destroyed the documents sent by the informers before his death, or had always sent those back to the informers themselves or that Macrinus later lied that there did not exist any list of informers. I believe, however, that the circumstantial evidence suggests that Caracalla actually organized an independently operating network of security personnel so that his Praetorian prefects would not learn of the contents of the messages received by the emperor. At a time when most of the people had strong superstitious beliefs, the very knowledge that the emperor was supposed to be using supernatural means to detect evil thoughts undoubtedly contributed to the creation of an atmosphere of fear among those harbouring such thoughts, which in turn lead them to behave in such a manner (i.e. use forbidden supernatural protective countermeasures) that would have aroused the attention of informers and spies. Considering Caracalla's quite manipulative behaviour and his sharp intellect, it is quite likely that he simply toyed with the people around him and acted as if he believed in astrology and prophesies in order to achieve the intended results.[28]

That sort of manipulation of people's conceptions would be entirely in keeping with Caracalla's very devious character. The four most important pieces of evidence to support this conclusion are: 1) the above-mentioned professions of the informer and spy chief Rufus; 2) those who had consulted oracles for the wrong reasons were executed; 3) according to Dio (78.15.5–7), Caracalla was in the habit of constantly sending prayers etc. to Apollo Grannus, Aesculapius and Serapis so that couriers were every day coming and going (these were likely to be important messages that appear to have included messages concerning the names of enemies that were shrouded as prophecies to hide the informers' true identities; this sending of couriers to shrines every day is particularly important for the analysis, because it proves that Caracalla was dispatching and receiving couriers daily, and when one remembers that he usually purged personnel after he had visited the shrines in person it becomes apparent that we are here dealing with a method to disseminate intelligence reports, which was disguised as something else; this also proves that it is very improbable that Caracalla would have sought some cure for himself or for his mother when he visited the shrines, even if one cannot exclude this possibility in its entirety); 4) after the murder of Caracalla, Macrinus claimed not to have found a list of informers from correspondence (i.e. the identities of informers were hidden by conveying the information as prophecies, if Macrinus's report was accurate and not self-serving).[29]

In short, it appears very probable (even if this is based solely on circumstantial evidence and probability) that Caracalla employed a network of semi-official or official seers and conjurors as informers, together with soldiers and other informers, and that he used to hide the identity of all of his informers by conveying their information to shrines as prophecies. This allowed him to hide the true identity of informers when these were not the seers themselves, while it also made it appear as if the emperor possessed supernatural means of detecting his enemies.

On the basis of the details concerning the assassination of Caracalla and other information provided by Dio, the system appears to have worked so that Caracalla used the *Praefectus Urbi* (Urban Prefect of Rome, a senatorial rank; Cilo 204–211, Marcellus 211, Asper 212 and Flavius Maternianus 214–217) and *Praepositus Sacri Cubiculi* (Head of the Imperial Bedchamber, who was a eunuch) as his principal spy chiefs. This means that Caracalla did not trust his Praetorian prefects. The Urban Prefect and *Praepositus* apparently collected evidence of plots and potential plots (through soldiers and informers, who included all sorts of people such as seers) and then dispatched couriers (*frumentarii*) to Caracalla directly. The Urban Prefect appears to have used the *Urbaniciani* as his secret service so that they reported back to him anything that was considered suspicious, and the *Urbaniciani* were located all over the empire to secure supplies for the city of Rome, just like the *Frumentarii* purchased and distributed grain (*frumentum*) for the troops – in fact it is probable that these two organizations sometimes cooperated and/or that the latter were subjected to the Urban Prefect at times when the Praetorian prefects were not in Rome. When Caracalla was in the East, all letters passed through his mother Julia Domna, who then sorted out important letters from the less important ones. Caracalla rightly considered her to have been a first-class administrator and a person whom he could trust. She was Caracalla's mother-in-arms in every sense of the word. Even though this is not specifically mentioned by the sources, circumstantial evidence suggests that it is probable that when the implicated plotter was himself in charge of security (as happened when Macrinus was implicated), Julia Domna (or someone else who had been delegated to the same tasks in the preceding years) dispatched two couriers with letters so that the plotter would not learn of the threat he was under: the first to Caracalla, in which she asked him to pray for her health in some particular shrine, and the second to the shrine, where Caracalla then learnt of the threat in such a manner that the message was presented as a prophecy. On the basis of the above, I would suggest that the division of labour among these spy organizations for internal security was two-fold: 1) all information was centrally dispatched to Rome when the emperor was located there; 2) when the emperor was not in Rome, he or his operatives received information directly from areas close to the emperor, while operatives in other areas still sent their reports to Rome, where the Urban Prefect read them and dispatched the relevant pieces of information directly to the emperor or to Julia Domna. In the latter case, this obviously meant quite long delays in the dissemination of information, because all information had to travel first to Rome, and only then on to the emperor.[30]

The obvious weakness of this organization is that the security of the information dispatched to Julia Domna should have been trusted only to men whose loyalty was beyond doubt, but in this case the *aggeliaforoi* couriers (presumably the *frumentarii*) had two commanders who were actually working for the conspirators. Consequently, if the messages were still hidden with a cipher, as during Julius Caesar's day, the contents did not remain a secret from the plotters because the messages were given in plain language to the disloyal commanders, who then ciphered the messages. An analysis of this can be found in Chapter 11.

It is possible that we should also see the favouritism showed by Caracalla towards the cult of Isis in the context of intelligence gathering. According to the SHA (Car. 9.10–11), Caracalla built magnificent temples for Isis at Rome and elsewhere. He was not the first emperor to do so (Commodus and Septimius also did that), but Caracalla is claimed to have shown greater reverence to Isis than any of his predecessors. Modern research has confirmed this and noted its potentially positive impact on Caracalla's standing among the populace, but in light of his use of religious places for the dissemination of intelligence, it is possible that he sought cults for this purpose which were not heavily infiltrated by members of the Roman upper classes (including equestrians and senators) who belonged to his traditional and potential enemies.

It should be noted that since Macrinus was himself Praetorian Prefect and a member of the *pontifices*, he was undoubtedly aware that some of the information came in the form of prophecies and that asking the wrong kinds of questions from the seers caused death, which means that he was somewhat insincere when he said that no information was found of any list of informants after the death of Caracalla. As prefect, he must have known the names of several informers, even if it is likely that he did not know those whose identity Caracalla and his closest associates hid. Considering Caracalla's use of several different services and officers for the gathering of intelligence, it appears probable that none of the prefects were entirely kept abreast of all intelligence-gathering activities. Rather, Caracalla seems to have used them all to spy upon each other. It appears probable that he had placed most of the secret internal intelligence-gathering on the shoulders of *Praepositus Sacri Cubiculi* Rufus and *Praefectus Urbi* Flavius Maternius. In hindsight, it is easy to see that it was unwise for Caracalla to anger any of the equestrian Roman officers in charge of the Praetorian cohorts, but even this would not have proved fatal had Caracalla himself paid more attention to reports he had been sent by his loyal friends or acted more promptly when suspicions of foul play were brought to his attention. Macrinus was already high on Caracalla's list of suspects well before the actual threat materialized.

The gathering of intelligence against external threats under Caracalla was based on traditional methods and consisted of the use of undercover spies (military officers and others who posed as traders, diplomats etc.), military spies/scouts in uniform (*speculatores*), scouting patrols (*exploratores*) along the frontiers, naval patrols, intelligence provided by traders and other private explorers, information obtained from double agents and deserters, and the use of military outposts, fortifications and walls. The dissemination of intelligence was facilitated by the road network, public post, and fire and smoke signalling. Messages could also be encoded to hide the contents. Counter-intelligence consisted of the use of scouts, patrols, sentinels, guard dogs, safety protocols, passwords etc., in addition to which the Romans employed various stratagems, ruses and the spreading of disinformation.[31] Caracalla was a master of the latter. As will be made clear, Caracalla always possessed first-rate intelligence of the internal situation and politics of foreign tribes and nations that enabled him to formulate his foreign policy goals in such a manner that exploited the weaknesses of neighbours to the hilt.

Contrary to the religious policies of his father, Caracalla's reign was marked by tolerance towards all religions, which included the much-maligned Christians and Jews. The only exceptions to this were the followers of Serapis in the city of Alexandria, but even in this case persecution was not extended to include other followers of Serapis (see Chapter 9). The change of policy occurred immediately. According to Bar Hebraeus (p.55) and Michael Syrus (Armenian version 60, g119), Caracalla allowed the return of exiles who had been banished because of their faith. Notably these included Alexander, who was appointed as Bishop of

Jerusalem (Michael Syrus 60, g119; Eusebius 6.8).[32] Eusebius (6.8) also implies that it was during the reign of Caracalla that those who had been persecuted during his father's reign found relief from their hardships. In other words, he followed a policy of religious tolerance that appears to have been buried under the hostile accounts of the senatorial class. Tolerance of Christianity was only likely to inflame the staunchly pagan senators even more.

Considering Caracalla's religious tolerance and his probable cynical use of superstitions for his own benefit, it comes as no surprise that his reign also marked the proliferation of various foreign religions at Rome and the increasing movement toward monotheistic views among the pagans. Just like Commodus and many other emperors before him, Caracalla paid particular lip service towards the Cults of Isis and Serapis. This probably had four purposes, as previously noted: 1) he wanted to endear himself with the populace who found these cults most appealing; 2) he may have wanted to bring both under the imperial control of information-gathering; 3) he may have wanted to use these cults to disseminate information; 4) he was fond of Egypt thanks to his idolization of Alexander the Great. By paying lip service to all possible religions, cults and deities, Caracalla also tried to canvass as much support from as great a number of people as possible. In addition, probably at the instigation of his mother, he may have started the pagan movement towards the monotheistic cult of the sun (the most important of these was the Sol Invictus), of whose Prophet/Messiah/Christ was the miracle worker Apollonius of Tyana,

Legionaries from three different British legions with swords in hand. Such a situation could theoretically take place when representatives of all three legions were (for example) foraging in Caledonia for their units at a time when the enemy suddenly attacked. All use cylindrical shields and ring-swords, but as regards other equipment these show typical variations attested for this period. The helmets show both simplified types and Imperial Italic helmets and footwear differs from one to another. One of them has shin-guards that front rankers were expected to have while the others are without.

The shield emblems are hypothetical because we do not possess definite information for the emblems of these legions for this period.

who lived during Domitian's reign.[33] This if anything was a very cynical move. The emperor needed to possess some control over religions in order to be able to gather intelligence from among the highly superstitious members of the upper-class senators. If all converted to Christianity or Judaism, such intelligence would stop. Hence he needed a pagan alternative for the eastern religions, and the best alternative was to use the eastern cult of the sun at its core, because the Imperial Family included a high priest and other priests of that particular cult. For example, Julia Domna's father had been one and Elagabalus was to become another.[34] Caracalla's general attitude towards all religions, however, was marked by tolerance.

Notes

1. The following account of the gaining of the military's support and Senate's reluctant approval etc. is based on: Dio 78.3.1ff., 79.36.2–3; Herod. 4.4.4ff. (with notes of Whittaker); SHA Car. 2.4ff., Geta 6.1ff.
2. As far as I know, other researchers have failed to take into account the other expenses besides the salary caused to the treasury by the army.
3. This list is based on Bohec's best educated guess and should therefore not be considered definite. However, it is still the best educated guess that we have available and gives us a rough picture of the differences in salaries. See Bohec (2000) pp.209–13; Bohec (2005) pp.185–87; Cascarino (2008/2010) p.84; Arguin, p.100.
4. Augustus had also similarly got rid off all opposition at the very beginning of his reign. This policy was later praised by none other than the famed Machiavelli. When the prince removed all his enemies and potential enemies at the beginning of his reign, he could later show clemency towards his opponents without having to fear for his own safety. However, in the case of Caracalla this was not to be. He was simply not given the chance. He was constantly under threat of being assassinated. Consequently, he felt it necessary to continue the string of murders, mass murders, executions and assassinations until the very end of his reign, which ended in his assassination. In a modern context, one may perhaps speculate that in Russia, where Putin has ruthlessly taken the reins of power in a chaotic situation requiring firm hand (one should note that with much less violence than was the case in ancient Rome), the situation may eventually become such (if Putin decides to stay in power so long that he can relax the controlling mechanisms) that Putin will be remembered as a sort of Russian Augustus in Russia. It should be noted that the neighbours of Augustus did not have a similarly positive view of his aggressive policies as the Romans did, and the same sentiment is of course shared by most of Russia's neighbours.
5. The following discussion of the purge is based on Dio 75.8.1 (Severus had 20,000 of Niger's supporters killed; an example for Caracalla or just conventional figure for many killed?), 78.1.1ff.; SHA Car. 2.25.7, 8.1–10; SHA Geta 6.1ff.;. Herod. 4.4.4ff.
6. This statement has usually been suspected as too high a figure, but considering the task at hand it is not quite as impossible as it might at first glance seem.
7. For the rivalry of these two units, see Herodian 1.12.6–9 with Whittaker's perceptive comments.

8. Dio 78.4. 1a ('certain things' is Cary's tr.): '*Hoti Antôninos Papianon kai Patrouinon tôn doruforôn epi tisi katêgorêsantôn autôn.*'
9. Gonzales (p.140) suggests that Cnaeus Marcius Rustinus Rufinus may also have served as Praetorian Prefect under Caracalla, but the PIR2 does not. According to the latter, the highest ranks for him were *Praefectus classium praetoriarum Misenatis and Ravennatis, Praepositus annonae imp. Septimii Severi et Antonini Augg* and *Praefectus vigilum* 205–207. Gonzales fails to note the appointment of Theocritus and Epagathus as supreme Praetorian Prefects in about 214. See the narrative.
10. The fact that the sources do not mention a separate trip to the *Castra Urbana* supports the view of Yann le Bohec (1994/2000) p.22 that the *Urbaniciani* moved to there in 270. This view is opposed by Arguin (p.81), who suggests that the new camp was built in late second century. If the latter view is correct, then Antoninus either did not visit the *Castra Urbana*, or his visit was not recorded by the sources, or he did not need to visit the camp because its commander was his very loyal relative. I prefer Le Bohec's view.
11. The other possibility is that these units received their titles under Elagabalus, but in light of the role of the *Praefectus Urbi* in the purge it is likely that the epithet was already rewarded under Caracalla.
12. Dio (p.288, Loeb ed., and 79.22.3, Loeb pp.386–87); PIR; Levick, pp.73, 90.
13. The Vestal Virgins were part of the College of Pontiffs, the head of which was Antoninus himself as *Pontifex Maximus*. Consequently, one possibility is also that he wanted to remove those members of the religious establishment that he considered potentially disloyal to himself (especially if he had previously had sex with them and then discarded the women in question) at a time when he wanted to use the religious establishment for espionage purposes (i.e. to spy upon those who consulted oracles, diviners, astrologers and seers). If the women in question had slept (also?) with Geta, then they were certainly considered suspect.
14. Dio 77.16.1–3; Herod.4.6.4 (with Whittaker's comments).
15. Note for example Caracalla's refusal to be called a god: Dio 78.5.1–2; SHA Car. 5.5. Note also Dio 79.8.3, 79.7.2. As will be made clear below, Caracalla used the supernatural as a means of internal control.
16. Julia's breast cancer in Dio 79.23.6.
17. Dio 78.9.17; Potter, pp.137–39.
18. The comparative unattractiveness of naval service is noted by Reddé, p.618, which obviously also holds true of the auxiliaries in general.
19. Herod. 4.6.4–5; Dio 78.10; Potter, pp.140–41.
20. Dio 79.20.1ff.
21. Telesphorus was originally a Celtic god, which the Galatians brought to Anatolia in the third century BC and which travelled back to the West in the second century ad and became particularly popular in Gaul as son of Asclepius, the god of healing.
22. Dio 78.20.1–2 (Xiph).
23. For religious policies and uses of imperial imagery, see: Grant (1996) pp.60–84 with Levick. For the building projects, see Garcia, p.89ff.
24. E.g. Dio 79.21.1–22.1, with scattered material in the narrative of this monograph.
25. E.g. Dio 78.3.3ff., 78.11.5ff., 79.23.4 (p.336, many people put to death because they had consulted an oracle) with the information included in the narrative after this. This section merely summarises the information included in the actual narrative.

26. Apollo Grannus was originally a Celtic god called Grannus, which was associated with healing and sun. The Roman version of Sarapis/Serapis was an Egyptian deity, which had been invented by Ptolemy I who wanted to unite his followers by creating a god which included both Greek and Egyptian elements. The Egyptian goddess Isis had originally been married to her brother Osiris, but in the Greco-Roman-Egyptian system Ptolemy's Serapis became the husband of Isis. This goddess Isis has nothing to do with the infamous terrorist organization Islamic State (ISIS, ISIL), but is a goddess with mystical and magic powers, which has followers even today. Aeculapius/Asclepius was a Greek god of healing, the son of Apollo.
27. Dio, 78.2.3, 78.3.3, 78.4.2–5, 78.5.3ff., 78.11.5–7, 78.12.4–5,78.15.5–7, 78.16.5, 78.16.1–4, 78.16.6, 78.17.1–3, 78.18.1ff., 78.20.4 (Exc. Val. 390), 78.22.1, 79.2; Herod, 4.8.4ff.; SHA (Car.); PIR2.
28. See the above endnote and the one below.
29. Dio 78.15.5–7, 78.20.4, 78.23.4, 79.2, 79.4.1 (the fact that a seer had announced in Africa that Macrinus was destined to become emperor suggests that the seer in question had been consulted by a supporter of Macrinus, which the seer duly reported to the authorities!), 79.4.4 (an Egyptian seer told Caracalla that Macrinus was destined to rule once again, which suggests that someone in his circle had consulted the seer), 79.7.2 (soothsayers warned Caracalla of the day on which he was to be murdered, i.e. they had been consulted by someone and they warned Caracalla of the plot, just like Julius Caesar was warned), 79.18.1–2, 79.12.1–2, 79.40.3–4. It is also possible that there existed no seers or oracles in this case who would have been consulted by fools, but that the identities of the real informers were hidden as prophecies.
30. Esp. Dio 78.17.1ff., 79.4.1ff., with the references of the previous endnote.
31. For a fuller discussion, see Sheldon (2005) and the introduction.
32. In light of Caracalla's idolization of Alexander the Great, it is probably not a coincidence that it was during his reign that Jerusalem obtained a bishop with the name Alexander. None of the sources suggest that Caracalla would have influenced the decision, but it would not have been impossible for him to make his wishes heard or for the Christians to attempt to influence Caracalla by appointing Alexander as Bishop of Jerusalem.
33. For the religious policies of Caracalla in general, see: Grant, p.74ff.; Levick. The connection between Sol and Apollonius of Tyana is uncertain. It is based on the fact that Caracalla visited Tyana, the birthplace of Apollonius.
34. At a later date this policy was most feverishly renewed by Emperor Aurelian, whose policies were then imitated by Constantine the Great, who finally came to the conclusion that it was wiser to join the Christian movement rather than try to fight it. By adopting this solution, Constantine was able to obtain the support of the whole Christian community, who thereby became the fifth columnists among the administrations and militaries of the competing emperors. I do not exclude with this statement the possibility that Constantine would have been a true convert. In my opinion, he was. The cynical use of religion for political purposes and personal beliefs are not mutually exclusive. A religious person can justify to himself the use of quite nefarious means by thinking that it serves the greater good when it promotes the goals of his religion.

Chapter Six

German Campaign 212–213: Antoninus Imperator, Germanicus Maximus, Pacator Orbis, Magnus

Background

Caracalla's plan from the very beginning of his reign was to wage war after war to gain unprecedented personal military prestige. His principal goal was to achieve what had eluded all previous Roman emperors and generals, which was the conquest of Persia/Parthia. He aimed to follow in the footsteps of Alexander the Great. Caracalla later bragged to the Senate that he started to lay the groundwork for the future conquest of Parthia at the very beginning of his reign by inciting the Parthian brothers (Vologaesus V/VI and Artabanus V) to war. His version is verified by circumstantial evidence. It is known that an ambassador from Parthia arrived on Roman soil in 210 or 211.[1] It is therefore quite probable that Caracalla's claim is correct.[2]

Caracalla started to plan his eastern campaign in earnest immediately after he had gained complete control over the empire. With this in mind, he raised new troops from among the Moorish tribes of Africa and transferred them and others to Europe and the East. The African frontiers were peaceful thanks to the efforts of the African Emperor Septimius Severus. Severus had pushed the frontier south both in Mauretania and Tripolitania, and had posted small military detachments in forts all over the area. In Mauretania Caesaria, he had built new fortifications in the desert and connected these with a road that paralleled the earlier road closer to the coast which had been built under Trajan. While he garrisoned the new forts, Severus still left garrisons in most of the Trajanic forts so that there was a military presence even in the interior. The presence of these small detachments all around enabled him to control the movements of semi-nomads so that they could be controlled and taxed. In Tripolitania, Severus established small isolated forts deep into the desert to observe and control the movements of nomads, and in particular the Garamantes. Once again, the spreading of small detachments of military forces to cover greater areas resulted in improved security for the region, so that the period from 197 until 235 saw an unprecedented economic prosperity in the entire Roman North Africa. This naturally meant more taxes and the recruiting of the restless tribal youth into the Roman army, which in turn ensured greater internal harmony for the region. The presence of observation posts deep in the desert ensured that the more prosperous areas closer to the coast could be warned in advance if nomads were planning to raid. That the same policy of building small forts to control the populace was continued by Caracalla is proven by the building of guard towers (*burgus speculatorius*) west of the Aures Mountains in Numidia during his reign.[3]

However, before Caracalla could bring that goal to fruition there were other more pressing things to deal with. In order to secure his own position, Caracalla needed a successful war to prove himself as a commander and emperor. He also needed to secure the northern frontiers, and recruit and train new men for the eastern campaigns. After the pacification of Caledonia, enemies and potential enemies along this very long frontier consisted of the Franks, Alamanni, Chatti, the tribes of the River Elbe, the Marcomanni, Vandili (Vandals), Quadi, Goths, Dacians, Sciri, Bastarnae and Sarmatians.

The Germanic Threat: The Society

The Germanic tribes can be divided into three major groupings: 1) the Scandinavian tribes (Saxons and other tribes in the south of Denmark and north of Germany can be considered to belong to this group); 2) the Western tribes and confederacies (Saxons etc. can also be considered to be part of this group, along with Franks, Alamanni, Suevi/Suebi, Marcomanni, Thuringians, Lombards, western branch of the Heruls etc.); 3) the Eastern tribes and confederacies (Goths, eastern branch of the Heruls, Burgundi, Vandals, Gepids, Quadi, Taifali, Rugi, Sciri, Bastarni etc.). The greatest problem for the Romans and Caracalla was that the Germanic tribes appear to have formed large confederacies of tribes by the end of the second century, which can be considered to have been roughly the equivalent of modern military alliances in which different nations (then different tribes) try to cooperate against their enemies. The Alamanni are for the first time mentioned at the time of Caracalla, but even though the Franks are mentioned in the sources for the first time only in the mid-third century, it is still probable that it was formed at the latter half of the second century just like the Alamanni. The reason for this conclusion is that the enemy who threatened the Rhine frontier from Mainz up to its mouth are likely to have consisted of one major group because both Caracalla in 212 and Alexander Severus in 234 had to make separate trips there with their armies. The two separate campaigns against the Germans of the Rhine and the Danube has also been noted by Whittaker (Herod. Vol.2, pp.126-127), and I have just taken the evidence a bit further by suggesting the existence of the Frankish confederacy for the Rhine frontier.

The Romans considered all German tribes to be fearless in hand-to-hand combat and therefore fearsome opponents, but there were significant differences between the tribes. The principal difference was that the Eastern tribes had been influenced by the steppe nomads, as a result of which they employed more horsemen than their Western cousins. The Eastern and Scandinavian tribes were also in the habit of using greater amounts of armour. Most Germanic cavalries avoided complicated manoeuvres and simply charged at a gallop straight at the enemy, which could be repeated if the enemy did not flee and there were enough spare horses for the fight to continue. This wild, undisciplined and impetuous cavalry attack was bound to frighten any poorly trained and disciplined infantry force.

Germanic societies valued freedom more highly than the Romans, so their kings did not possess similar powers to the Roman emperors. Despite the fact that some tribes possesed royal houses, the right to rule was always based on military ability, so much so that some of the tribes and confederacies could even elect temporary war-leaders. The kings were also graded according to their relative strength, so that tribal confederacies could have a single high-king or a temporary war-leader, below who were the lesser kings/princes. Some of the tribes were quasi-democracies ruled by a judge/president with the help of a council of elders.

The military elite of all Germanic tribes consisted of the wealthier nobles (*optimates*) and their retinues, so that the entire free male population was required to serve in the tribal army when called to do so. With this in mind, the male population was divided into age-groupings. The young ones had to prove their manhood in combat or in hunting before being allowed to marry a woman and have children. This meant that wars were usually fought by the young and by the military retinues of the nobles, while the older men usually stayed home. The principal weaknesses of most Germanic armies were the poorly organized logistical services, the lack of properly organized siege trains, lack of large-scale military training among the tribal levy, lack of protective armour and the relative weakness of the missile arm, but there were exceptions.

West Germanic Peoples
The fighting style of the West Germanic peoples was based on the use of infantry phalanxes and wedges. The infantry used an irregular unit order in difficult terrain and close or tortoise order in open terrain. Most of the footmen were armed with only spears, swords and shields. Only the tribal elite were equipped with armour and helmets. The numbers of horsemen remained small, but at the same time there were tribes who specialized in the use of cavalry. These included the Iuthungi and Lentienses, who belonged to the tribal confederacy of the Alamanni. The Alamanni were famous for their good quality cavalry who could also fight very effectively by using the tactic of having footmen riding pillion and then fighting on foot between the files of horsemen. The Tencteri (belonging to the Frankish Confederacy) were equally famous as horsemen as the Chatti were as footmen, which means that they fielded very disciplined cavalry forces able to use irregular and close orders as needed. Regardless of this, the vast majority of these forces, the Alamanni included, consisted of spear-armed infantry. The cavalry forces of these tribes consisted usually only of the tribal elite, equipped with spears, javelins, swords, armour, helmets and shields. The horses were usually unarmoured. Consequently, the vast majority of the Alamanni that Caracalla's forces faced would have consisted of footmen armed with spears and shields.

The Marcomanni were still considered a warlike people who could put into the field a mighty force of footmen and cavalry, but after their defeat during the

Antoninus Imperator, Germanicus Maximus, Pacator Orbis, Magnus 157

The Marcomannic infantry phalanx/shield wall on Aurelius' Column demonstrates how disciplined the Germanic combat formations could be. Source: Bartoli 1673.

Marcomannic Wars they no longer posed any real threat to the Romans. On the basis of Marcus Aurelius's Column, their armed forces consisted of unarmoured infantry and cavalry, primarily equipped with spears, swords and shields.

The Chatti (the Cenni of Dio?) were famed for their very high quality infantry, so much so that Tacitus (Germania 30–31) claims that they possessed similar military discipline to the Romans. Chatti footmen knew how to keep rank and carried supplies and entrenching-tools with them so that they could build fortified camps and stay in the field for a long time. They chose their leaders democratically and then obeyed their commands. They also planned their campaigns deliberately and engaged in combat only when it was advantageous. According to Tacitus, the number of men who sought to prove their manhood in combat and to make a living from fighting was greater among the Chatti than the other Germans. They presented a formidable enemy for Caracalla – far more so than any of the other German tribes.

It is unfortunate that we do not know for certain which tribes inhabited the mouth of the Elbe at this time. At the beginning of the second century, those inhabiting the Elbe region would have consisted mainly of the Chauci (at the mouth of the river), Angrivarii and Lombards, but one may make an educated guess that the Angles and Saxons would also have started to form up in this area because both confederacies emerge in the sources here later in the third century. The tribes in question possessed vast reserves of footmen and cavalry, just like the Chauci had in the second century, whom they could call into service when required. The illustrations of Germanic equipment in the Plates section are based on finds made at Thorsberger Moor in Schleswig-Holstein in 1858–1860. The equipment dates from the early third century and is representative of the type used by the tribes that Caracalla's forces met in the northern sections of the River Elbe. As can be seen, these Germanic warriors of the north could be quite well-equipped and armoured. On the basis of this, one can conclude that the reason why, for example, the Franks

Hedeby, c. 985, 54-62 men, c. 30.9 x 2.7 x 1.5m

Fotevik 1, c.1100, c. 16 men, 10.3 x 2.4 x 1.0m

A sample of Viking ships likely to be representative of the various types and sizes of ships used by the tribes occupying the coastline close to the mouth of the Elbe. (Drawn after Crumlin-Pedersen; Syvanne MHLR Vol.1)

Ladby, 900-950, c. 35 men, c. 22 x3.2 x 1.0m

Skuldelev 5, c. 1050, 26 men, 17.4 x 2.6 x 1.1m

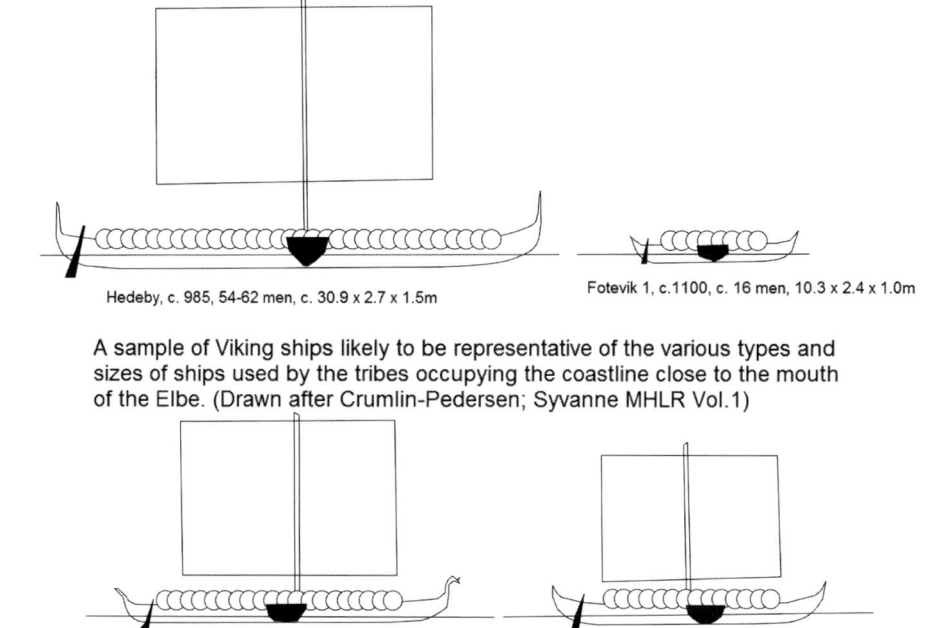

or Heruls wore so little armour was that they had consciously decided to do so for cultural/religious reasons.

The tribes that inhabited the mouth of the Elbe would also have possessed a navy of some sort, consisting of small Viking-style boats with crews typically ranging from around twelve to sixty or seventy men (at most perhaps 100–150 men), but most of the ships would have crews of just twelve to sixteen. These ships would not have posed any obstacle to the Roman fleet if they decided to oppose the ravaging of the coast mentioned by Dio.

East Germanic Tribes
The tribal forces of the East Germanic peoples differed from their cousins in that they had adopted the use of lancer/*contarii* cavalry and cataphracts from the Sarmatians and could employ armies consisting solely of horsemen. In addition to this, their armies could include mounted archers and multi-purpose troops equally adept at fighting with bows and melee weapons. The East Germanic peoples were also in the habit of using wagon laagers/fortresses for protection, a case not unknown among the West Germans either.

The principal emerging threats to the Roman interests in Eastern Europe were the Goths (with their subjects and allies the Alans, Sarmatians, Heruli, Taifali, Dacians, Sciri etc.) and Vandals, even if it were the Quadi, Sarmatians, Dacians, Bastarnae and Sciri who were actually their neighbours. These tribes could also ally themselves with the Sarmatians, Alans and Dacians. The Goths were the most Sarmatian-like of the East Germanic peoples. Their elite fighting force consisted of knights (*optimates*/nobles and their retinues) who were equipped as lancer-archers. Each of them had at least two or three spare horses. The Gothic cavalry was also the most armoured of the Germanic tribes, probably because they needed to face nomadic mounted archers (Sarmatians, Alans and others) on the steppes. I have estimated that the Gothic Greuthungi had a minimum of about 24,000 *optimates* and their fellow Goths the Tervingi perhaps about 12,000. Most of the Gothic and Sarmatian cavalry would still have consisted of the Sarmatian-style light (refers to equipment and not tactics) lancers/archers (*contarii*/*kontoforoi*). In contrast to the Goths, the Heruls and Taifali wore very little in the form of protective equipment and fought as light cavalry swordsmen or lancers. The vast majority of the Goths were not warriors, but common farmers and herdsmen, who were still required to serve as a general levy. The wealthiest of them could serve as horsemen (lancers and javelin throwers), and those who could not afford an extra horse served either as spearmen or archers.[4] At this time, the overall military potential of the Gothic tribes was probably only about 150,000–200,000 warriors, as they had not yet managed to conquer the territories that they possessed in the latter half of the third and fourth centuries.[5] It should be noted that the Goths could not put this entire force into the field against a single enemy because some of them had to be left behind to protect their homes and families. Regardless, it was still the host that formed the greatest threat to all of their neighbours.

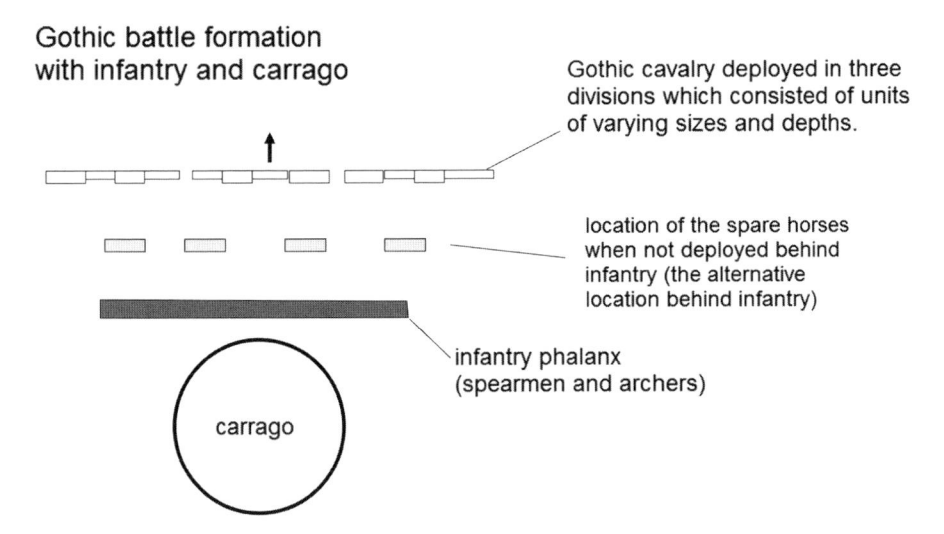

Gothic battle formation with infantry and carrago

Gothic cavalry deployed in three divisions which consisted of units of varying sizes and depths.

location of the spare horses when not deployed behind infantry (the alternative location behind infantry)

infantry phalanx (spearmen and archers)

carrago

The Gothic combat doctrine was based on a combination of Sarmatian and Germanic influences. The typical battle formation consisted of a single cavalry line, which was used aggressively with the attack at the gallop led by the king or commander in person. The attack was usually wild and impetuous, supported by mounted archers, and if the enemy did not flee, the Goths usually repeated the charge until the enemy gave way or the Goths ran out of spare horses. If the Goths employed infantry, it was usually placed in the rear to protect the cavalry. The largest Gothic armies possessed large numbers of wagons, which were formed into a defensive laager (*carrago*) when the army encamped.

Cavalry also formed the backbone of the armies of the Quadi and Vandals, but there were certain differences between them and the Goths. They possessed far fewer men, were less well armoured and had fewer mounted bowmen. The Quadi cavalry consisted primarily of non-armoured javelin throwers and the Vandal cavalry of non-armoured spearmen. Both nations also possessed a levy of footmen, but these were relatively unimportant in comparison with the cavalry. The Sciri ('pure' Germans) and Bastarnae ('Bastards' with mixed Celtic and Germanic blood lines) inhabited the north-west corner of the Black Sea area. Very little is known of their military practices at this time, but one can make an educated guess that they had been heavily influenced by Sarmatian cavalry tactics and by Dacian light infantry.

The Dacian Military *(below: Romans engaging Dacians in the Adamklisi Monument)*
At this time the Dacian military was a mere shadow of its former self. Trajan had crushed their power forever, and what remained of their former glory was now limited

to the areas possessed by the so-called Free Dacians (Carpi) outside Dacia proper, the latter of which was now a Roman province. Once again we know very little of their military practices, but on the basis of their place of abode it has been conjectured that the vast majority of Dacian forces would have consisted of very lightly equipped footmen with spears/javelins, swords and shields. It is clear that they did possess some archers and cavalry, but their role was minimal. It is not known with any certainty whether the Dacians still used their famous *falx* (scythe) in combat, but that is a possibility that cannot be entirely discounted. Consequently, it is possible that the Romans were forced to wear stronger armour, helmets and *manicae* (segmented armour for the arm) to counter this threat, just as they had done during the reign of Trajan. The attached drawings are based on the so-called Adamklisi Metope. It shows Roman legionaries in combat with Dacians during the reign of Trajan. Note the different ways of using swords and spears/javelins in close-range combat.

The Sarmatians and Alans[6]
The Sarmatians and Alans belonged to an Iranian-speaking group of steppe nomads. The former had achieved dominance on the European steppes in the third and second centuries BC, but were then subjected by the latter in the first century AD. They were particularly famous for their lancer cavalry (both *katafraktoi* and *kontoforoi*), which were equipped with the massive Sarmatian *contus/kontos* that could be used effectively only with a two-handed grip. The Alans in their turn had lost their dominance by the late second century, probably as a result of the arrival of the Goths, so that there were separate tribal groupings consisting of various Sarmatian and Alanic groups inhabiting barbarian Pannonia (mainly Iazyges and Roxolani, which later came to be called Argaragantes/Free Sarmatians and Limigantes, the slaves of the former), Dacia, Moesia and the steppes north of the Caucasus. The largest of the groups were the Alans inhabiting areas north of the Caucasus and Caspian Sea, who may have had about 200,000 mounted archers, just as their predecessors the Aorsi (Aurs – 'White') Sarmatians had in the same area. The royal family of the Bosporan kingdom was also originally Sarmatian, even if its blood lines had undoubtedly become mixed like the rest of the realm. The Sarmatians and Alans who were neighbours of the Romans and Germans continued to follow the *kontoforoi* traditions, but the importance of mounted archery practice increased among the Alans who lived east of the Don.

The Sarmatians and Alans had a hierarchy of tribes so that each grouping had its leading tribe (the 'royal tribe'), with the rest its 'subjects'. Regardless of the names, all men were considered free, and if there were any slaves they were prisoners of war. Each of the tribes was ruled by its own king, under whom could be several petty kings and below them tribal nobility/aristocracy (the *optimates* of the Romans), some of whom were magnates. At least some of the tribes had a senate of seniors to advise the king. The men were divided into age classes for military purposes so that only the young ones had the duty of proving their manhood through fighting. There were great similarities between the Germanic and Sarmatian societies.

162 Caracalla

The main striking forces of the Sarmatians and Alans were the cataphracts (*catafractarii/katafraktoi*), who consisted mainly of the rich nobles, and the *contus/kontos*-bearers (*contarii/kontoforoi*), who consisted of the commoners. These were true multipurpose troops because they carried missile (composite bows) and melee weapons (*contus Sauromatus*, ring-sword, dagger, long double-edged sword). It is possible that some of the subject peoples were required to contribute footmen, but their role was always minimal.

The Sarmatians usually avoided pitched battles with the Romans and rather concentrated on the exploitation of their great mobility to pillage Roman territory before they could mount an effective response and then flee back to their own territory when this happened. If they were forced to fight, the Sarmatians usually formed a single battle line in which every other unit consisted either of skirmishers, who lured the enemy to attack them and then feigned flight, or of close order troops, that charged at those who pursued the skirmishers. It is possible that the Sarmatians employed proto-stirrups, just like the Scythians before them, but this did not give them any decisive edge over their neighbours. Under Caracalla, the Sarmatians of the Danube appear to have been considered part of the Roman Empire as allies, just as they were in the fourth century (see Syvanne MHLR Vol.1). It is quite possible that some sections of the so-called Devil's Dykes were built during the reign of Marcus Aurelius to represent the extent of his new conquests in the area. The only referral to any fighting between Sarmatians and Romans comes from the SHA (Geta 6.6), but there does not exist any other evidence for this. Regardless, it is still probable that some fighting between Sarmatians and Romans took place because the former almost always fought in the Dacian and Gothic armies.

The so-called Kossika vase (Russia) 1-3rd Century AD (drawn after Brzezinski & Mielczarek, 15). It is usually thought that the men represent duelling Sarmato-Alans, but it is possible that the man on the left would be Goth and the man on the right an Alan. Note the fact that the *contus*-bearer had shot at least two arrows before he charged.

Background to the Troubles in Pannonia and Dacia: The Gothic Menace and the Crimea
The Gothic tribes originated from south of modern Sweden (Götaland, Gotland), from where they had crossed into Northern Germany and from there to what is modern Poland. In the course of the second century AD, Gothic tribes, together with other tribes such as the Heruls, migrated to the modern Ukraine. Small numbers of Goths under the name Lugii may have already participated in the invasion of Roman territories during the reign of Marcus Aurelius, but the principal contribution of the Goths to the troubles was that their movement towards the Black Sea and Dacia caused a domino effect among other tribes towards the Roman frontiers.[7]

We do not know for certain how early the division of the Goths into two major groupings was (the Greuthungi Confederacy in Ukraine and on the steppes, and the Tervingi to the north of the Danube), but it appears likely that the division already existed in some form thanks to the different directions taken by the tribes. Regardless, it is still likely that the tribes formed a confederacy, possibly even under the same king. The fact that there were Gothic and Alanic settlers on the Roman side of the Danube during the reign of Septimius Severus proves that the Romans had managed to defeat the Goths at some point and resettle some of them as farmer soldiers, with the requirement to contribute cavalry lancers when required in the same manner as the late Roman *laeti*. Note for example the origins of Maximinus Thrax whose father was a Goth Micca and mother an Alan Ababa (Jord., Get. 83; SHA Max. 1.5-7).

Dio (75.3.1) also refers to troubles with the Goths in the reign of Severus; he states that only the lucky coincidence of lightning killing three chieftains in c. 196 prevented their direct invasion of Roman lands. As a result of this the Goths became allies of Rome. However, this did not prevent some of the Goths from attacking the Roman client kingdom of Bosporus in the Crimea. The Bosporan kingdom was originally composed mainly of Greeks, but from the early first century onwards it was ruled by a Sarmatian (Alan?) dynasty. The Bosporan military organization was based on a combination of Sarmatian cavalry (mounted archers and *contarii/kontoforoi*), Roman style infantry with archers and Greek military organization. From the reign of Claudius onwards, the Romans also supported the Bosporans with expeditionary or garrison forces as needed. At some point in time between 191-235 (likeliest dates 196-215) there was a bellum Bosporanum which was won with the help of detachments drawn from *Legio I Italica* and cohors I Thracum. Consequently, it is possible that the war in question was fought under Caracalla.[8] We know that Rheskuporis II or III began his reign under Caracalla in 211, and that he received the acceptance of Caracalla and his successors because he received the title Friend of the Romans. It is therefore quite possible that he received the title because of the above-mentioned war.[9] It is unfortunate that we do not know whether Rhescuporis had any role in Caracalla's plans, but considering the fact that the Romans had used the Bosporans against the Goths and Parthians before, and were to do so in the future, this is quite possible, even if it is not provable. The following map shows the locations of Roman garrisons and naval detachments in the area. It is clear that even if Caracalla would not have envisaged any role for the Bosporans in his war against the Scythians or Parthians, he would still have understood the commercial importance of the area and kept it well garrisoned so that this important commercial hub would not be threatened by the Goths or any other tribal grouping in the area. The western part of the Crimea with the city of Chersonesus was probably officially part of the Roman Empire at this time and could be used to keep the Bosporans in check.[10] The following coin from the reign of Caracalla demonstrates well the close connection between the Roman Empire and Bosporan kingdom. The Bosporan kings minted their coins with the heads of the Roman emperors. The Roman presence remained strong until the mid-third century, when the endemic civil wars sapped Roman strength to such an extent that the Goths were able to force the Bosporan kingdom to become their tributary state.

Caracalla in the Coin of Rhescuporis III

A Bosporan lancer from Panticapaeum. The Sarmatians, Alans and Goths fielded similar cavalry forces.

© Dr. Ilkka Syvänne 2013

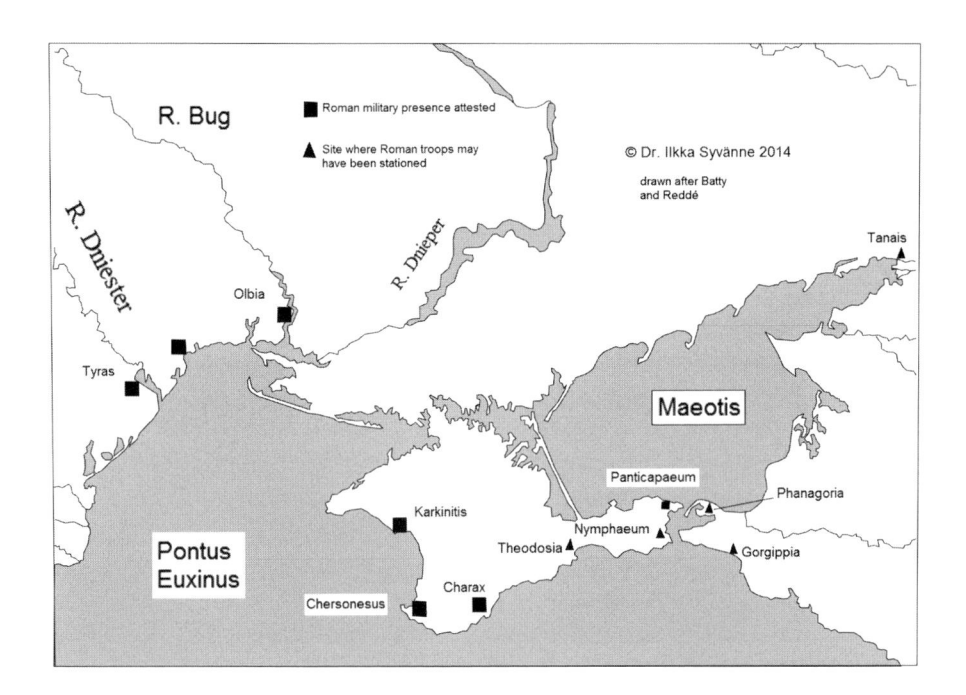

Caracalla vs the Germans in 212–213
Caracalla's first object was to secure the Danube and Rhine frontiers. This he set out to do in stages during 212–214. He is attested to have travelled to *Germania Superior* at the beginning of 212, evidently immediately after the issuing of the *Constitutio Antoniana* (Christol, p.41), and to have been in Raetia in 213 and Pannonia in 214. The documentary evidence proves that Caracalla repaired roads and repaired or built new forts in *Germania Superior* during 212. Most of this activity was naturally concentrated in the strategically important River Main region, so the city of Mainz (Mogontiacum) served as imperial/military headquarters. It is possible that Caracalla's route to Mainz would have gone through *Gallia Narbonenis*, because he is known to have removed the local governor.[11]

The problematic part of the evidence is that we know next to nothing about the military side of his activities in this area. All we know is that Caracalla achieved a great victory by the River Mainz in 212–213, fought against the Alamanni and then the Chatti and tribes of the mouth of the Elbe, was hailed *Germanicus Maximus* by the *Fratres Arvales* at Rome on 20 May 213 and also acclaimed imperator twice during 213.[12] Consequently, it would have been possible for Caracalla to have defeated the Alamanni by the River Main either in 212 or 213, when he is known to have been in Raetia. Similarly, it is possible that Caracalla would have moved first to *Germania Superior* in early 212 through Gaul, from there to Pannonia to defeat the barbarian invaders (Vandals and Carpi) in late 212 or early 213 (this victory is usually attributed to Caracalla's commanders)[13] and from there to Raetia in 213, from where he would have advanced against the Alamanni and the rest of the tribes north of them. Similarly, it would not be impossible for Caracalla to have defeated one of the Germanic tribes opposite *Germania Superior*, of which the only record would be the title *Germanicus Maximus*. The problem with this is that it is also possible that Caracalla received this title as a result of the successes of his generals against the invaders in Pannonia. Fitz (p.98ff.) has detected that one of these successful legates was Caius Julius Septimius Castinus. As a result of the victorious war in Pannonia, several units in the area also received the honorific title *Antoniniana*.

My own educated guess is that Caracalla moved to *Germania Superior* through *Gallia Narbonensis* in early 212, at which point he ordered military detachments to be sent at least from Pannonia for the forthcoming campaign against the Alamanni, Chatti and other Germanic tribes of the north. The result of these vast military operations was that the tribes opposite *Germania Superior* and *Inferior* (the tribes of the Frankish Confederacy) were cowed into signing new peace treaties and handing over new hostages and recruits for Caracalla's army. This is proven by the fact that the sources do not contain any references to hostilities in this region. However, I need to add a note of caution here. The fact that the sources are silent about military action in the lower Rhine region opposite what I would call Proto-Franks does not necessarily mean that there would not have been any military campaigns in the area. In fact the following can be used to prove that Caracalla fought a campaign in the region: it is possible that Caracalla received the title *Germanicus Maximus* for the campaigns he undertook both in 212 and 213; he can be attested to have been in *Germania Superior* in 212; forts and fortifications were constructed and repaired, which can have taken place only when the enemy did not pose a threat to these operations. My own educated guess is that Caracalla did indeed concentrate his forces in the area to force the tribes opposite to conclude peace agreements/alliances and that this may have included some military action of which we know nothing about. However, in the absence of any definite evidence for military action my working assumption here is that the tribes were cowed by the mere threat of military action. The other result of the transfer of forces from Pannonia to *Germania Superior* and Raetia was that the defences in Pannonia were weakened, which was then exploited by the Vandals and Carpi, who attacked *Pannonia Superior* and *Dacia Porolissensis* in 212. There may have also been a separate invasion of *Pannonia Inferior* by barbarians (Sarmatians or Vandals?) in 213, or it was a continuation of the previous attack. The Quadi appear to me to have let the invaders through their lands in order to avoid hostilities, or they may have sided with the enemies (the view taken e.g. by Fitz).[14] In contrast to the Quadi, the Marcomanni appear to have sided with the Romans, because they were not punished later. In my opinion, it was probably then that Caracalla demonstrated his noted celerity by riding c.150km per day (Dio 78.11.3) to reach the Pannonian frontier in six to seven days. It was probably as a result of this operation that Caracalla received his title *Germanicus Maximus* by late 212 or early 213, which was recorded by the Arval Brethren at Rome

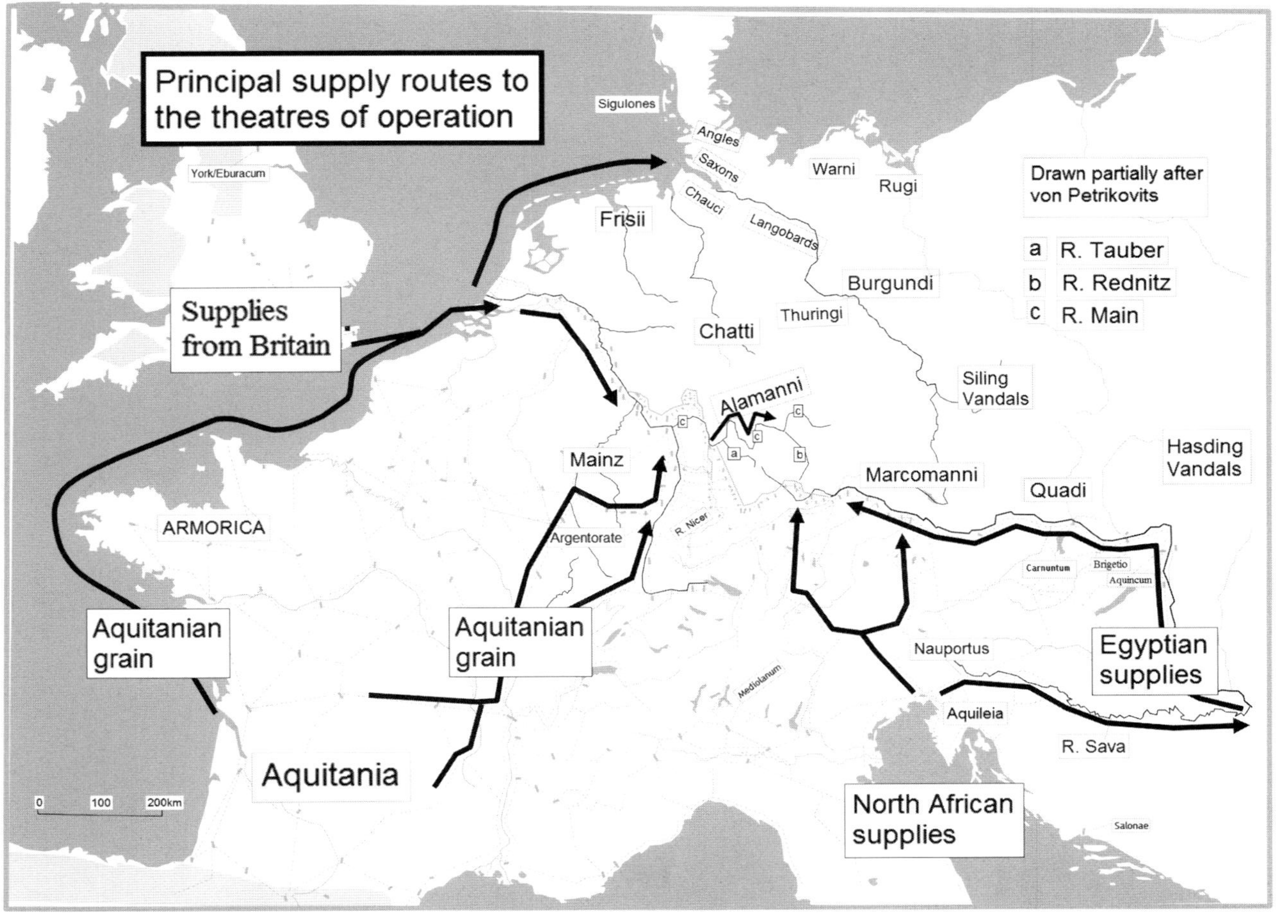

Principal supply routes to the theatres of operation
Drawn partially after von Petrikovits
a R. Tauber
b R. Rednitz
c R. Main
Sigulones
Angles
Saxons
Chauci
Langobards
Warni
Rugi
Frisii
Burgundi
Thuringi
Chatti
Siling Vandals
Alamanni
Hasding Vandals
Marcomanni
Quadi
York/Eburacum
Supplies from Britain
Mainz
Argentorate
R. Nicer
ARMORICA
Carnuntum
Brigetio
Aquincum
Aquitanian grain
Aquitanian grain
Nauportus
Egyptian supplies
Mediolanum
Aquileia
R. Sava
Aquitania
0 100 200km
North African supplies
Salonae

168 Caracalla

on 20 May 213. The other possibility is that there had been military action along the Rhine of which we know nothing about, or that the title was received thanks to both events.

On the basis of the speed with which Caracalla travelled (150km/day), it is quite easy to understand that he and his bodyguard cavalry could have reached the threatened frontier within a week to defeat the invaders with the forces at hand, and then return to Raetia to continue the preparations for war. If Caracalla took regular cavalry and infantry with him, it would have taken thirteen to fourteen days for the cavalry to march from Mainz to the scene of operations in fighting condition, if each horseman had at least one spare horse, and twenty-five to thirty days for the infantry with forced marches. However, since it would have been possible to take detachments en route from the forces posted there, it would not have necessarily taken more than fourteen to sixteen days for Caracalla to join the local forces with his reinforcements.

Caracalla's preparations for the Germanic war were very thorough. The milestones attest that he initiated road-building projects and repairs in Noricum, Raetia and Pannonia. He built an entirely new road in Noricum (Alföldy, Noricum, p.169) running from Boiodurum along the Danube towards Linz to improve the communications against possible Alamannic attack. As regards the provisioning of the army, it is quite obvious that the Rhine frontier would have been supplied mainly from Aquitania and the rest of Gaul, and possibly also from Britain. Most of the Aquitanian corn would have been transported by land to the Rhône and then shipped as close to Lake Geneva as possible, then loaded onto wagons for transport to the Rhine and Mainz. British (and part of the Aquitanian) corn may have been transported in ships to the mouth of the Rhine and then along it to the supply depots. The Romans would also have used ships to transport supplies to the Elbe. The Danubian frontier (Raetia, Noricum, Pannonia) would have been supplied partly from local resources and partly from outside (North Africa and Egypt). The North African corn would have been shipped to Aquileia, and from there either by land via roads leading up to the north or by land to Nauportus, where the wheat would have been loaded onto ships and then shipped along the Save to the Danube, and from there to the supply depots. The Egyptian corn would have been shipped to the Black Sea and along the Danube to the supply depots. It is also quite possible that part of the Egyptian corn would already have been shipped to Seleucia/Antioch in preparation for the eastern war.

The following quote shows how Caracalla financed the pay rise of his army and his Germanian campaign (Dio 78.9.1–15, tr. by Cary, pp.295–99, with additions in square brackets):

'Now this great admirer of Alexander, Antoninus, was fond of spending money upon the soldiers, great numbers of whom he kept in attendance upon him, alleging one excuse after another and one war after another [*i.e. Caracalla made it difficult for the senators to assassinate him, because he was constantly surrounded by loyal soldiers*]; but he made it his business to strip, despoil, and grind down all the rest of mankind, and the senators by no means least. In the first place, there were the gold crowns [*donativa*] that he was repeatedly demanding, on the constant pretext that he had conquered some enemy or other; and I am not referring, either, to the actual manufacture of the crowns – for what does that amount to? – but to the vast amount of money constantly being given in the name of the cities for the customary "crowning", as it is called, of the emperors. Then there were the provisions that we were required to furnish in great quantities on all occasions, and this without receiving remuneration and sometimes actually at additional cost to ourselves, all of which supplies he either bestowed upon the soldiers or else peddled out; and there were the gifts which he demanded from the wealthy citizens and from the various communities; and the taxes, both the new ones which he promulgated and the ten per cent tax that he instituted in place of the five per cent tax applying to the emancipation of slaves, to bequests, and to all legacies; for he abolished the right of succession and exemption from taxes which had been granted in such cases to those who were closely related to the deceased. This was the reason why he made all the people in his empire Roman citizens; nominally he was honouring them, but his real purpose was to increase his revenues by this means, inasmuch as aliens did not have to pay most of these taxes. But apart from all these burdens, we were also compelled to build at our own expense all sorts of houses for him wherever he set out from Rome, and costly lodgings in the middle of even the very shortest journeys; yet he not only never lived in them, but in some cases was not destined to see them [*i.e. these lodgings were intended to disguise the line of march Caracalla and his army would take*]. Moreover, we constructed amphitheatres [*these were needed to keep the soldiers amused*] and race-courses [*to keep the soldiers amused and also to keep them and their horses in combat readiness*] wherever he spent the winter or expected to spend it [*i.e. once again Caracalla disguised his intentions from potential external and internal enemies*], all without receiving any contribution from him; and they were all promptly demolished [*there is nothing strange about this. The army always built temporary lodgings etc. in which they spent their winters*], the sole reason for their being built in the first place being, apparently, that we might get impoverished [*Dio complains simply because Caracalla made the rich pay the costs of the military campaigns, which was actually far more humane than making the poor pay for the costs. The rich senators could easily afford the extra costs*].'

The above quote from Dio shows how extensive Caracalla's preparations were before he took to the field. This meant that the costs of the war were shouldered mainly by the rich and wealthy, and secondly by the cities near the theatres of operations. This ensured that everything was in readiness for Caracalla's soldiers to come to the scene and launch their campaigns. Considering the very great disparity between the wealthy and poor in the Roman Empire, Caracalla's decision to fund his campaigns out of the pockets of the wealthy can be considered a very wise and humane policy.[15] Unlike some other emperors, he did not confiscate the property of senators by resorting to some trumped-up charges or make the poor shoulder the cost of the wars he was waging. We should also remember that in the mind of Caracalla, it did not hurt to make the senators pay for the upkeep of the army. He clearly considered them directly or indirectly guilty of the death of his brother and of the subsequent bloodbath. He even rubbed the guilt in the face of the senators by forcing them to take part in ceremonies praying for the *manes* (soul) of his brother Geta![16] It is also noteworthy that Caracalla misled potential enemy spies observing his military preparations by simultaneously making preparations to take another route of march.

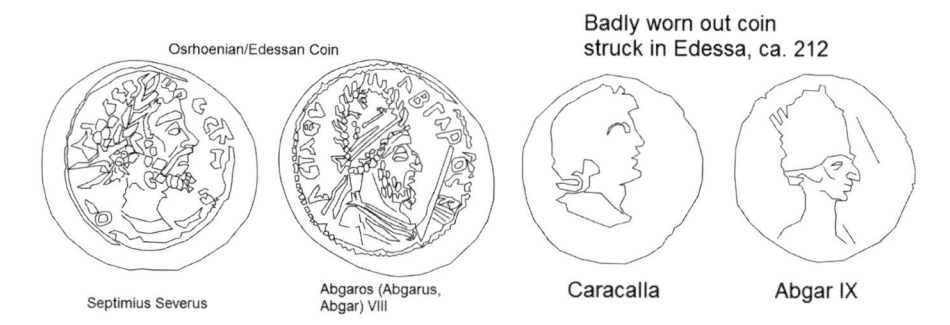

Osrhoenian/Edessan Coin

Septimius Severus

Abgaros (Abgarus, Abgar) VIII

Badly worn out coin struck in Edessa, ca. 212

Caracalla

Abgar IX

Preparations for the forthcoming wars included the simultaneous removal of the King of Osroene/Oshroene Abgar (Abgarus/Abgaros) IX from office and the annexation of his realm in late 212 or early 213. Abgar was eliminated with a trick. Caracalla invited Abgar to visit him but was then imprisoned.[17] The arrest can be dated on the basis of inscriptions, which state that Edessa and Osroene were already formally part of the empire in 213. The fact that the Osroenian cavalry performed well in the subsequent campaign proves that the annexation of their lands was not entirely unwelcome to them.

The first objects of Caracalla's German war were the Alamanni (meaning All-men) and after them the Cenni (the Chatti?), after which he intended to follow up his success by advancing to the mouth of the Elbe. As an excuse for the war, he appears to have used hostilities between the Cenni (Chatti?) and Alamanni, and pretended to side with the latter. Contrary to what is usually stated by modern historians, it is quite clear that the Alamanni were at the time allies of Rome and had called the Romans to their assistance.[18]

There are many theories regarding the origins of the Alamanni, who are for the first time mentioned during the reign of Caracalla. Even the existence of the Alamanni is contested, because it is possible that the later epitomators have inserted the name to the text. The most commonly accepted version seems to be that the Alamanni were probably not arrivals but had rather emerged in situ. The claim goes that the Alamanni consisted at least of the members of the tribes of Semnones (part of the Suebi/Suevi) and Iuthungi (Young Ones), and possibly of the Hermunduri who previously occupied the same area and the Marcomanni, and of other smaller tribes nearby. John F. Drinkwater has also suggested that the Alamanni and Iuthungi originally probably consisted of groups of young male warriors from various tribes (Germanic tribes habitually sent their young sons away from their homes to earn their fortunes) who had become attached to the retinue of a particular chieftain or warlord, and that as a result of the successes of these war-bands other groups also adopted their name.[19]

I agree with this basic view, but would suggest that there must have existed one initial war-band consisting of the young-ones under some king which grew in power with each military success, so that thousands grew into tens of thousands of warriors, consisting of various tribes. It is also unlikely that the Alamanni would have emerged in situ, but rather that the local tribes were subjected by the newly arrived war-band and were later strengthened by other newcomers. It is also possible that we should see the origins of the Alamanni in the young-ones of the Marcomanni. It is in this context that one should see the statement in the SHA (Aurelian 18.1–21.5) that it was the Marcomanni who invaded Italy during the reign of Aurelian, while all other sources claim that the invaders consisted of the Alamanni and Iuthungi. This suggests the possibility that the Alamanni, whom Caracalla now targeted, were actually just an offshoot of the Marcomanni, the young-ones who had separated from them. It is quite possible that the Alamanni consisted of those who had allowed other tribal warriors into their forces, while the Iuthungi were the direct and pure descendants of the original youth of the Marcomanni. The Iuthungi even bragged to Aurelian of their pure undiluted descent. The later sources prove that the Alamannic Confederacy included at least the Iuthungi and Lentienses, and six other tribes. If this is the case, then the Alamanni who had sought Caracalla's help were probably closely connected with the Marcomanni and therefore not expecting anything hostile, since Caracalla had already assisted their kinsmen against the Vandals and Carpi in Pannonia. The creation of this new tribal confederacy so close to Italy was obviously potentially at least as dangerous as the powerful Confederacy of the Marcomanni had been. Consequently, it is no wonder that Caracalla decided to crush the power of the new confederacy in the bud with a pre-emptive strike.

True to his nature, Caracalla decided to resort to a ruse. Since he also planned to wage war against the Cenni/Chatti and North Germanic tribes occupying the mouth of the Elbe in order to secure the rest of the northern frontier with a lightning campaign, it was in his interest to appear as if he would be willing to assist the Alamanni against their neighbours the Cenni/Chatti. Consequently, Caracalla called for the Alamanni to provide him with allied forces for this purpose, a request they agreed to. It is probable, even if the sources do not mention it, that Caracalla intended to conduct the operation against the North Germanic tribes in conjunction with the fleets previously used during the British campaign. This is likely, because he needed supplies and ships for the river crossings.

Caracalla's northern campaigns had several goals, which included: 1) a show of force to pacify the Germanic tribes before the eastern campaign; 2) the recruiting of soldiers and allies for the eastern campaign; 3) the securing of Raetia with new Germanic farmers, walls and forts; 4) the securing of the northern frontier; 5) the establishment of camaraderie between Caracalla and his soldiers. Preparations for campaigns in the Balkans and the East were also already taking shape.

Consequently, in the early spring of 213, Caracalla was ready to launch his well-prepared Germanian campaign from Raetia. It is not known whether the initial operation also included the use of a separate army and fleet along the Main, but that is very likely in light of Caracalla's preparations in the area in early 212. He would not have needed to worry that the Alamanni would attack the second division, because he was officially coming to help them.

Caracalla's army included the *Legio II Parthica*, at least nine cohorts of the *Praetoriani* with their cavalry and one cohort of the *Urbaniciani*, *Equites Singulares Augusti* and *Aulici/Protectores*, and full legions or detachments from the Rhine and Danube.[20] In addition to this, his army would have included units (legionaries, auxiliaries, marines/sailors, Moorish *numeri* and other *numeri*) and detachments from all over the empire, Osroenian and Armenian cavalry and probably also some Germanic allied forces. Since his army is known to have included a legionary detachment from *Legio II Traina* stationed in Egypt (Southern 2001, p.53; Farnum, p.105; Cowan 2002, p.151), it is possible that he may also have taken detachments from other eastern legions. The other legions attested to have taken part in this campaign include *III Augusta, II Adiutrix, II Parthica* and *III Italica* (Farnum, p.105; Cowan 2002, pp.150–51). The presence of the Egyptian forces suggests the possibility that Caracalla may have also drawn naval detachments from all over the empire, just like his father had for the British campaign. It is probable that most of the forces consisted of those collected previously for the British campaign, so these forces would have been billeted along the Rhine and Danube frontiers during 211 and 212 in preparation for the planned war.

Thanks to the existence of two inscriptions, we know the name of one of the commanders of these forces. He was the senator Caius Octavius Appius Suetrius Sabinus, legate of the *Legio XXII Primigeniae* stationed at Mainz. It is probable that he served as Caracalla's confidant, commander and companion (*comes*) during the campaign. He served with distinction, because he was afterwards rewarded with the governorship of Raetia.[21] The fact that Sabinus was the commander of the legion stationed at Mainz supports the previously mentioned possibility that the Romans may have had a second corps at Mainz that advanced along the Main to meet Caracalla's Raetian corps. What is notable about this is that, contrary to Dio's diatribes, there were also able and loyal senators whom Caracalla could fully trust.

When the preparations had been satisfactorily finished, Caracalla set out to accomplish his aims at three stages: Firstly, he dealt with the threat of the Alamanni with a stratagem; secondly, he followed up the success with an attack against the Cenni/Chatti, the neighbours of the Alamanni; and thirdly, he directed a joint army-fleet attack against the tribes of the mouth of the Elbe. The use of the fleet is proven by circumstantial evidence and by Dio's text, which refers to the ravaging of coastal territory. In light of this, it is probable that when Caracalla advanced against the tribes of the mouth of the Elbe, his Roman fleets would have advanced simultaneously along the Frisian coast up to the mouth of the Elbe and then some way upstream, where they would have met Caracalla's army and supplied it with victuals and arms. If Caracalla had left part of the Imperial Fleet of Misenum (and Ravenna?) in Britain or the north of Gaul, for example at Bononia, which is a distinct possibility if he planned to conduct a campaign in Germania, the Roman naval assets in the area would have consisted at least of detachments of the fleets of Misenum, Britain and Germany, and possibly also of detachments that had previously taken part in the Caledonian campaign.

The quotes below show that Caracalla had called the Alamanni to ostensibly contribute allied contingents to his forthcoming war against the Cenni/Chatti, who are likely to have been tribal enemies of the Alamanni. Thereby, he lured the flower of the Alamanni forces to be butchered.[22] The ploy worked like a dream.

> 'The Germanic nations, however, afforded him neither pleasure nor any specious claim to wisdom or courage, but proved him to be a downright cheat, a simpleton, and an arrant coward [*these are all lies of Dio*].
>
> 'Antoninus made a campaign against the Alamanni and whenever he saw a spot suitable for habitation, he would order, "There let a fort be erected. There let a city be built." And he gave these places names relating to himself, though the local designations were not changed; for some of the people were unaware of the new names and others supposed he was jesting [*this actually suggests that Caracalla advanced beyond Raetia and Agri Decumates into Alamannia proper and subjected it to Roman rule – a new conquest of territory*]. Consequently he came to feel contempt for these people and would not spare even them, but accorded treatment befitting the bitterest foes to the very people whom he claimed to have come to help. For he summoned their men of military age, pretending that they were to serve as mercenaries, and then at a given signal – by raising aloft his own shield [*note the similarity of Caracalla's signal to what had happened in Britain*!] – he caused them all to be surrounded and cut down, and he sent horsemen round about and arrested all others [*in other words, Caracalla used a ruse to destroy the flower of the enemy manhood, after which he sent out his cavalry to round up prisoners that he then used as slave farmers or half-free warrior settlers in Raetia, or subsequently as his elite slave soldiers of Germanic origin*].
>
> 'Antoninus sent a letter to the Senate commending Pandion, a man who had formerly been an assistant of charioteers, but in the war against the Alamanni drove the emperor's chariot and thereby became both his comrade

and fellow-soldier. In this letter he asserted that he had been saved by this man from an exceptional peril; and he was not ashamed at feeling more gratitude toward him than toward the soldiers [*note how Carcalla was prepared to show his gratitude towards even the lowly commoners, unlike the haughty Dio and his ilk*], whom in their turn he always regarded superior to us (senators).' (Dio 78.13.3–6 (exc. Val. 372–74), tr. by Cary, pp.309–11, with additions in square brackets.)

'Antoninus maligned himself when he claimed that he had overcome the recklessness, greed, and treachery of the Germans by deceit, since these qualities could not be conquered by force [*once again Dio shows his hostility and lack of understanding*].' (Dio 78.20.2 (exc. Val. 388), tr. by Cary, p.329, with additions in square brackets.)

'He [*Caracalla*] crushed the Alamanni, a populous nation who fight wonderfully well from horseback, near the River Main.' (Sextus Aurelius Victor 21, tr. by Bird, p.25, with addition in square brackets.)

Caracalla had fortified every suitable spot in *Agri Decumates* with forts to secure the area for the new settlers, who consisted of the captured Alamanni. The first quote also suggests that Caracalla may have subjected part of Alamannia proper outside the Raetian *Limes* under Roman rule, in the same manner as the British tribes outside Hadrian's Wall continued to be Roman subjects. At the same time, he also obtained large numbers of Germanic mercenaries and recruits for his forthcoming eastern campaign.

Caracalla's ploy to destroy the Alamanni was a truly masterful piece of generalship, and when one judges the character and policies of Caracalla in this context, it is only proper to cite the views of the ultimate realist Machiavelli's views regarding the use of such tricks (Machiavelli, *The Prince*, XVIII, tr. Bull, pp.99–100):

'… one must be a fox in order to recognize traps, and a lion to frighten off wolves. Those who simply act like lions are stupid. So it follows that a prudent ruler cannot, and must not, honour his word when it places him at a disadvantage and when the reasons for which he made his promise no longer exist. … But one must know how to colour one's actions and to be a great liar and deceiver. Men are so simple, and so much creatures of circumstance, that the deceiver will always find someone ready to be deceived.'

The initial success was exploited fully by advancing deep into Alamannia. The army corps that advanced northwards under Caracalla from Raetia probably marched either along the Tauber or more likely the Regnitz. Since it is known that the Alamanni had been surprised, it is quite possible that Caracalla could have even divided his army into a greater number of marching columns so that there would have been three columns marching along all three rivers – the Main, Taube and Regnitz – which were then united by the Main to crush the remnants of the Alamanni, who had by then apparently managed to rally their forces. The fact that Caracalla fought a major battle by the Main makes it certain that the Alamanni had managed to assemble some sort of force by the time Caracalla reached the scene. The battle ended in a major Roman victory, which secured the area for the next twenty years (see map: Caracalla's German Campaigns 212–214). It is probable that the Rhine fleet would have sailed along the Main to assist in the crossing of the river by building a pontoon bridge of boats. According to Whittaker's calculation, the battle on the Main against the Alamanni took place either in late August or September 213, as a result of which Caracalla was saluted *imperator* and given the title *Germanicus maximus*.[23]

Furthermore, contrary to Dio's claims, it is clear that Caracalla was no coward, but a man who put his own life on the line; it is quite possible that the incident in which his life was saved occurred in the battle of the Main River. I would suggest that since it was the driver Pandion who saved Caracalla's life while driving the emperor's chariot, Caracalla was emulating the British custom and advanced before his army in a chariot to challenge the enemy leader to a duel, as he was in the habit of doing during the German campaign according to Dio (78.13.2, p.312 in Loeb ed.). It is strange that Dio admitted this because it proves that Caracalla was no coward but a very good and brave duellist. It is not known whether Caracalla used a *quadriga* (four-horse) chariot or the British-style *biga* (two-horse). It is not at all surprising that the Alamanni did not accept the challenge in such circumstances, but attacked en masse when the person who was responsible for the butchery of their people had foolishly advanced in front of his army. The same quote also makes it quite apparent that Caracalla had a healthy self-esteem. He was quite ready to show his personal gratitude to those who served him well, despite the person's lowly position in society.[24] It is no wonder that soldiers trusted him. It is quite clear that the haughty attitude shown by Dio and other similar-thinking upper-class figures was something that would not endear them to the soldiers, as did Caracalla's camaraderie, but in this he was only following the example set up by his father (Herodian 2.11). The war against the Cenni is described as follows by Dio (78.14.1ff., tr. by Cary, pp.313ff., with additions in brackets):

> 'He [*Caracalla*] waged war also against the Cenni [*Chatti?*], a Germanic tribe. These warriors are said to have assailed the Romans with the utmost fierceness, even using their teeth to pull from their flesh the missiles with which the Osrhoëni [*this proves that the annexation of Osroene was not overly unwelcome news to the Osroenian soldiers – it is likely that Caracalla had bribed them with money*] wounded them [*note that Caracalla knew that the mounted archers were particularly useful in wars waged against the Germans; the earliest examples of the use of mounted archers occurred when Tiberius and Germanicus used Parthian mounted archers in their wars*],[25] so that they might have their

176　Caracalla

hands free for slaying their foes without interruption [*it is a natural reaction to pull arrows with teeth when both hands are needed to grasp the shield and sword/spear pair*]. Nevertheless, even they accepted a defeat in name in return for a large sum of money and allowed him to make his escape back into the province of Germany [*most likely another dishonest comment from Dio; the probable truth of the matter is that Caracalla defeated a large section or all of the Cenni, while he paid other noblemen or tribes for their support in order to divide the enemy*]. Some of their women who were captured by the Romans, upon being asked by Antoninus whether they wished to be sold or slain, chose the latter fate [*would there have been such prisoners, if Caracalla had really been forced to buy a peace?*]; then upon being sold, they all killed themselves and some slew their children also [*this is a standard topos in ancient texts, but still very probably true, except that it is very unlikely that all of the women would have killed themselves. Regardless, many or even most would have preferred to die free rather than live in slavery, and there is nothing improbable in that*].

'Many also of the people living close to the ocean itself near the mouths of the Albis [*Elbe*] sent envoys to him asking for his friendship, though their real purpose was to get money [*another dishonest comment; in truth, the tribes appear to have sent envoys to Caracalla to beg for peace*]. This was made clear by the fact that, when he had done as they desired, many attacked him [*and were evidently defeated*], threatening to make war, and yet he came to terms with all of them [*i.e. after having defeated them, Caracalla dictated new, harsher terms of peace*]. For even though the terms proposed were contrary to their wishes [*sic! this once again proves that Caracalla defeated the tribes of the Elbe*], yet when they saw the gold pieces they were captivated [*some of the tribes were evidently punished while others were bribed in a game of divide and rule, and the men who were considered loyal were placed on the throne, together with a sizeable bribe*]. The gold that he gave them was of course genuine [*Caracalla wanted to show himself a man worthy of his word*], whereas the silver and the gold currency that he furnished to the Romans was debased; for he manufactured the one kind out of lead plated with silver and the other out of copper plated with gold.

'... Antoninus devastated the whole land and the whole sea and left nothing anywhere unharmed [*this sentence once again shows the dishonesty of Dio. Caracalla clearly attacked the Germans from at least two directions simultaneously, by employing his fleet against the North Sea coastline while he himself advanced northwards along the Elbe to meet his fleet somewhere along it. Note that Dio's text states that the whole land and sea was devastated, and may also imply some sort of naval battle. This was a major achievement not achieved since the days of Germanicus in* AD *16*].

'The enchantments of the enemy had made Antoninus frenzied and beside himself; at any rate, some of the Alamanni, on hearing of his condition, asserted that they had employed charms to put him out of his mind. For he was sick not only in body, partly from visible, and partly from secret ailments, but in mind as well, suffering from certain distressing visions, and often he thought he was being pursued by his father and by his brother, armed with swords [*on the surface this text sounds credible. It is entirely possible that Caracalla could have suffered from feelings of guilt for having killed his brother, but in light of the tendentious reporting of Dio, it is still quite probable that this is not true, but that Caracalla had just caught a flu of some sort, as a result of which he saw feverish nightmares, which the enemy exploited by spreading disinformation to lower the Romans' morale, or that someone had managed to poison Caracalla*]. Therefore he called up spirits to find remedy against them, among others the spirit of his father and that of Commodus. … But to Antoninus no one even of the gods gave any response that conducted to healing either his body or his mind, although he paid homage to all the more prominent ones [*Antoninus did all of this in order to calm his superstitious men; i.e. he calmed the superstitious men by using "magic" against the enemy's evil eye*]. … He received no help from Apollo Grannus, nor yet from Aesculapius or Serapis, in spite of his many supplications and his unwearying persistence. For even while abroad he sent to them prayers, sacrifices and votive offerings, and many couriers ran hither and thither every day carrying something of this kind [*I would suggest that the real reason for this traffic was the conveying of intelligence reports in the form of prophecies. It is easy to see why Caracalla could have suspected a poisoning attempt.*]; and he also went to them himself, hoping to prevail by appearing in person, and did all that devotees are wont to do [*by doing this, Caracalla endeared himself with the followers of those religions, while he could also claim to receive messages from gods regarding the names of his enemies*]; but he obtained nothing that contributed to health [*it is of course possible that despite all the apparent cynicism in the use of religion, Caracalla may still have felt the urge to pray for his mother's well-being when she was suffering from the breast cancer*].'

The above proves that, after Caracalla had defeated the Alamanni, he moved north against the Cenni/Kennoi (i.e. the Chatti?) and then up to the mouth of the Elbe. Caracalla seems to have used a joint/combined arms approach by having his navy operate along the coast up to the mouth of the Elbe while he advanced towards the same locale (see map: Caracalla's German Campaigns 212–214). The whole operation shows the mastery of Caracalla's plans. He had used ruses to defeat the Alamanni, force to crush the Chatti and others, and money to buy the support of some. In addition to dividing his enemy by means of ruses, diplomacy and bribery, Caracalla also prevented the enemy from joining forces by engaging them separately and then by advancing from several directions simultaneously. The fact that Caracalla challenged the enemy leaders to single combat ('*monomachia*', Dio 78.13.2, p.312 in Loeb ed.) suggests the possibility that he may actually have fought duels with enemy leaders that had ended in the defeat of the latter.[26] Caracalla was clearly an expert duellist and unbelievably brave. He wanted to demonstrate to his men that he was taking great personal risks at their behest – now they had a commander who was not carried on a litter. This was heroic leadership in the extreme, and it is no wonder that the soldiers loved Caracalla. From the point of view of generalship, this was a very dangerous practice, but it was certainly a very cost-effective way of fighting. On top of that, if the enemy commander refused to fight a duel, he was bound to lower the morale of his own army while boosting that of the Roman army.

As a result of all this, Caracalla appears to have been able to divide his enemies so that he was able to defeat them piecemeal. Caracalla's campaign had been a huge success. He dictated the terms of peace and the frontier remained peaceful for two decades.[27] This was probably the first time since Tiberius ended Germanicus' campaigns in AD 16 that the Romans had managed to penetrate so deep into enemy lands. Caracalla fully deserved his titles *Germanicus Maximus* and *Magnus*.

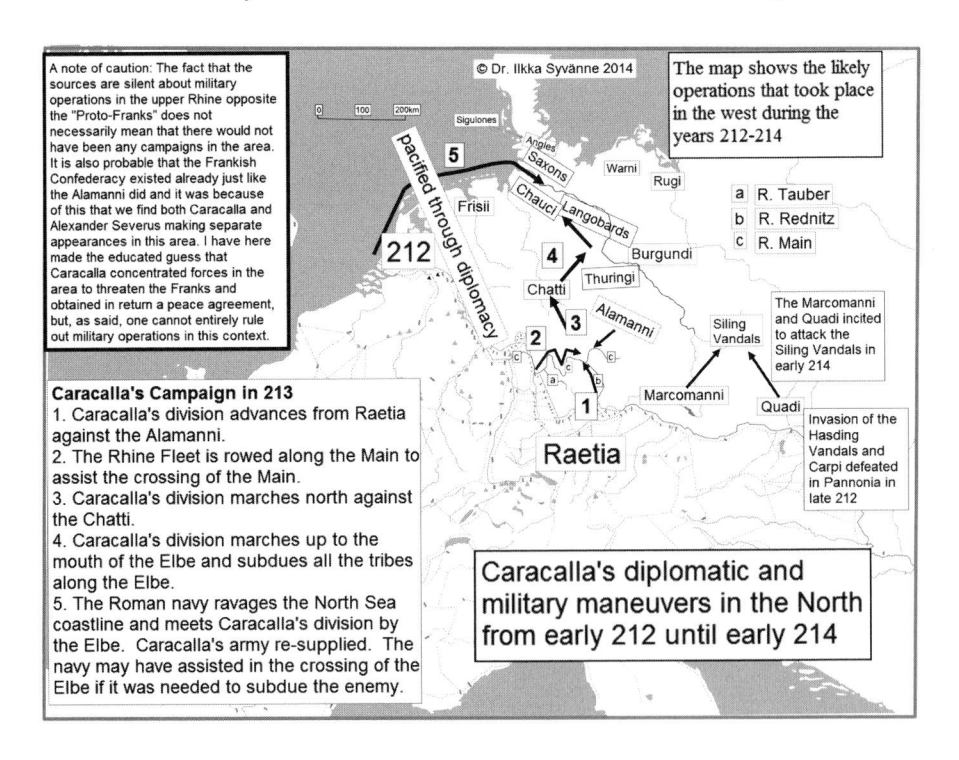

A note of caution: The fact that the sources are silent about military operations in the upper Rhine opposite the "Proto-Franks" does not necessarily mean that there would not have been any campaigns in the area. It is also probable that the Frankish Confederacy existed already just like the Alamanni did and it was because of this that we find both Caracalla and Alexander Severus making separate appearances in this area. I have here made the educated guess that Caracalla concentrated forces in the area to threaten the Franks and obtained in return a peace agreement, but, as said, one cannot entirely rule out military operations in this context.

The map shows the likely operations that took place in the west during the years 212-214

a R. Tauber
b R. Rednitz
c R. Main

The Marcomanni and Quadi incited the Siling Vandals to attack the Siling Vandals in early 214

Invasion of the Hasding Vandals and Carpi defeated in Pannonia in late 212

Caracalla's Campaign in 213
1. Caracalla's division advances from Raetia against the Alamanni.
2. The Rhine Fleet is rowed along the Main to assist the crossing of the Main.
3. Caracalla's division marches north against the Chatti.
4. Caracalla's division marches up to the mouth of the Elbe and subdues all the tribes along the Elbe.
5. The Roman navy ravages the North Sea coastline and meets Caracalla's division by the Elbe. Caracalla's army re-supplied. The navy may have assisted in the crossing of the Elbe if it was needed to subdue the enemy.

Caracalla's diplomatic and military maneuvers in the North from early 212 until early 214

It is unfortunate that we do not possess a detailed description of this magnificent German campaign and the tactics used by the Romans, but certain educated guesses can be made on the basis of the tactics the Romans had used against the Germans before and after this date. Germanicus' standard marching and combat formation against the Germans in AD 13–16 had been the hollow square/oblong with a vanguard and rearguard consisting of cavalry and auxiliaries. The baggage train and mobile field artillery were placed inside the hollow square. The army was deployed in a lateral formation of two combat lines (auxiliaries in front, legions behind) only when the terrain was suited to this.[28] Julius Africanus (Appendix 2) states the same. The hollow square was the standard Roman battle formation during the early third century. The descriptions of Maximinus Thrax's hollow square array by Herodian (8.1ff.) and the SHA (Max. Duo 21.1ff.) support the same conclusion. The archaeological finds from Harzfeld which date from the reign of Maximinus prove that the Romans continued to use the concentrated fire of ballistae against the Germans to create points of breakthrough in battle, just like they had during Germanicus' campaign.[29].

It is also likely that the size of the force Caracalla took to Germany was about the same as that fielded by Germanicus, because both faced similar obstacles and needed to cover similar distances. Germanicus had two cohorts of Praetorians, picked cavalry (Praetorians and *Corporis Custodis?*), eight legions and slightly more auxiliaries, and a fleet of 1,000 ships. When one remembers that (unlike Germanicus) Caracalla would have had full-strength legions, this would add up to a minimum of 89,000 footmen and 12,000 cavalry (with the *Praetoriani, Equites Singulares Augusti* and *Aulici*), and 1,000 ships. The size of the cavalry contingent, however, is likely to have been considerably larger, because Caracalla is known for his use of cavalry, in this case the Osroenians.

Consequently, my educated guess, which is based on the probability that the Roman army and Caracalla would have followed the same principles demonstrated previously and after, is that the standard marching and combat formation used by Caracalla was as shown below (not in scale) and that it was adapted to the terrain and situation as needed (as was also required by Roman combat doctrine), for example by adopting the lateral phalanx/line, double phalanx/line or hollow oblong for open terrain. Readers should keep in mind that this conjecture is solely based on the known features of the Roman combat doctrine and that there is no definite evidence for this in the extant sources. For the different ways of deploying and using this hollow square/oblong array, see my presentation available at academia.edu, Appendix 2, *The Age of Hippotoxotai,* and my forthcoming volumes of the *MHLR* (esp. vol. 2).

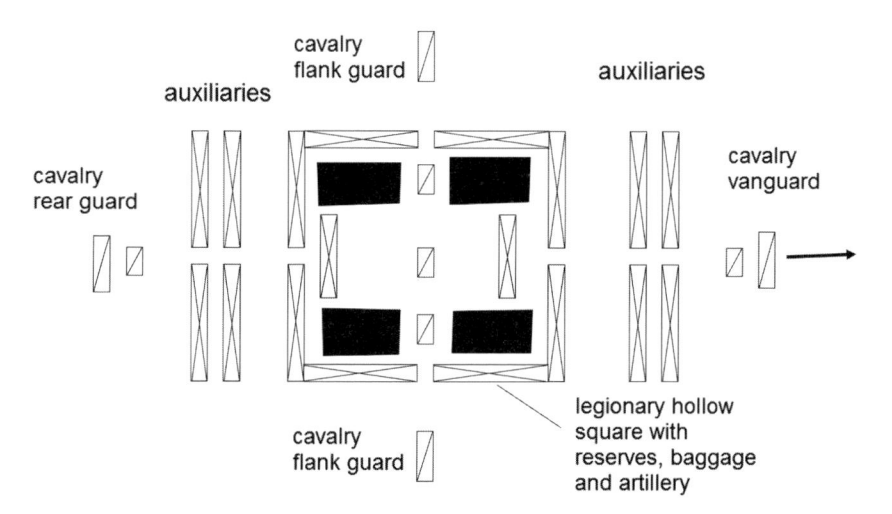

180 Caracalla

It is also probable that the Roman army demonstrated the same type of behaviour as during other periods for which we possess better evidence. I have already mentioned the killing, murder, rape, pillaging and capturing of prisoners and booty, but this was not the only unbecoming form of behaviour demonstrated by soldiers then and now.[30] Trajan's Column shows auxiliaries performing a form of headhunting to demonstrate their military prowess. It is probable that the Roman high command encouraged this by giving each soldier a sum of money in return for each kill. This sort of behaviour was also demonstrated by Praetorians and legionaries, as is well demonstrated by the separate attachment taken from the Trajanic relief incorporated into the Arch of Constantine (source: Bellori). This behaviour (the taking of heads, scalps, ears, hands, fingers etc.) has always been used and continues to this day, as recent events in Afghanistan prove. War was and is a cruel business, and soldiers need to be motivated to kill by whatever means possible. From the point of view of military effectiveness, it is a mistake to prevent this.

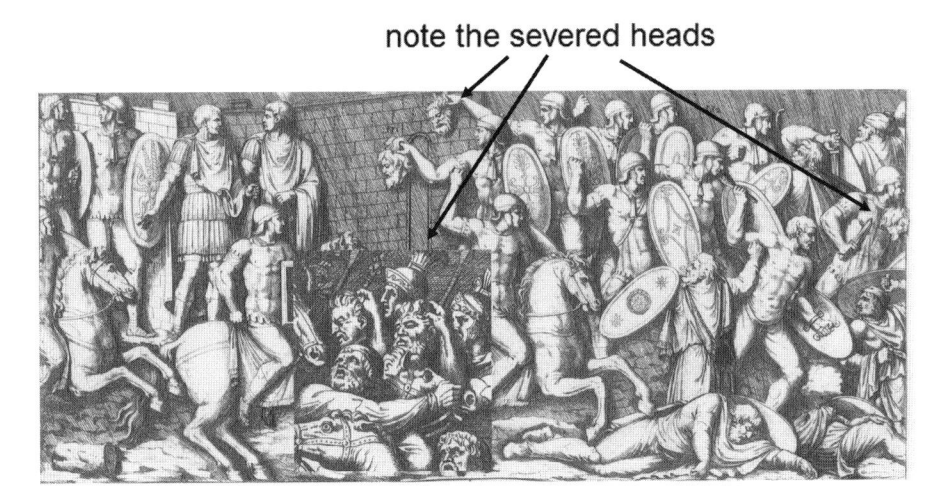

Rome's armed forces possessed the best medical service available in antiquity, and the soldiers would have received immediate medical treatment on the battlefield. Those who needed further medical attention would have been transported to receive treatment in medical facilities. It is practically certain that Caracalla must have paid particular attention also to this side of military life, because he was so loved by his soldiers. The following scene (seventeenth-century drawing) from the column of Trajan shows field medics doing their duty.

After the northern tribes had been subdued, Caracalla returned in late 213 to Roman territory, where he apparently visited the temples of Apollo Grannus in Raetia, and also the temples of Aesculapius and Serapis to find a cure for his unknown illnesses (probably a flu or poisoning). It would have been in these shrines that Caracalla received his intelligence reports. Thanks to the confused

Antoninus Imperator, Germanicus Maximus, Pacator Orbis, Magnus   181

state of the sources, modern historians have not found a consensus regarding the sequence of events after the victory over the Germans. Some are of the opinion that Caracalla proceeded immediately via Pannonia (where he supposedly induced the Marcomanni and Vandals to fight against each other, and executed the king of the Quadi) to Dacia, while others believe that he first visited Rome to celebrate a triumph, after which he travelled via Pannonia to Dacia. Unless new evidence surfaces, there is probably not going to be universal agreement on this. What is certain, though, is that Caracalla was hailed *Imperator* for the third time and was again called *Germanicus Maximus*, in addition to which soldiers and others called him *Hercules*, *Magnus* and *Pacatus Orbis*. It should be noted, however, that given Caracalla's habit of riding 100 miles a day, it would not be surprising if he called at Rome to celebrate a triumph. If Whittaker's conclusions are correct, and I believe that they are, then Caracalla celebrated his victories in grand style at Rome. Among the gifts given to the populace was a hooded Gallic cloak that Antoninus had lengthened to ankle length and which was called Caracalla/Caracallus hence his nickname Caracalla, the name by which history knows him. However, those who did not like him or wanted to jest gave Caracalla the deprecatory name of Tarautas, who was an insignificant, ugly, reckless and bloodthirsty gladiator. After this, in early 214, Caracalla proceeded along the so-called *Itinerarium Antonini*, along which mansions (stopping places and military magazines/arsenals) were at Rome, Mediolanum, Aquileia, Sirmium, Nicomedia, Antioch and Alexandria.[31] Meanwhile, the walls opposite Alamannia were strengthened with new forts and repairs to secure the territory in case the Alamanni did not respect their treaty (e.g. Herodian, Whittaker, p.409).

The following illustration by Montfaucon (a copy of a scene in Titus' Arch) shows what kind of spectacle Caracalla presented to the people and soldiers. The triumph was a PR exercise meant to gather support for the victorious emperor.

Whittaker suggests that it was probably during the autumn of 213 that Caracalla reorganized and divided Asturia-Gallacia away from the province of Hispania and divided the province of Britannia. I do not believe that Hispania would have been divided at this time, but when Caracalla was at Nicomedia in 214. However, Whittaker is probably correct in dating the changes in Britain to this time. Caracalla's goal would have been to remove all potential rebels, divide the military forces in the provinces so that these could not so easily revolt and to secure the western provinces with new appointees while he moved east against the Parthians. Caracalla made certain that none of the governers had more than two legions per province.[32] Perhaps the removal of some of the governors and the reorganization of the provinces were the result of investigations launched as a result of the 'illness' of Caracalla, the reports of which he would have read at the shrines.

Caracalla as General
The above has already proved that, despite all the hostility of Dio, Caracalla seems to have been very well schooled in the art of generalship. After all, Dio, Herodian and the SHA note Caracalla's admiration of Sulla, Tiberius, Hannibal and Alexander the Great. Just like any good general, Caracalla wanted to present himself as a comrade-in-arms of the soldiers. He marched, ran and worked with the soldiers and ate the same food as them – the last was obviously a good way to avoid being poisoned. He had been well schooled in the military arts, including riding (even as emperor he daily rode 100 miles = c.150km) and swimming in rough water. In order to prove his own manhood and to encourage the troops, he would also often challenge enemy leaders to single combat.[33] The soldiers just loved him, which is well proven by Herodian 4.7.3–7.

The SHA (Alexander Severus 9.1–2, tr. by Magie, p.193, with additions in square brackets) also inadvertently admits that Caracalla was a very brave and courageous commander, as one in fact would expect from an imitator of Alexander the Great:

> 'If you think of righteousness, who was more holy than [*Antoninus*] Pius? If of learning, who was more wise than Marcus [*Aurelius*]? If of innocence, who more honest than [*Lucius*] Verus? If of bravery, who more brave than Bassianus [*Antoninus Caracalla*]?'

While Dio 78.13.1–2 (tr. by Cary, p.313 with additions in square brackets) claimed:

> 'On necessary and urgent campaigns, however, he was simple and frugal, taking his part scrupulously in the menial duties on terms of equality with the rest. Thus, he would march with them, neither bathing nor changing his clothing, but helping them in every task and choosing exactly the same food as they had [*this made it more difficult for Caracalla's enemies to poison him*]; and he would often send to the enemy's leaders and challenge them to single combat [*he was a brave man*]. The duties of a commander, however, in which he ought to have been particularly well versed, he performed in a very unsatisfactory manner [*a hostile and untrue comment based on a very limited understanding of generalship*].'

The only thing deserving criticism is Caracalla's apparent unwillingness to listen to the advice of his officers and to follow only his own judgment, but it is possible that he simply refused to ask the advice of mediocre senators such as Dio and rather confided with those whom he could trust, which would not have been apparent to Dio, whose opinions were clearly not valued at all. However, it is still unlikely that Dio would have mentioned the existence of such an informal advisory council, even if he knew of its existence. That would have been contrary to his purposes.[34]

Indeed, contrary to the claims of Dio, Caracalla was actually a very gifted and devious general and supreme commander, regardless of the fact that he seems to have ignored advice given to him. Instead of engaging the enemy in the field of battle, he usually resorted to the more effective means of obtaining the peace, booty or victory through the use of cost-effective diplomacy and stratagems. The treacherous way in which Caracalla achieved his victories simply seems not to have been to the taste of the upper-class Romans, even if the soldiers loved him for the very same reason! On the basis of Caracalla's actions and what we know of his education, he seems to have been very well schooled in the arts of war and foreign policy.

The sources show Caracalla to have been an avid admirer of Sulla, Tiberius, Hannibal and Alexander the Great, who all well-deserved his and our admiration as military leaders.[35] The former three were particularly noted for their use of stratagems and trickery, while the last-mentioned inspired Caracalla to invade Parthia to gain immortal fame. It is therefore not surprising that, according to Dio, Caracalla rejoiced particularly for his successes in dividing his enemies with clever diplomacy. On the basis of the above list of great men and Caracalla's actual policies, one may make the educated guess, very much contrary to Dio's hostile claim[36] that Caracalla forgot his intellectual training completely, that Caracalla in fact modelled much of his own policies after the historical models. Firstly, Caracalla clearly modelled the purge of his enemies on Sulla's proscriptions, which mirrored the similar policy of his father Septimius. Secondly, it is probable that he imitated Tiberius when he used the divide and rule approach in Germania. Thirdly, just like Hannibal, he employed foreign mercenaries and favoured ruses. Fourthly, on the basis of his successful battles, he seems to have studied the battles of both Hannibal and Alexander in great detail to improve his tactical skills. Fifthly, he seems to have adopted the offensive military strategies of both Hannibal and Alexander when he decided to invade Parthia. However, instead of following blindly Alexander's rather straightforward and simple offensive strategy, Caracalla combined it with the use of stratagems, for which Hannibal was particularly famous. Sixthly, he showed particular attention to the cavalry arm (German, Scythian, Osroënian and Macedonian cavalry) and also the type of infantry (Macedonian phalanx) best suited to facing enemy cavalry. Finally, Caracalla paid particular attention to counter-intelligence and intelligence operations, for which the practices of Hannibal, Sulla and Tiberius provided plenty of examples to imitate.

In sum, Caracalla seems to have picked and chosen the best-suited model for each and every occasion from the historical precedents, which he then adapted to the circumstances. He was not such a simpleton as Dio claims him to have been. He was quite prepared to learn from history. In fact, the claim that Caracalla did not listen to advice should be seen as a complaint probably resulting from the fact that Caracalla was not prepared to listen to advice presented by the quite incompetent and vainglorious generals close to Dio and his senator friends. The downside was that Caracalla hurt their conceited pride with this. On the basis of Caracalla's successes in the use of ruses, it is not surprising that he would have come to despise the advice from such unmanly men who did not understand that true generalship meant much more than fighting pitched battles in the open.

The fact that Caracalla's camaraderie with the soldiers received so much attention from the sources shows that it was probably not the usual practice among the officers of the senatorial and equestrian classes at the time. They may even have seen such behaviour as being below their dignity. In great contrast to them, Caracalla seems to have been well-versed in the art of generalship. He knew full well the importance of showing to the soldiers that their commander shared their toils and dangers. The knowledge of this worked wonders, improving the fighting spirit of the men. The instances in which the source(s) claim that the soldiers had become mutinous because a particular general was a disciplinarian should be seen as examples in which the aristocratic or equestrian general had acted arrogantly and haughtily while demanding discipline from his men. Note, for example, Dio 78.9.1–3. It is probable that the men would not have mutinied if the generals in question had shared their hardships. Note also that Arrian does not disparage Alexander the Great because he always held athletic contests during his campaigns, whereas Dio (78.9.7) angrily accuses Caracalla for the very same practice. Perhaps the real reason for the hostility was the fact that Caracalla forced senators to build and pay for the construction of amphitheatres and (horse) race-courses wherever he and his troops spent the winter. As noted above, the principal grievances of the senators always appear to have been the fact that Caracalla forced them to pay for the upkeep of troops during the campaigns (Dio 78.9.1–7), which made some of them insanely hostile towards him. It was quite impossible for them to praise Caracalla.

In the field of military appointments, Caracalla eased the way for men of the lower classes to reach the top commands, much to the ire of senators. The appointment of men of low origins to top commands is the best proof of this. He seems to have had three demands which his appointees had to fulfil: 1) the most important was the demand of absolute loyalty; 2) they must have ability; 3) if possible the appointee would have to come from the lower classes so that he would be less likely to try to usurp him. This meant that Caracalla even appointed foreigners like Adventus and freedmen such as Theocritus to high-ranking military posts at the same time as he appointed senators to hold important provincial commands. In fact, excluding Macrinus, Caracalla's other appointees served with distinction. It should be remembered, though, that Caracalla's intention was not to use Macrinus in any military capacity. He was the lawyer Prefect of the Guard, while Adventus was the military Prefect of the Guard. The appointment of Macrinus as Praetorian Prefect at some unknown time was probably intended to court the support of the defeated African clique so that the entire Roman military elite would stand united under Caracalla. Caracalla appears to have underestimated the potential danger posed by Macrinus on the basis of his effeminate appearance and behaviour.

On the basis of the information given of Caracalla's behaviour during military campaigns, it is important to note the information which claims that the common soldiers did not bathe or change clothes often. This was not good from the point of view of battlefield survivability of the Roman soldiery. Dirty clothes mean that it was quite likely for most wounded soldiers to have suffered from infected wounds after combat. It is to the great credit of the Roman doctors that so many of the wounded survived to fight another day. If the soldier was not already suffering from wound fever, Greco-Roman medicine required that the doctor induced it in a controlled manner in order to speed up the recovery process. As regards Caracalla's own behaviour, it must have been considered beneath the pompous dignity of most of the period commanders. At least from the early Principate onwards, Roman commanders were always accompanied by bath servants, whose duty it was to build hot and cold baths daily for the commander's use. In contrast, the soldiers bathed

186 Caracalla

Caracalla.

Caracalla's coin celebrating his victory over the Germanic peoples (drawn after Cohen).

only when the circumstances allowed it (when encamped by a river, lake or sea). One of the forms of giving thanks to soldiers during campaigns was for the commander to let the soldier be rewarded with the use of his own bathing equipment, servants and bath/ersatz sauna.[37]

The *Caracalla*-cloak affair shows that from the very beginning of his reign, Caracalla was ready to adopt whatever he considered useful and improve existing designs if needed. In this case, it appears likely that the long hooded cloak was a very useful piece of clothing for soldiers in the field, better in fact than the standard cloak. Therefore, it is not surprising that the *Caracalla*-cloak became popular among the soldiers and populace.

Notes

1. The arrival of the Parthian ambassador in Birley (2000) p.176.
2. Dio 78.12.2a–3 (Exc. Val. 370, Xiph. 332).
3. LeBohec (2005) pp.74–80. This same policy was later used by Diocletian on the Arabian frontier. For Diocletian, see MHLR Vol.1.
4. For further info about the Goths, see Syvanne/Syvänne (2004; 2010; MHLR vols.1–2) together with Hernández's analysis of the Gothic military, pp.147–91).
5. The Goths had at least 300,000–400,000 warriors after they had conquered the Crimea. See Syvanne MHLR vols.1–5.

6. The following account relies heavily on Kouznetsov and Lebedynsky (2005) and Lebedynsky (2001) pp.35–49, 109ff.; (2002); (2007) pp.60–75; (2010); and Syvanne MHLR. For the Sarmatians and Alans in general, see especially: Lebedynsky (2010, 2007, 2006, 2002); Kouznetsov and Lebedynsky; Kazanski and Mastykova.
7. For the movement of the Goths, Heruls etc., see Heather, pp.30–50; Wolfram, p.42ff.; Koutnetzov and Lebedynsky, p.57ff.; Lebedynsky (2002) p.50ff.; Lebedynsky (2007) pp.62, 70; Kazanski, esp. p.29ff.; Kazanski and Mastykova, p.49ff.; Brzezinski and Mielczarek, pp.8–11; Mielczarek, pp.82, 99–100; Syvanne (2011) MHLR.
8. Ivantchik; Mielczarek, p.79ff., esp. p.99. It is also quite possible that the war was fought under Septimius Severus roughly at the same time as the Goths threatened the Roman Empire. For the Sarmatian and Bosporan militaries, see: Mielczarek; Brzezinski and Mielczarek; Koutnetzov and Lebedynsky.
9. The researchers are divided in their opinion regarding the dates of the reigns of the so-called Rhescuporis II and III. Some historians think that Rhescuporis ruled during the Flavian period, while others (e.g. Rostovtsev) date him to the reigns of Caracalla, Elagabalus and Alexander Severus. Others think that both Rhescuporis II and III reigned simultaneously, so the latter would have been the son of the former.
10. Mielczarek (1999) pp.28–29.
11. One would like to know whether the replacement for the disloyal governor was M. Clodius Pupienus (of humble origins but who rose in rank thanks to his great gifts), who became the co-emperor of Balbinus (one of Caracalla's *amici* and of noble birth), because we know that he served as governor of Narbonesis at some time. It is also possible that he served under Caracalla against the Sarmatians, because he served as a legate in Illyricum. For the career of Pupienus, see PIR. He was one of the most gifted commanders of the third century and the man behind the strategy that resulted in the defeat and death of Maximinus Thrax in 238.
12. Fitz, pp.100–01; Christol, pp.41–43.
13. For example Fitz, p.98ff., Mócsy (Pannonia), p.198 and Gonzales, p.100, give credit of this victory to the generals. We only know of this war and victory thanks to the inscriptions which mention it.
14. For alternative views, see Gonzales, p.100, with Fitz.
15. It should be noted that Caracalla was able to do this because the Roman upper classes could not move to another country to avoid taxes. The fleecing of the rich in this manner is no longer possible in the Western world thanks to free trade agreements and free movement of people and goods. If any single country or economic area decides to fleece the rich, these will only move themselves and their money and investments to another location which offers them a safe haven from these taxes. In the modern world, the most successful countries usually attempt to lure the rich into their own territory. It is not a question of right and wrong (this is always subjective), but what is the reality, and Caracalla certainly knew what the reality was and where he could get the money for his military campaigns.
16. Dio 78.12.6.
17. Dio 78.12.1ff. These events were so humiliating that the late Edessan Chronicle is silent about them.

18. The conclusions of this chapter and in the following chapters are based on the sources which are quoted later.
19. In general, for the emergence of the Alamanni, see Drinkwater (2007) pp.43–79, with the MHLR.
20. For a list of these (with the exception of *Aulici*), see for example Pollard and Berry, p.52ff.
21. Saxer, pp.49–50, includes the inscriptions with comments: CIL X 5398 at Aquinum C(aio) Octavio App(io) S[ue]/trio Sabino – legato [Aug(usti)]/ pr(o) pr(aetore) provinciae/ Raetiae, praeposit(o) vexi[ll(ariis)]/ Germ(anicae) expedit(ionis), comit(i) Aug(usti) n(ostri), legat(o), l[eg(ionis) II]/ et vicensim(ae) Pri[mi]g(eniae) – ; CIL X 6178 at Casinum C(aio) Octavio App(io) Suetrio Sabino – leg(ato) Aug(usti) pr(o) pr(aetore) provinciae/ Raetiae, praeposito vexillari(i)s Germanicae expeditionis, legato/ leg(ionis) XXII Primigeniae p(iae) f(idelis). Sabinus commanded therefore detachments from the legions II (which one?) or III Italica (according to Mommsen) and XXII Primigeniae.
22. The incident bears an uncanny resemblance to Caracalla's later ploy to kill the Alexandrians and may therefore (theoretically) be a duplicate in the epitome. However, I have here chosen to take it at its face value because there is no really good reason to doubt that. It is not inherently impossible that Caracalla would have employed the same ruse again later, since he seems to have done that on other occasions. It should also be noted that the news of such actions did not travel as fast and accurately as today.
23. Date and title: Whittaker in Herod, pp.408–09, n.1.
24. There is a distinct difference in the behaviour of the famed general George Patton and Caracalla towards a person who had saved their lives. Whereas Patton refused to recognize the man who had saved his life during the First World War in the 1930s (which shows that Patton had a low self-esteem which he needed to bolster with various means), Caracalla was quite prepared to do so in public. I do not intend to show any disrespect with this towards Patton – only to note the one character flaw he had – because I consider George Patton to have been the greatest tank/armoured force commander of the Second World War and one of the greatest commanders of all time.
25. My Germanicus presentation which is available online at academia.edu summarises the information.
26. Caracalla was certainly not the only man to show his heroism. Caracalla rewarded Titus Aurelius Flavinus with 75,000 sesterces and promotion for his outstanding bravery against the Cenni and other exploits. See ILS 7178/AE (1961) p.208, included in Campbell, p.52. This once again proves that Caracalla was always ready to reward bravery when he saw it.
27. For other views, see also Herod. 4.7.1ff., with comments of Whittaker; Potter, p.141. Despite noting the hostility of Dio, Burns, pp.273–79, has reached almost the exact opposite conclusions from mine. His view is that Caracalla did not take any sizeable forces with him to the north and that his campaign consisted only of the showing of the flag, and that it was only a diplomatic mission meant to shore up Rome's network of treaties among its client kingdoms. Furthermore, he claims that Caracalla's recruiting campaign was a small-scale affair involving only those directly along the frontiers. According to him, there is no evidence of concentrations of Caracalla's coinage deep

in *barbaricum*, whereas there is evidence in abundance for his father's and later reigns. In fact, if one reads the sources with care, this proves the exact opposite, since Dio (78.14.3–4) specifically claimed that Caracalla paid the barbarians with real gold while he paid his own soldiers with debased silver and gold coinage. This statement proves that Caracalla had used his father's coinage (which can be found in abundance deep in the *barbaricum*) for paying the barbarians, while he reserved his own debased coinage for his own troops. As regards the rest of the claims put forth by Burns (and others), the above suffices to put those claims at rest.

28. See Syvänne (2009, 2011), academia.edu.
29. I have visited the battle site under the guidance of the archaeologists who have conducted the digs.
30. This obviously refers only to those who do not really understand the way humans behave in violent situations. It is the animal side that takes over most of us, and an unfortunate fact of life is that this behaviour has been and probably should be tolerated in certain circumstances, but naturally not among friendly populations. It is always a dangerous thing to attempt to moralize the behaviour of people in war and violent situations when one lives in civilized, peaceful surroundings.
31. Christol, pp.41–43; Levick, p.100ff; Whittaker, pp.412–13.
32. Whittaker in Herod., p.409, n.3.
33. For example Dio 78.11.2ff. 78.13.7 (p.310) with Loeb ed. index; Herod 4.8.5; SHA Car. 2.2, 4.10, 5.4.
34. Dio 78.13.3–14.4; Herod. 4.7.1ff., with comments of Whittaker.
35. Dio 78.7.1–4, 78.9.1, 78.13.7; Herod. 4.8.15; SHA Car. 2.1–3, 4.10, 5.4.
36. For example in 78.11.3–4.
37. I have discussed this and other matters relating to the water supply in greater detail in Syvänne (2007) and in the research paper presented at the IWHA Conference in 2007.

Chapter Seven

Caracalla's Anabasis Phase 1: Caracalla the *Geticus* and the Preparations in 214

In 214, Caracalla appears to have had four goals to accomplish before he was ready to march against Parthia, the main objective of his career: 1) he wanted to secure the Pannonian and Dacian frontiers; 2) he wanted to recruit more Germans, especially cavalry, into his army to counter the Parthian cavalry; 3) he wanted to recruit a new Macedonian phalanx to counter the Iranian horsemen; 4) he wanted to secure Armenia through a ruse.

According to Dio (Exc. Val. 78.20.3, Loeb ed. p.328), Caracalla bragged later presumably at Nicomedia during the winter of 214–215 that he had managed to stir up enmity between the Silings Vandals (in Silesia) and Marcomanni (in Bohemia), and that he had executed Gaiobomarus, the king of the Quadi, on the grounds of accusations laid against him. On the basis of this, I would suggest that Caracalla's solution to the security problems in Pannonia was to foment a war between the Marcomanni and their neighbours the Vandals either in 213 or 214. It appears probable that both the Quadi and Marcomanni were allied with Rome at the time, and both were ready to fulfil their obligations. See for example SHA Elagabalus 9. The enemies of Gaiobomarus exploited the situation and got rid of him with Caracalla's help. In sum, Caracalla used very successfully the military strategy of 'stick and carrot' to obtain allies and client tribes among the Germanic tribes, new recruits and mercenaries for his upcoming eastern campaign, while also securing the frontier with military operations conducted by others on his behalf, combined with a show of force bolstered with new fortifications.

It is possible that it was after this that Caracalla reorganized the Pannonian provinces so that neither had more than two legions, because he feared the possibility of a revolt like his father had initiated in this region. The previous division of the forces had placed three legions in Pannonia Superior, while Pannonia Inferior had only one. This system had made it easier for the enemy to pass through the former into the territory of the latter, or vice versa, without having to fear anything because it was improbable that the governor of Pannonia Superior would come to the assistance of the neighbouring province.[1] The other alternative is that this division was made in late 212 or even by his father. It took several months for Caracalla to achieve the securing of the frontier, but this was not the end of his troubles because he also needed to secure Dacia and recruit even more men.

Caracalla the *Geticus* and the Preparations in 214   191

As in previous occasions, Caracalla combined military operations with a recruiting campaign. He both secured the frontier and enrolled into his army new recruits and mercenaries in preparation for his Parthian campaign, as the sources reveal:

'Then he made ready for a journey to the Orient, but interrupted his march and stopped in Dacia. In the region of Raetia [*possibly a confusion of campaigns resulting from the condensing of events*], he put a number of natives to death and then harangued his soldiers and made them presents … He did not, however, as Commodus had done, permit his men to call him by the names of the gods, for many of them had begun to address him as Hercules because he had killed a lion and some other wild beasts [*note that unlike Alexander, Caracalla did not want to be called a god or semi-god. He was too aware of its silliness and bad political associations*]. Yet he did call himself Germanus (in truth *Germanicus Maximus*) after defeating the Germans … Then he journeyed through Thrace accompanied by the prefect of the guard.' (SHA Car. 5.4–8, tr. by Magie, pp.13–15, with additions in square brackets)

'It is not out of place to include a certain gibe that was uttered at his [*Caracalla's*] expense. For when he assumed the surnames Germanicus, Parthicus, Arabicus, and Alamannicus (for he conquered the Alamanni too), Helvius Pertinax, the son of Pertinax, said to him in jest, so it is related [*it is possible that this is an invented discussion, but which still seems to show the nations which Caracalla defeated even if he did not actually bear all of the titles*], "Add to the other, please, that of Geticus Maximus also"; for he had slain his brother Geta, and the Getae is a name for the Goths, whom he conquered [*since Caracalla was in truth sorry for the fate of his brother, he probably didn't want to take such a title that would have reminded him and others of the fact*], while on his way to the east in a series of skirmishes ["*tumultuariis proeliis devicerat*", *i.e. Caracalla defeated the Gothic tribes in 'Dacia'. Thanks to the fact that the Goths were in the habit of absorbing new tribes either as allies or as full members of the Gothic nation, it is probable that the Goths/Getae included the real Getae, the Dacians/Carpi/Free Dacians and also Sarmatians*].' (SHA Car. 10, tr. by Magie, pp.27–29, with additions in square brackets)

'It was at this time, too, it is said that Helvius Pertinax, the son of Pertinax, afterwards killed by Bassianus, remarked to the Praetor Faustinus, who was reading aloud and had uttered the titles Sarmaticus Maximus [*there is no evidence that Caracalla held this title, but it is quite clear that the Goths were also supported by some Sarmatian cavalry, as a result of which we can say that this claim is also at least partially true*] and Parthicus Maximus, "Add to these also

192   Caracalla

Geticus Maximus," that is to say, Gothicus.' (SHA Geta 6.6, tr. by Magie, p.45, with additions in square brackets)

'Antoninus came into Thrace, paying no further heed to Dacia [*i.e. Caracalla's campaign in 214 was in Dacia*] … For the emperor kept Scythians [*Goths*] and Celts [*Germans*] about him, freemen and slaves alike, whom he had taken away from their masters and wives and had armed, apparently placing more confidence in them than in the soldiers; and among various honors that he showed them he made them centurions, and called them "Lions" [*Leones, the new cavalry bodyguards of Caracalla*].' (Dio 78.16.7, 79.6.1, tr. by Cary, p.351, with additions in square brackets)

'[S]etting out from Italy he arrived on the banks of the Danube where he saw to the business of the northern section of the empire [*this is a very short summary of the Raetian and Pannonian campaigns and includes actually the events after it*]. He took his physical exercise by chariot-racing and fought all kinds of wild animals at close quarters. He spent little time over legal cases but he was straightforward in his perception of an issue and quick to make a suitable judgment on the opinions expressed [*this actually proves the great intellectual capacity of Caracalla; Whittaker, p.409 n.2, also notes that contrary to Dio the period inscriptions suggest that Caracalla was patient and easy-going in the judicial hearings that he held everywhere he stopped. He did not leave all of these cases for his "mother" to decide, as claimed by Dio*]. He also won the loyalty and friendship of all the Germans north of the frontier; so much so, that he drew auxiliary forces [*symmachoi*] from them and created his bodyguard [*the Leones*] from specially selected men of strength and fine physical appearance. On many occasions he took off his Roman cloak and appeared wearing German clothes, including the surcoat they usually put on embroidered with silver. He also used to wear a wig of blonde hair elaborately fashioned in the German style. The barbarians were delighted and absolutely adored him [*this sort of behaviour was undoubtedly seen as demeaning among the pompous upper classes, but this is an example of first-class diplomacy. Just by wearing Germanic clothes and a wig, Caracalla was able to obtain the loyalty of the barbarian auxiliaries. This ploy Caracalla had clearly learnt from Alexander the Great, who wore Persian dress*]. So did the soldiers, mostly because of the donatives he paid out to them, but also because he shared their duties as an ordinary soldier. His table was laid inexpensively and there were occasions when he even used wooden utensils for eating and drinking [*this was clearly unheard of among the senatorial commanders!*]. [*The wooing of the regular soldiers by being their comrade-in-arms was a very sensible thing to do when Caracalla was also wooing the barbarian auxiliaries. If he had favoured only the barbarians, the Romans could have taken offence. Caracalla was clearly a first-class general as far as the maintenance of morale was concerned. The fact that the sources constantly refer to the heavy physical exercises and physical labour performed by the men and Caracalla also proves beyond doubt that Dio lies when he claimed that the soldiers were not trained].*' (Herodian 4.7.2–8.1, tr. by Whittaker, pp. 409–13, with additions in square brackets)

According to the SHA (Car. 10.4, see above), Caracalla defeated the Getae in a series of battles. On the surface, one could interpret that Caracalla defeated the real Getae (the Free Dacians/Carpi), but the details make it clear that he beat the Goths together with the Free Dacians and Sarmatians. On the basis of the very few references in the sources, most of the actual military campaigning and recruiting of new troops appears to have been conducted in Dacia or the neighbourhood of Dacia, possibly at least initially inside Roman territory.[2] The only pieces of evidence for the location are that Caracalla fought in Dacia, from which he then marched to Thrace. This leaves three possibilities: 1) Caracalla marched to Dacia as response of a joint attack by the Goths, Dacians and Sarmatians, forced them to retreat and then pursued and defeated the fugitives repeatedly in a series of improvised battles during the advance; 2) he defeated the above-mentioned invaders inside Roman Dacia; 3) he invaded Gothic lands from Dacia or Sarmatian lands from Pannonia/Sirmium to Dacia, and then marched towards the Dniester, defeated the Goths and their allies in a series of encounters and from there back to Thrace. In light of Caracalla's tendency to conduct pre-emptive surprise attacks, the likeliest alternative is that he invaded enemy territory without any warning or provocation, so he would probably have advanced from Sirmium to Dacia, from there up to the mouth of the Dniester or even to the Bug or Dnieper (just like he had advanced previously from Raetia to the mouth of the Elbe), and from there to Thrace. The list of defeated foes Sarmatians, Dacians and Goths suggests that he engaged each separately in succession. This would have secured the entire length of the frontier, from the mouth of the Rhine up to the mouth of the Danube, which appears to have been Caracalla's goal. It is probable, but not certain, that the Roman army would have consisted of both infantry and cavalry, and that the fighting march would have been conducted in a hollow infantry square or infantry squares/oblongs (fortified with *carroballistae*), which would have served as a base or bases for cavalry charges. It is also highly likely that the fleets were used to support operations, for example by providing ships for river crossings and provisions where feasible. There were Roman naval bases located at the mouths of the Dniester and Bug, which could have served as logistical hubs. It is unknown whether the citizens of Cherson or the Bosporans had any role in these events, as they had before and were to do later (see MHLR Vol.1). However, the fact that Rhescuporis III received the name Friend of the Romans does suggest that he had made a great service to them. One possible reason for the title could have been an attack from behind against the Goths when Caracalla attacked from the front. In this case Caracalla would certainly have

194 Caracalla

advanced to the city of Olbia, which served as a naval base at the mouth of the Bug, or even up to the Dnieper.

In spite of the fact that we do not know the exact details, we know that Caracalla's campaign was still a huge success. In order to obtain peace, the 'Dacians' (i.e. the Goths and Free Dacians) had to give hostages to Caracalla (Dio 79.27.5). According to Herodian (4.7.2–3), Caracalla won the loyalty and friendship of all Germans north of the frontier and drew auxiliary forces from them. As noted, he also wore German clothes and a wig of blonde hair, which made him all the more popular among the northerners. The best of the new 'Scythian' (mostly Goths) and the Germanic recruits of the previous year, possibly together with the *Equites Singularis Augusti*, were formed into a new cavalry bodyguard unit called the Lions (*Leones*). Even the rank and file Lions held the prestigious position of centurions. The future Emperor Maximinus Thrax served in this corps. The northerners who were recruited into the elite cavalry *equites extraordinarii* were adjoined to the *Legio II Parthica* and placed under the command of its prefect, Aelius Decius Triccianus, a military man who had begun his career as a private in Pannonia. It is uncertain whether we should equate the *equites extraordinarii* of the SHA with the *Leones*

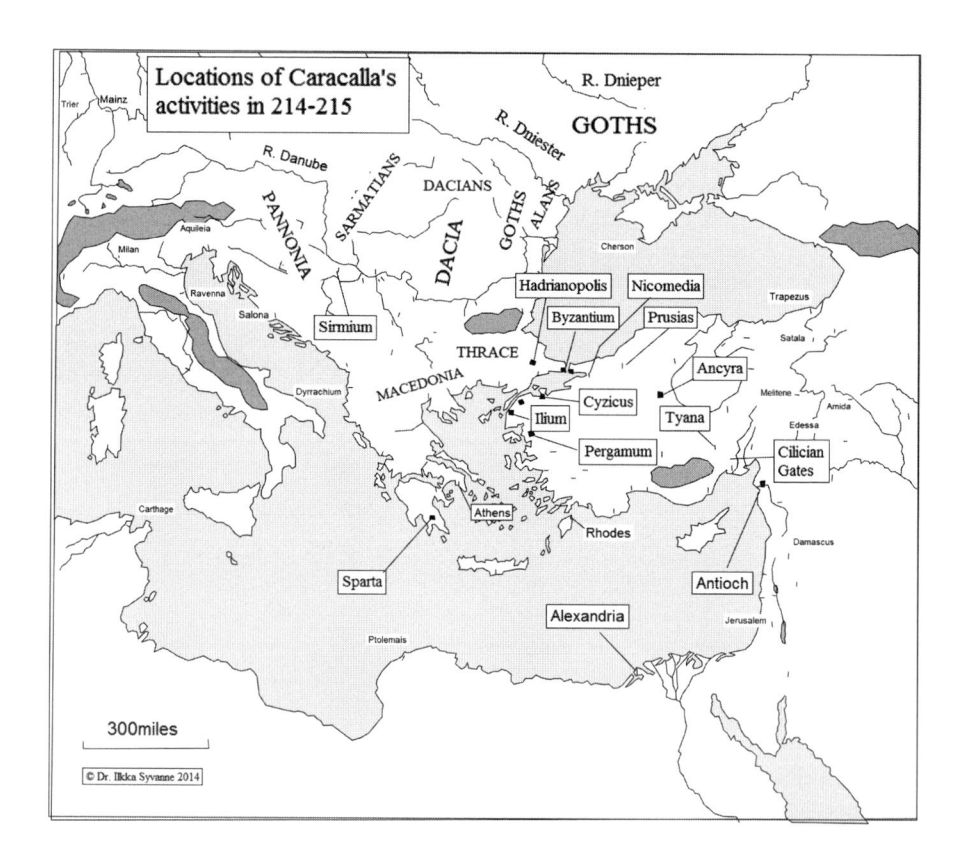

of Dio, but in light of the meaning of the *equites extraordinarii* in the Republican period (Polybius 6.26), which was that these formed the elite component of the consul's cavalry, it is probable that we should.[3]

The joining of the barbarian auxiliary cavalry with the *Legio II Parthica*, which had its own cavalry component, is also curious because we possess information of similar groupings of auxiliary units with the *Legio II Italica*. For example, according to the PIR, Q. Herennius Silvius Maximus served as *legatus legionis II Italicae et alae Antoninianae* either under Caracalla or Elagabalus. In light of this, it appears quite probable that under Caracalla the auxiliary cavalry forces were always placed administratively under the legionary commanders, so we should consider it probable that when on a campaign the legions always possessed sizeable cavalry forces to support them. Similar instances can be found in the SHA (Vopiscus of Syracuse, Aurelian 11).

As noted, according to the SHA (Car. 9.12.6), in the course of his life Caracalla assumed the surnames *Germanicus*, *Parthicus*, *Arabicus* and *Alamannicus*, in addition to which he also defeated the Getae/Goths while en route to the east. According to David Magie (SHA 2, Car., pp.27–28, n.6), the cognomen *Arabicus* is not found on coins or official inscriptions, but is still on some provincial inscriptions dated to the years 213–214. Consequently, if the dating of these inscriptions is correct, it is possible that Caracalla's generals secured the desert frontier and/or Yemen in 213–214 in preparation for the campaign, so Caracalla obtained the cognomen *Arabicus*. The aim would obviously have been to secure the southern flank for the campaign against Parthia. Alternatively, if the dating of the inscriptions is not correct, it is

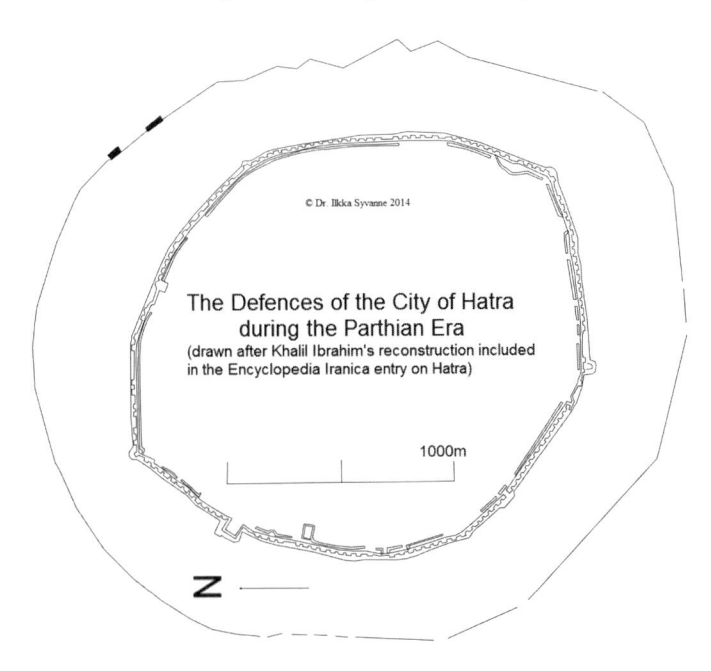

© Dr. Ilkka Syvänne 2014

The Defences of the City of Hatra during the Parthian Era
(drawn after Khalil Ibrahim's reconstruction included in the Encyclopedia Iranica entry on Hatra)

1000m

possible that Caracalla secured the desert himself when he was moving southwards to Alexandria in 215, but it is more than likely that the dating is accurate. We do not know what the military action was that earned Caracalla the title, but one possible explanation would be the conquest of Hatra, which had eluded both Septimius Severus and Trajan. It is known that Hatra possessed detachments of Roman soldiers during 238–240 (REF 1, 33), which has led to speculation that Severus still managed to install his own forces inside the city despite his failure to take it (thereby also earning the title *Arabicus* for the father and son), or alternatively that the Hatrans asked for Roman help during the reign of Alexander Severus, Maximinus Thrax or Gordian III. My own tentative suggestion, which is equally unprovable, just like the above, is that the Romans conquered Hatra now and that it was this that earned Caracalla his title *Arabicus*.

The army Caracalla had taken to the Balkans included detachments and entire units drawn from the western provinces, detachments and units he had previously taken from the Balkans, numerous Moorish light cavalry and infantry units (both auxiliaries and allies),[4] Germanic allied cavalry and most of the imperial reserve units consisting of Praetorians, 300 *Speculatores*, *Equites Singulares Augusti*, *Legio II Parthica*[5] and *Aulici*. As noted above, it was only after his victory over the Goths and others that Caracalla added a new elite unit called *Leones* to his forces, which included select individuals chosen from the ranks of the Germans and Scythians (mainly Goths), but he was not yet satisfied with the number of forces he had. Before going to the East, Caracalla planned to recruit even more forces from Macedonia and Greece. Considering the fact that the northern border remained calm when he moved east, it appears probable that he took only the absolute minimum in detachments from European units, as a result of which there was no power vacuum left behind. Caracalla appears rather to have formed the majority of his expeditionary forces from new recruits and allies, and from the forces already posted in the East. The recent memory of Caracalla's campaigns in the area and the removal of soldiers from *barbaricum* to serve in Caracalla's army obviously helped too.

According to Dio (78.12.1–3, esp. 2a–3), Caracalla unjustly took credit for himself for the fact that after the death of Vologaesus IV/V in c. 207, his sons began to fight for the throne. In fact, if the modern dating of the revolt of Artabanus IV/V against Vologaesus V/VI to 213 is correct, then, contrary to Dio's claim, Caracalla may indeed have induced Artabanus to revolt. Consequently, there is quite strong circumstantial evidence to back Caracalla's claim.

Caracalla had in all probability held discussions with an ambassador of Artabanes either in 211 or 212. It is also quite clear that he was already preparing an eastern campaign against Vologaesus V/VI at least from 212 onwards, of which the support of the pretender to the Parthian throne formed only the first part. Caracalla had also made other preparations. As we have seen, he was already recruiting men for the eastern campaign as early as 212 and 213. He was also making preparations in the future theatre of operations.

Firstly, as we have seen, Caracalla had induced Abgar IX (Abgarus), king of the Osroeni, to visit him, only to arrest and imprison him. The ploy had been to call the king and his men to join the campaign against the Alamanni and Cenni in early 213, because the Osroeni mounted archers took part in that campaign. As a result, the client kingdom of Osroene, with its capital Edessa, was annexed without a fight. Edessa was to serve as the main forward base of operations for the Persian campaign.

Secondly, according to Dio (78.12.1–2, Xiph 332.7, tr. Cary): 'When the king of the Armenians was quarrelling with his own sons, Antoninus summoned him in a friendly letter, pretending that he would make peace with them; but he treated them as he had treated Abgarus. The Armenians, however, instead of yielding to him had recourse to arms and no one thereafter would trust him in anything whatever.' Once again, Dio can be proven to falsify the truth when one compares his account with Armenian and Georgian sources. It becomes immediately apparent that Dio (or his epitomator Xiphilinus) had purposefully confused the events occurring in Armenia. Furthermore, this was not to be the last time Caracalla fooled his enemies. He did not play by the rules; he changed them! The Armenian incident, including the capture and then flight of Tiridates, must have also happened during 213 or 214 for it to serve as a *casus belli* for Caracalla. The problem with this is how to connect these events with the events and reigns mentioned by the Armenian sources, which do not specifically mention any of Caracalla's operations. What follows is my attempt to reconcile the sources.[6]

The Armenian historian Moses (Chorene) Khorenats'i (2.64–65) names three kings for this period: Tigran, Valarsh and Khosrov the Great. The last was the father of the famous Trdat/Tiridates (the first Christian King of Armenia). Khosrov can be dated securely to have ruled at least from c. 220/224 (or before) until 252/259, but we do not have accurate and reliable information regarding the other dates.

According to Moses (2.64), Tigran (Tigranes?) became King of Armenia in the twenty-fourth year of Valegesos Peroz (Victor). It is usually thought that the Valegesos in question was Vologaesus III/IV (c.148–192), but this is uncertain because it is probable that Moses has confused several different Vologeseses and Tigrans. However, if true, this would date the beginning of Tigran's reign to 172. Tigran is claimed to have lived for forty-two years and died without exhibiting any brave deeds. If Moses has confused the lifespan with the length of the reign, then this would put the death of Tigran right on the date 213/214 when Caracalla apparently removed the Armenian king from office. This appears to be the case. We can connect this with the information provided by the epitomator of Dio (78.19.1–2), who claims that Antiochus (an operative employed by Caracalla) and Tiridates fled from Roman territory to the court of Vologaesus V/VI and that Caracalla demanded their return. I would suggest that this Tiridates/Tigran was the King of Armenia who had been deposed by Caracalla, and that Caracalla had foolishly made the untrustworthy Antiochus the guardian of the deposed Tiridates. I would also suggest that Dio gives both Tigran and Khosrov the Great the name Tigranes, which has caused the confusion of identity.

Therefore, Caracalla's choice as successor appears to have been Tigran's son Valarsh (Vologaesus), but the problem with this is that Moses (2.65) claims that Valarsh became king in the thirty-second year of Peroz, the King of Persia. It is usually thought that in this case, Moses' Peroz was Vologaesus III/IV and that he was crowned in c.180.[7] I would suggest a date of 20 years after the death of Vologaesus III, which would give the year 212, which in turn is quite possible if he was made king during the lifetime of his father. This is also confirmed by the dating of the reign of Valarsh's son Khosrov (the second Tiridates of Dio 79.27.4), who came to the throne in the third year of Artabanus/Artavan, King of Persia. Artavan is usually identified with Artabanus V (213–224), who was King of Parthia before he was overthrown by Ardashir, the son of Sasan. This would mean that Valarsh died at the latest in 215/216. The problem is that Moses also states that Valarsh ruled for about twenty years, but this is likely to be a mistake for the beginning of his reign after the death of Peroz.

The key event of Valarsh's reign was the war against the northern nomads. According to Moses 2.65, the Khazars (Turks) and Basilk (Hunno-Bulgarians), in other words the tribes north of the Alans or the Alans themselves,[8] passed through the Derband/Daruband Pass under their king Vnasep Surhap. Valarsh defeated the invaders after they had crossed the River Kura, and then pursued them through the Daruband Pass, where the enemy regrouped and formed a battle line. Valarsh defeated the Alans/nomads once again, only to die at the hands of these expert archers. The death of Valarsh can be dated to 215/216. According to Moses and Thomas Artsruni (1.8), Valarsh's squires Babgean and the great Aspet Ashot were able to escape from the battle, and when they returned to Armenia they installed Khosrov the Great on the Armenian throne with the help of Artavan (Artabanus V). If the Romans had accompanied the Armenians, it is possible to think that the death of Valarsh would have been one of the setbacks suffered by Theocritus. In sum, it appears probable that Artabanus was able to exploit the situation and install Khosrov the Great on the throne without Roman involment in the winter of 215/216, which would have angered Caracalla beyond reason as it would have been a breach of previous agreements.

It also seems likely that Tigran was the King of Armenia deposed by Caracalla and that Tigran was succeeded by Valarsh, who had been co-ruler since 212 (if not earlier), and the king who subsequently revolted against the Romans must have been Khosrov the Great.

According to Dio (78.19.1–2), when Caracalla made an expedition against the Parthians, his pretext for war was that Parthian king Vologaesus had not surrendered Tiridates (who on the basis of the above analysis must be Tigran/Tigranes/Tiridates) together with a certain Cilician Antiochos/Antiochus. Dio tells us Antiochus had pretended to be a philosopher of the Cynic school[9] and had in the past proved himself invaluable to the Roman army as a man who could motivate soldiers to fight in a war. As a result, both Severus and Caracalla had showered him with money and honours, but he had become disillusioned and together with Tiridates deserted to the Parthians. This means that Antiochus had achieved some unnamed successes in the East under Caracalla before his desertion. The possible candidates for such successes include the campaign that earned Caracalla the title *Arabicus* and the plot to capture Tirdat/Tiridates, but since Antiochus actually betrayed Caracalla after the latter event it is probable that Antiochus did not approve it. Antiochus may also have served with distinction if Vologaesus V/VI had invaded Roman territory prior to Caracalla's campaign, but we do not have any concrete evidence for this.

From the point of view of analysis of the diplomacy of Caracalla, it is of interest to note that Tiridates and Antiochus fled to the court of Vologaesus. This makes it very probable that Tiridates had been Vologaesus' supporter and that Caracalla removed him from power to make certain that Tiridates and his Armenians would not support Vologaesus in the civil war against Artabanus. In short, it is probable that Caracalla purposefully weakened Vologaesus just before Artabanus attacked him. This makes it very likely that Caracalla had incited Artabanus to rebel in 210–211 and had then concluded an alliance with him, which in turn made it easier for Caracalla to negotiate with Artabanus in 215–216.

In sum, it appears quite probable that Caracalla had been in communication with Artabanus before the latter began his revolt against Vologaesus V/VI, and was making painstaking (especially for the senators) preparations that on the surface may have appeared as if he would join Artabanus in his war against his brother Vologaesus. These preparations were also connected with Caracalla's operations in Osroene and Armenia. Caracalla's aim was clearly to secure these two strategically important areas for his forthcoming campaigns against Parthia. Caracalla's primary intention was to achieve his initial goals through stratagems and diplomacy which would secure him direct control over Osroene and Armenia and the alliance of Artabanus against Vologaesus.

To a certain extent it is fair to say that Caracalla's eastern campaign sought to emulate and follow the route of Alexander the Great's eastern Anabasis, but there are quite a few differences as well. According to Dio (78.7.4), Caracalla imitated Alexander the Great by taking numerous elephants with him, but this is misleading because Alexander had obtained his elephants only after he had begun his campaign. Similarly, unlike Alexander, Caracalla sought to obtain his military goals mainly through the use of ruses and stratagems, and only secondarily through military force. He clearly considered himself more clever and devious than the rest of mankind and seems to have held the rest of humanity in contempt.

The inclusion of elephants in the emperor's entourage suggests the likelihood that Caracalla familiarized his cavalry and infantry with the beasts in case they faced them during the eastern campaign. It also suggests that he intended to continue his march all the way to India. The following illustration of elephants pulling the emperor's wagon shows one of the ways in which the elephants were used to enhance the emperor's prestige among the populace and soldiers. It is quite probable that Caracalla used them in like manner. The Romans obtained elephants both from

India and Africa (e.g. Claudian, Stilicho's Consulship 3.349ff), even if the former source was more important. The illustrations taken from Ginzrot's book show the use of such wagons by Claudius and Pertinax.

After completing his military campaign in 'Dacia', Caracalla moved to Thrace, where he began to emulate Alexander the Great in earnest. He began to wear the Macedonian dress, including the *kausia* (a sort of beret) on his head and *crepidae* (calf boot, footwear of a phalangite) for shoes. He also enrolled selected young Macedonian men into a 16,000-strong Macedonian phalanx and named it Alexander's phalanx. It seems likely that regular soldiers originating from Macedonia were transferred into this phalanx to form its veteran core. These men were in charge of drilling the new Macedonian recruits. The overall strength of the phalanx was 16,384 men.[10] They were equipped with helmets of raw ox-hide (*kranos ômoboeion*), a three-ply linen *thorax*-breastplate (*thorax linous trimitos*), bronze shield (*aspis chalkê*), long spear (*doru/dory makron*), short spear (*aichmê bracheia*), high boots (*krepides*) and sword (*xifos*). Ross Cowan has suggested that the triple linen *thorax* would not have been the Greek linen *thorax*, but in all probability the standard legionary *thoracomachus* or *subarmalis*, the padded linen garment worn under armour.[11] I disagree. It is inherently more likely on the basis of what the sources state that Caracalla did indeed equip his men as the people conceived Alexander the Great to have done. In other words, Caracalla equipped his phalangites with lighter linen and leather protective equipment, which was also cheaper than legionary equipment. The pairing of the long and short spears resembles the legionary practice of using the *hastae* against cavalry and *pila* against infantry, but with the difference that Caracalla appears to have equipped his new Macedonian phalanx with the real *sarissae*. The officers of the Macedonian phalanx were also told to adopt the names of Alexander's generals. In addition to his Macedonian phalanx, Caracalla recruited young men from Sparta and called the resulting formation a Laconian or Pitanetan *lochos* or Spartan phalanx. Some of the

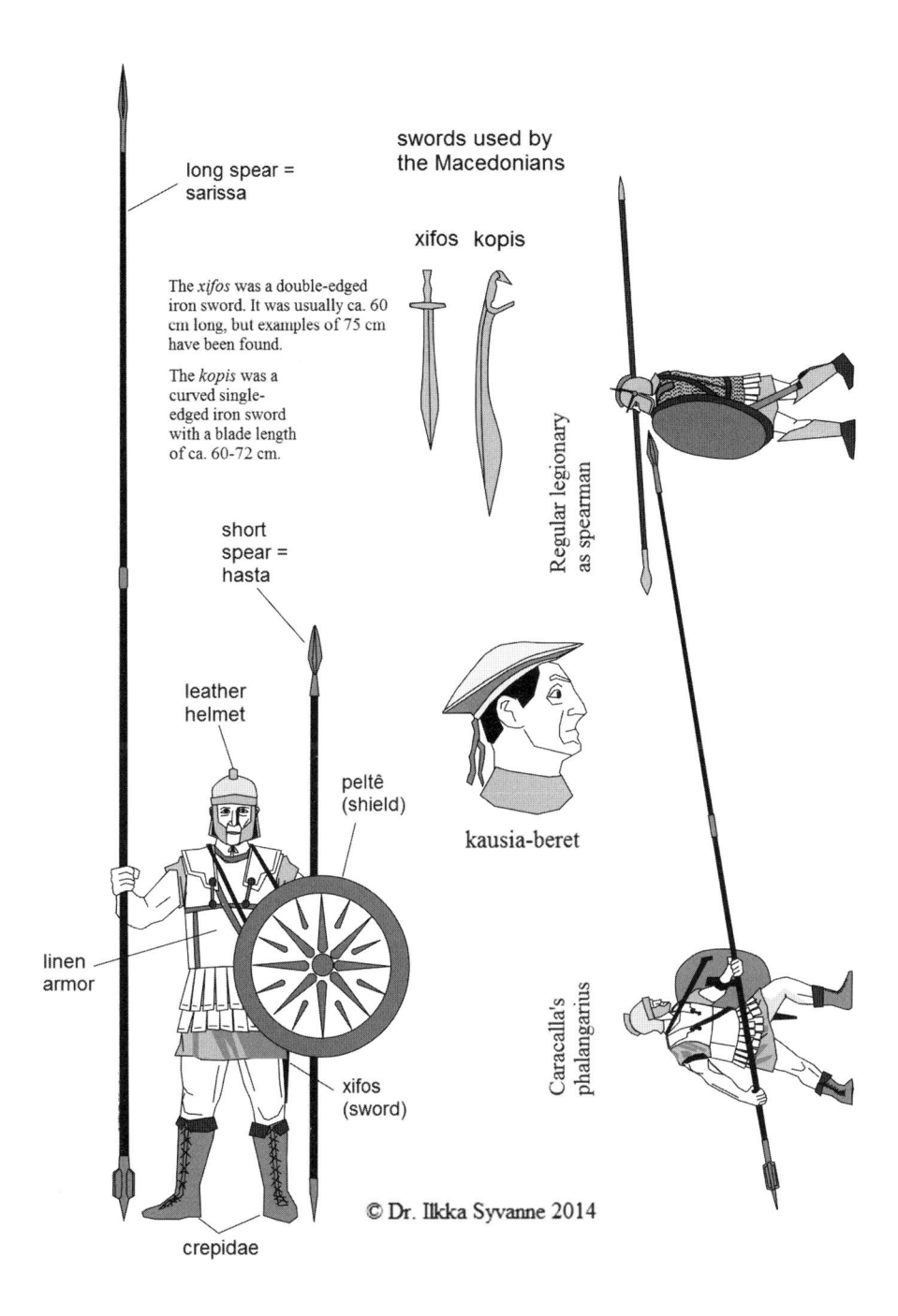

Caracalla the *Geticus* and the Preparations in 214

Spartan unit seem to have been equipped as anti-cataphract specialists armed with clubs/staves, while, in my opinion, the majority of the Spartan phalangites were equipped as hoplite/legionary spearmen.[12] See the illustrations.

It is unfortunate that we do not know which of the versions of Alexander's phalanx Caracalla adopted, because there were three variants: 1) one in which the Macedonian *phalangarii*, with some other units on their flanks, formed the front line (depth of eight *sarissaforoi* and four light infantry), behind which were placed the Greek hoplite phalanx as a second line; 2) a second version, which did not have the Greek hoplite phalanx behind it and which was therefore deployed sixteen deep, with eight light infantry behind; 3) a third version, which included the javelin throwers and Persian archers inside the phalanx (one form of the hollow infantry square/oblong).[13]

In light of the fact that Caracalla also recruited Spartan phalangites, it is possible that he placed Spartan/Laconian hoplites behind his Macedonians, so he would have used the first version. The problem with this interpretation is that the tombstone of Alexianus includes Hercules' club, which is indicative of the use of the Spartans just behind the Macedonian phalanx, from which they would have charged out together with the *lanciarii* and other lightly armed troops to engage the enemy cataphracts before the phalanx. The clubs would have been used to pummel the heavily armoured enemy with blows, and the men using this tactic would have been deployed in open order so that they could avoid the enemy spears and horses. The other tactical variant used with this system was to place a wedge or wedges of *lanciarii* in kneeling position in front of the Macedonian phalanx proper, with the clubmen just behind the *lanciarii*, and then send the clubmen forward when the enemy cavalry were brought to a halt before the wedge with thrust and thrown *lanceae*. In light of this, it is not certain what Caracalla's intentions were in this

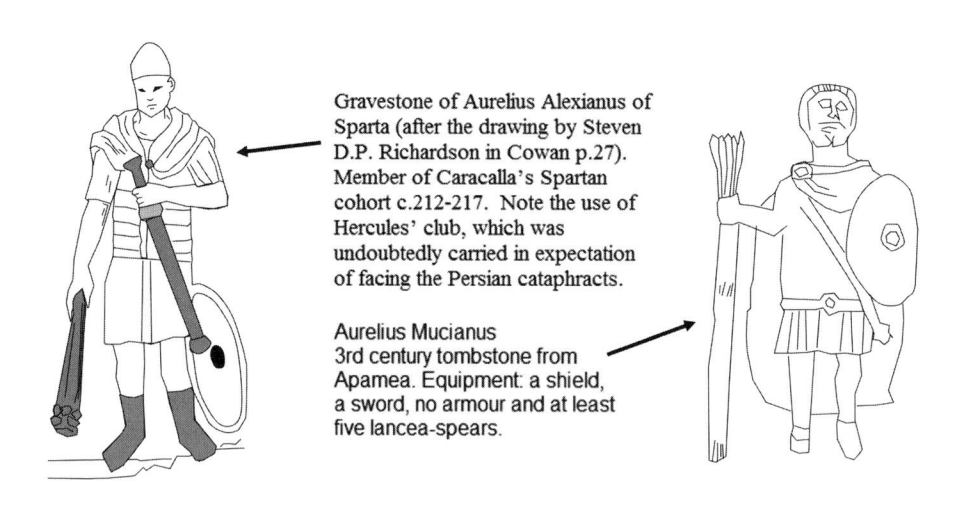

Gravestone of Aurelius Alexianus of Sparta (after the drawing by Steven D.P. Richardson in Cowan p.27). Member of Caracalla's Spartan cohort c.212-217. Note the use of Hercules' club, which was undoubtedly carried in expectation of facing the Persian cataphracts.

Aurelius Mucianus
3rd century tombstone from Apamea. Equipment: a shield, a sword, no armour and at least five lancea-spears.

Caracalla the *Geticus* and the Preparations in 214   203

Left: Coin of Septimius Severus Imp. IIII = AD 194-195
Right: Coin of Caracalla Reverse Cos. II = AD 207 (drawn after Cohen)

Left and below right: Medallions of Caracalla found at Aboukir, Egypt, 1902. The hoard consists of 20 medallions, two of which are included here, and of 600 gold coins issued by various emperors from Alexander Severus (222-235) to Constantius I (293-306). One of the medallions bears an inscription Olympic Games 274 (AD 242-243), which may mean that the medallions were issued as prizes. However, it is also possible that both medallions were minted under Caracalla, perhaps in ca. 214-217.
Right: Coin minted at Hadrianopolis AD 198-217. My educated guess is that the coin was minted in 214 at a time when Caracalla was in the region.

A beardless Caracalla imitating Alexander the Great on a medallion (perhaps AD 215-217?)
Note the sideburns and the hoplite style shield. Note also the eagle grip of the sword and the spearhead. The spearhead suggests the use of some sort of cavalry spear in which the purpose was to avoid the danger of the spear penetrating too deep when thrust so that the spear could be drawn back if necessary. My own tentative suggestion is that the spear in question is the cavalry *xyston* of Arrian (*Technê Taktikê* 40.4), which was the name of the spear used by Alexander the Great. It is also probable that we should equate the *xyston* with the *lancea pugnatoria* which was also used as a throwing and thrusting weapon.

case, but my educated guess is that the Spartans were intended to be more versatile forces than the phalangites, and could therefore be compared with the hoplites and *hypaspistai*. Consequently, the first alternative is the likeliest. Further support for this conclusion can be found in the deployment pattern of forces at the Battle of Nisibis fought under Macrinus in 217. The Romans definitely used a second line in this battle, which I interpret to have been the equivalent of the Greek hoplite phalanx of Alexander – but with the difference that the second line consisted of regular legionaries and auxiliaries, and of the Spartan hoplites, not solely of the Greeks/Spartans. The probable composition of the first line would have been the pike phalanx in the centre, with legionaries on both flanks.

The use of the Macedonian phalanx indicates that Caracalla probably organized it according to the Macedonian system, so that the *dekarchia* (*decanus*/*contubernium*) of eight fighting men (plus one recruit and one servant for a total of ten) formed the core of the system. Consequently, the phalanx would have consisted of units of eight (ten), sixteen (two 'tens'), thirty-two, sixty-four, 128, 256, 512, 1,024, 2,048, 4,096, 8,192 or 16,364. The basic building block was the 256-man unit, which would have been deployed with a depth of either eight (if the rear was protected by a second phalanx, terrain, baggage train or camp etc.) or sixteen (if there was no second phalanx or other protection behind) men. The 256-man units were used to build up the larger units. The light-armed troops would have been deployed behind the *sarisoforoi*/*sarisaforoi*, and would have consisted of similarly divided units up to 8,192 men. The overall size of the Macedonian phalanx would have been 24,756 men (16,364 phalangites and 8,192 light-armed) plus the supernumeraries. The *sarisae*/*sarissae* were approximately 6m long, so that spearheads of five to six of those protruded out of the phalanx to present an impenetrable wall of spearpoints to the enemy in front. Caracalla's intention was undoubtedly to use the *sarisae* against the Parthian cavalry. The use of the shorter spear enabled him to deploy his new forces in the same manner as the rest of his army. It is unfortunate that we do not know whether the short spear meant the regular cavalry spear of c. 3.74m (later called as *kontarion*, i.e. the short Gallic *kontos*/*contus* of Arrian) or the even shorter spear of c. 2.5m, because there would have been a slight difference in its usability as a throwing weapon. Both could be used for thrusting and throwing, but the shorter version was naturally better suited to this. Regardless, it is still clear from the weaponry that Caracalla wanted to have the option of using his Macedonians like regulars or like the *hypaspistai* and other units that Alexander the Great usually posted on the flanks of the Macedonian phalanx.

The use of the phalanx as such was not novel, because it had always been employed by the Romans, but what was unique was the use of the *sarisoforoi*/*sarisaforoi*/*sarissaforoi* (*sarissa*/*sarisa*-pike-bearers). The older variant with the heavy-armed spearmen in the front (3.74m *kontarion*/*kontos* or longer than average *pilum*) and the javelin (*lanceae*) throwers behind can also be found in the earlier *Ektaxis kata Alanôn* and *Techne Taktike* of Arrianos and later *Peri Strategikes*/*Strategias* of Syrianus Magister (16.40–50, esp. 45ff.).[14] However, in Syrianus' version, the length of the spear/pike was shorter than the traditional Macedonian *sarisa* only the spearheads of the first four ranks stuck out of the formation, whereas in the traditional Hellenistic manuals it was stated that the spearheads of the first five ranks stuck out.[15]

Reconstruction of the Macedonian phalanx in Dodge, Alexander

Caracalla's phalangarii vs. Parthian cataphracted camel-rider

The length of the original *sarisa* was already a topic of hot debate in antiquity and later. I would suggest that Dio's '*dory makron*' (78.7.2) meant the real Macedonian *sarisa* (c. 6–7m) rather than the Late Roman 3.74m cavalry/infantry spear (*kontarion* = Gallic *kontos* of Arrian). The use of the longer spear/pike was advantageous when one wanted to engage cavalry. Similarly, it was advantageous to wear lighter linen armour and leather helmets in the heat of Mesopotamia, which was recognized by Caracalla – the fact that it was also cheaper to equip the men with these cannot have been seen as any drawback in a situation in which there was already a dearth of money thanks to the pay rises of the army.

Caracalla may also have recruited similar numbers of hoplites and light-armed troops from Greece/Sparta to serve in his Laconian phalanx as a substitute for the mercenary Greek hoplite phalanx used by Alexander at the battles of Granicus, Issus and Gaugamela behind the Macedonian phalanx, but the evidence for this is less certain because it is possible that Caracalla recruited only a smaller number, such as 1,024 Spartans to serve as clubmen, but I would still suggest that he recruited far greater numbers of these as hoplites than that – even the use of the word phalanx suggests this. This would mean that Caracalla envisaged an infantry force of at least about 50,000 footmen (two phalanxes with light infantry), but it is possible that he may have sought to use an even larger force because Alexander the Great had a hollow square array at the Battle of Gaugamela[16] and he had access to greater numbers of men. It is very likely that Caracalla used his regular legionaries and auxiliaries as spearmen on both sides of his Macedonian phalanx and behind it. It is quite probable that some of the spearmen (e.g. the Spartans) were equipped with the hoplite shields and spears shown in the coins and medallions of Septimius Severus and Caracalla.

Though not mentioned by our defective sources, there is also quite a strong possibility that Caracalla, while en route to the East, may have recruited cavalry from Macedonia and Thrace. According to the Epitome of Dio (78.8.1–2), on one occasion when he congratulated a *chiliarchos* (tribune?) on the agility with which he had leaped upon his horse, he asked: 'What country are you from?' When he learnt that he was from Macedonia and his name was Antigonos, and his father's name was Philippos, he immediately advanced him through the military ranks to the position of *strategos* (*dux*) and not much later appointed him a senator with the rank of an ex-praetor.[17] Since the extant sources do not mention all the details, it would not be too far-fetched to assume that when Caracalla recruited his *pezhetairoi* (Foot Companions, i.e. the phalangites), he would also have recruited *hetairoi* (Macedonian Horse Companions). It is clear that our extant sources are full of omissions. A good example of this is that while the Byzantine epitomator of Dio mentions the Macedonian phalanx, he fails to mention the Spartan/Laconian phalanx. In fact, without Herodian and some inscriptions we would know nothing about it. The extant sources are by no means perfect, and when Caracalla went to such lengths in his imitation of Alexander, why would he not have copied his cavalry too? If Caracalla did so, he probably followed the Hellenistic theoretical model and added 4,096 horsemen to his phalanx (were these the *Leones*?).

While Caracalla was recruiting, equipping and training the Macedonian and Spartan troops, he also made administrative arrangements in the Greek cities and reorganized the defences in the Balkans. After these had been satisfactorily performed, Caracalla, in the company of the Praetorian Prefect (not named), crossed the Hellespont in a ship. The yard-arm of the ship broke, so he and his bodyguards (*cum protectoribus*) were forced to climb first into a lifeboat/boat (*scapha*), from which he was then rescued into the trireme of the prefect of the fleet (not named).[18] Unfortunately, the sources do not mention the cause of the breaking-up of the yard-arm and shipwreck, which allows the making of all sorts of speculations. It is entirely possible or even probable that the construction of the ship had been manipulated to break up. The likeliest culprit is the Praetorian Prefect Macrinus, and the attempt on Caracalla's life can be equated with Nero's similar attempt to kill his mother, with equally poor results. It appears probable that the breaking-up of the yard-arm was indeed an attempt on Caracalla's life and that he held one of his spymasters guilty of either negligence or ill-will (see the next chapter). The crossing was celebrated in coins struck at Cyzicus/Kyzikos. See the drawing of the coin of Caracalla with a war galley.

It is also clear that part of Dio's unhappiness about being forced to pay for the upkeep of the troops and building of *mansiones* included this eastern campaign, because Dio himself accompanied the emperor at least up to Nicomedia, which suggests that he, as a Greek, had been ordered to take part in the preparations for war in the area. Consequently, it is clear that Caracalla was taking every possible step to ensure the success of his eastern campaign well in advance of the actual undertaking. Dio is just not prepared to accept the level of sophistication and thinking ahead involved in his pre-campaign preparations. Dio's account (78.21.1–4, esp. 3–4) also shows that Caracalla appointed Theocritus, his freedman, dance teacher and a member of his household staff, as *eparchos/praefectus* (Supreme Praetorian Prefect?), who held supreme position over the two Praetorian Prefects Adventus and Macrinus, and who was also conducting special operations while in charge of collecting supplies in the East. In this capacity, Theocritus had toured back and forth, probably in 214–215, to gather supplies for the upcoming campaign, just like the Late Roman prefects who had been put in charge of provisions. While he was performing his duties, he put to death many people in connection with the gathering of provisions or for other reasons. In Egypt, he is said to have killed *procurator Alexandri* Flavius Titianus because he offended him. However, Whittaker/Herodian (p.423) has suggested the possibility that Flavius Titianus may have been a relative of Pertinax's wife Flavia Titiana, and could therefore be considered a potential threat. Another possibility is that Titianus was involved in some sort of plot against Caracalla or that he simply refused to obey Theocritus, and that Caracalla's subsequent visit to Alexandria was somehow connected with this (see next chapter). Consequently, it is

208   Caracalla

clear that while performing his duties as the man in charge of supplies, Praetorian Prefect Theocritus was also performing internal security functions in the East.

Dio also noted that another imperial freedman, Epagathus, was his equal in powers and lawlessness, but unfortunately he (or the Byzantine epitomator) fails to specify what position Epagathus held in the imperial administration and what he actually did. The circumstantial evidence, however, suggests that he was also appointed as *eparchos*/Supreme Praetorian Prefect, because he was clearly in charge of the Praetorians at Rome under Alexander Severus. The logical solution therefore would be to see him as the Supreme Prefect of the Praetorian Guard in the West while Theocritus was the Supreme Prefect in the East. The problem with this is that Epagathus was in the East in 218, because Macrinus, after his defeat at Immae on 8 June, sent his son to him so that he would take him to the court of Artabanus to seek a place of refuge. In light of this, it might be reasonable to suggest that Epagathus probably served as the Praetorian Prefect of Julia Domna at Antioch in the same manner as Theocritus served under Caracalla until he was dispatched to Armenia. The fact that Epagathus was executed only after Alexander Severus became ruler, together with the fact that Macrinus' son was executed, proves that Epagathus duly handed over the son to Elagabalus' men in order to survive still another change of ruler. Epagathus was clearly a man who changed sides fast and easily, which made him untrustworthy in the eyes of the Severan women, who had him executed after they had themselves got rid off Elagabalus.[19]

Notes

1. The provinces reorganized: Fitz, pp.99–104.
2. I am not alone in thinking that it is quite possible that Caracalla did indeed encounter the real Goths rather than the Dacians. See Batty's comments, pp.385–90, 568.
3. Dio 78.16.7, 78.20.2–4, 79.6.5–6; SHA Car. 5.4, 6.6; Polybius 6.26. For the career of Triccianus, see PIR with Dio 79.13.4. For the horse guards, see also Speidel (1994) p.66. My reconstruction of the organization, however, differs from Speidel's view. As regards the possible strength of the *equites extraordinarii* and the number of barbarian cavalry recruited by Caracalla, one can make very speculative comments on the basis of the Republican practice and the known strength of the typical cavalry contingent of each legion. We know that the *equites extraordinarii* consisted of a third of the cavalry forces provided by the *socii*, so the *Leones* may have had something like 500–600 fighters (typical cavalry contingent of a legion) chosen from the forces provided by the *socii* (allies), which would mean that the German and Scythian cavalry would have consisted of about 1,000–1,200 horsemen, but there are several points which make this improbable. Firstly, the sources would not have made such a fuss over the recruiting of such small numbers of barbarian cavalry. Secondly, we do not know the size of any of the forces in question, so it is pointless to make such detailed speculations. Thirdly, the *Legio II Parthica* had its own cavalry contingent, which means that one cannot use the standard size of legionary cavalry as the starting point for such speculations. Fourthly,

the *equites extraordinarii* and *Leones* clearly had so many men that the sources thought these to be important also from the military point of view, which means that they had at least the same number of troops as the *Equites Singulares Augusti* (c. 2,000 at this point in time). Fifthly, none of the sources that mention the recruiting of barbarians into the Roman army before or after has made a fuss over the recruing of small numbers of men, but all refer to such only when large numbers were recruited. All in all, I would suggest that the barbarian allied cavalry consisted of a minimum of 10,000–16,000 men, while the *Leones* consisted of about 2,000 men.

4. For the Moorish units, see Hamdoune in general and esp. pp.156–57 for the Eastern campaign.
5. The fact that there were still elements at Rome when Caracalla had been murdered shows that he left some bodyguard units behind to secure the capital. For the bodyguard units in general, see the introduction with: Speidel (1994); Bohec (2009) pp.24–26, 30; Rankov (2000); Jallet-Huant; Durry.
6. For other attempts, see for example Garsoïan, pp.70–73, who summarizes the current theories. Most seem to agree, however, with Toumanoff's conclusion that Khusrov I is the father of Trdat/Tiridates II.
7. See Moses/Thomson, pp.210–13. The same problems in dating can also be found in Thomas Artsruni 1.8–9, who has used Moses as his source.
8. The Khazars and Basilk are naturally the names of the tribes that inhabited the areas north of the Caucasus at a later date, but one cannot exclude the possibility that some of their ancestral tribes would have lived north and north-east of the Alans and who would then have passed through Alanic lands to invade Armenia. Of note is the fact (Moses 2.65) that this Valarsh built a fortified city called Valarshapat where he settled the first colony of Jewish captives in Armenia to create a commercial town. One would like to know if this favouritism of the Jews was somehow connected with Caracalla's policies.
9. In other words, Antiochus was a Cynic. Dio's hostile diatribes are not worth much.
10. Cowan (2003b) pp.27–28 has made the educated guess that the *phalangarii* were formed out of the *Legio II Parthica* and Praetorians. As proof of this, he cites the instance of one member of the *Legio II Parthica* being a *phalangarius* in the phalanx of Alexander Severus. I do not see any reason for going this far in contradicting the evidence presented by the narrative sources. The existence of *phalangarius* in the *Legio II Parthica* for the reign of Alexander Severus does not prove that Caracalla would not have recruited a separate Macedonian phalanx out of new recruits. Regardless, since all new recruits would need drilling, it is still likely that some veterans from existing legions were transferred to the new phalanx to perform this function. In addition, the figure in Dio 78.7.1 is 16,000 ('*myrious kai hexakischilious*') men and not 15,000, as claimed by Cowan in his effort to try to prove that Caracalla actually formed his Macedonian phalanx out of the *Legio II Parthica* and *Praetoriani*.
11. As suggested by Cowan (2003b) p.28.
12. Dio 78.7.1–4 (esp. 78.7.1–2); SHA Car. 5.48; Herod. 4.8.2–3, 4.9.4–5. The *Pitanei* were a group of Spartans who may have been organized as a *lochos* in Sparta. Note also that Herodian equals the Spartan *lochos* with the Spartan phalanx. Cowan (2003) p.27 has suggested that the Spartan *lochos*/phalanx consisted of only about 500–1,000 men. The

evidence gathered by Cowan (2003) pp.27–28 of the equipment of the Spartan unit shows that at least some of them wore the regular *lorica segmentata* armour while they carried medium-length swords, oval shields and spears. I disagree with the estimated size in Cowan and also disagree with his conclusions regarding the equipment. The second-line hoplites of Alexander the Great had to cover the same width of ground as the frontline phalangites, and Caracalla was certainly aware of thise because he formed the *Pitanei*/Spartan *lochos*/Spartan phalanx. Note that the length of the Macedonian *xifos* was actually quite close to the period *spatha*, but with the difference that the entire sword was made out of iron. On the basis of my limited fencing experience, the longer quillons would have been very beneficial in actual combat fencing and one may speculate that the introduction of these swords would also have entailed a change in fencing style that would have exploited the presence of these more fully and also the change in balance of the weapon (the *xifos* was better suited to cuts than the *spatha/gladius*). It should still be noted that the use of shields was a better tactic than the use of quillons in directing the enemy weapons in the desired direction. Furthermore, the fighting spirit and morale of the unit was always more important than the equipment and tactics combined. Regardless, my own opinion is that the Macedonian/Greek style *xifos* was a better sword than the *spatha* and that the all-iron *kopis*-sabre was also better as a cavalry weapon than the period swords; the best evidence for both comes from the modern period analyses of the advantages of different kinds of swords in eighteenth-century treatises. The fact that the militaries (the Roman one included) are often conservative in their preferences and are also prone to follow military fashions (note e.g. the adoption of certain types of camouflage or the adoption of the beret etc. by the different armed forces of the world) means that the best and most efficient solution to the problem has not been (and will not be) adopted, despite evidence to the contrary. Soldiers have quite often been peacocks in the past, and this is in evidence even today. Ross Cowan (2009) pp.33–35 has also drawn attention to the fact that Dio calls Caracalla's Macedonian spears *doru* and not *sarrissa*. On the basis of this, he suggests that Caracalla's phalangite was not armed with a pike (*sarissa*) and short spear, but with a spear and javelin. I disagree in the strongest terms. All sources make it quite clear that Caracalla imitated Macedonian equipment and also the Macedonian unit structure and tactics (contrary to what Cowan states). The use of the *doru/dory* by Dio in this context is by no means conclusive. Dio's military terminology is not exact and it is easy to see that a spear was just a spear for this man. Contrary to what Cowan states, the events of the reign of Alexander Severus cannot really be used to counter the information in the same sources that refer to the reforms of Caracalla. The sources state one thing for the reign of Caracalla and another for the reign of Alexander. It is clear that the Romans abandoned Caracalla's reforms after the Battle of Nisibis. See Appendix 2. As regards the equipment of the Spartan phalanx, it is quite easy to understand that the vast majority of its members would also have been equipped as Spartan hoplites, as implied by the sources, and not as legionaries or clubmen with *lorica segmentata*. The new recruits would have needed drill masters and officers, which means that Caracalla would have transfererred such from the old units to the new ones. It is quite obvious that they would have kept their old equipment because its replacement would have been expensive.

13. Syvanne (2010), *The Macedonian Art of War*, available online at academia.edu.
14. Usually assumed to date either from the sixth century or from the Middle Byzantine period. See my entry on Arrian in *Philosophers of War*, which also refers to Wheeler's outstanding studies of the Roman and Late Roman phalanx. It should be noted that even the cohortal tactics can be seen as a phalanx with a different number of lines. It should also be stressed that the Macedonian pike phalanx was not so difficult to manoeuvre as all too often assumed. Each unit was entirely capable of performing multiple manoeuvres, the only difference with the typical Roman cohorts being that the pikes were slower to reposition than the shorter *pila* or *hastae*.
15. There was a lot of confusion among the ancient authors of the details relating to Alexander's conquests, his army and his appearance. For example, Herodian (4.9.3) claims that Alexander, like Achilles, was a very strong and tall man.
16. See Syvanne, *The Macedonian Art of War*, available online at academia.edu.
17. Dio (78.8.3) also notes a trial in which Antoninus acted as a judge in a case involving a criminal whose name was Alexander. In this case, Caracalla ordered the prosecutor not to associate the name of Alexander with the crimes committed by the person. Note that this was not the first time the Romans imitated the Macedonian phalanx because, for example, Nero created his own.
18. Herod. 4.8.3; SHA Car. 5.8; Dio 78.16.7. It is improbable that the Prefect of the Fleet would have been the Prefect of the Praetorian Fleet or Fleets, because the flagship is a trireme. The extant evidence suggests that the flagships of the Prefects of the Praetorian fleets were either sixes or fives. The triremes were the typical flagships of the provincial fleets. The fact that the prefect rescued Caracalla supports the same. It is very likely that the person is the Prefect of the Fleet of Pontus, because Cyzicus (which minted a series of coins to celebrate the crossing, one of which is included in the text as an example) was the HQ of the *Classis Pontica*. The Prefect of the Praetorian Fleets appears to have supported Macrinus in his attempt to murder Caracalla. See chapter 11.
19. Dio 78.21, 79.23.1–2, 79.39–40.5, 80.2.2–4 (Loeb ed. pp.480–82); PIR Epagathus. The facts that the Praetorians killed Ulpian, and Epagathus was considered to have been chiefly responsible, means that the Praetorians had killed Ulpian on behalf of Epagathus. In light of this, it is probable that Epagathus served as Praetorian Prefect from the reign of Caracalla up to the reign of Alexander Severus.

Chapter Eight

Caracalla's Anabasis Phase 2: Caracalla Arrives in Asia to make Further Preparations

After the crossing, Caracalla went first to Pergamum to find a 'treatment' for his ailments at the shrine of Aesculapius (Asklepios) or those of his mother, and/or to show his thanks for his salvation when crossing. While at Pergamum, there were people who argued amongst themselves who was the author of a verse which called Caracalla the Ausonian Beast (Dio 78.16.7ff.). According to Dio, the man who had composed the verse was particularly proud of it. Dio also claims that Caracalla was equally proud and pleased to be called a beast, and that the great number of people that Caracalla put to death while at Bergamum proved him as such. What is of note is that Caracalla was pleased at a joke, which suggests a very strong self-esteem; and even more importantly, the visit to the shrine of Aesculapius was once again followed by a purge of suspected plotters. These were the people put to death at Bergamum. After the shipwreck, Caracalla had every reason to suspect a plot against him. In this case, it is uncertain whether he received any letters at the shrine or whether he just visited it so that his enemies would believe that he obtained supernatural assistance to find out who the culprits were. Both are possible, but considering the use of Caracalla's daily use of couriers to visit the shrines, it is once again more likely that he suspected some persons and then obtained confirmation from his intelligence operatives through these couriers.

It was only after this that he went to Troy/Ilium, where he emulated Alexander by honouring Achilles with sacrifices and races in armour. According to Herodian (4.8.4ff.), while there Caracalla sought out someone to be his Patroclus so that he could then bury him in a funeral. Does Herodian imply that Caracalla had a homosexual encounter with this Patroclus or with some unknown Hephaistion, the friend of Alexander? This is very unlikely on the basis of the incident that took place at Alexandria (see Chapter 9) and because it would be very strange if he had left out such a hostile versions of events. The referral to Patroclus simply means that Caracalla killed Festus so that he could be the Patroclus. The name of this Patroclus removes the last shred of doubt. Herodian claims that Caracalla found his Patroclus when one of his favourite freemen, Festus, *a cubiculo et a memoria*,[1] died. Herodian notes that some accused Caracalla of having poisoned Festus while others stated that Festus had died of disease. Herodian claims that Caracalla made himself the object of derision when he threw a lock of his hair upon the fire, because

Caracalla was supposedly almost bald. Does this rather mean that Caracalla wore his hair short in the military manner, as is represented for example in the bust in the Metropolitan Museum, or that he was older than the official version would have it?

What is notable about this episode is that Caracalla was once again imitating Alexander the Great with his visit to Troy, and also recreating the funeral of Patroclus by Achilles. It is quite probable that Festus had been Caracalla's spymaster and that he had been put to death with a poison (as Caracalla was accused to have done), because he had either not found out the plot to kill Caracalla with the defective ship or had been party to the plot, the latter being the likelier alternative. It is unlikely to be a coincidence that Festus was a close friend of Macrinus (SHA Macr. 2–5). It is more than likely that we should also connect Caracalla's visit to the shrine of Aesculapius with the death of Festus – Caracalla always visited the shrines before he eliminated someone. It is quite probable that it was there that he once again received a report from one of his spies in the form of supernatural advice. Unfortunately, it is impossible to know whether the report was accurate. What is certain, however, was that this was not the end of the cabal to kill Caracalla.

Festus' replacement appears to have been the eunuch Sempronius Rufus (the *cubicularii* were typically eunuchs, because they also looked after the empress' bedchamber), who according to Dio controlled the soldiers who spied upon the senators and their access to the emperor. In other words, it appears probable that one part of Caracalla's internal security apparatus operated under the jurisdiction of the *Praepositus Sacri Cubiculi* (Head of the Sacred Bedchamber), whose staff consisted of the staff of the sacred bedchamber, the *cubicularii*, and its secretaries, as during Late Roman times. In addition, it appears probable that, also just like during Late Roman times, the head of the *scrinia memoria* and his staff issued the letters of appointments to the *frumentarii* (in Late Roman times to the *agentes in rebus*) and the commanders of the *alae* and cohorts (i.e. the auxiliaries).[2] Consequently, I would suggest that in the case of Festus and Rufus, they not only issued the appointments to the *frumentarii*, but also controlled their activities, just as they did the activities of the soldiers used for security purposes. However, since these matters were not institutionalized until the fifth century, it is possible that Caracalla had given his freedmen even wider powers than their successors held.

Caracalla moved from Ilium to the winter quarters at Nicomedeia. There he received reports from his informers that were so detailed that they listed even the most insignificant matters. At the same time, Caracalla ordered his soldiers to keep their ears and eyes open for any dissenting voices. He also ordered the eunuch Sempronius Rufus to take control of the informers who were used to spy on the senatorial class and their opinions. Caracalla was clearly nervous after the probable attempt against his life. According to Dio (78.18.4–19.2), the governor of Baetica in Spain, Caecilius Aemilianus, was put to death because he had consulted an oracle of Hercules at Gades and was therefore suspected of conspiring against Caracalla. His text implies that this took place when Caracalla was at Nicomedia in 214, but

Whittaker (Herod. p.409, n.3) suggests that this took place while Caracalla was organizing the northern frontier in the autumn of 213, because the new governor of Baetica, Caius Julius Cerealis, can be attested to have been in office in 214, but this is not conclusive because it is possible that there could have been two governors in the same year, the one who was killed and a new one. I would suggest that it was only after this that Caracalla divided the provinces of Hispania because of the suspected usurpation. Before this there had not been any fear that a governor of a province with a single legion would contemplate any usurpation. This shows that Caracalla had a long grip over the whole extent of his vast empire. In my opinion, it is probable that the news of Aemilianus' disloyalty reached Caracalla at one of the shrines mentioned above, and from which he then sent the order via couriers to kill the ingrate.[3]

I would suggest that on the basis of the SHA (Car. 10.6) and Herodian (4.6.4) there is a possibility that the execution of Helvius Pertinax the younger (son of the like-named emperor) and Flavius Titianus (possibly a relative of Pertinax's wife Flavia Titiana) took place at about this time or already before that in late 214 after the Goths had been defeated. The reason for this is that the Pertinax Jr. is claimed to have joked that Caracalla should add *Geticus Maximus* to his title because he had killed Geta and had defeated the Gothic Getae. The reason for the execution was Pertinax Jr.'s alleged support of Geta. In light of the Hellespont incident it is also possible to speculate that the conspirators could have contemplated the possibility of nominating Pertinax as emperor instead of Caracalla and if this was brought to Caracalla's attention it would have sealed Pertinax' fate. However, the perceived support of Geta, which implied that Pertinax did not accept Caracalla's right to rule, would have been reason enough. On the basis of this it is also easy to see that there could have been a connection between Pertinax and the city of Alexandria with its organized citizen body that could be seen to conspire against Caracalla at least in the mind of the latter. Caracalla's behaviour at winter quarters towards the members of his official Imperial Council is also curious. According to Dio (78.17.3ff.), Caracalla was in the habit of convening his council for public business after dawn, but then, when the councillors, including Dio, came, he would keep them waiting until noon or even evening. They were not even allowed into the vestibule, but forced to stand outside. While this was going on, Caracalla spent his time driving chariots, fighting as a gladiator and drinking, the last of which caused him hangovers. He would mix great bowls of wine and pass it round in cups to the soldiers guarding him. All of this took place before the eyes of the distinguished councillors, most of whom were senators, who were forced to stand outside the palace. On the surface, this would seem a childish game meant to humiliate the senators belonging to his official council, which could also be considered unwise as it angered the men in question. However, this is only the surface. In truth, Caracalla had already angered the senators with the monetary demands he had made, which meant that he could not obtain their goodwill. The case for the equestrian councillors is less clear. Caracalla's power rested solely on the loyalty of his soldiers, and the public humiliation of the senators before them undoubtedly strengthened the loyalty of the men towards him. The high and mighty aristocrats were forced to stand outdoors, just like the rank-and-file soldiers. Furthermore, it is quite clear that the advice offered by these distinguished senators was quite worthless, if Dio's own comments can used as evidence of the views held by the other councillors. It was clearly a waste of time to listen to these men.

However, there is one problem with the above, which is that according to Danuta Okon's article, Caracalla's official council is known to have included his real friends and supporters, the careers of whom he also promoted, and some of whom are also known to have been good generals. These men included Aelius Coeranus, M. Antonius Gordianus Semprosianus Romanus (the future Gordian/Gordianus I), M. Antonius Iuvenis (a very old man who did not hold any offices under Caracalla and *frater Arvalis*), *comes expeditionis Orientalis* T. Quir. Aurelianus (or two separate Aureliani, if the *consul suffectus* Aurelianus killed in 217 is a different person; a favourite of Caracalla), D. Caelius (Calvinus) Balbinus (a favourite and the future emperor), L. (Claudius) Cassius Dio Cocceianus (the historian and councillor to several emperors), P. Catius Sabinus (favoured by Caracalla), C. Iulius Avitus Alexianus (husband of Julia Maesa and therefore relative), C. Julius Septimius Castinus, C. Octavius Appius Suetrius Sabinus, Q. Maecius Laetus (Praetorian Prefect c. 205–214), T. Messius Extricatus (ordinary consul in 217, civil servant under Caracalla and Praetorian Prefect under Elagabalus), M. Oclatinius Adventus (Praetorian Prefect) and M. Opellius Macrinus (Praetorian Prefect, incompetent as general). These are the only *amici* and *comites* that are known with certainty. According to Okon (p.259), the case for Q. Hedius Rufus Lollianus Gentianus and C. Ovintius Tertullus is unproven. Out of these, only four belonged to the old aristocracy (Balbinus, Dio, Catius Sabinus and Suetrius Sabinus), seven were *homines novi* (Coeranus, Avitus, Castinus, Laetus, Extricatus, Adventus and Macrinus) and the status of the rest is unknown. It is still important to recognize that even if the majority of these men were 'new men', most of them had started their careers well before Caracalla came to power. The sole exception appears to have been the Egyptian Coeranus, who had been demoted during the Plautianus affair, but who became consul in 212 and then Caracalla's advisor. The Egyptians were so hated in Rome that Coeranus became the first Egyptian ever to hold the consulate.[4]

This begs the question: who were the persons that Caracalla humiliated in public at Nicomedia? We know that these included at least Dio, who was certainly not competent in military matters and it is unsurprising that Caracalla did not value his views. The others who definitely accompanied Caracalla to the East were Iulius Avitus, Adventus, Macrinus, *comes expeditionis Orientalis/consul Suffectus* Aurelianus and possibly also Catius Sabinus (nominated for a second consulship in 216) and Extricatus (nominated ordinary consul in 217, presumably because of his services). Gordianus served as governor of Lower Britain in 216, which means that he probably did not accompany the emperor. We also know that the experienced military commanders and close and loyal friends of Caracalla, Castinus and Suetrius Sabinus, did not accompany him to the East. Caracalla wisely chose these two men to look after the Dacian and Pannonian borders. We do not know what Balbinus did. Okon suggests that he was made governor of Asia in 214, which would mean that he would have accompanied Caracalla, but would then have been dispatched to Africa, presumably in 215. Balbinus, however, was not known for his military experience and would not have contributed anything to the discussion.[5] This means that only two of the men, Aurelianus and Adventus, can be considered to have been military men. Caracalla did not need their advice, because he could always convene his military council (used by all commanders) where both men would have been present, if the emperor so desired. Even more importantly, the high-handed treatment appears not to have affected their loyalty – it is also possible that Caracalla did not even call all of them to attend the humiliating sessions, because the Late Roman equivalent of the Imperial Council did not have military commanders as permanent members. Consequently, with the exception of Macrinus, all of the councillors stayed loyal to Caracalla despite the apparently humiliating treatment. In light of this, it is possible that Dio's bitterness was not shared by all of the councillors. Furthermore, Caracalla did not need their advice, even in the civilian field, as often as Dio would have liked, because Julia Domna was in charge of the daily administration at least from 215 onwards.

Gladiators fight as horsemen. Drawn after Mazois' reconstruction of a painting in Pompeii.

While at winter quarters, Caracalla drilled his Macedonian phalanx and had two very large war engines built for the Armenian and Parthian wars. As noted, his other pastimes were the driving of chariots, the slaying of wild beasts, the fights as gladiator and the drinking in the company of his guards with the consequent hangovers.[6] It is unfortunate that the sources fail to mention whether Caracalla tilted the gladiatorial fights in his favour like Commodus did, or fought like any gladiator. In light of Caracalla's readiness to fight duels with enemy chieftains, it is possible that he fought honest fights, but I would still suspect that the fights in question were performed with training weapons rather than real ones. It seems quite probable that one of the reasons for the love that the soldiers had towards Caracalla was his ability as a fighter and duellist. The accompanying illustration from Pompeii by Mazois shows how gladiators fought on horseback, which is much less well-known than the fights on foot or on chariots. The regular cavalry would have used a similar fighting style when using the shorter spears and javelins. It is unfortunate that we do not know what fighting styles were employed by Caracalla in his training and what types of gladiatorial combats he held in his own honour at Nicomedia on his birthday on 4 April 215 (Dio 78.19).

The drinking, games and the driving of chariots were again forms of Alexander imitation, but just like under Alexander, they had also a military function.[7] The soldiers were kept busy and in training, while the drinking bouts with the soldiers showed Caracalla's camaraderie.

The two war engines were built in such a manner that these could be taken apart and carried in ships to Syria, to the city of Seleucia, the port of Antioch. Unfortunately, Dio does not tell us what these '*mêchanêmata*' were, which leaves open three possibilities: large siege towers (*helepoleis*); siege rams; or some sort of large stone-throwers. The likeliest alternative is the battering ram of the kind used by Septimius Severus, which the sources prove to have been the principal means of bringing down walls during the third and fourth centuries (see Syvanne MHLR). The following illustrations drawn by Montfaucon after the Arch of Septimius Severus show the two battering rams used by Severus against the Parthians during his campaign. It is probable that Caracalla's two '*mêchanêmata*' were based on those. Caracalla's Eastern campaign forces included the field army that he had previously employed in Germany, so it included the entire fighting strength of the regular bodyguard units (*Praetoriani, Equites Singulares Augusti, Speculatores, Aulici*) and *Legio II Parthica* (Albanum), at least one cohort of the *Urbaniciani* (*cohors XIV*), the entire *II Adiutrix* (*Pannonia Inferior*, probable) and detachments from the legions *I Adiutrix* (Pannonia Inferior; in my opinion it may have been included in its entirety), *I Minervia* (Germania Superior, possible), *III Augusta* (Africa), *III Italica* (Raetia), *III Cyrenaica* (Arabia), *III Gallica* (Syria Phoenicia), *IV Flavia* (Syria Coele), *IV Scythica* (Syria Coele), *VI Ferrata* (Palestine, uncertain), *VII Claudia* (Moesia, possible but not securely so), *VIII Augusta* (Germania Superior, probable), *X Fretensis* (Palestine, uncertain), *XIII Gemina* (Dacia), *XIV Gemina* (Pannonia Superior), *XVI Flavia* (Syria Coele), *XXII Primigenia* (Germania Superior, probably) and *XXX Ulpia* (Germania Inferior, probably). The Mesopotamian legions *I Parthica* and *III Parthica* would have naturally fought in their entirety. There is no evidence for the presence of any detachments from the Moesian legions *I Italica* and *XI Claudia* for this campaign.[8]

The complete fighting strength of the bodyguard units, *II Parthica*, *II Adiutrix*, *I Parthica* and *III Parthica*, would add up to a minimum of 30,000 footmen and 6,000 horsemen, plus the *Leones*. Since the typical legionary detachment consisted of 1,000 or 2,000 footmen, it is impossible to make an exact estimate for their size, beyond the general statement that the legionary detachments consisted of 17,000 to 34,000 men. There is also the additional complication that we do not know how many legionary horsemen were deployed alongside the footmen. It is possible that the detachments had the same number of foot and horse as the units which were included in their entirety. But this was not the entire armed strength fielded by Caracalla. In addition to this we should include the Moorish/Berber auxiliaries and allies, other auxiliaries from Europe and auxiliaries that had previously been fighting in Europe, such as Osroenian mounted archers. Furthermore, the navy was not only used for the transporting of men and supplies, but detachments also accompanied the land forces on campaign.

As noted above, Caracalla had not been satisfied even with these but had recruited large numbers of Germanic and Scythian mercenary allies, the bodyguard unit of the *Leones* and the Macedonian and Spartan phalanxes. The Macedonian phalanx alone would have added an additional 24,000 men to the figure. The barbarian mercenaries recruited by Caracalla would have consisted of at least the same number of men. And we should not forget that the Eastern front possessed its own garrison forces that had not taken part in the previous European campaigns. These consisted of nine legions, of which the above-mentioned Mesopotamian legions and detachments from the other eastern legions would have been preserved for the campaign against Parthia, while the Galatia-Cappadocian *XII Fulminata* and *XV Apollinaris* would have been delegated to the Armenian theatre, and we should not forget that there was also at least an equal number of auxiliary and allied units (Armenians and Arabs). The eastern auxiliaries and allies would have added a minimum of 45,000 troops to the men available for use. Caracalla's campaign army was huge by any standards. Cowan (2002, pp.154–155) has estimated that Caracalla's field army consisted of 80,000–90,000 men, in addition to which came the men detailed for the Armenian theatre, but on the basis of my calculations it is quite possible that he may have had even more – considerably more, with the allies perhaps c. 150,000 men plus the non-combatants. Caracalla had come well-prepared for any eventuality and could easily divide his massive army into two very large armies that could fight offensive campaigns simultaneously in Armenia and Parthia.

Notes

1. The identification of Festus as Marcius Festus with the titles in Whittaker/Herodian, p.417 n.3. Note the unification of offices.
2. For the Late Roman memoriales, see A.H.M. Jones, p.576ff.; Delmaire, p.69.
3. Dio 78.17.1ff.
4. List of councillors and their careers in Okon. See also PIR. The SHA (Gordiani 4.1-3) claims that Gordian (future emperor) held consulship simultaneously with Caracalla in 213 and that Gordian's consulship was envied by Caracalla because Gordian had better looking togas with broad stripes and because Gordian held games that surpassed Caracalla's own games. If this is true, then it did not affect Gordian's standing in Caracalla's eyes. Gordian belonged to his amici and was also promoted by him.
5. Iulius Avitus was the governor of Asia who then accompanied Caracalla to Mesopotamia, from where he was sent to Cyprus, where he died of old age and illness (Dio 79.30.2ff.). Castinus was governor of Dacia and Sabinus of Pannonia in 217 (Dio 79.13.2). For the careers of the rest, see Okon and PIR.
6. This and the following is based on Herod. 4.8.3–6; Dio 78.16.7–18.1.
7. Alexander's charioteering, for example in Alexander Romance 1.18-19 (notably in some of the texts the Olympic contest occurred at Rome).
8. List of legions in Whittaker/Herodian, pp.435–37, after Debevoise, pp.263–64); and Cowan (2002) pp.135–55; (2009) p.30ff. *Aulici* etc. are my additions.

Chapter Nine

Caracalla's Anabasis Phase 3: Campaigns in Armenia and Alexandria, 215

In the spring 215, Caracalla left Nicomedeia for Antioch, probably following the eastern route of Prusias to Ancyra, Caesarea Mazaca, Tyana, Cilician Gates and Antioch.[1] His purpose was to invade Parthia via Armenia and/or Mesopotamia and to secure the return of the King of Armenia, Tiridates/Tigran, and Antiochus. While still en route to begin the campaign, however, Caracalla received from Vologaesus a peace proposal. According to Dio (78.21.1), Caracalla's preparations had frightened Vologaesus, with the result that he surrendered both Tiridates and Antiochus. This is not surprising, because Caracalla seems to have fielded a truly huge army (bodyguard units, German and Scythian auxiliaries, Moorish auxiliaries, the phalanxes, eastern regulars and detachments from western units). As a result of Vologaesus' very conciliatory moves, Caracalla immediately disbanded the expedition against him.

On the basis of the very defective evidence it is possible that Theocritus campaigned together with Valarsh, the new King of Armenia, but it should be stressed that the evidence for this is far from conclusive. However, what appears to be more certain is that Valarsh fought against nomadic invaders in 215 and then pursued them to the north of the Caucasus, where he was killed by an arrow. This was then exploited by Artabanus, who installed Khosrov the Great on the throne. What is practically certain is that the Armenian campaign of Theocritus against the Armenians mentioned by Dio did not take place in 215 but in 216.

At Tyana, Caracalla and his mother appear to have honoured the famous miracle worker Apollonius of Tyana, who lived at the time of Domitian and was said to have performed similar miracles to Jesus Christ. It appears very likely that they were seeking a cure to Julia's breast cancer from the shrine or that they were there as tourists. In fact, in the religious battleground of third-century Rome, the pagans seem to have promoted Apollonius of Tyana as their counterpart for Jesus Christ of the Christians.[2] As will be shown in my forthcoming book dealing with his reign, Aurelian (Aurelianus) was the first one to try officially the expedient of having a single supreme god *Sol Invictus* and Apollonius of Tyana as its Christ.[3] Aurelian's experiment ended in failure. However, it served later as a model for none other than Constantine the Great, who realized that it was futile to make ersatz gods when one could instead invoke the support of the real Christian God.

Since the campaign against Parthia via Armenia was now off the books, Caracalla was again free to follow the route taken by Alexander the Great. He first stopped at Antioch, where he stayed for a while. While there, he emulated Alexander the Great by shaving off his beard (Dio 78.20.1). The beardless face or short beard helped in a melee because the enemy could not take hold of the beard, as had also been recognized by Alexander the Great. See the drawing of the medallion with Alexander's face in Chapter 7. After this, Caracalla marched his army to Alexandria. He left his mother at Antioch to receive petitions. She was also in charge of Caracalla's correspondence in Latin and Greek, except the most important cases. According to Dio, Caracalla did not heed anyone's advice, including that of his mother, but this is clearly incorrect, as this instance shows. Julia Domna was clearly placed in charge of daily governance of the empire while the son took care of military campaigns. It is probable that it was then that Julia Domna reproached Caracalla that he was spending too vast sums upon soldiers, with the result that 'There is no longer any source of revenue, either just or unjust, left to us.' Caracalla replied to her, while exhibiting his sword (Dio's *xifos* can mean either the Roman *gladius* or *parazonium* or the real *xifos*, because Caracalla had adopted Macedonian equipment), 'Be of good cheer, mother; for as long as we have this, we shall not run short of money.'[4] In other words, since Caracalla was running out of money, he decided to obtain it with the help of his sword.

It is probably not a coincidence that Caracalla introduced his famous double *denarius* in which he wore the radiate crown in early 215, which modern numismatics call *Antoninianus*. This double *denarius* had a silver content of one and a half of what two *denarii* would have had, so Caracalla saved silver if he paid his troops with these coins. This proves that Caracalla really needed new sources of revenue and income. The further diluting of silver content also suggests that Caracalla did not want to anger the senatorial class more than he already had with his extra taxes – the senators were already paying money and provisions to cover the costs of Caracalla's eastern campaign. Caracalla needed to use his sword. Military conquests and pillaging of enemy territory would enable him to pay for the upkeep of his army.

Caracalla already had a suitable candidate in store for his project to obtain extra revenue for his soldiers. He had heard from his informers that the population of Alexandria was intensely hostile towards him.[5] In addition, according to Dio (78.21.1–4), when Theocritus had been travelling and gathering provisions for the campaign (either his own, Caracalla's or both), Flavius Titianus, procurator at Alexandria, was put to death because he had offended Theocritus. To me, this suggests that there had been some problems in getting the necessary provisions from Alexandria. It is also possible that Theocritus had detected the existence of a plot against the emperor in the city and that the executions of Pertinax Jr. and Titianus formed part of this purge. In my opinion, it is probable that Caracalla's original intention was to punish the Alexandrians with extra taxes and other measures meant to secure the city, and that it was only the subsequent behaviour

Caracalla Antoninianus, 215 AD.
ANTONINVS PIVS AVG GERM, radiate & draped bust/ PM TR P XVIII COS IIII PP, Sol driving a galloping quadriga (four-horsed chariot). Another common type of Antoninianus had naked Apollo driving a quadriga. Note, however, that Caracalla and Julia Domna naturally aimed to please as large an audience as possible with the godly images included in the coins and they did not limit their gods or goddesses to these two. The radiate head became one of the standard coin types for the emperors of the third century.

of the Alexandrians that turned this into something much more violent. Garcia (p.68ff.) suggests that the reason for the visit was that the Alexandrians had revolted against Caracalla's extra war taxes and that Caracalla needed to punish them so as their fate would serve as a warning example to others. This sounds quite correct.

Herodian (4.9.1ff., with Dio 78.22.1ff.), however, claims that Caracalla's plan had all along been to massacre large numbers of Alexandrians as a form of punishment after continuous reports that he had received from 211–215 which stated that the Alexandrians were making fun of him. Whittaker (Herod. pp.424–25) suggests that Caracalla may have considered the Serapeum of Alexandria, the temple complex of Serapis, to have been the centre of opposition against him thanks to its pro-Geta stance and therefore potentially dangerous to his rule. He also suggests that the same was true of the philosophic schools (probably connected with Aristotle) and that their public mess halls were closed due to this. These conclusions appear quite sound. Whittaker also thinks it improbable that the original reason for the troubles would have been Caracalla's decision to expel the native Egyptians (*xenoi*, foreigners) from the city, but that this would have taken place only after the troubles, so Caracalla's intention would have been to prevent the occurance of similar problems in the city in the future, especially on the festival of Serapis on 25 April. In this case it is impossible to be certain, because both versions are possible, even if the latter is more likely. I would suggest that it is probable that Caracalla's original intention was just to purge his enemies from the Serapeum, close the mess halls of the Aristotelean school, impose heavy taxes on the Alexandrians who had opposed his prefect and possibly to expel the 'foreigners' from the city, and when his plans were then violently opposed and the angry mob attacked him, he changed his mind. However, there is a distinct possibility that initially the main targets were the tax contractors who had failed to deliver their due and that the punishment became more violent as a result of popular unrest, and that it was as a result of this that the purge was extended to the rest of the citizen body. For example, according to Banchich's edition of Peter the Patrician (frg.162), Caracalla targeted in particular Alexandrian contractors, while according to Synkellos (AM 5701) Caracalla massacred a multitude of Alexandrians because of riots.

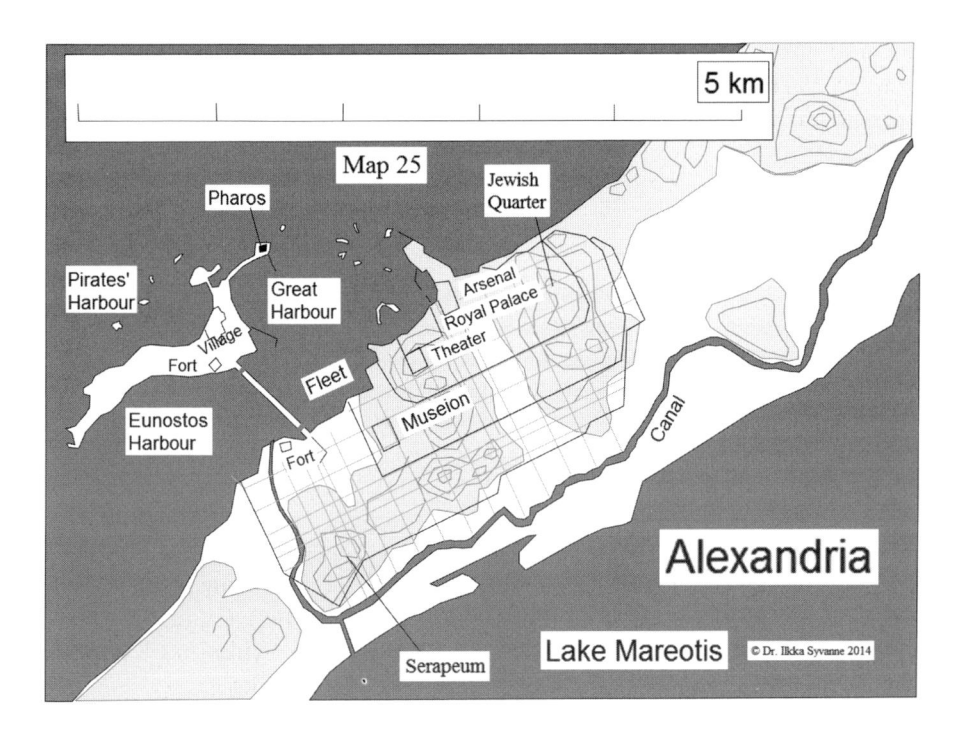

According to Herodian (4.8.7ff.), Caracalla entered Alexandria with his army and marched to the temple of Serapis, where he was enthusiastically greeted. It is probable that Caracalla visited the temple twice – first when he entered the city and then again when he launched his massacre – because all accounts suggest that Caracalla spent at least a day or more in the city before he began his attack and that he performed rites of purification in the temple when the massacre was ongoing. Herodian (4.9.3) states that Caracalla had received reports that the Alexandrians jokingly gave Julia Domna the name Jocasta, but he may also imply that they did that when Caracalla arrived as it was in their nature to joke. At about the time of Caracalla's visit there were certainly riots in the city where such insults could have taken place, even if it cannot be proven that these riots took place when Caracalla was there (Whittaker, pp.422–23). In his translation of the relevant part, Whittaker (p.423.n.3) notes that this insult had a double meaning. Jocasta had two sons called Eteocles and Polynices, one with a legal claim to power and the other an illegal claim. The other point was naturally that Jocasta was also the mother of Oedipus. This suggests that Caracalla was the illegitimate son of Julia. Perhaps their joking was too close to the truth. In addition to this, the Alexandrians jeered Caracalla for imitating Alexander and Achilles because they were claimed to have been tall while Caracalla was a small man. This was silly because Alexander was a short man, but the intention is still clear. It did not hurt Caracalla to make an example of the city dwellers who had not shown him and his mother due respect. Dio (78.22.) states that when Caracalla entered the city, he was at first greeted by the locals, who welcomed him with mystic and sacred symbols (clearly followers of Serapis). They were then greeted cordially by Caracalla, who entertained them at a banquet and only after this put them to death. This suggests that Caracalla had indeed learnt that some members of the local upper classes belonging to the cult of Serapis were consipiring against him, and that he entertained these persons to lull them into a false sense of security, which enabled him to use a ruse against them. One can say with great confidence that the need to pay up for the upkeep of the army and his security needs dominated Caracalla's policies both at home and abroad. It is unfortunate that we do not know what was the role of the Egyptian *amicus* and *comes* Coeranus in these events.

Christer Bruun's outstanding analysis of the inscription found at Albano Laziale has proved that the people of Alexandria did more than just insult Caracalla when he arrived in the city. It is also clear that Bruun's conclusions are supported by Synkellos' text. The *pericula Alexandriana* was so serious that the acting temporary centurion from the *Legio II Parthica* had taken a vow to dedicate thanks to a god if he could return safely back home. Unless this refers to the subsequent street fighting, it suggests that the Alexandrian mob had attacked the emperor and his retinue when it entered the city in opposition to his policies, and that the emperor and his followers were lucky to get away with their lives. It is probable that it was then that Caracalla went to the temple of Sarapis/Serapis (the Serapeum of Alexandria) for the first time, as stated by Herodian. In my opinion, it is probable that Caracalla and his retinue actually sought a place of refuge in the temple when attacked by the Alexandrian mob during the *pericula Alexandriana*, and it was after this that Caracalla entertained those who had greeted him with mystic rites. Dio's general explanation for the visits was that Caracalla wanted to pray for relief from his supposed physical and mental ailments,[6] but in this case Dio (78.22.1ff.) thinks that Caracalla prayed for the purification of the city and used the killing as human sacrifices to the god. Dio implies that the visit took place only after the soldiers were launched at the city, but I would suggest that there were two visits. The visits may also have had other more subtle reasons, such as to offer public thanks to the god for the safety of the emperor, but the principal reasons appear to have been to imitate the tradition that linked Alexander the Great to the god Sarapis and to purge local enemies in the Serapeaum, as suggested by Whittaker.[7] According to the sixth-century Rufinus' *Historia Ecclesiastica*, the statue of Sarapis was made to hover in mid-air by the use of magnets.[8] The sight must have been breath-taking and well worth a visit, but was not the principal reason for Caracalla's visit. He also left the sword with which his brother Geta had been killed in the temple. We do not know the reason for this, but the symbolic deed may have had something to do with the fact that the Alexandrians, in particular the followers of Serapis, had favoured Geta and had now attacked Caracalla. It was now the Alexandrians' turn to taste the sword. Caracalla appears not to have made any distinction between the different classes of Alexandrians who were killed, even if the principal targets were the local followers of Serapis and the Aristotelians.

After this, Caracalla went to the tomb of Alexander. It was now that he again used one of his trademark ruses, apparently this time modelled on the trick previously employed by Ptolemy VII Physcon Euergetes (died 116 BC). Caracalla ordered all the young men to assemble on open ground, possibly in the gymnasium as claimed by the SHA, in order to be enrolled into a phalanx in honour of Alexander, just as he had previously done in Greece. The young men were enthusiastic; after all, pay in the army and 'fringe benefits' appear to been particularly good under Caracalla. When the young men, their parents and brothers were all assembled, Caracalla had them surrounded by his army and butchered without mercy. It is probable that most of these men would have been native Greeks attending the philosophical schools and who trained in the gymnasium, but one cannot exclude the presence of native Egyptians and others. After the order had been given, Caracalla and his bodyguards left (Herod. 4.9.5–6), presumably to the temple of Serapis, where he then performed rites of purification with animal and human sacrifices, as stated by Dio. It seems very probable that this purification included the priests and followers of Serapis in the temple district of the city, including those who Caracalla had entertained at a banquet.

After this, the soldiers were let loose on the city. The inhabitants were ordered to stay indoors while the soldiers occupied all the streets and roofs. One possibility is that if Caracalla's intention was to target a particular group or groups of inhabitants, the order to stay indoors was given only to those parts of the city which Caracalla intended to leave unmolested, while the other parts were subjected to attack, but there is no specific evidence for this. Following this, the soldiers were ordered to kill the citizens of Alexandria. Even though the soldiers were told not to kill outsiders together with the citizens, some of these became 'collateral damage' as people were being murdered by night and day in all parts of the city. The murdered people were buried in mass graves or thrown into the Nile each day so that diseases would not spread. The soldiers looted the city and pillaged some of the shrines (presumably those opposing Caracalla). After this, all foreigners (*xenoi*, mostly native Egyptians), except merchants, were expelled from the city and the remaining inhabitants were divided by a cross-wall, with guards posted along it, to prevent free movement, and the mess halls were closed and public spectacles forbidden. This begs the question: why were the foreigners/natives expelled? Had they been behind the troubles or were they just expelled to prevent further troubles during the festivities of Serapis? It is probable that Whittaker is correct that the latter is true. It is unfortunate that the sources do not tell which groups of people were killed and then divided from each other with the cross-wall, but one possibility is that Caracalla separated the pagans, Jews and Christians from each other with his wall so that they would not kill each other. The location of the walls inside the city suggest that this was Caracalla's intention. It is therefore very unfortunate that the sources merely mention the killing of the followers of Serapis and Aristotle, the youths (presumably mostly Greeks) with their relatives and the indiscriminate killing of the citizens of the city with some unintended outsiders. Whatever the exact details, it is clear that one of the intentions was to restrict the movement of people in order to make it more difficult for them to assemble and revolt, but in such a manner that Caracalla tried to limit potential damage to the economy by protecting foreign merchants.[9] In other words, Alexandria became a walled ghetto in order to prevent future trouble.

The Exc. Val. 394–396 fragments of Dio (Loeb/Cary ed. 78.24) preserve a problematic piece of text which follows the above if it is placed in the right place. According to these, Caracalla gave 25,000 sesterces (Cary's emended version) as a reward to the regulars of the Praetorian Guard, and to the rest 20,000 as prizes for their campaign. The problem with this is that there is a lacuna after this. Consequently, we do not know whether this was a reward for the Alexandrian campaign (or the Balkan campaign if the text is placed in the wrong place) or it was an advance payment for the Eastern campaign to secure the loyalty of the troops. It is also possible that Caracalla wanted to make certain that the soldiers would stay loyal after the assassination attempts and the Alexandrian killings. Whatever the purpose, the soldiers received a handsome sum of money.

Thanks to the gap in the sources, we also do not know exactly what it was that angered Caracalla after this, despite the fact that he 'considered himself as a temperate man'. Dio simply states that Caracalla rebuked licentiousness in others, but now that something really outrageous took place before his eyes he only pretended to be angry but did not follow it with punishment. Instead of doing that, he allowed the youth to act as if they were courtesans among women or buffoons/jesters among men, and thereby corrupted the youth. This would suggest that the outrage that angered Caracalla was homosexual behaviour, but despite his anger he chose not to do anything about this. In other words, Dio accused Caracalla that he corrupted the youth by not punishing the homosexuals. If his purpose was to accuse Caracalla of homosexual behaviour, it is odd that he failed to state this clearly. What is certain, however, is that Dio's text proves that this sort of behaviour was not approved of by people like him. Dio and his ilk were bigoted ultraconservatives who hated homosexuals, Jews and Christians. Caracalla was far more open minded than them. I would once again see this as an instance in which Caracalla acted wisely. He must have known that there were homosexuals and bisexuals in his army and had he punished such behaviour severely he would have angered these. He wanted to be loved by all soldiers, regardless of their sexual orientation. Consequently, it sufficed for him to demonstrate his personal disapproval of such behaviour – it was only natural for a heterosexual like Caracalla to feel disgust, as it is for a homosexual to feel disgust at heterosexual behaviour. This also proves that it was not this behaviour that caused the massacre at Alexandria, even if it angered Caracalla.

It is difficult to estimate the overall damage done to the economy of the empire and the city of Alexandria, which was one of the most important economic hubs of the empire. In spite of the fact that the merchants were not among the principal sufferers, it is still clear that the damage must have been very considerable. One can estimate that a minimum of 100,000 Alexandrians were killed indiscriminately.[10] However, the proceeds of the loot acquired in the course of the following campaign season must have been more than enough to pay for the costs incurred as a result of this attack against a Roman city.

The butchery and looting in Alexandria appears to have served many purposes for Caracalla. Firstly, he exacted vengeance on the population for their disrespectful remarks of him, his mother and his orders, and for the rioting and violence which may have endangered his life. In other words, the massacre can be seen as a punitive measure intended to intimidate other communities and cities into unquestioned obedience towards Caracalla. Secondly, this act of pillage provided his troops, especially his barbarian auxiliaries, with some booty. This was needed because the Parthian war had been unexpectedly called off. Thirdly, with the loot taken from Alexandria, Caracalla could finance his planned military campaign against Parthia the next year. Fourthly, it is probable that Caracalla eliminated all those who were reported to have been disloyal towards him, which included in particular the followers of Serapis and Aristotle. Fifthly, it is possible that Caracalla also wanted to punish the Alexandrians because they had enthusiastically participated in the persecution of Christians[11] and he wanted to protect the Christians and Jews of Alexandria from the pagans, but the only evidence for this is the location of the walls which clearly separated the Jews (inner ring) and pagans (their temples were in the outer ring), presumably with the Christians in-between. This receives support also from the fact that there were not many Jews among the citizens of Alexandria that were targeted. Sixthly, it is possible that the massacre of Alexandrian youth was meant to act as a pre-emptive strike against similar troubles that faced Trajan in 116–117 when the Jews of Cyrene, Cyprus and Alexandria revolted. It should be noted, however, that the sources show Caracalla to have had a soft spot towards the Jews and Christians, and it is unlikely that these groups would have been the youth enrolled into the army and among the followers of Serapis or Aristotle. Furthermore, the foreign traders are likely to have included large numbers of Arabs, who certainly included Jews at this time. It is therefore more than likely that the punitive measures were directed mainly against the local pagans of Greek and Egyptian origin. In sum, in my opinion the likeliest reason for Caracalla's pre-emptive strike against the city of Alexandria was to prevent the recurrence of similar problems as had taken place during the reign of Trajan by eliminating those Alexandrians (mainly the Greek followers of Serapis and Aristotle) who were opposed to his rule, and then by restricting the ability of the people to assemble together. The official version, however, may have been the punishment of contractors because they had not delivered the taxes. This massacre would certainly have made others quite willing to pay their taxes.

The Red Sea Route
On the basis of the information provided by the inscriptions found in Yemen and material included in the SHA (Macr. 12.6, Diad. 8.1–9.3), it is very likely that Caracalla's Eastern campaign also included diplomatic and military operations along the trade route to India to weaken the Parthian hold on international trade.

At the end of the second century, ancient Yemen consisted of four kingdoms: Saba, Himyar, Hadramawt and Qataban. The Hadramawt conquered Qataban at some point between 160 and 210, while the Sabaeans fought against the Himyarites. According to the inscriptions, the Sabaean King Alhan Nahfan was unable to defeat the Himyarites on his own, and therefore allied himself with Gadurat/Gadarat, king of the Abyssinians (*nagashi* of Aksum/Axum). This event is usually dated to have taken place towards the end of the second century or at about 200. After this, the inscriptions record that Nahfan's successor Shairum/Shair Awtar (his reign is usually dated to the period c. 210–230) broke up the alliance with the Aksumites. Awtar's army consisted of the *Khamis* of Saba and the *Khamis* of Himyar, which means that he controlled both realms, so the Himyarite king was his client king. The Ethiopians were expelled from the Himyarite capital Zafar, but still managed to retain control of part of the coastline. The other inscriptions record that Awtar defeated Hadramawt in about 215 or 217–218.[12] It is possible that this referred to the revolt of the Hadrmawt against their ruler, who was married to the Awtar's sister, or to the final defeat and capture of the ruler of the Hadramawt. The researchers do not agree on the interpretation of the inscriptions. The inscriptions also mention wars in which Awtar fought with the Hadramawt against the Himyarites and with the Himyarites against Hadramawt, and in which Awtar subdued or raided the areas of the Kinda Kingdom in Central Arabia. These wars included fighting between brothers – something that Caracalla knew all about.[13]

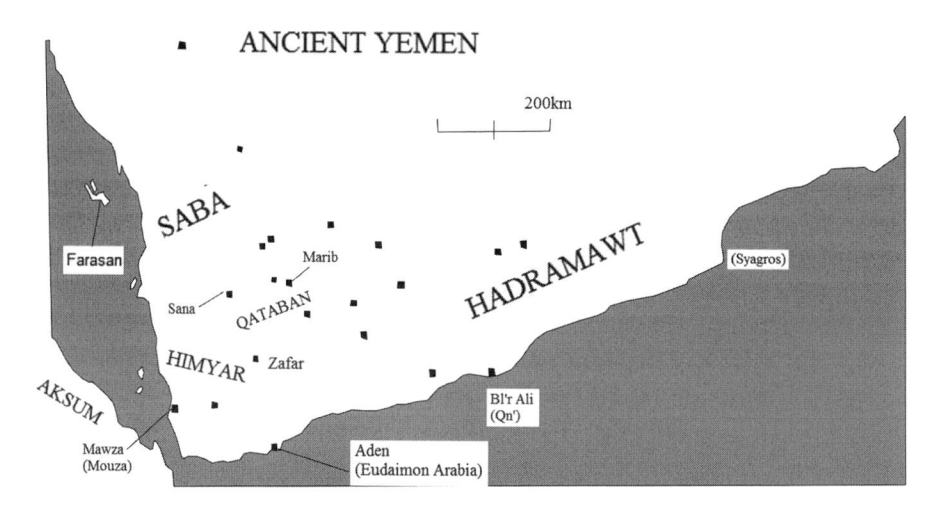

It is very unfortunate that the extant Roman sources fail to pay any detailed attention to these events, but one may assume that this results only from the fact that we possess an abridgement of Dio. Regardless of the general silence, the abridged Dio still includes one very important reference to the events that took place during the reign of Septimius Severus (76.13.1). According to Dio, after Severus had ended his Persian campaign in 200, he marched to Egypt with the aim of marching to Ethiopia, but this campaign was abandoned as a result of pestilence. It is very easy to connect this planned campaign against Ethiopia/Aksum with the Ethiopian alliance with Saba against the Himyarites. In short, it appears probable that Saba and Aksum were acting against Roman interests in the area and Severus intended to punish them. The other alternative is that the Ethiopians were actually pressured to join the Sabaeans with the threat of military action so that they would cooperate with Saba against Himyar, but the former appears more likely.

It is also possible to connect the events of the reign of Awtar with the policies of Caracalla. It is unlikely that Caracalla would have ignored Ethiopia and Yemen at the same time as he paid great attention to the events in Osroene, Armenia, Arabia and Alexandria. It is likely that his visit of Alexandria in 215 was also connected with events taking place in the Red Sea theatre of operations. It is very unfortunate that we do not know whether the Romans still maintained a naval base on the island of Farasan at the mouth of the Red Sea, as they did during the period 120–166,[14] but since the Romans continued their aggressive policies against Parthia under Severus and Caracalla, it is very probable that they would have retained an advanced naval military base on the Red Sea. My own educated guess is that the Romans were directly involved in all of the wars that took place in Yemen, and this is supported by the information provided by the SHA, which states that Macrinus was fighting wars against Armenia, Parthia and the Eudaemones of Arabia Felix.[15] It is clear that all of these wars had started under Caracalla. It is unfortunate that we do not know which side Caracalla backed, but since the sources fail to make merry about failures in Arabia Felix, it is probable that Caracalla backed the winning side – but this does not preclude the possibility that the side Caracalla backed would not have lost the war after Macrinus concluded peace with Artabanus in 218, because the Romans would have then probably withdrawn their forces from Yemen. The reference to the Eudaemones is interesting in this context, because Eudaemon was the ancient name for the city of Aden, which lay in the territory of Himyar. This would suggest that the Romans were fighting against the Himyarites. Unfortunately, this does not prove that Caracalla would have fought against their ally Awtar, or that he would have fought as an ally of Awtar against the Himyar. It all depends on the timing of the different wars, on top of which it is possible that the SHA could easily have mistaken the two different tribes, Himyarites and Hadramawt, with each other and called either of the tribes Eudaemones. Regardless, it is still probable that Caracalla supported Awtar against the Aksumites and Hadramawt, both of which would have been in possession of strategic commercial harbours at the time, rather than the other way around, but obviously we cannot know this with definite certainty. The fact that no action is mentioned in Ethiopia could be taken to mean that Caracalla acted as their ally in Yemen. Caracalla would certainly have been in position to prevent the Aksumites from sending any help to their forces in Yemen or to assist them in transporting forces to Yemen, because the strong-nailed Roman war galleys were the superior weapons-system in the area, especially if the Romans still had a naval station at Farasan. The other peoples in the area used dhows too weak to withstand encounters with nailed ships that were equipped with rams/ram-spurs.

230 Caracalla

My tentative reconstruction of the likeliest course of events is that Caracalla formed an alliance with Awtar against Awtar's brother[16] and helped him against the Aksumites (Septimius had planned to attack them), and then helped Awtar against the Kinda at the same time as he is recorded as having defeated the Arabs and received the title Arabicus in about 213. It is easy to see that the Kinda could have been the target of Roman aggression at a time when the Romans were in complete control of the west of the Arabian Peninsula. It would have been after this that Caracalla would have supported the alliance between the Sabaeans and Himyarites against the Aksumites so that the Roman fleet prevented the dispatch of reinforcements from Ethiopia, with the result that the Aksumites were evicted from Zafar and forced to conclude a peace with Saba. The purpose would have been to force the Aksumites to sign a more favourable trade treaty with Rome. The next step in the campaign would have been the invasion of Hadramawt to secure its harbours for Indian trade. The Himyarite harbours would already have been secure. This was achieved either in 215 or 217/218, but it is possible that the Himyarites then revolted against Saba at the same time as the Hadramawt, so the Romans were fighting against the Eudaemones/Himyarites together with the Sabaeans and Hadramawt in 218. The presence of a legate or legates in Arabia Felix during the reign of Macrinus means that Caracalla had probably also dispatched land forces to support his ally or allies. Thanks to the fact that the Romans possessed a superior navy and were supported by a powerful local ally, it is obvious that the help provided by the Romans would have been more than sufficient to tilt the balance of power in favour of their ally. The hostile sources would not have passed a chance to accuse both Caracalla and Macrinus of failure if their Yemenite campaign ended in defeat. The rest of the campaigns would obviously have taken place well after the reign of Caracalla and are therefore not discussed here. However, I will return to this topic at a later time. As regards the type of enemy the Romans would have faced in Yemen, see my MHLR Vol.1 pp.133–36.

Relief of soldiers wearing elephant helmets, Tell el-Herr (Egypt), 2nd-3rd century AD (source: D'Amato 2009a). According to D'Amato, the horsemen and footmen in this relief belong to the *numeri* defending the *praesidia* of the Egyptian desert. This relief is a good example of the great variety of equipment used by the soldiers of this era. The use of the rectangular shields and small targets by the cavalry is noteworthy as is the apparent use of the cylindrical shields by the infantry *numeri*. This suggests that the cylindrical shields could also be used by non-legionary forces. D'Amato suggests that the helmets belong to the class of animal leather helmets mentioned by Pliny the Elder.

The sources do not provide any specific concrete evidence for all of the above speculations, but since such operations were standard procedure for the Romans in these regions both before and after Caracalla's reign, it seems fair to assume that the events in Yemen did not take place in a vacuum in an area that had strategic importance for Rome, which is also proven by the referrals to such operations in the SHA. Caracalla clearly understood the importance of the profitable long-distance international trade between Rome and Parthia, and thereby also with India and Africa which bypassed Parthia (Herodian 4.4) – even those Romans who were interested in gladiatorial games (Caracalla certainly was) would have known that beasts were exported from Ethiopia and India to Rome (e.g. Herodian 1.15.4–5) and Caracalla is known to have possessed elephants of his own. It is very probable that the Syrian Julia Domna had an important and overlooked role in the formulation of these policies.

Notably, according to Majundar and Altekar (pp.335–37, esp. p.337), Alexandria and Palmyra and trade with India flourished under all Severans, including Septimius Severus, Caracalla, Elagabalus and Alexander Severus. It was also during this era that Roman interests in India were at their height. This suggests strongly that Caracalla paid close attention to matters on the Red Sea, especially at a time when he was himself planning to conduct military campaigns in the East. On the basis of this, it is difficult to assess what damage Caracalla's actions in Alexandria caused to the India trade. The fact that Alexandria remained prosperous suggests that the destruction was not severe, but at the same time it is clear that it must have caused some harm. It is in fact possible that one of the reasons for the butchery at Alexandria was to destroy that clique within the city that had opposed Caracalla's trade policies towards Yemen and India. It is also possible that the butchery may even have helped the trade if this was true. The real breakup in the trade network between Rome and India was caused by the rise of the Sasanians after 226. The most serious blow to the trade was the conquest of Sind by the Sasanians in about 246–249.[17] This blocked the most important part of the Silk Route from Central Asia to India.

Troubles Arise: The Rise of Artabanus V and the Revolt of Armenia in late 215
The peace agreement concluded with Vologaesus had given Caracalla a free hand in Armenia and Caucasus. It had also enabled Caracalla to sack one of his own cities without having to worry about Parthian intervention behind his supply lines in 215. It seems very likely that the fight between Artabanus and Vologaesus ended in the defeat of the latter in the summer or autumn of 215, because the next time Caracalla negotiated with the Parthians it was with Artabanus, who subsequently came to meet him at Arbela in 216. After his defeat, Vologaesus seems to have retreated to his capital Ctesiphon, because the mint there still minted coins bearing his name in the early 220s. Artabanus' forces appear to have consisted of the Parthians based in the province of Parthia and of their neighbours. On the basis of the subsequent

232 Caracalla

hostility of the Suren family to the plea of the Armenian Arsacid king Tiridates/Khosrov for support against the Sasanian usurper Ardashir, it appears very likely that Vologaesus' supporters consisted mainly of the eastern Saka tribesmen under the mixed Parthian/Saka house of Suren and of the Parthians, Persians, Medes, Babylonians and Greeks of Mesopotamia centred around the capital Ctesiphon. On the other hand, the Kushans, who at this time were also related to the Arsacid house, may actually have supported Artabanus, because they were subsequently attacked by the joint armies of the Suren and Ardashir. The presence of the army of Suren would have served to keep the Kushans at bay while Artabanus and Vologaesus fought their civil war. On the other hand, the Kushan threat behind the Suren was bound to keep them at bay.[18] The grand alliance between the Romans on the one hand, and Artabanus and the Kushans on the other, worked like a dream. On the basis of this, it appears probable that Vologaesus had to face the armies of Artabanus with his mixed forces of Parthians, Greeks, Persians, Arabs and Babylonians which were based in the cities of Mesopotamia. Vologaesus did not have a chance in open terrain against the superb cavalry forces of Parthia and their neighbours when the armed strength of the Saka-Parthians of Sakastan/Sistan were tied up by the Kushan threat.[19]

As noted above, it is probable that the Armenians revolted in late 215 or early 216. The sources fail to tell any reason for the revolt of Armenia, but this must be connected with the events mentioned by the Georgian Chronicles and Moses and with the arrival of Artabanus and defeat of Vologaesus V. In light of the fact that Artabanus did not initiate hostilities with Rome, it is quite probable that he enthroned Khosrov (Tiridates of Dio) only to distract the Romans and obtain a possible bargaining chip for negotiations so that he would not have to fear Roman intervention while he completed his operations against Vologaesus by besieging him in Ctesiphon.

Notes

1. The probable route in Whittaker/Herod., pp.418–19, n.2.
2. Dio 78.18.4; Whittaker/Herod, pp.416–17, n.1. Caracalla was evidently quite aware of the religious trends in the empire. For example, he was familiar with the religion of the Jews (SHA Car. 1.6).
3. I have discussed this matter before, for example in the *MHLR* Vol.1.
4. Dio 78. The quotes are from Gary's translation of Dio, p.299ff.
5. The account of the Alexandrian troubles is mostly based on Dio 78.7.3, 78.21.2ff. (Loeb, p.332ff.); Herodian 4.8.6ff.; SHA Car. 6.2–3. Other sources are mentioned in the text.
6. If Caracalla prayed for a medical relief at all in the temple, it was because he wanted a miraculous cure either for his impotence and/or for his ailing mother, the latter being likelier. However, as noted, the temple visits may have had another more sinister goal.
7. See Herod. 4.8.6ff.; Arrian, Anab. 7.26.2; Alexander Romance 1.30–33; Stoneman (2008) pp.60–62, 119. Considering Caracalla's interest in chariot races and Sarapis, it

is possible that he was already more familiar with the romantic version of Alexander the Great than with the real-life Alexander. It is perhaps no coincidence that the first extant A-text of Alexander Romance dates from the third century. The various versions of the Greek Alexander were already quite fabulous in content. The Greek Alexander Romance was subsequently translated into Latin, Syriac, Armenian, Persian and other languages, but in the course of its history its contents became ever more fabulous. For a study of the history of the various Alexander Romances, see Stoneman (1991; 2008) together with Minoo S. Southgate (Alexander Romance/Iskandarnamah). The reference to the Alexandrian danger by the legionary discussed by Bruun is not the only extant period record of the visit. There exists a papyrus P. Got. 3 (Levick 2, pp.219–20) in which a resident of the Phenebythus riverside district of Panopolis vows to stand as surety that a fisherman would prepare fish sauce, fine preserved fish and fresh fish for the visit of Caracalla in 215–216. Such preparatory steps were always taken when the emperor and his armed forces were on the move.
8. Stoneman (2008) pp.62, 119 (Rufinus 2.23).
9. Herod. 4.8.6–9.8; SHA Car. 6.23; Dio 78.22.1–23.4.
10. If Caracalla claimed to enrol 16,000 men in Macedonia, as is likely, this would give us only the minimum. In practice, far greater numbers of would-be soldiers would have turned up only to be butchered with their families. In addition to this, we should also include those who were then killed in the city.
11. The role of the Alexandrian mob is mentioned by Eusebius (Church History 6.1ff.).
12. In this case the date is relatively secure, but some historians date the revolt to 217/218 and the conquest to 215.
13. The evidence is presented and discussed by Bafaqih, esp. p.365ff., Schipmann, pp.60–61, Hoyland, pp.46–48, and Munro-Hay, esp. Chapter 4.4). The key point here is that these historians translate and interpret the evidence differently thanks to the fact that the interpretation of the lacunose inscriptions is an art form in itself.
14. Discussed in greater detail in Syvanne (MHLR 1–2); McLaughlin, pp.131–33.
15. The SHA (Aur. 33.7) lists the Arabes Eudaemones as follows: Blemmyes, Axomitae, Arabes Eudaemones, Indi, Bactriani etc. This means that it is more than likely that the Eudaemones were the next in line after the Aksumite Ethiopians sailed as one to India. On top of this, the ancient name of the city of Aden was Eudaimon. In short, the Eudaemones were one of the Yemenite tribes, probably the Himyarites.
16. It would certainly have been in character for Dio to hide still another instance of Caracalla's treacherous behaviour that brought results, especially if it had once again been done on behalf of one brother vs. another. Note, however, that there is no definite and concrete evidence for any of this in the sources. This represents my best educated guess of what is likely to have happened. The picture will hopefully become clearer with new archaeological finds.
17. For details, see the forthcoming Syvanne, *A Military History of Sasanian Iran* Vol.1 with MHLR vol.1.
18. It was for this reason that Ardasir and his son Shapur I subsequently had to crush the Kushans. In order to be able to operate freely in the west against Rome, the Sasanians needed to remove the Kushan threat. For the Kushans and Sacae/Saka/Saca/Sakai/

Sakas and their relations with neighbors in general, see Lebedynsky (2006) p.58ff. (for the military, see p.188ff.); Lebedynsky (2007) pp.78–85, 109–16; Raychaudhuri p.381ff. (with Mukherjee, p.691ff.); Nikonorov vol. 1, p.58ff. with illustrations vol.2; Puri (1999a, 1999b); Litvinsky et al.; Koshelenko and Pilipko. Note that they do not necessarily share my views and reconstruction of the events. For the other peoples inhabiting those areas, see Lebedynsky (2007).

19. This is based on Moses, p.210ff.; Tabari, p.i.813ff.; Thomas Artsrunik, pp.120–21; and the studies mentioned in the previous note, but in such a manner that I have reinterpreted the evidence partially. The Parthian Confederacy had been formed by a union of Parni/Parthians with the Saka tribesmen arriving from the east. They had united their forces against the Yuezhi/Kushans in a joint effort to protect Iran. The first to join the Parthians was the Saka family of Sam and Rustam of the *Shahnameh* of Firdawsi. The Saka were settled in Sakastan/Sistan under their own king belonging to the house of Sam. The same conclusion that the house of Sam in the Shahnameh belonged originally to the Saka tribal nobility has also independently been reached by Patryk Skupniewicz (exchange of e-mails) and even before someone else, according to Skupniewicz. However, to my knowledge, the following has not been noted by others. Subsequently, the House of Sam was also joined to the House of Seleucids (demons in *Shahnameh*) through the marriage with the daughter of the Greek king of Kabul and then also to the family of Arsacids themselves, when the daughter belonging to the House of Sam was married to a Suren, forming thereby the House of Suren. Similarly, the House of Karen was formed as a result of a union of the two family lines by marrying a Karen to a daughter of the Saka king. Subsequently, the House of Suren also conquered northern India from the Greeks. The Greeks (called demons in the *Shahnameh*) used poisons to defeat the invasion force of the Parthian king, but Rustam arrived in time to save his king. The area passed then to the House of Rustam/Suren, who ruled it independently of the Parthians. The House of Suren and other Saka/Parthians were in their turn expelled by the Kushans, who took over the north of India from them. The Kushans in their turn were allied with the Romans, at least from the reigns of Trajan and Hadrian onwards. Regardless of this, the Kushans also married into the Arsacid house and their kings were related to Artaban and Khosrov. It was this pattern of intermarriage that caused the family feuds among the kings.

Chapter Ten

Caracalla's Anabasis Phase 4: Campaign Against Artabanus in 216

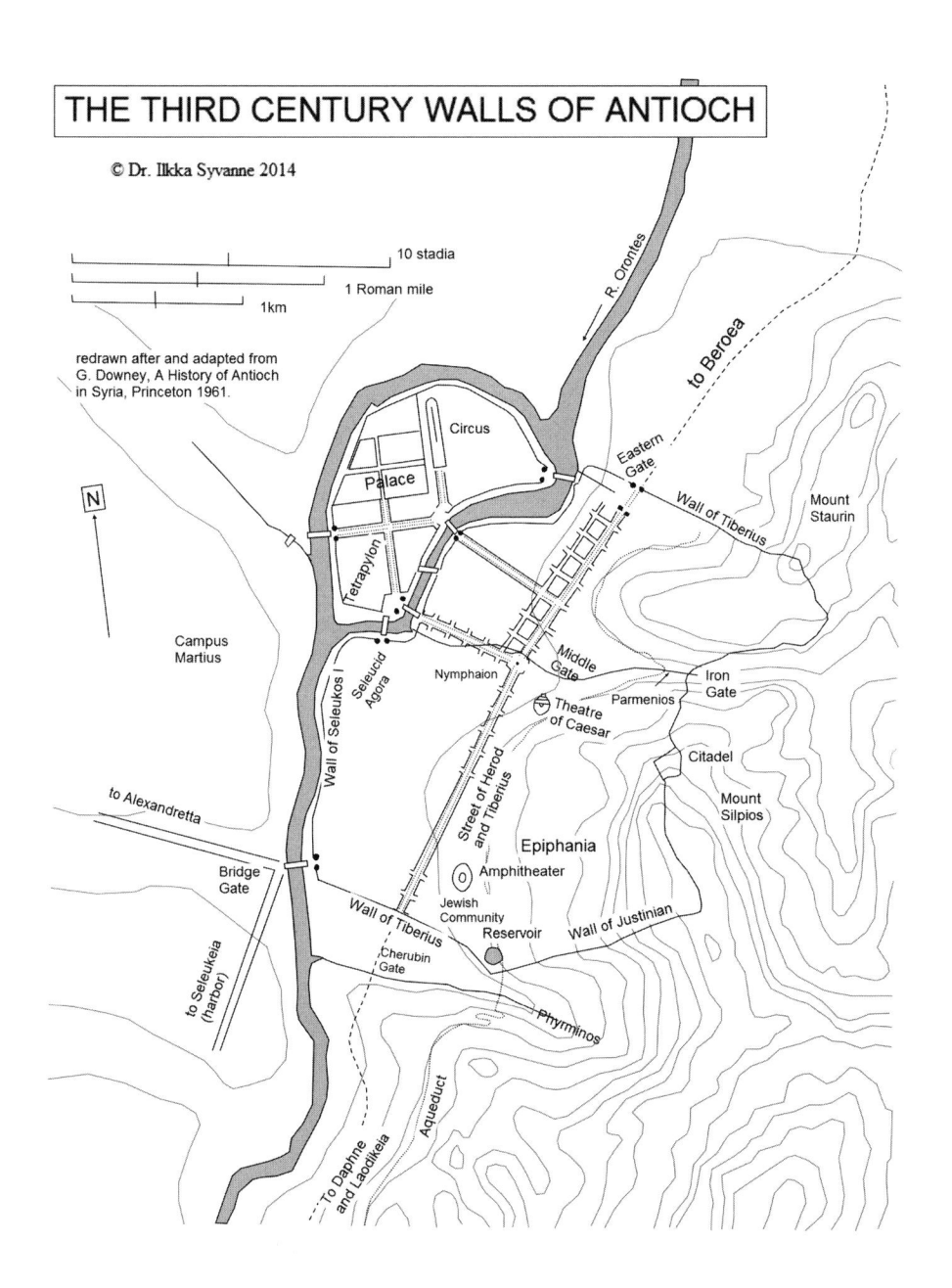

236 Caracalla

After having pillaged Alexandria, Caracalla returned to Antioch, where he spent the spring of 216.[1] Antioch served as Caracalla's logistical base for the eastern campaigns, just as it had been for the previous Roman generals and emperors and was to be for future generations. The logistical network consisted of the following: 1) the Romans shipped corn and other supplies from Egypt to Seleucia; 2) supplies and provisions that could not be obtained from Egypt were obtained locally and collected in arsenals, or were transported from elsewhere in ships to Seleucia; 3) the supplies stored at Seleucia were first transported to Antioch and from there to forward-based logistical centres such as Edessa.

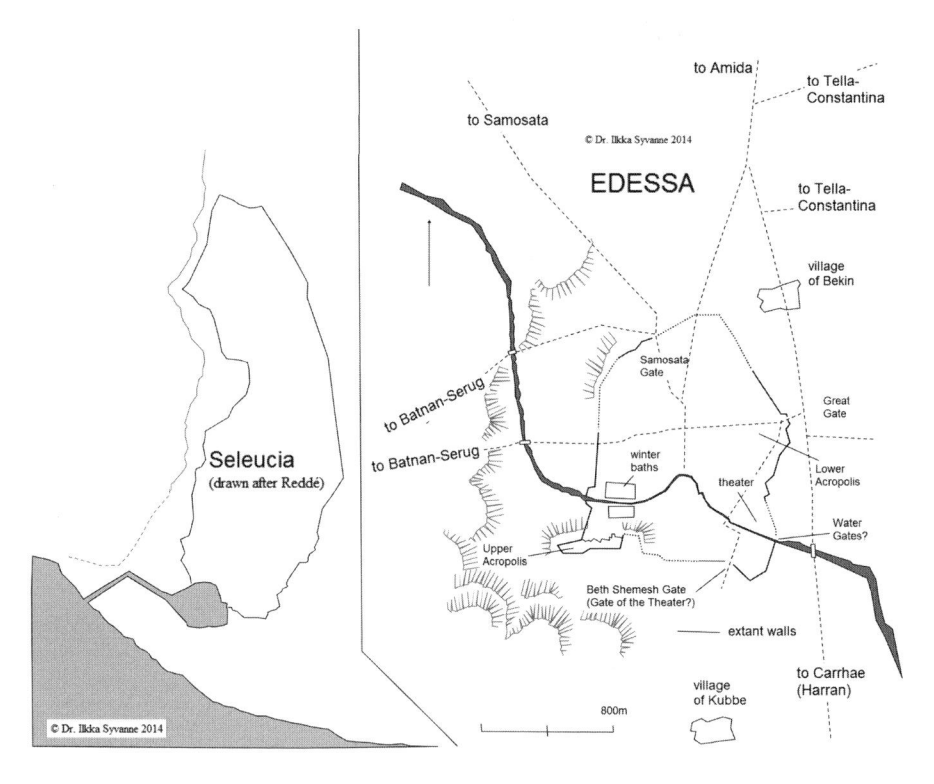

Caracalla had no intention of maintaining peace with Artabanus, and one may suspect not with Vologaesus either, because his ultimate goal was to conquer Persia/Iran, but the way in which this was to be achieved was still open. If my reconstruction of the events in the Caucasus, Iberia and Armenia is correct, then it is quite possible that one of the reasons for Caracalla's eagerness to proceed against Artabanus V was the crowning of Khosrov the Great as King of Armenia without Caracalla's permission, which was effectively a declaration of war. The problem was how to proceed against both the new King of Armenia and the Parthian King Artabanus, because both possessed huge armies. The Parthian army was truly awe-inspiring and had been the cause of many defeats in the past.

The Parthian Military² (see the maps in the Maps Section)
The Parthians were originally part of the Dahaean Tribal Confederacy that asserted its freedom in the third century BC. The Parthians under their Arsacid leadership conquered Iran from the Seleucids and Sakas (the so-called eastern Scythians)³ and after this they siezed large tracts of Kushan and Indian territories. The conquest of Syria brought the Parthians into contact with Rome. The initial contacts were hostile, but eventually the empires found a way to co-exist through a compromise achieved during Nero's reign that divided the spheres of interest. The key clause was the compromise according to which Armenia was to be ruled by an Arsacid king crowned by a Roman emperor. Both empires were in the habit of violating the peace whenever it suited their interest, but in general Rome behaved more aggressively/opportunistically. It was quite typical for the Romans to attack when the Arsacids faced a civil war or other conflicts. The fact that the imperial aspirations of Parthia were usually oriented towards the east and its trade routes naturally eased pressures on the eastern Roman border and made it easier for the Romans to pick and choose the time of their own attacks.

Parthian society was a feudal one with its own hierarchies. The power of the Arsacid King of Kings was limited by the vast armies possessed by the great noble families of the realm (Mihrans, Karins, Surens, Ziks, Kanarangiya, Ispahbudhans, Spandiyadhs, Jusnafs and Andigans). Most of these families were Parthian by origin, but there were also a great number of non-Parthian noble houses. These included the Surens of the *Sakai/Sacae* tribe of Sistan, the native Persian nobility in Fars and an unknown Greek family whose only traces in history can be found in Ferdowsi (probably the demon king of Kabul who married into the Suren clan), Tacitus (Hiero, possibly from Kabul: Tacitus Annals 6.42–3) and the later Sasanian sources. By the third century, all of these families were related to each other through marriage, so all possessed Arsacid blood in their veins. The most powerful of the clans were the Mihrans, Karins and Surens. The last had the hereditary right of crowning the king (Tacitus, Annals 6.43), which they retained even under the Sasanians. In addition to the high nobility, the hierarchy consisted of the Greek and Persian cities that retained their self-rule under the Parthians, various Persian satrapies with their own traditions, and various semi-independent tribes. Basically, the only glue that kept the Parthian Empire together was the prestige of the King of Kings as well as the self-interest of the nobility in maintaining the status quo.

The core of the Parthian military consisted of: 1) the feudal/tribal levies provided by the aristocracy (Parthian, Sakas, Greek); 2) militia provided by the free cities; 3) contingents provided by various subject tribes; 4) the allies and mercenaries. The flower of the Parthian military consisted of its feudal cavalry. The popular view is that the Parthians followed the steppe practice and divided their cavalry into decimal units (about 10,000, 1,000 and 100 men), but it is probable that these rounded figures included servants and recruits, just like in the Roman army.[4]

The cavalry force under Suren at Carrhae has also falsely been taken to reflect a typical cavalry army of the Parthian realm.[5] In truth, Suren's forces were not

Parthians at all but Suren's personal retainers, which consisted mainly of the Saka tribesmen. This force consisted of 10,000 horsemen, which was divided into the elite unit of 1,000 heavy cataphracts (man and horse fully armoured with scale or lamellar armour, armed with a long composite bow, two-handed version of the *kontos/contus*-lance, long sword and dagger) and the 9,000 regular Saka light cavalry archers (with long composite bow, long sword and dagger). This force was supported by a baggage train of at least 1,000 camels carrying arrows etc. In addition to this, there were 200 concubines loaded in 200 wagons for Suren's personal pleasure. This means that Suren's army consisted of the typical number of men for a steppe people, but that was as far as similarities go. Furthermore, we should assume that there were additional personnel detailed to take care of the baggage train and concubines. The 1:10 proportion of the heavy cavalry was not the same as among the actual native Parthian contingents. The sources state quite clearly that when the King of Kings took to the field, his forces consisted solely of the fully-armoured cataphracts and/or *contarii*.[6] It is therefore clear that most of the lightly equipped mounted archers fielded by the Parthians always consisted of their subject and allied tribes like the Sacae.

Regardless, it is still clear that Suren's grand tactical deployment was the same as among the Parthians proper, because it was based on standard Indo-Persian practices followed by all peoples in the area before and after Suren. The narrative sources prove that Suren used two lines, with a light cavalry vanguard as his first line and a support line of cataphracts and rest of his light cavalry. This was one of the standard ways to form cavalry, then and later. The first line was to be used for skirmishing at a distance. The intention was to either defeat the enemy through archery, or if this failed, then induce it to follow the first line, which would perform a feigned flight while peppering the pursuers with arrows by using the so-called Parthian shot, after which the second line (especially the cataphracts in the centre of the second line) would attack the pursuers, while the light cavalry wings surrounded them in loose formation. These same practices can be detected in Achaemenid times, in Indian Arthasastra and in Sasanian and Muslim military treatises. This was the famous five-part array (outer left, left, centre, right and outer right) that could be divided into two lines. All of these divisions could be used independently of each other, as required by the battle plan and situation. The battle tactics consisted of four basic variants: 1) a crescent to outflank the enemy; 2) the outflanking of the enemy on one flank; 3) the use of the convex array to break through the enemy's centre; 4) the use of a combination of feigned flight/retreat with an ambush or ambushes. The following diagrams (Gotha Ms. originals and my reconstructions) show the arrays in question, as well as the two ways in which the crescent was used. My reconstruction of the units is an oversimplification meant to demonstrate the principle. In truth, there would have been considerably greater numbers of smaller units deployed in various unit orders (depending on the nationality and tactic used) than shown in the illustrations. The baggage train and infantry are not shown.

Campaign Against Artabanus in 216   239

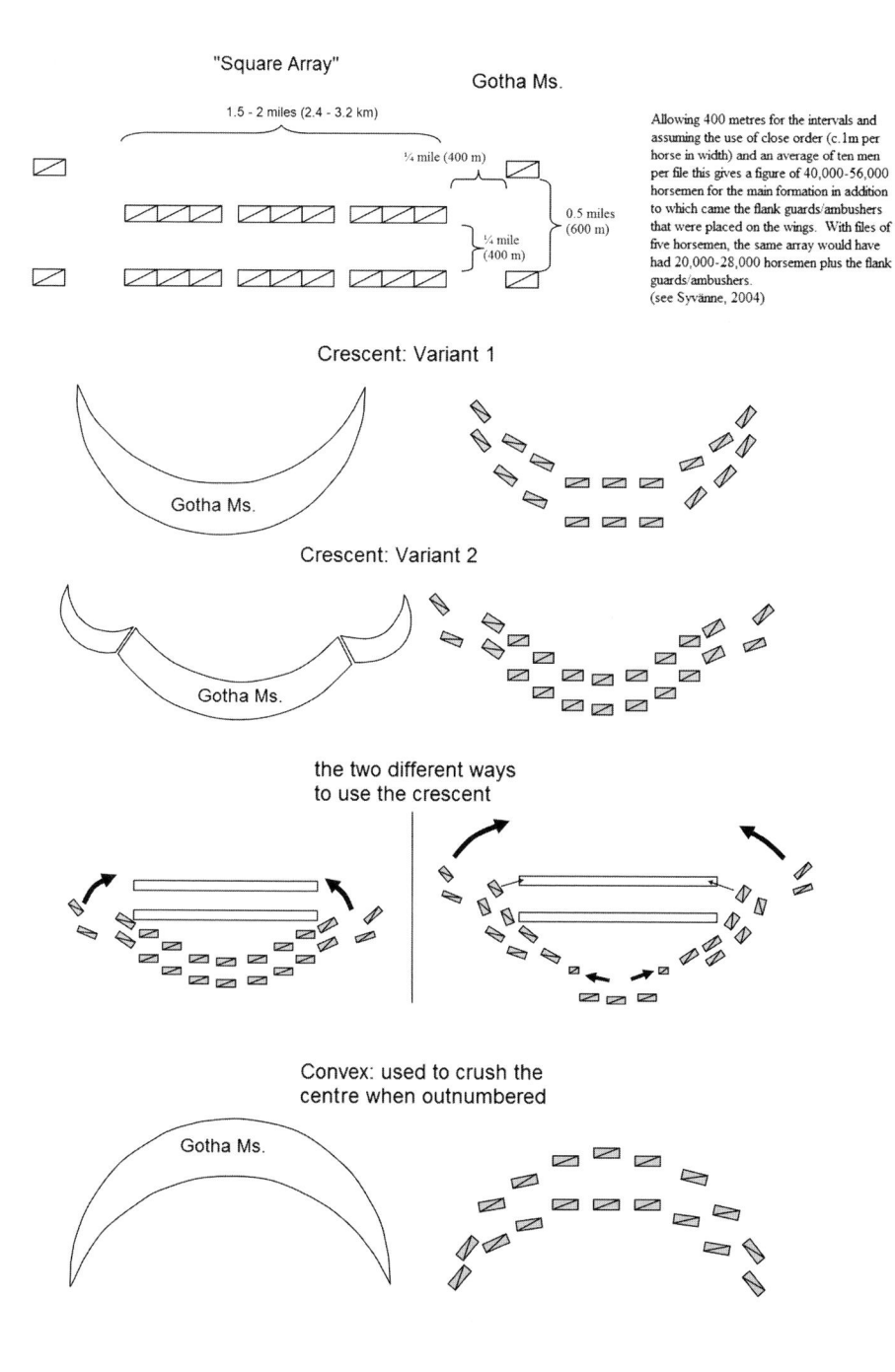

"Square Array"   Gotha Ms.

1.5 - 2 miles (2.4 - 3.2 km)

¼ mile (400 m)

0.5 miles (600 m)

¼ mile (400 m)

Allowing 400 metres for the intervals and assuming the use of close order (c.1m per horse in width) and an average of ten men per file this gives a figure of 40,000-56,000 horsemen for the main formation in addition to which came the flank guards/ambushers that were placed on the wings. With files of five horsemen, the same array would have had 20,000-28,000 horsemen plus the flank guards/ambushers.
(see Syvänne, 2004)

Crescent: Variant 1

Gotha Ms.

Crescent: Variant 2

Gotha Ms.

the two different ways to use the crescent

Convex: used to crush the centre when outnumbered

Gotha Ms.

The information regarding the unit orders employed by the Parthians is scanty. According to Aelian (18.4) and its Byzantine Interpolation (45.1–2), the Scythians employed the wedge formation, the Armenian and Parthian mounted archers employed the rhombus (128 men)[7] and the Persians used the square formation (apparently with a frontage of eight and depth of four for a total of thirty-two men). This means that the Parthian mounted archers used at least the rhombus, but we can go further than this. Since the Western sources consider the Sakas (*Sakai*) to be a Scythian tribe, it is possible to speculate that the Sakas could have used the wedge. Similarly, since we know that the Achaemenid Persians and Sasanians were using the traditional Persian square/oblong unit order, it is probable that the Parthians did as well. In sum, it is probable that the Parthians and their subjects employed all unit orders mentioned by the Greek military treatises. We do not know for certain what type of formation was used by the cataphracts, but on the basis of sources that describe their use, the use of either the wedge (sixty-four men) or the square (eight by four) or oblong (four by eight, or eight by eight etc.) would appear very likely. All of these were very useful for a frontal charge. Since the cataphracts also used bows, one can make the educated guess that they could also have used the rhomboid array. The Persian square/oblong array was used as a skirmishing formation with javelin throwers, so that one to four files at a time charged out of the array, threw their javelins and returned, which was repeated until it was decided to use the whole formation for a frontal attack.[8]

Justin's (41.2) figures confirm that the native Parthian army and its units of cataphracts were formed into rhomboids of 128 men. He claims that Mark Antony faced 50,000 Parthian horsemen commanded by 400 men. This would give each leader 125 men to command. It is quite easy to see that this 125 men actually means the 128 men required by the rhomboids, and that Justin has just used the nearest round number in his text.[9] It is also important to note that all of these men were fully armoured cataphracts. Plutarch agrees. He implies the same (Antony 45.3) by stating that the Parthians put aside their bows and advanced to close quarters with *kontoi* when they mistakenly thought that the Romans had become fatigued, but Plutarch makes one mistake. He claims that the Parthians had only 40,000 horsemen. This mistake is easy to explain. He has made the typical mistake of assuming that each of the 400 nobles led 100 men. Therefore, it is Justin who is closer to the truth in this case. The same campaign shows the Medes and Parthians employing the discussed methods. They used the crescent formation, rapid-firing archery volleys to decimate the enemy, feigned retreat and closing in with the *kontoi*-lancers. These same tactics were also used by the last of the Parthian King of Kings, Artaban V, with the exception that he experimented with cataphracted camels (Herodian 4.14.3ff.).

Thanks to the prevalence of cavalry in Roman accounts, the quality of the Parthian infantry has not received adequate attention. This has been noted by Patryk Skupniewicz. It is easy to see that, even if the feudal cavalry formed the backbone of the Parthian armed forces, the Parthians would not have been able to besiege and conquer so many cities and fortresses in Iran, Central Asia, India and Mesopotamia if they did not possess infantry forces of some kind. It is probable that the bulk of these would have consisted of forces provided by the subject peoples, so that the best footmen would have been Armenians, Greeks, Indians and mountain peoples (e.g. of the Daylami). After the victory of Septimius, the Parthians would also have possessed some Roman infantry, because Septimius' enemies fled to Iran. However, thanks to the fact that the Parthians concentrated on the use of cavalry in battle, the Romans would usually have faced Parthian infantry only when they stormed their camps or attacked their forts, towns or cities. As regards the Roman deserters, it is very probable that their descendants and the persons who they taught became the *Murmillones* of the Sasanian era mentioned by Ammianus Marcellinus, because a *murmillo* was armed with a curved rectangular *scutum* and short sword (see my illustration of Caracalla as a duelist in the Plates section).[10] It seems probable, however, that Caracalla's army did not face these Roman deserters in battle, because it is difficult to believe that the sources would not have mentioned it. On the basis of this, it is probable that the Roman deserters served under Vologaesus V, which is only natural because he would have inherited these soldiers as the sole legitimate ruler before the revolt of Artabanus.

In short, it is clear that Parthian equipment and tactics varied according to the circumstances and were not as uniform as usually assumed. The reason for this was that the Parthian army was quite heterogeneous. The Parthian commanders had to take this into account. For example, when the nomadic groups contributed large numbers of lightly equipped mounted archers, the commander had to adopt entirely different tactics than would have been the case with the fully armoured Parthian or Median cavalries.

Furthermore, thanks to the heteregeneous nature of the Parthian Empire, there was no uniform type of bow or shooting technique, but both varied from one nation to another.[11] Most Parthians appear to have used the so-called Sasanian bow (long composite bow with long ears), but other nations used the Hunnish bow (long composite bow that could be asymmetric), and still others used variants of the Scythian short composite bow. It is apparent even to the casual reader that the names of the bows given by researchers are very misleading. Each of the types of bow had its advantages and disadvantages. The Sasanian bow was particularly well-suited to delivering rapidly shot volleys of arrows, either with the Sasanian draw/lock or the thumb/Mongolian draw/lock. The Hunnish bow was best suited to delivering powerful long-range shots with the thumb draw/lock. Both of these bows were good in a prolonged archery barrage at long range when the intention was to avoid contact with the enemy until the time was right. In contrast, the effective shooting range of the Scythian bow was much shorter, and it was therefore usually used by those who sought to charge with lances immediately after one to three arrows had been shot to disorder the enemy.

Even this is an oversimplification of the facts. It was not only the nationality of the archer that affected the length and the stiffness of the bow. The bow had to be suited to the height, muscle-power and arm length of its user. Additionally, there existed several other variants of the locks/draws. Each variant of the thumb lock had its advantages (and supporters) and disadvantages (stressed by its opponents). The most important factor affecting which type of lock one could use was the size of the hand and the length of the fingers. Archery effectiveness was also not dependent solely on the type of bow and lock used. The materials and quality of construction of the bow, and the material of the cord, also mattered and affected the bow's performance. The type of arrow, its length, weight and material, and the type of arrow-head all affected the performance of the bow. The length of the arrow depended on the length of the bow and length of the arms of the user. It would require a full-length study of each of the different types of bows and arrows, which is beyond the scope of this book, but the general rule of thumb is that the longer and heavier the arrow and narrower the head, the shorter its range would be and the greater its penetrative power; and the lighter the arrow and the wider the head, the longer its flight, but with the cost of a loss of penetrative power.[12] By varying the type of arrow and lock, the Parthians could either use the shower archery tactic or the more powerful single shot tactic if it was necessary to penetrate the armour worn by opponents.[13]

Despite their heavy concentration on archery, the Parthian melee techniques were very sophisticated. The Parthian *katafraktoi* (cataphracts) and *kontoforoi* (lancers with less or no armour) could use their long *kontoi* with different types of two-handed grips like polearms or as lances.[14] Plutrach's account of the Battle of Carrhae in 53 BC proves that in the right circumstances, the Parthian/Saka cataphracts could even spear two of their static opponents simultaneously. The Parthians also possessed very high quality two-edged Indian-steel longswords that they used with the 'Italian grip', and used pick-axes and maces against armoured and helmeted opponents. Besides their bow, light cavalry also employed close-quarters weapons like swords, axes and daggers (and probably also javelins). Parthian infantry units employed all known tactical variations of antiquity, so different types of units were armed with different weapons (bows, swords, spears and javelins) for different tactical uses, and one should not underestimate the fighting skills of these men.

It is also well-known that the Parthians institutionalized wrestling, weightlifting and archery training. The heterogeneous nature of the Parthian Empire meant that there also existed other martial arts traditions. The Iranian tribes of Fars, the tribes of Central Asia and India, and the descendants of the Greek settlers (with Pankration, wrestling and boxing) and the Roman turncoats all continued to practise their own styles of martial arts, and it is possible that some sort of cross-pollination occurred between these different styles of fighting. In sum, the Parthians possessed very sophisticated melee techniques that they could employ very successfully when they decided to close with the enemy.

Campaign Against Artabanus in 216 243

Left: Parthian light cavalry mounted archer. Note the use of three arrows simultaneously, which was one of the forms of shower shooting (the Sasanians and Muslims considered it the weakest version of shower shooting). Right: Relief at Tang-e Sarvak in Elymais. Probably King of Elymais dating from c. 75–200 AD. Drawn after von Gall, 15. © Dr. Ilkka Syvänne 2009.

As we have seen, the Parthians were a worthy adversary for the Romans on strategic, operational and tactical levels. The principal strategic problem facing the Romans when invading Parthian territory was that the Parthians could avoid having to fight a decisive battle. The Parthians could use their cavalry forces to fight a guerrilla war while their infantry protected the fortified cities. This in turn made life difficult for the Romans on the operational and tactical levels. Therefore, the principal goal for all Roman commanders was to find a way to neutralize the Parthian cavalry-based field army or armies so that they could attack the cities without having to fear attacks from the rear or against their lines of communication.

At the time of Caracalla's first advance against the Parthian realm in 215, it was divided into three hostile blocks, partly thanks to Caracalla's intervention in their affairs. The east was ruled by Artabanus V and the west by Vologaesus V/VI, and the Sasanians were beginning their rise in the province of Fars. The Suren, Mihran, Spandiyadh and Ispahbudhan families appear to have supported Vologaesus, while the Karins (Karen), Andigan, Kanarangiya, Jusnafs and Ziks backed Artabanus.[15] The Parthians were weakened, but by no means helpless, as Macrinus was to learn to his great dismay. It required a skilled diplomat and general of the calibre of Caracalla to deal with the threat posed by the Parthians. He knew that he had to neutralize the enemy's field army and/or force it to fight a decisive battle.

The Armenian Military *(see the Map of Armenia and Caucasus in the Map section)*[16]
Armenia was ruled by the Arsacid Royal House, which was also the Royal House of Parthia. After the reign of Nero, the superpowers had followed up the practice in

which the Romans enthroned a member of the Arsacid House as ruler of Armenia so that both superpowers could consider Armenia as their satellite.

Armenian society consisted of three estates: 1) nobles (magnates and lesser nobility); 2) clergy; 3) commoners, non-nobles (*an-azat*), *ramik* (townsmen, traders) and the peasants (*shinakan*). The Arsacid king and his queen (*bambishn*, *tikin*) and immediate family formed the uppermost tier of society. Below them were the magnates, who consisted of the *nakharars* (*vitaxae*, princes/dukes; *nahapets/tanuters*/heads of *nakharar* families; *sepuhs*/members of the nobility) that were further classed as seniors (*awag*, *barjereck*, *gahereck*, *mecameck*) and juniors (*krtser*). Thanks to their vast hereditary domains, the magnate families were practically independent and the king needed their support just like his relative in Parthia. The most important offices were considered to be hereditary in these families. The Armenian nobility consisted of at least 120 autonomous families, below whom were the lesser nobles.

The Armenian defensive and administrative system was based on the fourfold division of the empire, so that there were four Gates/Armies (Gates of North, South, West and East) to defend the approaches from which the enemies could be expected to come. This system was ancient and can be found in use for example during the first century (Moses 2.54). In addition to this, there were four *vitaxae* (viceroys), which apparently reflected an earlier defensive division in which the viceroys faced a different set of the kingdoms.[17]

Thanks to the feudal system of defence, the Armenians possessed truly huge reserves of manpower. We do not have exact figures for the second and third centuries, but we do have detailed information from the fourth century onwards. At that time, all of the fourfold defensive zones had 18,500–23,600 heavy cavalry (mostly cataphracts and lancers also equipped with bows), in addition to which there were 35,900 knights under the king and his supreme commander settled in Ayrarat. This latter force served as the Royal Army. Consequently, the overall size of the Armenian feudal cavalry force was at least 120,000 horsemen. In addition to these, the Armenians had professional footsoldiers and the extraordinary levy of footsoldiers and cavalry. It should still be remembered that Armenian kings could not put this entire armed strength in the field for a single battle, because some of the men would always have been left behind to defend the cities, towns, forts, fortresses and castles. Regardless, it is easy to see that the Armenians could field truly sizeable armies of at least 60,000–80,000 horsemen when facing a serious military threat, and with the addition of allies (e.g. Alans), client states (Iberia and Albania at the beginning of the third century) and infantry militia, they could put into the field at least 100,000–120,000 horsemen and perhaps 60,000 footmen. The forces that the Armenian king had at his disposal, together with his allies, were just staggering and posed a significant risk to any invader.

The sources for the Armenian combat doctrine and tactics are either earlier or later, but the evidence such as it is suggests that they relied mostly on their heavy cavalry which was equipped with bows to win their wars. Depending on the situation, the Armenians relied on either guerrilla or regular warfare. The Armenian multipurpose cavalry was ideally suited to both. The cavalry could avoid close contact by fleeing and using mounted archery, and could seek to engage the enemy at close quarters fighting with spears. The cavalry was so heavily armoured that it could withstand showers of arrows and even engage footsoldiers in combat. The infantry was usually used only to protect and support the cavalry, either in hollow square array or as a phalanx. Descriptions of cavalry battle formations suggest that the Armenians always divided their first line into three divisions, but it is possible that they also used separate outer wings which would have protected the flanks, just like the Parthians. The second line had either one, two or three (or possibly five with outer wings) divisions, depending on the size of the army.

In light of the fact that the Romans were clearly able to advance deep into Armenian territory and capture Tiridates' mother and plenty of booty, it seems probable that some of the Armenians may have sided with Rome. It would otherwise have required a truly huge army to defeat the Armenians at the same time as Caracalla intended to engage the Parthians, even in a situation in which he aimed to achieve his goals primarily through stratagems. Regardless, the Romans must have sent at least 50,000–60,000 footmen and horsemen to Armenia for them to be able to advance deep into the Armenian heartland, even with the help of native turncoats. The Romans relied on their infantry to win battles, and this was certainly the right thing to do when one faced cavalry, but the fact that the Romans were able to do so proves that they had sufficiently large numbers of cavalry to support their infantry. Otherwise, the Armenian rebels/freedom fighters could have encircled and annihilated the Roman armies through hunger and thirst.

Iberia and Colchis
Iberia was heavily influenced by Iranian culture and military practices. Consequently, just like Armenia, Albania and Parthia, Iberia was a caste/class society with four or five distinct classes: nobles, priests, petty nobles, common levy of footmen and agricultural tenants. The Iranian influence was equally strong in the military organization. The Georgian Chronicles (pp.34–36) even states that the Iberians consciously used the Parthian military system as a model for their own military organization. It was thanks to this that the Iberian king appointed eight regional *eristavis/pitiaskhshi* (generals, governors, dukes, viceroys/*vitaxae*) to act as regional armies, and the commander-in-chief *spaspet* (*erismtavari* = Arm. *sparapet*) to command the Royal Reserve Army.[18] The Royal Army was located in the Inner Kartli (around Tpilisi/Tbilisi and Mcxeta/Mtskheta). The eight *eristavis* were further divided into Eastern *eristavis* (Kaxeti, Xunan, Samshwilde) and Western *eristavis* (the two *eristavis* of Egrisi = Egrisi and Margvi, Ojrhe, Klarjeti, Cunda).

The military hierarchy consisted of the above-mentioned *spaspet* and *eristavis*. The next ranks consisted of the *spasalarni* (generals), *khliarkhni/atasistavni*

(= quartermaster? in charge of collecting taxes and gathering of troops) and lesser officers/magnates, each in charge of his own contingent. The cavalry consisted of the feudal *azaurni* (fully armoured multi-purpose cataphracts) and the regular *tskhentartsani* (*kontoforoi*, spear-bearers, javelin-throwers and mounted archers). The infantry (*mkvirtskhlebi/tadzdreulni*) consisted of spearmen, swordsmen and light infantry. The *azaurni*-knights were fully armoured (both rider and steed) men equipped with a lance, axe, sword, bow and, at least during the fifth century, a shield.

My educated guess regarding the size of the Iberian armed forces is that it consisted of about 20,000 horsemen under the *eristavis* and of the Royal Army of about 5,000–7,000 horsemen under the *spaspet*. The infantry contingent available to serve in the Royal field army would have consisted of 30,000–60,000 men at most. In practice, the size of the Royal Army in the second and third centuries appears to have been about 16,000 cavalry and 30,000 infantry (see Appendix 3). The Iberians could bolster their numbers with forces provided by their tribute-paying or allied tribes of the Caucasus (mostly lightly equipped infantry with some cavalry) and nomadic groups (Ossetes/Alans, Bosporans) who lived north of the Caucasus. The Iberian combat doctrine encompassed all forms of warfare; the sources demonstrate them using guerrilla, siege and regular warfare, as required by the situation. On the basis of the scanty information available regarding Iberian battle tactics, they usually used their cataphracts in the front line to spearhead their attacks, with regular cavalry in the second line and the probably un-armoured infantry in the third line.

It is not known whether Iberia sided with Armenia or Rome in 216, but in light of the fact that the sources do not advertise its revolt against Caracalla as another instance of his failures, there is a strong probability that Iberia stayed loyal to Caracalla during this war. If this was the case, then it is probable that the Iberians contributed allied contingents together with nomadic reinforcements for the Roman army that advanced into Armenia in 216 or attacked Armenia from the north at the same time.

The information regarding Colchis-Lazica is even scantier than that regarding Iberia, but as far as we know this area was firmly in Roman hands during this era. It is quite possible or even probable that they provided allied contingents for the Roman army when it fought in Armenia. The later evidence suggests that the Lazi-Colchian nobility had both infantry (which fought as a phalanx) and cavalry forces (which fought as heavy cavalry). It is probable that the Colchian military organization resembled the Iberian one.

Albania
The details regarding Albania are very scanty and also either early or late, but as far as it is possible to make any conclusions on the basis of such evidence, the Albanian army appears to have resembled the Armenian and Iberian feudal armies. The

flower of the army was its feudal cavalry (light and heavy), which was backed up by infantry (light and heavy). Strabo (11.4–5) claims that the Albanians had a field army of 60,000 infantry and 22,000 cavalry when Pompey invaded Albania, which he claimed to have been stronger than the Iberian field army, but in truth it was only fractionally so. Like other nations in the area, the Albanians could also bolster these figures with nomadic allies. Albanian martial equipment consisted of javelins, spears, swords, bows, armour, shields and helmets, but only the wealthiest could afford to wear metal armour. The Albanians were at this time a client state of Parthia and/or Armenia, so the Romans could expect to find at least some Albanians in all of the armies they faced in the East.

Caracalla's Master Plan

In the course of the late 215 and early 216, Caracalla seems to have come up with a masterful idea that would provide him with another excuse for war, or if that failed at least with a stratagem to pillage Mesopotamia at his leisure. Caracalla asked the hand of Artabanus' daughter in marriage to seal an alliance between the empires. It is probable that this idea had been inspired by Alexander the Great's marriages with Persian princesses. If Caracalla conceived the ruse in the spring of 216, it is clear that the revolt of Armenia must have influenced his views of how to achieve his goals with the least risks. It is very likely that Caracalla dispatched his supreme *Praefectus Praetorio* Theocritus to Armenia to crush the revolt at about the same time as he implemented his plan in Parthia.

Theocritus' Armenian Campaign in 216

It is possible to date Theocritus' Armenian campaign to the spring of 216 because Dio (79.27.4) states that Caracalla had kept Tiridates' (Khosrov the Great) captured mother as prisoner for eleven months. This means that the capture must have been in May/June 216, and since it is clear that it took place somewhere in Ayrarat, the campaign must have begun at the latest in April or early May. Dio claims (78.21.1) that the Armenians defeated Theocritus severely. This is a complete lie, or at least an oversimplification of facts, because the war continued in late 217 and the Romans were then in possession of Tiridates' mother and had a vast amount of booty – none of which is a sign of defeat.

Consequently, one has to seek motives for Dio's claim from other reasons, the likeliest of which are his intense dislike of all things connected with Caracalla and people of the lower classes. Dio explains that the reason for Theocritus' failure was that he was an imperial freedman (a former dancer) and a civil servant, and therefore supposedly lacked military experience. His only recommendation to the post seems to have been his loyalty to Caracalla. The also pro-senatorial SHA has similar sentiments. According to the SHA (Car. 6.1), Caracalla appointed as commander of the Armenian war a man whose character resembled his own. In fact, this can be taken to be evidence of the very high quality of Theocritus' generalship.

248 Caracalla

If Theocritus resembled Caracalla, then he must have achieved similarly glorious military successes as Caracalla, which most of the very hostile sources falsely claim to have been defeats.

It is also easy to see why Dio would have criticized Theocritus' military abilities, if Theocritus resembled Caracalla as stated by the SHA. Dio undoubtedly thought only in terms of using the blunt instrument of naked military force to subdue the Armenians, whereas Caracalla and Theocritus considered the art of war to encompass much more than that. One should see the capture of Khosrov/Tiridates' mother by the Romans (undoubtedly at the behest of Theocritus) in May–June 216 in this light. The intention was undoubtedly to use the mother as a bargaining chip in future negotiations. Dio and his like did not really understand that the use of naked military force was just one of the instruments that could be used to bring about a desired outcome.

The likeliest explanation for the 'defeat' of Theocritus is actually that he was unable to beat Tiridates decisively because Tiridates resorted to guerrilla warfare. The reason for this conclusion is that the vast amount of booty and the capture of Tiridates' mother prove that the Romans had penetrated deep into Armenian territory, which together with the fact that the Romans were still inside Armenian territory in late 217, suggests that Tiridates could not defeat the Romans decisively in a pitched battle and could not prevent them from occupying the Armenian heartland. Since we know that the Armenians and their allies possessed huge reserves of manpower, it is likely that Tiridates did not have the support of all of the Armenian noble houses. Otherwise it is difficult to see how the Romans could have simultaneously faced the huge numbers of Armenians and the vast army of Artabanus in 216. The details of Caracalla's campaign in Parthia suggest that he conducted a simultaneous operation in Media Atropatene so that the Armenians could not receive any support from and seek safety there.

Consequently, Dio is probably correct in that Theocritus suffered some sort of minor reverses in skirmishes, but not such a crushing defeat as he claims. As noted, Dio's careless claims (79.27.4) that the Romans were in possession of booty captured in Armenia and that they were still fighting against the Armenians during Macrinus' reign both show that Theocritus had not suffered any serious defeat – *au contraire*. In other words, Theocritus was a considerably better general than Dio was ready to admit and Caracalla's judgment of his military capabilities better than Dio was ready to acknowledge. As a pompous senator, Dio was overly hostile towards all officers and officials who did not come from the ranks of the old and respected senatorial families. He and his ilk were always hostile towards emperors like Caracalla who supported men of such lowly origins. It seems probable that Theocritus' only failure was that he was unable to crush the Armenian revolt with one swift military action – if the Armenians resorted to guerrilla warfare, it is quite obvious why this was so. Since Theocritus' army was able to capture Tiridates' mother, it is probable that he also conquered a number of fortresses and cities, which in all probability included Dariwnk, Artaxata and Valarshapat (the Royal Residence).

It is also unfortunate that we do not know the composition of Theocritus' force. Did it consist mainly of the new and at least partially green and untested Macedonian and Spartan phalanxes, or did it contain significant numbers of regulars? My own guess is that Caracalla took his new phalanxes with him, but if the former is true, then Theocritus' inability to crush the revolt could be explained away by the presence of green soldiers in the army, but the sources are silent in that respect. On the one hand, it would be incomprehensible that the hostile Dio would have passed by an opportunity to blame the setback or defeat on Caracalla's foolish use of inexperienced Greek phalanxes. In the same breath, if the phalanxes trained by Caracalla in person performed admirably in combat, it is unlikely that these successes would have been mentioned by Dio or by the other similarly hostile period writers. Julius Africanus' comments (Appendix 2) suggest that these new recruits of Caracalla had fought with distinction during the military campaigns of his reign. The only culprits in the sources for the 'defeat' in Armenia are Theocritus and the man who appointed him, but as noted, any reverses suffered by Theocritus are magnified beyond their actual proportion and importance by the hostile sources.

If one compares the opposing forces, it is clear that Caracalla had arrived well prepared for the type of enemy he was facing. The principal fighting forces of the Parthian and Armenian armies were the feudal horsemen that consisted of large numbers of mounted archers and super-heavy cavalry cataphracts. The pike phalanxes were particularly well-suited to fighting against these, while the more traditionally equipped legionaries were not quite as good for these tasks. The Germanic and Scythian cavalry lancers (mostly *kontoforoi*; *kontos/contus*-bearers) recruited by Caracalla were also well-suited to facing this type of enemy. The Alans and Sarmatians had used this type of horsemen with great success against the Parthians, as had Alexander the Great against the Achaemenids. In addition to this, Caracalla may have followed up the example of Trajan (and his own father Severus?) when he recruited large numbers of light Moorish javelin-armed cavalry and infantry to act as his skirmishers and scouting troops.[19] It should be noted that in addition to the lancers and Moorish javeliners, Caracalla's cavalry included regular Roman legionary and auxiliary cavalry, which also included specialist *kontoforoi* and *hippotoxotai* (mounted archers) units besides multipurpose cavalry. Caracalla had brought with him an army that could take on any enemy, and if there had been any weaknesses in the army, Caracalla had emended them through his own additions and modifications. Consequently, it can be said with great confidence that Caracalla had come very well prepared for any obstacles his enemies could throw in his way.

Caracalla's Persian War: The Ruse in 216

Caracalla's stratagem was to ask the hand of Artabanus' daughter in marriage and thereby form a confederacy of the two peoples. His proposed alliance also included commercial dimensions, allowing merchants from both sides to practice their trade unhindered without having to resort to smuggling. The interesting part of this suggestion is that it proves that at the time the Parthians and Romans had placed high customs tariffs for traders crossing their mutual borders. This would have encouraged smuggling, especially among the Arabic peoples occupying borderlands, as well as the use of the Red Sea route to India. The use of the sea route cut off the Parthians from the lucrative trade of the Silk Road passing through the Kushan lands and India, and from the spice trade of India. It should be noted, however, that Caracalla had no intention of keeping his word! Dio (or rather the extant portion of Dio) claims that Artabanus refused the request, because he realized full well the potential danger this could pose. Caracalla could claim Parthia as his dowry. The refusal offered Caracalla the excuse for war that he was seeking. However, Herodian provides an entirely different account. He states that Caracalla managed to persuade the King of Kings that his offer was made with true intentions. Herodian claims that Caracalla's persistence and his gifts and promises, that must have included the promise of an alliance against Vologaesus, convinced Artabanus.[20] The beginning of the revolt of the Sasanian Ardashir (Ardašir) I in the province of Persis and the possibility of the Romans siding with Vologaesus may also have influenced Artabanus' sudden willingness to ally with the quite untrustworthy Roman. Caracalla's admiration of Alexander may have played its part in making the proposed marriage contract appear more plausible. After all, the real life Alexander did marry Persian and Sogdian princesses. The location Caracalla suggested for the meeting and marriage was also chosen in imitation of Alexander. It was Arbela-Gaugamela, and was to be the place where Caracalla would defeat Artabanus with far greater ease than Alexander had Darius.

Dio (79.1.1–4, tr. by Cary, pp.341–43, with my comments in square brackets) tells us:

> 'After this Antoninus made a campaign against the Parthians, on the pretext that Artabanus had refused to give him his daughter when he sued for her hand; for the Parthian king had realized clearly enough that the emperor, while pretending to want to marry her, was in reality eager to get the Parthian kingdom incidentally for himself. So Antoninus ravaged a large section of the country around Media ['*polla men tês chôras tês peri tên Mêdian*'] by making a sudden incursion, sacked many fortresses [*which proves the effectiveness of the 'machines'*], won over Arbela, dug open the royal tombs of the Parthians, and scattered the bones about. This was the easier for him to accomplish inasmuch as the Parthians did not even join battle with him [*this actually suggests that Herodian's account is correct; Caracalla had managed to neutralize the Parthian field army with his ruse*]; and accordingly I have found nothing of especial interest to record concerning the incidents of that campaign except the following anecdote. Two soldiers who had seized a skin of wine came upon

Campaign Against Artabanus in 216   251

him, each claiming the booty as his alone; upon being ordered by him to divide the wine equally, they drew their swords and cut the wine skin in half, apparently expecting each to get a half of the wine in it. Thus they had so little reverence for their emperor that they troubled him with such matters as this, and exercised so little intelligence that they lost both the skin and the wine [*this account bears some resemblance to the story of Solomon's judgment in the Bible and it raises two questions: has Dio or the epitomator recorded the incident correctly?; if the event took place actually as in the Bible, it may suggest that Caracalla was familiar with the story of Solomon like the women in his family were and like one of Caracalla's childhood friends who converted into Judaism*]. The barbarians took refuge in the mountains beyond the Tigris in order to complete their preparations, but Antoninus suppressed this fact and took himself as much credit as if he had utterly vanquished these foes.'

Herodian (4.10.1–11.9, tr. by Whittaker, pp.429–41, with my comments in square brackets) adds:

'Soon after this Antoninus wanted to have the title "Parthicus". So although there was in fact complete peace, he formulated the following plan. He wrote to the Parthian king, called Artabanus ... in letters he alleged that he was anxious to marry the king's daughter ... The Romans had an infantry force which was invincible in close-quarter fighting with spears [*note the implication that the Roman infantry fought with dory-spears, i.e. they may have imitated the Macedonians as the recreation of its units by Caracalla suggests; note, however, this does not mean that all Romans would have been equipped in like manner*], while the Parthians had a large cavalry force who are highly skilled in archery. If these forces united they would have no difficulty in ruling the whole world ... On the receipt of this letter the initial Parthian reaction was to say that a Roman marriage to a barbarian was not suitable [*e.g. just like Dio, Herodian states that Artabanus refused initially. To me this suggests the probability that the extant compilation of Dio is either incomplete because the compiler has failed to understand the text, or that Dio purposefully hid the use of a successful ruse by Caracalla*]. But when Antoninus pressed his case ... the barbarian king was convinced. He advanced until he ... was now near Artabanus' palace. But then Artabanus ... came out to meet him on the plain before the city and greeted him as the bridegroom. ... The entire barbarian population celebrated the occasion [*note that Antoninus had managed to lure the king to an unsafe place, just like Crassus had been lured by Suren to peace negotiations; poetic justice undoubtedly in Caracalla's mind*]. ... After all the people came together, they dismounted from their horses and, laying aside their quivers and arrows. ... They expected nothing out of the ordinary. ... This was the point at which Antoninus gave the signal to order his army to set upon the barbarians and kill them [*note how securely Caracalla's plan*

252 Caracalla

had been kept secret within the Roman army; the enemy had been completely taken by surprise. If one compares this one-sided butchery with Alexander the Great's battle at Arbela, it becomes quite obvious that Caracalla was the better general of the two]. Artabanus himself was snatched from danger by his bodyguard and placed on a horse. ... But the rest of the barbarians ... after letting the horses out to graze, were cut down. And so, after a great massacre of the barbarians, Antoninus retired unopposed, loaded with booty and prisoners. On the way he burned down villages and towns, giving his troops permission to loot. ... Antoninus, however, marched throughout the length and breadth of the Parthian territory [*note the extent of ravaging suggested by this statement*], until even his soldiers were exhausted from looting and killing, and he returned to Mesopotamia.'

Thus, Artabanus made preparations to welcome the Roman emperor at Arbela. Caracalla crossed the Euphrates and Tigris without opposition and was everywhere greeted with sacrifices made in his honour.[21] When Caracalla was nearing Arbela, Artabanus came out to meet him on the plain before the city. The whole population celebrated the arrival of the bridegroom and the Romans. The entourage of Artabanus dismounted from their horses, laid aside their quivers and arrows, and began to make libations with their wine cups for the success of the marriage of two peoples. The Parthians were in complete disorder, because they were lulled into believing that the Romans would arrive in peace. They were only waiting to get a view of the bridegroom. According to Herodian, it was at this point that Caracalla ordered his troops to attack and kill the unsuspecting Parthians. However, Artabanus was saved as a result of the quick thinking of his bodyguard, who immediately placed the King of Kings on a horse. It was only with great trouble that Artabanus, together with a few followers, managed to flee the butchery on horseback. But his children and relatives were among those who perished.[22]

Caracalla had managed to destroy with a single masterful stroke most of the Parthian nobility supporting Artabanus.[23] It is likely that Caracalla's treacherous behaviour towards Artabanus saved Vologaesus from utter defeat, and influenced the great Sasanian King of Kings Shapur I to use similar tricks. When the Romans now engaged Artabanus' army, Vologaesus got his chance to regroup his scattered forces and renew the war against his brother. In other words, one of Caracalla's goals was probably to keep the enemy forces divided. This had far-reaching consequences for the future, because Caracalla had seriously weakened the Parthians at a time when the Sasanian Ardashir had raised his flag of revolt. In the short term, however, the treacherous behaviour of Caracalla meant that the Romans could pillage and plunder the length and breadth of Parthian territory until the soldiers were utterly exhausted from the looting and killing. The remaining Parthians either withdrew to the mountains, where Artabanus began to assemble his forces, or engaged the Romans in a relatively unsuccessful guerrilla campaign, proven by the fact that the Parthians were unable to prevent the pillaging. It is very likely that Caracalla's army followed the policy of systematic destruction of cities, forts, crops, fields, water wells and fruit trees in the manner described by Julius Africanus in his *Kestoi* (Appendix 2). This is the only logical explanation for the huge quantities of poisons stockpiled by Caracalla.

The sources are not very specific as regards the details or extent of Caracalla's operations. Dio (79.1.1ff.) merely states that he ravaged a large section of territory 'around Media' and sacked many fortresses, gained possession of Arbela without struggle and destroyed the royal tombs there. The Parthians avoided combat and withdrew to the mountains 'beyond the Tigris' to regroup. Since Arbela was in Adiabene, which lay east of the Tigris, and Media lay east of Arbela, it is clear that Dio's text means the Elburz Mountains. This would mean that Caracalla had encountered the Parthian *shahanshah* near Arbela like Alexander the Great and had then pursued him to the Elburz Mountains, which was located just west of the Parthian heartland. The sacking of many fortresses proves that Caracalla put his siege machines to good use.

According to Herodian (4.11.1ff.), Caracalla advanced peacefully up to Arbela, after which he pillaged the Parthian territory widely until his soldiers became exhausted from looting and killing. The permission to loot and pillage at will was very generous, because the emperor and the state did not receive their share of the booty. The soldiers were undoubtedly very happy as a result. Herodian's statement is even less specific than Dio's, but proves the great extent of damage inflicted on the enemy.

The SHA (Car. 6.4ff.) states that Caracalla advanced through the territories of the Cadusii and the Babylonians and fought against the Parthian satraps. This suggests four possibilities: 1) that Caracalla divided his army in three, with one army advancing to Armenia, the second under Caracalla to the Elburz Mountains while still another marched to Babylonia (this is the least likely); 2) that Caracalla advanced first to the Cadusian territory in the Elburz Mountains through Media Atropatene, then south to Rayy or Media and from there westwards up to Babylonia; 3) that Caracalla marched to the Cadusian territory, retreated back to the Tigris and then marched south to Babylonia; 4) or that the SHA uses Babylonia inaccurately. What is notable about this is that the SHA's information is not contradicted by the other sources, even if they do not specifically mention Babylonia. Alexander the Great's connection with Babylon actually suggests that Caracalla would have had a particular interest to visit the ruins. Dio's text supports the advance up to the Elburz Mountains (Cadusii), and his unclear statement about the pillage of large areas around Media can be used to support an even greater area covered by Caracalla's forces than stated by the SHA. It is difficult to see any reason to contradict the information of the vast extent of damage inflicted when these statements are made by very hostile sources. Consequently, there are strong reasons to think that the SHA is correct in stating that Caracalla or one of the Roman divisions advanced up to Babylonia, which would actually have been easy to accomplish because Vologaesus V (VI) did not possess adequate forces to oppose them and was also officially at peace with Caracalla, and therefore his ally against Artabanus. There are

ABOVE: A nineteenth century Persian horseman employing the famous Parthia shot. The archer uses a *siper* ("shield") in the left hand to increase the length of the draw. It was probably invented in the fifth century AD. Drawn after Drouville. The Parthian shot would have seen widespread use during Caracalla's 216 campaign against Artabanus because the latter did not have enough men to engage the Romans in the open. Excluding the stirrups, the rest of the equipment is very close to the equipment worn by the third century Parthians and Persians. Note the use of the javelin-quiver for short javelins below the arrow quiver, a practice which is quite similar to the one employed by the Romans.
BELOW: Two nineteenth century Persian light cavalry horsemen. Drawn after Drouville. This illustration demonstrates well how the short javelins/darts would have been used during pursuit also by the Romans.

similarly quite strong reasons to accept that Caracalla also pillaged some of the areas surrounding Media, because this piece of information comes from the intensely hostile Dio. Of note is also the claim in the SHA (Car. 6.4) that when Caracalla advanced through the lands of the Cadusii and Babylonians and fought a campaign against the Parthian satraps he let loose wild beasts against the enemy. It is very likely that these were the pet lions of Caracalla mentioned by Dio (79.1.5–2.1, 79.7.2–3). According to Dio, Caracalla violated all precedents in his campaigns (and also invented his own costume), but unfortunately a lacuna in this part prevents us from knowing what he meant. However, before the lacuna Dio states that Caracalla himself told in his writings that he was particularly elated because a lion who had run down from a mountain and fought on his side. Dio considered this as one of the instances that violated the precedents. I would suggest that it is probable that the lion in question was Caracalla's pet lion Akinakes and that this referred to Caracalla's use of his pet lions (wild beasts) against the Parthians also mentioned by the SHA. This certainly struck fear in the enemy and was apparently purposefully advertised by Caracalla possibly for the very same reason. According to Dio, Caracalla always kept many pet lions around him, but it was only his favourite Akinakes (named after the Persian short-sword) that Caracalla caressed in public and had as a bedfellow and table-companion. It is clear that this had a security function as well and it is also notable that Caracalla called his barbarian bodyguards with the same name, lions. This is not the only instance of an emperor keeping wild animals for his own protection. For example, Valentinian I kept two female bears for the very same reason (see *MHLR Vol.2*). It is quite clear that the presence of these lions would have frightened most of the guests of Caracalla senseless, much to his own amusement and to the amusement of his barbarian bodyguards. The guests would have been quite aware that the domesticated wild animals could be unpredictable. In fact, Dio gives us an instance in which Akinakes seized Caracalla when he going out and tore his clothing to shreds.

To sum up, the evidence suggests that Caracalla inflicted horrible damage to the Parthians at very little cost to his army, and used his siege engines to very good effect.[24] He achieved far greater success with far fewer losses than Trajan and his father Septimius Severus ever did, and one can only guess at what he would have achieved if he had been given a few more years to live. The treacherous actions of Caracalla caused such intense anger in Artabanus and his followers that Artabanus planned to give Caracalla his chance to fight a decisive pitched battle next year. In other words, Caracalla's actions caused Artabanus to behave in a manner that was in the Roman interest.

My own educated guess is that Caracalla timed his invasion of Armenia to occur at about the same time as he surprised Artabanus, so that his actions in Armenia would not cause any alarm. The Armenian division under Theocritus would have advanced to Ayrarat only after Artabanus had been surprised, either from: 1) Satala; 2) or he stayed with Caracalla until they reached Lake Urmia and then advanced north; 3) or he stayed with Caracalla up to the Ganjak/Tabriz region and attacked Armenia from an unexpected direction usually used by the Parthian/Persian invaders, which at the same time cut off the Armenians from Parthia. I would suggest that the third alternative is the likeliest. Caracalla in his turn would probably have advanced along the main road skirting the southern frontier of Armenia (Adiabene, Persia, Media Atropatene) up to the lands of the Cadusii, and from there to Media (despite what

Dio says) or Tabaristan, because it would have been difficult for Caracalla to return via the same route that he had just pillaged. If Caracalla's attack followed this logic, and I would suggest that it did because it was the standard military doctrine, then he would probably have marched along one of the main roads to Rayy, the capital of Artabanus (or through Hamadan straight to Nihavand), and from Rayy through Nihavand (which was in Media), past Ctesiphon and Seleucia and on to Babylonia. Note that there was officially peace between Caracalla and Vologaesus after 215. The fact that Caracalla did not pillage Media proper (Dio's version) may suggest that this area was under Vologaesus, or that Caracalla sought to add it to the territories of Vologaesus. It is even possible that Vologaesus could have provided supplies for Caracalla's army in Media, because the Romans were fighting against his enemy Artabanus. However, it is equally clear that we should not accept any claim of Dio at face value. It is entirely possible that Caracalla also pillaged Media proper.

I would therefore consider it probable that Caracalla's forces sacked at least the cities of Ganzak and Tabriz en route to the lands of the Cadusii, and that they may also have sacked Rayy for its symbolic importance it was the capital of Artabanus, and his flight to Parthia had left the city undefended. The looting of the Fire Temple, which was located either in Ganjak or at Takt-e Solayman, was also symbolically very important because it was the locale of the most important Fire Temple of 'Media', or rather Media-Atropatene (the later Temple of the Warrior Class under the Sasanians), and its desecration was a terrible blow to the prestige of Artabanus. It is possible that this sacrilege, together with the butchery of relatives at Arbela, incited the Parthians under Artabanus to even greater anger against the Romans. The defilement of the sacred temple would also have eased the rise of the Sasanians, who were the keepers of the competing Fire Temple of Anahita in Fars/Persis.

The other alternative is that Caracalla avoided Media completely and marched from the lands of the Cadusii straight back to the Tigris (despite having pillaged the area previously),[25] and then along it south past Ctesiphon (where he could have negotiated with Vologaesus) to visit Babylon. In my opinion, the fact that there were detachments from *IV Scythica*, *III Cyrenaica*, *XVI Flavia*, *III Gallica* and *vexillatio Antoniniana* at Dura Europus in 216[26] makes it very likely that Caracalla did indeed visit Babylonia as claimed by the SHA, and that these detachments were left at Dura by Caracalla when he retreated from Babylonia. In short, it is probable that Caracalla also visited the city of Babylon in Babylonia because of its connection with Alexander the Great, who died there. Since the Romans had occupied Babylon under Trajan in 116, Lucius Verus in c. 165 and Septimius Severus in c. 198, it would be surprising if Caracalla had not done the same when his forces reached Babylonia. The city, however, was a mere shadow of its former self, because most of it was already in ruins when Trajan visited it (Dio 68.30.1).

The marching through Babylonian lands and the fighting against the satraps in the SHA also suggests the possibility that Caracalla fought as an ally of Vologaesus against the Satrap of Babylonia and the Arabs of that area (al-Hira was in this area), and possibly also against the Satrap of Mesene (the swamps of modern Iraq), whose territory lay just east of Babylonia and where there was a city founded by Alexander the Great called Alexandria, Antiochia or Spasinou Charax, close to the modern city of Basra. What appears probable is that Caracalla devastated the area just south of Ctesiphon/Beth Aramaye on behalf of Vologaesus. It would otherwise be very difficult to explain why there were no hostilities between the Romans and Vologaesus during the reigns of Caracalla and Macrinus. The ease with which the first ruler of Sasanian Persia, Ardashir I, crushed the forces of the Satrap of Mesene in 223, when Artabanus was still strong, could easily be explained by the fact that Caracalla had engaged and crushed the forces of this satrap at the same time as he devastated Babylonia in 216.[27] It is unfortunate that we do not know this with any certainty. All that we have is circumstantial evidence that points in this direction. The following maps show some of the major cities and fortresses that Theocritus conquered during this campaign and Caracalla probably conquered.

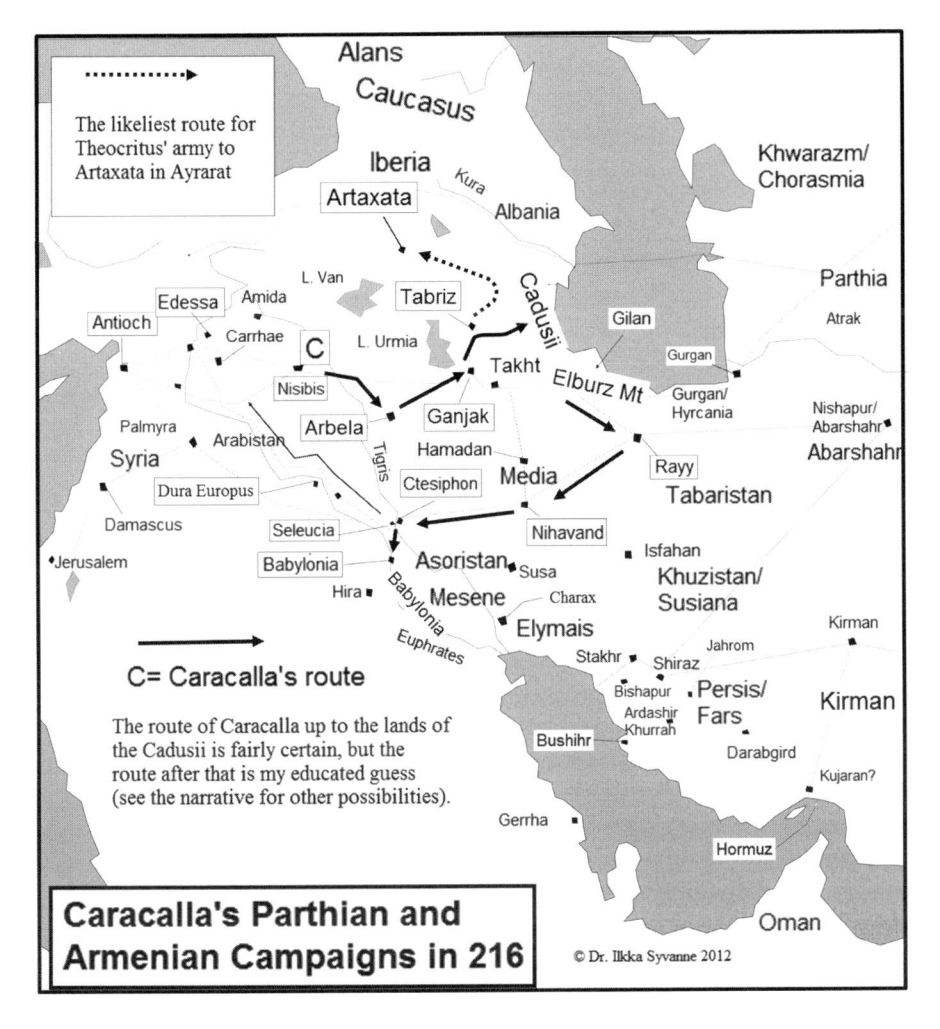

258 Caracalla

It is worthwhile to compare Dio's treatment of Trajan's Parthian War (68.17.1ff.) with that of Caracalla's campaign. It should be stressed that all of Dio's descriptions

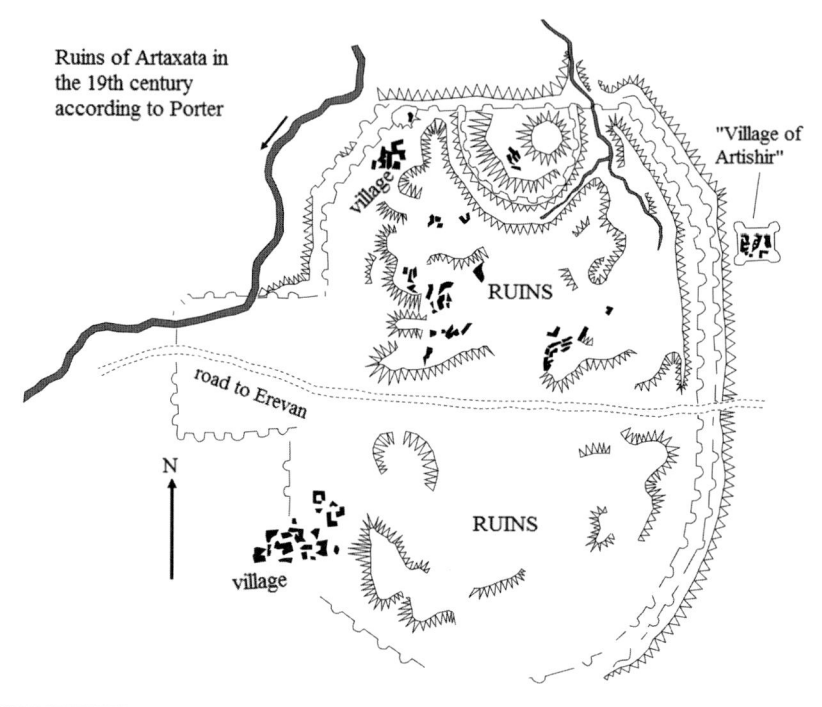

Ruins of Artaxata in the 19th century according to Porter

"Village of Artishir"

RUINS

road to Erevan

N

village

RUINS

source: Jane Dieulafoy

The type of massive mud brick walls Caracalla's army would have needed to level or penetrate in the course of the campaign

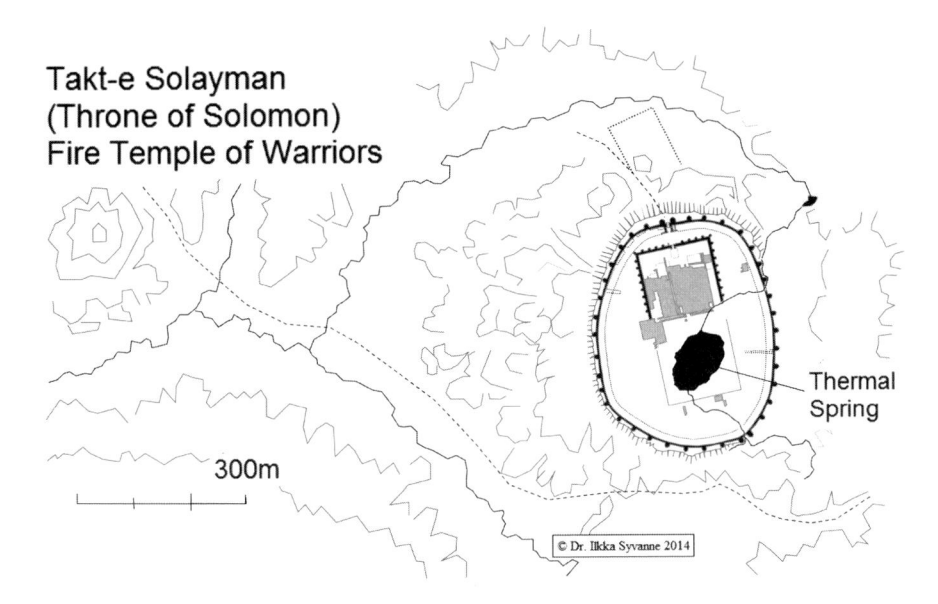

Campaign Against Artabanus in 216   259

Takt-e Solayman (Throne of Solomon) Fire Temple of Warriors

Thermal Spring

300m

© Dr. Ilkka Syvanne 2014

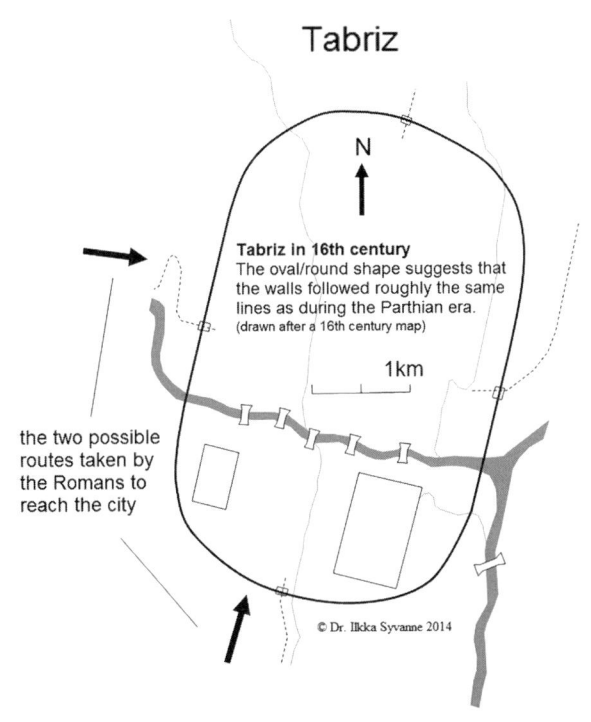

Takt-e Solayman: The current theory is that one of three most revered fires of the Sasanian period, the Fire of the Warriors (Adur Gushnasp), was originally located at Ganzak (Ganja, Ganjak, Haza, Ganzaca) from which it was then relocated to the nearby Takt-e Solayman (Throne of Salmon) in the 5th century (Boyce and Huff). The confusion of the places took place apparently already in antiquity or during the medieval times. In my opinion it is actually possible that the Fire was already located at Takt-e Solayman during the Parthian era, and that the confusion would rather have resulted from the nearness of this location to Ganzak. It is considerably more likely that the Fire was located in this place because it possessed a thermal spring lake (21°C) that would have made it an ideal location for the Temple rather than in a city with no such connections with the forces of nature. It should also be noted that Takt-e Solayman was already fortified with mud brick walls during the Parthian period, but the extent of these is not known with certainty. The illustration above (adapted from Rawlinson and Huff) shows the Sasanian Walls, which were built in many stages: 1) the mud brick wall was a massive 12m thick construction (the inner dotted line shows the inner portion) with many periods of rebuilding (in my opinion this included the Parthian perdiod); 2) the razing of the top of the mud brick wall and its replacement with stone and baked brick wall after 528, which is shown with the black wall. The location of the fortress on a hill of 60m above the valley shows well what type of forts Caracalla's forces were able to take on the go. This demonstrates how impressive the siege train he possessed was. © Dr. Ilkka Sycanne 2014.

Tabriz

N

Tabriz in 16th century
The oval/round shape suggests that the walls followed roughly the same lines as during the Parthian era.
(drawn after a 16th century map)

1km

the two possible routes taken by the Romans to reach the city

© Dr. Ilkka Syvanne 2014

The City of Rayy
– The citadel and the wall of Shahrestan were built during the early Parthian period (ramparts consisted of mud bricks; construction style was the same as in Balkh), which continued to be occupied during the Sasanian period. The small castle Qal'a Gabr/Qal'eh Gabr was probably built by the Sasanians and then incorporated into the latest wall during the Islamic period and came to be called the Gate to China. The city was enlarged during the early Abbasid period with a new town called Mohammadiya (not shown on the map). Before this, the original Ray (Citadel and Shahrestan) had already been enlarged with Bibi-Zobayda (Zubaideh), Hosaynabad (Husseinabad), Chasma-ye (Cheshmeh Ali), Chal Tarkan, Tepe Mill, Eshqabad, Nezamabad (Nasrabad?) and still later by Varamin (some of these are not shown on the map). The earliest Muslim construction was the quarter of Azdan south of the fortified city into which was added Nasrabad and Mehdiabad (built for the occupants of Shahrestan so that the mosque could be built there). Source: Rocco Rante and the accompanying maps, which are slightly at variance with the text.

– My own educated guess is that the late Parthian and early Sasanian city would have encompassed the Citadel, Shahrestan, and the area just behind the 8th–9th century ramparts (it is probable that it was built by incorporating earlier material into it) so that it would have encompassed the area just north of Azadan, but would have included Nasrabad. Husseinabad, Bibi Zubaideh and Cheshmeh Ali. Qal'eh Gabr served probably as an outpost to make it more difficult to approach the main fortifications. It may have existed already under the Parthians, but certain evidence for its existence dates only from the Sasanian period. The reason for this educated guess is that Rayy served as the HQ and capital for Artaban as a result of which it is unlikely that it would not have been a major city at the time. Since the Azadan was founded south of the city walls for the occupying garrison of Arabs, the walls must have been located north of it.

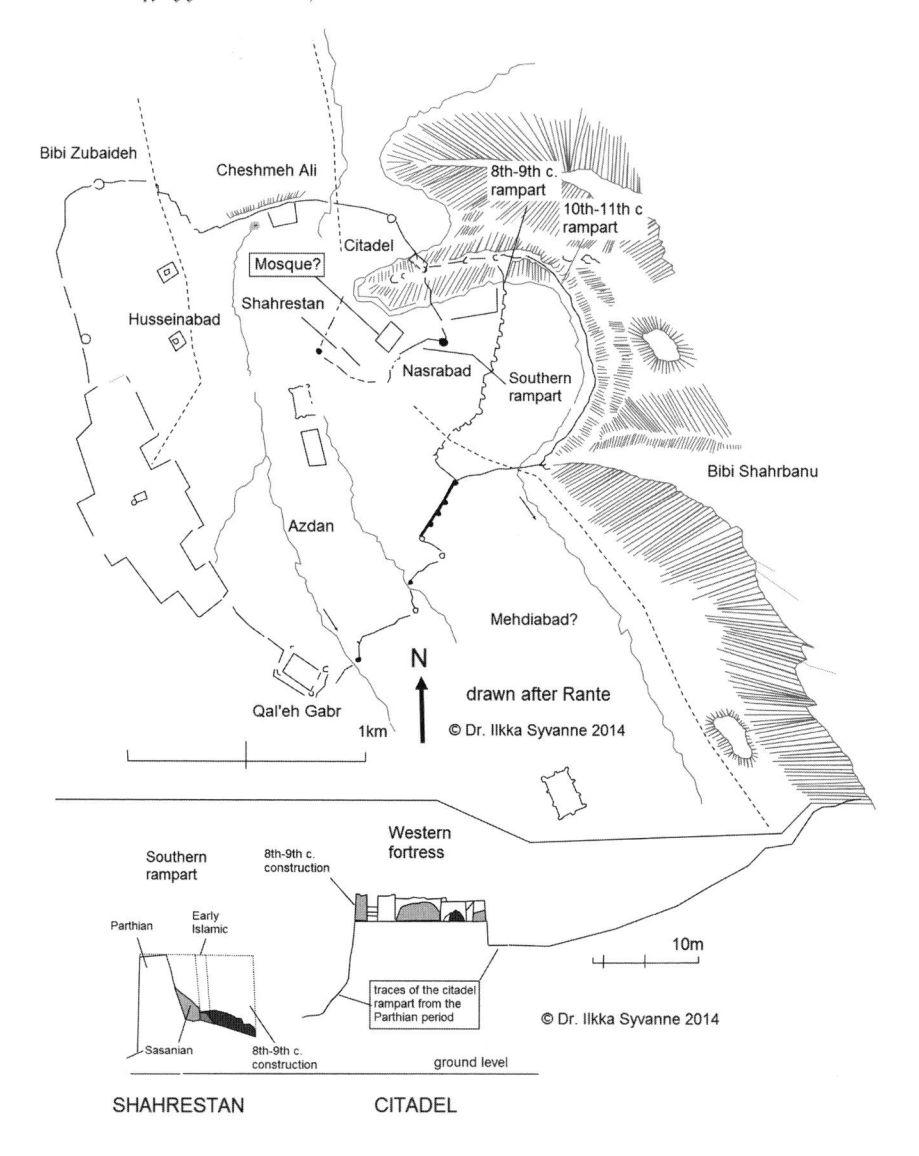

of the Parthian Wars were coloured by the fact that he was opposed to the wars of conquest in the East and considered all wars against Parthia – most of which actually resulted from Parthian invasions, which in my view definitely required some sort of punishment if Rome wanted to remain a superpower – as vainglorious exercises meant to bolster the emperor's standing among the troops.

Trajan began his campaign in 113 with thorough preparations. The cause of the war was the nomination of the nephew of the Parthian king as king of Armenia without Roman permission, as would have been required. The Parthian King Khosrov tried to negotiate, but with no result. Trajan's intention was to secure the border regions in 114 with a combination of force, diplomacy and stratagems. Consequently, when Trajan began his invasion all local satraps and kings, with the exception of the kings of Osroene and Armenia, immediately showed their obeyance by appearing before Trajan. The Armenian king required a little more persuasion before he too agreed to come before Trajan to accept the throne back from him. This, however, was a stratagem: the king was deposed and exiled. Dio does not include any long diatribes against treacherous behaviour in this case, but notes that the soldiers hailed Trajan *imperator* because of his bloodless victory. Dio clearly reserved an entirely different set of comments against Caracalla when he employed a similar trick against the king of Armenia. On top of this, Dio praises Trajan for his readiness to march on foot with the rank-and-file and for fording all the same rivers as the troops. Once again, Caracalla received completely different treatment when he engaged in similar behaviour.

After this, Trajan conquered Nisibis and Batnae and marched to Edessa. Trajan would have disposed of Abgar as well, but Abgar's shameless pimping of his handsome young son to the gay Trajan turned Trajan's head. In 115, Trajan secured Mesopotamia and raided Adiabene, and in 116, forced a crossing of the Tigris, subdued Adiabene and then fought his way to Seleucia, Ctesiphon, Babylon and the Persian Gulf. Parthian resistance was weak because the realm was wrecked by civil war. In this case the exploitation of the Parthian civil war is not called a lucky break, as it was for Caracalla. Trajan's campaign ground to a halt when the conquered territories and the Jews of Cyrene, Cyprus and Egypt revolted. No such thing happened under Caracalla, who followed a policy of religious tolerance. The granting of Roman citizenship must have had a role in this too. The massacre of the Alexandrian (probably pagan) youth and the creation of the walled ghetto ensured peace in this city. Furthermore, the Arabs had been pacified with the unknown military action that had earned Caracalla the title of *Arabicus*. Caracalla faced troubles only in Armenia, and these were not his fault, because the king he had installed on the throne died in combat.

After Caracalla's victorious army had reached Babylonia, it began its long homeward trek, which the enemy was powerless to oppose. Consequently, the Roman army reached its winter quarters in Mesopotamia and Syria in a state of joy.[28] The coins announced *Victoria Parthica* with good reason, but Caracalla knew that the war was not over and made preparations to continue his campaign next year. The headquarters of the army was placed at Edessa in the territory of Osroene. In other words, the army was spread out in order to ease its provisioning, which was the unenviable duty of their quite unwilling host families in the cities. The events of the following spring prove that, despite being settled in winter quarters, the army was still concentrated in so small an area that it was easy to collect together at a moment's notice. The placing of the headquarters at Edessa shows that Caracalla intended to continue the campaign next year, as Edessa was ideally located for both defence and offence because it was in a forward position from Antioch but still behind the defensive bulwark of Nisibis. Unsurprisingly, the city of Edessa served in this very same capacity during the following centuries. Caracalla knew well where to place his HQ. The enemy was about to commit his army to a decisive battle, which was something that Caracalla desired to happen after 200 years of inconclusive fighting between the powers. This once again proves Caracalla's skills as a general.

It is unfortunate that we do not know how Caracalla intended to achieve his conquest of Persia. There are basically three different ways in which he could have hoped to achieve this after the defeat of the enemy's field armies: 1) the occupation of the territory with enough men to garrison the entire country after people had been terrorized with a killing spree (this could mean that Caracalla intended to settle inside his new territories like Alexander); 2) the annihilation and/or mass deportation of the people; 3) the setting up of client kings to rule the territory. There was also the option of a combination of all of these methods. The Romans lacked adequate numbers to occupy the territory with garrisons, because they used a professional army, so one may guess that this was not Caracalla's plan, unless he intended to settle barbarians from other territories inside Persia to act as his occupying army. Caracalla implemented the second policy during his 216 campaign, but it is unlikely that he would have dreamed of attempting to kill so many people as there were inside so vast an empire as Persia. There is no firm evidence for the use of client kings to rule the territory, because Caracalla had just annexed the previous kingdoms inside the Roman Empire. However, the setting up of client kingdoms had been Trajan's goal and had also been used by Alexander the Great to limit the number of garrisons needed. Consequently, it is possible that Caracalla's intention was to follow this policy while removing some of the previous client kingdoms so that their number would remain limited. The likeliest alternative is that Caracalla intended to use all three methods. There is obviously no definite proof for this, but this appears to have been the model used by Alexander the Great and by Caracalla himself in Britain and therefore the one that Caracalla would probably have imitated. It should also be remembered that Caracalla had already demonstrated his readiness to please foreigners he had defeated by adopting their dress, which was also one of the key methods used by Alexander the Great to make it easier for his Persian subjects to accept him as their ruler. It is very likely that this would also have been one of the means that Caracalla would have used.

Notes

1. According to Whittaker/Herodian, p.428, an inscription at Alexandria proves that Caracalla was still there in late January 216. However, by 27 May 216 he was definitely at Antioch.
2. This is based on Syvänne (2004) and Syvanne (2013; MHLR Vol.1; *Mil. Hist. of Iran*, forthcoming).
3. Saka/Sakai/Sacae = an ancient nomadic tribe who spoke an Iranian dialect. The Suren were descendants of Sam and Rustam in Ferdowsi. They had a very important role in the conquest of Greek-held territories in Bactria (Kabul), Mesopotamia and India. The demons in Ferdowsi are the Greeks, but the Suren also married themselves into Greek families, as their marriage with the daughter of the king of Kabul proves. It should be noted, however, that the story in Moses (2.28, 2.68) that the Surens, Karins and Isbahbudhans (Aspahapets) all descended from the Armenian branch of the Arsacids may well be at least partially true. It is quite possible that the so-called brothers 'Suren' and 'Karin' married girls from those families (and changed their family names? or were they also girls?) while their sister Koshm married a general from the Isbahbudhan family during the reign of the Roman emperor Tiberius.
4. For other views of the Parthian military, see Shahbazi (2011) and Wilcox, pp.6–24. See also my *The Age of Hippotoxotai* and the forthcoming *Military History of Iran Vol.1* for a discussion of figures.
5. The following discussion of Suren's army is based on Plutarch, Crassus 21.6ff.
6. Note for example, Justin (41.2: Parthian horses and men using 'feathered-armour', i.e. scale or lamellar), and Plutarch (Antony 44.1–45.3: the king had sent his personal retainers to the combat, so there were 40,000 Parthians and Medes that were armed with *contus*-lances and bows).
7. Aelian's 113 men is to be amended to 128. Being an armchair philosopher/theorist, he has made the mistake of assuming that the array was an exact rhombus while still noting the sizes of cavalry units being sixty-four (wedge), 128 (rhombus), 256 etc. and that the wedge was one half of the rhomboid.
8. I have discussed these matters at greater length e.g. at Historicon 2010 and in the Saga Newsletter (see: academia.edu). The Greeks/Macedonians appear to have copied the cavalry square formation and its uses from the Persians, and the wedge from the Scythians. The invention of the rhombus is credited to the Thessalians, but it is possible that they could have copied it from the Armenians and Dahae while serving under the Persians. However, on the basis of our current knowledge and sources, it appears probable that the Armenians and Dahae actually copied their rhombus array from the hated Greeks.
9. Note also that the eighth-century fighting tactic of the Muslims in the so-called *karadis*-formation (plural for the sing. *kardus* of 128 men) means that they had restarted using the old rhomboid formation. The use of rhomboids was particularly useful for cavalry

units deployed on the flanks as it gave them an ability to face attacks from all directions. For earlier use of the rhomboids by the Dahae (Parthians were originally part of the Dahae confederacy) in the Seleucid armies, see Syvanne (2009–2010) (available on Academia.edu).
10. Skupniewicz, e-mails. Herodian (3.4.7–9) refers to the desertion of the Romans who had previously served under Niger and who then taught the Parthians how to use the spear (*doru*) and sword (*xifos*) in combat, and how to construct Roman equipment. It should be noted, however, that Herodian makes wild generalizations in the same context, which should not be taken at face value. The Parthian military and its tactics were not as one-sided as he gives us to understand, as even he later proves. For the *Murmillones* mentioned by Ammianus, see MHLR vols.1–2.
11. The following discussion on archery is based on my earlier articles and presentations and on my MHLR Vol.1 and *Military History of Iran* Vol.1.
12. The arrow-guide with its short darts appears to have been invented by the Sasanians for use against the Turkish multi-layered shields only later, in the fifth (or sixth) century. See *Arab Archery*, pp.125–26 with Syvänne (2004) MHLR; *Reign of Bahram V Gur* (academia.edu and History of the World).
13. Fakhr-i Mudabbir contains a particularly useful list of types of arrows to be chosen against particular defences. For further details, see my analysis of the Battle of Hurmuzjan in *Military History of Iran* Vol.1 and MHLR1. In MHLR Vol.1 and *Military History of Iran* Vol.1 I speculate on the basis of the existence of a drawing of Ardashir I that he invented a new version of the shower archery technique which may have given his men a slight edge over their enemies until they too learnt the technique. It should be noted that such an advantage would have been very slight and that the real differences between the Sasanian and earlier Parthian armies were the higher morale (the result of religious indoctrination) and better leadership.
14. For the great variety of two-handed spear/lance techniques, see Munuyatu'l-Ghuzat, which provides a good overview of the several possible ways of placing the hands, even if it dates from the fourteenth century. The Sasanian reliefs (some of which are included here as line drawings) also give a good indication of such variants.
15. See Syvanne, *A Military History of Iran* Vol.1.
16. This chapter is based on MHLR Vol.1 and *Military History of Iran* Vol.1.
17. Note that this chapter corrects the timing in MHLR Vol.1 by showing that the four-partite system was already in use before the third century AD.
18. It is probable that there were originally only seven principalities, each of which was ruled by a magnate appointed by the king: Shida Kartli, Kakheti, Khunami, Samswilde, Tsunda/Cunda, Cholarzene/Klarjeti and Odzrkhe/Ojrhe. The king added a ninth Persian *eristavi* Peroz to the Eastern *eristavis* in c. 277/8. The original domains of the Western *eristavis* also included the Black Sea coastline and part of Greater Armenia, but these had been lost to the Romans and Armenians before the birth of Christ.
19. Dio 79.32.1.
20. The following account of the war is based on: Herod. 4.9.8–11.2; Dio 79.1.1–5.5; SHA Car. 6.4ff. The very hostile description by Dio is not a reliable source for these events. According to Dio (79.1.1ff.), Artabanus refused to give his daughter in marriage to

Caracalla, with the result that Caracalla ravaged a large portion of the country around Media by a sudden invasion, in the course of which he sacked many fortresses, won over Arbela and dug open the royal tombs of the Parthians. The Parthians did not put up any serious resistance, but resorted to the use of guerrilla warfare. I consider Dio's account, or rather Xiphilinus' epitome of it, less reliable than Herodian's account of events. Herodian's version makes a lot more sense, since it explains why it was possible for Caracalla to loot and pillage far and wide without having to face any serious resistance, as well as the reason for the unforgiving anger of Artabanus because of the way he had been treated (Dio 79.26.2). The same fact has also been noted by Whittaker (Herod, pp.434–35, n.1). Dio was very reluctant to admit that Caracalla's treacherous and cruel behaviour brought results. In fact, it appears very likely that Dio simply glossed over the successes of Caracalla with outright false claims or half-truths.
21. The account of this war is based on the quotes provided together with the other endnotes provided.
22. Herodian 4.14.6.
23. For other analyses of Caracalla's last campaign, see Choisnel, pp.191–93), DeBevoise, pp.262–67, Sheldon (2010) pp.171–73, Verstandig, pp.338–44, and Wolski, pp.192–93. Unsurprisingly, my analysis of the war is far more favourable to Caracalla than any of the above.
24. For a completely different view of the accomplishments, see Barnett, p.26. His view is that the army advanced only as far as Adiabene.
25. The fact that none of the hostile sources suggest any problems with supplies implies that Caracalla did not use the same route, but marched through some other enemy territory as required by military doctrine – hence my suggestion that he marched south from the Elburzt Mountains and from thence west past Ctesiphon.
26. The presence of these detachments together with the *cohors XX Palmyrenorum* are mentioned by Cowan (2002) pp.140–42.
27. Tabari i.818 with my forthcoming *A Military History of Sasanian Iran* Vol.1, which contains full analysis of the sources referring to Ardashir's conquests and also of his strategy.
28. Dio 79.1.1–3.4, 79.11.5–6.

Chapter 11

Caracalla's Anabasis Phase 5: Army at Winter Quarters and the Death of Caracalla, 216–217

According to Dio (79.1.1–12.4), Caracalla's bribery of the soldiers, the great amount of booty obtained so far without much trouble, the favour shown to the barbarian troops and the quartering of soldiers in houses during the winter had demoralized the army to such a point that it was unwilling to fight. As a result of this, Caracalla then supposedly hid from his soldiers the fact that the angered Parthians and Medes were assembling a great army in the mountains beyond the Tigris. For the most part, Dio's account is once again entirely untrue. The only true parts of this account is that the favouritism of the German and Scythian bodyguards had angered some of the Praetorians and that some members of the high command had started to fear for their lives as they had witnessed how Caracalla was in the habit of fooling enemies, but that is all.

Dio's own account of Caracalla's actions contradicts his hostile diatribe. The fact that he (79.4.1) mentions that Caracalla was making preparations to carry on the war against the Parthians (he was by no means frightened and hiding) and Dio's subsequent claims (79.11.5–6) regarding the supposed unwillingness of soldiers to fight are contradicted by his own hostile version of events. The soldiers were fully aware that they would have to fight against the Parthians in 217 and Caracalla was making preparations for the coming war, even if it was not his destiny to carry on the war. The very same thing is also mentioned by the SHA (Car. 6.6): Caracalla's intention was to renew the war against the Parthians next spring. Caracalla was not hiding anything, except perhaps from Dio. The fact that the soldiers had obtained a very significant amount of booty was also known to boost the morale of the army rather than the opposite.

The fact that Caracalla was constantly aware of the war preparations made by the enemy also proves that he possessed first-rate intelligence of enemy plans and operations deep inside enemy territory. This suggests the presence of some high-ranking Parthian and/or Armenian turncoats in Artabanus' army, who are likely to have consisted of supporters of Vologaesus. The availability of such first-rate intelligence can be used to suggest that Caracalla must have cooperated with Vologaesus.

Dio (79.3.2–3) also accuses Caracalla, quite unjustly, of the fact that he supposedly could no longer bear great heat or the weight of armour, and therefore wore sleeved tunics fashioned like a breastplate (i.e. the linen breastplate). According to Dio, Caracalla did not only wear this dress in battle, but also at other times as a protection against assassins. In other words, Dio inadvertently once again admits here that the supposedly cowardly Caracalla participated in battles and smaller fights against the Parthians. This also proves that Caracalla began to wear the Macedonian-type linen breastplate before the winter of 216–217, because it would have otherwise been impossible for him to wear it in battles. The use of the linen breastplate was just another instance of Alexander imitation. However, as noted above, the use of the linen armour may in fact have been a good idea in the heat of Syria and Mesopotamia. Even more importantly, it is clear on the basis of Dio's statement that Caracalla was acutely aware that there was a plot to kill him. In addition, his use of German clothing and shoes in Syria and Mesopotamia, which he probably ordered his men to wear too, and the introduction of the long Celtic hooded cloak called Caracalla/Caracallus (he modified it to reach the ankles) to his army, can be seen as innovative improvements in clothing to make his army better prepared to the circumstances it was facing in the East. The German clothing and Caracalla-cloak obviously protected the men from the effects of the sun. Caracalla was clearly quite prepared to introduce foreign clothing, equipment and tactics, if these were better than the older traditional gear and fighting methods.

Caracalla did not forget the importance of good pastimes and entertainment in the keeping of morale while the army was billeted in cities. In the midst of all the war, killing, death and military drills, the soldiers also needed amusements so that they could cope better with the darker realities of army life. Consequently, just like his model Alexander, Caracalla held games, hunts of wild animals and chariot races to improve the morale of his soldiers. The games encouraged the soldiers to compete amongst themselves for excellence and thereby improved their fighting skills.[1] The hunting of wild animals was doubly beneficial: soldiers were trained in mass movements and the animals could be used to supplement the provisions given to the men. The competitions were a good way to make the soldiers train harder without having to resort to the use of harsher disciplinary measures. It is also notable that Caracalla did not make any attempt to continue the war against Artabanus during the harsh winter, which might have given him the opportunity to exploit the chaos in the interior after his ruse. He rather kept his soldiers happy and prepared for future fighting. Caracalla's willingness to please his soldiers was wiser than the short-term exploitation of military opportunity. If he had not let his men enjoy the rewards of war, he could have risked a mutiny of the army, as later happened for example to Emperor Maurice. The break in hostilities enabled soldiers to recuperate from the previous fighting so that they were better prepared to continue it.

Even in the midst of war preparations, Caracalla did not forget the importance of maintaining peace along the Rhine and Danube frontiers. He took care of the former by meeting the German and Scythian ambassadors with only interpreters present. The contents of these discussions were kept secret from the Romans and, according to Dio, the interpreters were killed to maintain that secrecy. However, according to Dio, the barbarians themselves later told the Romans that Caracalla had instructed them to invade Italy if anything happened to him.[2] It is impossible to verify this accusation, but if Caracalla really said that to the envoys, his purpose must have been to endear the barbarians to him and make them desist from any invasion attempts while he was waging war in the East. According to Dio (79.27.5), the Dacians (probably the Goths) did invade Roman Dacia after the death of Caracalla, but then retreated when the hostages given to Caracalla were returned to them. This gives some support to Dio's claim, but it may have been a coincidence that Dio merely used to blacken Caracalla's fame. Regardless, it is still clear that Caracalla had already to a large extent secured the European frontier with the double measure of his campaigns (that brought hostages) and his recruitment of barbarian troops, which he now sought to solidify even further with his diplomatic promises, and with the favouritism of barbarian troops and by wearing Germanic clothes. In other words, he sought to endear himself further with the German and Scythian allies he had made during those campaigns. For the immediate future, it is important to note that this favouritism of the barbarian bodyguards, the *Leones*, and barbarian troops in general seems to have angered a very small number of tribunes (only two are mentioned) of the Praetorian Guard, while most of them remained steadfastly loyal!

Neither did Caracalla forget the importance of internal security. According to Dio (79.2.1ff.), Caracalla understood full well how the senators hated him, and consequently continued to employ informers and assassins. In addition to these, he had the slaves, freedmen and intimate friends of all of those whom he suspected arrested and then tortured in order to find out what their patrons or friends thought of him. Dio also claims that Caracalla (tr. by Cary, p.343) 'used to judge, as he said, even by the charts of the stars under which any of the prominent men about him had been born, which one was friendly to him and which was hostile; and on this evidence he honoured many persons and destroyed many others'.[3] The key pieces of text in this quote are Dio's statement that it was Caracalla who claimed to believe in astrology and that careers were built or destroyed on the basis of this. This proves beyond any doubt that Caracalla did not believe in astrology at all, at least on the conscientious level. The date of the birth of a person does not change, so if Caracalla would really have trusted someone on the basis of his birth date when he appointed him to high office, he would not have been as suspicious of them as he was later. It was just one of Caracalla's ploys to frighten superstitious fools to seek supernatural protection against Caracalla's 'supernatural powers' to detect the evildoers, which in turn allowed the informers (seers, augurs, conjurors, haruspices, astrologers etc.) to inform Caracalla that someone had resorted to the use of such measures. Had Caracalla really believed in any of the stuff he claimed, he would not have needed to capture people for interrogation and torture them for evidence. Regardless, I would still not completely rule out the possibility that Caracalla believed in the supernatural on some subconscious level, because it is entirely possible for a person to be simultaneously rational and irrational.

These security measures did not help Caracalla, however, because the men who formed the cabal against him belonged to the security apparatus. He evidently did not consider it possible that a usurper could rise from outside the ranks of the elite. Furthermore, Macrinus, the leader of the conspiracy, was an effeminate Moor of lowly origins with a pierced ear. On the surface, it must have appeared impossible to even think that he would aspire to rule. As is usual in the case of conspiracies, we do not know all the details of the cabal in question, because these were hidden even from the period sources, but enough is known to understand the main features. There are still as many versions of the details of the conspiracy as there are authors (and some more), and it is the historian's job to try to untangle fact from fiction.[4]

Despite the fact that Dio does not specifically mention the existence of a plot against Caracalla whose *primus motor* would have been the Praetorian Prefect Macrinus, on the basis of his account it is clear that there was a large conspiracy afoot. According to Dio's version (79.4.1ff.), there was a seer in Africa who had declared that Macrinus, the prefect, and his son Diadumenianus were destined to become emperors. When the local authorities learned of this prediction, the seer was promptly sent to Rome, where he revealed the same prophesy to Flavius Maternianus, the commander of the soldiers in Rome (Urban Prefect). He immediately sent a letter to Caracalla to warn him of the plot. We do not know how the seer came to know of the plot, but his prophecy turned out to be correct. It is possible that he had heard that something was afoot, that someone had made inquiries regarding this or that he simply made a good guess with dire consequences. A more likely alternative is that the information was purposefully shrouded as a prophecy (by a seer who never existed) to cover up the identity of the real informant and to give the impression that the emperor had supernatural means of acquiring information of his enemies' activities. The fact that Macrinus subsequently did not find any secret documents naming the informants from the royal residence also suggests that the reports and documents sent by the secret agents and informants to Caracalla were shrouded in the form of mysterious prophecies – it is of course possible that Macrinus just claimed this to be so. In other words, I would consider it more than likely that Caracalla simply manipulated his more superstitious fellow citizens with his supposed use of seers. Unfortunately for Caracalla, Ulpius Julianus and Julianus Nestor, who were in charge of the couriers (both were *archê ... tôn aggeliaforôn*, which can be interpreted to mean commanders of the *Frumentarii* and/or *Peregrini*, or centurions of the *Frumentarii/Peregrini*), were privy to the plot. Maternianus' letter meant for Caracalla was delayed because it was sent to his mother at Antioch and not directly to him. She read all correspondence and dispatched only the important ones to Caracalla. Macrinus, on the other hand, received a warning from Ulpius Julianus in a timely manner, because this letter was dispatched directly to

270 Caracalla

him by other couriers.⁵ This was the key weakness of Caracalla's internal security apparatus. The persons who were in charge of delivering the messages were not loyal to their employer. One wonders why Caracalla, Julia Domna and their key security officers like Maternianus trusted the officers in charge of the couriers, who had presumably previously worked under Macrinus (and did not use ciphers to hide the contents of the messages from them), when they went to such lengths as to dispatch the messengers to the shrines for security purposes?⁶

In addition, according to Dio (79.4.4ff.), a few days before this, an Egyptian seer called Serapio had told Caracalla that he would be short-lived and that Macrinus would succeed him. According to this version, Serapio had been killed for the insult he had laid on the prefect, but in the same breath Dio says that Caracalla had suddenly removed Macrinus' companions, with various pretexts, away from the prefect's surroundings. In other words, Caracalla had imprisoned Macrinus' companions for the purpose of interrogation, which has nothing to do with prophecies! Macrinus had to act fast if he wanted to live. Caracalla's intention to visit the shrine at Carrhae must have panicked Macrinus. Even though this connection is not made implicitly by the sources, the previous examples clearly show that whenever Caracalla visited a shrine, a purge, execution, poisoning, murder or assassination followed. Macrinus would have been acutely aware of this. Consequently, Macrinus secured the services of two brothers, Nemesianus and Apollinaris (*Apollinarios*), who were tribunes (*chiliarchoi*) of the Praetorian Guard, and one Julius Martialis (*Martialios* enrolled among the *evocati*), who had a private grudge against Caracalla because he had been denied the position of centurion by him. It is uncertain what is meant by this, because the *Evocati Augusti* usually carried a baton just like the centurions and could therefore be seen as such.

On 8 April, Caracalla left Edessa for Carrhae to visit a shrine in the company of his cavalry bodyguards. It appears likely that Caracalla's public intention was to make a prayer in the temple for the successful outcome of the war. Artabanus' cavalry army was approaching fast. The apparent purpose would have been to encourage the men. The second and less apparent purpose would have been to visit the shrine to obtain the 'divine' intelligence report that named Macrinus, which would have been dispatched by Julia Domna to this temple. When Caracalla dismounted from his horse to relieve himself, Martialis approached him as if he wanted to tell him something, and then stabbed him with a small dagger. This was the only way that the expert martial-artist emperor could be killed by a suicidal coward. Martialis fled immediately, but was caught because he did not throw away his dagger. One of Caracalla's Scythian (i.e. Gothic) bodyguards, who was always in attendance with his beloved emperor, noted the bloody dagger and ran Martialis through with his *contus*-spear. After this, there is an unfortunate lacuna in the text, which has resulted in two different translations. According to Cary's interpretation of Dio (pp.347–49), Martialis had only wounded Caracalla, so the tribunes Apollinaris and Nemesianus pretended to come to the rescue, but killed Caracalla. According to Whittaker's view (Herodian p.451) the Scythian was killed by the tribunes (i.e. by Nemesianus and Apollinaris), who pretended to come to his help. Whittaker's translation is probably better, but thanks to the lacuna it is impossible to know this with certainty. Whittaker's translation, however, is also more likely for another reason – the plotters appear to have planned to blame the *Leones* for the murder.

According to Dio (79.6.4), at the time of Caracalla's murder, the soldiers (*stratiôtai*, i.e. the Praetorians) had become estranged from Caracalla, because in their opinion he preferred the barbarians over them. As a result, when Caracalla was killed, they did not come to his aid. Caracalla then died as a victim of a plot formed by the high-ranking members of the Praetorian Guard and because his Roman bodyguards failed to protect him. However, on the basis of Herodian and Dio's own account, which is full of inconsistencies, it is very unlikely that the rank-and-file Praetorians would have been hostile towards Caracalla. This appears to have been Dio's own opinion or purposeful lie. It was unfortunate for Caracalla that his loyal Supreme Praetorian Prefect, Theocritus, was not present, because the Armenian war had become protracted. It was because of this that Macrinus was in a position to act in the way he did. Otherwise, it would have been Theocritus who would have accompanied Caracalla, not Macrinus and his men.

According to Herodian (4.12.1ff.), there were two Praetorian Prefects: one called Adventus, who was an elderly military man of humble origins with a background in military intelligence, and another called Macrinus, who was a lawyer with a liking for luxurious living. As a result of this, Caracalla was in the habit of insulting Macrinus for his unmilitary background. In addition, Caracalla sometimes called Macrinus a coward and an effeminate, and threatened to execute him. The SHA (Macr. 4) gives further details. It claims that Macrinus had been a public prostitute and servant in the imperial palace of Commodus, and that Septimius Severus had initially banished him to Africa, but thanks to the help of his freedman colleague Festus he was made a pleader for the Privy Purse, presumably also under Severus. Contrary to the common view among modern historians, I see nothing improbable in this. This version explains why Caracalla continually called Macrinus an effeminate and why Caracalla had poisoned Festus. It is very probable that the plot to kill Caracalla had been formed already when all the key plotters (including the officers in charge of the couriers) were at Rome. Macrinus had also been the protégé of Plautianus and then of Cilo.[7] It would not be at all surprising if Macrinus held a grudge towards Caracalla, because of the treatment he had received in public and the fate of his patrons and friends. In sum, it is quite probable that Macrinus had from the very beginning of Caracalla's reign been forming a plot against Caracalla with like-minded men, who all had similar lowly backgrounds and character, and it was a terrible mistake for Caracalla to underestimate these men.

According to this version, Caracalla suspected that his seers, astrologers, oracles and sacrificial interpreters were not telling him the truth, but were just flattering him. In my opinion, this should be interpreted as that these seers etc. claimed that nobody had approached them with the wrong kinds of questions that would have put the heads of the curious ones on the block, or that Caracalla thought that his intelligence apparatus (which had dispatched the information to the shrines) had not found out all of the plotters. It is clear that Caracalla feared a plot, because he started to wear linen armour constantly in the spring of 217.[8] Consequently, he sent a message to Flavius Maternianus to consult the seers there to find out the truth. Then, either because the seers had told him so or because Maternianus had come to the same conclusion by other means, he sent a letter to Caracalla in which he warned him that Macrinus was plotting to gain the throne. According to this version, the letter duly arrived at Edessa, but at a time when Caracalla was about to drive his chariot in races. As a result, he supposedly told Macrinus to read his mail. When Macrinus read the letter, he became frightened for his life, because he realized that Maternianus would eventually send a second letter with the same information. In other words, Herodian was unaware of the role that the plotters had in diverting the letters. The other possibility is that Maternianus had indeed dispatched two letters because of the urgency of the situation, one to Julia Domna and another directly to Caracalla, with the result that the latter ended in the hands of Macrinus. Whatever the truth, Macrinus then obtained the services of his former client centurion Martialis, who held a grudge against Caracalla because his brother had been executed just a few days before, and because Caracalla had insulted him with accusations of cowardice, low birth and for being a friend of Macrinus. In Herodian's version Martialis was a centurion, whereas in Dio's version he had been denied promotion to this rank. As has been noted by Whittaker, if the denial of promotion mentioned by Dio is correct, this may have been caused by Martialis' friendship with his patron Macrinus.[9] In my opinion, Herodian's version does have one advantage over Dio's, which is that it gives a more plausible reason for the irrational fanatical hatred shown by Martialis. The grudge must have been very great for him to commit suicide by killing Caracalla.

Consequently, when Caracalla left the camp at Carrhae to visit the temple of Selene[10] in the company only of his cavalry bodyguards so that he would not disturb the whole army, which had apparently already been assembled for the campaign, the plotters were ready. The cavalry bodyguards consisted presumably of the German and Scythian *equites extraordinarii* of the SHA (these were either Caracalla's *Leones*, or alternatively the *Leones* formed a select elite corps belonging to the allied cavalry *equites extraordinarii*), the *Equites Singulares Augusti* and the Praetorian cavalry. When Caracalla felt a stomach ache and dismounted to relieve himself, and the bodyguards turned their heads away, Martialis was ready. He acted as if the emperor had nodded for him to come to him, and then stabbed Caracalla in the back when he was lowering his pants. The wound was fatal. After this, Martialis mounted his horse and fled, but the German bodyguards, who were not standing as far away as the rest, noted Martialis' act, pursued him and ran him through. When the rest of the army saw what had happened, they hastened to the spot. The first to reach the emperor was Macrinus, who supposedly stood over the body, pretending to cry and lament. This would presumably have happened while his two accomplices named by Dio killed the Scythian bodyguard. According to Herodian, the entire army was bitterly angry about the murder, and thought that they had not only lost an emperor but their comrade. The soldiers were unaware of Macrinus' role in the murder. Consequently, it is clear that Dio's account of the hostility of the Praetorians is a fabrication. In addition, it is clear that Herodian was unaware of the role of the tribunes and of the whole scale of the plot.[11]

According to the SHA (Caracalla 6.6ff.), when Caracalla was travelling from Edessa to Carrhae to honour the god Lunus,[12] he stepped aside to relieve his bladder and was thereby assassinated thanks to the treachery of Macrinus. Macrinus' accomplices were Nemesianus and his brother Apollinaris, and Aelius Decius Triccianus, who was the prefect of *Legio II Parthica* and commander of the (German) *equites extraordinarii*. The commander of the fleet, Marcius Agrippa,[13] and many members of the staff who had been told by Martialis, were also privy to the plot. It is possible that this commander of the fleet was the prefect of both Praetorian fleets and thereby the supreme commander of all fleets. The involvement of the commander of the fleet is quite plausible in light of the previous sinking of Caracalla's ship. In other words, the information in the SHA supports the existence of a wide plot and adds other names to the above-mentioned list. This version also differs from the others in other ways. According to the SHA, when Caracalla had dismounted to empty his bladder, he was surrounded by the bodyguards, who were all accomplices in the murder. When his equerry (*strator*)[14] was helping Caracalla to remount his horse, he stabbed him in the side with a dagger, and when this happened all shouted that it had been done by Martialis. The shout must have either been started by someone who believed that he saw Martialis carrying the bloody dagger, as was stated by Dio, or he was one of the plotters (possibly one of the tribunes or the equerry) who then instigated the Scythians to kill Martialis. According to this version, the Praetorians were particularly fond of Caracalla. It was because of this that Macrinus subsequently deified Caracalla and even named his son Antoninus in honour of Caracalla. On the basis of this account, it might be possible to conclude that the murder was committed by the German bodyguards, the *equites extraordinarii*, at the behest of their commander Triccianus, who then framed Martialis as the assassin and promptly killed him to cover up the actual plot, but this is not believable.

The SHA (Macr. 4.7–8) also includes a slightly different version of events. According to this version, Macrinus managed to bribe an imperial equerry, through whom he managed to hide his own role in the murder of Caracalla while spreading the disinformation that Caracalla had been killed in a conspiracy of soldiers because of their dislike of his fratricide and incest. This suggests that the *equites extraordinarii* had nothing to do with the murder, and that it had been committed by the bribed equerry, who may have been Martialis.

In sum, I would suggest that the principal plotters to kill Caracalla were Macrinus, Nemesianus, Apollinaris, Triccianus, Julianus, Nestor and Agrippa, and the deceased Festus. All of the plotters appear to have been freedmen, commoners or equestrians. Agrippa had been one of the exiles whom Caracalla had foolishly allowed to return, and Macrinus had been a protégé of Plautianus. It was a terrible mistake to trust these men. The irony of all this is that the high-ranking military commanders of the senatorial class appear to have remained steadfastly loyal to Caracalla – he clearly feared the wrong class of men. Most of the senators appear to have been poor or mediocre military leaders thanks to their upper-class behaviour (the result of this was the high-handed treatment of the rank-and-file), but if Caracalla had taken the trouble of finding out who were the loyal and competent ones, he would have been far better off than he was with those that he had as his advisors during his final campaign – after all, the equestrian Macrinus was not a competent commander, but Caracalla still kept him in the ranks as a lawyer prefect. The army was full of senators who served as generals, some of whom were actually very competent or were also included among the closests friends and supporters of Caracalla, but thanks to the tradition of not using senators as commanders of the bodyguards, these were not among those who protected the emperor. The senators whose loyalty had been tested would actually have been far better as commanders of the bodyguards. It should still be kept in mind, however, that the social standing or birth of the person does not make a person loyal or disloyal. It is a matter of personality and upbringing, and Caracalla should have paid closer attention to those with whom he surrounded himself. Did he want to keep his potential enemies close by in order to keep a closer watch over them? This was certainly the case with the senators who followed him in the campaign. If this was the case, he clearly miscalculated.

The role of Martialis in the events is not absolutely certain. He may have been used as a suitable idiotic assassin (he is likely to be the equerry), but may equally well have been used as an innocent idiotic scapegoat. The former alternative, however, is the likelier.

The sources also give conflicting information regarding the role of the Germanic/Scythian bodyguards in Caracalla's immediate vicinity. It is possible that they (or one of them, or that the equerry fooled them) were privy to the plot and as a result covered up the existence of a larger plot by killing Martialis. But it is even more likely that they had no foreknowledge of the plot to kill Caracalla, because they had the most to lose if he died. Rather, it is likely that the Scythian or Scythians simply killed Martialis because they thought that he had killed their beloved employer. It is probable that Maximinux Thrax's behaviour would have been quite typical for the members of this corps. He served among the centurions (i.e. among the *Leones*) and left the service when he became aware that Macrinus was Caracalla's successor and killer (SHA Max. 4.4). This does not preclude the possibility that Triccianus and Macrinus could have bribed some of the *Leones* to join the plot, but nonetheless this is the least likely of the alternatives. Their commander Triccianus, however, was definitely privy to the plot to kill the emperor and may have contributed to the success of the plot, for example by organizing the cavalry entourage in such a manner that it was possible for Martialis to get close to Caracalla. At the beginning of Caracalla's reign, the *Legio II Parthica* had been hostile to Caracalla; the presence of their prefect among the plotters shows that Caracalla had miscalculated when he had placed Triccianus in command. However, in contrast to their commander, the *Legio II Parthica* had become to adore Caracalla by the end of his reign. This is proven by their support for Elagabalus, who claimed to be the son of Caracalla.

The lacuna in Dio makes it difficult to know with absolute certainty whether the tribunes Nemesianus and Apollinaris were the real murderers of Caracalla, or whether they just killed the Scythian who had killed Martialis, but the latter is more likely. The plotters seem to have planned to accuse the Scythian *Leones* of the murder, but this failed when one of the Scythian bodyguards saw the bloody dagger of Martialis (or because someone fooled the Scythian to believe it to be so), and it was because of this that the SHA includes the two contradictory claims: 1) the murder had been committed by the *equites extraordinarii* (*Leones*), which is likely to be the intended fictitious story, and the soldiers (i.e. the Scythians) were used as scapegoats by Macrinus; 2) The equerry killed Caracalla.

The presence of the *strator* (Martialis?) in the immediate vicinity of the emperor suggests that the *stratores* (equerries) and grooms of the Imperial Stables formed part of the Imperial Cavalry Bodyguards (as *Stablesiani*?), and that their commander,

Caracalla AR Denarius. January–April 217
ANTONINUS PIUS AUG GERM/VIC PART P M TR P XX COS IIII P P
The reverse side has Victory crowning Caracalla. This coin celebrates Caracalla's Parthian Victory, which unlike Macrinus' subsequent claim was well founded in reality. The soldiers and populace knew this so this coin merely represented matters of fact even if it was still minted for propaganda purposes.

the *Tribunus Stabuli* (Tribune of the Stables), ranked very high in the imperial hierarchy. This position became so important that it was a stepping stone to higher ranks. The best example of this is the rise of Aureolus as Gallienus' *Hipparchos* (*Magister Equitum?*) in the 260s (see MHLR, vols.1–4).

Notes

1. Herodian (4.11.9) mentions chariot races and hunts as Caracalla's pastimes. However, it appears likely that there were also games just like there had been during the previous winter break.
2. Dio 79.6.1–2.
3. Dio 79.2 (Xiphilinus, p.342).
4. In the following discussion I will give only the most important versions in Dio, Herodian and the SHA.
5. Dio 79.4.1–4, 79.15.1, 79.21.1–4 (no documents of informers found from the royal residence: 79.21.1–2).
6. As noted above, the daily sending of couriers to the shrines and back proves that the shrines were used for the dissemination of information, and the executions that took place after the visits to the shrines prove that Caracalla obtained the prophecies (the name of the enemy) on site.
7. See Whittaker's comment (Herod, p.441, n.2).
8. Dio 79.3.2, Loeb ed. pp.344–45.
9. Herod. 4.12.1ff. with the comments of Whittaker.
10. In truth Sîn, a male moon god as noted by Whittaker (Herod. p449, n.3).
11. Herod 4.13.3ff. with the comments of Whittaker.
12. As noted above, the Semitic male moon-deity Sîn.
13. This Marcius Agrippa had been one of the exiles that Caracalla had allowed to return.
14. It should be noted that the SHA doesn't specifically name Martialis as the *strator* as is usually claimed, even if it is possible that he was the *strator* mentioned. It is probable that the *stratores* (equerries) performed the same functions as the Late Roman ones, so that the *stratores* together with the grooms served under the *tribunus stabuli* (Tribune of the Stables). They were responsible for the levy of the horses for the imperial court and the cavalry as a whole. See A.H.M. Jones for the Late Roman *stratores*.

Chapter Twelve

The Apogee of Rome: The Reign of Caracalla Magnus, 'The Ausonian Beast' (211–217)

As we have seen, Caracalla's achievements have largely been covered up by the hostile sources, while his failings or rather his supposed failings have received much attention. This does not mean that we should not see him for what he really was. He was still a ruthless and harsh ruler and a mass murderer, but all the same this should not blind us from his greatness and great achievements, which included such enlighted policies as tolerance of other religions and homosexuals. It was not for nothing that he was loved by the people and the army, and by significant numbers of senators as well.

There is one Latin source that gives Caracalla his due merit as a military leader and emperor. His name is Sextus Aurelius Victor. In his *Liber de Caesaribus* 24.8, Sextus Victor says that Rome had grown through its struggles from the times of Romulus to Septimius, and then because of the successful policies of Bassianus (i.e. Caracalla) it had reached its peak of success. In other words, Victor saw Caracalla's successful foreign policy and military campaigns for what they were really worth. War is an art of deceit; Caracalla was certainly the greatest deceiver of all Roman commanders, and therefore perhaps even the greatest commander of all. The speech to the soldiers put into the mouth of Macrinus by Herodian (4.14.4–5, tr. by Whittaker, p.457) also supports the same inescapable conclusion that Caracalla had been very successful in his military ventures:

> 'Naturally you all are sad about the loss of an emperor of this calibre – or perhaps it would be true to call him a fellow soldier.... We shall preserve the memory of Antoninus in our hearts and pass it on to future generations; it will be glorious for ever because of his important and noble achievements and also of his affection and goodwill towards you and the way he shared in your labours.'

Had Caracalla lived, it is quite possible that he could have achieved the unthinkable, the conquest of Persia, because Persia was at the time divided into three hostile factions, partly thanks to Caracalla's efforts: the Parthians were fighting a civil war amongst themselves; while the Sasanians had raised the flag of revolt in Persis. Artabanus was certainly playing into Caracalla's hands by committing his army to a pitched battle. The situation was never more opportune for aggression as then. It is not a great surprise that the militarily incompetent Macrinus could not defeat Artabanus decisively, but had to settle on buying the peace with money and concessions. Caracalla's judgment of the man was spot on: Macrinus was an effeminate coward. Consequently, the next two emperors, Elagabalus (Heliogabalus) and Alexander Severus, can at best be considered to have been utter military incompetents, and the actual result of Caracalla's potentially successful Parthian policies was the serious weakening of the Roman position, because as a result of his murder the beneficiaries of his policies were the Sasanians and not the Romans, and the new Persian Empire proved to be much stronger and more dangerous as a foe than the Parthians had ever been. Caracalla's immediate successors simply could not match his deftness and skill in the handling of military matters. They were foolish enough to let pass by the once-in-a-lifetime (or once-in-a-century) opportunity resulting from Caracalla's masterful manipulation of the situation. The stability of the Rhine and Danube frontiers until the reign of Severus Alexander also prove how successful Caracalla was in his endeavours.

Excluding the enemy invasions in Pannonia at the very beginning of Caracalla's reign, which required emergency measures, he was otherwise very successful in the securing of all of his frontiers with diplomatic manoeuvres and stratagems, while he conducted major pre-emptive wars which progressed from west to east. This meant that under his rule, the Romans did not face the difficulty of having to concentrate forces from far-flung places to meet major enemy invasions. Under Caracalla, the Romans usually chose when and where the wars took place. He was clearly the best strategist of his day.

Caracalla belongs to the class of great Romans who were murdered by those who were closest to them. These men include such greats as Julius Caesar, Gallienus and Aurelian. In contrast to them, however, he has not received the same level of admiration in modern times as they have, thanks to the influence of the biased sources – it is also not fashionable among cultured historians to shower praise on a person who achieved his successes through treacherous behaviour and mass murders. However, for a military historian like myself it is a great pleasure. The soldiers certainly appreciated the fact that they were able to butcher helpless foes without having to take unnecessary risks themselves. The goal of all good commanders should be the saving of the lives of their own soldiers.

It is also a great delight to see a man who was able to use historical models in period context, but it should still be acknowledged that Caracalla understood that the historical models were only to be used as sources of inspiration and not blindly – he copied what was useful and modified those to the period circumstances, and invented new ruses and equipment. This is actually what the military treatises required from a good general. It is a great pity that far too many modern leaders lack knowledge and understanding of even basic history, which is no wonder in light of the scanty resources given to the teaching and study of history. At the risk of sounding banal, I will state this again: one cannot really understand today's world unless one understands history. Caracalla understood this.

As regards the *Constitutio Antoniana*, the granting of Roman citizenship to all free citizens of the empire, it had one very important long-term outcome. Henceforth, the provincials living within the borders of the Roman Empire actually came to see themselves as Romans and not as their subjects. The fact that the populace considered themselves Romans made native tribal revolts less likely – the Roman identity made all the difference in the world. In the short term, Caracalla's religious tolerance towards Christians also brought good results in the form of stopping the needless persecution of people who did not pose any real threat to the empire or its emperor.[1]

Caracalla's introduction of new clothing for the army and reintroduction of the Macedonian phalanx also paved the way for future developments, just like his recruitment of large numbers of German, Scythian (mainly Gothic) and Osroenian cavalry. He clearly sought to make the Roman army better suited to facing the Parthians/Persians. Subsequent events of the reign of Severus Alexander, and in particular the devastating criticism by Julius Africanus of the Roman shields and helmets when facing the Sasanian Persians, stand as the best proofs of Caracalla's foresight (see Appendix 2). It was because of these facts that Caracalla had reintroduced the Macedonian phalanx with different shields, helmets and spears. The use of large numbers of Germanic lancers (*kontoforoi/contarii*, bearers of the *contus*-pike/spears) against the Parthians finds support from the sixth-century *Strategikon*, which regarded the cavalry lancer charge as particularly effective against the cavalry of Sasanian Persia. The sixth-century sources also prove this to have been a matter of fact. The Gothic *contarii* of the sixth-century East Roman army were particularly effective against the Persian cavalry and much feared by them just like Alexander the Great's Companion cavalry with its spears.[2]

There is also a reference in Dio (79.6.3) to the requisitioning and buying of large quantities of various poisons (worth 7.5 million *denarii*) for the secret killing of high-ranking men. Since the existence of this stock of poisons was published by Macrinus and then duly burned, it is possible that it was pure propaganda to make the senators grateful towards him, but, considering the huge quantity of poisons, there is an even more likely alternative, namely the military use of poisons against the Parthians. The best clue to such usage comes from the period military treatise of Julius Africanus, which mentions the use of the hellebore in the making barren of enemy territory, as well as the use of poisons and germs against enemy soldiers.[3] In other words, it appears very likely that Caracalla was also a pioneer in the field of bacteriological, biological and chemical warfare. He was one of the most devious and inventive Roman military leaders ever.

However, it is quite clear that Caracalla's internal security measures proved inadequate for the task at hand. Despite his vast network of spies, informers and bodyguards, Caracalla's enemies still managed to form a plot that involved relatively large numbers of people and then to assassinate him. Caracalla had wisely employed various tricks, such as the use of seers, astrologers and visits to the shrines to obtain intelligence reports to fool his enemies, but he had failed to understand that the lowly born freedmen and equestrians within his security apparatus could pose a similar threat to his rule as the senators whom he kept under tight watch. Most importantly, Caracalla seriously underestimated the effeminate Macrinus, whom he ridiculed in public. Caracalla was a roughshod soldier who despised men like Macrinus. He did not realize that even such men could pose a threat if they employed the services of other more manly (suicidal) men. Caracalla's second and greatest mistake was to keep Martialis among his immediate entourage, even after he had killed his brother and/or refused to promote him.

There is no better way to finish the analysis of the reign of Caracalla than to cite Niccolò Machiavelli's judgment of the man (Machiavelli, Prince 19, tr. by Bull, pp.110–11, with my comments in square brackets):

> 'Now Antoninus Caracalla, his [*Septimius Severus*'] son, was also a man of splendid qualities which astonished the people and endeared him to the soldiers; he was a military man, capable of any exertion, and he scorned softness of any kind, at the table or elsewhere. This won him the devotion of the troops. Nonetheless, his ferocity and cruelty were so great and unparalleled (after countless individual murders, he put to death great numbers of Romans and all the citizens of Alexandria) that he became universally hated [*as we have seen, this is not true; the only group of people who hated him intensely were the most conservative elements within the senatorial class and the men of low birth and character who joined Macrinus in the plot to kill him, but even then the senators actually remained loyal*]. Even those closest to him started to fear him [*this is true; Caracalla's treacherous actions against enemies undoubtedly caused fear among those closest to him, which clearly included the two commanders of his own bodyguards, Macrinus and Triccianus*]; and as a result he was killed by a centurion, when he was surrounded by his troops. Here it should be noted that princes cannot escape death if the attempt is made by a fanatic, because anyone who has no fear of death himself can succeed in inflicting it; on the other hand, there is less need for a prince to be afraid, since such assassinations are very rare. However, the prince should restrain himself from inflicting grave injury on anyone in his service whom he has close to him in his affairs of state. That was how Antoninus erred. He put to death, with disgrace, a brother of that centurion, whom in turn he threatened every day even though still retaining him in his bodyguard [*a grave mistake indeed, made by a person who believed in his own superior martial and intellectual qualities*]. This rash behaviour was calculated to bring him to grief, as in the end it did.'

Notes

1. The pagan historians show a constant dislike towards those emperors who did not persecute Christians, with the result that their bias can sometimes be found even in the Christian chroniclers who had used these same texts as their sources.
2. For the *Strategikon* and Gothic *contarii*, see Syvänne, *The Age of Hippotoxotai*, Tampere (2004).
3. I have discussed these matters briefly already in Syvänne (2004) pp.287–88; Syvänne (2007a); Syvänne (2007b). Julius Africanus recommended the use of rotten corpses of snakes in hermtically sealed ceramic vessels and poisons. The use of bacteriological warfare in very rudimentary form appears very likely since the 'poisoning' was said to have transferred from one person to another.

Akinakes
(Persian short sword c.40-45 cm)

According to Dio (79.7.2-3), Caracalla kept many pet lions. His favourite was called Akinakes (named after the Persian short sword). Akinakes even slept and ate beside Caracalla so that Caracalla would often caress him in public. This undoubtedly made it very difficult and dangerous for anyone to approach Caracalla when Akinakes was nearby. The presence of the lion would also have frightened senseless most of those who were brought before Caracalla. This ploy is not entirely unknown even today as is well proven by President Putin's use of his pet dog in a meeting with Chancellor Merkel.

© Dr. Ilkka Syvanne 2016

Caracalla training to fight as a hoplomachus in 216, but with the exception that he has a regular large hoplite shield. At this stage he is already imitating Alexander the Great by having sideburns.

Chapter 13

An Epilogue: The Reign of Macrinus the Effeminate, 217–218

Macrinus Consolidates his Position[1]

After the death of Caracalla, the Roman Empire was without a ruler for two days, because Macrinus did not yet dare to make a move for the throne. He was a Moor of lowly origins with a pierced ear. He needed to gather support for the move before attempting it, in addition to which it would have been extremely unwise to play his hand immediately, because the soldiers had loved the dead emperor dearly. According to Dio, during these two days, Macrinus' henchmen travelled back and forth between the garrisons of Mesopotamia, promising money and peace if they would declare their support for Macrinus. He did not want to appear to have been behind the plot to kill the emperor. The situation, however, favoured his rise to power. The vengeful Artabanus was fast approaching at the head of his vast army. The empire needed an emperor, even if he was of lowly origin. According to Herodian, the throne was first offered to Adventus, because he had military experience and was considered a good prefect, but he refused the offer, giving as his excuse his old age. In truth, he must have been aware of the extent of the plot and feared for his life if he accepted the throne in a situation in which he had not secured the support of the army. After this, the tribunes working for Macrinus persuaded the Praetorians to choose Macrinus as their emperor, which they duly did after they had been bribed with promises.

- Macrinus's coin which still resembles Caracalla's coins.
- The aim was not to upset the army (drawn after Cohen)

An Epilogue: The Reign of Macrinus the Effeminate, 217–218

Macrinus pretended to be grateful to his colleague Adventus, whom he appointed as City Prefect of Rome and placed in charge of burying Caracalla with due honours. Officially, Adventus' mission was to take Caracalla's cremated body first to his mother at Antioch (presumably with the mission to test the loyalty of the Praetorians and their prefect Epagathus there), and from there to Rome, where his mission was to replace and kill Maternianus, who had been loyal to Caracalla. In truth, Macrinus' only purpose was to remove his sole potential rival from potential supporters, the Praetorians and the field army. On top of that, he sent his rival into a lion's den. Adventus had a lowly birth and had served in the security services of both Septimius and Caracalla, the latter of whom had appointed him as consul, all of which made him hated in the Senate. Adventus had very few supporters in Rome. The murder of Maternianus would have also angered the only significant military forces in the capital, the Urban Cohorts and the Vigiles. According to Dio (79.17.4), nobody in the city of Rome dared to declare Caracalla a public enemy because the *Urbaniciani* loved Caracalla and would have killed anyone suggesting such. It is quite easy to see that they would not give their support for a man who had killed their commander. Consequently, it was then easy for Macrinus to replace Adventus with his own man, Marius Maximus. However, even his successor could not put any trust in the loyalty of his soldiers towards himself or Macrinus, because the soldiers stationed in the city of Rome adored Caracalla. Adventus' career began to blossom again under the next emperor, Elagabalus, and one can make the educated guess that he had also been working towards that goal through his former associates and contacts.

Macrinus appears to have initially kept in office most of the men appointed by Caracalla, and the purge of those began only after the Battle of Nisibis. This was undoubtedly a wise decision, because it was not wise to disorder the military just before a decisive battle.

The Battle of Nisibis, 11 April 217 and the Parthian War

Macrinus had to act in haste, because Artabanus' powerful army, composed of vast numbers of mounted archers, cataphracts and armoured camel riders, was fast approaching.[2] According to Herodian, Artabanus had assembled his entire eastern force, which must mean that it consisted mainly of the Dahae tribesmen, native Parthians and possibly of the Sakas. The fact that Artabanus was collecting his forces in the Hyrcanian Mountains makes it clear that most of the easterners were native Parthians and Dahae or other local nomads, and also probably included Medes. It is unclear from which part of the realm originated the camel corps employed by Artabanus. At first glance, it appears likely that they were Arab tribesmen, but one cannot exclude the possibility that they would have been Central Asian tribesmen mounted on Bactrian two-humped camels. Macrinus may at this stage have already tried to avoid fighting through negotiations, but to no avail.[3] Artabanus was in no mood for negotiations after the death of his children and relatives.

284   Caracalla

Macrinus had no chance to deliberate the matter further, because, according to Dio (79.26.5), the armies came to loggerheads over water supply while they were encamped opposite each other near Nisibis. This suggests very poor use of scouts and patrols to observe enemy activities, and similarly poor advance planning by Macrinus and his staff officers. Caracalla was clearly a head above these men, and it would have required a man of his calibre to do these things correctly. According to Herodian, Artabanus instigated the encounter. Artabanus hailed the sun at sunrise and then ordered a general attack. According to Herodian, the barbarian mounted archers, cataphracts and cataphracted camels charged the Romans at a gallop while shouting loudly. The Parthian battle formation is described to have been disorderly, but this hides the fact that there was order hidden inside the outward appearance of chaos. The Parthian cavalry units galloped and retreated in such manner that, to the untrained Roman eye, it appeared a disorderly chaos. On the basis of this it is impossible to make any reconstruction of the array, but other descriptions of the Parthian tactics and wall paintings of Central Asia allow us to make a guess that the battle formation consisted of several divisions (probably five, with a reserve placed behind), each of which was divided into wings consisting of mounted archers and centres of cataphracts.[4] My own guess is that camels were used in front of the cavalry to disorder the Roman cavalry formation just before the units engaged each other when the Parthians had decided to fight the Romans at close quarters. However, the Romans were ready to receive their attack.

Plaision:
The 10 c. AD Byzantine Interpolation of Aelian (Dain M1, M ad fig., Scholium 32, p.106; tr. by A.M. Devine, Aelian's Manual of Hellenistic Military Tactics 48.1, 48.4, Ancient World 19, 1989, p. 63): "This formation [plaision] has a depth much greater than the length or a length much greater than the depth, and is called "an oblong-formation [plaision] when all its sides consist of heavy infantry, with archers and slingers inside... It is called an "oblong-formation" [plaision] when the deployment takes place on the four sides of a formation not in the shape of a square but in that of an oblong" The diagram is drawn after Codex Burney 108 f.22 ("p.43").

↑ a file-leader (*lochagos*); a misleading term since in all of the diagrams the *lochagos* is clearly a higher ranking officer (probably a *falangarchês* or in some cases the *kerarchês* or even *strategos/hypostrategos*) usually posted in the front center or in the front right flank of the formation

↓ spear-bearing (*kontos*-bearing) heavy infantryman (*hoplitês kontaratos pezos*); *kontos* was a c. 3.6 m long (cavalry) spear that could be used for both thrusting and throwing.

targeteer or light-armed slinger (*peltastês ê sfendonêtês psilos*); the 10th c. AD infantry peltast seems to have been a javelin thrower.

archer (*psilos toxotês*)

According to Herodian (4.15.1, 4.15.4), the Roman battle array was orderly and its phalanxes were deployed in depth (this implies a double phalanx *difalangia*); light-armed and well-armed troops were placed in the empty hollow spaces between the

An Epilogue: The Reign of Macrinus the Effeminate, 217–218   285

phalanxes (probably intervals), from which they made powerful sallies against the enemy; and the cavalry and Moorish soldiers (cavalry) were placed on both flanks. The description allows the making of four different reconstructions of the Roman battle array: 1) a single hollow/oblong infantry square (*plaision/plinthion*) with cavalry wings;[5] 2) a phalanx in which light and heavy infantry units alternated[6] with cavalry wings; 3) a double phalanx with cavalry wings; 4) a double phalanx with cavalry wings, in which each of the individual 6,000-men phalanxes/divisions (4,000 heavy and 2,000 light infantry) was arranged as a hollow oblong/square. On the basis of the third day's events, the traditional double phalanx or double phalanx with divisional hollow oblongs appears the most likely, because the constant lengthening of the line implies this. In fact, it appears likely that Macrinus used the standard battle array of Alexander the Great (at the battles of Granicus and Issus), in which the phalangites and heavier legionaries were placed in the front phalanx while the 'hoplite' phalanx (possibly the *hypaspistai* of Dio, see below) and other similar units bearing lighter equipment were placed in the second line. This basic structure of the double phalanx could be modified into a hollow square/oblong if the army was forced to fight against numerically superior enemy in the open plain. The Battle of Gaugamela/Arbela is the best example of this: Alexander simply arrayed part of his wing units into columns to form an all around defensive formation that he used offensively.[7] In other words, it appears likely that Macrinus was using the deployment devised by Caracalla for the upcoming battle, but did not understand that the double phalanx was to be used in such terrain that the enemy could not outflank the Romans and the hollow oblong/square (or hollow oblongs) in the open plain. Furthermore, Macrinus seems not to have understood that Alexander the Great always employed his battle arrays offensively and not defensively, and never used his second line to lengthen the front line. Macrinus proved himself to be just as incompetent a general as Caracalla claimed him to be.

In my opinion, the large-scale use of Moorish light infantry and use of the *lanciarii* – for example among the elite *Legio II Parthica* and similarly lightly equipped men behind or between the phalangite units for powerful sallies in front of the infantry phalanx – also appears to have been conceived by Caracalla, because an army almost always fights like it has been trained to do. The *lanciarii* received their name from the spear/javelin called *lancia/lancea*, which came in at least two sizes: the small light javelin called *lancea* (lance) and longer *lancia pugnatoria*, the fighting lance. Both could be thrown or thrust, although the latter naturally saw more use in the second way. It is usually suggested that the light infantry fought either as individuals in front of the phalanx, in the manner of the ancient *velites* or *antesignani* (those who fought in front of the standard), or in the manner of the Spanish legionaries of Pompey during the Civil War. According to Caesar (*Civil Wars* 1.44), the Pompeians first charged at full speed and seized some advantageous position without taking any particular care to preserve their ranks, and fought singly in loose order, and if they were hard pressed did not consider it a disgrace to retreat and abandon their position. Ross Cowan has speculated, in my opinion quite correctly, that the *lanciarii* and *antesignani* could also fight in close order. In other words, the *lanciarii* and other similarly equipped Roman troops were all-purpose elite fighters who could be used as light or heavy troops as needed.[8] The other standard way of using the light-armed troops was to place them behind the phalanx, so that when the heavy infantry stopped the cavalry charge the light troops charged out to engage the disordered horsemen. It is probable that this tactic was used during the three-day battle.

There were other likely ways in which the light troops may have been used in front of the phalanx: 1) as a wedge in which the front rank or all men kneeled and pointed their spears at the enemy horses, behind which were archers and slingers; 2) men armed with clubs, maces or staves in really loose order in front of the array to break up the cohesion of the enemy cataphract attack, or after the enemy cavalry had been brought to a standstill by the spears of the phalanx. There is period support for these procedures: they are described by Arrian and Aelian almost a century before, and there is a relief of a man belonging to the Spartan phalanx which shows him with a club.[9] In addition, we can find the same type of club/stave/mace-armed men opposing the Palmyrene cataphracts about sixty years later.[10] Consequently, there are very strong reasons to believe that there were troops specifically designed for use against the Parthian cataphracts, which included the *lanciarii*, some men of the Spartan phalanx (clubbers) and probably also Moorish javelinmen.

The battle began as a clash of cavalry. The superior numbers of the Parthian cavalry told immediately. The barbarians caused heavy casualties among the Roman horses and camels with a combination of showers of arrows shot by the horse archers and the *contus*-spears wielded by the cataphracts and camel riders. This suggests that the Romans were employing camels in like manner to the Parthians, with riders using long *contus*-pikes at distance. The men belonging to this camel corps must have come from the Arabic auxiliary units. The Romans are said to have fared better in the hand-to-hand combat at close quarters. If this description is correct, then it would suggest that Macrinus failed to exploit to the maximum the presence of Gothic *contarii* recruited by Caracalla. However, even if this were the case, the Germanic cavalry would still have been at a disadvantage when facing the fully armoured Parthian cataphract knights. Herodian's account makes it clear that the Parthians wisely targeted the vulnerable Roman horses and thereby dismounted their opponents. The same tactic was impossible for the Roman cavalry because the horses of the Parthian cataphracts were armoured. The Romans did not possess enough cataphracts or horse archers of their own to withstand this sort of attack. According to Herodian, when the size of the enemy host and the number of their camels began to cause trouble, the Roman cavalry feigned flight, during which they threw down caltrops and other iron implements with sharp spikes sticking out of them. This ploy seems to have worked well, as Herodian claims that the horses and

An Epilogue: The Reign of Macrinus the Effeminate, 217–218

THE TWO DIFFERENT WAYS OF USING LIGHT INFANTRY IN FRONT OF A HOLLOW SQUARE

1. Light infantry deployed in front of the hollow square (plaision used as a generic hollow square) as a wedge so that some of the lanciarii kneeled and pointed their spears at the horses while other lanciarii threw their spears when the enemy was close enough. The clubmen stayed behind until the very last moment and then charged out to pummel the enemy.

2. Light infantry (lanciarii and clubmen) used in front of the hollow square in a scattered array so that they could dodge and jump to avoid enemy attacks. Some of the light infantry would have stayed behind inside the square because it would have been impossible to deploy all light-armed troops in the front when in open order.

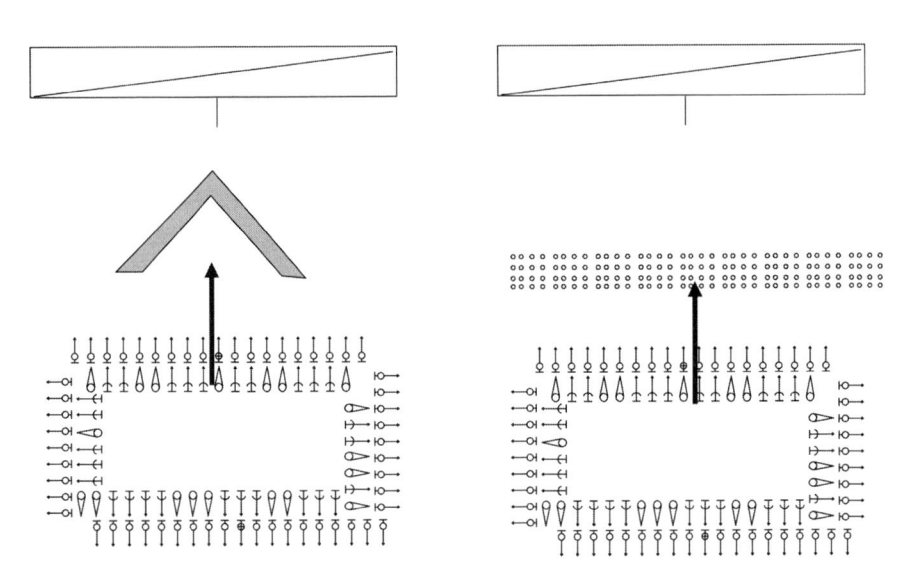

The two different deployment patterns of light infantry in front of the regular phalanx to break up the cavalry charge

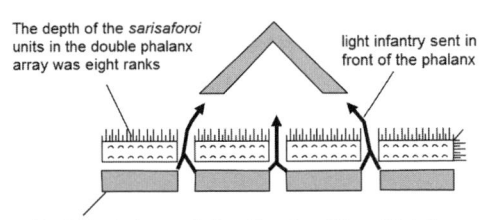

The depth of the *sarisaforoi* units in the double phalanx array was eight ranks

light infantry sent in front of the phalanx

open order (shows only the principle and is not in scale)

The light infantry was deployed four deep if it consisted of archers and/or javeliners. If there were slingers, the light-armed were deployed two deep and the slingers separately in a location where they could use their slings.

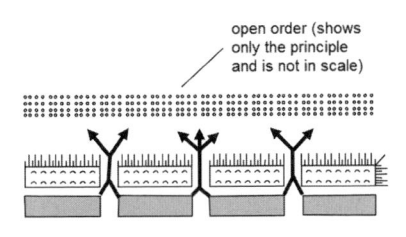

When the light infantry was deployed in open order before the phalanx, the slingers and archers would have been posted behind the *lanciarii* and clubmen or behind the phalanx.

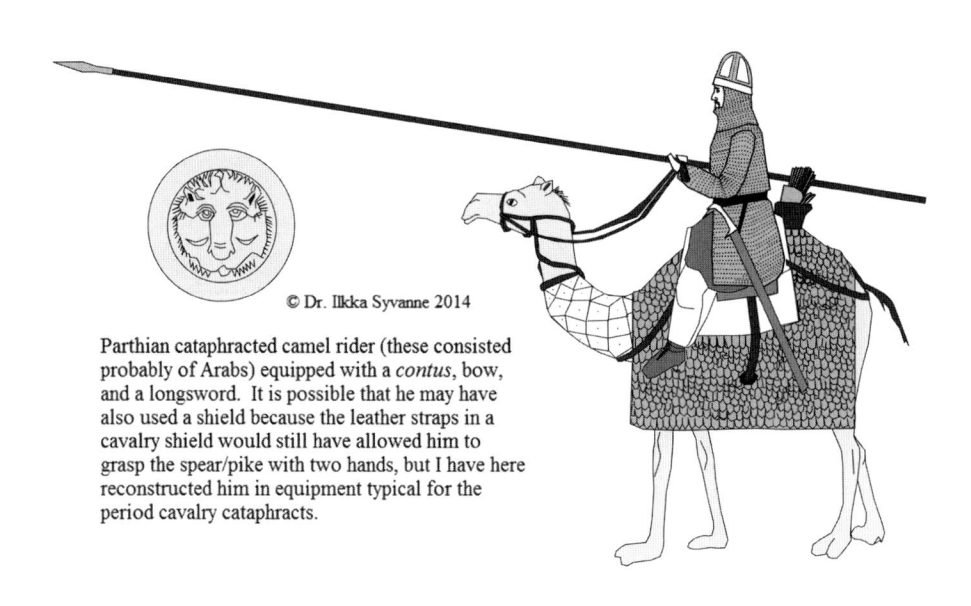

Parthian cataphracted camel rider (these consisted probably of Arabs) equipped with a *contus*, bow, and a longsword. It is possible that he may have also used a shield because the leather straps in a cavalry shield would still have allowed him to grasp the spear/pike with two hands, but I have here reconstructed him in equipment typical for the period cavalry cataphracts.

A procession of Palmyran nobles about AD 100-150
Note the bow-cases and quivers attached to the rear of the saddles as well as the ends of the spears between the legs (shown with the darker colour). This group was clearly equally well adapted for long and short range combat. The equipment is clearly copied from the Parthians. This is how the Arab/Bedouin armies (when lightly-equipped) would have looked when they came out of the desert to assail the settlements of the sedentary peoples. The wealthier Arab and Bedouin tribes could also bring armour with them (placed in saddle bags carried by the camels) so that they could then put on their armour when needed.

Note that the Persian mounted archers could also be as heavily armoured as their 'lancers'. The horse-armour was primarily used as a defence against enemy arrows.

Dura Europus, cataphract (drawn after von Gall)

Dura Europus, mounted archer on armoured horse (after fig. 17D James)

The Battle of Nisibis, April 11-13, 217

The Likely Battle Formations (simplified by reducing the number of divisions)

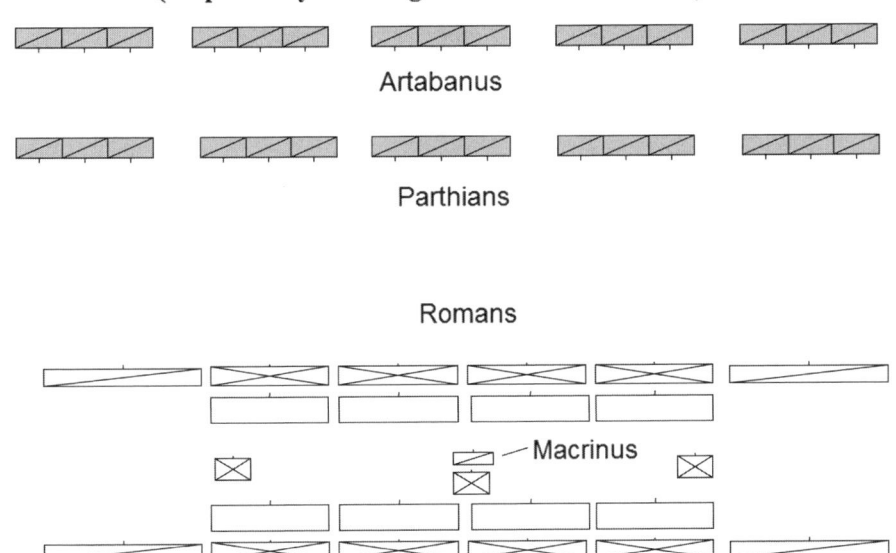

Artabanus

Parthians

Romans

Macrinus

camels of the pursuers were lamed and their riders thrown to the ground. According to Herodian, the fight continued like this for two days from dawn to dusk. The effective way of employing the Germanic *contarii* and other Roman cavalry would have been to use them as one part of the combined arms tactic in the same manner as Alexander the Great. The double phalanx of infantry (or rather hollow oblong) should have been used offensively in support of the attacking cavalry. It was this that Macrinus did not understand at all. The cavalry simply operated on its own against numerically superior foes until it was forced to retreat inside the infantry formation for safety.[11] The tactic of using caltrops suggests that the Romans had equipped their own cavalry with metal slippers to enable them to charge again through the field of caltrops.

On the third day, however, the barbarians changed their tactics and tried to encircle the Romans with their superior numbers. According to Herodian, the Romans responded by not forming their phalanxes in depth, but continually extending their to prevent encirclement.[12]

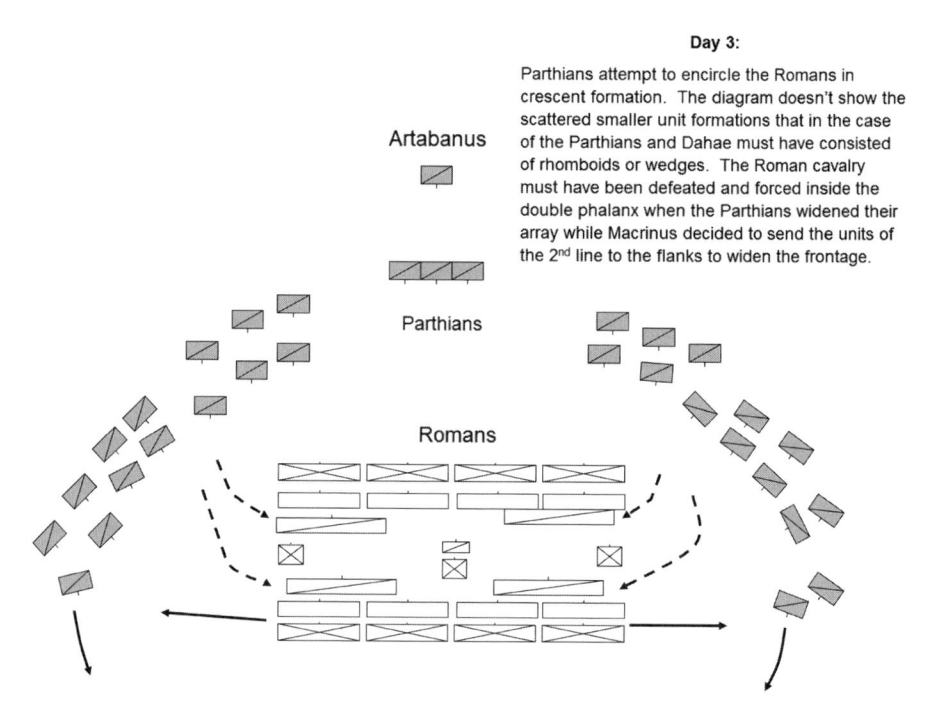

Day 3:
Parthians attempt to encircle the Romans in crescent formation. The diagram doesn't show the scattered smaller unit formations that in the case of the Parthians and Dahae must have consisted of rhomboids or wedges. The Roman cavalry must have been defeated and forced inside the double phalanx when the Parthians widened their array while Macrinus decided to send the units of the 2nd line to the flanks to widen the frontage.

This must also be the instance described by Dio in one of the surviving fragments (79.26.5–7), in which he claimed that Macrinus came very near to losing his camp thanks to the enemy's superior numbers and his own flight from the battle, and was only saved by the *hypaspistai* (shield-bearers)[13] and baggage carriers who happened to be there. These men rushed out of the camp and charged the unsuspecting barbarians, taking them by surprise. I take this to mean that Macrinus' manoeuvre to widen the frontage ended in failure because it was quite impossible to widen it indefinitely against the more mobile enemy cavalry on a flat plain. As a result, part of the Parthian cavalry force was able to ride past the outer infantry flanks, while Macrinus with his widening of the array had blundered away from his reserves and

An Epilogue: The Reign of Macrinus the Effeminate, 217–218

thereby removed the protective second support line from the rear of the Roman formation. The route lay open for the enemy to attack simultaneously the rear of the Roman infantry phalanx and their camp. However, the timely counter-attack of the Roman baggage-carriers against the outlying Parthian cavalry saved the day. The flight of Macrinus from the battle when the Parthians outflanked his line demoralized his forces, which appear to have begun to retreat to their camp at the same moment as they had been outflanked. The contrast between the cowardly Macrinus and manly Caracalla could not have been any greater.

As regards the meaning of the word *hypaspistai* in this context, there are two alternatives. The first is that Dio (or his epitomator) did not understand that the *hypaspistai* were actually the second line that Macrinus had used first to widen the frontage, and that it was only after this had ended in failure that the armed baggage-carriers charged out of the camp. This does not mean, however, that there would not have been regular guards in the camp who would have taken part in the counter-attack. It is also possible to equate the *hypaspistai* with the *triarii* of Vegetius' third book. In this case, the *hypaspistai* would indeed have been stationed behind the battle line proper, together with the servants, for the protection of the camp, in the same manner as Julius Caesar posted his two legions at the Battle of Bibracte in 58 BC.

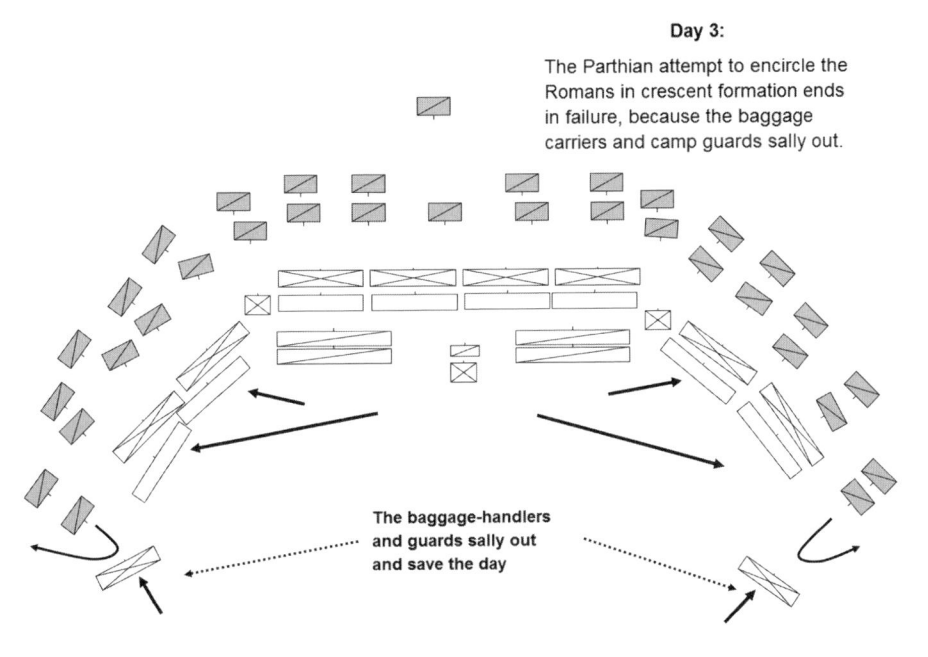

Day 3:
The Parthian attempt to encircle the Romans in crescent formation ends in failure, because the baggage carriers and camp guards sally out.

The baggage-handlers and guards sally out and save the day

According to Herodian, the widening of the frontage balanced out the odds and apparently resulted in great carnage on both sides, but especially among the enemy camels. Macrinus had been lucky that his mistake had not led to defeat. The quick-thinking Camp Prefect had saved the day. It was basically impossible for the Parthian cavalry to defeat the Roman infantry so long as it maintained its close order formation and presented an orderly front towards the attacking cavalry. The infantry units could march through enemy cavalry with impunity if they assumed either the *amfistomos/orbis* (two-fronted array) or *plaision* (hollow square/oblong) formations.[14] The only Roman units likely to suffer were those that were equipped with the shorter spears or with *pila*, because the enemy cataphracts could reach them with their pikes before the Romans could, unless the spears were thrown. If the legionary threw his *pilum* to outreach his enemy before he could land a thrust with his pike, he lost his only long-range weapon and had to resort to the use of sword, which was disadvantageous if the approaching enemy still had his pike, but this disadvantage would not become apparent so long as the rear-rankers had enough spears/javelins to hand over to the front-rankers. Furthermore, if the sword-armed legionary had the courage to attack, he could gain an advantage by advancing close enough to make the *contus* useless. The fact that the bodies of men and animals, especially those of camels, piled up high enough to prevent the men from fighting suggests that the Parthians suffered most of the casualties. Their attack had been blocked by the tight Roman infantry formations bristling with *sarisae*, *hastae*, *pila* and *lanceae*, which were supported by the regrouped cavalry. The *sarissae* introduced by Caracalla would have been particularly effective when facing the enemy, but it is obvious that the volleys of *pila* and other javelins must have caused plentiful carnage among the horsemen and camel riders who approached too close. Every mount that fell with its rider made it ever more difficult for the Parthians to attack. Consequently, after the presence of piles of corpses made fighting impossible, the armies withdrew to their camps for the night.

The fact that the Roman infantry was able to withstand the onslaught speaks volumes about the effectiveness of Caracalla's training methods and for the high morale and discipline of the Roman army in a situation in which Macrinus had made the very serious miscalculation of sending his infantry reserves to the flanks. The ancient military manuals are unanimous that the second line of the double phalanx formation was meant to be used as a safety measure against threats from the rear and for the reinforcement of the front line and protection of its flanks, not for the widening of the frontage, in particular when the enemy consisted of more mobile mounted units who could easily reposition themselves to outflank the new flank unit. If the Romans had fortified their camp, as the use of the word 'ditch' by Dio in this case implies, it would have been in no danger of being taken, despite what Dio says. If the Parthian cavalry had made the mistake of going to the space between the camp and the Roman double phalanx, the Romans could simply have gradually withdrawn to their camp and all Parthian units foolish enough to stay in the way would have been crushed. However, the inexperienced Macrinus was foolish enough to send his second line to the flanks, with the result that his whole formation became vulnerable from rear attacks. In these circumstances, it was necessary for the baggage-carriers to charge out. Consequently, the third day also ended in stalemate.

According to Herodian (4.15.6–8), it was only now that Macrinus realized why Artabanus and the Parthians fought so desperately in a situation in which the Parthians typically gave up the fight if their initial encounters had not been met with success. The reason was obviously that they did not realize that Caracalla was dead. Consequently, Macrinus informed them of this and promised to return the prisoners and booty in return for peace.

After receiving this information, and having been effectively stopped from advancing, Artabanus decided to withdraw back across the Tigris while Macrinus retreated towards Antioch. The armies were kept in readiness while both heads of state resorted to the use of diplomacy to settle matters.[15] According to Dio (79.27.1), Macrinus, both because of what he called his natural cowardice resulting from his Moorish race and the soldiers' lack of discipline, did not dare to continue the war. If there is any truth to this statement at all, it is that Macrinus' tactical mistakes in the battle may have angered the professionals to such an extent that he had no other alternative but to seek peace through diplomacy rather than military means. I would also dare to say that the stark contrast between the brave Caracalla, who fought single combats with enemy leaders, and the flight of the cowardly new emperor made the soldiers less than willing to fight for the latter, and Macrinus must have been aware of this.

Regardless, it is still clear that the situation was not as stark as it may have seemed to some. Even though Macrinus was an incompetent military commander, he must still have known from the advice given by those who were competent that by having merely withstood and survived the enemy onslaught and invasion, he was now in a good position to end the war through negotiations without having to take any more chances. The Parthians could be defeated without taking any major risks by resorting to the use of guerrilla warfare from within the fortified cities. The Parthians, who did not come with vast resources of supplies, would soon run out of their supplies and be forced to retreat. On top of that, the feudal cavalry did not expect to stay in the field for prolonged periods of time. In short, the fact that it was possible to defeat the Parthians without running any serious risks by resorting to the defence of the cities made it easier for Macrinus to negotiate a face-saving peace settlement. The Parthians knew this too.[16]

Even Dio contradicts his own claim that Macrinus had been defeated with the statement that the soldiers subsequently caused greater harm to the state than the Parthians, because 'while the Parthians killed a few soldiers and ravaged portions of Mesopotamia, these men cut down many of their own number and also overthrew their emperor; and what is still worse than that, they set up a successor just like him, one by whom nothing was done that was not evil and base'.[17] In other words, even Dio was forced to admit that the Parthians caused only a few casualties. Despite his tactical blunders and cowardice at the Battle of Nisibis, Macrinus, or rather the soldiers of Caracalla, had clearly defended Roman territory successfully.

Settlement of the Parthian and Armenian Wars, 217–218

Despite having effectively been defeated, Artabanus seems to have tried to exploit the situation. He demanded that the Romans rebuild the destroyed forts and cities, abandon Mesopotamia and pay reparations for damage done to the royal tombs and for other damage caused. He knew that in order to consolidate his position, the new emperor would need to end the war as soon as possible in order to be able to go to Rome. Macrinus' peace offer and the return of prisoners must have encouraged Artabanus to seek even more. However, he overplayed his hand. Macrinus was happy to prolong the negotiations, because he knew that the Parthian feudal armies were difficult to provision with supplies and keep together for long periods of time. However, Macrinus had his own troubles too, which he failed to address in time. In order to secure his own position, he would have needed to disband the restless and dissatisfied army to its home garrisons and himself go to Rome to secure his position among the senators and populace. In other words, there were very pressing reasons for him to conclude a peace as soon as possible, but the harsh demands put forth by Artabanus made this impossible. After all, contrary to Dio's claim that he had been defeated, Macrinus had in truth effectively defeated Artabanus simply by stopping the enemy invasion in front of Nisibis. The feudal Parthian forces did not carry adequate supplies with them, and the Romans had destroyed whatever stores there were close by in Parthian territory during Caracalla's invasion. It was also impossible to live off the land, because the Romans had stored their provisions safely inside their fortresses. The Parthians could do very little so long as they could not defeat the Roman field army, which they had not achieved. If the Romans had a capable leader, the dissolving of the feudal Parthian army would have allowed them to advance into Parthian territory again to continue the looting and pillaging of the last year, but two things prevented this. Macrinus was a coward and the dissatisfaction of the field army over his combat performance made it very dangerous for him to attempt to lead them again. In the end, both rulers saved face with a peace settlement, according to which the Romans would pay 50 million *denarii* and return all surviving prisoners in return for peace.[18]

In addition to concluding a mutual peace, Macrinus and Artabanus agreed that the Armenian war would be settled so that Macrinus would send a crown to Tiridates (Khosrov), together with his mother who had been held hostage by Caracalla and the booty taken in Armenia. Tiridates was also seeking to regain all the territory formerly held by his father in Cappadocia, as well as the annual payment made previously by the Romans.[19] Future events proved that Tiridates was to become one of the greatest Armenian kings ever, and therefore it is not surprising that the Romans had not been able to subdue him in the course of their two-year war.

An Epilogue: The Reign of Macrinus the Effeminate, 217–218 295

My own educated guess is that Macrinus also ended the Arabian war in *Arabia Felix* (modern Yemen) mentioned by the SHA (Macr. 12.6 with Diad. 8.4–9.3) at the same time as he ended the Persian and Armenian wars. It is unfortunate that we do not know the result of the war waged in Yemen and on what terms the war was ended, or what was the relationship between the revolt of the commanders of these armies (*dux* of Armenia, and legates of Asia and Arabia) against Macrinus with the peace concluded.

After having concluded the peace, Macrinus and Artabanus appear to have been on quite friendly terms, because subsequently Macrinus was even prepared to send his son Diadumenianus to Artabanus for safety.[20] The killing of Caracalla must have endeared Macrinus to Artabanus in a manner that was uncommon between enemies.

Dacian War, 217

With the death of Caracalla, the Romans had lost their most gifted military commander, and their neighbours knew it. The death of the emperor had also nullified the treaties concluded with Caracalla. According to Dio (79.27.5), the next in line to challenge the weak Macrinus were the 'Dacians', i.e. the Goths. They invaded Dacia, apparently in order to receive back the hostages Caracalla had taken from them in the name of an alliance. Macrinus complied and sent back the hostages, and the Dacians duly stopped their ravages. This was the third time in a year that Macrinus showed distinct weakness in the face of foreign aggression, and it did not endear him to the soldiers.

It appears probable that the future Emperor Maximinus Thrax, whose father was a Goth and mother an Alan, had a role in the Gothic invasion. He had joined the cavalry, from which Severus raised him to the rank of *stipatores corporis* (bodyguard, probably belonging to the Germanic cavalry). Under Caracalla, he was promoted as an officer in the Centuries or of the Centurions. This probably means that Maximinus was made an officer of the *Leones*, which served as Caracalla's personal unit of bodyguards. When Caracalla was murdered, Maximinus left the army in disgust and returned to Thrace, where he was considered a friend of the Goths and Alans, which strongly suggests that he was one of the persons behind the attack of the Goths against Macrinus.[21] One can see the attack of the Goths as an operation meant to lend support for the revolt of Elagabalus, who also seems to have received backing from other 'centurions'.

Internal Affairs 217–218

Before the Battle of Nisibis, Macrinus did not dare to openly show any disrespect towards Caracalla because he feared the reaction of the soldiers who loved Caracalla.[22] However, as soon as the Battle of Nisibis was over, Macrinus began a purge of Caracalla's henchmen, spies, informers and slaves at Rome and in the provinces.[23] In other words, Macrinus' purge was no different from that of Caracalla, but it did not receive the same condemnations from Dio or Herodian: the empire was simply purged of 'criminals'. The only thing that received Dio's outright condemnation was the killing of Maternianus and Datus.[24] They had performed their duties loyally and were punished because of that. As a former commander of the Praetorian Guard, Macrinus relied heavily on his *frumentarii* to maintain internal security (SHA Macr. 12.4ff.), but as we shall see this proved insufficient in circumstances where he was just too unpopular among the rank-and-file.

At the same time as Macrinus purged his enemies, he also tried to endear himself to the opponents of Caracalla among the senators and equestrians by having their sentences annulled. In the same vein, he also promised not to kill any senators. However, at the same time Dio notes that when the soldiers demanded the death of the ex-consul (*suffect*) and senator Aurelianus, who had angered the soldiers in the course of many previous campaigns (had he been a disciplinarian?), Macrinus, despite having first saved his life, was eventually forced to accept the request. What was the reason for this change of heart? I would suggest that the original demand was made immediately after the death of Caracalla, when Macrinus was still strong enough to oppose the soldiers because they did not yet know the character of the man. But when Macrinus had then shown himself a very poor commander and his role in the killing of Caracalla was becoming more apparent, he could no longer protect Aurelianus. The soldiers needed someone to vent their anger against and it was not in Macrinus' interest to be that man. The SHA (Macr. e.g. 2.3–4, 7) claims that the senators were glad to accept Macrinus as their ruler because they hated Caracalla so intensely because of his murder of Geta, incestuous behaviour and murder of senators and people, but typically contradicts itself (Diad. 6.10) by stating that the army, people and Senate all loved Caracalla. The latter suggests once again the existence of an alternative tradition, according to which even the Senate included vast numbers of supporters of Caracalla. It was not without reason that Macrinus associated himself and his son with the dead emperor by assuming the name of Antoninus, and that he also gave as gifts Caracalla cloaks/mantlets to the people (SHA Diad. 2.6–10).

In order to consolidate his position, Macrinus also replaced a large number of provincial governors with his own supporters and rewarded his fellow conspirators with high offices.[25] Triccianus was made governor of Pannonia and Marcius Agrippa of Dacia. Despite being unqualified for so high a position, Ulpius Julianus and Julianus Nestor, the men who had diverted the letter accusing Macrinus, were rewarded with Praetorian prefectures. Their only qualification was their unquestioned loyalty and support of Macrinus. The SHA (Diad. 8.1–9.3) claims that Macrinus kept the *dux* of Armenia and the legates of Asia and Arabia in office because of their former friendship. This author claims that Macrinus spared their lives even though they had been involved in a plot to seize the imperial power, and then claims that their lives were spared because of the former friendship. It also claims that Diadumenianus, or rather his teacher Caelianus, demanded that these men be put to death, most importantly because they still possessed armies.

An Epilogue: The Reign of Macrinus the Effeminate, 217–218   297

In the same context, the text includes three names Arabianus, Tuscus and Gellius as examples of Macrinus' senseless mercy. It is not known whether or not these unknown names should be connected with the *dux* and legates. In my opinion, it is probable that Theocritus is the *dux* of Armenia and that he had been kept in office to continue the war thanks to his former friendship with Macrinus, and that the legates of Asia and Arabia are likewise governors appointed by Caracalla who were kept in office for the same reason. The problem with the claims made by the SHA is the revolts of these commanders against Macrinus. Did these men revolt when Macrinus concluded the peace with Artabanus on the humiliating terms that also spelt an end to their military commands, or at a time when Elagabalus began his own revolt? If the former is true, then the fact that Macrinus failed to punish the men would certainly have caused these armies to side with Julia Maesa and Elagabalus when they raised their revolt. What is certain is that they had been loyal to Caracalla, but were not to Macrinus, despite their former friendship.

As regards the Severan family, Macrinus at first left things as they were and even left the retinue of Praetorians attending Julia Domna intact, but when he heard that Julia had tried to win over her bodyguards to begin a revolt against the hated new emperor, he ordered her to leave Antioch as a private citizen. This seems to have happened when Macrinus had already reached Antioch. The depressed Julia, who was already suffering from breast cancer, starved herself to death. However, Macrinus had not taken into account all possible matters. Julia Domna had a sister, Julia Maesa. She used to live with her sister in the royal residences and did not take kindly that she and her sister had been thrown out of their home. After the death of her sister, Macrinus ordered Julia Maesa to return to her own country. This she must have done quite willingly, because it gave her the opportunity to gather around her supporters in Emesa. She had two daughters: Julia Soaemias Bassiana, also called Sohaemias (the elder), and Julia Avita Mamaea. Soaemias had a 14-year-old boy called Bassianus (according to Herodian) or Avitus (Dio), later better known by the name Elagabalus/Heliogabalus, while Mamaea had a 9-year-old boy called Alexianus (Herodian) or Bassianus (Dio). It appears likely that both were also called Bassianus, because both were claimed to be sons of Bassianus/Antoninus Caracalla. It was the former of these sons that Julia Maesa had thoughts of raising to the throne. Julia Maesa was a very wealthy old woman with a lot of influence on her home ground, which luckily for her also had a garrison of soldiers, namely the *Legio III Gallica*, stationed nearby at Raphaneae. The other garrisons were at Antioch and Apamea.[26] Consequently, despite having been exiled from the imperial court, she was still in a superb position to gather support for her family among the local nobility and soldiery.

298 Caracalla

The Battle of Immae, 8 June 218, and the Overthrow of Macrinus
Meanwhile, Macrinus was making himself deeply hated among the soldiers and populace at Rome. Since the new emperor was nowhere to be seen, there were already public demonstrations against him. In addition to this, in order to be able to pay for his peace agreements and donatives, Macrinus needed money. Since Macrinus had chosen to buy the support of the senators by removing the extraordinary taxes and other burdens from them, he desperately needed cash from other sources, while he also needed to lower the cost of the upkeep of the army to the level it was before Caracalla's reforms. Most of the money needed to pay the donatives and peace agreements must have come from the loot gathered by Caracalla and from confiscations of the property of Caracalla's supporters, but in order to finance the army in the future without military campaigns, he needed to drastically reduce the cost of its upkeep. This he decided to do by keeping the salary of currently serving soldiers intact, while reducing the salaries of future recruits. As noted by period sources, this ploy could have worked if the soldiers had already returned to their home garrisons, but as peace negotiations with the Parthians continued in the winter of 217–218 and the soldiers were kept in the field, it was bound to result in trouble. Now it only made the soldiers suspect that their salaries would also be lowered once they returned to their home garrisons. Consequently, the soldiers began to entertain mutinous thoughts.

all coins drawn after Cohen

The bearded Macrinus imitating Marcus Aurelius signified a break with Caracalla's coins and medallions. It is no wonder that when the soldiers got their first bearded versions of Macrinus that they started to feel anger building up. The medallion on the right proclaiming Parthian Victory would not have fooled the soldiers who knew Macrinus' cowardly behaviour at the battle of Nisibis and who knew that the peace had been bought with concessions.

In addition, Macrinus began to grow a beard to associate himself with the philosopher Emperor Marcus Aurelius while disassociating himself from the shaven Caracalla. This can be seen on medallions from the time. The equestrian Macrinus wanted to endear himself to the senators by adopting the appearance of their favourite emperor. At the same time, he also lived in the lap of luxury at Antioch in the company of philosophers, while the soldiers were kept under canvas, at times even without the necessary supplies. According to the SHA (Macr. 12),

Macrinus made the situation worse with his strict military discipline, and harsh and cruel punishments which he meted out to soldiers, officers and his staff. He also seems to have foolishly lowered the rations given to the soldiers.[27] The contrast with Caracalla could not have been greater. Caracalla had avoided all luxury and lived spartanly, while he had allowed his soldiers to spend their winters inside cities in the houses of their hosts. Furthermore, Macrinus appears not to have kept the soldiers busy with training and work, with the result that they had too much time to gossip and form plots.[28] It is not surprising that the soldiers began to long for Caracalla. It was not long before their prayers would find an answer in the form of 'False-Antoninus/Pseudo-Antoninus'.

Both grandchildren of Julia Maesa were dedicated to the service of the local sun god of Emesa which was worshipped under the Elagabalus, which was a local manifestation of the originally Phoenician cult of Baal. At the heart of the temple there was no man-made statue of the god, but a conical rounded black stone.[29] The local and neighbouring inhabitants, satraps and barbarian princes all tried to outdo each other in the annual sending of costly offerings. Unsurprisingly, the priests of Elagabalus possessed considerable influence over the locals. Consequently, it was a great advantage that Avitus/Bassianus, the elder of the grandchildren, had been made the chief priest of this god, as it was possible for Julia Maesa to influence the local people through her local connections, money and her grandchild. Bassianus' good looks, youth and impressive clothing were not a bad thing either when he appeared in public to perform his religious functions. The soldiers of the local garrison were obviously particularly interested in this youth because he belonged to the imperial family. Some of the soldiers were also clients of Julia Maesa or refugees like Festus, Gannys, Eutychianus and Marcianus[30] who had sought her protection. Julia Maesa told the soldiers through her accomplices that despite being officially the son of Varius Marcellus, Bassianus was actually the natural son of Antoninus Caracalla. It did not hurt that Bassianus seems to have borne some physical likeness to Caracalla, or at least the portraits of the young Antoninus/Bassianus that Julia Maesa's henchmen showed to the soldiers did. According to Julia Maesa's story, Caracalla had slept with both of her daughters (Julia Soaemias and Julia Mamaea) when they were young and able to bear children at the time they were living in the palace. The portraits of both daughters are shown in the Plates section (source: Bernouilli). Julia Maesa's claim has been suspected both in antiquity and today, but it is not as far-fetched as it at first may appear. Julia Maesa and her daughters were indeed present at the court, while their husbands were not. And when we remember Caracalla's notorious womanizing, it is not impossible that he may have slept with both of them, and as noted previously there were almost always witnesses to the sexual acts of the nobility, and that would have been true in this case. Even Herodian (5.3.10) was hesitant to make a final judgment of Julia Maesa's claims, which he said may or may not have been true.

Left: Julia Maesa on a medallion
right: Julia Maesa on a coin
(drawn after Cohen)

Regardless of what the truth was, the soldiers believed the claims. They also had another good reason to believe the story. They were told that Julia Maesa possessed wealth beyond their wildest dreams and that she was ready to distribute it to the soldiers freely, if they would just restore the empire to her family. According to Dio (79.31.1–4), it was one Eutychius who, with the support of a few freedmen, soldiers, equestrians and senators of Emesa, brought Avitus/Bassianus dressed in Caracalla's clothes into the legionary camp at night, supposedly without the women's knowledge. We can be certain that the latter claim of Dio is his own fabrication. The decisive move to rouse the soldiers to revolt was undoubtedly done with the full knowledge of Julia Maesa and at her behest. The coin and medallion from the reign of Elagabalus show Julia Maesa's profile.

At dawn of 16 May, the soldiers garrisoned at Raphaneae (*III Gallica*) near Emesa acclaimed Avitus/Bassianus as emperor and moved all their supplies, children and wives inside the camp for safety.[31] The first to react to the news was *Praefectus Praetorio* Ulpius Julianus, who seems to have been stationed closest to Raphaneae and Emesa.[32] He first put to death both a daughter and son-in-law of Marcianus, who was probably the husband of Julia Mamaea. After this, he led his forces against the camp. The attack was spearheaded by Moorish auxiliaries, who distinguished themselves by breaking through some of the gates. They fought with particular élan for Macrinus, because he was their fellow-countryman. For some unknown reason, Julianus did not exploit the short window of opportunity, causing Dio (79.32.1) to speculate that he was either afraid to charge inside or still hoped to induce the mutineers to surrender. The rebels exploited the impasse and rebuilt the gates during the night, and Julianus was forced to renew the attack, but this time to no avail. The rebels carried Avitus/Bassianus, whom they now called Marcus Aurelius Antoninus, around the ramparts and at the same time displayed portraits of Antoninus Caracalla to show the besiegers the likeness of the two. The rebels also promised sizeable bribes to turn the heads of the attacking forces. This brought the attack to a halt and caused the attackers to change sides. The likeness between

Caracalla and Elagabalus must have been quite obvious even to the casual observer, because the attackers (e.g. Praetorians) included men who had seen Caracalla in person in his youth. When some of their centurions and other officers tried to restrain the soldiers, Eutychius sent Festus outside to incite the soldiers to kill those officers who opposed them with promises of handing over the property of the killed to the killers. As a result, with the exception of Julianus, who managed to flee to Apamea, the soldiers killed all of their commanders. So powerful was the fame of Caracalla, even among the Moors, that they willingly served his supposed son, even against their fellow-countryman.[33] In addition, it appears very likely that Macrinus lost approximately half of his Praetorian corps at this same debacle, because Julianus had been their prefect. It is probable that these Praetorians would have consisted of those who had formerly served under Adventus. The debacle at Raphaea would have meant that Macrinus lost control of the *Legio III Gallica* and its auxiliaries, and a part of the Praetorian Guard (4,000–5,000 men?) and some of the Moorish auxliaries/bodyguards (c. 2,000?).

Since it was clear that the Praetorians at Antioch would stay loyal to Macrinus until the bitter end, the securing of the loyalty of the *Legio II Parthica*, the garrison force of Apamea, was now of utmost importance. The other units housed in Apamea consisted of the *cohors XIV Urbana* and detachments from the *III Gallica, IV Scythica, IV Flavia, XIII Gemina, XIV Gemina* and auxiliaries. Ross Cowan (2002, p.139) has estimated that Apamea housed about 20,000 troops at the time.[34] Julianus had fled there to regroup his forces against the usurper, but contrary to his expectations, the legion joined the revolt and killed him. The lustre of Caracalla's fame was just too much for him to oppose. Thanks to the lacuna in Dio's text, we do not know the full details of how this happened. The lacunose text mentions that someone had been put to death by a man supporting Macrinus, because Marcellus was already dead, but that this man had not enough courage to proceed further without orders. The person killed may have been Gessius Marcianus, the husband of Julia Mamaea and official father of Alexander Severus. Consequently, Macrinus proceeded there on the double while also appointing his own 10-year-old son Diadumenianus as *Autokrator/Imperator/*emperor to court favour from the soldiers with a successor to the throne. Diadumenianus was officially made only Caesar, but his coins declared in Greek that he was *Autokrator* (*Imperator*) and *Sebastos* (*Augustus*).[35] He was also named Antoninus to court the troops. The existence of a successor had a great potential significance because this entailed the promise of further donativa every five years to the troops. When Macrinus arrived at Apamea, he promised each of the soldiers 5,000 *denarii* (*drachmae*), distributing 1,000 immediately and restoring to the soldiers their full rations. In addition, he gave the local populace a lavish dinner in honour of his son before revealing to them anything about the revolt in the army camp. However, while he was thus engaged, one of the soldiers who had revolted brought the head of Julianus, who had been found and duly killed, wrapped in cloth, pretending that it was the head of Pseudo-

Antoninus. Then the soldier ran away. When Macrinus opened up the baggage, he became so frightened that he no longer entertained any thoughts of assaulting the camp and immediately returned to Antioch. Consequently, the *Legio II Parthica* and other troops wintering in the area were free to join the revolt. This means that Elagabalus had at least about 30,000 troops at his disposal.

When Macrinus arrived at Antioch, he wrote a letter to Maximus, the Prefect of the City, so that he could secure the capital before news of the revolt arrived. In addition, he wrote letters to the Senate to secure its loyalty and support. Fulvius Diogenianus, who was an ex-consul and in the opinion of Dio not of sound mind, said that the senators had all prayed for the death of Macrinus. This statement may imply that the Senate was divided between supporters and enemies of Macrinus. This strong opposition in the Senate against Macrinus once again suggests that Caracalla had feared the wrong persons – it is quite obvious that the upper-class senators were more loyal to Caracalla than Dio is ready to admit. Immediately upon arrival, or even before, Macrinus sent messages to all troops in Syria and elsewhere to assemble at Antioch.[36] Elagabalus, or rather his handlers, also sent their own messengers to the legions and auxiliaries to join the revolt, but most of them appear to have been captured and put to death by the governor of Egypt, Basilianus, who had been appointed prefect in place of the dead Julianus, and by Marius Secundus, governor of Phoenicia. After the defeat of Macrinus, both governors paid with their life for their misplaced loyalty.

When the *Legio II Parthica* and the detachments and auxiliaries accompanying it joined Elagabalus, his army marched immediately towards Antioch to engage the emperor before his reinforcements could arrive.[37] It appears likely that one of the reasons for the success of the revolt with so few forces was that part of the army had been sent to (or was on its way to) the Balkans to oppose the Gothic invasion. Despite this, Macrinus' forces seem to have outnumbered his enemy, so he advanced immediately towards them. The sources do not mention other units besides the Praetorians, but his army must have included at least the Germanic bodyguard units and some auxiliaries, and probably detachments of legionaries, in order to cause the reaction in the enemy army that his approach produced. Macrinus had clearly enough men (probably cavalry) to threaten Elagabalus' flanks. Macrinus had about two weeks to assemble his forces, which means that he had probably recalled the forces billeted in Isauria and other locations nearby. It is also quite probable that Macrinus' army included marines taken from the fleet anchored at Seleucia. It is also possible that Elagabalus received reinforcements from the other garrisons during the lull, so that both armies would have had about 40,000 men at their disposal. For the strategic situation facing the opponents, see the accompanying map.

When Gannys, the commander of Elagabalus' army, learned of the approach of Macrinus, he made haste to occupy a pass in front of the village of Immae and drew up his army in good order, despite being entirely without military experience. The second-in-command in Elagabalus' army appears to have been Comazon

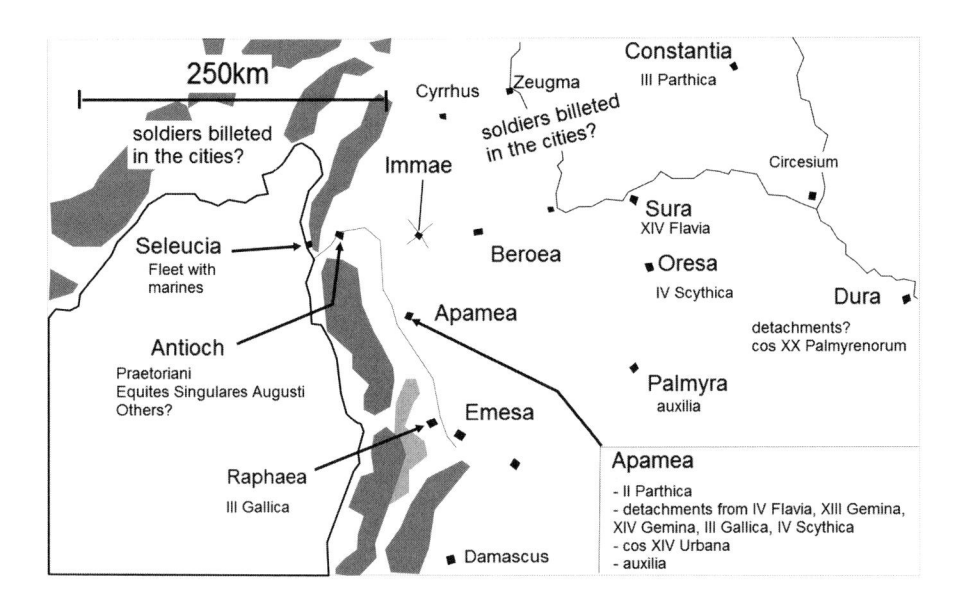

An Epilogue: The Reign of Macrinus the Effeminate, 217–218

Map

- **Constantia** – III Parthica
- **Cyrrhus**, **Zeugma** – soldiers billeted in the cities?
- **Immae**
- **Circesium**
- **Sura** – XIV Flavia
- **Beroea**
- **Oresa** – IV Scythica
- **Dura** – detachments? cos XX Palmyrenorum
- **Apamea**
- **Seleucia** – Fleet with marines
- **Antioch** – Praetoriani, Equites Singulares Augusti, Others?
- **Palmyra** – auxilia
- **Emesa**
- **Raphaea** – III Gallica
- **Damascus**
- **Apamea**:
  - II Parthica
  - detachments from IV Flavia, XIII Gemina, XIV Gemina, III Gallica, IV Scythica
  - cos XIV Urbana
  - auxilia
- soldiers billeted in the cities?

(Kômazontos). Consequently, the armies came into contact with each other 38.4km (24 miles) from Antioch at Immae on 8 June 218.[38] The locale chosen by Gannys for the battle shows that Macrinus' army probably outnumbered him, at least in the number of horsemen and also probably in footmen. According to Herodian, Elagabalus' forces fought bravely while Macrinus' troops were only half-hearted in their efforts and changed sides, with the result that the emperor became frightened that all his troops would desert. Consequently, towards evening, Macrinus took away his imperial insignia and fled in the company of a few trusted centurions. Macrinus' personal bodyguards and Praetorians (Herod. 5.4.8: *sômatofulakes kai doryforoi*), however, continued the desperate fight and did not give up even when the rest of the army had deserted to the enemy. Their futile resistance continued until they noticed that neither Macrinus nor his imperial standards were anywhere to be seen.

Dio gives an entirely different account. According to him, Gannys' men made a very weak fight and would have fled had not Julia Maesa and Soaemias leaped from their chariots to restrain the fleeing soldiers, while Elagabalus on his horse, with a drawn sword, rushed among the fugitives to stop their flight. In Dio's opinion, even this bravery would have proved futile had Macrinus not proved a coward and fled. The imperial women and Elagabalus were clearly more manly than Macrinus. On the basis of Dio's account, one can make the educated guess that Macrinus had placed his trusted Praetorians in the centre and the rest of the troops on the flanks. According to Dio, Macrinus had also ordered the Praetorians to take away their breastplates of scale-armour and their cylindrical shields in order to make them lighter for battle. Another likely purpose not mentioned by Dio for the use of the lighter equipment would have been to enable the men to march faster. On the basis of Dio's comment, however, we can deduce that Macrinus' purpose was to equip his Praetorians in the same way that Caracalla had his Macedonian phalanx. In other words, Macrinus' action verifies the veracity of Caracalla's decision to use the lighter equipment in the summer heat of the Middle East. The abandonment of the curved rectangular or cylindrical shields in favour of the flat oval or round shields suggests the same. Caracalla's analysis of the relative strengths and weaknesses of combat mechanics was correct.

On the basis of what both Dio and Herodian state, it is clear that Macrinus' Praetorians performed admirably and pushed through the enemy centre, and it was only the timely interference of the women and Elegabalus that saved the day – note that the women and a 14-year-old boy who was a bisexual cross-dresser were braver than Macrinus! Macrinus' plan, however, makes tactical sense. When the enemy had deployed their forces in a pass, the wisest course was to break its centre if one decided to fight a frontal battle. The use of the flat oval or round shields would have enabled the men to use the massed shoving action to push the opposition backwards, which was impossible with the cylindrical shields. It is probable (even though this is not mentioned by any source) that Gannys had also deployed the Praetorians in the middle, and that the success of Macrinus' Praetorians resulted at least partly from their eagerness to take revenge against their comrades. The bravery of Macrinus' Praetorians was in vain, because while they fought with great determination, the rest of the army deserted to Elagabalus. This happened when the example of the imperial ladies and Elagabalus had steadied the centre. When

LEFT: Macrinus (Louvre) (source Piranesi 1805)
CENTRE: Macrinus (Louvre).
RIGHT: Elagabalus (Louvre) (drawn after Bernoulli)

An Epilogue: The Reign of Macrinus the Effeminate, 217–218   305

towards evening Macrinus noted that only the Praetorians remained, he panicked and fled, and when they saw that he had fled they surrendered to Elagabalus.

Macrinus sent his son Diadumenianus, together with Epagathus, to seek a place of refuge from Artabanus, while he tried to reach Rome with his trusted centurions to gather support there. He pretended to be a courier and came very close to succeeding in his flight. He managed to reach Chalcedon unnoticed, but then his whereabouts became known when he foolishly sent a man to one of the procurators to ask for money. Consequently, he was arrested while still in Chalcedon, after which he was handed over to centurion Aurelius Celsus, who had been sent by Elagabalus in pursuit of the fugitive. His son was also captured by centurion Claudius Pollio of the *Legio IV Scythica* stationed at Zeugma, presumably with the help of Epagathus, who appears to have retained his position as Praetorian Prefect until the reign of Alexander Severus. Macrinus was sentenced to death and killed by centurion Marcianus Taurus in Bithynia.

Thus began the reign of the assumed son of Caracalla. Elagabalus (Heliogabalus) was not quite what the soldiers expected from a son of Caracalla. A bisexual cross-dresser, when he also started to show signs of being a transsexual (he wanted a sex change) the women of the family got rid of Elagabalus and his wife and replaced him with his cousin Alexander Severus. In order to make the usurpation legitimate, the women claimed that Alexander was also an illegitimate son of Caracalla. It is quite clear that the soldiers truly idolized Caracalla and considered him to be an ideal ruler. However, the hopes of the soldiers were once again betrayed. Alexander Severus was a 'mama's boy' – the real power was in the hands of his mother, Julia Mamaea, who even intervened in military matters and accompanied her son on campaigns. This fact was exploited by the barbarian Maximinus Thrax. He overthrew the legitimate ruler and killed both the mother and son. The memory of the military qualities of Caracalla was so powerful that the soldiers were ready to overthrow his supposed descendant and replace him with a military man of Caracalla's calibre.

However, before their overthrow, the son, mother and their supporters had managed to institute several key reforms, the most important of which was probably the introduction of the first true imperial cavalry reserve for Rome, which consisted of the former bodyguard regiments, the eastern cataphract cavalry (Parthians, Osroenians and Romans equipped as cataphracts), the eastern mounted archers and the German cavalry regiments. Some of these had already been formed under Caracalla, but their numbers were significantly increased under Alexander. It was with these forces that Maximinus defeated the Germans. This proves that the example set up by Caracalla regarding the reform of the armed forces was well-founded. The only problem was that Caracalla set up an impossible model for his successors to follow. He had been too good a general and comrade-in-arms. It required a barbarian for the soldiers to be happy, but he was unacceptable to the native Romans, who showed their disapproval soon enough by revolting. The Italians and the Roman upper classes were not ready to accept an emperor who was

306   Caracalla

a descendant of Alans and Goths. The rise of Maximinus, however, was the sign of times to come. The rest of the third century was dominated by soldier emperors, most of whom came from humble origins. The granting of Roman citizenship to all freeborn men had set in motion great social mobility, which was detested by the old upper classes. Despite being a short man, Caracalla had cast a very long shadow.

Notes

1. The entire chapter on Macrinus is based on: Dio 79.9.1ff.; Herodian 4.13.8ff.; SHA Macrinus and Diadumenianus.
2. The following account of the war and the Battle of Nisibis is based on: Dio 79.26.1ff.; Herod. 4.14.3ff.
3. I have here chosen to follow Herodian's dating of the events and accepted an early date for the Battle of Nisibis. According to the surviving fragmentary text of Dio, there were negotiations before the battle in which Macrinus tried to convince the vengeful Artabanus to desist from attacking because the emperor who had betrayed him was dead, but to no avail. Artabanus trusted in the strength of his army. In light of the general hostility of Dio towards the equestrian Macrinus, it appears probable that he is again guilty of falsifying the facts in order to blacken the enemy of the senatorial class as much as possible. The negotiations cannot have lasted long.
4. I have discussed this matter in a research paper presented on 3 October 2008.
5. Julius Africanus' text implies that the Romans always used the *plinthion* (brick) array (hollow square) to face the Parthians. See Appendix 2. In other words (to reiterate), I do not agree with Cowan's suggestion (2009) pp.30, 35, of a *triplex acies*.
6. This would have been the array first devised by Pyrrhus to make his pike phalanx more flexible. However, the standard practice of placing the light infantry behind the phalangites appears more likely.
7. See Syvanne, *Macedonian Art of War*, on the web at academia.edu.
8. Cowan (2003) pp.24–27, 62–63; Cowan (2008). In 2009 (p.35), Cowan added a cautionary note regarding the *lanciarii*, *phalangarii* and clubmen, which is to a point and I include it here for the same reason. Herodian does not identify the light troops the Romans used as *lanciarii* and he does not mention the *phalangarii*. On the basis of this, Cowan notes that his suggestions should be seen as suggestions and not facts. He is right. On the other hand, it is still equally clear that his speculations are very likely to be true, because his suggestions are supported by other evidence. All sources (including military treatises) suggest that the types of units referred to were used in the manner he speculates that they were. However, there is one point with which I disagree. It is his suggestion that the Romans would have used the *triplex acies* in this battle. This is unlikely in light of Caracalla's preoccupation with Alexander the Great's tactics. It is inherently more likely that the Romans fought in the way Caracalla had trained them to do.
9. The man with a club in Cowan (2003) p.27; see also the introduction with the redrawn figure.
10. See also Syvänne (2004) p.190. This was the same tactic as employed by the menavlatoi in the tenth century.

An Epilogue: The Reign of Macrinus the Effeminate, 217–218   307

11. The other way to employ the more lightly equipped Roman cavalry and Germanic lancers would have been independently of infantry, which would have placed them somewhere out of harms way, as was later done by the Emperor Aurelian against the Palmyran cataphracts in 272. He placed his infantry behind the Orontes River and deployed his cavalry on the other side. He ordered his cavalry to perform feigned flight until the Palmyrene horse, which were burdened by heavy armour and heavily armoured men, would be exhausted by the heat and weight, after which the Roman cavalry was to attack them. The deployment of cavalry separately from infantry enabled them to perform a longer retreat, which made the use of this tactic possible. See Zosimus 1.50.3–4. Macrinus could not use this tactic, because he used a combined arms approach and in that case he should have adopted the offensive tactic with hollow square.
12. This widening of the frontage by Macrinus has also been noted by Cowan (2009) p.30.
13. Dio uses the word *doryforoi* for the Praetorians, and therefore it is clear that he did not mean them.
14. For a later example of this, see Syvanne MHLR Vol.2 which describes the instances in which the Sasanian cataphracts and elephants penetrated the Roman hollow square, but failed to inflict any serious casualties to the infantry units.
15. Dio 79.26.2ff.; Herod. 4.15.6–9. The *Chronicle of Arbela* (8. Bishop Hairan) describes the same war briefly.
16. This has also been noted briefly by Cowan (2009) p.30.
17. Dio 79.29.2; English tr. by Cary, p.407. There is a lacuna in the text at this point. I accept the emendation and translation based on it in the Loeb edition. The text must have included a reference to the Parthians (the word Parthians is not mentioned in the extant text) killing soldiers and ravaging Mesopotamia at this point as a contrast to the damage caused by the Roman soldiers.
18. Dio 79.26.2ff.; Herod. 5.1ff.
19. Dio 79.27.4.
20. Herod. 5.1.4; Dio 79.39.1.
21. Jordanes 15, pp.83–88, esp. 87–88; SHA Maximi Duo 2.1ff. When Elagabalus had overthrown Macrinus, Maximinus rejoined the army to serve under the son of his beloved Caracalla. When it became apparent that Elagabalus was a degenerate (Maximinus' view), Maximinus did his best to avoid any contact. However, when Alexander assumed power, Maximinus was again ready to lend his helping hand to the new ruler, who readily promoted so loyal a supporter through the ranks, only to pay the price for such foolish trust when Maximinus usurped the throne.
22. The following account is based on Dio 79.11.4ff.; Herod. 5.1.1ff.
23. According to Dio (79.21.1ff.), despite the demand of the Senate, Macrinus did not send any documents of the informers to the Senate, because he claimed not to have found any in the royal residence. Dio speculated that Macrinus did this either because Caracalla had destroyed the greater part of the documents or sent them back to the senders, or alternatively because Macrinus wanted to avoid great commotion. As I have noted before, it is also possible that Caracalla received the information in the form of prophecies that hid the identity of the informer.

308 Caracalla

24. Dio does not tell us who Datus was and what he had done, but the association with *Praefectus Urbi* Maternianus in this case does suggest a role in internal security.
25. This and the following is mostly based on Dio 79.13.1ff. The other sources are mentioned at the beginning of the chapter.
26. The garrison cities named by Whittaker in Herod., pp.22–23, n.1. It should be noted that both Antioch and Apamea had originally been built by Seleukos Nikator to garrison his soldiers (at Antioch and Apamea) and elephants (at Apamea).
27. Dio 79.34.3.
28. According to Dio's opinion (79.28.1), it had been Caracalla who had not trained the soldiers, with the result that the soldiers became mutinous against Macrinus, who supposedly ruled them with a firmer hand. This is utter rubbish. Even Dio himself mentioned that Caracalla trained his men. This is again a typical instance of his hostility towards Caracalla. Subsequently, Dio contradicts himself by telling us that the soldiers had enough free time on their hands to visit the temple of Elagabalus to see Avitus/Bassianus (better known as the Emperor Elagabalus). See Syvänne (2004) for the dangers of not keeping the soldiers busy during the winters.
29. In other words, it resembled the conical stone that was worshipped at the temple of Aphrodite at Paphos in Cyprus.
30. Dio 79.31.1–4, 79.32.4, 79.38.3. In the extant fragmentary account, Dio (79.31.1–4, 79.38.3) mentions separately Eutychianus, Marcianus and Gannys. Marcianus is likely to be Gessius Marcianus, the husband of Julia Mamaea. The subsequent killing of Marcianus' daughter and son-in-law suggests that Marcianus had found a place of refuge probably from Julia Maesa. However, it is possible that he was subsequently dispatched to Apamea where he may have been the unknown man killed by a supporter of Macrinus (Dio, Loeb ed., pp. 414–16).
31. The following account is only in Dio 79.31.4ff.
32. It is probable that he was stationed at Emesa proper or very near it, which was the reason for the transfer of the families of the soldiers away from Emesa and the neighbourhood inside the garrison itself at Raphaneae.
33. Note that Whittaker's comment (Herod. 5.4, pp.30–31, n.1) about the likelihood that Macrinus still had Moors among his forces at the Battle of Immae, is uncertain. Dio (79.32.3) states quite clearly that all soldiers accompanying Julianus had been corrupted by the enemy, the Moors included! Regardless, I am still inclined to agree with Whittaker. It is probable that there were also other Moorish troops that stayed loyal to Macrinus.
34. Cowan (2002) pp.137–39.
35. Magie's note in the SHA Macr. (vol.2, p69, n.4).
36. Note that the locales of the legions listed by Whittaker in Herodian 5.4 (pp.30–31, n.1) are not correct but refer to the situation prior to Septimius Severus' reign. The *Legio IV Scythica* was now garrisoned at Oresa and not Zeugma, as in Whittaker, and the *Legio XIV Flavia* at Sura and not Samosata.
37. The following account of the end of Macrinus is based on: Dio 79.37.3ff.; Herod. 5.4.5ff.
38. The date and locale in Whittaker/Herod. 5.4, p.31, n.2.

Appendix I

The Family of Caracalla

FAMILY TREE OF CARACALLA

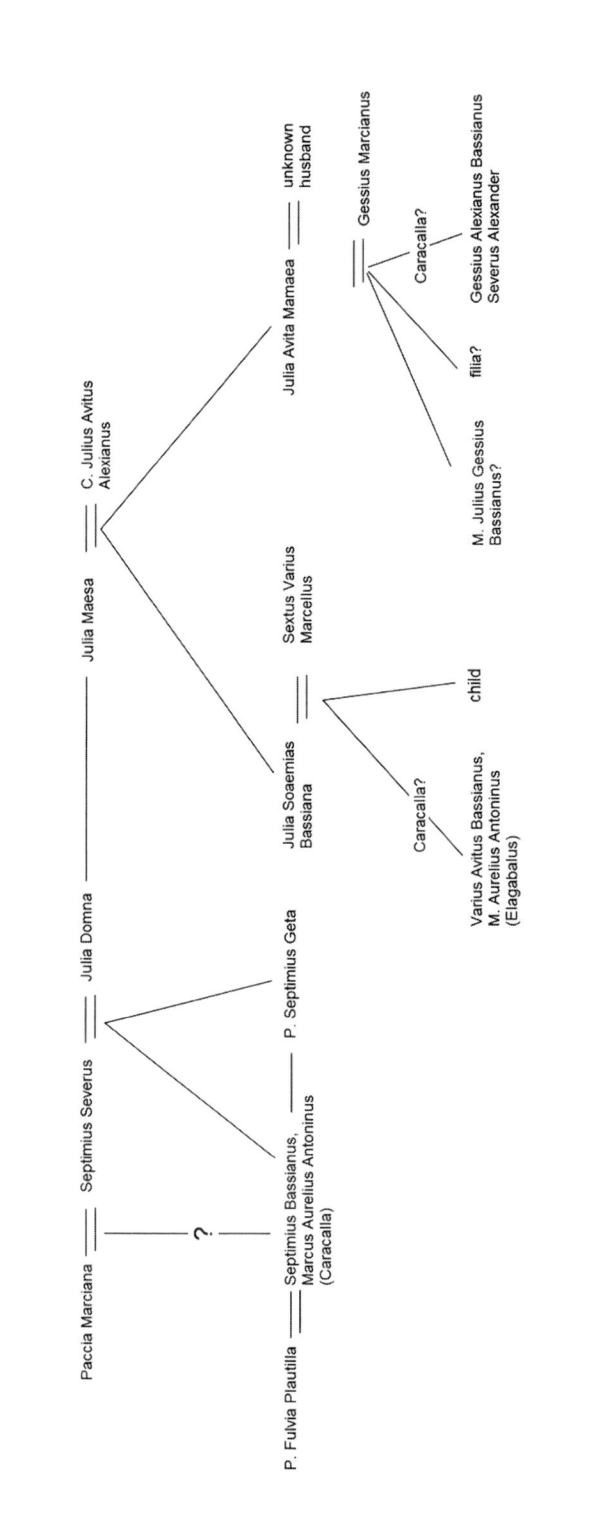

Paccia Marciana === Septimius Severus === Julia Domna ─── Julia Maesa ─── C. Julius Avitus Alexianus

P. Fulvia Plautilla === Septimius Bassianus, Marcus Aurelius Antoninus (Caracalla) ──?── P. Septimius Geta

Julia Soaemias Bassiana === Sextus Varius Marcellus

Julia Avita Mamaea === unknown husband / Gessius Marcianus

Caracalla? / Varius Avitus Bassianus, M. Aurelius Antoninus (Elagabalus)

child

M. Julius Gessius Bassianus?

filia?

Caracalla?

Gessius Alexianus Bassianus Severus Alexander

Appendix II

Julius Africanus and Severan Military Science

Julius Africanus' Kestoi

Julius Africanus was a Christian with access to the highest circles of Roman society. He was the architect of Severus Alexander's new Pantheon library. He is famous for having written the first Christian chronicle of world history and for being a correspondent of Origen. It is also possible that he arranged the famous meeting between Julia Mamaea (Alexander Severus' mother) and Origen in 232.

His military treatise, the *Kestoi* (Amulets or Embroideries), was written during the reign of Alexander Severus (222–235), but after 227, because he mentions the building of the bath and library of Alexander. Both J-R. Vieillefond and E.L. Wheeler have speculated that Julius Africanus wrote the first nine books of the *Kestoi* in the spring of 231 to serve as a guide to the emperor, who was about to depart to the East to fight against the Persians. This is a possible date for the treatise, but in my opinion it is also possible (or even preferable) to see it as an analysis of the reasons for the failure of the war of 231, so it would have been written after that. The reason for this is that the treatise criticizes the standard Roman equipment and the use of the hollow square/oblong in combat, and with this exonerates Alexander Severus. The setbacks suffered against the Parthians had not been the fault of the emperor, but that of his predecessors and officers who had introduced faulty equipment and tactics. Most importantly, the treatise includes instructions on how to engage elephants and then congratulates such *basileios* who are able to capture these, just like Alexander did. Whatever the date, it is clear that Julius Africanus promoted the equipment and tactics adopted by Caracalla, and when one remembers that the SHA (Sev. Alex. 50.5) claims that Alexander Severus' 30,000-strong phalanx consisted of six legions equipped like the others, it is quite possible that Julius' criticism was directed against the re-adoption of the older standard Roman equipment after Caracalla's death.

Julius Africanus proposed a series of reforms for the Roman army so that it could defeat the Persians (always called Parthians) in battle. After the quite evident failure of the Emperor Macrinus (and Alexander Severus) against the Parthians, Africanus naturally concluded that the infantry-based Roman army could not defeat the Persian mounted archers. Regardless of the intention to offer advice against the Persians, the treatise was also clearly intended to be universally applicable, because Julius devoted only the fragment 1.1 to the Eastern question. The rest of the treatise is devoted to a wide variety of matters that could be used in many different theatres of war. On the basis of the fact that Julius Africanus' treatise found its way to the imperial archives of both Rome and Byzantium, it had a profound impact on the military thinking of the Romans.[1] The following discussion is a short summary of the contents of the *Kestoi*.

As already noted by Wheeler, in his discussion Africanus does not distinguish legionaries from auxiliaries. This is the natural result of the granting of citizenship by Caracalla to all men in the empire. Consequently, according to Julius Africanus, the Roman infantryman wore a mail breastplate, single greave, helmet, carried a large shield held by a single-handed grip, and used as weapons the *spatha* and several javelins. According to Africanus, the Roman shield (*thyreos*) was not suitable for the *synaspismos* formation (i.e. the *testudo* shield wall in which the shields were interlocked rim-to-boss), because the soldier could not press his entire shoulder against the shield. Julius presumably meant the traditional legionary curved rectangular shield, which was not suited to rugby shoving and which left the right shoulder unprotected when one used spears.

Julius Africanus' observation is also important for another reason. It proves that the Romans were using the offensive rim-to-boss/shields overlapping *synaspismos* version of the *testudo/foulkon* array against the Parthian cavalry together with the defensive version in which the front rank kneeled, which had been the favourite tactic to face a cavalry charge with infantry throughout the history of the Roman Empire. The curved rectangular shield was definitely unsuitable for this tactic. It would have been better to use the standard kneeling version and then charge forward after the cavalry had been stopped before the Roman formation, as described for example by Arrian in his *Ektaxis kata Alanôn*. In my opinion, Julius Africanus criticizes correctly the adoption of the unit order suited for the flat shields when the men were using the curved rectangular shields. The Romans used a great variety of shields and the commanders should have taken into account what type or types of shields each unit had. It is quite clear that this critical mistake must have taken place during Alexander Severus' eastern campaign – perhaps the destruction of the southern army corps resulted from this. The decision to use the interlocking of shields universally by all units (even by those using the curved rectangular shield) to face enemy cavalry can only have been made at the very top. Therefore, it is very likely that Alexander Severus' campaign stands as one of those rare examples of gross military incompetence in which the military doctrine adopted by the high command contributed to the defeat of the army at unit level. It is very likely that the mistake in question had been made by the senatorial commanders who acted as Alexander Severus' military advisors.[2]

In Julius' opinion, the lightness of Roman equipment allowed them mobility in attack and retreat, which they could use to their advantage against the Greeks, but these very same attributes worked against them when they faced the Persians. The Romans were unable to use their mobility against the more mobile Persian cavalry,

Plinthion:
10 c. AD Byzantine Interpolation of Aelian (tr. by A.M. Devine, Aelian's Manual of Hellenistic Military Tactics 42.6, Ancient World 19, 1989, p. 62): "It is called a plinthion whenever the formations on the four sides are drawn up identically, so as to be square in shape." The diagram is drawn after Codex Burney 108 f.20 ("p.39").

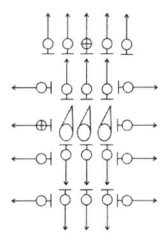

because their own mobility was hindered by the use of the hollow square formation (*plinthion*), inside which they placed their baggage train and beasts of burden. It should be noted that it is probable that Julius means with this *plinthion* both the four-sided hollow square *plinthion* and the oblong-shaped *plaision*. The illustration in the Byzantine Interpolation of Aelian also suggests the possibility that the *plinthion* could have meant a unit of sixteen men by sixteen men, but on balance it is more likely that Julius (and the Interpolation) did indeed mean the grand tactical hollow square with four equally long sides. The inclusion of the slingers inside the diagram of the array suggests a hollow space, because the light infantry slingers would have required enough room to use their slings or staff slings.

The mobility of the Roman soldiers was hindered even further by the use of the kneeling *testudo*-order that was used as a defensive measure against Persian missiles. Consequently, Julius Africanus thought that the Romans were impotent against the Persians thanks to their use of the hollow square formation and *testudo* unit order. The use of these formations enabled the Romans to withstand the showers of arrows and stones initially, but in the end the stationary array would still succumb to exhaustion as a result of the successive waves of attacks by the Persian bands/tribes (*ethnoi*).

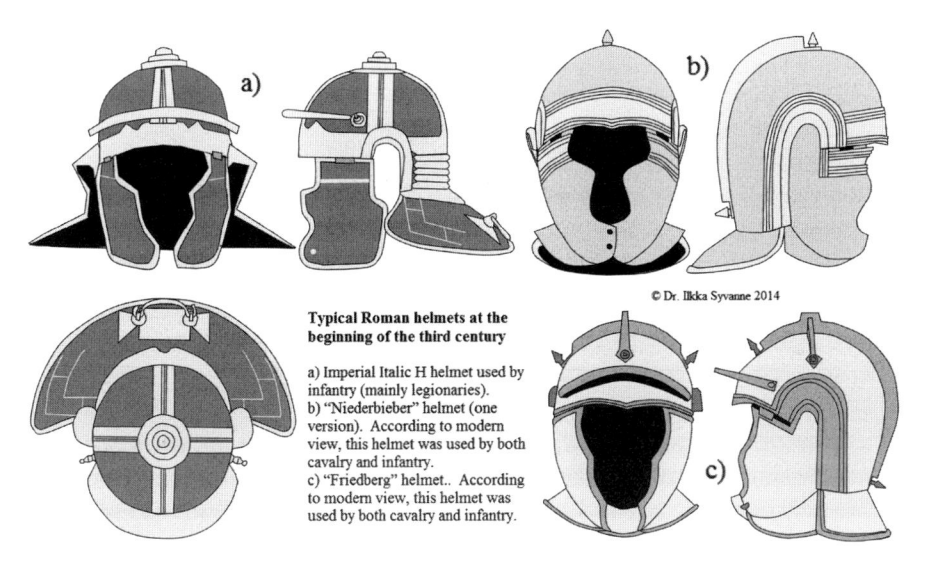

Typical Roman helmets at the beginning of the third century

a) Imperial Italic H helmet used by infantry (mainly legionaries).
b) "Niederbieber" helmet (one version). According to modern view, this helmet was used by both cavalry and infantry.
c) "Friedberg" helmet.. According to modern view, this helmet was used by both cavalry and infantry.

© Dr. Ilkka Syvänne 2014

Julius thought that it was a weakness that the Romans never fought as individuals, nor used champions,[3] which limited their ability to cause damage to others. Julius Africanus also claimed that the Roman helmet (probably the Roman Imperial-Italic H-type, Niedermörmter and Niederbieber types, as noted by Wheeler) did not provide adequate protection against slingshots, so that the shots penetrated the skull. The helmet also prevented free movement of the head and hindered vision so that it was difficult to evade the incoming missiles. In his opinion, this made the Roman soldier vulnerable to projectiles. In other words, he thought that the Roman soldier could not dodge incoming missiles when arrayed in the *testudo* formation. This is definitely inaccurate, because the soldiers could have just lifted up their shields to block the attack, even if it is still clear that the structure of the helmet did indeed prevent free movement of the head and neck. It is a matter of opinion whether one considers the peak/visor of the helmet useful, as someone evidently had, or harmful, like Julius did. It did hinder the view upwards, but at the same time it protected the eyes from dropping missiles and the head from cuts with weapons. One may perhaps think that some of the men and officers found a ready excuse for their defeats by blaming the type of equipment rather than admitting poor generalship, and that this criticism then found its way into Julius' treatise. Venditius Bassus, Corbulo, Trajan, Septimius Severus and Caracalla certainly did not have any difficulties in dealing with the Parthians, even if it is still clear that Caracalla appears to have had similar views of the equipment as Julius. There is no doubt that he introduced new equipment and tactics that corrected the precise failings mentioned by Julius Africanus. Note also the implication that the Parthian and Sasanian cavalries carried stones and slings, just like the Roman forces and the later Abbasids and Mamluks. Additionally, Julius Africanus claimed that the Roman infantry was ineffective because it could achieve only one kill per ten thrown javelins and because the Roman *kontos*-spear (which presumably means the *hasta* or *pilum*, rather than the 3.74m cavalry *kontos*-spear) was too short to stop a cavalry charge. Caracalla agreed.

According to the *Kestoi*, the Romans had defeated the Greeks, and the Greeks had defeated the Persians, but the Romans had not been able to defeat the Persians. Consequently, Julius Africanus proposed to equip the Roman army with the Greek kit. These newly equipped soldiers would then be deployed as individuals in the Greek manner to attack the enemy *kontoforoi* cavalry. According to Africanus, the Greek hoplite equipment consisted of doubly protected helmet, *aspis*-shield (a round concave bronze shield with arm and wrist grips), scale armour, two shin-guards, a javelin (*akontion*), cavalry spear (*doru*) for close quarters fighting and a short sword. Note that with the exception of the scale armour, this set of equipment is what Caracalla used for his Spartan and Macedonian phalanxes, but with the difference that the Spartans would have presumably used the Roman 3.74m cavalry *hasta/kontarion*-spear and the Macedonians the *sarisa/sarissa*-pike. This equipment was so heavy that the hoplites could only charge a short distance forward, but it gave them the ability to weather the showers of arrows and stop the attack of the *kontoforoi* cavalry. Caracalla's Macedonian-style force was naturally less heavily equipped and more mobile. According to Africanus, while one part of the hoplites withstood and stopped the attack of the spear-armed cavalry with the *synaspismos* (shields placed rim-to-boss) array, the others sprang forward to disperse the enemy. According to a possibly later interpolation (1.36–7 based on 2.16) to the text, the Greeks could also spray hellebore from large syringes to stop enemy cavalry charge.[4] The Greeks also employed peltasts and slingers, who could operate at their leisure behind the rampart of hoplites. The double helmet can be interpreted to mean that the Greeks wore a protective cap underneath the actual helmet. Should this be interpreted that the Romans did not have similar protective caps beneath their helmets, which would be odd when the extant evidence suggests that they did? This would mean that Julius actually meant doubly thick helmets. The other possibility is that he meant that the Romans would not have worn any real helmets at all in the encounters he criticized, but would have used mail or scale hoods as shown in some of the third- (e.g. in Dura Europos) to fifth-century paintings, or that he just accused the equipment to exenorate Alexander Severus from any blame.

According to Julius Africanus, the Macedonians had modified the Greek system only slightly by introducing the Lacedaemonian helmet[5] to their armies and having the beards shaven so that the enemy could not seize them by their beards.[6] In other words, Julius thought that the Greek *doru* was as long as the Macedonian *sarisa*. His note on the beards can be seen as criticism of the current military fashion of having beards. Caracalla had shaved off his beard to emulate Alexander the Great. Should this be seen as a statement of the same?

What is notable about the above list is that it recommends the very same measures that had been undertaken by Caracalla against the Parthians, and which had apparently been abandoned after him thanks to the influence of the conservative senatorial block within Roman society. It should be stressed that this was not decisive if the soldiers had good morale and the commanders did not make the mistake of ordering the men to assume the wrong fighting formation.

However, Africanus' proposed series of reforms did not only deal with military equipment and battle tactics. He also provided a long list of precautions, instructions and ruses, which were to be combined with 'magical tricks' to make the Roman army invincible. His treatise pays particular attention to the health and training of Roman horses and pack animals, but unfortunately he does not state how these were to be used effectively on the battlefield.[7] Nevertheless, the attention Julius gives to the horses in warfare suggests that he favoured increasing the number of cavalry, which had found favour with Caracalla and also under Alexander Severus.

According to the *Kestoi*, the superiority in the numbers of swords, men, arrows and walls could be overcome by advantageous wind, sun and terrain, as well as by ruses, stratagems and spectacles, and by the raising of a bold and loud war-cry. Julius Africanus' models included for example: the use of the wind and sun in the battles of Cannae and Trasimenus; the use of restricted terrain at the Battle of Thermopylae; the use of the war-cry at the Battle of Marathon; the use of poisoned arrows; the placing of the army in a forest; the use of the retreat and destruction of pastures; and the poisoning of wells. Notably, he also mentions (1.2.2) that Alexander [the Macedonian?] became master of the Alans by destroying their fields with hellebore.[8] This shows that the hellebore was also useful when invading enemy lands. Note also that it is very probable that Caracalla intended to fight with poisons.

Julius Africanus promoted the use of guerrilla warfare, night attacks, poisons, diseases and stratagems against barbarians in his first and second books, because he considered the waging of war an unpredictable proposition. He expected Roman commanders to procure all possible advantages for their own side.[9] The general first took care of the supplies and safety of his army, without which it would have been impossible to win. The general was expected to place his marching camp in a healthy place that had an abundant supply of safe water. Not surprisingly, Julius Africanus also noted the importance of having a doctor to accompany the army and the inherent dangers of heat and physical exhaustion to the health of the army. Notably, food and drink were also to be distributed to the soldiers in small portions with absinthe throughout the day, which in the opinion of modern nutritional science was very beneficial to their general health.[10] As a result, the soldiers were lean, mean fighting machines that always possessed energy to endure physical labour or combat. However, just in case the soldiers had not had the chance of eating and drinking before the battle, Julius Africanus recommended (1.3) the use of *gastrasia* (*alectorias*, belly stones of cocks?[11]) placed below the tongue, that were, according to him, used by soldiers, athletes and gladiators to alleviate fatigue and thirst. I personally do not know whether the *gastrasia* produced the hoped-for results, but at least their presence in the mouth would undoubtedly produce saliva that would in turn alleviate the feeling of thirst and fatigue. The problem is accentuated by the fact that the *Kestoi* claims that the *gastrasia* had magical qualities. It is probable that Julius Africanus and other period people claimed magical qualities to all things and practices that they did not fully understand, but which apparently had some positive or negative consequences.

The *Kestoi* includes a long list of instructions on how to treat wounded or otherwise ill men, horses and draught animals (see fragments 1.4–13, 1.17, 2.6–11, 3.1ff). Most of the medical treatments of the *Kestoi* are based on some combination of first aid procedures, surgery, herbal medicine and magic. Consequently, it is difficult to assess the effectiveness of these without practical experiments. As regards the magical component in the treatments, some of these would have produced the desired effect if the patient believed in them while others would have been entirely useless. In addition, some of the magical treatments, like the placing of 'magical things'/amulets on a horse, would also have worked because they distracted the horse so that it would not behave in an unwanted manner – a practice which is still used to change the behaviour of horses and dogs. Regardless of their actual effectiveness, these prove that in the minds of his contemporaries, magic (or rather things that seemed to work in a magical manner) was a very potent force to be reckoned with.

Unsurprisingly, Julius Africanus demanded that the Roman commander paid attention to use of the dominant terrain, ditches, advanced guards (*profylakai*), night marches (*nyktoporiai*, i.e. night attacks), cavalry vanguards (*prohippasiai*), patrols/scouts (*diereunéseis*), spies (*kataskopai > kataskopoi*), light-armed troops (*euopliai*, i.e. to be well-armed), reconnoitring (*pronomeiai*) and adequate sleep/rest. The general was required to maintain a mistrustful attitude towards the enemy at all times. The army was required to carry with it antidotes in the form of pills against poisoned arrows and infectious water.[12] The horses and draught animals were similarly fed with a concoction of herbs and other substances that supposedly protected them against pestilence (1.12). Trees and woods were to be cut down in order to prevent the enemy from hiding in the forests. In order to be particularly effective, every possible tree and piece of vegetation was to be cut down. Julius' aim was therefore nothing less than the total destruction of any type of vegetation that could provide cover for the enemy, which reminds one of Agent Orange in the Vietnam War. On campaign, the army was also required to carry with it enough fodder and supplies so that it would not have to rely on foraging. It was thanks to this practice that the Roman general could wear out the enemy by subjecting it to hunger and epidemics. In offensive warfare, the general was to destroy fields and pastures with hellebore and cut down trees so that the enemy would not find any subsistence and cover. This strategy was obviously also very useful in defensive warfare.

Julius Africanus endorsed the harnessing of the air and wind, food and water for military purposes. He promoted the use of poisons and an early form of germ warfare. He did not separate the use of poisons from bacteriological warfare. Both were used to 'poison' enemies. Regardless, it is still clear that in practice Julius understood the difference between the two, because whereas real poisons affected only those who were directly in contact with them, he understood that germ-poisons spread from one human to another. Julius includes several different ways for the spreading of poisons and germs. Firstly, both types of contaminants, poisons and germs, could be spread by baking the substances into bread or other food. Secondly, these could be added to wine or other drinkable substances. The contaminated food or drink would then be left behind for the enemy to consume. If this did not work, then it was possible to have prisoners eat the infectious food and drink, and then send them back to their own camp or lands. According to Julius, this system enabled the Romans to spread the disease first to the enemy's comrades, and from them to their families, villages, army and finally to the whole enemy nation. This proves that Julius understood the theory behind germ warfare, even if he failed to separate poisons and germs conceptually. If all of the above failed because the enemy refused to be 'poisoned', the final method was to harness the power of the wind, which was impossible to avoid. This was done by placing certain poisonous snakes in hermetically sealed clay vessels that were first dried and then opened up when the wind blew from the right direction. According to Julius Africanus, it was possible to stop and kill a horse in the middle of a gallop, and likewise men and birds, by releasing poisonous fumes at them. Unsurprisingly, Julius also promoted the contamination of the earth, wells and ponds. This was to be done by throwing garbage or poisonous or infectious substances into them. He also noted that one should not expect the eastern barbarians to be ignorant of these very same devious methods. As an example, he gave the instance in which the Pharisees (Jews) had destroyed a Roman phalanx (legion?) through the use of feigned flight and poisoned wine. It is not known when this event occurred. There were Jewish revolts during the reigns of Trajan, Hadrian and the original Antoninus Pius, all of which are possible candidates.

The *Kestoi* also promoted the use of night attacks with light infantry and cavalry. The expected results varied, from harassment and capture of advance guards all the way up to the total destruction of their forces. When the attackers reached the enemy camp, they used arrows, javelins and stones to cause confusion and panic inside the camp, while horsemen equipped with trumpets circled around the enemy to confuse them over the direction of the attack. If this attack failed to destroy the enemy, it was to be repeated several nights in succession to deprive the enemy of sleep, which would enable the Romans to defeat the sleep-deprived and therefore ineffective enemy force.

As noted above, the *Kestoi* pays particular attention to the use of horses in warfare. Julius Africanus wrote that all horses have their own personal qualities and faults that needed to be addressed if the horse was to be used in combat (1.6). Some horses were rapid, but amorous; some were good hunters/fighters, but biters; some others were good trotters, but too ardent; some did not allow the rider to mount his horse; some threw their riders; some rode against walls or trees; some were vicious by nature, and so forth. He noted that there were horse trainers who corrected these faults by various means, but also suggested one particular remedy to put a stop to neighing. He noted quite correctly that the neighing of horses in ambush was very bad (fr.1.7). The typical reason for neighing was the odour of mares, which was bound to cause stallions to neigh loudly. Consequently, according to the treatise, when one travelled in lands infested by brigands or when one intended to ambush the enemy with cavalry, one was to resort to the following remedy, that was also used by the Parthians: place the tendon of an ox to the painful spot behind the horse's tail in such a manner that it penetrated deep. The pain caused by this kept the horse silent and ready for combat. This sounds like an effective ploy, but requires practical experimenting.

Julius Africanus claimed that Roman cavalry officers were ignorant of the 'prophesying qualities' of horses, which manifested themselves in the movements of a horse's head, its attitude, neighing and silence. Consequently, according to the *Kestoi*, it was possible to foretell thunderstorms, good hunting, abundant harvests, birth of foals and the attack of enemies, and to discover hidden brigands (the horse either moved its ears, was hesitant or breathed with open nostrils) just by observing the behaviour of the horse. Africanus noted the well-known fact that by observing the behaviour of animals, in this case horses, it was possible to 'foresee' future events that animals had already detected with their heightened senses. It would be very odd that Roman cavalry officers did not know of this, but this is what Julius Africanus claimed. On the basis of this, one can conclude that most of the upper-class Roman cavalry officers had become quite ignorant of the behaviour patterns of animals, which would suggest that these officers considered horses as just expendable tools that could be ridden to death if needed, so there was no sense in growing too fond of any particular animal. Obviously, one should not include all officers in this class of ignorance. Despite what Julius Africanus claimed, it is obvious that some Roman cavalry officers would still have been empathetic enough to observe the behaviour of their mounts. However, Julius Africanus goes even further in his claims. He claims that horses could not only discover human criminals, but also evil spirits, and the demons that inhabited particular crossroads (is this sentiment to be taken for real or as a metaphor for the presence of ambush at crossroads?) – a 'fact' of great importance according to Julius! This sort of claim raises serious doubts regarding his own observatory capabilities, unless he meant the general potential of the place for ambush, which would then have been personified as a demon in his thinking.

The *Kestoi* (1.8.19ff.) also claimed that horses should abstain from sex, just like athletes, before battle. He claimed that this could be achieved by giving them the plant of Bacchus (i.e. wine). I do not personally know whether this was in any way beneficial to the combat efficiency of the horse. However, one may speculate that if the stallions were keen to mate with the enemy's mares, this could be used in a cavalry attack to induce the stallions to charge the enemy.

The treatise also includes stratagems to negate the impact of enemy cavalry charges. According to Julius, there were people who offered a prayer or sacrifice to Poseidon before battle to obtain his help, but he himself favoured another method that he claimed to have discovered. Firstly, a certain poisonous drug was placed in large syringes carried by lightly equipped men. These men were then placed just behind the first rank of heavily equipped men, who protected them with their shields. When the enemy *katafraktoi* (cataphracts) charged, the first rank sustained their attack behind their shields, while the second rank syringe-bearers launched the drug onto the nostrils of the horses and their riders. As a result, the horses would immediately stop and rear up, and the riders would fall onto the ground, where they could be captured or killed. According to Julius, the use of this poison and syringes was more effective than the use of arrows. In later Byzantine texts, the syringe was replaced by *cheirosiphona* (hand-held siphons) that were also used to shoot Greek Fire.

Julius Africanus did not stop his instructions at this, but also claimed that horses could be felled by wetting their nostrils with the gall of turtles or by a mixture of herbs and other substances. He also claims that the sting of a tarantula and salamander could kill a horse, but I cannot see how this could be used unless one collected huge numbers of the creatures that were then either spread on the battlefield well before any action took place or shot at the enemy in clay vessels during battle. He also claimed that the burning of women's period linen could be used to stop horses. According to Vieillefond (p.341), this method had Jewish origins and had therefore been used in practice. It is impossible to verify the effectiveness of the above instructions without practical experiments, but Julius Africanus included one verifiably effective ruse borrowed from Polyaenus (2.2.9). This was the use of infantry in a *plinthion*/brick formation (presumably also including the *plaision*, hollow rectangle or square) to build a marching camp, so that the rear-rankers dug a ditch while the front-rankers protected them. When the ditch was finished, the hoplites retreated behind the ditch. This method had definitely been used by Romans ever since antiquity.

Like other ancient military treatises, the *Kestoi* promoted the use of hunting as a form of military training (1.14). However, Julius Africanus' instructions bear no real resemblance to the others, because he describes only using infantry in lion hunting and not the use of cavalry. In spite of this, it is certain that his instructions for the lion hunt reflect actual Roman military training practices, because mosaics and paintings depicting scenes of lion hunts can be found all over the empire, particularly in North Africa. When the army commander (*polemarchos*) wanted to train his army, he first ordered the infantry to equip themselves for combat and then led them to hunt the big cats. The hunters first located the lair of the lion, and then the infantry marched silently to the place. After this, the infantry closed its ranks, formed a circle, interlocked the shields rim-to-boss and formed a roofed *testudo* (an array likened in the text to a tiled roof). Then the trumpets (*salpigges*) were sounded and the men let out a very loud war-cry. As a result, the beast would rush out from its den, only to found itself trapped by the wall of hoplites, shields and torches (if the men carried one instead of a spear). If the lay of the land allowed, the soldiers used a large cage to catch the lion. In this case, cataphracts (*andres katafraktoi*) on foot moved behind the lion, and with cries and by striking dried-up skins (i.e. drums/tambourines) with sticks, they frightened the lion towards the cage. When this happened, the hoplites from both sides of the cage (*mêchanês*) moved up to close the cage behind the beast. This method trained the infantry to cooperate with the scouts (the hunters) and with each other collectively. They learned how to manoeuvre the battle line, to close ranks, form the *testudo*, withstand the approach of a very frightening big animal and operate separate sections of the line independently of others (the cataphracts and those who captured the lion in the cage). The presence of cataphracts among the infantry is very interesting. This means either that part of the infantry wore the full panoply of armour, or that parts of the cataphract cavalry could be dismounted to stiffen the infantry line.

The two illustrations (see next page) copied by Bartoli (1706) from a Roman grotto show this military-style hunting taking place during the Late Roman period.

Julius Africanus did not forget the importance of possessing the necessary skills in the use of the dioptre to estimate the width of a river or height of a wall (1.15). Consequently, the *Kestoi* includes a discussion of the mathematical methods based on the principles of Euclides that were used for this purpose.[13] This was absolutely necessary, because a commander and his engineers needed to know how many boats would be needed for the building of a pontoon bridge. Similarly, it was necessary to know the height of a wall so that one could bring against it a *helepolis* (city-taker, mobile siege tower) or ladders of the right height for its scaling. This proves that in the third century AD the *helepolis* still meant a siege tower and not yet a large stone thrower of the trebuchet type, as it usually did from the sixth century onwards.

The *Kestoi* also notes the importance of the senses in warfare (1.16). According to Julius Africanus, the Mauritanians/Moors had the keenest eyesight. They could see a person at a very great distance. However, the eyesight could also be trained, and this was of great use for the military. According to him, the Moors had another practice that was to be emulated, namely that when they slept, they dug a small hole in the ground, in which they placed a piece of wood. The wood was placed beneath the ear as an aid to hearing. According to Julius Africanus, this method was also used by Gallic brigands.[14] If a large army wanted to find the hiding places of the enemy, he recommended the digging of a deep hole into which descended one soldier, who then covered the hole with any kind of fabric to listen to tremors in the ground.

In Julius Africanus' opinion, war elephants were virtual super weapons of antiquity (1.18). This is not surprising, considering the fact that Alexander Severus appears to have faced considerable numbers of them in the East when he fought against the Sasanians. According to the SHA (Sev. Alex. 55–56), the King of Kings Ardashir/ Artaxerxes had 700 pachyderms in his army, of which the division commanded by Alexander Severus in person claims to have killed 200, captured 300 and sent eighteen to Rome. Contrary to common opinion among historians, I consider these facts and numbers reliable.[15] Ardashir had sought to emulate his prestigious models, the Achaemenids, in all respects, the army, scythed war-chariots and elephants included. He even wrote a military treatise to serve as a book of guidance both to his commanders and his successors. However, the first experience of the reality of period battlefield ended the experiment of using large numbers of war-elephants. Henceforth, elephants were regarded by the Sasanians as symbols of the king, or as baggage animals and workhorses of the army, rather than super weapons. The prestige of the elephant, however, persisted among the Sasanians, and there were periods in which elephants were still used against the Romans on the battlefield. It is therefore no wonder that Caracalla had taken elephants with him to the East. He clearly understood that he needed to train his men and horses to face these beasts on the battlefield. See the following illustration of the Sasanian war elephant.

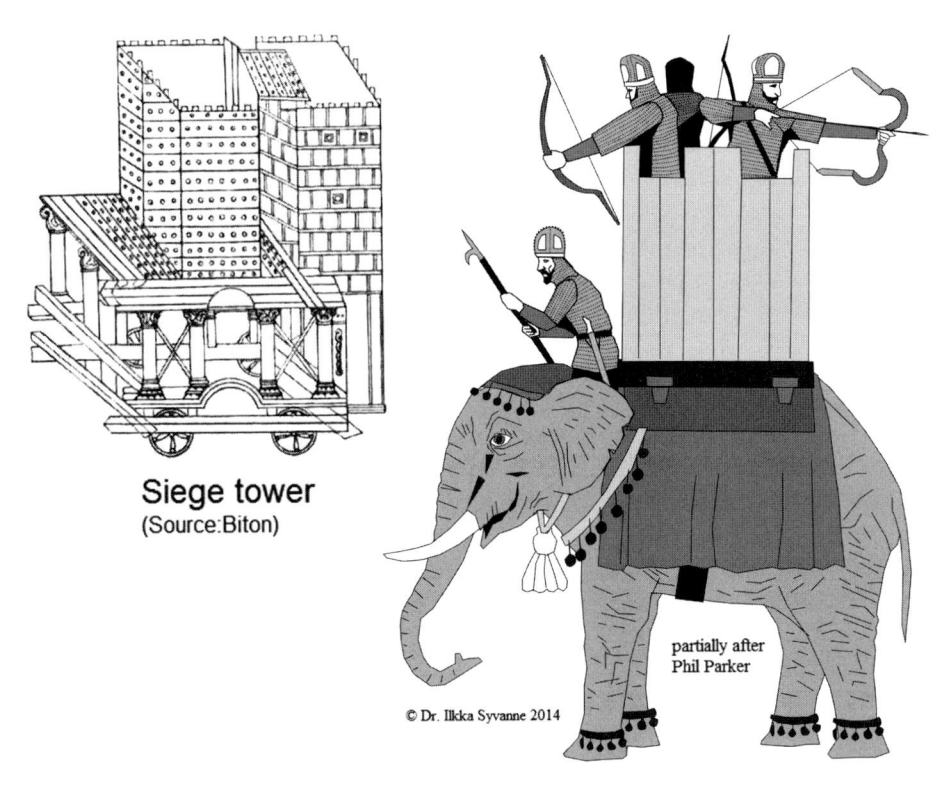

Siege tower
(Source: Biton)

partially after Phil Parker

© Dr. Ilkka Syvanne 2014

According to the *Kestoi*, the ancients considered elephants to be of great use in battles: both men and horses feared them if they were not familiar with the beast; towers carried by elephants were a cause for added terror; and, in combat, elephants formed a kind of rampart that advanced in front of the phalanx. It was supposedly impossible to bear their trumpeting and their impact in battle. Elephants were protected by a thick skin, trunk and spear-like tusks. According to Julius Africanus, elephants dominated the battlefields. All that was needed was that they shattered the formation of interlocked shields (*synaspismos*), and the army was as good as destroyed. When an elephant faced an infantry phalanx, it was like the bronze ram of a trireme crushing a ship. The war-elephant had an appearance of a mountain; it knocked down its opponents; it caught horses, men and chariots/wagons (*harma*) in its trunk, and it knocked them violently down, rolled them and trampled them; it frightened horsemen; and from the height of its tower, archers shot charioteers/ drivers (*harmatēlatas*) from distance. It is possible that elephants were the super weapons as portrayed by Julius Africanus, but the Romans knew how to counter them. I would suggest that Julius refers to elephants only because Severus Alexander had faced them with great success, even if elephants had probably caused plenty of problems for Romans who had not faced them in a long time – the extant evidence suggests that Parthians did not usually use elephants against Romans.

Unless Julius simply borrowed the above from an ancient source, the text implies that Romans would also have used chariots/wagons against elephants in battle. Unfortunately, the word *harma* allows many interpretations: it can mean supply wagons or war chariots. However, since the text refers to archers in the towers killing charioteers at distance, the latter option appears more likely. Could this mean that the Romans used scythed chariots against the elephants with poor results? The fourth-century *De rebus bellici* XII.1 includes a cataphracted scythed chariot *currodrepanus* driven by two fully armoured men that owed its invention to the exigencies of battle with the Parthians. It had two variants: *currodrepanus singular* (XIII.1), which was a single-horse chariot driven by a single fully armoured man; and *currodrepanus cliepatus* (XIV.1), that had a mechanism in the rear that lashed the horses on and spiked shields for its protection, and was driven by a single man. Vegetius (*Epitome* 3.24) lists similar counter-measures against elephants: the cutting off of the trunk; the use of a chariot drawn by two cataphracted horses, from which *clibanarii* threw *sarisae* at the elephants; the use of light javelin-armed infantry *velites*; and the use of *carroballistae* (artillery mounted on wagons). Therefore, the shooting of drivers at distance could actually refer either to drivers of war chariots or drivers of *carroballistae*, because the sources clearly prove that the Romans used both (see Syvanne MHLR Vol.2). The different possibilities are shown in the illustrations (source: Schneider, 1908, *De Rebus Bellicis*).

After Julius Africanus had shown the power of war-elephants, he detailed the ways in which they could be opposed, firstly, in his opinion, with light infantry javeliners and archers. Cavalry was not to be used against them anymore, because the horse's fright of unfamiliar beasts could disorder the entire army. If the text had been written after 231, does this mean that Alexander Severus had first sent his cavalry against the elephants of Ardashir with such disastrous results for the cohesion of the army that it was only saved from complete defeat by the timely arrival of reserves under Alexander? The attack against the elephants was to be accompanied by the loud sounding of the trumpets to scare off the beasts. The javeliners were to aim at the elephant, while archers were to send their fire arrows at the wooden towers. It was enough that even one of the missiles penetrated the skin to cause the elephant to become enraged, and in rage the elephant was usually more dangerous to its own side. The use of iron caltrops in very large quantities in the path of the elephants was also considered a very effective counter-measure. Julius Africanus noted that the captured elephant or hide of an elephant was more glorious than the shield of a general or the armour of a dead champion[16] to the victorious *basileus* (emperor). If the text was written after 231, which is probable, he flattered Emperor Alexander Severus with this statement, because Alexander brought with him numerous elephants as war booty, but evidently not any equipment taken from the nobility of the Sasanians, who evidently all managed to escape on horseback.

Julius Africanus also took into account the fact that the army needed different kinds of supplies in different theatres of war (1.19) at different times of year. There was a great variety of climates and terrains, ranging from the Saharan and Syrian deserts to the forests of Germany, steppes of Pannonia, the Alps, the Caucasus and so forth. In those areas that did not produce wine, one had to do with ersatz produce called *zythos* in Egypt (barley beer), *camum* in Pannonia (barley beer), *kerbesion* (*cervoise*) by the Celts (barley beer), *sikera* by the Babylonians (either barley beer or palm wine) or fig wine. Julius also includes a discussion on how to produce vinegar by different methods, how to make different kinds of oils (olive, lent, pistachio) and how to produce *garum*, all of which were considered necessary for military campaigns. The sixth-century military treatise the *Strategikon* makes it clear that the filters (which were used to make oils in the *Kestoi*) could also be used to purify drinking water (see Syvänne, 2006).

Considering its importance in third-century AD warfare, it is not surprising that Julius Africanus concluded his first book with anecdotes of archery (1.20), all of which, he claims, he had personally witnessed. One of the anecdotes concerned the arrow flight speed experiment conducted by an unnamed party. According to this ancient test, the flight speed of an arrow was 185km/h, which is very close to the experiment conducted in 1969 that measured a speed 160km/h.[17] According to Julius Africanus, when he was in the court of Abgar VIII (ruled 179–211/2) at Edessa, he had witnessed the excellent archery skills of Mannos/Manou, the son of Abgar IX (ruled 212, 217–242). When hunting, the cavalry escort of Mannos, which included Julius Africanus, was surprised and frightened by a bear. However, Mannos blinded the bear by shooting out both of its eyes so that the bear was at their mercy. Another example provided by Julius Africanus concerns Berdasane the Parthian (154–222, a poet and philosopher who spent a large part of his life at

Edessa), who demonstrated his skill by shooting arrows at a shield held by a man in such a manner that the arrows showed the outline of the man. The last example concerns the trick shooting skills of Syrmos the Scythian (a Goth?), who fought against an arrow with another arrow. He placed an archer opposite himself at some distance, who then shot an arrow at him. Syrmos used a regular arrow while the other used a headless arrow. When the other archer shot an arrow at Syrmos, he shot his arrow at the approaching arrow, with the result that it penetrated and destroyed the unarmed arrow. Obviously it is impossible to verify these stories, but the gist of them is to portray to the Roman audience the great military importance of archery and also the special archery skills of the Edessans, Parthians and Scythians. The exploits of the modern Danish archer Lars Andersen prove that all of the trick shots mentioned by Julius can be replicated when the archer has enough talent and practice behind him. For example, Anderson has proved that it is possible to shoot three arrows in just 0.6 seconds and to shoot down an arrow shot at him. The Hungarian János Kassai has similarly demonstrated the foolishness of earlier historians who have doubted the stories told of mounted archery in the sources.

In his second book (2.5), that survives only in later Byzantine compilations, Julius Africanus also includes a recipe for making poisoned arrows, which has clear military implications. It is not for nothing that the Romans were required to possess antidotes against poisons (2.7) – they also used them!

The second book of the *Kestoi* (2.11) also includes a discussion of how to produce automatic fire, the equivalent of sixth-century AD automatic fire and seventh-century Greek fire. The concoction was to be preserved in an airtight vessel that could then be thrown at the target, which would catch fire on contact with the substance. Despite the fact that the fragments of the second book come from later Byzantine treatises, this automatic fire appears not to be a later interpolation, because there is plenty of evidence for the use of fire-bombs from earlier Hellenistic and Late Roman periods. If it were a later interpolation, it would also have included a discussion of the siphons used to deliver the actual Greek fire during the Byzantine period. Rather, it describes an automatic fire that had in all probability been invented during the Hellenistic period and later copied, for example by Marius the Syrian at the turn of the sixth century (see Syvänne, 2004).

A light-armed man armed with a syringe full of poison as described by Julius Africanus. The use of the Macedonian shield and equipment is my educated guess, because it is a known fact that some of the light-armed carried shields. The shield would have been quite necessary for a man deployed in the second rank.

Appendix III

The Georgian Chronicles and Caracalla's Campaign in Armenia

The history of Georgia/Iberia during the reign of Caracalla is particularly difficult to reconstruct because the Classical sources are silent on its history and the Georgian Chronicles offer a chronologically very confused account. This appendix offers my attempt to date the evidence provided by the Georgian Chronicles. See also the analysis of Moses Khorenatsi in the narrative.

The relevant portion of the list of kings of Iberia in the Georgian version of the Chronicles (pp.65–70) has eight prior to the the reign of Alexander Severus (222–235). These are P'arsman, Amazasp, Rev/Vroyn, Vač'e, Bakur, Mirdat, Bakur and Asp'agur, the last of whom was overthrown by the Sasanian king Ardashir I.[18] The Armenian version includes only P'arsman, Amazasp, Rev/Vroyn, Vač'e and Asp'agur. This list is likely to be more accurate, so Bakur, Mirdat and Bakur were added to the list only to fill up the chronological gap resulting from the misdating of the rulers in the Georgian Chronicles, because no details of their reigns are given. The Chronicles jump to the reign of the Persian *shahanshah* Khosrov Anushirwan, who ruled from 531–579 (even though all versions actually describe the events of Ardashir I's reign in Khosrov's name), with the result that the author(s) has added three kings to the list to fill the chronological gap. It is clear that the author has realized that something was amiss with the chronology without realizing that the text gave Ardashir the name Khosrov. It is in fact probable that even Vač'e was added to the list, because some of the manuscripts do not contain his name.[19] These persons can be discarded immediately. Those who are of particular interest here are therefore P'arsman, Hamazasp/Amazasp, Rev/Vroyn, Vač'e and Asp'agur, because it appears very likely that their reigns coincided with the Severan era. What remains to be done is to find out who ruled during Caracalla's reign.

According to the Georgian Chronicle (pp.65–69), P'arsman ruled without incident and was succeeded by his son Amazasp/Hamazasp, who was a strong and powerful ruler. It was during his reign that the Ossetes (i.e. Alans) managed to surprise the Iberians and cross the Caucasus (in 214?). They marched along the road of Dualet/Dvalet'i and rested their army for eight days on the River Leax/Liaxvi, then marched against the capital Mtskheta. In the meanwhile, the king had summoned reinforcements from all his *eristavis* and from Armenia. Amazasp had managed to assemble 10,000 horseman and 30,000 footmen, but he still played for time by challenging enemies to single combat. When on the third day the number of cavalry reached 16,000,[20] Amazasp launched a general attack and defeated the invaders. The next year (in 215?), the Armenians joined Amazasp and their combined forces descended on Ossetia (Alania) north of the Caucasus range. Amazasp plundered Ossetia and returned home in triumph. As a result, Amazasp became haughty and intolerable to his nobles, killing many of them, and also became an enemy of the Armenians, and thereby an ally of Persia (Parthians?).

When Amazasp revolted against the Armenians, five *eristavis* of the West (two *eristavis* of Egrisis, Ojrhe, Klarjeti and Cunda) revolted and allied themselves with the King of Armenia. The King of Armenia received a force from Roman territory and formed an alliance with the Alans. The King of Armenia invaded and joined forces with the rebels and Alans, while Amazasp brought to Iberia his Parthian allies. The armies met in combat. Amazasp and his army were annihilated and the Armenian king installed his son Rev (nephew of Amazasp) as King of Iberia. Rev was married to a Roman woman called Sepelia. She was a daughter of a Roman *logothete* (official in charge of finances). She brought with her an image of Aphrodite, which was set up at the entrance of Mtskheta (Mc'xet'a). The king and his wife followed a policy of religious tolerance, forbidding the sacrifice of children to gods and the persecution of Christians. Human sacrifices were replaced by animal sacrifices. Notably, the policy of religious tolerance was typical for the reigns of Caracalla, Elagabalus and Alexander Severus

It is also possible to connect the marriage of Rev and Sepelia with the Armenian campaigns of Theocritus, who was an imperial freedman put in charge of the logistics and finances prior to the Armenian campaign, from which he progressed to the position of commander of the Armenian campaign as a Praetorian Prefect. However, it is more likely that this event took place later so that Amazasp's revolt against Armenia and Rome should be dated to the period after 224. It is likelier that Amazasp's campaign in Ossetia should be connected with Valarsh's campaign in the same area in 215. It is also probable that Rev and Aspagur were contemporaries with Alexander Severus and possibly also with his successors.[21]

Notes

1. A copy of it was preserved in the imperial archives at Constantinople and was used as a source for the tenth-century Byzantine military treatises *Apparatus bellicis*, *Geodesia* of Heron of Byzantium, *Excercitationes*, *Sylloge tacticorum* and *Taktika* of Nikephoros Ouranos. It was also used as a source during the sixth century, at least by Cassianus Bassus, who had used as his sources two fourth-century treatises by Vindanius Anatolius of Beirut and Didumaios of Alexandria. See Vieillefond, pp. 67–70, 189–98, 342–43.
2. See my forthcoming study of the reign of Alexander Severus.
3. Is this a form of praise for Caracalla's behaviour?

4. See Vieillefond's note, p.106a. Note that the syringe is not really the same as the later flame-thrower invented during Leo VI the Wise's reign, which makes it quite possible that the syringes to shoot hellebore were the original piece of equipment invented by the Greeks and that these inspired Leo to invent his more effective flame-thrower.
5. The use of the Lacedaemonian helmet did not find favour during the third century, but by the end of the sixth century these were used, if the David Plates can be taken as evidence of this. However, it is always possible that these plates did not reflect the actual reality, but an artistic imitation of earlier works. The David Plates can be accessed online on the home page of the Metropolitan Museum of Art.
6. It was Alexander the Great who ordered his men to shave their beards so that the enemy could not grasp the beard.
7. These very same questions have also been noted by E. Wheeler in his excellent brief analysis of Julius.
8. As far as I know, Alexander the Great had not fought against the Alans, but the instruction to use hellebore to poison pastures was still a very usable and effective means of fighting through indirect means. However, it is possible that the Alans are in fact the Saka against whom Alexander the Great fought in the East. This obviously raises the possibility that the Saka and Alans, who all of a sudden appear in the West at about the time of the birth of Christ, were one and the same people, and that the Alans had learned the use of *kontus* from the Macedonians. There is also the possibility that the word Macedonian was added to the text by the later Byzantine commentators, who did not realize that Julius Africanus had meant Alexander Severus and not the famous Alexander the Great (i.e. the Macedonian). This conclusion finds support from the fact that 1.2.16 mentions only Alexander while the word Macedonian is to be found only in the fragment 2.2.3 that comes from later Byzantine excerptors. This raises the possibility that Alexander Severus (and other Romans) may have used hellebore to poison the fields and pastures of the Alans.
9. This advocation of total war has also been noted by E. Wheeler.
10. The possible health benefits of the use of absinthe are obviously controversial. In large quantities it causes hallucinations, but in small portions it helps the digestive system, and in herbal medicine its daily use is seen to be beneficial to the general health of its user. I have discussed this matter also in a book chapter (2006, Water).
11. See also Vieillefond's translation, p.124 and note 42.
12. The same requirement can also be found in the sixth-century military treatise the Strategikon and in the Late Roman and Byzantine treatises that included borrowings from the Kestoi. The recipe for the pill is to be found in Kestoi 2.7 (Viellefond ed.).
13. Similar discussion can also be found in the tenth-century military treatise of Heron of Byzantium. See also the discussion in Vieillefond, pp.342–43.
14. Vieillefond, p.343, notes that according to the Mémoires du Général Baron de Marbot, the French used quite similar methods even in 1799.
15. For the different views, see: Scullard, p.302 (he suspects that there may be something behind the claims); Rance (2003); Kistler, pp.170–71 (claims a Sasanian victory with elephants); Charles (2007) (also has some suspicions that there may be something behind the claims). However, I do agree with both Philip Rance and Michael B. Charles, that

after the initial failure, the Sasanians used the elephants mainly as baggage animals, siege towers, battering rams, aids in the crossing of rivers, cranes or as symbols of the power of the king etc., rather than for actual field battles. In these roles the elephant proved to be relatively useful. Regardless, it is still quite clear that the Sasanians continued to use elephants also on the battlefield, but usually with poor results when they faced the Romans.

16. Note the inclusion of champions in this part of the text. It was a typical feature of Iranian culture to fight single combats between champions before battle. Hence the reference to the equipment taken from dead champions.
17. See Vieillefond, p.180, n.152.
18. Asp'agur opened up the passes of the Caucasus and helped his kinsman Khusrov the Great/Tiridates against the Sasanians, and was therefore a contemporary of Khusrov and Ardashir I.
19. The omission of Vač'e and others in some manuscripts is mentioned by Thomson.
20. The Armenian text has 16,000 cavalry and the Georgian version 10,000. The likely reason for the difference in the figures is that the Armenian version preserves the final number of cavalry after the reinforcements had arrived, and the Georgian version the original strength.
21. As noted above, Vache is likely to be an addition to the list to fill-up the chronological gap resulting from the jump to the reign of Khosrov Anshirwan.

Select Bibliography

Select Primary Sources Online:
Available online: Aelian; Arrian; Scriptores Historiae Augustae (SHA 'Aelius Spartianus': Severus, Antoninus Caracallus, Antoninus Geta; Opellis Macrinus by 'Julius Capitolinus'); Dio; Herodian; Nennius; Bede; Geoffrey of Monmouth; Sextus Aurelius Victor, Epitome de Caesaribus 21; Sextus Aurelius Victor, Liber de Caesaribus; Eutropius, Historiae Romanae Breviarium; Festus, Breviarium Rerum Gestarum Populi Romani; De Rebus Bellicis; Itinerarium Provinciarum Antonini Augusti; Orosius; Zosimus; Synkellos (Syncellus) AM 5701ff; Bar Hebraeus; Michael Syrus; Moses Khorenat'si; Georgian Chronicles (Georgian and Armenian versions); Eusebius, History of the Church, Chronicle; Edessan Chronicle/Chronicle of Edessa; Chronicle of Arbela; Alexander Romance. The best places to seek these sources are the internet archive and Robert Bedrosian's home page. I recommend the latter site in particular for those interested in Armenian sources. Many university library websites, like that of Heidelberg (highly recommended), offer access to old manuscripts, and old and new studies. There is also a plentiful supply of sources on the web which include numismatic studies, information regarding auctions and photos of coins – all of this warms the heart of a former coin collector like me. Good places to start a search for numismatic information are George Depeyrot's studies (including those on the web, e.g. on the academia.edu website) and simple 'googling'.

Select Sources:
Alexander Romance (Greek version), *The Greek Alexander Romance, Translated with an Introduction and Notes Richard Bateman*, Penguin Books. London (1991); Collected Ancient Greek Novels, edited by B.P. Reardon, University of California Press. Berkeley, Los Angeles, London (1989), Pseudo-Callisthenes, Alexander Romance, 650ff.
Alexander Romance (Persian version), *Iskandarnamah. A Persian Medieval Alexander-Romance*. Translated by Minoo S. Southgate, Columbia University Press. New York (1978).
Alföldy, G. (1974), *Noricum*. London.
D'Amato, R. (2009a), *Arms and Armour of the Imperial Roman Soldier from Marius to Commodus, 112 BC–AD 192*. Illustrations by G. Sumner. Barnsley.
—— (2009b), *Imperial Roman Naval Forces 31 BC–AD 500*. Ill. by G. Sumner. Oxford.
Andersen, Lars, a superb Danish archer who proves the effectiveness of the shower archery technique on YouTube.
Arguin (Argüin), A.R.M. (2011), *El ejército romano en campaña De Septimio Severo a Diocleciano (193–305 D.C.)*. Sevilla.
Artsruni, Thomas (1985). *History of the House of the Artsrunik*. Translation and commentary Robert W. Thomson. Detroit.

Select Bibliography 331

Austin, N.J.E., and Rankov, N.B. (1995), *Exploratio*. London and New York.
Bafaqih M. A. al-Q. (1991), *l'unification du Yemen antique*. Paris.
Bar Hebraeus (1932) (Reprint Amsterdam 1976), *The Chronography of Gregory Abû'l-Faraj 1225–1286*. Tr. by E.A.W. Budge. London.
Banchich T.M. (2015), *The Lost History of Peter the Patrician*. Oxon and New York.
Barker, P. (1981 4th ed.), drawings by Ian Heath, *Armies and Enemies of Imperial Rome*. A Wargames Reasearch Group Publication.
Barnett, G. (2009), 'Father and son invade Iraq. The Parthian wars of the first Severi', *Ancient Warfare II.6*, 22–28.
Batty, R. (2007), *Rome and the Nomads. The Pontic-Danubian Realm in Antiquity*. Oxford.
Bender, S. (2013), 'Der Feldzug gegen die Germanen 213 n. Chr.', in *Caracalla – Kaiser, Tyrann, Feldherr*, Archäeologisches Landesmuseum Baden-Württemberg. Darmstad/Mainz, 104–131.
Birley, A.R. (2000), *Septimius Severus, the African Emperor*. London and New York.
—— (2006) *BBC TimeWatch* (April 2006).
Bird, H.W. (1995), *Liber De Caesaribus of Sextus Aurelius Victor*. Liverpool.
Bishop, M.C., and Coulston, J.C.N. (2nd ed. 2006), *Roman Military Equipment From the Punic Wars to the Fall of Rome*. Oxford.
Bohec, Yann Le (2009), *L'armée romaine dans la tourmente*. Paris.
—— (2005), *Histoire le Afrique romaine*. Paris.
—— (1994, 2004), *The Imperial Roman Army*. London and New York.
Boyce, M. (2012), 'Ganzak', in *Encyclopaedia Iranica* (available online).
Breeze, D.J., and Dobson, B. (2000), *Hadrian's Wall* 4th ed. London.
Bruun, Christer (1995), '*Pericula Alexandrina*: The adventures of a recently discovered centurion of the *legio II Parthica*', in *Arctos 29*, 9–27.
Brzezinski, R., and Mielczarek, M. (2002), *The Sarmatians 600 BC–AD 450*. Oxford.
Burns, T.S. (2003), *Rome and the Barbarians, 100 BC–AD 400*. Baltimore and London.
Campbell, B. (1994), *The Roman Army 31 BC–AD 337: A Sourcebook*. London and New York.
Cascarino, G. (2008), *L'esercito romano. Armamento e organizzazione. Vol. II da Augusto ai Severi*. Il Cerchio.
Cary, E. (ed. and tr.), *Dio's Roman History*, Loeb (1927).
Charles, Michael B., 'The Rise of the Sassanian Elephant Corps: Elephants and the Later Roman Empire', in *Iranica Antiqua* XLII, 2007, 301–346.
Choisnel, E. (2004), *Les Parthes et la Route de la Soie*. Paris.
Christol, M. (2006), *L'empire romain du IIIe siècle. 192–325 apr. J.-C*. Paris.
Coulston, J. (1986), 'Roman, Parthian and Sassanid tactical developments', in P. Freeman and D.L. Kennedy (eds), *The Defence of the Roman and Byzantine East*, BAR Int. Ser. 297. Oxford, 59–75.
Cowan, R. (2002), *Aspects of the Severan Field Army. The Praetorian Guard, Legio II Parthica and Legionary Vexillations, AD 193–238*. PhD. Thesis, University of Glasgow.
—— (2003), Ill. by Angus McBride, *Imperial Roman Legionary AD 161–284*. Oxford.
—— (2008), 'Lanciarii. Elite Legionary Light Troops?', in *Ancient Warfare* Vol. II, Issue 1, Feb/Mar 2008, 18–23
—— (2009), 'The Battle of Nisibis, AD 217', in *Ancient Warfare* 3.5, 29–35.

Dando-Collins, Stephen (2010), *Legions of Rome.* London.
Daquet-Gagey A. (2008), *Septime Sévère.* Paris.
Dawson, T. (2007), '"Fit for the task": equipment sizes and the transmission of military lore, sixth to tenth centuries', in *BMGS* 31.1, 1–12.
Debevoise, N.C. (1938/1968), *A Political History of Parthia.* New York.
Delmaire, R. (1995), *Les institutions du bas-empire romain de Constantin à Justinien.* Paris.
Dio, Cassius, *Dio's Roman History*, 9 vols. Tr. by Cary. Loeb.
Drinkwater, J.F. (2007), *The Alamanni and Rome 213–496. Caracalla to Clovis.* Oxford.
Drouville, G. (1825), *Voyage en Perse fait en 1812 et 1813.* 2 vols. Paris.
Durry, M. (1938), *Les cohortes prétoriennes.* Paris.
Eadie, J.W. (1967), 'The Development of Roman Mailed Cavalry', in *JRS 37*, 161–173.
Elliot, P. (2014), *Legions in Crisis.* Fonthill Media.
Farnum, J.H. (2005), *The Positioning of the Roman Imperial Legions. BAR Int.Ser. 1458.* Oxford.
Feugere (Feugère), M. (1993/2002), tr. by D.G. Smith, *Weapons of the Romans.* Charleston.
Fitz, J. (1962), 'A Military History of Pannonia From the Marcomann Wars to the Death of Alexander Severus (180–235)', in *Acta Arcaeologica Tomus 14*, 25–112.
Fraser, J.E. (2005), *The Roman Conquest of Scotland. The Battle of Mons Graupius AD 84.* Stroud.
Fuhrmann, C.J. (2012), *Policing the Roman Empire.* Oxford.
García, Paloma Aguado (2013), *Caracalla. La configuración de un tirano.* Madrid.
Ginzrot, J.C. (1817), *Die Wagen und Fahrwerke der griecher und römer.* München.
Goldworthy, A. (2009), *The Fall of the West.* London.
Gonzales (González), J.R. (2010), *La dinastía de los Severos. Comienza del declive del Imperio Romano.* Madrid.
Grant, M. (1996), *The Severans. The changed Roman empire.* London and New York.
Guhl, E., and Koner, W. (1882), *Das Leben der Griechen und Römer.* Berlin.
Hanson, W.S. (1978), 'Roman campaigns north of the Forth-Clyde isthmus: the evidence of the temporary camps', *Proc. Soc. Antiq. Scot. 109* (1977–1978), 140–150.
—— (1987), *Agricola and the Conquest of the North.* London.
Hamdoune, C. (1999), *Les auxilia externa africains des armées romaines.* Montpellier.
Heather, P. (2002), *The Goths.* Oxford.
Hekster, Olivier, *Commodus. An Emperor at the Crossroads*, J.C. Gieben, Dutch Monographs on Ancient History and Archaeology Vol. 23, Publisher Amsterdam (2002).
Herrnándes, F.D. (2010/2011), *Los Godos desde sus origines Bálticos has Alarico I.* Spain.
Herodian, *Herodian in Two Volumes*, tr. by C.R. Whittaker. Loeb (1969).
Historia Augustae, see SHA.
History of civilizations of Central Asia (HCCA). Volume II. The development of sedentary and nomadic civilizations: 700 B.C. to A.D. 250. Editor János Harmatta. Co-editors: B.N. Puri and G.F. Etemadi (UNESCO 1994). New Delhi (1999).
Hoyland, R.G. (2001), *Arabia and Arabs from the Bronze Age to the Coming of Islam.* London and New York.
Huff, D. (2002), 'Takt-e Solayman', *Encyclopaedia Iranica* (available online).
Isaac, B.H. (1990), *The limits of empire: the Roman army in the East.* Oxford.

Ivantchik A. (2014), "Roman Troops in the Bosporus. Old Problem in the Light of a New Inscription Found in Tanais", in Ancient Civilizations From Scythia to Siberia 20, 165–194.
Jallet-Huant, M. (2009), *La garde prétorienne dans la Rome antique*. Paris.
James, S. (2011), *Rome & the Sword*. London.
Jeffreys, E., Jeffreys, M., Scott, R. et al. (tr. and ed.) (1986), *The Chronicle of John Malalas*. Melbourne. This is actually a better edition than the Greek text because it contains translations of both Greek and Slavic verions with comments. Highly recommended.
Jones, A.H.M. (1964/1986), *The Later Roman Empire*. 2 Vols. Oxford.
Kamm, A. (2009/2012), *The Last Frontier. The Roman Invasions of Scotland*. Neil Wilson Publishing.
Kassai, János, a superb Hungarian mounted archer who has proved possible all stories regarding mounted archery. Available online on YouTube.
Kazanski, M. (1991), *Les Goths (Ier-VIIe après J.- C.)*. Paris.
Kazanski, M., and Mastykova, A. (2003), *Les peuples du Caucase du Nord*. Paris.
Kistler, J.M. (2006), *War Elephants*. Westport Connecticut and London.
Koshelenko, G.A., and Pilipko, V.N. (1994/1999), 'Parthia', in *HCCA*, 131–150.
Kouznetsov, V., and Lebedynsky, I. (2005), *Les Alains. Cavaliers des steppes, seigneurs du Caucase Ier-XVe siècles apr. J.-C.* Paris.
Lebedynsky, I. (2010), *Sarmates et Alains face à Rome, Ier Ve siècles.* Clermont-Ferrand.
—— (2007), *Les Nomades*. Paris.
—— (2006), *Les Saces*. Paris.
—— (2002), *Les Sarmates*. Paris.
Le Bohec, see Bohec.
Lenoir, M. (ed.), *Pseudo-Hygin. des fortifications du camp*. Paris (2002).
Levick, B. (2007), *Julia Domna. Syrian Empress*. London and New York.
—— (Levick 2), *The Government of the Roman Empire. A Sourcebook*. Beckenhamn and Sydney (1985).
Lindenschmit, L. (1882), *Tracht und Bewaffnung des römischen Heeres während der Kaiserzeit*. Braunschweig.
Litvinsky, B.A., with the contributions of M. Hussain Shah and R. Shabani Samghabadi (1994/1999), 'The Rise of Sasanian Iran', *HCCA*, 473–484.
Machiavelli, N., *The Prince*. Tr. by George Bull. London (1961).
Magie, *SHA (Scriptores Historiae Augustae)* (1924), English tr. by David Magie. Loeb.
Maxwell, G.S. (1989), *The Romans in Scotland*. Edinburgh.
Majumdar, R.C., and Altekar, A.S. (1967/2007), *The Vakataka-Gupta Age*. Delhi.
Mettesini S. (2006/2008), *Les Légions Romaines*. Rome.
McHugh, J.S. (2015), *The Emperor Commodus: God and Gladiator*. Barnsley.
McLaughlin, R. (2014), *Roman Empire and the Indian Ocean*. Barnsley.
Michael, Syrus, *Chronicle*, Armenian version, tr. by Robert Bedrosian. New York (2013).
Mielczarek, M. (1999), *The Army of the Bosporan Kingdom*. Łódź.
—— (1993), *Cataphracti and Clibanarii. Studies on the Heavy Armoured Cavalry of the Ancient World*. Łódź.
Mócsy, G. (1974), *Pannonia and Upper Moesia*. London.

Moses, Khorenatsi, *History of the Armenians*, tr. by R.W. Thomson. Cambridge and London (1978).
Munro-Hay, S. (1991), *Aksum. An African Civilization of Late Antiquity.* Online, ed. by Alan Light.
Nikonorov, V.P. (1997), *The Armies of Bactria 700 BC–450 AD.* 2 Vols.
Okon, D. (2013), 'Caracalla and his collaborators', in *Mnemon 13*, 253–262. St Petersburg.
Patterson, L.E. (2013), 'Caracalla's Armenia', in *Syllecta Classica 24*, 173–199.
Peter the Patrcian, see Banchich.
Pollard, N., and Berry, J. (2012), *The Complete Roman Legions.* London.
Porter, K. (1822), *Travels in Georgia, Persia, Armenia, Ancient Babylonia.* London.
Potter, D.S. (2004), *The Roman Empire at Bay AD 180–395.* London and New York.
Puri, B.N. (1994/1999a), 'The Sakas and Indo-Parthians', in *HCCA*, 191–207.
—— (1994/1999b), 'The Kushans', in *HCCA*, 247–263.
Rance, Philip, 'Elephants in Warfare in Late Antiquity', in *Acta Antiqua, Academiae Scientiarum Hungaricae 43*, Budapest (2003), 355–384.
Rankov, B. (2000), *Guardians of the Roman Empire.* Oxford.
—— (1986), *The* beneficiarii consularis *in the western provinces of the Roman Empire*, Unpublished Dissertation, University of Oxford (1986) (available online).
Rawlinson, G. (1841), 'Notes on a Journey to Takhti Soleïmán and on the Site of the Atropatenian Ecbatana', *JRGS 10*, 1–158. Identifies falsely Takt-e Solayman with Ecbatana.
Raychaudhuri ,H. (7th impression, 2006), *Political History of Ancient India. Commentary B.N. Mukherjee.* New Delhi.
Reed N. (1976), 'The Scottish campaigns of Septimius Severus', in *Proc. Soc. Antiq. Scot. 108* (1975-1976), 92-102.
Ref 1, The Roman Eastern Frontier and the Persian Wars (AD 226–363), compiled and edited by M.H. Dodgeon and S.N.C. Lieu. London and New York (1991).
Salway, P. (1993/2001), *A History of Roman Britain.* Oxford.
Saxer, R. (1967), *Epigraphshische Studien 1. Untersuchungen zu den Vexillationen des römisches kaiserheeres von Augustus bis Diokletian.* Köln and Graz.
Schippmann, K. (2001), *Ancient South Arabia.* Princeton.
Schneider, R. (ed.) (1908), *Anonymi De rebus bellicis liber.* Berlin.
Schönberger, H. (1969), 'The Roman Frontier in Germany: An Archaeological Survey', in *JRS* 59.1, 144–197.
Scullard, H.H. (1974), *The Elephant in the Greek and Roman World.* London.
Skupniewicz, P., Personal communication; See also his articles in AW 1.4 and 5.3.
SHA, Scriptores Historiae Augustae, 3 vols, tr. by D. Magie. Loeb (1921–1932).
Sheldon, R.M. (2010), *Rome's Wars in Parthia.* London and Portland.
—— (2005), *Intelligence Activities in Ancient Rome. Trust in the Gods, but Verify.* London and New York.
Southern, P. 2001 (reprint 2003), *The Roman Empire from Severus to Constantine.* Routledge London and New York.
—— (1989), 'The Numeri of the Roman Imperial Army', in *Britannia 20*, 81–140.
Speidel, M.P. (1994), *Riding for Caesar. The Roman Emperors' Horse Guards.* London.

—— (2006), *Emperor Hadrian's Speeches to the African Army – a New Text*. Mainz.
Starr, C.G. (2nd ed., 1960), *The Roman Imperial Navy 31 B.C.–A.D. 324*. London.
—— (1943), 'Coastal Defense in the Roman World', in *The American Journal of Philology*, 56–70.
Stepheson, I.P. (2003), *Roman Cavalry Equipment*. Stroud.
—— (2001), *Roman Infantry Equipment*. Stroud.
Stoneman, R. (1991), see *Alexander Romance*
—— 2008, *Alexander the Great. A Life in Legend*, Yale University Press. New Haven and London.
Syvanne (Syvänne/Syvaenne), Ilkka, MHLR *A Military History of Late Rome*, Pen & Sword, Barnsley. Vol. 1 published in 2015. Vol. 2 due to be published in 2017 and vols 3–4 in 2017–2018. ASMEA 2015 = "The Eyes and Ears: The Sasanian and Romans Spies ca. 222-450", Historia i Swiat 5, 2016, 107-131. The writing of this research paper/article was generously supported by ASMEA research grant.
"The Reign of Bahram V Gur", in Historia i Swiat, 71–102.
—— (2014a) research paper 'An Overview of the Late Roman Naval Warfare AD 365–565', *The 10th Maritime Heritage Conference (Norfolk, Virginia, September 17–20, 2014)*
—— (2014b) research paper 'Rome's Eastern Foreign Policy 324–450', *Asmea Conference 2014, October 30 November 1, 2014*.
—— (2013), 'Arrian/Arrianus', *Philosophers of War 2 vols*, eds D. Coetzee and L.W. Eysturlid. Santa Barbara, Denver, Oxford.
—— (2013), research paper 'An Overview of the Late Roman Naval Warfare 284–395', in *2013 McMullen Naval History Symposium*.
'Water Supply in the Late Roman Army', in *Environmental History of Water*, eds P.S. Juuti, T.S. Katko and H.S. Vuorinen, IWA Publishing. London (2006), Chapter 6 (pp.69–91).
—— (2004), *The Age of Hippotoxotai, Art of War in Roman Military Revival and Disaster (491–636)*, Acta Universitatis Tamperensis 994, Tampere University Press, Tampere – other articles and presentations are available online at academia.edu.
Tabari (1999), *The History of al-Tabari Volume V*, tr. C.E. Bosworth. New York.
Verstandig, A. (2001), *Histoire de l'Empire parthe*. Brussels.
Viellefond, J.-R. (1970), *Les Cestes de Julius Africanus*. Firenze, Sorbonne-Paris.
Webster, G. (1998), *The Roman Imperial Army* 3rd ed. Introduction by Hugh Elton. Oklahoma.
Wheeler, E. L. (1997), 'Why the Romans can't defeat the Parthians: Julius Africanus and the Strategy of Magic', in *Roman Frontier Studies 1995*. Oxford.
Whittaker, *Herodian* 2 vols. (1969), English tr. by C.R. Whittaker. Loeb.
Wolfram, H. (1990), *History of the Goths*. Berkeley, Los Angeles, London.
Wolski, J. (1993), *L'Empire des Arsacides*. Louvain.

Index

Abernathy, capital of Picts, 113
Abgar (Abgarus/Abgaros), ruler of Osroene under Trajan, 261
Abgar (Abgarus/Abgaros) VIII, King of Osroene/Oshroene, 170, 324
Abgar (Abgarus/Abgaros) IX, King of Osroene/Oshroene, 170, 197, 324
Abyssinia, Abyssinians, *see* Aksum
Achilles, hero, 211–13, 223
Adamklisi Metope, 22, 160–1
Aden, 229, 233
Administration (Roman), 3–6, 143–51, 182, 190, 208, 214
Adventus, *see* Oclatinius Adventus
Aelius Coeranus, Egyptian senator and Caracalla's councillor, 215, 224
Aelius Decius Triccianus, prefect of *Legio II Parthica*, accomplice of Macrinus, 194, 208, 273–5, 280, 296
Asclepius/Aesculapius, 143, 145, 147, 152–3, 177, 180, 212–13
Agri Decumates, Upper Germany, Baden-Württeberg, Germany, 173–4
Africa (with North Africa), 3, 6–7, 61, 63–4, 72, 77, 95, 113, 127, 153–4, 168, 200, 216, 218, 231, 269, 271, 320–1
  see also Egypt, Blemmyes, Aksum, Mauretania, Tripolitania, Cyrene, Sahara
African Clique/Faction (supporters of Geta), 126, 135, 185
Agentes in Rebus, 213
  see also Frumentarii, Intelligence gathering, Peregrini
Aggeliaforoi, see Frumentarii
Agricola, famous Roman commander, 98, 105
Agrippa, *see* Marcius Agrippa
Aksum, Aksumites (Ethiopians), 227–30, 233
Alamanni, Germanic tribal confederacy, 93, 155–8, 165–8, 170–9, 181, 188, 191, 195, 197
Alans/Ossetes, Sarmatian tribal confederacy, 53, 123, 158–9, 161–2, 187, 198, 209, 244, 246, 249–5, 306, 316, 326–8
  see also Sarmatians

Alaric, Gothic king, 40
Alban, St, 112
Albania/Albanians, 244–7, 257
Alba Longa/Albanum, city, Latium, Castel Gandolfo, Italy, 38, 44, 133, 139, 218, 224
Albany (the area north of Hadrian's Wall), 119–20
Albinus, *see* Clodius Albinus
Alexander, accused criminal, 211
Alexander, Bishop of Jerusalem, 149–50, 152
Alexander the Great, king of Macedonia, ix–x, 48, 81, 149–50, 153–4, 168–9, 182–5, 191–2, 199–206, 209–13, 217–19, 221, 223–5, 232–3, 247, 249–53, 256–7, 262–3, 267, 279, 285, 290, 306, 315–16, 328
Alexander Severus, *see* Severus Alexander
Alexandria, city, Egypt/Alexandrians, vii, xi, 37, 61, 80, 146, 149, 181, 188, 196, 207, 212, 214, 220–7, 229, 231–3, 236, 261, 263, 280, 327
Alexandria, Mesopotamia, also known as Antiochia or Spasinou Charax, close to modern Basra, 257
Alexianus, 202, 215, 297
Alfenus Senecio, L., 92
Allies Roman (contingents provided by allies also known as *Foederati*/Federates or *symmachiarii*), 7, 27–35, 53, 118–19, 141, 162–3, 170, 172, 190–2, 196, 208, 218–19, 230, 268
Almond, river, 100
Amida, city, 194, 257
Ancyra, Galatia city, Ankara, Turkey, 194, 220
Andersen, Lars, 325
Angrivarii, Germanic tribe, 155–8
Annona militaris, 42, 152
Antioch, city, xi, 81, 168, 181, 208, 218, 220–1, 235–6, 257, 262–3, 269, 283, 293, 297–8, 301–303, 308
Antiochia, *see* Alexandria, Mesopotamia
Antiochus, cynic, 197–9, 209, 220
Antoniniana, (a title given to a military unit for their loyalty or bravery by Caracalla or Elagabalus), 93–4, 133, 139, 166, 195, 256

Antonine Wall, UK, 92, 95, 99–101, 119
Antoninianus, a modern name for a coin of two denarii, 221
Antoninus Magnus, the Great (in official documents Magnus was used to separate Caracalla from Antoninus Pius), *see* Caracalla
Antoninus Pius, emperor, (Caracalla named after him to join Caracalla with this emperor and Marcus Aurelius), 2, 27, 183, 318
Antonius Gordianus Semprosianus Romanus, M. (the future Gordian/Gordianus I, councillor of Caracalla), 37, 70, 215–16, 219
Antonius Iuvenis, M. (councillor of Caracalla), 215
Antony, Mark, 240, 263
Apamea on the Orontes, Coele Syria, Qalaat al-Mudik, Syria, 297, 301, 303, 308
Apollinaris, *see* Aurelius Apollinaris
Apollo Grannus, Celtic god, 145, 147, 153, 177, 180
Apollodoros, architect, 100
Apollonius of Tyana, 150, 153, 220
Aquileia, city, Italy, 167–8, 181
Aquitania (major source of grain), 96, 167–8
Arabia Felix, *see* Yemen
Arabia/Arabs/Saracens, 3, 33, 47, 51, 63, 96, 186, 191, 195–6, 199, 218–19, 227–33, 250, 257, 260–1, 264, 283, 286, 288, 295–7
Arabianus, commander 297
Arbeia (South Shields), 93, 96
Arbela, city and battle of, 231, 249–53, 256–7, 265, 285, 307, 330
Archers, archery, x, 9, 15–17, 20, 23, 27–9, 33, 51, 53, 59, 65, 75–6, 158–63, 175, 197–8, 202, 218, 238, 240–3, 245–6, 249, 251, 264, 283–4, 286, 305, 311, 323–5
see also Mounted Archers
Ardashir I, ruler of Persia, 198, 232, 250, 252, 257, 264–5, 321, 324, 326, 329
Ardoch, xi, 107
Argaragantes, *see* Sarmatians
Armenia/Armenians, vii, xi, xviii, 53, 172, 190, 197–9, 208–209, 216, 219–21, 229, 231–2, 236–7, 240–9, 253, 255–6, 261, 263–4, 266, 271, 294–7, 326–7
military, 242–5
see also Civilian Police
Army, *see* military
Arrenianus, Sulpicius, senator and informer, 145
Arrian/Arrianos 23, 27, 52–4, 185, 204–205, 211, 232, 286, 312

Arsacids, 232, 234, 237, 243–4, 263
Artabanus/Artavan V/VI, King of Parthia (c.213–224), vii, x, 154, 196, 198–9, 208, 220, 229, 231–2, 234–6, 240–1, 243, 247–60, 265–7, 270, 277–8, 282–95, 297, 305–306
Artaxata, city, xi, 249, 257–8
Asoristan, satrapy in Parthia, 257
Asturia-Gallacia, 182
Augustus, title, 3, 83, 89, 99, 110, 112, 116, 301
emperor Octavian, 4–6, 9, 36, 48, 121, 134, 151
Aulici (*Corporis in Aula, Protectores, Scholae/Ostensionales*), (imperial bodyguards), 4, 11, 15, 17, 37–9, 75, 98, 113, 122, 128, 139, 145, 172, 179, 188, 196, 206, 218–19, 295
see also Bodyguards, Lions
Aurelian, emperor, 153, 171, 195, 220, 278, 307
Aurelianus, T. Quir. (*comes expeditionis Orientalis* and councillor of Caracalla, or two separate Aureliani), 215–16, 296
Aurelius Alexianus of Sparta, 202
Aurelius Apollinaris, minion of Macrinus, 270–1, 273–5
Aurelius Celsus, centurion, 305
Aurelius, Marcus, emperor, (Elagabalus and Caracalla both named after him to connect them with his family), 2–3, 8, 23, 75, 79–80, 83, 100, 138, 157, 162–3, 183, 298, 300
Aurelius Nemesianus, minion of Macrinus, 270–1, 273–5
Aurelius Victor, historian, v, 70–2, 130–1, 143, 174, 277
Aureolus, *hipparchos* and usurper, 276
Auxilia/Auxiliaries, ix, 7, 10–11, 15–16, 18–19, 22–4, 27–35, 50–9, 64–9, 73, 76, 98, 101, 114, 141, 152, 172, 178–80, 192–6, 204, 206, 213, 218–20, 227, 249, 286, 300–302, 312
Awtar, Shairum/Shair, Sabaean king, 228–30

Babylon, city in Babylonia, Parthia, Iraq, 232, 253–4, 256–7, 261, 324
Baetica, 213–14
Bahram V Gur, Persian ruler, 264
Balbinus, *see* Caelius
Ballistae/Carroballistae/Arcuballista/Manuballista, 11, 13, 17, 23–4, 56, 59, 67–8, 179, 193, 324
Ballistarii, 17
Bandon (pl. *banda*), 52
Basilianus, Praef. of Egypt, 302

338 Caracalla

Bassianus, *see* Caracalla, Elagabalus
Bastarnae/Bastarni, mixed tribe, 155–6, 158–60
Batnae, city, 261
Beneficiarii, 42–3, 47, 65, 73, 75
Berbers, *see* Moors
Beroea, city, Aleppo, Syria, 303
Bervie Water, 108
Bewcastle, 118
Birdoswald (Banna), 93
Blemmyes (modern Beja tribe), 233
Bodyguards/Bodyguard (word), 4, 7–8, 11, 17, 29, 36–8, 44, 48, 51, 54, 73, 75, 85, 94, 97, 110, 114, 117, 121–3, 125, 127–30, 132, 135, 138–9, 144–5, 168, 192, 194, 206, 209, 218–20, 225, 252, 255, 266, 268, 270–5, 279–80, 295, 297, 301–303, 305
  see Aulici, *Equites Extraordinarii*, *Equites Mauri*, *Equites Singulares Augusti*, *Evocati Augusti*, *Leones*/Lions, *Praetoriani*, *Stratores*
  see also Urbaniciani, *Frumentarii*, *Peregrini*, *Vigiles*, Intelligence Gathering, *Statores*, Festus, Rufus, Theocritus, Epagathus, Flavius Maternianus
Boiodurum, 168
Bononia/Boulogne/Gesoriacum, 94, 97, 173
Bosporan Kingdom/Bosporans, 161, 163–4, 187, 193, 246
Boulogne *see* Bononia
Brigantes, a tribe south of Hadrian's Wall, 92–3, 120
Britain/Britannia, xi, 61, 74, 92–123, 168, 173, 182, 216, 262
Bug, river, 165, 193–4
Bulla, bandit, 94
Burgundi/Burgunds, Germanic tribe, 155–8
Byzantium, city, Constantinople, Istanbul, Turkey, 81, 194, 312, 327–8

Cadusii, ancient people in Iran, 253–7
Caecilius Aemilianus, 213
Caelianus, teacher of Diadumenianus, 296
Caelius (Calvinus) Balbinus, D. (councillor of Caracalla and future emperor), 38, 187, 215–16
Caesar, *see* Julius Caesar
Caesar, title, 83, 87, 89, 112, 301
Caledonia/Caledonians, tribal confederacy in 'Scotland', x–xi, 92–3, 95, 98, 101–21, 155, 173
Caligula, emperor, 111
Caracalla/Caracallus, emperor, [original name: Lucius Septimius Bassianus or Julius Bassianus, renamed Marcus Aurelius Antoninus in 195/6; full name: IMPERATOR CAESAR MARCUS AVRELIVS (SEVERVS) ANTONINVS AVGVSTVS, but is better known with his nickname Caracallus/Caracalla], i–xii, 4, 6–7, 15, 27, 29, 38, 47, 54, 64, 70–2, 77–280, 282–6, 291–302, 304–12, 314–16, 322, 325–7
  Youth, 79–111
  Duelling and Gladiatorial fights, ix, 87, 143, 175, 177–8, 181, 214, 216–17, 231, 241, 281, 316 (gladiators use gastrasia)
  Incest and sexual behaviour, 79–80, 111, 120, 128–9, 140, 223–4, 227, 232, 273, 296
  Military campaigns under,
    Military education Middle Danube or Raetia/Britain, 92–123
    Pannonia/Dacia 212–13, 93–4, 165–8
    Against Geta, 124–31
    Against Geta's supporters, 132ff
    Africa, 154–5
    German in 212–13, 165–81
    Pannonia, Dacia 214: Dacians/Sarmatians/Goths, 180, 190–5
    Arabia/Yemen, 195–6, 227–31
    Alexandria, 207, 221–7
    Osroene, 170, 197
      see also Osroene
    Armenia, 197–9, 219–21, 231–2, 236, 244–9, 255–6, 266–7
    Parthia, 154, 196–207, 216–21, 231–2, 236, 243, 246–7, 249–63, 266–7
  Idolization of Alexander the Great and other great men like Sulla, Tiberius and Hannibal, ix–x, 81, 135, 149–50, 153–4, 168–9, 182–5, 191–2, 199–206, 209–13, 217–19, 221, 223–5, 232–3, 247, 249–53, 256–7, 262–3, 267, 279, 285, 289–90, 306, 315–16
  Caracalla as General, 182–6
  Council, Councillors, 127, 138, 183, 214–16, 219
    see also Council
  Military reforms, 134, 141, 168–9, 196, 199–211, 216–19, 221, 254–5, 278–9, 285–6, 289–90, 292, 303–304, 311–12, 314–16, 322
    see also Macedonian Phalanx, Sparta, Lions, Osroene
  Titles, vii, 94, 154, 165–6, 175, 178, 181, 190–2, 195–6, 199, 214, 230, 251, 261, 277

Propaganda and Religious Policies, 141–51, 222–7
  see also Asclepius, Apollo Grannus, Apollonius of Tyana, Isis, Mars, Sarapis
  Astrology, Oracles, Seer, Prophecies, Fortune Tellers, Internal Security, 48, 76, 143–53, 177, 213, 268–72, 276, 280, 307
    see also Intelligence Gathering
  Taxation, 168–9, 207, 221–7
    see also Constitutio Antoniana, Taxes, Trade
  Murder of Caracalla, 268–76
  Father of Elagabalus and Alexander Severus(?), 87, 91, 111, 126, 297, 299–301, 305, 307
Carlisle (Luguvallum), 113, 122
Carpi, see Dacia
Carrhae, Mesopotamia city, Haran, Turkey, and battle of, 237, 242, 257, 270, 272–3
Carroballistae, see Ballistae
Carthage, city, Tunis, Tunisia, 37
Cassius Dio, historian, councillor of Caracalla (a biased major source), iii, 12–14, 36, 48, 65, 70–2, 75, 78–9, 82–3, 85–93, 96, 101, 103–106, 108–11, 113, 116–18, 121–3, 128–32, 135–8, 140, 143, 145–7, 151–3, 157–8, 163, 166, 168–9, 172–7, 182–90, 192–9, 205–22, 224–6, 228, 232–3, 247–51, 253–6, 261, 264–73, 275–6, 279, 282–5, 290–7, 300–304, 306–308
  see also Caracalla, Council
Cataphractarii (Equites Cataphracti)/ katafraktoi, x, 16, 28, 51–3, 69, 76, 158, 161–2, 202, 238, 240, 242, 244, 246, 249, 283–4, 286, 288–9, 292, 305, 307, 319–20, 323
  see also Archers, Cavalry, Clibanarii, Parthia, Contarii, Mounted Archers, Armenia, Osroene
Cataphracts, see above
Catius Sabinus, P. (councillor of Caracalla), 215
Cavalry, ix–x, 8–20, 22–4, 26–59, 73–5, 98, 113, 122, 156–63, 168, 170, 172–3, 178–9, 184, 190–6, 199–200, 202, 204–206, 208–10, 217, 232, 237–47, 249, 251, 263–4, 270, 272, 275–6, 279, 284–95, 302, 305, 307, 312, 314–15, 317–20, 324, 327, 329
  see also Cataphractarii, Archers, Legions, Auxilia, Aulici, Praetoriani, Equites Singulares Augusti, Lions, Clibanarii, Contarii, Osroene, Equites Mauri,

Armenia, Parthia, Goths, Sarmatians, Alans
Cenni, see Chatti
Central Asia, 231, 241–2, 283–4
Chalcedon, city, 305
Channelkirk, 99
Chariot (wagon), war chariot, charioteer, driver, 50, 57, 87, 91, 101, 103, 109, 125, 142, 158, 160, 168, 173, 175, 192, 199–200, 214, 216–17, 219, 232, 238, 267, 272, 276, 303, 321, 323
Chatti (the Cenni of Dio?), 155–8, 165, 168, 170–1, 173, 175–7, 188, 197
Chauci, Germanic tribe, 155–8, 178
Cheirosiphon, see Syringes
Cherson/Chersonesus/Chersonites, (city and inhabitants of the Crimean city state), 164–5, 193
Chesters (Cilurnum), 93
China, 3, 260
  see also Silk Route
Christians, Christianity/Christ, 42, 48, 52, 70, 78, 92, 112–13, 118–21, 149–51, 153, 197, 220, 225–7, 264, 279, 281, 311, 327–8
Cilician Gates, 220
Cilo, see Fabius Cilo
Circesium, city, 303
Circus Maximus, 124, 141
Circus Factions/Chariot Races (Blues and Greens), 87, 91, 124–6, 141–2, 173–5, 192, 214, 216–17, 219, 232–3, 267, 272, 276
City Prefect, see Praefectus Urbi
Civilian police/paramilitary forces/militia, 7, 40–3, 47, 63
  Armenian militia, 224
  Parthian militia, 237
  see also Urbaniciani, Vigiles, Statores, Stationarii, Beneficiarii, Intelligence Gathering
Classis, Classes, see Fleets
Claudius, emperor, 37, 111, 163, 200
Claudius II, emperor, 70
Claudius Piso, 93
Claudius, Pollio, centurion, 305
Clibanarii, 17, 323
  see also Cavalry, Cataphractarii, Contarii, Mounted Archers
Clodius Albinus (emperor in 193–197), 92
Clodius Balbinus, (emperor in 238), 38, 187, 215–16
Clodius Pupienus Maximus, M. (emperor in 238), 38, 187
Cohortes Urbanae, see Urbaniciani
Colchis, 245–6

Comes (companion, count, general), 172, 215, 224
Comitatenses/Comitatus, 14
Commodus, emperor, 29, 38, 75, 77, 122, 142, 148, 150, 177, 191, 217, 271
Consilium (Emperor's Council), *see* Council
Constantia, city, 303
Constantine I the Great, emperor 306–337, 14, 70, 72, 75, 153, 180, 220
Constantinople (Byzantium), city, *see* Byzantium
Contarii, Kontoforoi, Lancers, 23, 27, 51, 53–4, 158–63, 238, 240, 242, 244, 246, 249, 279, 281, 286, 289, 307, 314–15
  see also Clibanarii, Cataphractarii, Lions, Parthia, Armenia, Goths, Sarmatian, Alans, Osroene
Constitutio Antoniana, 141, 165, 279
Corbridge (Coria), 93
Corbulo, famed Roman commander, 48, 314
Cormac mac Art, Irish High King, 121
Corn *see* Grain
Cornificia, daughter of M. Aurelius, 138
Corporis in Aula, see Aulici
Corporis custodis, Germanic bodyguards of Augustus later replaced by *Equites Singularis Augusti*, 179
Council (Emperor's private *Consilium*), 4, 71, 97, 127, 138, 183, 214–16, 219
Council (Military), 183, 216
Council (City), 3, 6, 77
Council of Elders, Senate (Barbarian), 156, 161
Cramond, 96, 99–100, 105
Ctesiphon, Parthia city, Iraq, Voloagesus' capital, 231–2, 256–7, 261, 265
Curiales, see Decurions
Customs, *see* Taxes
Cyprus, 64, 219, 227, 261, 308
Cyrene/Cyrenaica, 63, 77, 218, 227, 256, 261
Cyzicus, 194, 207, 211

Dacia/Getae/(Free) Dacians (Carpi), 155, 158–63, 165–6, 171, 181, 190–4, 200, 208, 216, 218–19, 268, 295–6
Dacia Porolissensis, 166
Dacian War AD 217, 295
Damascus, 194, 257, 303
Danube, river, 35, 62, 77, 93–4, 97, 100, 155, 162–3, 165, 167–8, 172, 178, 192–4, 267, 278
Decurions, cavalry, x, 9, 11, 13, 28, 36
Decurions (class of *curiales* in cities), 2–3, 6
Deira (south of Hadrian's Wall), 119

Devil's Dyke, 162
Diadumenianus, son of Macrinus, x, 143, 269, 295–6, 301, 305–306
Dio, *see* Cassius
Diocletian, emperor, 15, 186
Dnieper, river, 165, 193–4
Dniester, river, 165, 193–4
Domestici, see Aulici
Domitian, emperor, 134, 151, 220
Domna, *see* Julia Domna
Dover (Dubris), city, 95, 97
Drusus, Roman commander, 48
Duces, see Dux
Duke/Dukes, *see Dux*
Dux (general), 95, 112, 117, 121, 206, 295–7
Dura Europos, Coele Syria city, Syria, 20, 89, 256–7, 303, 315
Durno, 105

Eboracum, *see* York
Edessa, Osroene city, Urfa, Turkey, xi, 170, 187, 194, 197, 236, 257, 261–2, 270, 272–3, 324–5, 330
Egnatius Victor, 93
Egypt/Egyptians, 2, 6, 10–11, 42, 61–4, 77, 150, 153, 168, 172, 207, 215, 220–31, 236, 261, 270, 302, 324
  see also Alexandria, Blemmyes, Aksumites, Yemen, Moors, Arabs
Elagabalus/Heliogabalus, emperor, 70, 123, 126, 130, 151–2, 187, 190, 195, 208, 215, 231, 275, 278, 283, 295, 297, 299–305, 307–308
Elburz Mt., 253, 257, 265
Elephant/Elephants/War Elephants, 57, 95, 199–200, 231, 307–308, 311, 321–4, 328–9
Eleutherius, Pope, 119
Elbe, river, 62, 155, 157–8, 165, 167–8, 170–1, 173, 176–8, 193
Elymais, satrapy in Parthia, 243, 257
Emesa, Homs, Syria, 297, 299–300, 303, 308
Epagathus, freedman and supreme praet. pref. with Theocritus under Caracalla, 152, 208, 211, 283, 305
Ephesus, Ionia city, Turkey, 95
Equestrian Order/Equestrians/Upper Classes, 1–6, 10–12, 28–9, 48, 64, 82–3, 90, 135, 140, 144–5, 148–9, 183–5, 187, 192, 214–16, 224, 274, 280, 296, 298, 300, 305–306, 319
  see also Senate
equites extraordinarii, (elite Imperial bodyguards, probably to be identified with the *Leones*), *see* Lions (*Leones*)

equites itemque pedites iuniores Mauri, (a mixed unit of cavalry and infantry with the *iuniores* title proving the existence of *seniores*), 29
Equites Mauri, (elite imperial cavalry bodyguards, and mixed infantry and cavalry *numeri*), 29, 38–9, 51, 75–6, 98, 172, 196, 209, 218, 220, 249, 285–6, 300–301, 308
see also Bodyguards
equites singulares, (elite cavalry auxiliaries protecting commanders), 54, 73
see also pedites singulares, Bodyguards
Equites Singulares Augusti, (imperial bodyguards of barbarian origin), 36, 38–9, 98, 113, 117, 139, 145, 172, 179, 194, 196, 209, 218
see also Aulici, Bodyguards, Lions, *Praetoriani*
Esk, South, North, rivers, 108–109, 114–15, 118
Ethiopians, *see* Aksum
Ethiopian soldier, Ethiopian *numerus*, 113
Eudaemon, *see* Aden
Eudaemones of Arabia Felix, *see* Yemen
Euodus, Caracalla's teacher, 85, 97, 110, 116
Euphrates, river, 252, 257
Euprepes, famous charioteer, 125–6
Eusebius, Church historian, 150, 233
Eutychianus, supporter of Elagabalus, 299–301, 308
Evocati/Evocati Augusti, (veterans called back into service and bodyguards of the emperor), 36, 42, 81, 122, 128, 138, 144–5, 270

Fabius Cilo, L., City Prefect, 75, 85, 125, 135–7, 139, 147, 271
Festus (possibly Marcius Festus, *a cubiculo et a memoria*), friend of Macrinus, 146, 212–13, 219, 271, 274
Festus, accomplice of Elagabalus, 299, 301
Flame-thrower, *see* Syringes
Flavia Titiana (wife of the emperor Pertinax), 207, 214
Flavius Titianus, Procurator in Alexandria, 207, 214, 221
Flavius Maternianus, City Prefect, 147, 149, 269–70, 272, 283, 296, 308
see also Praefectus Urbi
Fleets (navy, naval, ships, shipping, *classis/* classes), x, 6, 38, 47, 50, 60–9, 77–8, 96–100, 103–106, 108–109, 114–15, 118, 134, 141, 149, 152, 158, 164, 168, 171–3, 175–7, 179, 193–4, 206, 211–13, 218, 229–30, 236, 273, 302, 323 (metaphor)
Briton/Irish/Scandinavian Fleet, 104, 120
Germanic Fleets, 158
see also Praetorian fleets, *Vexillationes*
Foederati (Federates), *see* Allies
Fortifications/Fortresses/Forts/Fortified Camps/Walls, xi, 7, 17, 42, 47, 50, 59, 62–3, 92–3, 96, 99–101, 104–109, 113–15, 117–20, 122, 125, 133, 149, 154–5, 157–8, 165–6, 172–4, 181, 190, 195, 209, 218, 223, 225–7, 235–6, 241, 243–4, 247–8, 250, 253, 258–61, 265, 292–4, 315, 318, 321
see also Antonine Wall, Hadrian's Wall
Fratres Arvales, 145, 165
Free Dacians, *see* Dacia
Franks, Germanic confederacy, 155–8, 166, 178
Frumentarii, 7, 36, 42, 48, 98, 114, 123, 138–9, 145, 147–8, 213, 269, 296
see also Intelligence Gathering, *Peregrini, Speculatores*
Fulvia Plautilla, wife of Caracalla and daughter of Plautianus, 80, 83–4, 91, 138, 140
Fulvius Diogenianus, ex-consul, senator, enemy of Macrianus and hence supporter of Elagabalus, 302
Fulvius Plautianus, C., Praet. Pref., ix, 81, 83–7, 90–1, 126, 215, 271, 274
Fulvius Plautius, brother of Plautilla, 138

Gadurat/Gadarat, king of the Aksum, 228
Gaiobomarus, the king of the Quadi, 190
Gallia Narbonesis, 165–6, 187
Gallienus, emperor, 9, 11, 14–15, 52, 70, 72, 276, 278
Ganjak, city, 255–7, 259
see also Takt
Gannys, supporter of Elagabalus, 299, 302–304, 308
Garamantes, Berber tribe, 154
Gaugamela, *see* Arbela
Gellius, commander, 297
Georgia, *see* Iberia, Colchis
Gepids, Germanic tribe, 155–6, 158–60
Germania Superior, 165–6, 218
Germans, Germanic peoples, 12, 22, 36, 38, 94, 117, 122, 139, 155–61, 163, 165–81, 184, 188, 190–2, 194–6, 208, 218–20, 249, 266–8, 272–4, 279, 286, 289, 295, 302, 305, 307, 324
see also Alamanni, Chatti, Chauci, Franks, Goths, Marcomanni, Quadi, Vandals
Germanicus, Roman commander who campaigned in Germania in AD 13–16, 48, 175–6, 178–9, 188

342 Caracalla

Germanicus/Germanicus Maximus, title, vii, 94, 154, 165–6, 175, 178, 181, 191, 195
Gessius Marcianus, husband of Julia Mamaea, 299–301, 308(?)
Gesoriacum, *see* Bononia
Geta, *see* Septimius Geta
Geta, emperor, brother of Caracalla, iii, vii, xi, 70–1, 79–90, 93, 99, 101, 110, 112–13, 116–18, 120, 124–30, 132, 134–40, 144, 151–2, 162, 170, 177, 191–2, 214, 222, 224, 228, 233, 296
   Youth, 79–89
   Britain, 93, 99, 101, 110, 112–13, 116–18, 120
   Final Power Struggle and death, 116–17, 124–30
Getae, *see* Dacians and Goths
Gloucester, 119
Greek Fire, *see* Syringes
Gold/Gold Content in Coins and Medallions, 10, 169, 176, 189
Gordian I, *see* Antonius Gordianus
Gordian III, emperor, 196
Goths, Germanic tribal confederacy (also called Getae), 22, 122–3, 155–6, 158–64, 186–7, 191–6, 208, 214, 268, 270, 279, 281, 286, 295, 302, 306, 325
Grain/Corn, 6, 42, 77, 93, 96, 147, 168, 236
Greek Phalanx, *see* Spartan Phalanx
Greuthungi Goths, *see* Goths

Hadramawt, *see* Yemen
Hadrian, emperor, 2–5, 23, 51, 74, 234, 318
Hadrian's Wall, UK, 92–3, 95–6, 99, 113, 118–9, 122, 174
Hamadan, 256–7
Hannibal, great Carthagian commander, 182–4
Hatra, city, Mesopotamia, Iraq, xi, 195–6
Heliodorus, rhetor, 90
Heliogabalus, *see* Elagabalus
Helios, *see* Sun
Hellespont, 206, 214
Herennius Silvius Maximus, Q. *legatus*, 195
Hermunduri, Germanic tribe, 171
Heruli/Heruls, Germanic tribe, 155, 158–60, 163, 187
High Rochester, 118
Himyar, Himyarites, *see* Yemen
Hippotoxotai, (mounted archers), *see* Mounted Archers
   see also Archers, Bodyguards, *Cataphractarii, Clibanarii, Contarii,* Cavalry, Armenian, Sarmatians, Goths, Osroene, Parthia
Hira, al–, city, 257

Hispania, 63–4, 182, 214
Homosexuals/Gays, 70, 78, 83–4, 212, 226, 261, 277
Honestiores, 2
Housesteads (Vercovicium), 93
Humiliores, 2, 144
Huns, 241
Hyginus (Pseudo-Hyginus), 9, 38, 64

Iazyges, *see* Sarmatians
Iberia (Caucasus), Georgia, vii, 197, 232, 236, 244–7, 326, Appendix 3
Ilium (Troy), 194, 212–13
Immae, city in Syria/battle of, 208, 298–305, 308
India/Indians, 3, 47, 63, 199–200, 227, 230–1, 233–4, 237–8, 241–2, 250, 263
Intelligence gathering, information gathering, disinformation, informers, couriers, spying, spies, (words), xii, 7–8, 11, 36–7, 44–5, 47–8, 68, 73, 75–6, 83, 86, 114, 123, 139–40, 144–53, 170, 177, 180, 184, 207, 212–13, 221, 266, 268–76, 279–80, 293, 295, 307, 317
   see also Frumentarii, Peregrini, Pontifex Maximus, Praetoriani, Aulici, Evocati, Speculatores, Beneficiarii, Urbaniciani, Praefectus Urbi, Praepositus Sacri Cubiculi, Festus, Rufus, Maternianus, Theocritus, Epagathus
Iran, *see* Persia
Irish/Scots/Scotti, 63, 119–22
Isauria/Isaurians, 302
Isis, Egyptian goddess, 48, 148, 150, 153
Lydus, John, 9, 14–17
Iuniores, *see Seniores, Equites*
Iuthungi, *see Alamanni*
Itinerarium Antonini, 181

Jerusalem, 149–50, 153, 257
Jews, 42, 70, 81, 113, 149, 209, 225–7, 232, 261, 318, 320
Julia Domna, mother or stepmother of Caracalla, ix, 71, 79–81, 84, 86, 101, 111, 120, 124, 126–30, 137, 140, 147–8, 150–1, 177, 192, 208, 212, 216, 220–1, 223–4, 227, 231, 269–70, 272, 283, 297
Julia Maesa, sister of Julia Domna, 111, 126, 215, 297, 299–300, 303, 308
Julia Mamaea (daughter of Julia Maesa, wife Gessius Marcianus and mother of Alexander Severus), x, 87, 91, 111, 297, 299, 305, 311
Julia Soaemias also known Sohaemias, (daughter of Julia Maesa, wife of Varius

Marcellus and mother of Elagabalus), x, 87, 91, 111, 126, 297, 299, 303
Julian, emperor and usurper, 72
Julianus, Nestor, (minion of Macrinus), 269–70, 274, 296
Julianus, Ulpius, (minion of Macrinus), 269–70, 274, 296, 300–302, 308
Julius Africanus, Sex., historian, architect, vii, 179, 249, 253, 279, 281, 306, Appendix 2
Julius Asper, C., City Prefect, 139–40, 147
Julius Avitus Alexianus, C., (husband of Julia Maesa and councillor of Caracalla), 215, 219
Julius Caesar, Roman dictator, 48, 148, 153, 278, 291
Julius Cerealis, C., 214
Julius Septimius Castinus, C. (councillor of Caracalla), 95, 166, 215–16, 219
Julius, senator and informer, 145

Kair House, 108
Kassai, János, 325
Khamis, Yemenite military division, 228
Kinda Arabs, 228, 230
Khosrov Anushirwan, AD 531–579, 326, 329
Khosrov, Parthian King of Kings during the reign of Trajan, 261
Khosrov the Great, (King of Armenia c. 215–253/9), 197–8, 209, 220, 232, 234, 236, 245, 247–8, 294, 329
see also Tiridates
Kontoforoi, see *contarii*
Kushans, Central Asian empire and tribal grouping, 232–4, 237, 250

Laconian/Lacedaemonian *lochos*, see Sparta, *Macedonian phalanx*
Laeti, barbarian farmer soldiers, 163
Laenus, see Maesius Laetus
Laetus, see Maesius Laetus
Lancers, see *Contarii, Cataphractarii*, Cavalry, Lions
Langobards/Lombards, 155–8, 167, 178
Legions, legionaries, xi, xiv, 1–2, 6–30, 36, 38–9, 42, 44, 50–8, 64, 68–9, 74, 76–7, 93–6, 98, 101, 105–106, 115, 119, 122, 133–4, 139, 141, 161, 163, 172, 179–80, 182, 188, 190, 194–6, 200, 202, 204, 206, 208–10, 214, 218–19, 224, 233, 249, 273, 275, 285, 291–2, 297, 300–303, 305, 308, 311–12, 318
legio I Italica, xiv, 163, 218–19
legio I Adiutrix, xiv, 93–4, 218–19
legio I Minervia, xiv, 95, 218–19
legio I Parthica, xiv, 10–13, 115, 218–9

legio II Augusta, xiv, 95, 98, 106, 122, 188
legio II Adiutrix, xiv, 172, 188, 218–19
legio II Traiana (Egypt), xiv, 11, 172, 188
legio II Italica, xiv, 188, 195
legio II Parthica, xiv, 6, 10–13, 20, 38, 44, 98, 115, 133, 139, 172, 188, 194–6, 208–209, 218–19, 224, 233, 273, 275, 285, 301–302
legio III Gallica, xiv, 218, 297, 300–301, 303
legio III Augusta, xiv, 172, 218–19
legio III Cyrenaica, xiv, 218
legio III Italica, xiv, 172, 188
legio III Parthica, xiv, 10–13, 115, 218–19, 303
legio IV Scythica, xiv, 218–19, 301, 303, 305
legio IV Flavia, xiv, 218–19, 301
legio V Macedonica, xiv, 93
legio VI Ferrata, xiv, 218–19
legio VI Victrix, xiv, 95, 106
legio VII Macedonica (Claudia), xiv, 218–19
legio VII Gemina, xiv
legio VIII Augusta, xiv, 96, 218–9
legio X Gemina, xiv
legio X Fretensis, xiv, 218
legio XI Claudia, xiv, 218
legio XII Fulminata, xiv, 219
legio XIII Gemina, xiv, 218, 301
legio XIV Gemina (Flavia), xiv, 218, 301, 303
legio XV Apollinaris, xiv, 219
legio XVI Flavia, xiv, 218
legio XX Valeria Victrix, xiv, 95, 98, 122
legio XXII Primigenia, xiv, 95, 98, 172, 188, 218–19
legio XXX Ulpia, xiv, 95, 218–19
naval legions, 64, 68–9, 105, 303
Lentienses, see Alamanni
Leonards, St, 99
Leones, see Lions
Limes, 7, 93, 174
Limigantes, see Sarmatians
Limitanei, frontier troops, 7, 14
Linz, city, 168
Lions, Caracalla's pets, x, 255, 281, Plates
Lions, Caracalla's elite Celtic (German)/ Scythian (mainly Gothic) bodyguards, 38, 113, 122, 145, 184, 192, 194–6, 206, 208–209, 218–20, 249, 255, 266, 268, 270–5, 279, 281, 295, 325
Machiavelli's Lions, 174
see also *Aulici*, Bodyguards, *Equites Extraordinarii, Equites Mauri, Praetoriani*, Scythian
Logistics, see Supply
Lollianus Gentianus, Q. Hedius Rufus, (possible councillor of Caracalla), 215
Lucius, king of the Britons, 119–20

344   Caracalla

Macedonian phalanx/Macedonia/ Macedonian, 55, 64, 81, 184, 190, 194, 196, 200–206, 209–11, 216, 219, 221, 233, 249, 251, 263, 267, 279, 304, 306, 314–16, 328
Machiavelli, N., 151, 174, 280
Macrinus, M. Opellius, (Praet. Pref. and councillor of Caracalla, murderer of Caracalla, emperor), vii, 70, 85, 123, 138, 143, 146–9, 153, 185, 204, 206–208, 211, 213, 215–16, 229–30, 243, 248, 257, 269–75, 277–80, 282–308, 311
  reign, 282–308
Maesa, *see* Julia Maesa
Maesius Laetus, Q., (Praet. Pref. 205–214), 113, 116, 137–8, 215
Maetae, tribal confederacy in 'Scotland', 92–3, 100–104, 109–10, 113–14, 119
Main, river, 93, 165, 172, 174–5, 178
Mainz, city, 155, 165, 167–8, 172
Mamaea, *see* Julia Mamaea
Manilius, senator and informer, 145
Marcellus, *see* Varius
Marcianus, *see* Gessius Marcianus
Marcianus Taurus, centurion, 305
Marcius Agrippa, prefect of the fleet, accomplice of Macrinus, 273–4, 276, 296
Marcius Dioga, Q., (PIR claims that Marcius Diocles, name uncertain, was in charge of *Annona*), 125, 130
Marcius Rustius Rufinus, Cn., Praef. of the Praetorian Fleets, 64, 152
Marcomanni, Germanic tribe, 12, 18, 22, 120–1, 155–8, 166, 171, 178, 181, 190
Marcus Aurelius, emperor, *see* Aurelius
Marius, famous Roman commander, 9
Marius Maximus, historian and Urban Pref., 283, 302
Marius Secundus, governor of Moesia, 302
Marius the Syrian, philosopher, 325
Mars, Roman god of war, 93
Martialis, Julius, equerry and murderer of Caracalla, 144, 270, 272–6, 280
Maternianus, see *Flavius Maternianus*
Mauretania/Mauritanians, 61, 63–4, 154, 321
  see also Africa, *Equites*
Maximinus Daia, (emperor 310–313), 75
Maximinus Thrax, (C. Julius Verus Maximinus, emperor 235–238), x, 38–9, 113, 122–3, 163, 179, 187, 194, 196, 295, 305–307
Maximus, *see* Marius Maximus
Maximus, *see* Clodius Pupienus
Melitene, city, 194
Meros (pl. *mere*, military division, roughly the equivalent of legion 6,000–7,000 men), 14, 55

Mesene, satrapy in Parthia, 257
Mesopotamia, 205, 218–20, 232, 241, 247, 252, 261–3, 267, 282, 293–4, 307
Messius Extricatus, T. (councillor of Caracalla), 215
Milan (*Mediolanum*), city, 52, 181
Military, *see* allies, auxiliaries, bodyguards, cavalry, legions, *numeri*, fleets
  see also Equites Singulares Augusti, *Equites Mauri*, Intelligence Gathering, *Aulici*, *Evocati*, *Stratores*, *Praetoriani*, Lions, *Urbaniciani*, *Vigiles*
Military equipment,
  see Chapter Background, Legions, *Auxilia*, *Numeri*, Civilian Police, Bodyguards, *Cataphractarii*, *Clibanarii*, Archers, Macedonian Phalanx, Spartan Phalanx, Appendix 2
Militia, *see* Civilian Police
Misenum, city, Italia (HQ of the Fleet of Misenum), x, 38, 60, 64, 97, 152, 173
  see also Fleets, Praetorian Fleets
Mogontiacum, *see* Mainz
Mons Graupius, battle of, 105
Moray Firth, 104–105, 108–109, 112, 114–15
Moors (Mauri, Berbers), people and period views of the people, 61, 76, 98, 154, 269, 282, 293, 301, 321
Moors, Roman soldiers, *see Equites Mauri*
Mounted archers, 9, 15, 17, 27, 28, 33, 51–3, 76, 123, 158–63, 175, 197, 218, 238, 240–6, 249, 251–2, 283–93, 305, 311, 320, 325
  see also Archers, *Cataphractarii*, *Clibanarii*, *Contarii*, *Equites Singulares Augusti*, Leones, Osroene, Armenia, Parthia
Mounth, 108

Nahfan, Alhan, Sabaean king, 228
Narbonesis, province, Gaul, 165–6, 187
Naval Tactics, 66–69, 104, 158, 172–3, 175–6, 179, 193
  see also Fleets
Navy, *see* Fleets
Nemesianus, *see* Aurelius Nemesianus
Nero, emperor, 111, 206, 211, 237, 243
Nestor, *see* Julianus
Netherby, 118
Newstead, Newstead-type, 17, 96, 99, 123
Nicaea, *see* Christians
Nicomedia, city, 83, 181–2, 190, 194, 207, 213, 215, 217, 220
Niger, *see* Pescennius
Nigrinus, XI Urban Cohort, 39, Plates
Nihavand, 256–7

Nisibis, city, Mesopotamia, Nisibin, Syria, 204, 210, 261–2, 283–95, 306
  battle of, 204, 210, 283–295, 306
Noricum, province, 168
North Africa, *see* Africa
  see also Egypt, Blemmyes, Aksumites
Notarii/notarius (secretary/notary), 11
*Numeri (*arithmos, arithmoi, katalogoi*)*, national numeri, 7, 27–35, 50–1, 73, 75, 98, 172
  see also Ethiopian
Numerus of *Statores Augusti*, 36

Oclatinius Adventus, M. (Praet. Pref. and councillor of Caracalla), 113–14, 123, 138, 185, 207, 215–16, 271, 282–3, 301
Onager/Onagri, 11, 13, 17, 23, 56, 59, 67–8
Oresa, city, 303, 308
Osroene, Oshroene, Osroenian cavalry, x, 170, 172, 175, 179, 184, 197, 199, 218, 229, 261–2, 279, 305
Ostensionales, see Aulici
Ouse, river, 99
Ovinius Tertullus, C. (possible councillor of Caracalla), 215

Paccia Marciana, (Septimius Severus' first wife, the alleged mother of Caracalla in some sources), 79–80, 120, 128–9, 140, 223–4, 227, 273, 296
Palace/Palatine Hill (Palatium), xi, 4, 14, 81, 85, 124–5, 128, 130, 135–7, 271, 299
  palace at Nicomedia, 214
  Artabanus' palace at Arbela, 251
Palmyra, city, 231, 303, 307
Pandion, charioteer who saved Caracalla's life, 173–5
Pannonia (general area) with provinces Pannonia Superior and Inferior, 93–4, 97, 161, 163–8, 171, 181, 187, 190–4, 216, 218–19, 278, 296, 324
Paphos, city, Cyprus, 308
Papinian/Papianus, Aemilius, Praet. Pref., jurist, 97, 110–11, 113, 116, 128–9, 132, 135, 137
Paramilitary forces, *see* Civilian Police
Parthia/Parthians/Persia/Persians/Iran, xi, 22, 29, 38–9, 51, 75, 87, 105, 154, 161, 164, 175, 182, 184, 186, 190–2, 195–9, 202, 204, 216, 218–21, 227–9, 231–4, 236–45, 247–67, 277–9, 283–95, 298, 305–307, 311–15, 318, 323–5, 326–7, 329
  Parthian Military, 237–45
  see also Artabanus, Tiridates, Vologaesus, Valarsh, Arabs, Armenia, Osroene, Civilian Police, Legions (*I, II, III Parthica*), Appendix 3
Pathhead, 95, 99
Patroclus, 212–13
Patruinus, Valerius, Praet. Pref., 116, 132, 135, 137
pedites singulares, (elite infantry auxiliaries protecting commanders), 73
Peregrini, Princeps Peregrinorum, 7, 36, 48, 98, 114, 123, 128, 138–9, 145, 269
  see also Intelligence gathering, *Frumentarii, Speculatores*
Pergamum, city, Bergamo, Turkey, 194, 212
Peri Strategias/Strategikes, 204
Pertinax, P. Helvius, emperor, 14, 75, 191, 200, 207, 214
Pertinax Jr., Helvius, son of the emperor, 191–2, 214, 221
Pescennius Niger, rival emperor of Septimius Severus, 7, 81, 151, 264
Philip the Arab, emperor, 37, 51, 70
Picts, 103, 119–21
Pitanetan *lochos, see* Sparta, Macedonian phalanx
Plautianus, *see* Fulvius Plautianus
Plautilla, Publia Fulvia, *see* Fulvia Plautilla
Pompey the Great, famous Roman commander, 48, 247, 285
Pontifex Maximus, (high priest), 3, 48, 76, 145, 152
Praefectus Annonae, 75
  see also Praepositus Annonae, Annona, Supply
Praefectus classium praetoriarum Misenatis et Ravennatis (Prefect of the Praetorian Fleets Misenum and Ravenna), 64, 152, 211, 273
  see also Marcius Rustius, Marcius Agrippa
Praefectus Praetorio (Praetorian Prefect, Prefect of the Guard and acting Prefect), ix, 2–4, 35–6, 47, 75, 83, 85–6, 113, 116, 125, 132, 135, 137–8, 144–9, 152, 185, 191, 206–208, 211, 215, 247, 269, 271, 283, 296, 300, 305, 327
  see also Adventus, Macrinus, Laetus, Theocritus, Epagathus, Papinian, Patruinus, Plautinus
Praefectus Urbi/ Praefectus Urbis Romae (Urban Prefect of Rome, Prefect of the City), 5–6, 36–7, 72, 75, 85, 98, 125, 132, 135, 139, 145, 147–9, 152, 269, 283, 302, 308
  see also Urbaniciani, Cilo, Marcellus, Maternianus
Praepositus Sacri Cubiculi (Commander of the Sacred Bedchamber), 146–7, 149, 213

Praepositus Annonae, 152
  see also Praepositus Annonae, Annona, Supply
Praepositus/Praepositi (acting commanders for various purposes), 11, 13, 28–9, 66, 121, 152, 188
Praetorian Fleets, 38, 47, 60–9, 77, 97–100, 104–106, 108–109, 114–15, 118, 134, 152, 158, 171–3, 176, 179, 193, 206, 211, 273, 302
Praetoriani (Praetorians, Praetorian Guard), x, 10, 14, 16, 35–9, 44, 81, 85–6, 98, 113, 116–17, 121, 123, 125, 129–30, 132, 134–9, 142, 145, 172, 179–80, 196, 209, 211, 218, 226, 266, 268, 270–3, 282–3, 296–7, 301–305, 307
  see also *Aulici*, Bodyguards, *Equites Extraordinarii*, *Equites Mauri*, Lions, Scythian
Praetorians, *see Praetoriani*
Prefect of the City, *see Praefectus Urbi*
Prefect, *see Praefectus*
Princeps Peregrinorum, see Peregrini
Priscillianus, Lucius, senator and informer, 145
Proculus, Torpacion, killed at York, 116
Protector/Protectores/Protectores Domestici, see Aulici
Provisions, *see* Supply
Prusias, city, Turkey, 194, 220
Pseudo–Hyginus, *see* Hyginus
Pupienus, *see* Clodius

Quadi, Germanic tribe, 155–6, 158–60, 166, 178, 181, 190
Quaestor (fleet), 65
Qataban, *see* Yemen

Raetia, province, 92–4, 165–72, 180, 188, 191–3, 218
Raphaea, Raphaneae, Rafniye, Syria, 297, 300–301, 303, 308
Ravenna, city, Italy (HQ of the Fleet of Ravenna), 38, 60, 62, 64, 97, 152, 173
  see also Fleets, Praetorian Fleets
Rayy/Ray, capital of Artabanus V, xi, 253, 256–7, 260
Reconnaissance, *see* Intelligence Gathering
Regnitz, river, 174–5, 178
Rhescuporis III, king of Bosporus, 163–4, 187, 193
Rhine, river, xvii, xi, 62, 96–7, 155, 165–8, 172, 175, 178, 193, 267, 278
Risingham, 118
Rome, city, Italy, xi, 1, 5–8, 35–41, 48, 64, 75, 93–4, 124–30, 132–43, 145, 147–8, 165–6, 169, 181, 208–209, 219, 271, 283, 294–5, 298, 305, 312, 321
Roxolani, *see* Sarmatians
Rufus, (Sempronius Rufus), *praepositus sacri cubiculi* in charge of spying under Caracalla, 146–7, 149, 213
Rugi/Rugii, 155–6, 158–60

Saba, *see* Yemen
Sacae, 233, 237–8, 263
Sagittarii, see archers
Sahara, 324
Samosata, city, Samsat, Turkey, 308
Saracens, *see* Arabs
Sarapis/Serapis, Egyptian god, 128–9, 146–7, 149–50, 153, 177, 180, 222–7, 232–3
Sardinia, 64
Sarmatians, 22, 27–8, 51, 155, 158–63, 166, 187, 191–4, 249
  see also Alans, Goths, Dacia
Satala, city, 194, 255
Saturninus, tribune of the Guard, 85
Saxons, Germanic confederacy, 178
Scholae, see Aulici
Sciri, Germanic tribe, 155–6, 158–60
Scots, Scotti, *see* Irish
Scrinium Memoriae (Bureau of Memoire), 145–6
Scutarii, see Aulici
Scythian/Scythians/(Caracalla's Scythians are likely to mean mainly Goths, but could also include other tribesmen from the same area), 162, 164, 184, 192, 194, 196, 208, 219–20, 249, 266–8, 270–5, 279, 325
  see also Bodyguards, *Equites Extraordinarii*, Goths, Lions
Scythian Sacae/Saka/Sakai, *see* Sacae
Seleuceia/Seleucia Pieria, city, Coele Syria, Maharacik, Turkey, xi, 168, 218, 236, 302–303
Seleucia, Mesopotamia, close to Ctesiphon, 256–7, 261
Semnones, *see* Suevi
Senate/Senators/Upper Class, 1–12, 36, 48, 70–2, 80–3, 85, 117–19, 125, 127, 134–5, 137–40, 142–8, 150–1, 154, 168–70, 172–4, 183–5, 187, 192, 199, 206, 213–16, 221, 247–8, 268, 274, 277, 279–80, 283, 294, 296, 298, 300, 302, 305–307, 309, 312, 315
  see also Council, Senate (Barbarian), Decurions, Equestrians (Order)
Seniores (and *iuniores*), 29
Septimius Geta, P., brother of Septimius Severus, 85, 116
Septimius Severus. L. emperor and father of Caracalla, iii, ix, 2, 4, 6–10, 12, 15, 20, 29,

35–6, 38–9, 44, 50, 64, 70–1, 77, 79–89, 92–101, 103–106, 108, 110–20, 122, 124, 126–8, 134, 141, 144, 146, 151, 154, 163, 196, 198, 206, 218, 228–9, 231, 249, 255–6, 271, 280, 295, 308
Serapio, Egyptian seer, 270
Severus, Alexander, emperor, alleged son of Caracalla, x, 7, 38, 70, 89, 123, 126, 141, 155, 183, 187, 196, 208–11, 231, 278–9, 305, 307, Appendix 2
Shapur I, Persian ruler, 233, 252
Ships, *see* Fleets
Sicca Veneria, 95
Sicily, 6, 64,
Siege Warfare, 11, 13, 17, 23, 28, 50, 59–61, 63, 77, 92, 120, 156, 217–18, 241, 246, 253, 255, 258–60, 300, 321, 329
   see also Ballistae, Onager, Fleets
Silings, *see* Vandals
Silk Route, 231, 250
Silver/Silver Content in Coins, 141, 176, 189, 192, 221
Sirmium, city, Lower Pannonia, Srmska Mitrovica, Serbia, 181, 193–4
Soaemias, *see* Julia Soaemias
Society (Roman), 1–3, 87–8, 90–1, 140–51
Sol, *see* Sun
South Shields, *see* Arbeia
Sparta, Spartans, Spartan phalanx, Greek phalanx, 163, 194, 200, 202, 204–206, 209–210, 219, 225, 249, 286, 312, 314–15
   see also Macedonian phalanx, Aurelius Alexianus
Spasinou Charax, *see* Alexandria, Mesopotamia
Speculatores (detached scouts in units and detached service), *Burgus Speculatorius* (Guard Towers), *Speculatores Augusti* (imperial scouts, spies, bodyguards, assassins); in this book the usual meaning is *Speculatores Augusti*, x, 11, 35–6, 42, 47–8, 73, 85, 98, 114, 123, 128, 138, 145, 149, 155, 196, 218
Spice Trade, 250
Spying, *see* Intelligence Gathering
Stationes/Station, 11, 42, 47
Stationarii, 11, 42, 47
Statores military police/Stator/*Statores Augusti*, Emperor's military police, 11, 36
'*stipatores corporis*', unit of bodyguards, possibly the *Equites Singulares Augusti*, or the *Aulici/Scholae*, 122, 295
Stracathro camps, 107
Stratores (*Stablesiani*), 36, 73, 273, 275–6

Stratagems, ruses, 149, 171, 173, 177, 183–4, 188, 190, 199, 224–5, 245, 247, 249–52, 261, 267, 278, 315–16, 319–20
Strategikon (military treatise), iii, 52, 279, 281, 324, 328
Strategy/Diplomacy (goals and strategies very broadly conceived), xi, 3, 7–8, 10, 35–47, 60–3, 71, 75–6, 83–4, 86, 92–4, 96, 98, 103, 113, 116, 130, 132–51, 153–5, 165, 172, 177, 182–4, 187, 190, 192–3, 199, 229, 231–2, 236, 243, 245, 247, 252, 261–2, 265, 278, 283, 293, 302–303, 317
   see also Stratagem
Suetrius Sabinus, C. Octavius Appius, (councillor of Caracalla), 172, 188, 215–16, 219
Suevi/Suebi, Germanic confederacy, 155, 171
Sulgenius, Briton leader, 119–21
Sulla, Cornelius Sulla, L. dictator, 81, 135, 182–4
Sun (Sol, Helios), 46, 170, 255
   see also Elagabalus
Supply, Logistics, Supply Depots/Hubs/Bases, Food, Fodder, Wine, Water, Garum, Oil, Supplying, Supplies, Provisions, 6, 10, 28, 37, 42, 47–8, 50, 59, 63, 65, 75, 77, 86, 93, 96–7, 99, 101–103, 105, 109, 134, 147, 156–7, 167–9, 172–3, 182–3, 189, 193, 207–208, 214, 218, 221, 231, 236, 250–3, 256, 262, 265, 267, 284, 293–4, 298, 300, 316–19, 323–4, 327–8
   see also Grain, *Frumentarii, Praefectus Urbi, Annona*
Sura, city, 303, 308
Symmachiarii, see Allies
Syria, xi, 60–3, 218, 237, 262, 267, 302, 324
Syrian Faction/Clique (the supporters of Julia Domna and Caracalla), 126, 231
Syrianus Magister, 205
Syringes to shoot hellebore/*Cheirosiphon*/Greek Fire/Flame-thrower, 59, 61, 315, 319, 328

Tabriz, city, xi, 255–7, 259
Tacitus, emperor, 12
Tacitus, historian, 52, 103, 157, 237
Tactics, (word), 17–59, 71, 74, 77, 103, 159–60, 178–80, 182–6, 199–206, 209–11, 238–41, 244–6, 264, 267, 283–93, 298–305, 311ff.
   see also Chapter 1, Legions, *Auxilia*, Cavalry, Mounted Archers, Macedonian Phalanx, Spartan Phalanx, Caracalla Campaigns, Caracalla Military

Reforms, *Contarii, Cataphractarii*, Mounted Archers, Archers, *Clibanarii*, Bodyguards, Appendix 2
Tagmata (cavalry corps), 52
Taifali, Germanic tribe, 155–6, 158–60
Takt–e Solayman, xi, 257–9
  see also Ganjak
Tarautas, ugly and bloodthirsty gladiator, Caracalla named after, 131, 143, 181
Tauber, river, 174–5, 178
Taxes, tax, taxpayers, *donativa*, 1, 3, 6, 41–2, 50–1, 63, 77, 96, 119, 134, 141, 154, 169, 187, 221–2, 227, 246, 298
  see also Annona, Caracalla Taxation, Trade
Telesphorus, Celtic god, 142–3, 152
Tencteri, see Franks
Tervingi Goths, see Goths
Theocritus, supreme praet. pref. with Epagathus under Caracalla and commander in Armenia, 152, 185, 198, 207–208, 220–1, 247–9, 255, 257–8, 271, 297, 327
Theodosian Code, 65, 78
Theodosius I, emperor, 72
Thorsberger Moor, Schleswig–Holstein, 157
Thrace, 123, 191–4, 200, 206, 295
Thuringians, 155
Tiberius, emperor, 48, 81, 111, 175, 178, 182–4, 263
Tigran, King of Armenia until deposed by Caracalla in AD 214, 197–8, 220
  see also Tiridates 1, Khosrov the Great, Valarsh
Tigris, river, 96, 251–3, 256–7, 261, 266, 293
Tiridates 1/Tigran/(Tigranes?), 197–9, 220
  see Tigran, Khosrov the Great, Valarsh
Tiridates 2 (Khosrov the Great, king of Armenia), 197–8, 209, 220, 232, 234, 236, 245, 247–8, 294, 329
  see also Khosrov the Great, Tiridates 1, Valarsh
Tiridates 3, see Trdat
Titiana, see Flavia
Titianus, see Flavius
Trade, tolls, customs, tariffs, 3, 42, 47, 63, 149, 187, 227, 230–1, 237, 244, 249–50
Trajan, emperor, 8, 23, 51–2, 75, 96, 100–101, 154, 160–1, 180, 196, 227, 234, 249, 255–6, 261–2, 314, 318
Trapezus, city, 194
Trdat/Tiridates, king of Armenia c. 256–330, 197, 209
Tricciarus, see Aelius Decius Triccianus
Tripolitania, 154
  see also Africa
Troy, see Ilium

Turma (unit of 500/512 horsemen), 9, 14–15
Turma (Praetorian unit of 192 horsemen?), 35
Turma (unit of 32–36 horsemen), 9, 11, 28–9
Tuscus, commander, 297
Tyana, city, Kemerhisar, Bahçeli, Turkey, 150, 153, 194, 220

Urbaniciani (*Cohortes Urbanae*, Urban Cohorts, sing. *Urbaniacus*), x, 36–7, 39, 48, 75, 125, 130, 132, 134, 136–7, 139, 145, 147–8, 152, 172, 218, 283, 301
Urban Prefect, see *Praefectus Urbi*

Valarsh, king of Armenia c. 212–215, son of Tigran/Tiridates, 1, 197–8, 209, 220, 249, 327
  see also Tiridates 1, Tiridates 2, Khosrov the Great
Valarshapat, city, 209, 249, 257
Valens, emperor, 40
Valentinian I, emperor, 40, 255
Valerius Pudens, C., 92
Vandals, Germanic confederacy, 155–6, 158–60, 165–6, 171, 178, 181, 190
Varius Marcellus, Sex., official father of Elagabalus, 125–6, 130, 132, 139, 147, 299, 301
Vegetius, 9, 11–15, 56, 64, 68, 73, 75, 77, 291, 323
Verus, Lucius, emperor, 75, 183, 256
Vestal Virgins, 140, 152
Vexillationes (Vexillations), *Vexillarii* (legionary cavalry or any detachment), 7, 9, 14–16, 66 (naval *vexillation*), 98, 188, 256
Vicar/*Vicarius*, 15
Vigiles, 36–7, 39, 134, 139, 145, 152, 283
Vologaesus, king of Armenia, see Valarsh
Vologaesus/Vologeses III or IV/Valegesos Peroz, King of Parthia (c.145/8–192), 197–8
Vologaesus IV or V (c. 191/2–207), 196
Vologaesus V or VI, King of Parthia c. 207–222/4, x, 154, 196–200, 231–2, 236, 241, 243, 250, 252–3, 256–7, 266

Wagon, see Chariot
Wahram see Bahram

Yemen, 195, 227–231, 233
York/Eboracum, city, 92–3, 96, 98–9, 101, 112–13, 116–17, 120, 123–4

Zafar, Himyarite capital, 228, 230
Zeugma, city, 303, 305, 308
Zosimus, historian, 307, 330